NICHOLSON SCHOOL OF COMMUNICATION

BETWEEN
ONE
and
MANY

The Art & Science of Public Speaking | **Seventh Custom Edition**

Steven R. Brydon
Michael D. Scott
California State University, Chico

with contributions by

Jeff Butler | Stephan Ihde | Jim Katt | Burt Pryor
University of Central Florida

 Learning Solutions

Boston   Burr Ridge, IL   Dubuque, IA   New York   San Francisco   St. Louis
Bangkok   Bogotá   Caracas   Lisbon   London   Madrid
Mexico City   Milan   New Delhi   Seoul   Singapore   Sydney   Taipei   Toronto

BETWEEN ONE and MANY
The Art & Science of Public Speaking
Seventh Custom Edition

1 2 3 4 5 6 7 8 9 0 QDB QDB 13 12 11

ISBN-13: 978-0-07-759790-0
ISBN-10: 0-07-759790-7

Learning Solutions Consultant: Kimberly Wollschlager
Production Editor: Constance Kuhl
Cover Photos: Graduation speech © Comstock Images/JupiterImages; Taking questions from the audience © Jupiter Images; Town Hall Presentation on local environmental issues © CDC/Cade Martin; Company presentation © BananaStock/PictureQuest
Cover Design: Fairfax Hutter
Printer/Binder: Quad/Graphics

To our families for their support over the years:
Pamela, Robert, Julie, Randi, and Colin

Brief Contents

Contents

Chapter 3   A Communication Theory Sampler   51

4   CONTEXTS FOR PUBLIC SPEAKING   307

Chapter 13   Informative Speaking   309

Chapter 14   Persuasive Communication   329

Chapter 15   Thinking and Speaking Critically   359

Preface

Public speaking is a dynamic transaction "between one and many"–between the one who is speaking and the many who are listening. The meaning of the message emerges from the relationship between speaker and audience. Speakers cannot succeed without knowing their audience, and no audience member can benefit by just passively receiving a message. Both speaker and audience–and the transaction between them–are essential to the process. As teachers and as authors, we focus on the transactional nature of successful public speaking.

Public speaking is also an art, a science, and a skill–one that can be learned, improved, and polished. We encourage our students to think of public speaking as a learning experience, where their goal is steady improvement rather than perfection. We also encourage them to think of their speech transactions as a refined and more organized extension of their everyday conversations, and we offer them the tools to become the speakers they want to be. Public speakers can draw on a vast body of information, ranging from classical rhetorical theories to empirical communication research. In this book we include traditional topics, such as logos, ethos, and pathos, and current topics such as research on cultural diversity, the role of nonverbal communication in delivery, and the *appropriate* uses of technology in public speaking.

Today's students of public speaking will face many different speech situations in their lives, and they will face audiences of increasing cultural, demographic, and individual diversity. Throughout this book we focus on ways to adapt to audiences to have the best chance of being heard and understood. We stress the responsibilities and ethical issues involved in being a good public speaker. We focus on the importance of civic engagement and particularly *civil* engagement throughout the book. Finally, we discuss how to be a good audience member: one who knows how to listen, behaves ethically, and critically evaluates the message being presented. In sum, we attempt to provide students with a broad understanding of the nature of public speaking as well as the specific skills they need to become successful, effective public speakers, both as college students and throughout their lives.

Features of the Book

Bringing Visual Life to the Text   This seventh edition of *Between One and Many* continues the tradition we pioneered with our very first edition–bringing visual life to the art and science of public speaking. We have moved with innovations in technology from VHS tapes in the first three editions, to CD-ROMs in the fourth and fifth editions, to a fully developed online presence in the sixth edition. We have upgraded and improved that Web presence for this edition. With the popularity of YouTube, Facebook, and Hulu, today's students are accustomed to viewing their video content online–so we embrace this trend. In addition to the usual videos of sample speeches found with most texts, our innovative Web site provides video segments on the role of public speaking in the lives of people with whom students can identify, concrete skills for mastering speech anxiety, examples of introductions and conclusions, examples of delivery techniques, and concrete advice on the proper role of visual aids, including the frequently misused Microsoft PowerPoint software. The text and the Online Learning Center Web site are coordinated, and each of the seven sample student speeches outlined or transcribed in the text is *presented in full* on the Web site. Sample speeches range from a speech of introduction and storytelling presentation, to informative and persuasive speeches, to a pro–con set of speeches on the topic of the value of a college education. Our Web site also provides a wide range of learning tools, such as an Outline Tutor and a PowerPoint Tutorial. The Web content is an integral part of the learning package provided by *Between One and Many,* seventh edition. Visit our comprehensive Online Learning Center Web site at www.mhhe.com/brydon7e.

Integrated Pedagogy   Throughout the text, boxes are used to focus attention on subjects of special interest. Four different types of boxes appear. In Their Own Words boxes provide examples of speeches by students and public figures, including selected student speeches in outline form with annotations. Self-Assessment boxes allow students to evaluate their own skills and attributes (such as speech anxiety and overall communication apprehension). Considering Diversity boxes show how the topic of a chapter applies to today's multicultural, multiracial, and multiethnic audiences. More than an afterthought, these boxes not only add to the discussion of diversity throughout the book but also challenge students to think about diversity as it specifically applies to the topics covered in a given chapter. Speaking of . . . boxes contain current, topical information that relates to the text discussion.

Throughout the book, speechmaking skills are highlighted in special lists labeled "Tips and Tactics." A popular feature with students, Tips and Tactics make it easy to apply practical suggestions to speeches. Finally, Web icons in the margins call attention to corresponding video segments and other online features.

Help for Speech Anxiety   We recognize that students often come to a public speaking class with some trepidation. As we have done in every edition, we devote a full chapter early in the text to speech anxiety. The text offers many specific, concrete techniques students can use to productively manage and channel their anxiety, regardless of level. Several of these are visualized online. In keeping with the most recent research on speech anxiety and communication apprehension, we distinguish between generalized anxiety about communication and fears that are specific to public speaking and thus are responsive to the techniques we offer to students.

Emphasis on Adapting to Audience Diversity   We give significant attention to audience diversity and emphasize the fact that it encompasses more than one's cultural origins. Drawing on Geert Hofstede's work on understanding differences among cultures, we use Hofstede's dimensions of collectivism and individualism, power distance, uncertainty avoidance, masculinity and femininity, and long-term versus short-term orientation as starting points for analyzing and adapting to cultural differences and similarities between speaker and audience. In addition, we also offer specific Tips and Tactics students can use to recognize, analyze, and adapt to the demographic and individual diversity that their audiences exhibit.

Emphasis on Critical Thinking   Central to effective and ethical communication are the abilities to critically evaluate evidence, to present sound reasoning in speeches, and to detect fallacious reasoning in the speeches of others. *Between One and Many,* seventh edition, continues to provide a strong critical thinking component. Critical listening has been added to our discussion of types of listening.

Using Technology in Speaking   Two major technological innovations have had a great impact on public speaking in the last few years. Presentational software, especially Microsoft's PowerPoint, is a regular feature of presentations in corporations, military briefings, classroom presentations, and professional meetings. We wish we could say that this has been a completely positive development in the history of speechmaking, yet we cannot. For every presentation that uses PowerPoint well, we see many more that punish audience members with too much information, superfluous graphics, and overkill. As a result, we have focused in our text and the Online Learning Center Web site not so much on the mechanics of creating slides (although there is a tutorial to guide students unfamiliar with PowerPoint through the process) but on the dangers of over reliance and the potential benefits of the technology when used properly.

The other major technology, which also has a dark side, is the use of electronic resources for researching a speech. Rather than simply telling students how to find online information, we stress how to properly evaluate the information they find. We stress the importance of currency, relevance, authority, accuracy, and purpose in assessing the credibility of evidence.

Highlights of the Seventh Edition

Based on feedback from many instructors, we have incorporated a number of changes into this edition to strengthen the book.

New Focus on Civic and Civil Engagement   Beginning with the first chapter, and continuing in our discussion of ethics, listening, and critical thinking, we emphasize that public speaking is an important tool for becoming civically engaged. We especially stress that civic engagement should be *civil* engagement. It is important to speak up for what we believe, but it is equally important that we respect the right of all sides to be heard.

New Chapter on Introductions, Conclusions, and Transitions   We have divided the previous edition's chapter on organization into two parts—adding a new chapter focusing on introductions, transitions, and conclusions. Too often, introductions seem a mere afterthought and an audience loses interest before the speaker ever gets to the body of the speech. Poor transitions make even a well-organized speech hard to follow. And even a stellar speech can be undone by a weak conclusion. In addition, dividing organizational topics into two chapters allows us to give more attention to the body of the speech and the importance of outlining.

Expanded Discussion of Proper Use of PowerPoint   Our discussion of PowerPoint has been updated for this edition, with a new section discussing how to effectively present slides during a speech by avoiding common pitfalls, such as being tied to the computer, standing in front of a screen, or letting the slides overwhelm the spoken message.

New Material on Persuasive Speaking   Given its relevance to the narrative approach to persuasive speaking and the research it has spawned, we have added transportation theory to our discussion of persuasion. We also illustrate that while persuasion is in theory a rational process, in practice it often appears to be just the opposite. To help in this regard, we have also incorporated a discussion of audience personality traits, such as self-efficacy and risk-taking, to provide another tool to speakers in adapting to the rhetorical situations they face.

New Material on Special Occasion Speaking   Chapter 16, "Speaking Beyond the Classroom," has been significantly revised to include an extended discussion of small group communication, with an emphasis on avoiding the perils of "groupthink." A new section discusses the increasingly common "elevator pitch," a brief presentation designed to introduce a concept, product, or practice, often to potential investors. Finally, we've added a discussion on public speaking as a career—demonstrating that the marketplace can reward highly skilled public speakers.

New Sample Speeches   Five of the seven student speeches in this edition are new to this book. We have retained two speeches, but have added new samples of storytelling, organization, persuasive speech, and speeches for critical thinking analysis. As with previous editions, the full speech is available in video in the Speech Coach Video Library at www.mhhe.com/brydon7e.

Organization of the Text

We have made two changes in the chapter structure in this seventh edition. In addition to dividing the sixth edition's organization chapter into two chapters (now Chapters 8 and 9), we have combined and condensed the materials from the first two chapters of the sixth edition into one introductory chapter. Finally, as with earlier editions, the chapters are designed so that instructors may assign them in any order they find appropriate.

Part One deals with the foundations of the art and science of public speaking. Chapter 1 focuses on the personal and professional reasons for becoming an effective public speaker, as well as the role public speaking can play in making civic engagement a more civil process. We offer specific examples of people with whom students can identify who use public speaking in their daily lives. We also introduce a model of public speaking and "quick start" guide to students' first speeches. Chapter 2 provides students with the tools they need to cope with the nearly universal experience of speech anxiety. Chapter 3 deals with basic communication theories that inform the public speaking strategies you will learn and includes an important discussion of ethical norms for public speakers.

Part Two makes explicit the idea that focusing on the transaction between speaker and audience is the first key to success in public speaking. Chapter 4 presents a thorough treatment of listening, with a focus on listening to public speeches, and incorporating guidelines for providing constructive feedback. Critical listening has been included in this chapter. Chapter 5 provides the tools for analyzing the cultural, demographic, and individual diversity of audience members. In addition, we offer practical suggestions for adapting speeches to audiences once the analysis has been completed.

Part Three is about putting theory into practice. Chapter 6 covers researching the speech. In recognition of the fact that most students already use the Internet, but often without applying critical standards to the information they find, we have focused on the skills needed to distinguish reliable from unreliable Internet sources. Chapter 7 is devoted to supporting the claims we make in speeches with reliable evidence gathered from high quality sources. We have deferred discussion of Toulmin's model of reasoning, previously treated in this chapter, to Chapter 15. Chapter 8 is new to this edition and provides students with the tools to effectively introduce and conclude their speeches, as well as transition between main points. Chapter 9 treats organization from an audience-focused perspective. We include a variety of traditional organizational patterns, under three rubrics: rhetorical patterns, such as Monroe's motivated sequence, stock issues, and problem-solution; conventional patterns, such as categorical, time, and spatial; and organic patterns, such as star, wave, and spiral. Chapter 10 addresses language use, with particular attention to adapting to diverse audiences. We suggest ways to choose language that is inclusive rather than exclusive, nonsexist rather than sexist, and thoughtful rather than stereotypical. We also offer techniques for enhancing the effective use of language. Chapter 11 deals with delivery skills, again focusing on adaptation to the audience. This chapter provides both a strong theoretical foundation based in nonverbal communication research and solid, practical advice for the public speaker. Chapter 12 presents a comprehensive discussion of visual, audio, and audiovisual media that can be adapted to the audience and occasion to enhance most public speeches. Speech Coach online has a Power-Point tutorial that will enable students to learn the best practices in an interactive fashion.

Part Four addresses the most common contexts for public speaking that students are likely to face in the classroom and beyond. Chapter 13, on informative speaking, stresses audience adaptation, particularly in terms of diverse learning styles. Practical applications of learning theories are discussed in relation to speeches that explain, instruct, demonstrate, and describe. Chapter 14, on persuasive speaking, has been significantly revised to establish the basic theories of persuasion and then show students how to apply those theories in practice. Chapter 15 provides a detailed treatment of critical thinking, with a special focus on recognizing and responding to fallacies of reasoning. The Toulmin model is used to organize fallacies, but is explained in terms we believe students will find more understandable than in previous editions. Two speeches on a topic close to students' hearts—whether or not a college education is worth the cost—are compared, and students are invited to use their critical thinking skills to evaluate these speeches. Finally, Chapter 16 provides a discussion of speaking beyond the classroom. It includes guidelines for speeches of introduction, recognition, acceptance, commemoration, and to entertain. New sections deal with the "elevator pitch," answering audience questions, leading and participating in small groups, and public speaking as a career.

Supplements

Visit our Online Learning Center Web site at www.mhhe.com/brydon7e for comprehensive teaching and learning resources.

For Students Fully integrated with our text, the student resources include the Speech Coach Video Library, tutorials on PowerPoint and outlining, multiple-choice self-quizzes, detailed chapter outlines and overviews, plus key terms within each chapter and their definitions. Each video segment in the Speech Coach Video Library can be viewed independently of the others and is coordinated with a specific chapter in the text. Marginal text icons indicate where a particular video segment would be appropriate. The Speech Coach videos not only reinforce the text but also preview material to be covered later in more depth.

For Instructors The password-protected instructor section of the Web site includes the Instructor's Manual (IM), written by the text authors. This IM includes a variety of excellent resources for new and experienced teachers. These include strategies for managing multisectional courses, a primer for graduate assistants and first-time teachers, and quick references to the speechmaking skills highlighted in each chapter. The IM offers a number of in-class activities, sample syllabi for semester- and quarter-length terms, and sample evaluation forms. In addition, approximately 1,800 test items, including multiple-choice, true/false, and essay questions are available in the Instructor's Computerized Test Bank. PowerPoint lecture slides are also available to aid instructors.

Acknowledgments

We gratefully acknowledge the support and help of many people at McGraw-Hill who played a role in this book, including Meghan Campbell, managing editor; Craig Leonard, developmental editor; Sridevi Palani, media project manager; Jane Mohr, project manager; Margarite Reynolds, design coordinator and Brian Pecko, photo researcher. We also thank Wendy Nelson, manuscript editor, for her attention to detail.

We are especially grateful to Dr. George Rogers, Professor Emeritus at Chico State, who provided several photographs for the book and produced the video segments that appear in the Speech Coach Video Library. We also thank Aaron Bowen, reference/subject librarian at Chico State, for his advice in updating portions of Chapter 6 and Appendix A. Special thanks go to the speakers who shared their talents in providing sample speeches: the late Jonathan Studebaker, Kristin Wilhelm, Shelby Anderson, Trevor Morgan, Kathryn (Kate) Motroni, Greg Shafer, and Arjun Buxi. We would also like to thank Enrique "Rick" Rigsby and Russ Woody for generously consenting to contribute to our effort. They are friends, colleagues, former students, and role models; they have all enriched our book and our lives. We also thank Dr. Nichola Gutgold of Penn State Lehigh Valley Campus, for sharing her research on Hillary Clinton's rhetorical style and Professor Christine Hanlon of the University of Central Florida for her box on orally citing sources.

A grateful thank-you for the reviews and counsel of our peers in the classroom who graciously prepared careful critiques of our manuscript and videotape in various stages of development:

Jim Abbott, University of North Dakota Grand Forks

Linda Anthon, Valencia Community College

Christine Clapp, George Washington University

J. Douglas Lepter, Trevecca Nazarene University

Charles Falcon, Alamo Community College

Donald Goss, Valencia Community College

Nichola Gutgold, Penn State Lehigh Valley

Adam Jenkins, Millersville University

Joshua Lyman, Cuesta College

Dawn Muhammad, Calumet College of St. Joseph

Kelly Petkus, Austin Community College

Clifford Roth, California State University, Fullerton

Mara Singer, Red Rocks Community College

MJ Wagner, University of Central Florida

Christine Hanlon, University of Central Florida

Shari Hodgson, University of Central Florida

Stephan Ihde, University of Central Florida

Gino Perrotte, University of Central Florida

David Young, University of Central Florida

We appreciate the help of all these individuals in preparing this book, but we are, of course, ultimately responsible for its content. Any errors or omissions are solely our own. And last, but certainly not least, we wish to thank our wives, Pamela and Randi, who not only showed great patience as we worked on this project but often provided assistance in more ways than we can possibly list.

About the Authors

Steven R. Brydon
California State University, Chico

Steven Brydon is Professor Emeritus at Chico State and received his Ph.D. from the University of Southern California. He currently teaches courses in public speaking, small group communication, argumentation, and public opinion and propaganda. He coached speech and debate for 12 years and served as department chair for 10 years over three separate terms. He has coauthored three books and has also published in the areas of political communication, argumentation, and debate.

Michael D. Scott
California State University, Chico

Michael Scott is Professor Emeritus at Chico State and received his Ph.D. from the University of Southern California. He is coauthor of a handful of books and is widely published in academic journals in communication and health. For the past decade he has been part of a team funded by the National Cancer Institute whose purpose is to apply communication theory and research to persuasive campaigns targeted at reducing people's risk for skin cancer, the most common and most easily prevented form of cancer among college-age adults in the United States.

PART 1

FOUNDATIONS

This class will help you bridge the gap between one and many as you develop your public speaking skills.

PRACTICAL SPEAKING

Objectives  www.mhhe.com/brydon7e

After reading this chapter and reviewing the online learning resources at www.mhhe.com/brydon7e, you should be able to:

- Explain the personal, professional, and public reasons for studying public speaking.

- Demonstrate an understanding of the transactional and symbolic nature of the process of public speaking.

- Identify the general purposes associated with public speaking.

- Select an appropriate topic for your first speech.

- Construct a specific purpose for your first speech.

- Develop a clear thesis statement for your first speech.

- Prepare your first speech, using appropriate sources for information.

- Organize your speech to (1) open with impact, (2) focus on your thesis statement, (3) connect with your audience, (4) preview your main points, (5) organize your main points, (6) summarize your main points, and (7) close with impact.

- Deliver your speech in a conversational, extemporaneous manner.

- Understand and reduce public speaking anxiety.

Key Concepts

In each chapter we will introduce you to some key terms you need to know. We place these at the beginning of each chapter to alert you to important terms you will encounter. In this chapter look for the following terms:

B-R-E-A-T-H-E Process	main points
channel	message
content (of messages)	perception
credibility	preview
decoding	relational component (of messages)
encoding	signposts
extemporaneous delivery	specific purpose
feedback	symbol
general purpose	system
interdependence	thesis statement
invention	transaction

"If all my talents and powers were to be taken from me . . . and I had my choice of keeping but one, I would unhesitatingly ask to be allowed to keep the Power of Speaking, for through it, I would quickly recover all the rest."

—DANIEL WEBSTER

We begin each new semester with an admission to our students: "We are well aware of the fact that many of you seated here are in attendance only because our class is required for your degree." Next, we ask our students: "How many of you believe the time spent with us studying the art and science of public speaking could be more profitably spent in classes more relevant to your major and future success?" Not surprisingly, many students raise their hands to agree with this statement.

We make the admission because we know many students would excuse themselves from our class if given a choice. We ask the question because we've learned, through decades of teaching, that it's one students often ask themselves.

So why *is* public speaking required of students at most colleges and universities across the United States? Wouldn't it make greater sense for students to take an additional course in their major or one where the connection to their future success is obvious?

Not necessarily, we tell our students. If they are willing to make even a modest investment of their time and effort in our class, they will find that speaking effectively in public can (1) help them make better grades in other classes, (2) make a difference on their résumé, (3) increase their lifetime of success in their chosen profession, and (4) help them become more effectively engaged in the civic discourse of our democracy.

People admire those who can think on their feet and deliver a powerful presentation. This knowledge and skill is so valuable that, in fact, employers consistently rank it as one of the most desirable characteristics in their new and seasoned employees.[1] Knowledge and skill in public speaking is *that* important. Further, this is true whether we're talking about science and medicine, the law and public service, education and the social sciences, or even the fine arts. Consider the stories of the three people shown in the photos on page 5.

Sandi Young. Sandi began her professional life as an elementary school teacher. Before too long, however, she completed a master's degree and credential in special education and took on a new job as a resource specialist for children with special needs. Soon thereafter Sandi was being called on to lead training workshops for other teachers, school administrators, and even parents. "I was doing the very thing I dreaded most as a college student," Sandi says, "making presentations in public to audiences ranging from a few teachers to as many as 1,200 parents, teachers, and administrators."[2]

Jeff Johnson. As a part-time surfer and full-time brand manager and nutritionist at Kashi Company, Jeff has found a way to combine his love of surfing with his work. Kashi selected Jeff as their spokesperson in a nationally televised ad. He also speaks on behalf of Kashi, appearing for example, on the Food Network cable channel. "I now know firsthand what I didn't know while enrolled in my public speaking course," Jeff recounts. "Public speaking can take you places in the corporate world that would be otherwise closed. It's not a substitute but a complement to your degree. And it lets you share your expertise with the audiences you hope to reach with your products."[3]

Edna Morales. Mrs. Morales's son Alvin was infected with hepatitis C and needed a liver transplant that meant traveling from Puerto Rico to the United States and Cincinnati Children's Hospital. Although her son's transplant was a success, Mrs. Morales saw an unfilled need for many other Spanish-speaking families. After moving to Cincinnati she realized, "I needed to stay here because there was a huge need to help the Hispanic families, and that was going to be my goal."[4]

School principal Sandi Young

Kashi nutritionist and brand manager
Jeff Johnson

Medical translator and patient
advocate Edna Morales

She worked hard to improve her English proficiency, and has fulfilled her goal by becoming a medical translator. She now serves as a liaison between Spanish-speaking patients and hospital staff and is a member of the Family Advisory Board of the hospital. She speaks frequently to diverse audiences about her experience in the effort to empower them should they face a similar medical crisis.

What all these people have in common—whether a principal, brand manager, or patient advocate—is that public speaking has become central to their lives and to attaining both their own goals and those of others around them. Public speaking is an essential communication skill in today's world. It also is an extension and refinement of many of the skills you already practice in your one-on-one and group communication encounters.

Our goals in this initial chapter are threefold. First, we seek to persuade you of the personal, professional, and public reasons to study public speaking. Second, we describe public speaking as a system of communication, providing a basic model of the communication process. Finally, we offer a "quick start" guide to public speaking to give you an overview of the skills you will need to give your first speeches in class.

Why Study Public Speaking?

Personal Reasons

The first and most obvious reason to become a more effective public speaker is personal. At the end of each semester, we ask our students to write a brief paper reflecting on their experiences in our class. Students often describe how they once feared public speaking and now enjoy it. Often those who were most reluctant to take the class are the most appreciative. As most of our students learn, there is a personal satisfaction in receiving a positive reaction from an audience. There's also the opportunity to empower themselves and others.

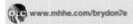

To view a video that shows the role public speaking can play in people's lives, click on the Speech Coach link in our Online Learning Center Web site and go to Segment 1.1.

Becoming a skilled public speaker is one of the surest paths to self-empowerment. Recently the individual voices of women in our community were being heard in the annual "Take Back the Night" event. In symposia and open public forums, speeches on once-taboo topics such as incest and rape were shared with the on- and off-campus community.

Just before the culminating event, an arm-in-arm parade marched down the main street of our city. Over 40 women took the microphone and told their personal stories to the crowded audience during Survivor Speak Out.[5] As they did, many of them also commented that hearing other women speak in a public setting had given them the courage to step up and speak out themselves, often for the first time in their lives.

Professional Reasons

Besides personal empowerment, there are many professional reasons for honing your public speaking skills. The ability to present an effective speech is one of the most desirable skills companies look for in a new hire. Ask any successful person in business or the professions and the chances are high that the person will tell you that skilled speakers are much more likely to fast-track up the rungs of their organization's ladder. People who speak well in public are better able to (1) promote their professional self, (2) present their ideas to decision makers, (3) create positive change in the workplace, and (4) contribute worthwhile ideas in meetings.

The chance to speak in public frequently presents us with an ideal opportunity to enhance our professional credibility and advance our careers. Some time ago Dr. Bonnie Johnson treated the authors of this text to a presentation where she spoke about work she had done for Intel, the world's largest silicon chip manufacturer. As someone trained in organizational communication, Dr. Johnson studied how well personnel were adapting to technological change in the workplace. When she had concluded her study, Intel offered her a position with the corporation.

Following her presentation, Dr. Johnson welcomed questions. One audience member asked her why she thought Intel had hired her. "Do you want to know candidly?" she responded. "Because initially they were more impressed with the public presentation I made to top management on the results of my study than with the study itself. They hired me because I not only knew my subject but could effectively speak about it and its implications for Intel." Surveys of personnel managers at top companies consistently demonstrate that they look for college graduates who not only can communicate interpersonally and in writing but also can deliver a speech with impact.

Your success depends not only on your ideas but also on how well you can present those ideas to people whose decisions will affect your career. When you think about it, every occupation and profession involves selling ideas to other people. Most corporations require managers to present reports or briefings describing their accomplishments and future plans and goals. For example, an Amazon.com software engineer tells us that although his workgroup was composed of several people, his speaking skills allowed him to be the face of the group to upper management. His skills in this regard won his group an award and ultimately helped him earn a promotion.

One of the most important tasks for any supervisor or manager is to be able to convince colleagues that proposed changes are desirable. To remain competitive, companies must implement new technologies and procedures. Yet many employees resist change. Often the best way to introduce change is to *sell* rather than *tell*. Fifty-plus years of empirical research demonstrate that opinion leaders are most effective in selling organizational change. You needn't be the CEO to lead opinion—you simply have to exhibit several of the qualities people recognize in opinion leaders. The ability to communicate effectively, especially through public speaking, is chief among these qualities.

Although small group communication is not the main focus of this book, many of the skills we discuss—ranging from active listening to critical thinking to making impromptu presentations—are directly applicable to functioning in group meetings. As communication professor Ronald Adler reports, the average business executive spends about 45 minutes out of every hour communicating, much of this time in meetings.[6] Further, surveys show that executives spend as many as 700 hours per year in meetings.[7] Your ability to speak effectively in meetings will be indispensable to your success in the workplace.

Public Reasons: Promoting Civic Engagement

In recent years there's been a renewed emphasis on preparing ourselves to be civically engaged in our communities and the world at large. Skilled public speakers serve as agents of change both in and outside of the workplace. Were it not for those who spoke out publicly, the voting age would still be 21 and only white male property owners would be able to vote. All the progress of the past century has resulted from people coming up with new and sometimes controversial ideas and speaking out to persuade others of the wisdom of adopting them. Among the public reasons for studying public speaking, therefore, are (1) becoming a critical thinker, (2) functioning as an informed citizen, (3) enhancing freedom of speech, and (4) promoting civil discourse.

As we discuss in Chapter 15, the ability to think critically about your own messages and those of others is essential to reaching sound conclusions about the issues of the day. Citizens who do not think critically about issues on which they speak can do more harm than good. Not only should speakers strive to base their persuasive efforts on sound reasoning, listeners need to take responsibility to detect unsound reasoning. Some arguments that seem valid actually contain flaws that render them invalid. Becoming a critical thinker will make you less susceptible to phony arguments and less prone to engage in them yourself.

Our democracy is based on the premise that for our country to thrive there must be a public forum for the free exchange of ideas. Thus, it is no accident that the First Amendment to the U.S. Constitution guarantees freedom of speech, as well as freedom of the press, religion, and peaceable assembly. Even if you don't have an immediate need to speak out on an issue of public policy, you will be the consumer of countless speeches on every issue imaginable—from atmospheric warming to zero-tolerance policies in college dorms for drug possession. The ability to forcefully and publicly present your thoughts to others—whether as a speaker or as an audience member questioning a speaker—is more than a desirable skill. It is also a responsibility you owe to others and yourself.

As the violent crackdown on dissent in Iran in the summer of 2009 demonstrated, freedom of speech is a right denied to millions around the world. Even in democratic nations, some people believe the way to deal with unpopular ideas is to invoke a quick fix: censorship. One of our goals in this book is to give you an appreciation for the importance of free speech and expression in a democratic society. The empowerment of more and more citizens to express their views publicly should lead to vigorous debate about those ideas. Those who have confidence in the truth of their own views should welcome the opportunity to debate, rather than suppress, opposing views.

Regrettably, much of the public discourse of recent years in response to controversial issues has degenerated into name calling and appeals to our basest emotions. Twenty-four-hour cable TV and talk radio shows prize verbal aggressiveness. Hosts shout down guests with whom they disagree, make outrageous and unsupported claims about politicians they don't like, and encourage their listeners and viewers to do the same.

Is it possible to agree to disagree without resorting to name calling and labeling people? We think it is. In fact, we believe almost any topic—from abortion to religious zealotry—can be debated without the debaters personally attacking each other's pedigrees. Even though he was in the political fight of his life, Senator John McCain defended his opponent when someone at one of his town hall rallies said he was afraid to raise his child under a President Obama. Even though his own supporters booed him, McCain called Obama a "decent person and a person that you do not have to be scared of as president of the United States."[8] Learning to focus one's public speaking skills on the substance of a controversy rather than the personality of an opponent is an important step in promoting civil public discourse. As more Americans learn how to make their views known rationally, and learn the critical thinking skills necessary to evaluate public discourse, the overall level of debate about issues in contemporary society is likely to improve.

The Public Speaking Transaction

Earlier we said that public speaking is an extension and refinement of the communication skills you use every day. This means public speaking is similar to, but different from, conversation and group discussion. The differences are most notable in terms of (1) planning, (2) organization, and (3) delivery.

To speak well, we need to plan well in advance of the actual transaction. We need to think about, analyze, and adapt to our intended audience. What do we know about our audience members, and what do we need to find out about them? We need to plan for the physical location where we will be speaking. If it's a room, does it pose constraints on movement or eye contact? Can we mediate our message? Will a microphone be necessary? It is crucial to plan for all the contingencies we may face.

Public speaking also requires a much more organized and coherent message than either conversation or group discussion. In conversation and discussion, communicators can interrupt each other, ask questions, gesture to one another, and ask for clarification when needed. This is not so easily done in the case of public speaking. As a result, we need to organize our message so its meaning is clear and its logic easily followed.

Finally, delivery is more formal with a public speech than with conversation and discussion. Please don't get us wrong—this should not be construed to mean that a speech is stilted or stuffy. Many of the best speeches are conversational in tone. But let's face it, there are some differences. We stand up when speaking, perhaps behind a lectern, whereas audience members are seated. We may use notes and visual aids to enhance our speech. We also may move about the room while speaking.

With this in mind, we can now turn to certain principles that reinforce the similarities between public speaking and its counterparts. Whether the focus is an intimate conversation between lovers, an informative speech before your class, or a speech at a political rally, the process of communication is best viewed as a transactional system.

A **transaction** involves an exchange of verbal and nonverbal messages between two or more people. A **system** is a collection of interdependent parts arranged so that a change in one produces corresponding changes in the remaining parts. Consider a mechanical system such as a car. Its parts show varying degrees of interdependence. **Interdependence** exists when things have a reciprocal influence on one another. Changes in some of a car's parts will produce subtle changes in others. For example, even minor tire tread wear will affect a car's handling. The change is so subtle, though, that most drivers don't notice it. In contrast, changes in other parts of the car can produce changes drivers cannot help noticing. Engine failure, for example, produces obvious changes throughout the hydraulic system of the car, including failure of the car's power steering and power brakes.

Perhaps this is why the public speaking transaction seems such a significant departure from the more familiar contexts of communication in which we engage. Whereas the changes that occur to the communication system when moving from an interpersonal to a small-group exchange are subtle, the changes that occur to the system when moving to an exchange between one and many can seem rather pronounced. Consider something as simple as the number of people. The lines of communication increase with the number of people. This may be one reason people are fond of the saying, "Too many cooks spoil the broth." As illustrated in Exhibit 1.1, the lines of communication increase geometrically

transaction
An exchange of verbal and nonverbal messages between two or more people.

system
A collection of interdependent parts arranged so that a change in one produces corresponding changes in the remaining parts.

interdependence
A relationship in which things have a reciprocal influence on each other.

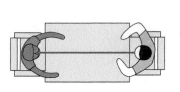

Dyad
(1 line of communication)

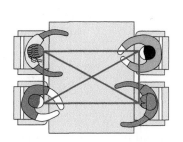

Group of 4
(6 lines of communication)

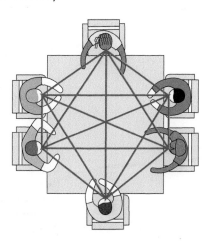

Group of 6
(15 lines of communication)

Exhibit 1.1

Lines of Communication.

The lines of communication increase with the number of people. This may be one reason people are fond of the saying "Too many cooks spoil the broth."

Exhibit 1.2

Public Speaking as a Transaction.

In this model of the speech transaction, messages are simultaneously conveyed between speakers and listeners, with both parties functioning simultaneously as sources and receivers of messages. Communication is bound by the situation, and each person's perceptions are significant in interpreting the content and relational components of messages.

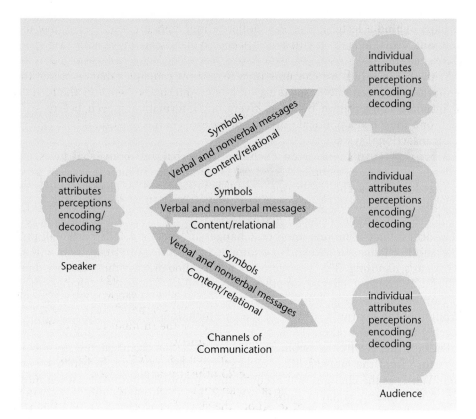

as the number of communicators increases. Whereas this change isn't especially dramatic as you move from two communicators to three or four, the change is staggering by the time you get to a group of even seven.

Exhibit 1.2 models the interdependent parts of the public speaking transaction as a system. Consider (1) the context in which the public speaking transaction takes place, (2) the speaker and the audience, (3) the messages they exchange, (4) the process of constructing and interpreting the symbols they use to convey their messages, (5) the channels through which the messages are sent, and (6) the role perception plays in the process.

The Context

Every speech takes place in a specific context. In Chapter 5, we will discuss this in more detail and introduce you to Professor Lloyd Bitzer's concept of the "rhetorical situation."[9] For now, however, it's sufficient to realize that every speech is called forth and constrained by a particular context of events, persons, relationships, and goals.

Consider first the physical situation that speakers face. It's one thing to speak inside a classroom and quite another to speak at an outdoor graduation ceremony. We can generally rely on our natural voice to speak inside a classroom, but we probably will need a microphone to be heard outside. Changes also may be required in our gestures, movements, and decisions about such things as visual aids.

Next consider the goal a speaker seeks to fulfill. What is it about the situation that moves us to speak? Are we speaking to impart important information to our audience, as teachers do on a daily basis? Are we speaking to organize our fellow citizens to fight a perceived wrong? Are we gathered to eulogize a beloved family member or friend? Are we speaking to entertain our audience with amusing stories or jokes?

The Speaker and the Audience

In contrast to early models of speaking, which implied the speaker first talks and the audience then responds, the transactional model tells us that the speaker and the audience simultaneously exchange verbal and nonverbal messages. Verbal messages are the actual words spoken, while nonverbal messages are wordless. Even as speakers share their messages with audience members, for example, individual members of the audience are sharing messages right back. Generally this **feedback** is nonverbal in nature and includes such things as eye contact, facial expressions, and applause. In some situations, these audience-initiated messages may be verbal, as is the case of opponents of health care reform who often shouted down members of Congress during the summer recess of 2009 at various town hall meetings throughout the country.

The sheer number of people in an audience also affects the overall speech transaction. It's one thing to speak with 25 other residents in the lounge of your dormitory. It's quite another to speak to an auditorium with hundreds of people. Thus, you can no more afford to ignore the size of your audience than you can afford to ignore their feedback, the environment in which the transaction takes place, or the purpose for which you have gathered.

feedback
Audience member responses, both verbal and nonverbal, to a speaker.

Messages: Content and Relational Components

The **message** is the meaning produced by the speaker and the audience members. In the transactional system modeled here, the message and the medium through which it travels are intentionally blurred. This is because the two are *interdependent*—not independent. What we would like to say to our audience is significantly affected by the manner in which we say it, and the way we convey the message is affected by what we want to say. This reciprocal process has a tremendous impact on how our message is perceived by our audience.

All messages are composed of two parts. The first part of the message is its **content,** the essential meaning, the gist or substance, of what a speaker wants to convey. For example, you might wish to convey your affection for another with the three words "I love you." The second part of a message, called its **relational component,** involves the combined impact of the verbal and nonverbal parts of that message as it is conveyed. Consider how you might use your voice, face, and eyes to alter the impact of the words "I love you." You could make these three words an expression of sincere endearment, a plea, or even a statement of wanton desire.

Meaning is derived from both the content and the relational parts of a message. Moreover, neither part is more important than the other in its contribution to meaning. What you say and how you say it contribute to the meaning in roughly equal parts.

message
The meaning produced by communicators.

content
(of messages)
The essential meaning of what a speaker wants to convey.

relational component
(of messages)
The combined impact of the verbal and nonverbal components of a message as it is conveyed.

Constructing and Interpreting Symbols

Public speaking, like other forms of communication, is symbolic.[10] Words are verbal symbols that we use to describe persons, places, and things. Gestures, too, can be nonverbal symbols, as when we wave our hand to signal good-bye or shake our fist at someone to signal that we are angry.

When we try to convey our thinking to other people, there is no way to directly communicate our ideas. Our thoughts must be converted into words and gestures whose meaning can be interpreted by those receiving the message. These words and gestures are really **symbols,** things that stand for or suggest other things by reason of relationship or association. This process of converting our thoughts and ideas into meaningful symbols is called **encoding.** These symbols are then interpreted when received by audience members, a process known as **decoding.** This is easier said than done. Whether an audience decodes a speaker's message as encoded depends on many factors, including but not limited to language, culture, age, and gender.

Although we deal with the symbolic nature of public speaking at length in Chapters 10 and 11, we mention it here because you need to understand that the meaning you attach to the verbal and nonverbal symbols you use to express yourself may not correspond to the meaning others attach to them. What's more, this may be the case even when you think you share a common language—what Americans call "gasoline," for example, is "petrol" to the British.

As you prepare your speeches, think about the degree to which you and your audience share meaning for symbols you commonly use. This means, at a minimum, checking out the degree to which you and your audience share a common language, come from a similar culture, and share a similar socioeconomic background.

Channels

A **channel** is the physical medium through which communication occurs. The transmission of the light and sound waves that make up the picture you see on your TV set requires a channel through which they can be signaled and received. Picture and audio are encoded into electronic impulses, which must be decoded by your television receiver. In human communication, we primarily use our senses as channels for the messages we send and receive. We use our voice, eyes, and body, for example, to channel our speeches, conversations, and group discussions. On occasion we also use our sense of touch, sense of smell, and even our sense of taste as channels of communication.

In the case of public speaking, we can also use supplementary channels of communication to augment the five senses. We can electronically amplify our voice so that it can be better heard or use visual aids such as poster boards, overhead transparencies, and PowerPoint slides.

Perception

The transactional system we've been describing demands that we both understand and appreciate the role of perception in public speaking. **Perception** is the process by which we give meaning to our experiences. This process begins

---

symbol
Something that stands for or suggests something else by reason of relationship or association.

encoding
The process by which ideas are translated into a code that can be understood by the receiver.

decoding
The process by which a code is translated back into ideas.

channel
The physical medium through which communication occurs.

perception
The process by which we give meaning to our experiences.

when we decide to pay attention to some stimulus that our senses detect. For example, our eyes pick up a smiling face as we walk from one class to the next. When we hear the words "What's up," also coming from the smiling face, this is what usually happens. First, we organize the facial expression and audible sound into a whole. Second, we give meaning to this whole. Third, we organize a response, smiling back and saying, "Nothing much." Such transactions not only take place in microseconds, but also require little or no conscious thought.

On one hand, the instantaneous way we make sense of and respond to the messages is essential to our survival. On the other, it also can make us overconfident and prone to making mistakes about what we sense, how we perceive what we sense, and how we respond to it. This tendency to perceive the familiar is both good and bad from the standpoint of public speaking. It is good because it enables us to quickly establish a reference point from which we can plan our own speaking behavior as well as interpret that of others. It's bad because it can blind us to other data that may be even more important to how we behave and interpret the messages of others.

As a public speaker, you can never assume that your perceptions of such things as the context, your audience, or the messages your audience feeds back to you are foolproof. Just because some person, some place, or some circumstance strikes you as familiar, that doesn't necessarily make it so.

Quick Start Guide to Your First Speech

To become a competent public speaker, you will need to get on your feet and speak to your classmates early and often. That's why we assign a brief speech in the first week or two of the term. These speeches are usually based on personal experience, such as a storytelling speech or a speech of self-introduction. Not only does this get students speaking early, it also helps classmates learn about each other, which will be important to them later as they match their speech topics to their audience. Some instructors have students create digital speeches of self-introduction, which are posted on YouTube for everyone in the class to see.

Recognizing that your instructor may also require a speech before you've had a chance to read the bulk of this book, this section takes a general look at the steps you need to follow to develop and deliver your first speech. This is not a substitute for the content to follow in later chapters, but a brief preview. The steps you need to follow in any speech are the following: (1) analyze the context and audience; (2) decide on a general purpose; (3) choose a topic; (4) construct a specific purpose; (5) develop a clear thesis statement; (6) prepare the substance of your speech; (7) organize your speech; and (8) deliver your speech.

Analyze the Context and Audience

In preparing for your first speech, you need to understand the situation and the expectations that come with it. For starters, you need to know who is in your audience. Typically you will be speaking to your classmates. You may already have come to know some of them in the first few days of class, but even if you have not, you can make certain assumptions about them based on their attendance at your university or college. Do you attend a small, rural, liberal arts

Today's public speakers need to adapt to multi-cultural, multiethnic, and multigenerational audiences.

college or a large, urban university? What are the common majors emphasized at your institution? Beyond knowing these general facts, you can also observe your classmates in the effort to discover things about them. Are most of them the same age as you, older, or younger? People of the same age tend to share many of the same experiences and cultural references. Sometimes it's helpful to visit your classmates' Facebook pages to get an idea of their interests and backgrounds.

Knowing the common experiences you share with your audience allows you to predict what topics are likely to elicit a favorable response. Factors such as the age, sex, and social status of your listeners may also help you predict audience response. Depending on who they are and what experiences they share, audience members come to any speech situation with a variety of expectations. For example, your classmates probably expect you to speak to them as a peer. If you violate that expectation, taking on an air of superiority, for example, you may not get the response you desire. Only after you thoroughly understand your speech situation, your audience, and their expectations should you begin to consider the purpose for your speech.

Choose a General Purpose

general purpose
The primary function of a speech. The three commonly agreed-upon general purposes are to inform, to persuade, and to entertain.

One of the first decisions a speaker faces is to decide on the **general purpose**—the primary function of the speech. The most common types of speeches seek to *inform* others about things they do not already know or to *persuade* others to believe or behave in certain ways. Persuasive speeches not only seek change, they also may seek to reinforce social values, as when someone gives a Fourth of July speech or a sermon. Other speeches seek to *entertain* by sharing an enjoyable experience. Obviously these general purposes are not mutually exclusive. A persuasive speech will also inform the audience, and an informative speech should be interesting enough that it encourages the audience to listen. Nevertheless, the general purpose you either have been assigned or have decided on yourself should tell you something about the topic you ultimately choose. Controversial topics, for example, lend themselves to a persuasive speech; they are less well suited to an informative speech. A speech of introduction is likely to be primarily informative—telling your classmates something about who you are. A storytelling speech, on the other hand, is often an opportunity to entertain your listeners with an amusing tale.

Choose a Topic

Once you've analyzed your audience, the situation you face, and selected a general purpose, one of the hardest things for many beginning speakers is the selection of a topic. Sometimes your instructor will do this for you, but it's just as likely you'll have to decide on a topic yourself. In many classes, the first speech you give may not require choosing a complex topic. However, even if you are simply introducing yourself or telling a story, you still need to choose what you will say about yourself or what experience you will share. Many of the same criteria that govern topic choice for research-based topics also apply to these early speeches. Like all speech topics, they should be interesting, appropriate, and worthwhile.

An obvious place to begin is with your own interests, experiences, and knowledge. Remember to look for topics as you go through your day. For example, you may see a television program, read a blog, or see a YouTube video that deals with a topic that interests you. A magazine or a newspaper may also suggest a topic. Other sources include campus publications, instructors, and fellow students. The number of places to find a good topic, in fact, is limited only by how aware you are of what's going on around you.

In addition to knowing *where* to look for a topic, it is important to know *what* to look for. First, the topic should be interesting to you. If you don't care about the topic, how can you expect your audience to care? Second, select a topic that will be interesting to the members of your audience—or at least one that can be made interesting to them. This is why it is crucial to know as much as possible about your audience. Third, your topic should be appropriate to the situation. If your instructor has asked you to speak on your pet peeve, she or he probably is thinking of topics like dorm food, roommates, or people who blow smoke in your face, not the destruction of the rain forests. Fourth, make sure your topic is appropriate to the time available. Time is a limitation facing all speakers, not just those in a public speaking class. Know what your instructor expects and stick to it. That's just one of many reasons why it is important to practice your speech in advance, making sure it fits into the allotted time. Fifth, make sure your topic is manageable. Don't pick a topic that is beyond your abilities or resources. One of your greatest assets in speaking is your own **credibility,** which is the degree to which your audience trusts and believes in you. Nothing will undermine your credibility faster than speaking on a topic with which you are unfamiliar. Know more than your audience. Why else would you speak to them? Finally, it is crucial that your topic be worthwhile. We treat time in our society as a commodity. We bank time, spend time, and buy time. You are angered if someone wastes your time, so don't waste your audience's time. If you pick a well-worn topic, then you must give it a different "spin" or focus.

credibility
The degree to which an audience trusts and believes in a speaker.

Tips and Tactics

A good speech topic should be:

1. interesting to you.
2. interesting to your audience—or at least be capable of being made interesting.
3. appropriate to the situation.
4. appropriate to the time available.
5. manageable.
6. worthwhile.

www.mhhe.com/brydon7e

To view a video of Jonathan Studebaker's Speech of Introduction, click on the Speech Coach link on our Online Learning Center Web site, and go to Segment 1.2.

specific purpose
The goal or objective a speaker hopes to achieve in speaking to a particular audience.

Construct Your Specific Purpose

You may be assigned a general purpose for your early speeches. But you will not be assigned a specific purpose. The **specific purpose** is the goal or objective you hope to achieve in speaking to a particular audience. For example, assume you are asked to introduce yourself to the rest of the class. What do you want your classmates to think and feel about you? As the speech in the In Their Own Words box "Speech of Introduction" on page 17 shows, one of our former students, Jonathan Studebaker, used the opportunity of a speech of self-introduction to inform his audience about his disability. More than that, however, he sought to educate them to understand that people with disabilities are really just like everybody else. Even in early speech assignments, you should try to articulate a specific purpose for your speech.

The specific purpose of a speech typically begins with "to." For example, Jonathan's speech had a specific purpose that could be phrased: "to inform my audience that my disability doesn't change the fact that I'm a person just like everyone else." A speaker might express a specific entertainment purpose as "to entertain my audience with the story of my worst blind date." Often our students use their storytelling speeches as an opportunity to entertain, as did one student who described her first date with a guy who showed up wearing a chicken costume and took her to dinner at KFC.

Whatever speech topic you select, therefore, you need to clarify in your own mind and for your instructor what specific purpose you intend to achieve through the speech. Make sure the specific purpose is realistic, is worthwhile for your audience, and helps you achieve your own goals as a speaker. It will make what comes next much easier.

Develop Your Thesis Statement

thesis statement
A single declarative sentence that focuses the audience's attention on the central point of a speech.

Every speech should have a central idea or point. Your **thesis statement** should help the audience understand what response you seek. For example, you might be opposed to further restrictions on what you can do in dorm rooms. Assuming you are speaking to a group of student colleagues, you may wish to focus your speech on what they can do to fight the restrictions. Thus, your thesis statement might be, "We need to lobby the board of trustees of the university to treat us like adults in

Speech of Introduction

In the 35 short years of his life, Jonathan Studebaker had an impressive list of accomplishments: honorary football coach for the East-West Shrine game (pictured here), kicking coach for the Chico State Wildcat football team, college graduate, television sports commentator, member of the Chico city planning commission, writer, motivational speaker, and founder of "Project Speak Out." Speaking was Jonathan's passion. When we interviewed him for the first edition of this book, he put it this way: "Speaking isn't broccoli; it's fun!" In the speech transcribed here, Jonathan introduces himself and explains that he is far more than a person with a disability.

WHO AM I?
by Jonathan Studebaker

Our former student, Jonathan Studebaker, is pictured here as honorary coach at the Shrine East-West game.

Good morning!

Who am I? Why am I here? Seems like I've heard that before. For myself, I've been asked these and other questions. Two of them I'd like to answer for you today.

I've been asked: "Are you a midget?" "What do you have?" "What's your disability?" "Why are you small?" But I'd really like people to ask me: "What do you like to do?" "What's your favorite color?" So what I'll try to do is answer both of these today.

I'm a nice guy. Don't worry, I won't bite. I like to do many things, except water ski. I've gone to school. I've gone to elementary school, high school, and I graduated from Cal State Chico. A lot of people ask, "So why are you here?" Well, I'm here because I want to educate others. I've coached football at Chico State University. I was the kicking coach for three years. And out of those three years I had two kickers make first team all-conference. So how do you coach football? You do it by simply telling people what to do. Well, how do you do that? You do it by doing a lot of the things that we all do—by studying, by reading, by listening to others. And that's what I've done throughout my life, and that is what made me who I am.

Like I said, I'm a nice person. I'm cheerful, I'm energetic. Okay, so I have a disability. I was born with osteogenesis imperfecta, a disease which causes my bones to be fragile. Have you ever accidentally dropped a glass on the floor? What happens? It breaks. Well, my bones kind of break like glass, which is why I tell people, when you carry me, treat me like your best crystal. I'm happy about being who I am. I wouldn't change a thing. I've done a lot of things in my life. Like I said, I've coached football, I graduated from college, things that people wouldn't think a person with my condition would do.

So who am I? Well, I'm Jonathan Studebaker, Jonathan Peter Charles Studebaker. Why such a long name? Well, my middle name is Charles, which came later. And Charles is kind of a symbol of a lot of things. My dad used to call me chicken when I was younger. And then it evolved to chicken Charles, and now Charles. Now, some of you might be offended by being called chicken. But, you know what, it doesn't matter to me. I like being who I am. I've been put here to educate others, not by teaching others, but by just being myself.

Thank you.

Excerpted from TWENTY-FIRST CENTURY SELLING. © Dr. Loretta Malandro. Taught in her program "Speak With Impact," offered by Malandro Communication, Inc., Scottsdale, Arizona.

our own homes." Notice that the thesis statement here is directly related to the specific purpose of your speech. In this instance, your specific purpose is "to convince other students to lobby the board of trustees to stop the proposed restrictions." The thesis statement, if accepted and acted upon by the audience, will fulfill your specific purpose. While the specific purpose expresses your goal for the audience's response to the speech, the thesis statement expresses the essential message that is designed to fulfill that purpose. The specific purpose is not normally stated explicitly to the audience, but the thesis statement should be sufficiently related to that purpose to allow the audience to know what you want to accomplish.

Prepare Your Speech

invention

The creative process by which the substance of a speech is generated.

The ancient Greeks called the creative process by which the substance of a speech is generated **invention.** It may seem odd, at first, to think of a speech as an invention. However, just as it was not enough for the designers at Apple to have the idea for the iPad, it is not enough for you just to have an idea for a speech. You need to invest time and effort in inventing the substance of what you plan to say. Where do you go for the substance of your speech? Here are some general suggestions, which we develop in more detail in Chapter 6.

Personal Experience

Particularly in your first speeches, a good place to begin is with your own experiences. Each of us has had experiences that make us unique. You may be able to rely on hobbies or past job experiences for an early informative speech; for example, one of our students who worked as a beekeeper gave a fascinating speech on honeybees.

Outside Sources

Even though your personal experience and knowledge are good sources with which to start, don't stop there. No matter how intense your experience or extensive your knowledge, there is always more to learn. For example, our student beekeeper supplemented his speech with quotes from a book he called "The Bible of Beekeeping."

When we are given a topic to research, most of us head immediately for our computer and access a free search engine such as Google or Bing. Unfortunately, most searches reveal millions of "hits," and there's no easy way to distinguish between reliable and valid sites, and those that are just popular.

One of the great benefits of being a college student is that you have resources available to you for research purposes that go beyond those available to the average person. For example, not only do you have access to a physical library, housing thousands—perhaps millions—of books, periodicals, and documents, you may also have access to innumerable proprietary computer resources. For instance, many students have access to databases such as *Academic Search,* which indexes over four thousand periodicals covering everything from the sciences and humanities to popular culture.

Finally, you may be able to gain information from interviews with experts. College campuses abound with faculty experts on topics ranging from anthropology to zoology. Check your college Web site for faculty with specialties related to your topic. You may be pleasantly surprised at how much information you can glean from a well-planned interview. In Chapters 6 and 7 we will cover the process of speech preparation in much more detail.

Regardless of where you find your information, whether from written sources, the Internet, or interviews, remember to carefully record the facts and quotations you discover. Note not only what was said but also who said it, when, and where. Orally citing your evidence for an audience will build your credibility, which will enhance the likelihood you will be effective in delivering your speech.

Organize Your Speech

Someone once said that every speech has three tell 'ems. First you tell 'em what you are going to tell 'em; then you tell 'em; and, finally, you tell 'em what you told 'em. Although a bit simplistic, this captures the basic idea of the three parts of every speech: the introduction, the body, and the conclusion.

Though there are many ways to organize your speech, one of the most helpful patterns we have found for our own students is an adaptation of a system developed by Dr. Loretta Malandro for the business executives she coaches.[11] According to Dr. Malandro, the traditional introduction, body, and conclusion of a speech should include seven important steps. Steps 1–4 are the introduction, step 5 is the body of the speech, and steps 6 and 7 are the conclusion.

Tips and Tactics

Seven Steps for Organizing Your Speech

1. *Open with impact.* In this step you capture your audience's attention.
2. *Focus on your thesis statement.* In this step you draw the audience's attention to the central point of your speech.
3. *Connect with your audience.* In this step you let the audience know "what's in it for them."
4. *Preview the body of your speech.* This is where you tell your audience what you are going to tell them in the body of the speech.
5. *Present your main points.* In this step you present the body of your speech. This step constitutes the bulk of your presentation.
6. *Summarize your main points.* In this step you tell the audience what you've told them.
7. *Close with impact.* In this step you leave your audience with a lasting impression.

Let's briefly examine each of these steps and how they relate to the traditional introduction–body–conclusion format of a speech. This relationship is illustrated in Exhibit 1.3.

Introduction

To present an effective introduction, you should follow four steps.

Open with Impact   Introduce your presentation dramatically or humorously. There's no surer turn-off than beginning a speech, "Uh, um, well, I guess I'll talk about dorm food today." Begin the speech with something that captures your

Exhibit 1.3

Organizing Your Speech
This seven-step organizational pattern relates closely to the traditional introduction–body–conclusion pattern.

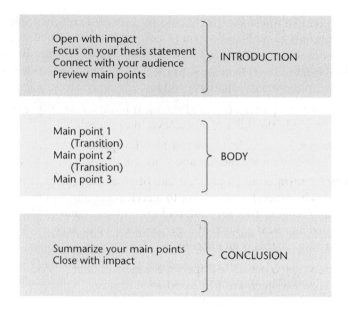

Open with impact
Focus on your thesis statement
Connect with your audience
Preview main points
} INTRODUCTION

Main point 1
   (Transition)
Main point 2
   (Transition)
Main point 3
} BODY

Summarize your main points
Close with impact
} CONCLUSION

audience's attention, such as an appropriate joke, a startling statistic, an anecdote, or a reference to current affairs.

Focus on Your Thesis Statement   As we noted earlier, the thesis statement captures the central point of your speech. For example, if you are opposed to a planned tuition hike on your campus, you should state clearly, "The students of this campus should not be forced to pay more for less."

Connect with Your Audience   Answer the questions "What's in this for my audience?" and "Why is it in their personal or professional interest to listen to me?" For example, will the proposed tuition hike keep some in your audience from completing their degrees? Make the connection to your specific audience clear in the introduction to the speech. This is also a good place to build your credibility as a speaker. Let the audience members know you understand their concerns and have their best interests at heart. If you have expertise on the topic, let your listeners know this now so that they can appreciate what is to come.

Preview   Generally, people like a road map of the territory they're entering. The **preview** provides your listeners with a forecast of where you are taking them. Although a preview of points is generally a good idea, there may be exceptions. For example, in a storytelling speech, a preview may destroy the impact of a surprise ending. Depending on the nature of the assignment, therefore, your first speech may not require a preview.

preview
A forecast of the main points of a speech.

Body

The majority of your speech should develop the thesis you are trying to convey. Usually, the body of the speech is divided into three to five main points that together develop the thesis of your speech.

Organize Your Main Points A speech that wanders off the topic or doesn't follow a logical pattern of development is likely to lose the audience. The same is true of an overly complex speech. Here are some basic patterns for organizing your **main points,** which are the key ideas that support the thesis of a speech:

- *Time pattern.* Most stories are arranged chronologically. The use of a narrative or time pattern is one of the most basic forms of speech making and is commonly the basis of any storytelling speech.
- *Spatial pattern.* Some topics are best dealt with spatially. A speech on the solar system might begin with the sun and work out to the most distant planets.
- *Categorical pattern.* Many topics fall into obvious categories. A teacher explaining the federal government to a civics class, for example, is likely to talk about the legislative, judicial, and executive branches. This is sometimes called a topical pattern of organization. If a topic lends itself to natural divisions, this is an excellent way to arrange your speech.

These three ways to organize a speech are summarized in Exhibit 1.4. Other ways to organize a speech are discussed at length in Chapter 9. For now, this

main points
The key ideas that support the thesis statement of a speech.

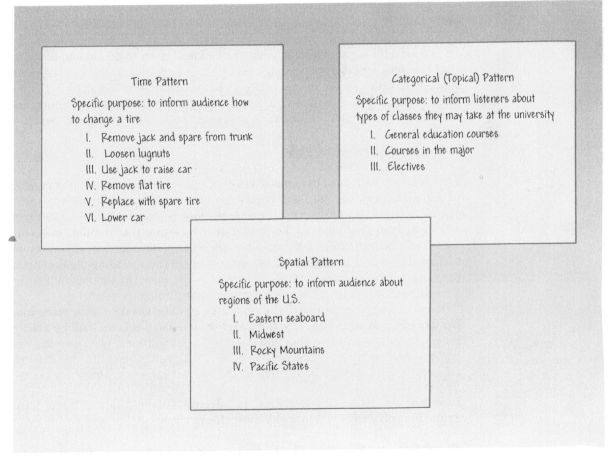

Exhibit 1.4
Common Patterns for Organizing the Main Points of a Speech

will give you a start. The key thing to remember in this regard is to pick a simple pattern and stick with it for the entire speech.

Provide Transitions   We also want to emphasize the importance of using transitional statements, sometimes called **signposts,** that bridge your main points. For example, you might say something as simple as, "My second point is . . ." or "Now that you understand the problem, let's examine some possible solutions." The goal in using transitions is to provide your listeners with guides along the path of your speech so that they will know where you have been, where you are, and where you are going next.

signposts
Transitional statements
that bridge main points.

Conclusion

All too often, speakers invest so much energy in developing the introduction and body of their speeches that they run out of gas at the end. The impact with which you conclude a speech is just as important as the impact with which you began. The key parts of a conclusion are the summary and the close.

Summarize   Tell 'em what you've told 'em. That is the first and most important function of a conclusion. Remind the listeners of what they've heard.

Close with Impact   Just as a salesperson doesn't like the customer to walk out the door without buying something, you don't want your audience to leave without at least thinking about doing what you've asked them to do. So find a way to reinforce your specific purpose. It's also your last chance to leave a favorable impression. Listeners are turned off by a poor conclusion, such as "Well, I guess that's about it." Finish with a flourish that is as powerful as your opening. So, conclude your speech by *summarizing* your main points and *closing with impact*.

Deliver Your Speech

Most important step!

There's a story told about the great speaker of ancient Greece, Demosthenes, who said that the first, second, and third most important things in rhetoric are—delivery, delivery, and delivery.[12] No matter how well thought-out your speech, or how many hours you put in at the library, or how elegant your outline, unless the speech is effectively presented, your message will not have its desired impact. In Chapter 11 we deal at length with the nature of delivery, including the important functions nonverbal communication serves for a speaker. In the meantime, the following guidelines will help you present your beginning speeches.

Keep in mind that you have three tools as a public speaker: your *voice,* your *face and eyes,* and your *body.* If you manage these effectively, you will be able to get your message across to your audience.

Use Your Voice Effectively

How you use your voice is critical to effective communication. Some basic guidelines will enable you to speak most effectively.

Speak Conversationally   Think of public speaking as heightened conversation. Don't attempt to emulate political orators: Most audiences are put off by their techniques. Speak as you do in conversation, but enlarge your voice sufficiently to be heard by all in the room. Avoid shouting. This not only strains your voice but can alienate your audience. It is certainly appropriate and even advisable to ask those in the back of the room if they can hear you, should there be any doubt.

Vary Your Voice   Nothing is more deadly to a speech than a monotone voice. Vary the rate at which you speak, the pitch (high or low) at which you speak, and the volume (loudness). The goal is to present your speech enthusiastically, sincerely, and energetically. Let the audience know you care about your topic and them.

Use Your Face and Eyes Effectively

The face is one of the most complex and expressive parts of our anatomy, capable of communicating thousands of messages. Use your facial expression to reinforce your verbal message. The eyes, in particular, convey a great deal. Consider a person who gazes at you without pause. This will tend to make you uncomfortable. On the other hand, in our mainstream North American culture, a person who refuses to look at us communicates a negative message. As a speaker communicating to a mainstream North American audience, therefore, maintain eye contact. This does not mean staring at just one portion of the room or shifting your eyes randomly. Rather, look at one member of your audience, then shift your gaze to another member, and so on. Be alert for audience responses to what you are saying. Are people restless, interested, puzzled? Such feedback can help you adapt to the audience as you speak.

Use Your Body Effectively

Your body is the third tool you use to communicate your message through *posture, movement, gestures,* and *dress.*

Posture   How do you want to stand during your speech? Some speakers are comfortable behind a lectern, whereas others prefer to move away from it or dispense with it entirely. Choosing not to use a lectern can be an effective way of lessening the physical and psychological distance between yourself and the audience. If your preference is to use a lectern, do not use it as a crutch or bass drum. Avoid leaning on or clutching the stand, as well as beating on it with your open palm. Instead, find a comfortable, erect posture and stand slightly behind the lectern. Keep in mind that to breathe effectively you need to have good body posture.

Movement   Movement should be spontaneous and meaningful. Though good speakers avoid pacing and random movements, it is perfectly appropriate–in fact, desirable–to move to emphasize an important idea or a transition between points. There is no reason a speaker's feet have to be nailed to the floor. Use your body to communicate your message whenever possible.

Gestures   It is common in everyday conversation to gesture with your hands. In fact, try this experiment: Give someone directions *without* moving your hands. You will find it virtually impossible. The key to effective use of gestures in a public speech is that they should be appropriate to the point you are making and clearly visible to your audience. The larger the room, the larger the gesture needs to be for your audience to see it. On the other hand, too many gestures, especially if they appear to be the result of nervousness, such as fidgeting, can be distracting to an audience. Finally, your gestures should be natural extensions of what you do in everyday conversation. They should never be or appear to be forced or rehearsed.

IN THEIR OWN WORDS

ARE YOU "SUIT"ED FOR SUCCESS?
By Gino Perrotte

"What should I wear?" You ask yourself this question as you look through your closet. The university's career fair is tomorrow and you want to be prepared to make a good first impression with potential employers. Perhaps the outfit you choose will give you a competitive advantage over other students at the fair. Can professional attire really make you stand out from the crowd? Yes, it can! According to Jacqueline Whitmore, author of the book *"Business Class Etiquette Essentials for Success at Work,"* clothes can either detract from or enhance a person's appearance (2005, p. 34).

Just as you would want to make a good first impression with potential employers at a career fair, it is equally important to do so when speaking to an audience. That is why I require students to dress professionally for their presentations. Dressing well increases an audience's perception of a speaker's overall competence.

It is important to note that being well dressed is not a substitute for planning and delivering a good, solid speech. What it does mean is that having an appropriate style of dress allows you to step up to the next level of credibility with your audience. Appropriate attire says that you respect yourself (p. 33). Companies develop strict dress codes in order to create a respectable professional image for their business. Young professionals realize quickly that a formal style of business attire projects competence (Cardon & Okoro, 2009).

Obviously, it is important that your speech day attire enhances your appeal and credibility for the audience. The following tips inform you of the most common things that college students need to be aware of when it comes to presenting a professional, competent image on speech day.

These tips provided by both professionals and students should be your guide for dressing appropriately on your speech day. Remember that your professional look will add to your credibility as a speaker. If you commit yourself to dressing well, then you are on your way to being well "suit"ed for success.

Mr. Gino Perrotte (M.A., University of Central Florida) is a public speaking and interpersonal communication instructor at the University of Central Florida's Nicholson School of Communication. Mr. Perrotte's professional experience includes several HR functions such as interviewing, hiring and policy making.

References

Cardon, P. W., & Okoro, E. A. (2009). Professional Characteristics Communicated by Formal Versus Casual Workplace Attire. *Business Communication Quarterly*, 72(3), 355–360.

Haefner, R. (2008, July 30). *How to dress for success for work.* Retrieved January 26, 2011 from http://www.cnn.com/2008/LIVING/worklife/07/30/cb.dress.for.success/index.html

Whitmore, J. (2005). Business Class etiquette essentials for success at work. New York, NY: St. Martin's Press.

Tips and Tactics

Workplace Professionals

What NOT to Wear:

- Worn/scuffed shoes
- Heavy perfume/cologne
- Stained/wrinkled clothes
- Excessive jewelry
- Sneakers
- Night club attire
  (Whitmore, 2005, p. 37)

- Flip flops
- Mini-skirts
- Sleeveless shirts
- Jeans
  (Haefner, 2008)

This group of business-people illustrates business casual dress appropriate for most public speaking situations.

Tips and Tactics

Tips from Students

Yes, Wear It!	Don't Even Think About It!
• Ties	• Stiletto heels
• Dress pants and a nice belt	• Excessive makeup
• 3 to 4 inch heels or flat dress shoes	• Distracting hair
• Collared shirts	• Hats
• Tailored skirts within 2 inches of the knee	• Too big or too tight clothing
• Suits	• Shorts

Dress Your dress as a speaker should be *appropriate* to the situation and the audience. A good rule of thumb is business casual in a classroom. As you can see in the photo above, business casual is a step above what you normally might wear to class, but a step below more formal dress. People make instant judgments about other people and, as one shampoo ad proclaims, "You never get a second chance to make a first impression." In no case should your dress detract from the message you want to convey.

Methods of Delivery

There are four common ways to deliver a speech:

- Write out a *manuscript* and read it to your audience.
- *Memorize* your speech and recite it from memory.
- Present a spontaneous, unrehearsed *impromptu* presentation.
- Combine preparation and spontaneity in an *extemporaneous* presentation.

extemporaneous delivery

A mode of presentation that combines careful preparation with spontaneous speaking. The speaker generally uses brief notes rather than a full manuscript or an outline.

Each type of delivery has its advantages and limitations, which we discuss in more detail in Chapter 11. However, for now we highly recommend an **extemporaneous** mode of delivery, a mode of presentation that combines careful preparation with spontaneous speaking. You generally use brief notes rather than a full manuscript or an outline. You avoid the challenges of speaking "off the cuff" while at the same time maintaining eye contact with your audience, something that often is lost when reading from a manuscript. Only the most experienced speakers should rely solely on memory when delivering their speeches. The extemporaneous method allows you to be prepared yet flexible. If you see from the audience feedback that people are lost, you can re-explain a point or add another example. If the audience seems bored, you might skip ahead to your most interesting example. An extemporaneous speech should be a true transaction between speaker and listener.

IN THEIR OWN WORDS

JUST B-R-E-A-T-H-E!
By Shari Hodgson

According to the National Association of Colleges and Employers (2009), the number one skill on employers' wish lists for college graduates is the ability to effectively speak publically. Unfortunately, speaking publically is also the number one fear of most people (Motley, 1997). While teaching public speaking at the University of Central Florida, I have helped students cope and reduce their speaker anxiety by incorporating a systematic process called "BREATHE" while preparing for speech assignments.

The B-R-E-A-T-H-E Process
B = Brain and the F.E.A.R. (false evidence appearing real) response process

Shari Hodgson has been an instructor at UCF, Nicholson School of Communication, for 22 years. She has taught several courses in Interpersonal and Organizational Communication, as well as the basic public speaking course. Ms. Hodgson has also been a private consultant to businesses and attorneys.

More than 100 billion nerve cells comprise a network of neural pathways that begin the process of everything we think, feel and do (LeDoux, 1991). The brain's fear response is autonomic so we don't know what's happening until it is too late to reduce (Behnke & Sawyer, 1999). The following sequence exhibits the physical phenomenon on our body during the fear response.

When you experience fear, the blood rushes to the parts of the brain that alert the body to take action; NOT, to the part of the brain that remembers your speech. To reduce this effect, you must **reframe** the way to think of yourself and the public speaking situation to reduce fear and produce successful results.

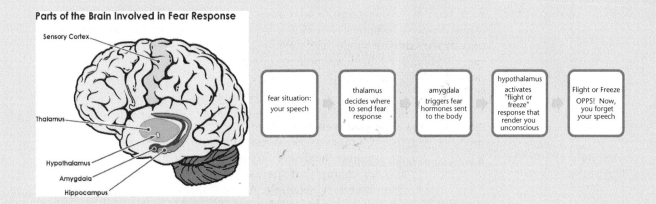

Parts of the Brain Involved in Fear Response

Sensory Cortex
Thalamus
Hypothalamus
Amygdala
Hippocampus

| fear situation: your speech | → | thalamus decides where to send fear response | → | amygdala triggers fear hormones sent to the body | → | hypothalamus activates "flight or freeze" response that render you unconscious | → | Flight or Freeze OPPS! Now, you forget your speech |

R = Reframe with new thoughts

You may not always choose <u>what</u> situations you face but you can choose <u>how</u> you will experience these situations. Your beliefs about giving a speech are scaring you, NOT, the actual upcoming speech event (Lefkoe, 2001). Your thoughts create your feelings that trigger actions that will lead to your demise.

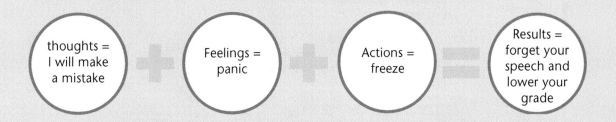

thoughts = I will make a mistake + Feelings = panic + Actions = freeze = Results = forget your speech and lower your grade

As you plan and practice your speech, use this 4-step process to help you **reframe** your thinking.

1. First, acknowledge you're fear thoughts and think, "Wow, I just scared myself."

2. Second, accept that these thoughts are based on old beliefs about being judged or ridiculed and think, "Is this fear really real for the speech situation today?"

3. Third, know that you have new skills and say, "I am prepared and ready to speak!"

4. Fourth, state these new beliefs and repeat 10 times a day, "I am a good speaker!" With this new thought your results will begin to change. Confident people simply *believe* that they are competent. While you are reframing old beliefs into new beliefs, you can further manage the brain's fear response by **envisioning** yourself as successful.

E = Envision yourself successful by reprogramming your brain

The next two techniques will help you reprogram the old vision of making mistakes during your speech to seeing yourself successful and confident (Bandler & Grinder, 1981).

1. *Relaxation Techniques:* Get into a relaxed state, preferably with eyes closed and in a quiet place. REPEAT the new message you used when reframing your thoughts, "I am prepared and excited about..." Because you are relaxed, the new message is

programmed directly to your sub-conscious mind. When you associate this positive message with speaking, the message will work at a deeper internal level to quickly alleviate your anxiety and increase your chances for success and a higher grade. (Lefkoe, 2001).

2. *Natural Programming:* Every day of your life you go through some natural programming of your brain. Can you ever get away from the messages constantly transmitted by the media, music, texting, your friends, family, and school outcomes? This constant barrage may be preventing you from engaging in the process of thinking positively about yourself. Monitor the messages you are listening and programming into your brain. By more carefully selecting messages, you will naturally create new positive thought patterns. However, this reprogramming does take **practice and repetition** (Butler, Chapman, Forman, & Beck, 2006).

A = Apply through practice

Repetition of a skill causes the brain to assign extra neurons to the practice of this skill (Sousa, 2001) much the same way that a computer assigns more memory for more complex software. If you want your speaking ability to improve, you will need to practice your speeches in a way that increases the effectiveness of your practice sessions. Here are a few tips:

1. Be motivated to practice and plan. I recommend 15 practice sessions and in front of classmates!

2. Your instructor will provide you with a grading rubric. Use this rubric to develop speech content and evaluate your progress during practice sessions.

3. Know what extemporaneous delivery components are required and practice <u>all</u> of them. For example, if your speech requires that you use PowerPoint or another visual aid, make sure you include appropriate gestures and movement associated with PowerPoint in your practice.

4. Get help and appropriate feedback to help you analyze your practice progress. Practice with classmates familiar with speech requirements and able to give constructive criticism that *tests* your level of anxiety.

T = Test your plan for speech day

Test all of your speech day activities to reduce any unexpected disasters. Plan your clothing, complete your note cards, and check your PPT slides the night before speaking. On the day of your speech, plan extra time for traveling to class. While in route, practice your new *positive self-talk and visualize* yourself giving a successful speech. When you arrive, check the classroom technology.

H = Handle your negative thoughts

But what if things don't go exactly as planned? Even the most planned speeches are not perfect. *While you are waiting to speak*, remember to reprogram your negative thoughts to positive: "I am prepared and excited about giving my speech. *During the speech* if something unexpected happens, acknowledge it and remind yourself: "No one knows what I don't know and I am well prepared." *After your speech*, if you think negative self-talk like, "I forgot my facts and looked dumb," *immediately reframe and repeat* positive thoughts: "I enjoyed giving my speech and I did my best. "No matter what happens, *CELEBRATE yourself*. Repeat this statement 15 times: "I did the best job possible when giving my speech!"

E = End your fear cycle

By understanding your <u>brain's</u> fear response, <u>reframing</u> your thoughts, <u>envisioning</u> your success, <u>applying</u> yourself through practice, <u>testing</u> your speech plan, and <u>handling</u> *negative* <u>thoughts</u> before, during and after your speech, you can <u>end the fear</u> response cycle. You will actually change your brain and reduce your fear of the public speaking experience.

(NOTE: If you experience severe symptoms of anxiety such as shortness of breath, disori-entation, heart palpitations, numbness, or nausea you may suffer from 'communication apprehension' which is estimated to affect about 16% of the American population. Communication Apprehension (CA) sometimes extends to other speaking situations like meeting new people or participating in class discussions. The next chapter includes a Self-Assessment of CA and an in-depth discussion of possible causes and coping strategies.)

References

Bandler, R., & Grinder, J. (1981). TRANCE-formations: *Neuro-Linguistic Programming and the structure of Hypnosis*. Salt Lake City, UT: Real People Press.

Butler, A. C., Chapman, J. D., Forman, E. M., & Beck, A. T. (2006). The empirical status of cognitive-behavioral therapy, *Clinical Psychology Review*, 26, 17–31.

Richmond, V. P., & McCroskey, J. C., (1995). Communication: Apprehension, avoidance, and effectiveness (4th Ed.). Scottsdale, AZ: Gorsuch Scarisbrick.

Behnke, R. R., and Sawyer, C. R. (1999). The prediction of a state of uneasiness as perceived by individuals. *Journal of Applied Communication*, 8, 98–102.

Cameron-Bandler, L., Gordan, D., & Lebeau, M. (1985). *The Emprint Method: a Guide to Reproducing Competence*. San Rafael, CA: The Future Press.

Clements, K., and Turpin, G. (1996) Physiological effects of public speaking assessed using a measure of palmar sweating. *Journal of Psychophysiology*, 10, 238–290.

"Fear and the Amygdala," http://www.sfn.org. Society for Neuroscience: Brain Briefings. Web. 10 December 2010.

LeDoux, J. (1991). Emotion and the limbic system concept. *Concepts in Neuroscience*, 2, 169–99.

Lefkoe, M. (2001a). Behavior change doesn't have to be difficult. *California Psychologist*, 34, 24–25.

Lefkoe, M. (2001b). Everyone knows that you can't eliminate fundamental beliefs: are you sure? *California Therapist*, May, 54–60.

Motley, M. T. (1997). *Overcoming your fear of public speaking: a proven method*. Boston, MA: Houghton Mifflin.

NACE (2009). *Employers site qualities, attributes of "perfect" job candidate*. Retrieved December 10, from http://www.naceweb.org/Press/Release/Employers.

Sousa, D. (2001). *How the Brain Learns (2nd ed.)*. Thousand Oaks, CA: Sage.

Summary

There are many good reasons to study and practice public speaking. Among them are these:

- Personal reasons, including personal satisfaction, empowering yourself and others.

- Professional reasons, including self-promotion, presenting ideas to decision makers, creating positive change in the workplace, and contributing worth-while ideas in meetings.

www.mhhe.com/brydon7e

To evaluate your understand-ing of this chapter, visit our Online Learning Center Web site for quizzes and other chapter study aids.

- Public reasons that help us become civically engaged, including becoming a critical thinker, functioning as an informed citizen, enhancing freedom of speech, and promoting civil discourse.

The public speaking transaction is an extension and refinement of everyday communication skills, including these important interdependent parts:

- The context or situation
- The speaker and the audience
- The message, including content and relational components
- Verbal and nonverbal symbols
- Channels
- Perception

In preparing for your first speeches, keep in mind the following:

- Analyze the context and audience.
- Choose a general purpose.
- Choose a topic.
- Construct your specific purpose.
- Develop a clear thesis statement.
- Prepare the substance of your speech.
- Organize your speech to (1) open with impact, (2) focus on your thesis statement, (3) connect with your audience, (4) preview the body of your speech, (5) present your main points, (6) summarize your main points, and (7) close with impact.
- Deliver your speech extemporaneously, using your voice, face and eyes, and body.
- Dress for Success suggestions
- B-R-E-A-T-H-E tactics

Check Your Understanding: Exercises and Activities

1. This chapter suggests that public speaking can empower you. How can public speaking skills empower you to satisfy your most pressing personal and professional needs? Write a short paper or give a brief speech explaining your answer and giving examples.

2. How important are public speaking skills in the profession for which you are preparing? If possible, interview either a practitioner of the profession or a professor in the appropriate department about the ways public speaking might be applicable in your field. Give a brief (one- to two-minute) presentation to your classmates, or write a short paper about your findings.

3. Attend a meeting of a local government agency, such as a city council, planning commission, or board of supervisors, or attend a student government meeting on your campus. Chances are you will see several

speakers present their views in a public forum. Write a short paper about one of the speakers. What impressed you most about the speaker, and what impressed you least? How did the ability to speak help this person achieve his or her goals?

4. Write a one- or two-page analysis of the audience for your first speech. What characteristics do your classmates seem to have in common? Are they similar to or dissimilar from you in age, social status, and background? What assumptions can you make about them based on their attendance at your university or college? How will what you know about your classmates affect your choice of speech topic and specific purpose?

5. Come up with three possible topics for your first speech. For each topic, consider whether it is (a) interesting to you, (b) interesting to your audience, (c) appropriate to the situation, (d) appropriate to the time available, (e) manageable, and (f) worthwhile. Based on this analysis, which topic do you believe is best for your first speech?

6. Once you have selected the best topic, determine what general purpose it would fulfill and phrase a specific purpose that you would hope to achieve in presenting the speech.

7. Make a list of appropriate sources for information about the topic you have chosen for your first speech.

8. Create a brief one- to two-minute digital speech of self-introduction. You will be paired with another student, and each of you will digitally record the other with a cell phone video or the new "flip" camera technology. All self-introductions are posted on YouTube and viewed in class. Guidelines of possible material for introductions include: *How long have you lived in the United States? Where are you from originally? What kind of person are you? Name one or two personal strengths. What are your future career goals? What majors interest you? What are some things or activities you like?* You may use note cards and are encouraged to practice several times before hitting the record button. You must also watch at least four classmates' digital self-introductions and comment on them using the course online discussion board. You will upload their speech to YouTube and send your instructor the link to the video. (Thanks to Dr. Nichola Gutgold for sharing this assignment.)

Notes

1. National Association of Colleges and Employers, "Employers Cite Communication Skills as Key, But Say Many Job Seekers Don't Have Them," 26 April 2006. [Retrieved from http://www.naceweb.org/press/display.asp?year[H11005]2006&prid[H11005]235, 12 November 2006.]

2. Steven R. Brydon and Michael D. Scott: *Between One and Many: The Art and Science of Public Speaking,* 6th ed. (New York: McGraw-Hill, 2008), 5.

3. Brydon and Scott: *Between One and Many,* 6th ed., 5.

4. Personal communication, 7 May 2007.

5. Kourtney Jason, "Chico State Takes Back the Night at Annual Event," *The Orion,* 25 October 2006. [Retrieved from http://media.www.theorion.com/media/storage/paper889/news/2006/10/25/News/Chico.State.Takes.Back.The.Night.At.Annual.Event-2407174.shtml, 12 November 2006.]

6. Ronald B. Adler, *Communicating at Work: Principles and Practices for Business and the Professions,* 3rd ed. (New York: Random House, 1989), 4.

7. Adler, *Communicating at Work,* 216.

8. Sam Stein, "McCain Faces Backlash over Rabid Crowds," *The Huffington Post,* 10 October 2008 [Retrieved from http://www.huffingtonpost.com/2008/10/10/mccain-defends-his-rabid_n_133710.html, 23 June 2009.]

9. Lloyd Bitzer, "The Rhetorical Situation," *Philosophy and Rhetoric* 1 (1968): 1–14.

10. W. Barnett Pearce and Vernon E. Cronen, *Communication, Action and Meaning: The Creation of Social Realities* (New York: Praeger, 1980).

11. The formula was originally developed by Dr. Loretta Malandro and is taught in her program "Speak With Impact," offered by Malandro Communication Inc., Scottsdale, Arizona. We have modified it to add a preview to the introduction.

12. George Kennedy, *The Art of Persuasion in Greece* (Princeton, N.J.: Princeton University Press, 1963), 283.

UNDERSTANDING COMMUNICATION APPREHENSION

— Dr. Jeff Butler

Objectives

After reading this chapter, you should be able to:

- Explain the differences between normal anxiety and communication apprehension.

- Identify and explain the four potential causes of communication apprehension.

- Explain how and why culture can affect a person's level of communication apprehension.

- Recognize the potential effects of communication apprehension, especially those that pertain to academic success.

- Understand and use the skills that have been shown to reduce the effects of communication apprehension.

Key Concepts

collectivistic cultures

communibiology

communication apprehension

environmental reinforcers

generalized anxiety

genetic contributors

individualistic cultures

kinesics

learned helplessness

negative self-talk

positive self-talk

proactive imagination

self-talk

SELF-ASSESSMENT

How Anxious Are You About Public Speaking?

The following scale measures communication anxiety in general, as well as anxiety resulting from communication in four specific contexts: (1) dyads, (2) small groups, (3) meetings, and (4) public settings. Upon completion of the measure, you may find that although your overall score is indicative of mild levels of communication anxiety, you are moderately to highly anxious about communicating in one or more specific contexts. Some research, for example, indicates that communicating in groups, meetings, and public settings is most anxiety arousing for students much like you. In any case, the techniques introduced in this chapter will help you cope with your communication anxieties, regardless of their contextual source.

Personal Report of Communication Apprehension (PRCA-24)

Directions: This instrument is composed of 24 statements concerning your feelings about communication with other people. Please indicate in the space provided the degree to which each statement applies to you by marking whether you (1) Strongly Agree, (2) Agree, (3) Are Undecided, (4) Disagree, or (5) Strongly Disagree with each statement. There are no right or wrong answers. Many of the statements are similar to other statements. Do not be concerned about this. Work quickly; just record your first impression.

_____ 1. I dislike participating in group discussions.

_____ 2. Generally, I am comfortable while participating in a group discussion.

_____ 3. I am tense and nervous while participating in group discussions.

_____ 4. I like to get involved in group discussions.

_____ 5. Engaging in a group discussion with new people makes me tense and nervous.

_____ 6. I am calm and relaxed while participating in group discussions.

_____ 7. Generally, I am nervous when I have to participate in a meeting.

_____ 8. Usually I am calm and relaxed while participating in meetings.

_____ 9. I am very calm and relaxed when I am called upon to express an opinion at a meeting.

_____ 10. I am afraid to express myself at meetings.

_____ 11. Communicating at meetings usually makes me uncomfortable.

_____ 12. I am very relaxed when answering questions at a meeting.

_____ 13. While participating in a conversation with a new acquaintance, I feel very nervous.

_____ 14. I have no fear of speaking up in conversations.

_____ 15. Ordinarily I am very tense and nervous in conversations.

_____ 16. Ordinarily I am very calm and relaxed in conversations.

_____ 17. While conversing with a new acquaintance, I feel very relaxed.

_____ 18. I'm afraid to speak up in conversations.

_____ 19. I have no fear of giving a speech.

_____ 20. Certain parts of my body feel very tense and rigid while giving a speech.

_____ 21. I feel relaxed while giving a speech.

_____ 22. My thoughts become confused and jumbled when I am giving a speech.

_____ 23. I face the prospect of giving a speech with confidence.

_____ 24. While giving a speech I get so nervous, I forget facts I really know.

Scoring

To determine your anxiety level, compute the following formulas. The higher your score, the more significant your level of anxiety. (The numbers in parentheses in the formulas refer to the numbered questions above.)

Group = 18 − (1) + (2) − (3) + (4) − (5) + (6)

Meeting = 18 − (7) + (8) + (9) − (10) − (11) + (12)

Dyadic = 18 − (13) + (14) − (15) + (16) + (17) − (18)

Public = 18 + (19) − (20) + (21) − (22) + (23) − (24)

Overall CA = Group + Meeting + Dyadic + Public

Making Sense of Your Score

Your combined score for all 24 items should fall somewhere between 24 and 120. If your score is lower than 24 or higher than 120, you need to recalculate it. A score above 83 indicates high communication apprehension; a score between 55 and 83 indicates moderate apprehension, which is the norm for most people. Low apprehension is anything less than 55. Your subscores indicate the degree to which you are anxious when speaking in public, talking in a meeting or group, or engaging in conversation with another person. These scores can range between 6 and 30. The higher your score is, the more anxiety you feel. A score above 18 on the public speaking subset suggests you feel a manageable level of speech anxiety. Regardless of your score on this subset, you can significantly benefit from the skills and techniques presented in this chapter. A score of 18 or above on the other three subsets also suggests you feel some anxiety about interpersonal, meeting, and group communication.

Source: James C. McCroskey, *An Introduction to Rhetorical Communication,* 7th ed. (Needham Heights, Mass.: Allyn & Bacon, 1997). Reprinted by permission.

Communication apprehension can affect all areas of our lives–academic, personal and professional. This chapter will introduce you to this common phobia, and explain the differences between communication apprehension and normal speaker anxiety. Next, it will examine some of the causes of communication apprehension, including genetic and environmental factors, cultural influences and personality traits. Then, it will discuss the effects it has on your academic career. Finally, you will learn some skills to reduce communication apprehension.

Is Speaking Anxiety Normal?

This chapter is about a common phobia called communication apprehension. Before discussing details about this phobia, it's important that we distinguish between normal speaking anxiety and communication apprehension.

Most people, even experienced communicators, feel some anxiety before (or during) a speech, presentation, or even just a normal conversation with someone new. This anxiety often takes the form of "butterflies" in your stomach, a quaver in your voice, or adrenaline-induced symptoms such as trembling hands or increased heart rate. These symptoms are usually comparatively mild and typically diminish. They are a bit like the chill you feel when you first jump into the water when you go swimming: it's a little uncomfortable at first, but the discomfort fades quickly. Most of the American population experiences some form of this mild anxiety in some circumstances. If these symptoms are similar to how you have felt, then you have experienced normal levels of anxiety about communication. The rest of this chapter will focus on the more severe form of anxiety called "communication apprehension."

Even if you don't experience communication apprehension yourself, you will encounter people who do. Consequently, the rest of this chapter is intended to promote an understanding of this condition. Such an understanding is important for two reasons. First, we often discount other people's phobias. A common reaction to another person's report of extreme nervousness about communicating is the reply, "Oh yeah, I get nervous, too." Non-phobic individuals who make this or a similar response often think they feel the same way as a genuine apprehensive, but they don't. Think of your own worst phobia (for me, the fear of heights). Perhaps you are afraid of flying, or snakes, or clowns. The stark terror these phobias inspire in affected persons is the same way most high apprehensives feel about communicating with others. It's not mild anxiety, it's gut-wrenching fear, and people who are not apprehensive need to understand how truly traumatic that fear is.

Second, forcing someone who has a phobia about communicating with others into a situation where they *must* communicate can actually increase the intensity of their phobia. This is important in light of another common response to persons who experience communication apprehension. Often, non-phobic people will urge the victims of apprehension to "just do it." While this sort of sink-or-swim approach may work for some activities, it usually doesn't work for high apprehensives and can make the apprehension worse. I often wonder how much damage has been caused by well-intentioned instructors who forced apprehensive students to "get up there like everyone else." Fortunately, those who have high communication apprehension can often be overcome it through the use of techniques discussed later in this chapter.

What Is Communication Apprehension?

Communication Apprehension
Fear and avoidance of communication with other people

Communication apprehension (CA) is a type of anxiety that involves the fear and avoidance of communication with other people (McCroskey, 1993). It's widespread, with various surveys identifying components of CA, such as fear of public speaking, as the most common phobia in the United States (Motley, 1997). Millions of Americans experience some form of CA. In fact, about 16% of the American population experiences high levels of communication apprehension (Daly & McCroskey, 1984).

Communication apprehension has many forms. For example, some people don't usually feel nervous about speaking, but may find a specific situation threatening. Such a person might normally feel comfortable talking with a supervisor, but would be anxious about conversing with that supervisor during an annual evaluation. Others might be relaxed during normal conversations but experience anxiety about a forthcoming public speech. In contrast to these situation-specific forms of CA, other people experience **generalized anxiety** about almost all communication in almost all settings with almost all people (Daly & McCroskey, 1984). This generalized anxiety is regarded as the most serious form of CA.

While, this chapter focuses primarily on anxiety related to oral presentations, please remember this fear is only one aspect of the phenomenon we label "communication apprehension." In other words, CA is not just a new term for "stage fright." It encompasses a fear of public speaking, but it also includes anxiety about other communication settings and situations.

Generalized Anxiety
Feelings of anxiety associated with communication in nearly all situations

What Are the Causes of Communication Apprehension?

The cause of communication apprehension is the subject of considerable debate among communication scholars. Although individual researchers may support certain causes and disagree with others, most would agree that the available evidence centers around four potential causes of apprehension: genetic contributors, environmental reinforcers, personality traits, and cultural factors.

Genetic Contributors

Researchers subscribing to **communibiology** as a cause of anxiety suggest that CA may have a predominantly hereditary basis. Studies of identical twins raised together as compared to identical twins who were separated at birth, have shown commonalities in personality and behavior which suggest people may inherit preferences (temperaments) to behave in certain ways. Temperament traits don't mandate specific behaviors (you aren't genetically destined for a certain occupation, for example) but combinations of inherited proclivities may exert powerful influences on our behavioral preferences. A person who inherits a tendency to be high in extraversion and low in self-doubt, for example, is unlikely to experience CA. On the other hand, someone who has inherited high introversion and high self-doubt has a higher probability of feeling anxiety about communicating (Beatty, McCroskey, & Valenic, 2001). Communibiology is a very new field of research and probably the most controversial, but it raises legitimate questions about the role of **genetic contributors** in human behavior.

Communibiology
The study of the biological bases of human communication

Environmental Reinforcers

Rewards, punishments, and negative **environmental reinforcers** are also likely contributors to communication apprehension. Researchers who believe that environmental factors contribute to the fear of communicating with others suggest that behavior that is rewarded is likely to be repeated while behavior that is punished will be decreased or extinguished (Richmond & McCroskey, 1998). Consider two children who were raised in different environments. Rita was raised in a home where communication was encouraged and rewarded. Because her communication ability was reinforced, she improved her communication

Genetic Contributors
Combinations of inherited tendencies that may exert influences on our behavioral preferences

environmental reinforcers
Factors within our environment that contribute to our fear of speaking

skills. Rita would be an unlikely candidate for high CA. Burt, on the other hand, was raised to believe that "children should be seen, not heard." His early attempts at communication were criticized and ridiculed. Because Burt's communication behavior was punished, he did not develop into a competent communicator. Frequently, competence and confidence are linked together so Burt would be more likely to develop high communication apprehension.

Another environmental contributor to communication apprehension involves uncertainty about the outcome of communication. **Learned helplessness** often occurs if a person's communication behavior is rewarded one time and punished the next. This uncertainty makes it difficult for the person to predict the consequences of communication (Richmond & McCroskey, 1998). Poor Jim never knew what reaction he would receive when he talked to his mother. One day he would be told how smart he was, but the next he would be called "stupid" and told to keep his mouth shut. Because he could not predict the outcome of his communication behavior, he withdrew from communication whenever possible and, consequently, failed to develop skill and confidence in his communication ability. These circumstances placed Jim at risk for developing high CA.

Researchers who believe environmental factors are primary contributors to communication apprehension probably represent the majority of communication scholars. Still, their findings are sometimes questioned because they offer only a partial explanation for the overall cause of communication apprehension. Critics argue that even their best research accounts for only a comparatively small percentage of the reasons people experience CA (Beatty, et al., 2001).

> **Learned Helplessness**
>
> A person feels unable to predict whether a behavior will result in a reward or punishment, therefore he or she avoids the behavior all together if possible

Personality Traits

Certain personality traits appear to be associated with high CA. When researchers compared mean scores of groups of people with high CA with mean scores of groups of people with low CA, they found high CAs tended to have lower tolerance for uncertainty, less self-control, less adventurousness, lower emotional maturity, higher introversion, lower self-esteem, and lower assertiveness (Richmond & McCroskey, 1998).

These results should be interpreted carefully. First, correlation alone can never imply causality. Sometimes something that is correlated with something else is actually a casual factor (people who smoke are more likely to develop cancer because cigarette smoking is one of the causes of lung cancer). At other times two phenomena can occur together and have nothing to do with each other (every serial killer in history has had a mother, but it does not follow that motherhood causes serial killers). Since all the research cited in this section is correlational, it would be dangerous to imply causality. Consider the research on high communication apprehension and self-esteem, for example. Research suggests a correlation between low self-esteem and high CA. However, we don't really know if low self-esteem causes high CA, high CA causes low self-esteem, some other factor causes both of them, or whether they occurred together but are totally unrelated.

Questions can also be raised about the framework of comparison used for this research. Although most researchers tend to argue that high CAs are disadvantaged when compared to their low CA counterparts, an equally good argument is that low CAs are uniquely gifted and high CAs are no different in personality than the normal population. There is credible research in support of this argument (Butler, 1986).

Cultural Factors

Scholars of intercultural communication argue that the culture in which we are raised can affect our level of CA. These researchers suggest that some cultures, such as those found in many Asian, Arab, and some South American countries, are comparatively collectivistic. **Collectivistic cultures** tend to discourage individual assertiveness and stress group harmony. Other cultures, such as those found in the United States and other western countries, are comparatively **individualistic cultures**, stressing individual assertiveness over group harmony. A growing body of research suggests a strong correlation between high CA and collectivistic cultures, probably because collectivistic cultures discourage assertiveness and often value silence (Zhang, Butler, & Pryor, 1996; Sarquisse, Butler, & Pryor, 2003).

collectivistic cultures
Cultures that discourage individual assertiveness and stress group harmony

individualistic cultures
Societies that stress individual assertiveness over group harmony

Communication apprehension is serious and can have a negative impact on your academic career

Most communication researchers would agree that the factors discussed in this section represent significant contributors to high communication apprehension but many would argue over which factors are most predominant. Controversies such as these are characteristic of scientific inquiry; competing claims are tested against each other until research reveals which are most strongly supported by the evidence. Also, these factors are not necessarily discrete. Culture, for example, can be viewed as a part of one's environment, and personality characteristics may contain an hereditary component. Nevertheless, most researchers would agree that heredity, environment, personality, and culture all contribute to communication apprehension.

What Are the Effects of Communication Apprehension?

The effects of communication apprehension have been widely studied, with research results generally painting a gloomy picture of the effects of high CA. These effects are widespread, affecting people in virtually every aspect of their lives, including self-perception, relationships, work satisfaction, occupational choices, and academic success (Daly & McCroskey, 1984). Because this chapter is designed for college students, we will forego discussion of the more general aspects and focus on the academic effects. From an academic standpoint, high communication apprehension appears to be detrimental to success.

CA and Standardized Test Scores

Although research has revealed no significant difference in intelligence between high and low CAs, scores on standardized tests such as the ACT tend to be significantly lower for high CAs than for their low CA counterparts (Daly & McCroskey, 1984).

CA and Grades

Some (but not all) studies have found that high CAs have lower mean grade point averages than low CAs. This is particularly true in courses that require oral participation (Daly & McCroskey, 1984).

CA and Class Selection

High and low CAs differ in their choice of classes. Low CAs prefer small classes with lots of participation while high CAs prefer large classes with little participation (Daly & McCroskey, 1984). High CAs also tend to select classes where they can use their seating preferences to avoid communication. While most low CAs choose seats in the front, middle section of a typical classroom, high CAs tend to select seats that are out of the instructor's normal zone of participation, such as seats in the back or on the sides of the room (Daly & McCroskey, 1984).

High CAs try to avoid classes that involve group projects and discussions. When they are required to take such classes, they choose obscure seating positions and minimize participation. Their comments are often irrelevant, and they seldom disagree with other group members. They are also less likely to engage in productive brainstorming (Daly & McCroskey, 1994).

CA and College Graduation

Perhaps as a result of the factors discussed earlier in this section, graduation rates for high CAs are lower than those for low CAs. Research by Ericson and Gardner (1992), for example, found that "high communication apprehensives had tendencies to not complete their degrees" (p. 132). In fact, 50% of the high apprehensives they studied failed to graduate, and incoming freshmen with high CA were more likely to drop out of school than those with low CA.

Cautionary Thoughts on CA Research

Research on the academic effects of high CA paints a bleak picture for those affected by this form of anxiety. Highly apprehensive students have comparatively lower test scores, grades, and graduation rates than their low apprehension counterparts. In spite of these findings, high CA students can take encouragement from three observations.

First, remember the previously cited research was comparative in nature. For example, high CAs have lower grades only when compared with low CAs. Such a comparison *could* demonstrate that low CAs average uniquely high grades, not that high CAs average uniquely low grades. A more telling comparison could have been made by comparing the mean GPAs of high and low CAs with the GPAs of students with normal levels of apprehension, but such comparisons were not examined in the research cited in this section. This lack of data makes it hard to determine whether high CAs truly are disadvantaged.

Second, the research cited in this section draws its conclusions by comparing mean group scores and is not designed to be applied to individual students. Pretend, for example, that researchers compare groups of engineering majors and computer science majors and conclude that engineering majors have higher mean IQ scores than computer science majors. Would this research prove that every engineering major is smarter than every computer science major? Obviously it would not. In spite of the differences in group means, there would still be plenty of engineering majors with low scores, and many computer science majors with high scores. Even though mean group GPAs differ, there are still plenty of high CA students with excellent grades. Research conducted on groups simply cannot be generalized to individuals. Researchers who make such generalizations are committing a classic research fallacy known as the *ecological fallacy*.

Can the Effects of Communication Apprehension Be Reduced?

The negative effects of high communication apprehension can be mitigated. In this section we will discuss ways individual students can reduce their anxiety. These are methods I have used and found to be effective in nearly two decades of working with highly apprehensive students. I will concentrate on the ones that do not require professional supervision and that have proven effective for most high CA students.

Use Positive Self-Talk

The first strategy focuses on a phenomenon called **self-talk.** We probably talk to ourselves more than we talk to other people and the nature of our self-talk often influences our perceptions of reality. Researchers have discovered

Self-talk
Silent communications with oneself that influence one's perceptions of reality

that persons with high communication apprehension often engage in **negative self-talk**, which is critical and negative (Bullard & Carroll, 1993). When thinking about a forthcoming speech for example, high CAs often bombard themselves with criticism. Typical thoughts include, "My speech will be boring," "People will think I'm stupid," or "I'll lose my place and people will laugh at me." Unfortunately, thoughts like these can easily turn into self-fulfilling prophecies, so many high CAs literally become their own worst enemies.

From a physiological standpoint, the thoughts we have about ourselves trigger interesting reactions in our brains. Physicists who study electrical activity in the human brain report that thoughts about ourselves trigger up to 100 times more neuronal firings than random thoughts. Moreover, thoughts about ourselves *spoken out loud* generate up to 1,000 times more neuronal firings than random thoughts (Bullard & Carroll, 1993). In other words, our brains devote considerable energy to processing our self-talk, especially when we say things about ourselves out loud. When we talk, our brains listen.

Most high CAs who engage in negative self-talk learned this self-destructive habit from someone else, usually parents, teachers, or even friends. Unfortunately, many high CAs incorporate these descriptions by others into their self-perceptions and come to believe them. They perpetuate these negative images by engaging in self-criticism and self-doubt. Over time, these people *become* their own negative descriptions. If you call yourself a loser enough times, chances are you will become what you say you are.

Luckily, self-talk doesn't have to be negative. Furthermore, *you* are in charge of how you talk to yourself! Picture yourself walking across campus. As you walk, you encounter a friend who greets you. Undoubtedly, you will respond with a "good morning" or some conventional greeting. It is unlikely that you would respond with a random utterance that makes no sense as a greeting. "Good morning" is seldom followed with a nonsensical response like "prune juice for dinner." This silly illustration demonstrates that you are in charge of what you say to other people. You have the ability to control your conversational responses. You also have the power to control what you say to yourself. If you are busily talking yourself into being a poor communicator, there is only one person on the planet who can reverse that trend. You see that person every time you look into the mirror.

This is not to suggest that reversing negative self-talk is easy. Old habits are hard to break–but they can be broken. The next time that inner voice says "I'm a loser", tell it to shut up! Replace negative self-descriptions with **positive self-talk**. Think, "I am an interesting person," or "People will enjoy what I have to say." Better yet, say these things to yourself out loud (your car is a good place for this, even if other drivers think you are crazy). Remember, when you speak, your brain listens, and you–not old habits–are in charge of what you say.

Use Positive Visualization

Positive self-talk mainly affects the verbal areas of the brain. Other parts of the brain are primarily influenced by visual images. Consequently, we can influence our visual perceptions with visualized images. One could label these images **proactive imagination**. Things that we imagine can have a very real impact on how our brain processes information. Remember, your brain receives visual data only in the form of electrical impulses, and these impulses seem real to your brain whether they come from actual or imagined events. That's why movies (or nightmares) can trigger strong emotional and physical responses in us even though nothing "real" is actually happening.

You can use this property of your brain to help overcome high CA. Let's say you are giving a speech. Picture yourself speaking confidently to a smiling, interested audience. Visualize yourself giving an articulate, informative presentation–the more detail, the better. Combining visualization with self-talk allows you to positively influence both the visual and verbal areas of your brain. Visualization is best practiced with your eyes closed while you are lying down. Closing your eyes helps eliminate most competing visual information, so it is easier for you to picture what you are trying to proactively imagine (Bullard & Carroll, 1993). It's also a good idea to prepare a "script" to guide your visualization (Bullard & Carroll, 1993). You might picture yourself standing and walking to the front of the room, then visualize yourself speaking articulately to a smiling, interested audience. Visualization is a powerful technique for reducing high CA, especially when used in conjunction with positive self-talk.

Many athletes use visualization to improve their game

Utilize Kinesic Inputs

Kinesics is the study of body movement and facial expressions. Researchers who investigate the impact of kinesics on our moods have made an interesting discovery: our facial expressions can influence how we feel. Most of us think that facial expressions are usually the result of our feelings, and we're right. In general, expressions are the result, not the cause, of emotions. But nonverbal reactions also perform a second, more subtle function. In addition to reflecting our feelings, they also influence them. Communication researchers have discovered that changing facial expressions can alter our state of mind (Kleinke, Peterson, & Rutledge, 1998). High CAs can use this discovery to their advantage. Never mind how you feel inside, when it's your turn to give a speech, interact with a group, or meet with your professor, smile, and walk confidently into the room, and then sound and act as if you are interested in your topic. You can literally reduce some of your anxiety by acting confidently.

> Kinesics
> The study of body movement and facial expressions

Change Your Perspective

Remember the last time you watched individual competitive events like diving or figure skating during the Olympics? The contestant would finish and then nervously wait for his or her evaluation. Eventually, the judges would each hold up a card with a number on it and the numbers would be tallied for a final score. That system works fine for Olympic competition, but it is not typical of most speaking situations. The trouble is that some high CAs don't realize this.

Changing your facial expressions can alter your state of mind. Smile!

Consider the plight of Sally, who needed to give a presentation to her classmates.

Poor Sally regarded her audience as a group of critics. She felt they were keenly focusing on every word she said and every movement she made. Any tiny error she committed would be recorded and deducted from her score. Since she regarded her audience as a group of hostile critics, she anticipated her presentation with trepidation.

Sally's classmate, Burt, cultivated a different attitude about his presentation. Instead of regarding it as a performance, he saw it as an opportunity to share information about his topic with his audience. He was excited to exchange information about his home state of Ohio and his favorite football team, the Buckeyes, with his classmates, and pictured them not as critics, but as interested receivers of his message. Burt wanted to do a good job, but he recognized that most human communication contains a few errors and figured that if he made a mistake, his audience would get over it. He wasn't too worried about his upcoming presentation.

As you can see from these examples, your attitude about the purpose of any presentation and the role of the audience can play a significant part in how much anxiety you feel. If you have unrealistic attitudes about your job as a presenter or the perspective of the audience, you will probably experience increased anxiety.

Let's go back and analyze Sally's position. Sally's first mistake was to regard her presentation as a performance. The truth is that most contemporary *presentations are not perfectly rehearsed performances*; they are more like enlarged conversations. In the early days of our country, speeches were seen as entertainment, and speakers were applauded for their oratorical skills. Renowned speakers like Daniel Webster and William O. Douglas gave flawless, moving performances–some over three hours long. We still have vestiges of that style. You see it in a few evangelists, and in the State of the Union Address. Most speeches though, are comparatively informal. Think of a presidential news conference, a Pentagon briefing, or a college lecture. These events just *aren't* performances.

Sally's second mistake involved her *misinterpretation of the audience's expectations.* As you listen to other student's presentations, monitor your own attentiveness and behavior. Are you listening with critical attention, ready to pounce on the smallest error, or are you listening in a more detached way, trying to understand the main points the speaker is trying to make? In fact, do you really care all that much about what the other speakers are saying at all? How much time do you spend agonizing over other students' presentations out of class? Do you discuss them in detail with your friends or lay awake at night thinking about them? Probably not.

Sally's classmate, Burt, was considerably closer to the truth. He recognized that if he offered his audience interesting, relevant information, delivered with reasonable articulation and enthusiasm, he would probably be okay. When it

SPEAKING OF . . .

Some Final Thoughts for Persons Who Experience High Communication Apprehension

Please don't mistake these suggestions about coping with apprehension for a panacea. The solutions offered here are the best answers we currently have, but they aren't miracle cures. There are at least three problems with what I've suggested.

First, the solutions I've proposed usually reduce apprehension, but they seldom eliminate it. If you experience uncommonly high anxiety about communicating with others, the methods I've discussed should lower your discomfort to tolerable levels, but you'll still probably experience some nervousness. Ideally, I'd like to offer you a method that would completely eliminate your discomfort, but it's probably more realistic for you to expect to reduce it. Even a *reduction* in anxiety can be important. It can make a significant difference in your college grades, your career success, and your relationships after you graduate.

Second, reducing anxiety can be a slow process. Don't expect one week of positive self-talk and proactive imagination to undo years of habituated anxiety. Your nervousness will decrease gradually, and you may not experience a meaningful decline in it for a while. Anxiety reduction is a bit like working out or losing weight. It works, but it's slow.

Third, these methods won't work effectively for everyone. Over the years, I've known a few people (probably fewer than 5% of my high CA students) who diligently used the methods I've recommended without much effect. These students lie at the extreme end of the high CA spectrum. They're the people who can't sleep for days prior to giving a speech, become physically ill before class, pass out while speaking, and repeatedly register for and then drop the basic speech class. I had one student who dropped the course three times before I met him.

If you think you are one of the students who fall into this extreme category, I strongly urge you to consider seeking professional assistance. This may sound like an extreme solution to overcoming apprehension, especially since college is so filled with short-term deadlines and obligations that it's hard to think of long-term consequences. When I admitted that we can't always help people with extremely high CA, I was speaking with a degree of candor that you don't often find in college texts or popular self-improvement manuals. I'm speaking with that same blunt honesty now. The consequences of high CA reach far beyond your college education. In this chapter, I restricted my discussion of the results of high communication apprehension to the college environment, partly because a complete discussion would have at least doubled the length of this chapter, but mostly because I didn't want to bury you under an avalanche of bad news. I won't bury you now either, but I want to make it abundantly clear that communication apprehension affects more things–and bigger things–than a few college classes. People with extremely high communication apprehension don't do well in relationships, in employment, in life. High CA is seriously bad stuff, and deciding to "just live with it" should only be a last ditch option. I'm not overstating when I say that if you don't overcome it now, you may pay for it for the rest of your life.

In the end, more than anything else, it comes down to courage. Are you going to give in to the apprehension monkey on your back, or are you going to go to war with it? The war isn't easy, but you'll carry the consequences of your choice for the rest of your life. Both Abraham Lincoln and Winston Churchill suffered from high communication apprehension. If they had lacked the courage to overcome it, I wonder if their names would mean anything to us today.

Make good choices and don't give up. And remember that you have plenty of good resources at your disposal–your instructors, your friends and fellow classmates are all there to help you. Good luck!

---

comes to your perspective on communication, you want to be more like Burt than Sally.

The bottom line is this: most of your small mistakes will hardly be noticed by your classmates, and even if you really blow it, other people won't think about it all that much. Thinking otherwise places you in an imaginary world–a place where presentations are like theater performances and audiences are like predatory tigers ready to pounce.

Be Prepared

This section is last because it is probably the least important component of anxiety reduction for high CAs. Still, it deserves some consideration. Most anxiety doesn't seem to be linked to how well-prepared a person is. You may recall that lack of preparation was *not* one of things discussed in the *Causes of Communication Apprehension* section of this chapter. There are two ways, however, that lack of preparation can lead to increased apprehension.

First, a person who is already nervous does not need any additional negative baggage. In other words, a person who is predisposed to be anxious about communicating, comes from a background that was punishing and critical, has personality characteristics associated with apprehension, or comes from a culture that discourages speaking, certainly doesn't need anything else to contribute to their anxiety. Being unprepared can do just that. I have won state championships for college impromptu and extemporaneous speaking (never mind what year), yet I still feel a little nervousness when I'm unprepared, so pity the poor high CA who is unprepared.

Second, one specific type of nervousness is clearly linked to the lack of preparation. Although it may sound tautological, lack of preparation definitely leads to nervousness about not being prepared. I personally cherish the fine art of procrastination and am an ardent practitioner, but if you're already nervous, putting off preparing for a presentation is a poor move. Likewise, if you have a meeting, you might benefit by finding out as much as you can about the people you are meeting. Think about the kinds of questions they might ask you and then prepare some answers for those questions. If you're going to an interview, have a mock interview with a friend to prepare. All of these activities can ease your anxiety.

Summary

In this chapter, you learned the following:

1. Communication apprehension is a type of anxiety involving the fear of communicating with others. It is not the same as normal speaker anxiety that many people have when they give presentations.

2. Most communication scholars agree that there are four potential causes of communication apprehension: genetic contributors, environmental reinforcers, personality traits, and cultural factors.

3. While communication apprehension impacts all areas of life, it affects student's academic careers in several ways.

   • High CAs tend to have lower scores in standardized tests, for example the ACT.

   • High CAs tend to have lower GPAs.

   • High CAs prefer larger classes that require little or no participation.

   • College graduation rates are lower for people with high communication apprehension.

4. There are several strategies students can employ to manage communication apprehension.

   • Changing self-talk from positive to negative influences your perception of yourself as a communicator.

- Visualizing yourself giving a successful presentation is especially effective when used in conjunction with positive self-talk.

- Looking and acting confident, regardless of how you feel, can reduce some of your anxiety.

- Perfection is rarely expected. Allowing yourself to be human and understanding that the people you're communicating with are not looking for every little mistake you make will change your attitude toward communication.

- Not being prepared can raise your level of anxiety. It's wise to plan ahead for any presentation.

5. Although deciding to tackle your fear of communication may seem daunting, your efforts will benefit you for the rest of your life.

Check Your Understanding: Exercises and Activities

1. Take the self-assessment survey called the PCA-24 found at the beginning of this chapter. What are your scores? Do they accurately represent your levels of communication apprehension?

2. Do you know any student who suffers from CA? Based on your observations, in what ways is their school experience consistent with the research on the academic effects of CA? In what ways is it inconsistent?

3. Based on what you have learned in this chapter, what are some specific steps you can take to prepare for your next presentation?

References

Beatty, M. J., McCroskey, J. C., & Valenic, K. (2001). *The biology of communication: A communibiological perspective.* Cresskill, NJ: Hampton Press.

Bullard, B., & Carnol, K. (1993). *Communicating from the inside out.* Dubuque, Iowa: Kendall/ Hunt.

Butler, J. F. (1986). Personality characteristics of subjects high and low in apprehension about communication. *Perceptual and Motor Skills, 62,* 895–898.

Daly, J. A., & McCroskey, J. C. (1984). *Avoiding communication.* Beverly Hills, CA: Sage.

Ericson, P. M., & Gardner, J. W. (1992). Two longitudinal studies of communication apprehension and its effects on college students' success. *Communication Quarterly, 40,* 127–137.

Kleinke, C. L., Peterson, T. R., & Rutledge, T. R. (1998). Effects of self generated facial expressions on mood. *Journal of Personality and Social Psychology, 74,* 272–279.

McCroskey, J. C. (1993). *An introduction to rhetorical communication,* 6th ed. Englewood Cliffs, NJ: Prentice-Hall.

Motley, M. T. (1997). *Overcoming your fear of public speaking: A proven method.* Boston, MA: Houghton Mifflin.

Richmond, V. P., & McCroskey, J. C. (1998). *Communication: Apprehension, avoidance, and effectiveness,* 5th ed. Boston, MA: Allyn and Bacon.

Sarquisse, V., Butler, J., & Pryor, B. (2003). A comparison of communication apprehension scores between Americans and Argentineans. *North American Journal of Psychology, 5,* 223–228.

Zang, Y., Butler, J., & Pryor, B. (1996). A comparison of apprehension about communication in China and the United States. *Perceptual and Motor Skills, 82,* 1168–1170.

A COMMUNICATION THEORY SAMPLER

— Dr. Jim Katt

Objectives

After reading this chapter, you should be able to:

- Recognize and define key attributes of the communication process

- Define the terms *logos, pathos,* and *ethos,* and understand what speakers can do to enhance each of them in their presentations

- Identify the variables in the SMCRE model of communication and explain how each of them functions in the public speaking context

- Recognize components of the Elaboration Likelihood Model (ELM) and explain what the model suggests about how listeners process and become persuaded by messages

- Appreciate the value and characteristics of ethical communication as expressed in the NCA Credo and explain how these apply to public speaking

Key Concepts

amorality

central route

channel

elaboration

environment

ethos

logos

message

message

NCA Credo

pathos

peripheral cues

pervasiveness

source

"He who loves practice without theory is like the sailor who boards ship without a rudder and compass and never knows where he may cast."

–LEONARDO DAVINCI

Although we have been communicating all of our lives, most of us have not put a lot of thought into how the process of communication works. In this course, you will have the opportunity to deliver several speeches. As you prepare for those speeches, knowing about the process of communication will be essential. Fortunately for you, there is a large body of knowledge just waiting to be tapped.

The study of communication has a theoretical basis that draws from contemporary empirical research as well as observations that date back centuries. This chapter makes no attempt to cover the body of knowledge that makes up communication theory, but instead looks at a few selected instances where some knowledge of communication theory can help be a more effective presenter and also be a more effective communicator in your everyday life.

What Is Communication?

Communication is a complex process that, many would argue, is extraordinarily difficult to define. So, rather than attempting to define communication, let's examine some of the attributes of this process. Specifically, let's look at how communication is pervasive, amoral, and necessary to advancing our life-agenda.

Communication Is Pervasive

pervasiveness
Communication takes place wherever humans are together because people tend to look for meaning, even when a message is not deliberately sent

Many argue that humans in the presence of other humans cannot <u>not</u> communicate. Even when we try not to send any sort of message it's likely that others will infer meaning from our lack of action. What do you think when someone doesn't call you back, doesn't look at you when you are talking, or doesn't answer your email? If you are like most people, you start making inferences about the other person's motives for not responding – she doesn't like me; he's just a rude person; she's afraid to talk to me; he's probably really busy; and so on. *People tend to look for meaning, even when there is no message.* It's human nature. The problem is that, much of the time, the meaning assigned to the lack of an overt message simply isn't correct. Your voicemail is full and all of a sudden people think you don't like them, or you're rude, or you're fearful, or too

What do you think when someone doesn't return your text message?

busy to talk. But what does this inability to turn off the communication process mean for us as communicators? If we cannot *not* communicate, if people are going to assign meaning to our lack of sending messages, then maybe we would be better off trying to send clear messages that have a better chance of being received accurately. If the process of communication is going to continue whether we participate or not, it's better that we become active participants.

Communication Is Amoral

The word *amoral* is often misused. People use it when they really mean *immoral*. Within the context of communication, the word **amoral** means ethically neutral; neither moral nor immoral. Perhaps a quick analogy will help. Think about those one-celled amoebas you studied in high school biology. You may recall they reproduced *asexually*. Does this mean that the amoebas are sexually deficient or inferior? No, it means they are sexually neutral; neither male nor female. Scholars as far back as Aristotle have argued that the communication process is amoral. The morality, or lack of morality, comes from the people engaged in the process. Perhaps you have tried to persuade a roommate not to go out with a person you know is "bad news." Or, maybe you have tried to talk a friend out of using prescription drugs illegally to stay awake and be more mentally alert for finals. These are examples of moral, ethical communication behavior. In fact, many would argue that *failure* to attempt to influence your friend in these cases would be immoral. Unscrupulous scam artists, who try to sell worthless insurance policies to people who are poor and unknowledgeable, or drug dealers, who try to convince your kids to try their products, may use those same methods of persuasion in immoral, unethical ways. The process is neutral. It is the people engaged in the process who provide the morality, or lack of it. This brings us to another aspect of communication: what exactly do we *do* with it?

amoral
The process of communication is ethically neutral

Communication Allows Us to Advance Our Life-Agenda

Communication is the means by which each of us advances our life-agenda. As infants, we cried to be fed. Ever since, we have used whatever communication skills we could muster to influence others to think, feel, or act in ways that we believe they should. While such a statement may spark connotations of manipulation or coercion (see the Persuasion chapter to help distinguish "persuasion" from "coercion"), we must remind ourselves that the *process* of communication is ethically neutral and that advancing our life-agenda can be an ethical pursuit, enriching (or, at least, not harming) those around us. Or, it could be an unethical exploitation, advancing our agenda at the expense of others. Which one it is depends on the morality that we, as individuals, bring to the process.

If we acknowledge that communication is a pervasive process that happens with or without our active participation; that it is by this process that we advance our life-agenda; and that it is possible to engage in agenda-advancing behavior in an ethical manner, then communication becomes more than a college course requirement: it is an essential life skill. Becoming a more effective communicator is about more than getting a decent grade in your speech class – it's about becoming more effective at *life*.

What Can We Learn from Aristotle?

Twenty-five hundred years ago, long before anyone dreamed of printing presses, telephones, radio, television, the Internet, or texting, people had lives to live and agendas to advance. Public speaking was the primary mode of communication. Aristotle was a student of Plato, and wrote prolifically on many subjects. He was a keen observer of human behavior and lived in a culture where laws and societal issues were debated and decided orally. It was a society where the most effective orators usually had the most influence, so effective oral communication was important. Among the many things he wrote about, Aristotle (trans. 1932) identified three types of appeals one might use when sending a message. He called them *logos, pathos and ethos*.

Logos - "Listen to my message because it makes sense"

logos
Logical appeals

First are logical appeals, or **logos**. Presenting a series of arguments supported by evidence can lead an audience to a "logical" conclusion. Some ways to increase the logical appeal of a message are to be well organized, to be sure that any claims you make are based on credible evidence, and to be clear in presenting that evidence. On a basic level, if a message does not make logical sense, an audience is unlikely to be moved by it. Consistency is also important. If we compose a mostly logical message that includes a few weak or illogical arguments, there is a danger that the weak arguments will cast doubts on the strong arguments and impugn the entire message. The *logos* you communicate will say to your audience, "Accept my message because it makes sense."

Pathos - "Listen to my message because of the feelings it evokes"

pathos
Emotional appeals

Aristotle also recognized the power of emotional appeals, or **pathos**. While logos attempts to influence what message receivers *think*, pathos is concerned with what they *feel*. Statistical data and facts help you to appeal logically, but specific examples and stories allow you to appeal emotionally – to make people receiving your message *feel* something about your topic. Some would suggest that while emotional appeals might be effective for some topics, informative or technical topics should not employ pathos. Although it would be difficult to imagine an effective presentation on a technical topic that used only emotional appeals, the absence of pathos would be of equal concern. Why should an audience care about a topic? How should they feel about the topic? Answering these questions provides an emotional component to go along with the logical one. The pathos in your message says to receivers, "Accept my message because of the feelings it evokes." Accepting it feels like the right thing to do, or rejecting it feels like the wrong thing to do.

Ethos – "Listen to my message because I am a competent, trustworthy, and well-intentioned person"

The Greek word for the third type of appeal is **ethos**. Today we call that same concept "credibility." At the most basic level, credibility (ethos) can be defined as a receiver's perception of a sender's competence, trustworthiness, and goodwill (McCroskey & Teven, 1999). That definition seems simple enough, but let's unpack it. Notice that it is the receiver's perception, not reality, which determines ethos. As a message sender, your credibility is based on how competent, trustworthy, and well-intentioned those receiving your message think you are, not on how competent, trustworthy, and well-intentioned you actually are. *The receivers assign credibility.* If you really are competent, but your receivers don't perceive you to be competent, they will not assign you high credibility. Likewise, if you really are trustworthy, but your receivers don't perceive you to be trustworthy, they will not assign you high credibility. Goodwill has to do with your receivers' perception of your intentions toward them. Do they feel you have their best interests in mind? Or do they perceive you as self-serving, or someone who just doesn't care one way or the other about them? To be a truly credible communicator, your audience must perceive you as competent, trustworthy, and well-intentioned.

> **ethos**
> The receiver's perception of a sender's competence, trustworthiness, and goodwill; credibility

How can you maximize your credibility? In the case of *competence*, if you have expertise, let people know about it. Let's assume you were making a presentation about computer animation software and you have been involved with computer animation since you were 13 years old. You have already taken several courses in animation and spent one summer interning for an animation company. If your audience knows about your experience, they will undoubtedly see you as more competent than they would if they had no knowledge of your expertise. But they will not know unless you tell them.

Some presenters are reluctant to mention their qualifications or experience for fear of being perceived as boastful. It is, however, quite possible to present your expertise in a humble manner, thus increasing your audience's perception of your competence without coming across as a braggart. "While some kids were busy conquering Dungeons and Dragons, I was glued to my computer, trying to conquer pixels and polygons. The animation bug caught me when I was 13 years old, and since then I have devoted most of my time to learning animation. Here at the University, I have completed several courses in animation and was lucky enough to have spent last summer interning at Acme Animation."

Being well-prepared, organized, and appropriately dressed for your presentation will increase your audience's perception of your competence.

Sometimes you may be speaking about a subject on which you are not an expert. In these cases, you may be able to "borrow" some expertise by citing the qualifications of the sources that you consulted in preparing your speech. For example, you might say, "I've been interested in growing my own herbs, but really didn't know very much about it until I read *The Secret Herb Garden* by Virginia Block, head of Harvard University's Herbal Horticulture Department." It's a way of saying, "I am competent to speak about this topic, because I have consulted expert sources."

In addition to their perceptions of your topical expertise, your audience may also have perceptions about your competence as a communicator. A speaker's delivery can affect the receivers' perception of that speaker's competence (McCroskey, 2001). Being well-prepared, organized, and appropriately dressed for your presentation will also help increase your audience's perception of your competence.

Perceptions of *trustworthiness* are a little more difficult to influence. Just saying "I'm really trustworthy" tends to have a hollow ring. Fortunately, most people will assume you are trustworthy unless you give them evidence to the contrary. Once you give them reason to doubt your honesty or reliability, however, it is difficult to regain their confidence. For this reason, effective communicators are careful to present everything in an honest, trustworthy fashion. Many attorneys have won cases by catching opposing witnesses in a lie. Even if the lie had no direct impact on the cases, once it has been established that certain witnesses do not always tell the truth, their trustworthiness is damaged and their testimony is perceived as unreliable.

The perception of *goodwill* occurs when your audience feels that you care about them, that you have their best interests at heart, and that you are concerned with them. If you are making a presentation at work and you are ill-prepared or use visual aids that are crudely produced, these factors may send a message that you just don't care that much about your audience. Presenters who value their audiences go to the trouble of being well prepared. Also, a dismissive, flippant, or arrogant attitude (during a presentation or in every day interactions) may say, "I really don't care about you." Thoughtful speakers show their understanding and concern by adopting a respectful, caring attitude toward those in their audience.

If you can tell people about your competence, avoid giving them any reason to doubt your trustworthiness, and demonstrate that you have their best interests at heart, you will maximize the possibility they will perceive you as credible. The ethos in your presentation says to your audience, "Accept my message because I am a competent, trustworthy, and well-intentioned person."

Over the years, there has been some disagreement over which type of appeal is most effective in different situations. Because no clear answer has emerged, perhaps the most practical advice is to utilize logos, pathos, and ethos in every situation. When making a formal presentation, keep your logic sound by making a series of clearly stated claims and by avoiding logical fallacies. Include credible statistics and other data to support those claims. Provide specific examples and stories to help your audience feel something about your topic. Be sure your audience knows about your personal expertise, avoid giving them any reason to doubt your honesty, and project a caring, respectful attitude. Appeal to your audience with logic, emotion, and credibility – logos, pathos, *and* ethos.

Advice from Aristotle for Increasing the Appeal of Your Message

Logos
- be well organized
- use credible evidence
- clearly present your evidence
- maintain consistency by using sound arguments

Pathos
- provide specific examples and stories
- tell your receivers why they should care about your message

Ethos
- if you have expertise in your topic, describe it to your audience
- clearly cite the qualifications of your sources
- present your message in an honest and trustworthy fashion
- present your message in a prepared, organized manner
- adopt a caring attitude toward those receiving your message

The SMCRE Factors

In an effort to study the complex process of communication, scholars have found it helpful to categorize or group the many factors involved. One grouping is the SMCRE model, which identifies five groups of communication variables: Source, Message, Channel, Receiver, and Environment. Although these categories can be applied to any communication situation, let's consider them within the context of public speaking.

In a public speaking situation, the ***source*** is the speaker (including the speaker's perceptions); the ***message*** is the speaker's intended message (as opposed to any other, incidental messages that might become part of the transaction); the ***channels*** are sound and sight (in-person and in real time); the ***receivers*** are the audience (and their perceptions); and the ***environment*** is the situation or context in which the transaction takes place. Remember that these are variables we would see if we could "freeze frame" the communication process and study it in only one direction. In reality, the process of communication is *transactional*, meaning we "are engaged in sending (encoding) and receiving (decoding) messages simultaneously" (Wenberg & Wilmot, 1974, p. 5). So the SMCRE model does not explain *how* the process of communication works, but it is very useful when studying what elements, or variables, make up the process of human communication. Below are brief descriptions of each category and some examples of variables that fit into each group. Bear in mind that the examples given are just a sampling. If we attempted to present an exhaustive list, there would be scores of variables for each category.

Source
The person initiating the communication

Message
The message the speaker *intends* to send

Channel
The means through which the message is sent

Receivers
The audience to whom the message is delivered

Environment
The situation or context in which the transaction takes place

*influenced by
source's characteristics
ex(gender, age)*

Source Variables

The source is the person who initiates the communication transaction. In the case of speeches, it is the speaker. This model suggests that the overall effectiveness of the communication will be influenced by source factors such as age, gender, intelligence, education, attractiveness, personality, and voice quality as well as perceptual items such as attitudes, prejudices, and values. Furthermore, how these variables affect the process will depend on the situation. Take age, for example. Being a senior citizen may be a positive factor when making a presentation about the impact of the Korean War and a negative factor when making a presentation about which video gaming platform is best. Aristotle believed that arguments should be accepted (or rejected) solely on their own merits, but he recognized that "external matters do count for much, because of the sorry nature of an audience" (Aristotle, trans. 1932, 3, 1, 1404a). Some twenty-three hundred years later, his observation is still accurate – audiences can still be swayed by external matters. Aronson and Mills (1965) presented identical messages attributed to either physically attractive or physically unat-tractive sources. The audience was more persuaded by the message when it came from an attractive source. Since the topic had nothing to do with grooming, fashion, or fitness, the attractiveness of the source should not have made any difference – but it did.

An email is probably not the best channel of communication for a marriage proposal.

Message Variables
(how message is presented)

All of the elements in a message can affect the communication process. Some of these variables would include length of message, organizational scheme, use of humor, types of appeals, types of arguments, or use of evidence. Again, the effects would vary with the situation. For example, using humor can often be an effective device, but it might be considered inappropriate and have a negative impact on a speech about world hunger.

Channel Variables

In older versions of this model, the channels were defined by the five senses: sight, sound, touch, taste, and smell. More recently, modalities (live, recorded, teleconference, computer-mediated, text-message, email) within the five senses have also been considered channel variables. Today, we have more choices than ever when it comes to communication channels. Certainly, some are preferable to others in a given situation. An email communication might be an effective way to announce an upcoming business meeting, but probably not the ideal channel for a marriage proposal. Most speeches are face-to-face endeavors featuring sounds and sights, but as businesses increase their use of internet and satellite technology, you may find yourself delivering an up-linked speech to an audience that is scattered across the globe.

5 senses + technology used to send message

Receiver Variables

In this model, the receivers are people receiving the message. During a speech, the receivers are the audience. Each member of the audience brings his or her own variables (such as age, gender, cultural background, prior knowledge of topic, listening ability, and mood) and perceptual items (such as attitudes, values, and prejudices). The same topic may require a different approach based on receiver variables. For example, a presentation about the importance of cancer screenings might emphasize screenings for prostate cancer to an audience of men and breast cancer screenings to an audience of women. Effective communicators tailor their messages specifically to the audiences who will be receiving them.

each person has their own variables / perceptual items

Environment Variables

Communication does not happen in a vacuum: it happens in places. Some places are noisy, some are crowded, some are attractively decorated, some have comfortable chairs, some are too cold, and some are messy. Research has shown that many of these "environmental" factors influence communication. Ask anyone who has tried to make a presentation on a hot, Florida afternoon in a room where the air-conditioning was not working, or tried to have a serious conversation with a close friend while a roommate's music was blasting at party levels – environmental factors make a difference.

surroundings

Which Variables Can You Control?

Although this question has implications for communication in any context, let's stay with our example of public speaking. If you are giving a speech, which of the variables in the SMCRE model would you be most able to control? Many would answer "source" variables because we like to think we have control over ourselves. While that is partially true, there are a lot of source variables, such as age, gender, height, ethnicity, and race, over which we have no control. Consider the source variable, attractiveness. Yes, we can spruce ourselves up a little, and even wear clothing that is appropriate to the rhetorical situation, but much of what others find attractive or unattractive in us is out of our control.

What about the channel? In real-world situations, we are usually assigned the channel through which we must communicate. Occasionally your boss may say,

"How do you think we can best get the message across?" but, more often, she'll say, "I'm sending you to Toledo to give a presentation to the sales force." Our communication environments are usually assigned as well. Once we get there, we may be able to adjust the thermostat or the lighting, or re-arrange the chairs, but at best we have only partial control over our environment.

The variables over which we have the *least control* are the receiver variables. Speakers rarely have the opportunity to choose audience members with certain characteristics. An exception might be during political campaigns, when a candidate may speak to an audience made up entirely of loyal constituents who were handpicked by the politician's staff. This scenario, however, is the exception, not the rule. Most speakers speak to an audience they did not choose.

The variables over which we have the *most control* are the message variables. Sometimes speakers are assigned a topic, but rarely are the elements of the message prescribed. The message is the invention of the speaker. The speaker generally gets to choose what to include, what to leave out, how to order the information, what evidence to provide, and what words to use. This is true in non-public speaking contexts as well. Whether speaking, writing, emailing, or texting, the sender controls the message.

So, there are many, many variables affecting the process of communication, but, as message senders, we have little control over any except those that make up the message. If communicating effectively is important to us (and it is), how can we focus more attention on our message and less on all of those other things we cannot control? How can we influence those receiving our message to pay more attention to our arguments and our evidence and less attention to our looks, the temperature of the room, or the fact that they are tired from partying last night? Another communication theory provides a possible answer to these questions.

The Elaboration Likelihood Model (ELM)

elaboration
The degree to which a receiver scrutinizes a message

The Elaboration Likelihood Model is one of the most thoroughly researched communication theories. First described by Richard Petty and John Cacioppo (1986), the ELM is a comprehensive theory of persuasion. What is described here is a just a portion of the model, but it is a portion that has particular relevance to everyday communicating, including public speaking. The Persuasive Communication chapter will cover the ELM in greater depth and examine how to apply the theory to persuasive presentations. For now, let's examine aspects of the ELM that generalize to almost any communication situation.

central route processing
Receivers mentally elaborate on the elements of your message and carefully scrutinize your arguments and evidence

Central Route or Peripheral Cues?

peripheral route processing
Receivers give brief attention to the message without elaborated thought

ELM researchers found that receivers expend a lot of mental energy processing some messages but very little energy processing others. More specifically, receivers sometimes mentally elaborate on elements of the message, scrutinizing the arguments and evidence, and at other times receivers give the message only cursory attention, often basing their decision to agree or disagree with the message on peripheral factors such as source attractiveness or the temperature of the room (Anderson & Pryor, 1992). Petty & Cacioppo (1986) termed the effortful scrutinizing of the message **central route processing**, and the casual, more cursory message reception **peripheral route processing**.

Their observation begs the question: "Why do receivers expend the effort to engage in central route processing sometimes, and other times process only peripherally?" Petty and Cacioppo (1986) suggest that people intrinsically want to hold correct attitudes, but don't have the time, inclination, or energy to carefully scrutinize every message they receive. Therefore, they must choose which messages they will process by the more effortful central route. According to their research, when people are motivated and able to scrutinize a message, they are likely to do so. Alternatively, people who lack either motivation or ability are more likely to be influenced by peripheral cues. The name "Elaboration Likelihood Model" is based on the premise that those who have both *motivation* and *ability* are more likely to engage in elaborative processing.

ELM research also found that receiver attitudes based on central route processing are more persistent, more predictive of behavior, and more resistant to counter-persuasion (Petty & Cacioppo, 1986). So, if you make a speech and your audience changes their attitudes in the direction you advocate based on central route processing, they are more likely to retain those attitudes, more likely to act in accordance with those attitudes, and less likely to be un-persuaded by someone with an

Why do receivers expend mental energy processing some messages but not others?

opposing view. If we think back to our examination of the SMCRE model, we notice that central route processing is focused primarily on the message variables, and peripheral route processing is focused more on sender, channel, receiver, and environment variables. If our audience is focused primarily on the message, they are basing their attitudes on the variables in the communication process over which we have the most control. If our audience is focused on peripheral cues, they are basing their attitudes on the elements over which we have very little control. All of this suggests that speakers who invent high quality messages have a better chance of being successful communicators if their audiences engage in central route processing.

Motivation and Ability

What can we, as speakers, do to increase the likelihood that our audience will engage in elaborative (central route) processing? Since we know that receivers are more likely to elaborate if they are motivated and able, the question becomes, "What can we do to maximize our audience's motivation and ability?"

Although a number of motivational factors have been studied, the factor most useful to message senders is *relevance*. If people believe a message is personally important (relevant) to them, they are more motivated to process that message carefully (Petty & Cacioppo, 1979). Anything that we, as speakers, can do to help our audience see how our message is important to them has the potential to increase their motivation. Aristotle observed that "people pay attention to things of importance, to their own interests, to anything wonderful, to anything pleasant; and hence you must give the impression that your speech has to do with the like" (Aristotle, trans. 1932, 3. 14. 1415b). If we can give that impression, and increase our audience's perceptions of relevance, we can increase their motivation, and thus their likelihood to elaborate. So, we should do what we can to make our messages relevant to our audience.

If you are making a presentation, tell your audience why your message will be important or useful to them. Moreover, tell them early, so the likelihood that they will engage in effortful processing of your entire message will be maximized. Sometimes the relevance of a message is unclear until late in the presentation. In these cases, it is too late for the audience to go back and re-process the message. When you send a message, make sure the answer to the "What's in it for me?" question is clear. If you are talking to your boss about an idea you have to make your job more efficient, help your boss see how it benefits the organization *and* how it benefits the boss. Even with something as simple as an email to a friend, a subject line that indicates why this email is important (as opposed to all of the others your friend receives that turn out to be unimportant) can help get your message read. To maximize your audience's motivation to process your message, make the case for relevance, and make it early.

Tips and Tactics

A Practical Application of Communication Theories

An interesting thing about communication theories is that there are often multiple theories at work simultaneously. For example, typing "**URGENT**" in the subject lines of emails that really aren't urgent may increase receivers' motivation to read your emails at first, but when they find out your claims of urgency are overstated, they may begin to doubt your trustworthiness, and that might motivate them to ignore your messages in the future. In this example, ethics, ethos, and the ELM are all happening at the same time, but they are not at odds with one another; a clear, truthful subject line can increase motivation without damaging your credibility.

Ability is the other variable that determines a receiver's likelihood to elaborate. But ability is a receiver variable and there is little we can do to change our audience's ability to process a message. We can, however, avoid doing things that might diminish their ability to process the message. For example, when a message includes a lot of jargon that is unfamiliar to listeners, we will lessen their ability to process the message. If a message is spoken in Russian, only those who understand Russian will be able to process the message. Jargon can be a foreign language to the audience who is unfamiliar with it, and its overuse can interfere with their ability to process the message.

Another impediment to message processing is the inclusion of too many behaviors that distract from your message. In a written message, misspellings and grammatical errors can distract your audience and interfere with their message processing ability. In an oral presentation, including an occasional "ah" or "um" will probably not diminish your overall effectiveness. Sometimes, however, speakers include so many "ah's" and "um's" that audience attention is drawn away from the message. When this happens, the audience's ability to process the message in diminished. So, while we cannot increase our audience's innate ability to process our message, we can maximize that ability by *not* doing things that interfere with their ability.

In summary, those receiving your message are more likely to focus on your message (instead of peripheral cues) if they are motivated and able. Perceiving the relevance of your message can increase motivation, and eliminating interfering elements (jargon, technical references, distracting behaviors, etc.) can maximize their ability. Once engaged in the central route, your audience will be more influenced by the message that you invented, and less influenced by peripheral items over which you have no control.

Before leaving the ELM, three items need to be clarified. First, be reminded that this discussion has covered only a portion of the Elaboration Likelihood Model. There is much more to the model, but in this chapter we have covered only the basics to emphasize the importance of making your messages relevant and accessible.

Second, although the "route" metaphor suggests a receiver either takes one route or the other – that is, relies on central message processing or peripheral cues – the ELM is *not* an either/or model. Motivation and ability will cause the effect of peripheral cues to be diminished, but not eliminated. Under conditions of high elaboration likelihood, non-message factors will still be a part of the process, but they will be less influential than the message factors.

Third, having your audience focused on your message does not mean they will necessarily accept your message. Increased scrutiny will favor strong messages and expose weak messages (Petty & Cacioppo, 1984). If those receiving your message are following the central route, they may accept *or* reject your message, but they will do so based primarily on the message itself, not on peripheral cues. So, to increase the likelihood for successful communication, make your message relevant, avoid doing anything to impair your audience's ability, and create a strong, logically sound message.

The Ethics of Communication

Earlier in this chapter, we talked about the process of communication being amoral (ethically neutral). We observed that the morality – or ethics – of communication comes not from the process but from the *people* involved in that process. So what does it mean to communicate ethically? The National Communication Association (NCA) has adopted a "Credo for Ethical Communication" which offers several principles to guide us in answering that question:

SPEAKING OF...

NCA Credo for Ethical Communication

Questions of right and wrong arise whenever people communicate. Ethical communication is fundamental to responsible thinking, decision making, and the development of relationships and communities within and across contexts, cultures, channels, and media. Moreover, ethical communication enhances human worth and dignity by fostering truthfulness, fairness, responsibility, personal integrity, and respect for self and others. We believe that unethical communication threatens the quality of all communication and consequently the well-being of individuals and the society in which we live. Therefore we, the members of the National Communication Association, endorse and are committed to practicing the following principles of ethical communication:

- We advocate truthfulness, accuracy, honesty, and reason as essential to the integrity of communication.

- We endorse freedom of expression, diversity of perspective, and tolerance of dissent to achieve the informed and responsible decision making fundamental to a civil society.

- We strive to understand and respect other communicators before evaluating and responding to their messages.

- We promote access to communication resources and opportunities as necessary to fulfill human potential and contribute to the well-being of families, communities, and society.

- We promote communication climates of caring and mutual understanding that respect the unique needs and characteristics of individual communicators.

- We condemn communication that degrades individuals and humanity through distortion, intimidation, coercion, and violence, and through the expression of intolerance and hatred.

- We are committed to the courageous expression of personal convictions in pursuit of fairness and justice.

- We advocate sharing information, opinions, and feelings when facing significant choices while also respecting privacy and confidentiality.

- We accept responsibility for the short- and long-term consequences of our own communication and expect the same of others.

(National Communication Association, 1999)

— plagiarism

The attitudes expressed in the NCA Credo extend to your classroom as well. Presenting the words or ideas of another person as your own constitutes plagiarism and clearly violates the "truthfulness, accuracy, honesty, and reason as essential to the integrity of communication" (NCA, 2009) clause of the NCA Credo. This applies to copying someone else's material verbatim as well as to failing to cite the source of ideas you have paraphrased. Ethical speaking also requires showing respect for the views of others, even (our founding fathers would say *especially*) when we disagree with those views. You'll notice that the Credo endorses "freedom of expression, diversity of perspective, and tolerance of dissent," but at the same time requires "respect for self and others." The NCA Credo does not suggest that everyone must agree; but it requires that we communicate our disagreements in a civil and respectful manner. The process of communication has no morality of its own. It is the responsibility of the people who engage in communication to bring morality to the process.

Does your communication measure up to the standards set forth in the NCA Credo? Consider how your life would be different if those with whom you regularly interact lived up to the standards it sets forth. How would your life be different if *you* always lived up to those standards? The process of communication is neutral. The rest is up to us.

64

SPEAKING OF . . .

Copyright

In addition to the ethical issues of source attribution, there is a legal issue as well. Most of the materials you find to support your speech, whether in books, periodicals, or on the Internet, are protected by the copyright laws of the United States, even if they do not carry a copyright notice. This is a complex topic. Although we are not lawyers, there are several guidelines that we recommend you follow in your speeches.

First, short quotations or other excerpts are generally considered "fair use" under the law. According to the U.S. Copyright Office's Web site, fair use for "purposes such as criticism, comment, news reporting, teaching (including multiple copies for classroom use), scholarship, or research, is not an infringement of copyright."[1] You should still acknowledge the source, both in your written outline and orally during your speech.

Second, just because something is on the Internet doesn't mean it's not protected by copyright. For example, the popular search engine Google has a feature that allows you to search for images. These can liven up a speech when shown with PowerPoint. But beware, because many of the images you find may be protected. Google states on its Web site: "The images identified by the Google Image Search service may be protected by copyrights. Although you can locate and access the images through our service, we cannot grant you any rights to use them for any purpose other than viewing them on the web. Accordingly, if you would like to use any images you have found through our service, we advise you to contact the site owner to obtain the requisite permissions."[2]

Third, be particularly cautious about the use of video from Web sites such as YouTube. As noted on the site, "It doesn't matter how long or short the clip is, or exactly how it got to YouTube. If you taped it off cable, videotaped your TV screen, or downloaded it from some other website, it is still copyrighted, and requires the copyright owner's permission to distribute."[3] In fact, many networks have asked YouTube to remove content they believed infringed on their copyright.

So how can you avoid copyright infringement? First, keep quotations brief and to the point. This is good advice for a speech in any event. As long as it's in a classroom situation, you should be fine. Second, with photos, limit your use to public domain sites. For example, photos from government agencies such as NASA are not copyrighted. If you can't find such photos, consider using ones you have taken. For example, one student gave a speech on modern dairy methods and illustrated her speech with photos from our university farm. Third, if you are using PowerPoint and are connected to the Internet, you may be able to put a hyperlink in your presentation, so that the material viewed is directly from the site that created the content. Thus, rather than showing a clip of *The Daily Show* from YouTube, go to the Comedy Central Web site itself.

When you leave the university and enter the workforce, the fair use exemption related to teaching will no longer apply. Learning the importance of respecting copyrights is important, not only ethically, but also to success in your career. In short, the best advice is when in doubt, leave it out. And if you absolutely must use something that is copyrighted in your speech, seek and obtain permission.

[1]United States Copyright Office, *Copyright Law of the United States of America and Related Laws Contained in Title 17 of the United States Code Circular 92* (n.d.) [Retrieved from http:// www .copyright.gov/title17/92chap1.html#101, 25 November 2006.]

[2]*Google.com,* "About Image Search: Frequently Asked Questions," 2005. [Retrieved from http://www.google.com/help/faq_images .html, 26 November 2006.]

[3]*YouTube,* "Copyright Tips," 2006. Retrieved from http://www .youtube.com/t/howto_copyright, 26 November 2006.]

Tips and Tactics

Ethical Guidelines for Speakers

- Provide truthful, relevant, and sufficient information to allow audience members to make informed choices.
- Show respect for the power of words. Recognize that offensive or divisive language reflects badly on your credibility as a speaker and can be hurtful to others.
- Reinforce and be consistent with democratic processes. Recognize the importance of free speech in a democratic society and the right of others to disagree.
- Be mindful of cultural diversity. This does not mean simply accepting the practices of other cultures that you find unethical, but it does mean treating other cultures with respect.

- Treat people as ends, not merely means to an end. Put yourself in the position of the listeners and treat them with the same respect you would expect were the roles reversed.
- Present "good reasons," not just those that may work. Appeal to the best, not the worst, in people.
- Take responsibility for your own work. Plagiarism is the ultimate in intellectual dishonesty.
- Demonstrate goodwill and trustworthiness toward the audience.
- Don't conceal your intentions from your audience, but reveal them at the appropriate point in your speech.
- Discuss both sides of controversial issues, recognizing that it is not only ethical but also more effective to do so.
- Utilize fear appeal with caution. Avoid exaggerated or unfounded fear appeals.

Summary

Although this chapter does not claim to offer a complete overview of communication theory, we have tried to bring together a number of theoretical elements that can be useful in preparing and delivering oral presentations. We have seen the important and pervasive role of communication in our lives. We have learned from Aristotle that our message might appeal to receivers' sense of logic, to their emotions, or to their willingness to accept a competent, trustworthy, and benevolent source. Rather than choosing among these three strategies, we suggested you look for ways to utilize all of them in your presentations. The SMCRE model reminds us that there are many factors that affect our attempts to communicate, but we have very little control over factors outside of the message itself. The Elaboration Likelihood Model helps explain why receivers sometimes focus on our message and sometimes focus on peripheral factors. Our discussion of the ELM also suggests some ways we might increase the likelihood of keeping our audience message-centered. Finally, we looked at the "NCA Credo for Ethical Communication" as a guide to communicating honestly and respectfully. It has been said that nothing is more practical than a good theory. As you continue communicating in college and later in your careers, you should find many practical applications for the theories introduced in this chapter.

Check Your Understanding: Exercises and Activities

Is it acceptable for a speaker to . . . ?

Read the following scenarios carefully. Put an A next to those that you think are acceptable for a public speaker. Put a question mark next to those that are possibly acceptable in some cases. Mark those that are unacceptable with a

U. Be prepared to present your responses in class and to discuss any differences between your responses and those of your classmates.

1. You are running out of time to write your speech. A friend who took the class last term offers you the outline of a speech that will fulfill the assignment. You decide to only change the name on the outline and a couple of subpoints, but otherwise give your friend's speech.

2. You are a United States senator. A staff member hands you the draft of a speech you are supposed to give that evening at a gathering of supporters. You jot a few notes in the margin and return the speech to the staffer to correct and put on the TelePrompTer for your address.

3. You find a Web site that has exactly the information you need for your speech. But there is no way to discover who is responsible for the content posted there or whether or not it's true. But it's exactly what you need, so you use it anyway, citing simply the URL (www . . .).

4. In researching your speech, you discover some very damaging statistics that undermine your case. Nevertheless, you believe firmly in the rightness of your cause. Thus, you ignore the contradictory evidence and focus only on statistics that support your point of view.

5. You take a class in which you are required to debate a controversial topic. You strongly believe in one side, but your teacher insists that everyone in the class has to debate once on each side of the resolution. You decide to go ahead and do the debate even though you don't agree with the position because you need a good grade in the class.

References

Anderson, S., and Pryor, B. (1992). *Speech fundamentals: A contemporary approach.* Needham Heights, MA: Ginn.

Aristotle (trans. 1932). *The rhetoric of Aristotle* (L. Cooper, Trans.). New York: Appleton-Century-Crofts.

McCroskey, J. C. (2001). *An introduction to rhetorical communication* (8th ed.). Boston: Allyn and Bacon.

McCroskey, J. C., & Teven, J. J. (1999). Goodwill: A reexamination of the construct and its measurement. *Communication Monographs, 66,* 90-103.

Mills, J., and Aronson, E. (1965). "Opinion change as a function of the communicator's attractiveness and desire to influence." *Journal of Personality and Social Psychology, 1,* 173-177.

National Communication Association (1999). *NCA credo for ethical communication.* Retrieved May 22, 2011, from http://www.natcom.org/Default.aspx?id=134&terms=credo

Petty, R., and Cacioppo, J. (1979). Issue involvement can increase or decrease persuasion by enhancing message-relevant cognitive responses. *Journal of Personality and Social Psychology, 37,* 1915-1926.

Petty, R., and Cacioppo, J. (1984). The effects of involvement on responses to argument quantity and quality: Central and peripheral routes to persuasion. *Journal of Personality and Social Psychology, 46,* 69-81.

Petty, R., and Cacioppo, J. (1986). *Communication and persuasion: Central and peripheral routes to persuasion and attitude change.* New York: Springer Verlag.

Wenberg, J., & Wilmot W. (1973). *The personal communication process.* New York: Wiley.

BETWEEN AUDIENCE
AND SPEAKER

In a successful communication transaction, listening is just as important as speaking.

LISTENING

— Stephan Ihde

Objectives

After reading this chapter, you should be able to:

- Define listening.
- Identify five ways to listen.
- Identify four listening styles.
- Understand how to improve your listening skill.
- Understand how to facilitate audience listening during a speech.

Key Concepts

action-oriented listening style

appreciative listening

comprehensive listening

content-oriented listening style

critical listening

decoding

discriminative listening

listening

people-oriented listening style

selective attention

therapeutic listening

time-oriented listening style

verbal cues

visual cues

vocal cues

"As speakers, men have become schooled in the arts of persuasion, and without the counter-art of listening a man can be persuaded—even by his own words—to eat foods that ruin his liver, to abstain from killing flies, to vote away his right to vote, and to murder his fellows in the name of righteousness. The art of listening holds for us the desperate hope of withstanding the spreading ravages of commercial, nationalistic and ideological persuasion."

—WENDELL JOHNSON

You might be surprised to find a chapter on listening in a speech textbook. You may be even more surprised to learn just how crucial listening is to the communication process. Face-to-face communication is the primary communication channel we use at school, at work, and in interpersonal situations (even though mediated communication channels such as e-mail and texting have increased in percentage) (Janusik & Wolvin, 2009). However, *successful* face-to-face communication requires that both the speaker and the listener are actively participating in the process. According to research by Janusik & Wolvin (2009) summarized in Exhibit 4.1 we spend more of our time listening each day (about 24%) than we spend speaking (about 20%) (see also Emanuel et al., 2008). But it is rare to find students who have had any formal training in listening. We spend the least amount of time writing (9%) and reading (8%) but those are the skills you have probably practiced the most in school.

College students tend to believe that they are naturally good listeners (Sargent & Weaver, 2003). In one study, students who received formal instruction in listening realized at the end of that instruction that their listening skills were not very strong (Zabava Ford, Wolvyn, & Chung, 2000). In this chapter we cannot provide extensive instruction in listening but we can help you understand the concept of listening the way listening scholars do. We will define listening, examine different goals of listening in different situations, look at four distinct listening styles, and discuss some specific strategies to help you become a better listener as well as a better speaker.

As you learned in the chapter on Communication Theory, one way to characterize communication is as a set of variables. According to the SMCRE model, receivers (R) have a significant part to play in the public speaking process because they decode the messages senders give to them. Decoding requires a listener to translate messages into understandable symbols. These symbols are interpreted as part of the listening process. You might be thinking at this point that decoding is just a matter of having a large vocabulary. In reality, we have more than one vocabulary. We tend to have different vocabularies for reading, writing, speaking and listening. For example, when was the last time you used the word "pulchritudinous" in a conversation? As a college student you could probably recognize the definition of this word or interpret it from the context of a story. You might have a harder time understanding it when listening to a lecture. The vocabulary, syntax, and grammar we use to write or read are usually larger than those we use to speak or listen. (By the way, this is one reason why writing out your speech word-for-word is not a good idea for most speaking situations. It doesn't sound natural.) In our early years, our primary vocabulary comes from listening to

Exhibit 4.1

Research indicates that we spend more of our time listening than in any other communication activity.

Source: (Janusik & Wolvin, 2009)

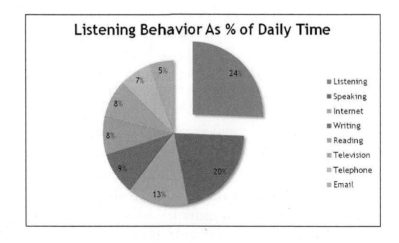

others speak and experiencing concrete forms (for example, "ball," "house," and "dog") (Nagy & Herman, 1987). But at grades 4 or 5, we shift from learning only concrete words to learning more abstract ones as our abstract reasoning capacities begin to develop (Chall, 1987). So in our childhood, our listening vocabulary is paramount, but then later our primary vocabulary comes from our reading and we learn terms that we don't always use in everyday speech. Interestingly, the average high school senior's vocabulary is probably somewhere around 40,000 words (Nagy & Herman, 1987). This is not very large given the fact that the Oxford English Dictionary catalogs upwards of 295,000 distinct English words! That does not even include many specialized and technical terms that would be considered the *jargon* of certain professions. Nor does it take into account the various **connotative meanings** of many words. So, it should be obvious that simply having a college-level vocabulary does not ensure that you are a good listener. Being a good listener requires an understanding of what listening is, how it is improved, and how it can be made easier during the communication transaction.

Denotative meaning
the literal or explicit definition of a word
Connotative meaning
the implied meaning of a word based upon its use within a given context

What Is Listening?

Andrew Wolvyn and Carolyn Coakley (1996), listening researchers at the University of Maryland, state that **listening** is "the process of receiving, attending to, and assigning meaning to aural and visual stimuli" (p. 69). *Receiving*: we take in lots of information, but we only *attend* to some of the information. Exercise 1 at the end of this chapter illustrates that sound and activity may be happening all around you, and your brain is aware of it at some level, but you only notice it when you literally pay attention to it. Listening requires mental energy. First, you must give selective attention. That is, you must decide what sound you want to hear. Second, you must *assign meaning* to the sound. And finally, you must decide how to associate it and store it if you want to recall it later. So the process might go something like this: sound waves hit our ears, we pay attention to the sound, we recognize it as the song of a mockingbird because we have heard these before, and then we decide what to do with it. In this case, we decide to listen and enjoy it. We can say we *listened* to the mockingbird. Note also that listening required more than simply *hearing,* which is only the physical process of receiving sound.

listening
the process of receiving, attending to, and assigning meaning to aural and visual stimuli

It is significant the Wolvyn and Coakley definition includes *visual stimuli.* Listening is not only done with your ears, but also with your *eyes.* Consider this example: through the evening news, you just found out that your best friend won the lottery. Then you see your friend enter the room where you are, and you exclaim, "Wow! Congratulations! I just heard the news! That's incredible!" Your friend replies with a sad, morose face: "Thanks. I'm really happy to have won." What do you conclude from this conflicting information? Your friend *said* they were happy, but their *nonverbal communication* says otherwise. Which do you believe? According to traditional research (e.g., Mehrabian & Ferris, 1967), you'd believe the sad face over the words spoken. Early research on contradictory messaging suggested that we tend to believe nonverbal communication when it directly contradicts the verbal message. However, some recent research has suggested that we decide whether to believe the verbal, vocal, or visual cues (Telfer & Howe, 1994) based on the situation. The more "dominant" channel of communication given the situation and context (Walker & Trimboli, 1989) will determine how we assign meaning to the message. Thus, maybe your friend truly *is* excited (verbal component—what was said) but you understand that the context of your friend's response allows for a flat emotional response (vocal component—how it was said) and also for a sad face (visual component—what was seen) due to the shock of the event. What's important to note here is that communication involves more than just *what* is said. It also involves *how* something is said. Good listeners pay attention to *all* channels of a message.

A Systems Model of Listening

The idea that listening occurs against a larger backdrop than simply the speaker-listener interaction is gaining traction with listening researchers. More than conceptualizing listening as simply information processing, researchers now see multiple factors in play, as illustrated by this process chart (Imhof and Janusik, 2006). This *systems model* characterizes listening as more than simply the interaction of a sender and a receiver. Factors such as personality, cultural norms, abilities, and goals are also considered. When any of these is altered, the listening process is affected.

As shown in Exhibit 4.2, listening *presage* includes the things listeners bring to a listening situation and the context in which listening occurs, including the listener's culture, the norms governing conversations in that culture, and the listening styles the person has. The *process* of listening is the actual mechanics of listening, including converting sound into electrical impulses and then into meaning (decoding), and accessing memories in order to prepare effective responses. Additionally, the behaviors of listening such as head nods and eye contact are seen here. Finally, the *product* of listening is the outcomes of the process, such as a strengthened relationship between friends, a personal feeling of satisfaction or accomplishment, or a deeper understanding of a particular concept or idea.

Five Ways of Listening

Wolvyn and Coakley (1996) identify ways to listen that anyone can do: people can listen discriminatively, cognitively, therapeutically, critically, and appreciatively. Each of these involves different goals and can be thought of as a different way of listening, much like there are different flavors of ice cream at an ice cream shop.

Exhibit 4.2

The *systems model* of listening characterizes listening as more than simply the interaction of a sender and a receiver.

Source: (Imhof and Janusik, 2006)

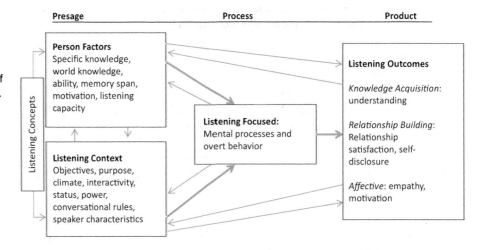

Discriminative Listening

We use Discriminative listening when we "distinguish the auditory and visual stimuli" (p. 152). We are able to distinguish the sound of a bird from a human voice, the sound of a fan from the sound of a car. Discriminative listening answers the question, "What is that sound?" Exercise 1 at the end of the chapter helps you focus and listen for different sounds. This type of listening is also used to identify languages. Discriminative listening allows us to know how a language *sounds*. You may not understand Spanish or Chinese but you can probably distinguish between these languages simply by the way they sound. Moreover, we recognize questions from statements in English given the speaker's inflection and tone of voice. Discriminative listening allows us to distinguish among sounds and stimuli.

Comprehensive Listening

Comprehensive listening is used to "understand the message in order to retain, recall, and, possibly, use that information at a later time" (p. 152). If you are actively listening to a lecture, you are utilizing comprehensive listening. That is, you are seeking to understand the information so you can pass the exam, gain personal knowledge, appeal to a personal interest. There are a whole host of other reasons why we listen in this way. Comprehensive listening refers to the process of information acquisition, storage, and retrieval.

Therapeutic Listening

Therapeutic listening provides "help to a person who needs to talk through a concern" (p. 153). Typically, therapeutic listening helps others process their feelings. Everyone faces a time when they need someone to help them through a difficult experience, and it can be invaluable to "be with" someone as they walk through those times. Therapeutic listening requires "being with" another person by reflecting thoughts back accurately to the other, sharing information without judging or "flinching," accepting the other person, or helping them make sense of difficult information (Myers, 2000). While trained counselors do this professionally for deeply troubling issues, friends and family do this quite often for much lesser ones. Therapeutic listening is a big part of the human experience: very often, we simply need to be heard and validated by another human being.

Critical Listening

We use Critical listening to "evaluate the merits of the message" (p. 154). Critical listening arrives at an informed judgment regarding an idea, situation, or argument. For example, suppose it is election time and you are evaluating the candidates in order to decide how to vote. This is the first election in which you can vote, so you want to make your vote count. You might listen to each candidate and, considering your own biases, evaluate your vote based on the merits of the candidates' arguments, the *messages* they offer. This kind of listening will be used when you and your classmates present persuasive speeches. You will need to listen critically to each one. Are the speaker's arguments sound? Are there logical fallacies? Does the message make sense? Does the message appeal to you? These are questions critical listeners employ when listening to a message. By the same token, as a speaker, you must be aware that others are using critical listening to process your arguments. You will want to make sure your arguments are sound and that there is no reason for anyone to dismiss your arguments on logical grounds. (For more on logical fallacies, see Chapter 15. For a more expansive treatment, see Warburton, 2003, which is available online through the UCF library or in print form).

Appreciative Listening

Finally, **appreciative** listening serves "to obtain sensory stimulation or enjoyment through the works and experiences of others" (p. 362). Appreciative listening is not simply putting on the headphones and listening to your favorite MP3 from "Petrified Remains." Sure, you can passively "veg-out" to music or mindlessly flop

Exhibit 4.3

Source: (Wolvyn and Coakley, 1996)

Appreciative, Critical, and Therapeutic listening

Comprehensive Listening

Discriminative Listening

in front of the television to watch a favorite show; but these aren't examples of listening actively. Appreciative listening is actively listening to and engaging with the sound, music, words, and the blends that the sounds produce. Imagine taking in the blends of sound that make up a musical piece: the drums, the singers and their specific harmonies, the guitars, the bass, and so on. As you listen to the music in your headphones, are you aware in which ear the person who mastered the mix put most of these sounds? Does it switch from ear to ear at given points? Can you make out the individual harmonies? Do the toms of the drums sound as if they were around you as the drummer fills in a measure with a drum riff? Of course, appreciative listening isn't limited to music: it can just as well be talk, sounds, song, music, theatre, or film. Wherever you go to take in listening for enjoyment and pleasure, you can listen appreciatively.

Exhibit 4.3 shows a model of listening developed by Wolvyn and Coakley (1996, p. 153) which illustrates the interdependence of different ways to listen. If we interpret this model in terms of the ways to listen described above we might substitute the labels as follows: Discriminative listening is at the root of the listening process; how we distinguish among stimuli orients us to what we do next with the stimuli. The trunk of the tree in this illustration reflects Comprehensive listening: we listen to understand across a variety of contexts, and need to understand a message before we can act on it appreciatively, therapeutically, or critically. Finally, the branches reflect Appreciative, Critical, and Therapeutic listening. These "higher order" levels of listening are possible only once a solid foundation of Comprehensive and Discriminative listening has been achieved.

By now, you should see that true listening is an active process. Yes, there is "couch potato" listening where messages go in one ear and out the other, but, in those cases, no real information typically lands anywhere to plant and take root. To listen actively to a friend, a lecture, a song, a sermon, or to distinguish among different sounds requires mental effort, and that is something we're not always ready to give. Let's face it: it's much easier to pretend as if we're listening than to truly listen. So, if you want to improve your listening habits, one of the first things you need to do is understand what kind of listener you are. This brings us to the concept of *listening styles*.

What Kind of Listener Are You?

Researchers have long wanted to have a way to measure differences in the ways people listen, to identify preferred individual *listening styles*, in order to help people improve their listening behavior. While everyone practices the five ways to listen, it is not difficult to see that some people prefer to listen to facts and figures; some prefer the content of a message; some prefer stories and illustrations; and some prefer concise, succinct information. While several tests have been created, one of the more recent and empirically grounded measurement tools is called the Listening Styles Profile-16 (LSP-16), developed by Kittie Watson at Tulane University and Larry Barker and James Weaver III at Auburn University (1995). These researchers wanted to help conceptualize differences in listening–"the how, where, when, who and what part of the information reception and encoding process" (p. 2). The research by Watson, Barker, and Weaver suggests that listening patterns can be characterized as four main *listening styles*: people-oriented, action-oriented, content-oriented, and time-oriented. Table 1 presents a modified version

What Kind of Listener Are You?

Table 1 The Listening Styles Profile (LSP-16) (Modified)

Circle the response next to the question that best reflects you.

Always	Frequently	Sometimes	Infrequently	Never	Questions
4	3	2	1	0	1. I look at my watch or clocks in the room when I have limited time to listen to others.
4	3	2	1	0	2. I focus my attention on the other person's feelings when listening to them.
4	3	2	1	0	3. When hurried, I let the other person(s) know that I have a limited amount of time to listen.
4	3	2	1	0	4. I prefer to listen to technical information.
4	3	2	1	0	5. When listening to others, I focus on any inconsistencies and/or errors in what's being said.
4	3	2	1	0	6. I interrupt others when I feel time pressure.
4	3	2	1	0	7. I am frustrated when others don't present their ideas in an orderly, efficient way.
4	3	2	1	0	8. I become involved when listening to the problems of others.
4	3	2	1	0	9. I ask questions to probe for additional information.
4	3	2	1	0	10. When listening to others, I quickly notice if they are pleased or disappointed.
4	3	2	1	0	11. I nod my head and/or use eye contact to show interest in what others are saying.
4	3	2	1	0	12. I begin a discussion by telling others how long I have to meet.
4	3	2	1	0	13. I jump ahead and/or finish thoughts of speakers.
4	3	2	1	0	14. I prefer to hear facts and evidence so I can personally evaluate them.
4	3	2	1	0	15. I am impatient with people who ramble on during conversations.
4	3	2	1	0	16. I like the challenge of listening to complex information.

(Adapted from Watson, Barker, & Weaver, 1995)

of the LSP-16 which you can use to assess your preferred listening style. So, what does your style mean?

If you have a **people-oriented** listening style you tend to have a high regard for another person's feelings and seek to find common ground with the speaker. These individuals respond keenly to the emotions of others and particularly enjoy harmony and commonality. Listeners with this style are often labeled as "relationally oriented." **Action-oriented** listeners like to receive concise, succinct information that is free from mistakes. These individuals are particularly frustrated by disorganized presentations since they get in the way of commencing action. Individuals with this style are often thought of as "task

Scoring the LSP-16

A.   Add scores together for questions 2,8,10,11:   _____

B.   Add scores together for questions 5,7,13,15:   _____

C.   Add scores together for questions 4,9,14,16:   _____

D.   Add scores together for questions 1,3,6,12:   _____

If you scored 12 or higher in category A above, you prefer a **people**-oriented style.

If you scored 12 or higher in category B above, you prefer a **content**-oriented style.

If you scored 12 or higher in category C above, you prefer an **action**-oriented style.

If you scored 12 or higher in category D above, you prefer a **time**-oriented style.

Note: You may have more than one listening style, or may have any of these particular styles.

See pages 78–79 for a discussion of what these styles mean and what the research reveals about them!

oriented." If you have a **Content-oriented** listening style you prefer challenging and complex messages. Someone who is content-oriented is more drawn to evaluate facts and strengths of arguments. These listeners are frequently called "unbiased" since they are willing to listen to both sides of an argument before rendering judgment. Finally, if you are a **time-oriented** listener, you prefer brief listening encounters. A time-oriented person will let others know they have limited time to spend in an interaction and prefer interactions to move along swiftly, sometimes even interrupting others in order to move the interaction along (Bodie & Villaume, 2003; Johnston, Weaver, Watson, & Barker, 2000; Watson, Barker, & Weaver, 1995).

What do we know about people who have these different listening styles? Many research studies have asked this question with interesting results:

- In a large survey done by Watson, Barker, & Weaver, 40% of respondents had two or more listening styles, 36% of respondents had only one listening style, and 24% had no particular listening style (Watson, Barker, & Weaver, 1995). Of those who had a single listening style preference, people-oriented was most popular (11.6%); followed by action-oriented (8.5%), content-oriented (8.3%), and time-oriented (7.7%).

- Listening styles may change depending on the situation. For example, a person may be more people-oriented when talking with friends, but more content-oriented when listening to a lecture (Imhof, 2004). So, don't be surprised if your LSP changes with a given situation.

- People-oriented jurors in a mock trial concerning a failed savings and loan found the plaintiffs less at fault, whereas time-oriented listeners awarded higher damages to the defense (Worthington, 2001).

- First-year medical students had a strong, majority people-oriented listening style upon entering medical school. At the end of their first year of medical school, however, people-oriented listening styles in those same students dropped dramatically. Also, at the end of schooling there were more students with no distinct listening style than with any one style (Watson, Lazurus, & Thomas, 1999).

- Bodie and Villaume (2003) measured nine dimensions of communication style (such as dominant, animated, and relaxed) against the four listening styles. They found that

  - People with a high people listening orientation are more relationally oriented. They attend to and affirm the other person and feel less receiver apprehension when speaking.

  - People with high content and action listening orientations tend to have a precise and attentive style of arguing the issues that leaves a strong impression on other people.

  - People with high time and action listening orientations tend to feel higher receiver apprehension and tend to be dramatic, forceful, and animated. Additionally, these individuals tend to dominate others in conversation.

- People- and content-oriented listeners are more conversationally sensitive than the other listening types (although the strength of the association found in this study was weak for content-oriented listeners) (Chesebro, 1999).

- People-oriented listeners are more extraverted (i.e., they are more sociable and have a positive self-concept); they are less psychotic (where psychotic individuals deviate from social norms and have a stronger, more independent sense of self), and also less neurotic (where neurotic individuals are more anxious and have a more negative self-concept) (Villaume & Bodie, 2007).

  - Additionally, they found that individuals with high time- and content-orientations more psychotic and have a friendlier communication style. "In other words, they seem to say what they want and do not necessarily worry about the effect on others that may run counter to their expectations" (p. 119).

- People- and content-oriented listeners have slightly less communication apprehension in group, meeting, and interpersonal settings (however, all styles were somewhat apprehensive about public speaking) (Sargent, Kiewitz, & Weaver, 1997).
- Content-oriented listeners are more likely to have a higher "need for cognition," or a greater tendency to think and enjoy the thinking process (Worthington, 2008).
- Content- and action-oriented listeners are more likely to question the information they hear than the other listening types (Kirtley & Honeycutt, 1997).
- A study of international students suggests that Israeli students favor the content and action listening orientations, German students favor an action listening orientation, and American students favor both people and time listening orientations (Kiewitz, Weaver, Brosius, & Weimann, 1997).

So we can see that there are quite a number of distinctions among these four listening styles. But how else does this relate to us as individuals? We can compare these styles to familiar personality characteristics, how we utilize empathy with others, and our gender.

Listening Styles and Personality

Some particularly fascinating relationships occur between these four listening styles and personality types. One familiar personality inventory, the Myers-Briggs Type Indicator (MBTI®), measures personality across five bipolar dimensions: introversion (e.g., you "recharge your batteries" by being alone) versus extraversion (e.g., you "recharge your batteries" by being around other people); intuiting (e.g., you gather and process information through a strong internal sense and awareness) versus sensing (e.g., you gather and process information most readily by the five senses); thinking (e.g., you make decisions by careful thought and logical processes) versus feeling (e.g., you make decisions by based on emotional sensitivity to others); and judging (e.g., you prefer structure and predictability) versus perceiving (e.g., you prefer open-enddeness and possibilities) (see, e.g., Quenk, 2000; Keirsey, 1998). These personality traits are often very consistent with listening styles. (If you don't know your Myers-Briggs personality type and you want to find out what it is, a reliable facsimile may be obtained via the Keirsey Temperament Sorter on-line at http://www.keirsey.com or at http://www.humanmetrics.com/cgi-win/jtypes2.asp.)

The results of Worthington's (2003) study [Table 2] show that Feelers and Intuitors are more strongly related to the people-oriented listening style while Thinkers have a small relation to action-, content-, and time-oriented listening styles. It makes some sense to think that those who are interested in relationships, community and harmony will have a listening style that reflects this while those who value efficiency and action will also reflect this in their listening. Similarly, Bommelje, Houston, & Smither, (2003) conducted a personality-listening styles study using different personality measures (intellectance, adjustment, prudence, sociability, likeability, ambition and school success) and using a different listening inventory (the Watson-Barker Listening Test). In their results, however, they found that only "school success," the degree to which a person values educational achievement and academics, was a predictor of effective listening.

Table 2 Listening Styles and Myers-Briggs Personality Types Associations

(Adapted from Worthington, 2003)

	People Orientation	Action Orientation	Content Orientation	Time Orientation
Introversion (I)				weak
Extraversion (E)	weak			
Intuiting (N)	moderate			
Sensing (S)		weak		weak
Thinking (T)		small	small	small
Feeling (F)	moderate			
Perceiving (P)	small			
Judging (J)		weak		

(Based on Pearson Product Moment Correlations significant at $p<.05$)

Listening Styles and Empathy

Another study looked at the LSP-16 and how people display empathy via empathetic responsiveness. Empathetic responses include *congruent emotional responses* (a friend feels sad, so you feel sad), *perspective taking* ("walking in the other person's shoes"), and *sympathetic responsiveness* (feelings of sorrow or compassion for others in distress). Weaver and Kirtley (1995) found that individuals with a people-oriented listening style showed a great deal of sympathetic responsiveness to others in difficult situations (that is, they generally have a great deal of concern and compassion for the well-being of others) but not much empathetic responsiveness. This seems to suggest that people-oriented listeners can feel pity and compassion for others but don't tend to feel the emotions that another may feel. Additionally, action and time listening styles showed the least amount of sympathetic responsiveness toward others in difficult situations, perhaps because in communication scenarios, they prefer a simple, get-to-the-point approach that doesn't deal so much with the feelings of others. Interestingly, however, there was a level of moodiness and nervousness to which action- and time-oriented listeners sympathized. Finally, content-oriented individuals (perhaps due to their objectivity) seemed to have an ability to interact with others who were emotionally upset without becoming emotionally upset themselves. As mentioned earlier, it could well be that empathy and listening styles are context dependent, so that an "active emotional commitment, acceptance of role-taking as a necessity, and identification with the other" (Walker, 1997, p. 134) may arise from any type of listener in a particular situation.

So, a variety of studies show links between the four listening styles and personality types and empathy styles. Hopefully, you will see these as more tools at your disposal to help you learn more about who you are and how you can become a more effective listener. It should be noted, however, that the research indicates it is somewhat difficult (but not impossible) to change your listening style once you have yours, even when you are presented with better and more efficient options of listening (Wolvyn & Coakley, 1996). Worthington's study suggests some links between personality and listening styles and we know that personality is something deeply ingrained in us. It would follow that our listening style would be resistant to change, although, as we saw earlier, some of your listening styles may well be context dependent. Before we look at some specific ways you might work to improve your listening skills, let's turn to another deeply engrained trait that shows some connections to our listening behavior–our gender.

Listening and Gender

It turns out that men and women are somewhat different when it comes to listening styles. The data summarized in Table 3 show that women tend to prefer conversations with others, particularly where feelings are involved and common ground is evident. Men tend to prefer listening for complex information that is to the point, free from error, and brief. Men make more errors in communication and are more likely to use "uh" and "um." Women use more body language and movement to communicate; however, they tend to perceive head nods in communication differently!

From where do all these differences come? Are we born with them or do we learn them? Johnston, Weaver, Watson, & Barker (2000) suggest that these listening differences may be a function of learning or socialization rather than biology. Maltz and Borker (1982) suggest that men and women perceive head nods differently due to the fact that they are from different *cultures*. Bryden (1980) argues that how men's and women's brains are organized could be as much biology or learning strategies. And finally, Canary and Hause (1993) would argue with all of these results, suggesting that very little gender difference can be accounted for statistically when communication research is taken

Table 3 Male and Female Differences in Listening Styles and Behaviors

Males	Females
Specialize in vocal communication: are better at judging and expressing information through the voice (Hall, 1984)	Specialize in visual communication: are better and judging and expressing information in the face and body (Hall, 1984)
Perceive head nods as feedback to be indicators of agreement (Maltz & Borker, 1982)	Perceive head nods as feedback to be indicators of "I'm listening" (Maltz & Borker, 1982; Doohan, 2007)
Interrupt more frequently in conversation (Hall, 1984)	Display more complexity and differentiation in how they describe emotional experiences (Barrett, Lane, Sechrest, & Schwartz, 2000)
Emit more errors in speech (such as filled pauses) (Hall, 1984)	Use more body movements to communicate involvement (Hall, 1984)
Favor the task-oriented listening styles (content-, action-, and time-oriented) (Johnston, Weaver, Watson & Barker, 2000)	Favor "communal" or people-oriented listening styles (Johnston, Weaver, Watson & Barker, 2000), but can also favor content-oriented (Watson, Barker, & Weaver, 1995)
Rate themselves as more content-oriented (Sargent & Weaver, 2003)	Rate themselves as more people-oriented (Sargent & Weaver, 2003)

as a whole. Well, it doesn't seem like researchers have much consensus on this particular question. What do *you* think? Do you think the difference in men's and women's communication and listening behavior is something innate, something learned, or both?

How Can You Improve Your Own Listening Skills? (Receiver)

Now that you have a good handle on what listening is; on different ways to listen; on what your particular listening style is; and how your style of listening relates to your personality, gender, and the way you display empathy; let's look at some ways you can improve your listening skills.

Poor listening skills can be costly. The space shuttle *Challenger* disaster can be traced, in large part, to communication breakdowns—spoken and listening— between managers and subordinates (Moore, 1992; Winsor, 1988). Unclear messages sent or received may result in such consequences as misunderstandings, loss of business, injury, or even death (Ihde, Katt, & Bosley, 2000). Even physicians who do not listen are more likely to be sued for malpractice if something goes wrong (Hickson, Clayton, Githens, & Sloan, 1992). Let's face it: the technical professions demand precision, and errors can be costly. Fortunately, there are proven ways to improve our listening skills, and these can have great benefits—for example, as Virshup, Oppenberg, and Coleman (1999) discuss, physicians who listen to their patients are less likely to be sued (see also Coy & Stratton, 2002) and patients are more likely to be happier with their doctors (Harris & Templeton, 2001).

Ask Pre-Questions

Listening researcher Margarete Imhof (2001) states that "intentional and meaningful learning can only take place when a person has identified a specific learning goal" (p. 4). Imagine coming to class with a list of questions for things *you* wanted to learn rather than simply writing down what the instructor or speaker gave to you! It would change your focus about what you learned for the class. King (1994) found that students who could ask their own questions about an upcoming lecture did better on a posttest than those who were simply given questions to consider. Look on the syllabus for this class and ask yourself: "What do *I* want to get out of this class today?"

Consider Your Interest Level

How much interest you have for a given topic seems to suggest a greater ability to recall that information at a later time (Schiefele & Krapp, 1996). Intuitively, this makes sense: we attend to things we want to learn, and so are willing to devote more mental energy to those things. You're less likely to retain information you're "forced" to learn. While there's little you can do to change the interest level you have for something, you *can* change your perception and evaluation of a given topic. Instead of saying, "How boring!" what would it be like to approach an uninteresting topic with, "What can I learn from this?"

Use Elaboration Strategies

Elaboration strategies (Imhof, 2001) involve relating new knowledge in some meaningful way to existing knowledge (such as creating new examples, contrasting the information, and mentally "seeing" the concept). Taking good notes with these elements in mind also falls into this category. According to Imhof, when these methods were used, "participants consistently reported more comprehensive understanding, deeper level of processing, more reflective assessment of the new material, facilitated integration of new information into existing knowledge structures, and improved processing characteristics (e.g., sustaining attention and selective focus, better retention)" (p. 16). Practice putting the information you hear into your knowledge framework in a way that makes it more meaningful for you.

As a Listener, Take 51% of the Responsibility for the Communication Transaction

Researchers Wolvyn & Coakley, (1996) have suggested that effective communication is more than half the responsibility of the listener. Imagine how different your communication interactions would be if you saw yourself as having slightly more responsibility than the speaker for clear communication! Rather than letting the speaker do all the work, imagine being actively engaged in the entire process. In this class, take 51% of the burden of communication during student speeches, during lectures, and when you speak to your classmates. If there's something you don't understand, ask questions!

Choose to Focus

This is easier said than done, but well worth the effort. Thinking speed (about 500 words per minute) is typically substantially faster than speaking speed (about 125 to 175 words per minute) (Wolvyn & Coakley, 1996; Foulke, 1968). The question, then, is what do we do with the difference in words and time? Our minds do something with the difference. For example, in the middle of a speaker's sentence, we might predict the end of the speaker's sentence and then devote our mental energy toward something else, figuring that we already know what the speaker will say. Instead, if we should choose to focus our full attention on the speaker and the message we might use our extra thought energy for elaborating on the message.

Be Aware of Logical Fallacies, Source Credibility, and Appeals

These are especially relevant for the persuasive speeches. Thinking critically will help you analyze a speaker's message and make you more likely to accept or reject it based on carefully-considered, well-reasoned grounds, rather than peripheral factors or fallacious arguments (Wolvyn & Coakley, 1996). Pay attention to that little voice inside you when it says that something isn't quite right with the speaker's message. Chapter 15 will discuss the logical fallacies in detail. In Chapter 14 you will learn more about persuasive appeals and what types of appeals are typically used to increase persuasion.

Keep a Listening Journal

Johnson, Barker, & Pierce (1995) suggest that you keep track of your listening behaviors by writing down what you did, assessing what you learned from those behaviors, and writing how you felt as a result. It can be an eye-opening experience to see what we actually do–and do poorly–as listeners. Also, it may make you more aware of how your listening style affects others and how others' listening styles affect you.

Be Willing to Listen

Researchers Roberts & Vinson (1998) found that a person's willingness to listen positively correlated with communication skills and negatively correlated with communication fears of receiving messages, sending messages, and always being right ("dogmatism"). It's possible that simply being willing to listen may make the whole process of communication work better.

How Can You Facilitate Increased Listening in the Audience? (Sender)

If you are struggling with extemporaneous delivery, take heart: Having a message that has high relevance to your audience also helps ensure that listeners will be less affected by areas of your delivery that still need improvement and may still respond positively to the highly relevant verbal content of your message (Marsh, Hart-O'Rourke, & Julka, 1997).

As speakers, we can also help our listeners make the communication transaction a more profitable experience for them. Here are some key strategies:

Have a Strong Message that Is Relevant to Your Audience

Let's be honest: Have you heard speeches in this class that you thought were a waste of time? Well, here's an even tougher question: Do you wonder if *your* speeches have wasted the class's time? More than likely, if you don't care about your message, your audience won't, either. Having a message that *you* care about and that has strong sources and utilizes good *logos* increases the chances that that your audience will care about the message also. Have you made your messages relevant to them? Did you use good audience analysis techniques discussed in Chapter 5? Recall that we tend to remember and process things in which we have an interest (Schiefele & Krapp, 1996). This is a good time to practice "perspective taking," one characteristic of empathy discussed previously: think about how your audience will perceive your message. And why not specifically refer to one or two members of your audience in your introduction and, topic permitting, show how your topic might be relevant to them?

Use Confident Language

In a study by Holtgraves & Lasky (1999), subjects used both central and peripheral routes to persuasion when the speaker used confident ("strong") language instead of hedging language (e.g., "I suppose that...", "It's kinda true that...", and frequent vocal pauses). Make sure your purpose and thesis statements are crystal clear for your speech so you know exactly what you want to say and how you want to say it. As you read Chapter 10 think about specific techniques and word choices that will make the language of your persuasive speech more confident and assertive.

Define any Unfamiliar Terms and use Standard English

Make sure you clearly explain any terms that your audience doesn't understand. Using vocabulary or concepts that your audience doesn't know is much like speaking a foreign language (Reimann, 2001). When asked how professors could improve speaking to foreign students, Chinese students responded with answers like, "avoid using colloquial and slang expressions," "speak clearly and loudly in the classroom," "use formal English to deliver lectures," and "try to get rid of strong accent and strange pronunciation" (Huang, 2004). Expressions and idioms are among the most difficult things for new speakers to a language to understand accurately (e.g., "It's raining cats and dogs!"). Consider your specific audience's language capacity and vocabulary base, and use terms with which they will be familiar.

Offer Opportunities for Clarification

While your speeches in this class may not have the time or format to do this, remember this when you're giving presentations in the "real world." Take the time to make sure your audience understands your message. If you are a people-oriented listener, you will know quickly if your audience doesn't understand your message by their reactions and nonverbal expressions to your message. Build in opportunities for feedback if the situation allows, and allow for questions. As we saw earlier, when students could generate their own questions regarding a topic, they did better on recall (King, 1994).

Assume that Your Audience May Not Have the Same Listening Style as You

You may enjoy connecting with an audience and making everyone feel good but there may be audience members who prefer a succinct and direct message. Similarly, if your points are not in logical order and you are speaking to content-oriented listeners who are strongly uncomfortable with disorganization, this will spell trouble. And if you are an action-oriented speaker whose audience is primarily people-oriented, you may need to relate to them on levels of connectivity. Utilizing good audience analysis skills is a key element of planning a strong message.

Summary

In this chapter, you have learned:

- listening is crucial to our communication patterns but it is a subject which is rarely taught in depth in the grade school or college curriculum

- listening is "the process of receiving, attending to, and assigning meaning to aural and visual stimuli" and it is distinct from hearing

- a systems model of listening (presage, process, and product) suggests that changing individual elements affects the entire process

- how to listen discriminatively, comprehensively, therapeutically, critically, and appreciatively, which define the differing listening goals we might have at a given time

- four styles of listening (people-, content-, action-, and time-oriented) which have direct correlations with personality, gender, and styles of empathy

- specific ways to improve listening habits both as a receiver and as a sender.

Check Your Understanding: Exercises and Activities

1. Do a listening experiment. Before you begin reading this chapter:

   > Close your eyes
   > Silently count to ten
   > Listen—Take in all the sounds around you.

   What did you experience? What did you notice? What did you hear? Did you become aware of any new sounds around you? Did you hear an air conditioning fan, a radio, a television, conversations, a bird, an automobile, your own breathing? Now, do the same thing one more time—close your eyes, silently count to ten, and listen—but this time, try to listen for a sound you *didn't* hear the first time. Were you aware of these sounds before you closed your eyes the first time? If not…how is it that you became aware of them now? Why did you notice them now and not before?

2. Keep a listening journal. For the next two weeks, keep daily accounts of how you listened, whom you listened to, and in what situations you chose to listen. Which ways to listen did you employ most frequently? Did you encounter people with different listening styles than you? What happened when there were differences? How did you feel about the ways that you listen? When you complete your two weeks, look back over your journal. Did you see any areas in which you need to improve?

3. Take the Jung Typology Test on http://www.humanmetrics.com/cgi-win/jtypes2.asp. Then take the Listening Styles Profile on Table 1, and score your results. Now look at Table 2 on page 83. Do your results match? If not, why do you think there are differences?

4. Rent a British/Irish/Scottish movie that has a strong dialect difference from American English. (Some examples include "Trainspotting," "Snatch," "Becoming Jane," and "About a Boy." The movie "About a Boy" has an "English to English" translation section in the special features of the DVD that highlights British English idioms and expressions that American audiences would probably not recognize.) Practice your discriminative listening skills by first watching the film without subtitles and then watching the film with subtitles.

5. Expand your critical and content-listening skills by visiting an open trial in a courthouse. Many courts are open to the public, and sitting in an actual trial can be quite instructive. Listen to the lawyers as they state their arguments, and listen especially when the opposing lawyer shouts "Objection!" and the judge responds. You can also read ahead to chapter 15 concerning logical fallacies.

6. Expand your therapeutic listening by practicing with a friend. Enlist a friend to tell a real story that either positively or negatively influenced them. Practice empathy simply by "being in the other person's shoes." As they are telling their story, what do you think they are feeling? How do you think they felt when the event happened to them? Test what you're feeling by asking your friend, "I can imagine when ___ happened, you felt ___. Am I right?" What else can you do to support what the person is feeling? *Special note to men: Avoid the stereotypical temptation to "fix" your friends, especially if your friends are female. For example, if a female friend says she is upset, a male might stereotypically respond "Well, here's what you need to do." Instead, try listening and validating what your friend is feeling. A better response might begin "I see how sad you are when you're telling your story."*

7. Scan the radio dial and stop on stations that you normally don't listen to. Practice appreciative listening by engaging with what you hear.

References

Barrett, L. F., Lane, R. D., Sechrest, L., & Schwartz, G. E. (2000). Sex differences in emotional awareness. *Personality and Social Psychology Bulletin, 26(11)*, 1027–1035.

Bodie, G. D. and Villaume, W. A. (2003). Aspects of receiving information: The relationship between listening preferences, communication apprehension, receiver apprehension, and communicator style. *International Journal of Listening, 17*, 47–67.

Bodie, G. D., Worthington, D., Imhof, M., & Cooper, L. O. (2008). What would a unified field of listening look like? A proposal linking past perspectives and future endeavors. *International Journal of Listening, 22*, 103–122.

Bommelje, R., Houston, J. M., & Smither, R. (2003). Personality characteristics of effective listeners: A five factor perspective. *International Journal of Listening, 17*, 32–46.

Bryden, M. P. (1980). Sex differences in brain organization: Different brains or different strategies? *The Behavioral and Brain Sciences, 3*, 230–232.

Canary, D. J. & Hause, K. S. (1993). Is there any reason to research sex differences in communication? *Communication Quarterly, 41*, 129–144.

Chall, J. S. (1987). Two vocabularies for reading: Recognition and meaning. In M. G. McKeown & M. E.Curtis (Eds.), *The nature of vocabulary acquisition* (pp. 7–17). Hillsdale, NJ: Lawrence Erlbaum Associates.

Chesebro, J. L. (1999). The relationship between listening styles and conversational sensitivity. *Communication Research Reports, 16 (3)*, 233–238.

Coy, K. & Stratton, R. (2002). Avoiding your greatest fear—malpractice. *Journal of the Oklahoma Dental Association, 93(2)*, 18–27.

Doohan, E. (2007). Listening behaviors of married couples: An exploration of nonverbal presentation to a relational outsider. *International Journal of Listening, 21 (1)*, 24–41.

Edwards, R. (2011). Listening and message interpretation. *International Journal of Listening, 25(1)*, 47–65.

Emanuel, R., Adams, J., Baker, K., Daufin, E. K., Ellington, C., Fitts, E., Himsel, J., Holladay, L., & Okeowo, D. (2008). How college students spend their time communicating. *International Journal of Listening, 22(1)*, 13–28.

Foulke, E. (1968). Listening comprehension as a function of word rate. *Journal of Communication, 18*, 198-206.

Hall, J. A. (1984). *Nonverbal sex differences.* Baltimore, MD: The Johns Hopkins University Press.

Harris, S. R. & Templeton, E. (2001). Who's listening? Experiences of women with breast cancer in communicating with physicians. *The Breast Journal, 7(6)*, 444.

Holtgraves, T. & Lasky, B. (1999). Listening power and persuasion. *Journal of Language and Social Psychology, 18(2)*, 196–205.

Huang, J. (2004). Voices from Chinese students: Professors' use of English affects academic listening. *College Student Journal, 38(2)*, 212–223.

Ihde, S. K., Katt, J., & Bosley, A. (2000). *Technically Speaking: A guide for technical communicators.* Dubuque, IA: Kendall-Hunt.

Imhof, M. (2004). Who are we as we listen? Individual listening profiles in varying contexts. *International Journal of Listening, 18,* 36–45.

Imhof, M. (2001). How to listen more efficiently: Self-monitoring strategies in listening. *International Journal of Listening, 15,* 2–17.

Imhof, M. & Janusik, L. A. (2006). Development and validation of the Imhof-Janusik Listening Concepts Inventory to measure listening conceptualization differences between cultures. *Journal of Intercultural Communication Research, 35,* 79–98.

Janusik, L. A. & Wolvin, A. D. (2009). 24 hours in a day: A listening update to the time studies. *International Journal of Listening, 23(2),* 104–120.

Johnson, I. W., Barker, R.T., & Pearce, C. G. (1995). Using journals to improve listening behavior: An exploratory study. *Journal of Business and Technical Communication, 9(4),* 475–483.

Johnston, M. K., Weaver, III, J. B., Watson, K. W., & Barker, L. B. (2000). Listening styles: Biological or psychological differences? *International Journal of Listening, 14,* 32–46.

Keirsey, D. (1998). *Please understand me II: Temperament, character, intelligence.* Del Mar, CA: Prometheus Nemesis.

Kiewitz, C., Weaver, III, J. B., Brosius, H. B., & Weimann, G. (1997). Cultural differences in listening styles preferences: A comparison of young adults in Germany, Israel, and the United States. *International Journal of Public Opinion Research, 9(3),* 233–247.

King, A. (1994). Autonomy and question asking: The role of personal control in guided student-generated questioning. *Learning and Individual Differences, 6,* 163–185.

Kirtley, M. D., & Honeycutt, J.M. (1996). Listening styles and their correspondence with second guessing. *Communication Research Reports, 13(2),* 174–182.

Maltz, D. N, & Borker, R. A. (1982). A cultural approach to male-female miscommunication. In J. J. Gumperz (Ed.), *Language and Social Identity* (pp. 196–216). Cambridge: Cambridge University Press.

Marsh, K. L., Hart-O'Rourke, D. M., & Julka, D. L. (1997). The persuasive effects of verbal and nonverbal information in a context of value relevance. *Personality and Social Psychology Bulletin, 23(6),* 563–579.

Mehrabian, A. & Ferris, S. R. (1967). Inference of attitudes from nonverbal communication in two channels. *Journal of Consulting Psychology, 31,* 33–41.

Moore, P. (1992). When politeness is fatal: Technical communication and the *Challenger accident. Journal of Business and Technical Communication, 3(3),* 269–292.

Myers, S. (2000). Empathic listening: Reports on the experience of being heard. *Journal of Humanistic Psychology, 40(2),* 148–173.

Nagy, W. E., & Herman, P. A. (1987). Breadth and depth of vocabulary knowledge: Implications for acquisition and instruction. In M.G. McKeown & M.E.Curtis (Eds.), *The nature of vocabulary acquisition* (pp. 19–35). Hillsdale, NJ: Lawrence Erlbaum Associates.

Quenk, N. L. (2000). *Essentials of Myers-Briggs type indicator assessment.* New York, NY: John Wiley & Sons.

Reimann, P. (2001). Jargon, abbreviations cloud message being conveyed. *Ophthalmology Times, 26(8),* 76.

Roberts, C. V., & Vinson, L. (1998). Relationship among willingness to listen, receiver apprehension, communication apprehension, communication competence, and dogmatism. *International Journal of Listening, 12,* 40–56.

Sargent, S. L., Kiewitz, C., & Weaver, J. B. (1997). Correlates between communication apprehension and listening style preferences. *Communication Research Reports, 14(1),* 74–78.

Sargent, S. L. & Weaver, III, J.B. (2003). Listening styles: Sex differences in perceptions of self and others. *International Journal of Listening, 17,* 5–18.

Schiefele, U. & Krapp, A. (1996). Topic interest and free recall of expository text. *Learning and Individual Differences, 8,* 141–160.

Telfer, K. E., & Howe, C. J. (1994). Verbal, vocal, and visual information in the judgment of interpersonal affect: A methodological limitation of some influential research. *Journal of Language and Social Psychology, 13(3),* 331–344.

Villaume, W. A., Bodie, G. D. (2007). Discovering the listener within us: The impact of trait-like personality variables and communicator styles on preferences for listening style. *International Journal of Listening, 21(2)*, 102–123.

Virshup, B. B., Oppenberg, A. A., & Coleman, M. M. (1999). Strategic risk management: Reducing malpractice claims through more effective patient-doctor communication. *American Journal of Medical Quality, 14(4)*, 153–159.

Walker, K. L. (1997). Do you ever listen? Discovering the theoretical underpinnings of empathic listening. *International Journal of Listening, 11(1)*, 127–137.

Walker, M. B. & Trimboli, A. (1989). Communicating affect: The role of verbal and nonverbal content. *Journal of Language and Social Psychology, 8(3,4)*, 229–248.

Warburton, N. (2003). *Thinking from A to Z.* New York, NY: Taylor & Francis.

Watson, K. W., Barker, L. L, & Weaver, III, J. B. (1995). The listening styles profile (LSP-16): Development and validation of an instrument to assess four listening styles. *International Journal of Listening, 9*, 1–13.

Watson, K. W., Lazarus, C. J., & Thomas, T. (1999). First-year medical students' listener preferences: A longitudinal study. *International Journal of Listening, 13*, 1–11.

Weaver, III, J. B. & Kirtley, M. D. (1995). Listening styles and empathy. *The Southern Communication Journal, 60*, 131–140.

Winsor, D. A. (1988). Communication failures contributing to the *Challenger* accident: An example for technical communicators. *IEEE Transactions on Professional Communication, 31(3)*, 101–107.

Wolvin, A. & Coakley, C. G. (1996). *Listening* (5th ed). Brown & Benchmark: Dubuque, IA.

Worthington, D. L. (2008). Exploring the relationship between listening style and need for cognition. *International Journal of Listening, 22(1)*, 46–58.

Worthington, D. L. (2003). Exploring the relationship between listening style preference and personality. *International Journal of Listening, 17*, 68–87.

Worthington, D. L. (2001). Exploring juror's listening processes: The effect of listening style preference on juror decision making. *International Journal of Listening, 15*, 20–37.

Zabava Ford, W. S., Wolvyn, A. D., & Chung, S. (2000). Students' self-perceived listening competencies in the basic speech communication course. *International Journal of Listening, 14*, 1–13.

Then Illinois State Senator Barack Obama electrified the Democratic National Convention with his keynote speech in 2004, setting him on a path that would lead to the presidency four years later.

ADAPTING TO YOUR AUDIENCE

Objectives  www.mhhe.com/brydon7e

After reading this chapter and reviewing the online learning resources at
www.mhhe.com/brydon7e, you should be able to:

- Define and apply the concept of rhetorical situation.

- Identify short- and long-term goals for speaking to a particular
  audience.

- Determine whether your audience is voluntary or captive.

- Analyze the cultural, demographic, and individual diversity of your
  audience.

- Adapt to the cultural, demographic, and individual diversity of your
  audience.

- Gather information to learn about your audience.

- Confront and adapt to constraints associated with the rhetorical
  situation.

Key Concepts

attitude

audience diversity

belief

captive audience

central beliefs

constraint

core beliefs

cultural diversity

deficiency needs

demographic diversity

demographics

growth needs

individual diversity

long-term goals

peripheral beliefs

rhetorical situation

short-term goals

socioeconomic status

values

voluntary audience

"There is not a liberal America and a conservative America—there is the
United States of America. There is not a Black America and a White America
and Latino America and Asian America—there's the United States of America."

—BARACK OBAMA, SPEAKING TO THE DEMOCRATIC NATIONAL CONVENTION, JULY 2004[1]

In the previous edition of this book, we drew attention to a young U.S. senatorial candidate from Illinois and the electrifying keynote speech he gave to the 2004 Democratic National Convention. The quotation with which we introduce this chapter was a central theme of that speech, which Obama adapted to a far wider audience than the convention delegates gathered that evening in Boston.

Much as we might like to think we are clairvoyant, we are not. Although we suspected that Barack Obama's political future had a major upside, we had no idea he would be president in just four more years.

Regardless of what you personally think about his policies, President Obama shares a skill in common with many of our presidents: he knows how to deliver a powerful speech. For the purposes of this chapter, however, it is not his delivery skills per se that make him an example. Rather, it is his background and the role it has played in helping him adapt those skills to the most diverse audiences, something that helped this son of a Kenyan father and a Kansan mother rise to a level that no one would have predicted.

Barack Obama's personal history helps explain his ability to connect with audiences from different cultures and groups, especially during his campaign. Born in Hawaii, he moved to Indonesia when he was six. At age 10, Barry (as he was then called) returned to Hawaii to be raised by his grandparents in one of the nation's most diverse states. As he wrote in 1999, "The opportunity that Hawaii offered—to experience a variety of cultures in a climate of mutual respect—became an integral part of my world view, and a basis for the values that I hold most dear."[2] Although his mother and grandparents were white, in his teen years Obama sought out African American mentors to help him understand his biracial identity—a struggle he chronicles in his book *Dreams From My Father*.[3]

At Harvard Law School, the signs of his ability to appeal to ideologically diverse audiences began to emerge. As Politico.com reported in June 2008: "Barack Obama's election in 1990 as the first black president of the Harvard Law Review . . . was . . . won in part by convincing the conservative minority of law students that he would treat them fairly."[4]

As president, Obama has continued to draw on his multi-cultural background to appeal to a variety of audiences. On June 4, 2009, for example, he delivered a promised speech to Muslims in Cairo, proclaiming, "I'm a Christian, but my father came from a Kenyan family that includes generations of Muslims. As a boy, I spent several years in Indonesia and heard the call of the azaan at the break of dawn and at the fall of dusk. As a young man, I worked in Chicago communities where many found dignity and peace in their Muslim faith."[5]

Putting political preferences aside, Obama's ability to adapt to the situation and audience, especially during his campaign, is an example from which we can all learn. It teaches lessons first taught by rhetorical scholars decades and even centuries ago, including :

- How public speeches emerge as a response to the rhetorical situation
- How to formulate attainable goals and specific purposes in light of the rhetorical situation
- How to adapt to audience diversity, including its cultural, demographic, and individual dimensions
- How to learn about audience characteristics
- How to adapt to the constraints that are faced in the rhetorical situation.

The Rhetorical Situation

There are times when we are faced with what Professor Lloyd Bitzer calls a **rhetorical situation,** "a natural context of persons, events, objects, relations, and an exigence [goal] which strongly invites utterance."[6] The hallmarks of such a situation are (1) some kind of goal that a speaker seeks to achieve, (2) an audience that is capable of helping reach that goal, and (3) a set of constraints that limits what the speaker can accomplish. It is likely that you will find times in your life—personally, professionally, and publicly—when the only way you can respond to a situation is through rhetoric, a concept with a long and storied history.

Although the specific term *rhetorical situation* wasn't coined until the late 1960s, its roots can be traced to ancient Greece and the fifth century BC. Then as now there was a need for public speaking skills because democracy requires that people talk about and debate public policy. Further, there were no lawyers, and people had to plead their own case in court. As we discussed in Chapter 3, a group of teachers of rhetoric, known as *Sophists,* taught the skills of speaking for a fee. Plato opposed their approach to rhetoric as dishonest. Plato believed that one should first discover the truth philosophically and then use rhetoric only in service to truth.

Plato's famous student Aristotle brought order and systematic focus to the study of rhetoric. Aristotle defined rhetoric as the "faculty of observing in any given case the available means of persuasion."[7] He specified that rhetoric consisted of three modes of proof: *ethos,* the personal credibility of the speaker; *pathos,* putting the audience into a certain frame of mind; and *logos,* the proof or apparent proof provided by the actual words of the speech (*logos* being the Greek word for "word"). In many ways this classification foreshadows much of contemporary communication research with its emphasis on source credibility *(ethos),* audience analysis and reaction *(pathos),* and message construction *(logos).*

The study and practice of rhetoric was further refined by Roman rhetoricians such as Cicero and Quintilian, who developed the canons of rhetoric: invention, organization, style, delivery, and memory. Invention is the creative process of developing a speech—from topic selection and research to choosing the ideas to use. Organization involves arranging those ideas in a manner that is easy to follow and compelling. Style deals with the language choices made to impact the audience. Delivery deals with the nonverbal channels—voice, body, and face—working together to communicate a message. Memory has been largely discarded as a tool of public speaking. Ancient speakers, lacking TelePrompTers and cue cards, memorized their speeches and developed many mnemonic devices to help them recall their words (some of which are taught today in memory improvement courses). Today memorized speeches are largely confined to competitive speech contests.

After the Roman period, the study and practice of rhetoric went into a period of decline. As Europe plunged into the Middle Ages, the need for a complete rhetoric was diminished, and human affairs were largely governed by church dogma. Eventually rhetoric came to be associated almost entirely with matters of style. It is also largely from this period that rhetoric was reduced to empty words, signifying nothing, as the often heard expression, "that's just rhetoric," suggests.

With the coming of the Enlightenment, rhetoric was rediscovered. There is not sufficient space here to chronicle all the theorists who revived rhetoric.

rhetorical situation
A natural context of persons, events, objects, relations, and an exigence (goal) which strongly invites utterance.

Particularly noteworthy, however, are the trio of Hugh Blair, George Campbell, and Richard Whately, who wrote in the late 18th and early 19th centuries. Blair concerned himself largely with style. Campbell was a proponent of a type of psychology emphasizing discrete mental faculties, returning rhetoric to a concern with the audience and pathos. Whately revived the concern with invention. His treatise on the *Elements of Rhetoric* gave a new importance to logic and reasoning in rhetoric.

By the early 20th century, departments of speech began to emerge as discrete entities on college campuses. Theorists again began writing about rhetoric and rhetorical theory, many of them returning to the subject's fifth-century BC roots in ancient Greece.

Given this rich history, rhetorical scholar Lloyd Bitzer was following well-established tradition when he sought in 1968 to ground rhetoric in situational factors. As you analyze your own rhetorical situations, remember that your goals and the audiences you speak to are central to preparing just the right speech. And, as you will discover later in the chapter, there are also factors that will constrain or limit your choices—everything from how much time you have to speak to the legal limits of slander and libel. Let's begin, then, by looking at your goals as a speaker and the specific purpose you seek to fulfill in any given speech situation.

Goals and Specific Purpose

All too often beginning speakers get ahead of themselves in the planning process: for example, they start with the challenges an audience poses without first considering their own purpose in speaking and the goal they hope to achieve. If you have no clear goal to start with, no amount of audience analysis is going to help. We want you to be able to reasonably predict how your audience is likely to respond to your speech. This begins with deciding on your goal and then selecting a specific purpose that will make sense in light of the audience you know awaits you and the goal you hope to achieve.

short-term goals
Those ends that we can reasonably expect to achieve in the near term.

long-term goals
Those ends that we can hope to achieve only over an extended period of time.

You can have both **short-term goals** and **long-term goals.** For example, Barack Obama's long-term goal in his Cairo speech was Middle East peace. Of course, this is a problem with a long history that has bested many presidents. Such a thorny problem cannot be solved by any speech or series of speeches. Thus, his short-term goal for this speech was to try to reframe how America is viewed in the Muslim world.

Although we should never lose sight of the "big picture," we should also recognize that the realization of short-term goals makes the realization of long-term goals more probable. Giving up a bad habit for a day, for example, makes giving up the habit for a week or longer much easier for people. It's in the speaker's best interest, then, to focus on what an audience would find palatable in the short run before tackling tougher long-term goals.

Your specific purpose, as discussed in Chapter 1, is the objective you hope to achieve in speaking to a particular audience on a particular occasion. Although your instructor will probably assign you a general purpose for each speech, such as to persuade, to inform, or to entertain, the specific purpose is up to you and should be chosen to fulfill a specific goal.

The Audience

Given the specific purpose and goals you have tentatively established for your speech, you now want to be able to predict whether they make sense in light of your audience. Analyzing your audience is an extension of the process we all go through when meeting and getting to know new people. It begins on a general level and then becomes increasingly specific. When we meet new people, we try to gauge the degree to which they are similar to us; for example, do they share our language and dialect? We then use this information as a basis for predictions about how to introduce ourselves and what topics of conversation and questions would be appropriate. As we get to know people better, we learn more about what makes them unique. We then use this new, more sophisticated knowledge to guide us in broaching more sensitive topics with them.

You do much the same thing with an audience. Instead of focusing on one person, however, you have the more difficult task of focusing on many. What you discover about them helps you decide what to say and how to say it. You can never know all there is to know about even a small audience. Still, if you are systematic in your analysis, you can learn a tremendous amount about the increasingly diverse people you encounter. You can profitably use what you learn about such people to adapt your purpose, goal, and eventual message so that they welcome rather than reject your speech.

Any hope you have of achieving your speaking goals, however, depends on whether there is an audience "capable of being influenced by discourse and of being mediators of change."[8] Audience analysis begins by knowing who your audience is.

Audience Choice

In looking at your audience, ask yourself two basic questions:

- Do I get to choose my audience?
- Does my audience get to choose whether to listen to me?

In some situations you will be able to choose the audience for your speech. But in many cases, including your public speaking class, you will have no choice. Short of changing class sections, you will not be able to select another audience. Once you leave the classroom, however, you are likely to have some degree of choice about which audiences to address.

When you choose an audience, think about two important questions. First, what do audience members think of my goals? If an audience is likely to support your goals, then your task is quite different than if its members are indifferent or dramatically opposed. Managers of political campaigns nearly always stage audiences by filling them with people who agree with the goals represented by their politicians. The last thing a campaign manager wants is an audience full of unpredictable "wildcards" who may or may not share the politician's goals.

Second, ask if and how your audience can help you achieve your goals. We've heard classroom speeches that urged the approval of an international treaty to reduce global warming. This is a noble goal, but aside from writing a letter to public officials there is very little class members can do to help achieve this goal. On the other hand, college students can personally do their part to fight global warming: take public transportation, ride their bikes, and purchase hybrid cars. The best public speakers ask not only whether their audience supports their goals but also how the audience members can realistically help them achieve those goals.

In addition to your choice of audiences, you need to consider the audience's ability to choose whether to hear you speak. Audiences can be broadly defined as voluntary or captive. A **voluntary audience** chooses to hear a speaker. A **captive audience** has no choice about hearing a speech. Whether audience members are present voluntarily can make a big difference in their response to a speech. For example, when controversial filmmaker Michael Moore came to our campus, a standing-room-only audience paid to see him. Although some audience members clearly came to heckle him, the vast majority was there to cheer him on. Compare this to the response of the captive audience that booed him when he used his Academy Award acceptance speech to denounce the war in Iraq. Academy members and guests were not there to hear Michael Moore's political views but to celebrate their industry.

When speaking to your classmates, it is important to remember that they are in the room not as volunteers but because they are required to be there. We regularly discourage students from selecting topics that might be offensive or hurtful to their classmates. Instead, we encourage them to select topics that potentially can benefit their classmates.

However you arrive at your audience—whether you choose them or they choose you—it is crucial that you learn as much as you can about them, beginning with an understanding of their diversity—culturally, demographically, and individually.

Audience Diversity

Audience analysis begins with recognition and acceptance of the fact that today's audience is more diverse than ever. **Audience diversity** represents the cultural, demographic, and individual characteristics that vary among audience

---

voluntary audience
Listeners who choose to hear a speaker.

captive audience
Listeners who have no choice about hearing a speech.

audience diversity
The cultural, demographic, and individual characteristics that vary among audience members.

There is a better than even chance that the student seated next to you comes from a different background than you do.

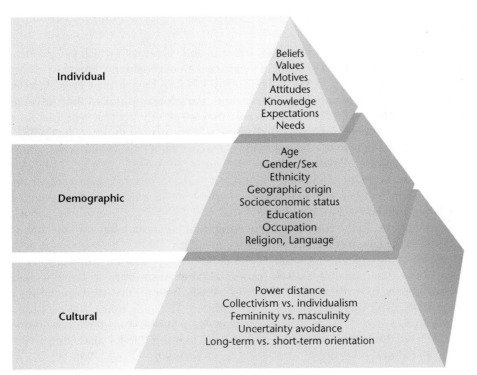

Exhibit 5.1
Levels of Diversity

members. According to an analysis of the 2000 U.S. Census by *USA Today*, "The nation's diversity increased dramatically over the past decade. . . . There is nearly a 1 in 2 chance that two people selected at random are racially or ethnically different."[9] We see this increasing diversity daily in the classes we teach, and it is in these classes that our students present their speeches.

Recently, for example, one of us taught a public speaking class whose members resembled a small United Nations assembly. There were 15 men and 9 women, although statistically most classes at our university have more women than men. While the median age was about 20, one class member was almost 50, and another was in his 30s. Five students were from Japan. One was from Indonesia, and two others were from Malaysia. Another student was from the former Soviet Republic of Kyrgyzstan. One native-born American student was of Chinese origin, and another traced her ancestry to the Philippines. A number of students were hard-core science majors, while others were pursuing music, public relations, and graphic design. Hobbies ranged from scuba diving and fishing to origami and batik. Although this class's diversity was more dramatic than most, we think it is a preview of a not too distant future.

Once you have recognized and accepted the fact that the people in your audience are not clones of each other, you need to learn about and adapt to their diversity. Three levels of audience diversity are depicted for you in Exhibit 5.1. We begin at the most general level, looking at the cultures to which members of your audience belong. Then we look at some differences in what are termed **demographics**—differences such as age, sex and gender, and ethnicity. Finally, we look at your audience members as individuals. The more you can learn about your audience at each level, the better you can predict their response to your speech.

demographics
Basic and vital data regarding any population.

Discovering Cultural Diversity

Culture is a learned system of beliefs, customs, and values with which people identify. Culture also is more a product of language than of geography. French-speaking Canadians, for example, think of themselves as more French than English, even though Canada has mainly English traditions. Barcelonians think of themselves as Catalonians rather than Spaniards because they speak a dialect that is distinct from the rest of their country. **Cultural diversity** refers mainly to differences among people in terms of beliefs, customs, and values—in a sense, their worldview.

cultural diversity
Differences among people in terms of beliefs, customs, and values—in a sense, their worldview.

Because culture is learned, what is appropriate in one culture may not be perceived as appropriate in another. The list of specific things that make one culture unique from another is inexhaustible. However, recognizing and responding to cultural diversity does not demand that you try to learn everything about a specific culture. To the contrary, discovering what is common but variable among cultures is the key to culturally responsive speaking.

Dutch communication scholar Geert Hofstede says that all cultures vary in terms of at least four dimensions: "power distance (from small to large), collectivism versus individualism, femininity versus masculinity, and uncertainty avoidance (from weak to strong)."[10] In addition, Hofstede notes that a fifth dimension has recently been discovered: long-term versus short-term orientation to life.[11] We think Hofstede's dimensions are a useful guide for analyzing an audience's cultural diversity.

Although Hofstede's work examined cultural diversity at the national level, it is important to realize that nations often have many cultural streams making up the larger culture. As Professors Peter Andersen, Myron Lustig, and Janis Andersen recount, when people relocate from one region of the United States to another, they often experience culture shock. "Stories of the slow and polite south, rude and fast northeast, materialistic and hedonistic southwest, or the workaholic and traditional midwest abound."[12] One must be careful, of course, to avoid overgeneralization and stereotypes about various regions of the country. As we review Hofstede's discussion of differences in dimensions like collectivism and individualism, keep in mind that some parts of the United States have a long history of rugged individualism (think of places in the southwest) while others may be more collectivistic in tradition. Some of this is simply due to the ancestral origins of the people who first settled in a region as well as patterns of immigration within the United States over the years.

Power Distance

Power distance is "the extent to which the less powerful members of institutions and organizations within a country expect and accept that power is distributed unequally."[13] All societies are unequal, some more than others. However, different societies handle inequality in different ways. For example, there are large power distances in countries in Latin America, Asia, and Africa and in some European countries such as Spain. On the other hand, countries such as the United States and Great Britain and some parts of Europe have smaller power distances. Sweden is an egalitarian country with a small power distance, whereas France has a large power distance.

Power-distance differences have important implications for you as a public speaker. Suppose you are a manager in an international organization announcing a major change in working conditions. You could not assume that an audience from a small-power-distance culture, such as Sweden, would react in the same way to your speech as would one from a large-power-distance culture, such as Japan. Similarly, teachers are treated with deference in large-power-distance cultures, whereas they are treated as near equals in small-power-distance cultures. For example, a professor from a Japanese university teaching in the United States might be surprised to be called by his or her first name, though such a practice is not uncommon at American universities. Conversely, a Japanese student studying in the United States might find it odd that professors expect students to treat them less formally than professors are treated in Japan. Interestingly, this respect is reciprocal. One of us was informed by a Japanese student that not only do students call their professors by last name as a sign of respect, but professors in Japan address students by their last names as well.

Collectivism Versus Individualism

The second dimension common to all cultures is collectivism versus individualism. "Collectivism stands for a society in which people from birth onwards are integrated into strong, cohesive ingroups, which throughout people's lifetime continue to protect them in exchange for unquestioning loyalty."[14] In an individualistic society, on the other hand, "everyone is expected to look after himself or herself and his or her immediate family only."[15] Some cultures, notably Asian and Native American, believe the good of the many far outweighs the good of the few. In these collectivist cultures, people shun the individual spotlight. Singling out a member of a collectivist culture while you're giving a speech is likely to embarrass the person.

In cultures where so-called rugged individualism is admired and encouraged, the opposite is true. In the United States, for example, the dominant culture is very individualistic. We champion lone-wolf entrepreneurs who strike it rich, the most valuable player in team sports, and politicians who march to the beat of a different drummer. There is evidence to believe, in fact, that the United States is the most individualistic nation on Earth.[16]

Appealing to enlightened self-interest is key when speakers face audience members from individualistic cultures. Even in the case where these audience members agree about a common goal, they are likely to perceive that the mechanism for achieving the goal is best left to individuals.

In speaking to a more collectivistic audience, one would emphasize the greater good rather than individual benefits. Venezuela's President Hugo Chavez drives people from individualistic cultures crazy with his plans to nationalize private industries. For the collectivist people who voted for Chavez, however, his public speeches reinforce their belief that these industries should benefit the population as a whole, not just the executives and stockholders of individual companies.

The highly individualistic orientation of Americans may be slightly changing given immigration patterns and birth rates. Census data show that more people from collectivist cultures such as Asia reside in the United States today than at any other time in history. American college students today find that people from collectivist cultures are an increasing part of their audience. To find out where you stand as an individual on this dimension, see the Self-Assessment box "How Collectivistic or Individualistic Are You?"

How Collectivistic or Individualistic Are You?

The purpose of this questionnaire is to help you assess your individualistic and collectivistic tendencies. Respond by indicating the degree to which the values reflected in each phrase are important to you: Opposed to My Values (answer 1), Not Important to Me (answer 2), Somewhat Important to Me (answer 3), Important to Me (answer 4), or Very Important to Me (answer 5).

_____ 1. Obtaining pleasure or sensuous gratification

_____ 2. Preserving the welfare of others

_____ 3. Being successful by demonstrating my individual competency

_____ 4. Restraining my behavior if it is going to harm others

_____ 5. Being independent in thought and action

_____ 6. Having safety and stability of people with whom I identify

_____ 7. Obtaining status and prestige

_____ 8. Having harmony in my relations with others

_____ 9. Having an exciting and challenging life

_____ 10. Accepting cultural and religious traditions

_____ 11. Being recognized for my individual work

_____ 12. Avoiding the violation of social norms

_____ 13. Leading a comfortable life

_____ 14. Living in a stable society

_____ 15. Being logical in my approach to work

_____ 16. Being polite to others

_____ 17. Being ambitious

_____ 18. Being self-controlled

_____ 19. Being able to choose what I do

_____ 20. Enhancing the welfare of others

To find your individualism score, add your responses to the *odd-numbered* items. To find your collectivism score, add your responses to the *even-numbered* items. Both scores will range from 10 to 50. The higher your scores, the more individualistic and/or collectivistic you are.

Source: "Collectivism/Individualism Self-Assessment" by William B. Gudykunst from *Bridging Differences,* 2nd Edition. Copyright © 1994. Reprinted by permission of Sage Publications, Inc.

Femininity Versus Masculinity

The third dimension of culture in Hofstede's scheme is femininity versus masculinity. Hofstede explains: "Femininity stands for a society in which social gender roles overlap: both men and women are supposed to be modest, tender, and concerned with the quality of life."[17] Masculinity, on the other hand, "stands for a society in which social gender roles are clearly distinct: men are supposed to be assertive, tough, and focused on material success."[18] The United States ranks relatively high on measures of masculinity, ranking 15th out of 53 countries. Despite traditionally being a highly masculine country, this is changing slowly,

The 2009 Nobel Prize in Physiology or Medicine honored Elizabeth Blackburn and Carol Greider, reflecting the increasing role of women in science.

as evidenced by 2009 Nobel Prize winners Elinor Ostrom in economics along with Elizabeth Blackburn and Carol Greider in medicine—the first women so honored by the Nobel Prize in these fields, which are traditionally dominated by men. The most feminine cultures are found in Scandinavia and tend not to assign one set of roles to men and another set of roles to women. In these cultures, the professional role a person assumes is a product of ability rather than biological sex. Thus, when imagining a physician or chief executive officer of a company, people don't automatically see a man. In imagining a nurse or secretary, they don't automatically see a woman.

The opposite is true for many other cultures. Some go to extremes in the degree to which one's biological sex decides one's role. Countries such as Austria, Venezuela, and Japan (which ranks highest on masculinity) have few women in positions of corporate or public authority. Women are assigned roles out of view and out of power. Thus an audience of Japanese men would be polite but predictably unreceptive to a woman speaking on a topic such as reengineering the Japanese corporation. By the same token, a Scandinavian audience would be wary of a male speaker suggesting women belong in the home.

This dimension can be a factor in a number of settings. For example, in masculine cultures, children in school tend to speak out and compete openly. Failure is viewed as a disaster and can even lead to suicide. Boys and girls tend to study different subjects. On the other hand, in feminine cultures, students tend to behave less competitively, failure is not viewed as a catastrophe, and boys and girls tend to study the same subjects. The more you know about which type of culture you are dealing with, the more effective speaker you will be. Even with an American audience, there are likely to be differences in masculinity and femininity based on cultural heritage, age, and progress in gender equity. For a discussion of how Hillary Clinton demonstrates the ability to move freely between feminine and masculine styles of speaking, depending on the rhetorical situation she faces, see the box "Speaking of . . . Secretary Hillary Clinton's Full Range of Rhetorical Skills."

Uncertainty Avoidance

The fourth dimension Hofstede discusses is uncertainty avoidance, which is "the extent to which the members of a culture feel threatened by uncertain or unknown situations."[19] As a student you know all about uncertainty and the feelings of discomfort that can accompany it. Instructors who are vague about assignments, tests, due dates, and evaluation not only create uncertainty but also are the ones you probably try to avoid. Just as people vary in terms of the amount of uncertainty they can tolerate, so it is with whole cultures. People who live in "low-uncertainty-avoidance cultures" have considerable tolerance for the kind of ambiguity that can drive some people nuts.

Among societies that *avoid* uncertainty are Greece, Portugal, Guatemala, and Japan. Societies that tend to tolerate uncertainty include Singapore, Jamaica, Denmark, Sweden, Great Britain, India, Philippines, and the United States. If you think about it, if it were not for the tolerance of a certain amount of uncertainty, it is unlikely that new businesses would ever secure the funding of venture capitalists. The United States is by and large a nation of immigrants and their descendants, people who came to the "new world" prepared to accept a very high level of uncertainty in their lives.

How is this important to you as a speaker? If you have an audience that can tolerate at least a moderate amount of uncertainty, you do not need to promise certainty. Highly probable outcomes may be sufficient to gain their support. On the other hand, total uncertainty is likely to result in rejection of your ideas, particularly in those societies that do not tolerate such ambiguity. You should tailor your appeals to the likely level of uncertainty that your audience is willing to accept.

Long-Term Versus Short-Term Orientation

The final dimension Hofstede discusses is long-term versus short-term orientation to life. "Long-term orientation stands for the fostering of virtues oriented toward future rewards, in particular perseverance and thrift."[20] "Short-term orientation stands for the fostering of virtues related to the past and the present, in particular respect for tradition, preservation of 'face,' and fulfilling social obligations."[21]

Asian countries, such as China and Japan, tend to rank very high on the long-term dimension. In fact, this dimension is sometimes called Confucian because

SPEAKING OF . . .

Secretary Hillary Clinton Exercises a Full Range of Rhetorical Skills

By Nichola D. Gutgold

Hillary Clinton was an active first lady turned elected senator from New York who almost won the Democratic nomination for president in 2008. She is the first woman presidential candidate in the United States who was not seen by voters and the media as merely a symbolic candidate. She is an especially interesting speaker to study because her trajectory is one of no other American woman. As first lady, Hillary Clinton traveled to more than 80 countries, meeting with foreign leaders and visiting isolated villages and health clinics. On her first trip as secretary of state, she traveled to Seoul, South Korea. Later that year Secretary Clinton presented a major foreign policy address where she called for "a new mindset about how America will use its power to safeguard our nation, expand shared prosperity, and help more people in more places live up to their God-given potential."[1] And upon her arrival in Kenya for an 11-day Africa tour, the South African children and women sang "Hill-ar-ree, Hill-ar-ree!" as they met her. This type of presentation of self is far different from the role that most people envision when they hear the words former first lady.

As secretary of state, Hillary Clinton has displayed many of the rhetorical skills evident during her first-lady tenure, Senate campaigns, and notable presidential bid. These skills should be seen as universally positive attributes as she travels the globe in her effort to improve international relations. They point to an ability to move freely between a masculine and a feminine style of speaking.

In my book Almost Madam President, Why Hillary Clinton "Won" in 2008, *I note that Hillary Clinton's style as a public speaker demonstrates a rhetorical agility that no other American woman has exercised. But the comfort level Hillary Clinton now enjoys as a public figure has been a long time coming. To the surprise of many in the state of Arkansas, when her husband became governor, Hillary Clinton did not limit herself to a traditional first-lady agenda. Instead, she used her strong rhetorical skills to lead a task force to reform the Arkansas education system. As America's first lady she stretched the rhetorical constraints of the role, becoming an extraordinarily important actor in her husband's administration. She went on to run and win elective office as senator from the state of New York, and she became the first front-runner woman candidate for the presidency of the United States. As first lady, first of Arkansas and then of the United States, she was often criticized for presenting herself in a way that "typically omits all of the discursive markers by which women publicly enact their femininity."[2] Hillary Clinton told Mark Landler of the* New York Times, *"I happen to believe that the transformation of women's roles is the last great impediment to universal progress—that we have made progress on many other aspects of human nature that used to be discriminatory bars to people's full participation. But in too many places and too many ways, the oppression of women stands as a stark reminder of how difficult it is to realize people's full human potential."[3]*

Dr. Nichola Gutgold

Though her political story is still unfolding, there is one certainty about Hillary Clinton that few would argue about: she has stretched women's roles in the United States and she remains an interesting research subject for rhetorical scholars.

[1]Hillary Rodham Clinton, "Foreign Policy Address at the Council on Foreign Relations," 15 July 2009. [Retrieved from http://www.state.gov/secretary/rm/2009a/july/126071.htm, 1 September 2009.]

[2]Campbell, Karlyn Kohrs. "The Discursive Performance of Femininity: Hating Hillary." *Rhetoric and Public Affairs* 1 (1998): 1, 3.

[3]Mark Landler, "A New Gender Agenda, *New York Times Magazine*, 18 August 2009. [Retrieved from http://www.nytimes.com/2009/08/23/magazine/23clinton-t.html?_r=1, 1 September 2009.]

Source: Nichola D. Gutgold is author of *Almost Madam President: Why Hillary Clinton "Won" in 2008* (Lexington Books, 2009); *Seen and Heard: The Women of Television News* (Lexington Books, 2008) and *Paving the Way for Madam President* (Lexington Books, 2006). She is an associate professor of communication arts and sciences at Penn State University—Lehigh Valley campus.

"Speaking of . . . Secretary Hillary Clinton Exercises a Full Range of Rhetorical Skills" by Dr. Nichola Gutgold. Reprinted by permission of the author.

many of the values, on both sides of the dimension, are the same as the teachings of Confucius. The United States is in the lower third of countries, and Pakistan is at the bottom of the list, meaning both have a short-term orientation.

Those cultures with a long-term orientation to life tend to adapt long-standing traditions to modern situations, are willing to save and persevere to achieve long-term goals, are willing to subordinate themselves for a purpose, and are thrifty in their use of resources. Short-term-oriented societies respect traditions, are willing to overspend to maintain their lifestyle, and expect quick results. If this scenario sounds familiar it is because we live in a culture that is largely short-term in its orientation. As a group, Americans save less and spend more than any other modern culture in the world.

Thus, knowing whether your audience members share a short- or a long-term culture can significantly affect the content of your speech. Appeals to thrift and patience are likely to be effective in societies with a long-term orientation, whereas appeals to instant gratification are more effective in societies that have a short-term view of the world. The current debate in the United States over the rising budget deficits and the cost to future generations reflects the results of years of a short-term orientation on the part of American society. That this issue is now being seriously debated suggests that both short- and long-term orientations are competing within the American culture.

Adapting to Cultural Diversity

All five of Hofstede's dimensions are important to analyzing cultural diversity. You shouldn't automatically give one greater credence than another. Rather, tailor your speech to fit with those dimensions that are most relevant to your topic. For example, a speech encouraging students to avoid accumulating credit card debt while in college is going to be better received by those with a long-term orientation than a short-term one.

Further, in a world where cultural diversity is the norm rather than the exception, you can count on audience membership that is not only culturally diverse but also variable with regard to such dimensions as femininity versus masculinity. Thus developing and delivering a speech that appeals to a majority of the cultures represented in your audience is tougher than ever. The wider the range of reasons you present for your position, therefore, the better your chances of success.

Demographic Diversity

demographic diversity
Variations among people in terms of such attributes as socioeconomic background and level of education.

After cultural diversity, the second major factor you will want to examine to better understand your audience is how people vary in terms of demographics, which are the basic and vital data regarding any population. Demographic factors include age, gender and sex, ethnicity, geographic origin, socioeconomic status, education, occupational role, religion, and language usage. **Demographic diversity** refers to the differences among people in terms of such factors. Many of these, such as age and ethnicity, are sometimes readily observable. Others, such as religion, occupation, and socioeconomic status, may be less obvious. We'll start with some of the easier ones to observe and move to the less obvious.

SPEAKING OF . . .

The Millennials

Every generation is a little different and possesses a "culture" of its own with unique beliefs, customs, and values. The current generation of young adults, aged 18–29, has been labeled the "Millennial Generation." The beliefs, values, and customs of this group are significantly different from those of earlier generations. A series of studies by the Center for American Progress found that their attitudes are more progressive than those of earlier generations at the same age on a variety of economic and social issues. They are more likely to support gay marriage, racial and gender equality, and religious tolerance than earlier generations. This generation is more racially diverse than earlier generations of youth—60 percent white, 18 percent Hispanic, 14 percent Black, 5 percent Asian, and 3 percent other.[1]

What this means to you as a speaker is that many of the old social issues that divided Americans are no longer as divisive as they once were. And the assumption of one dominant majority culture shared by virtually all has disappeared in an increasing multicultural and multiethnic society.

[1]David Madland and Ruy Teixeira, *New Progressive America: The Millennial Generation*, Washington, DC: Center for American Progress, May 2008 [retrieved from http://www.americanprogress.org/issues /2009/05/pdf/millennial_generation.pdf, 7 September 2009], and John Halpin and Karl Agne, *The Political Ideology of the Millennial Generation: A National Study of Political Values and Beliefs Among 18- to 29-Year-Old Adults,* Washington, DC: Center for American Progress, May 2009 [retrieved from http://www.americanprogress.org/ issues/2009/05/pdf/political_ideology_youth.pdf 7 September 2009].

Age

We both began teaching college students in our twenties. As a result, our experience was not that much different than many of our students. Although not identical, our tastes in music, TV, and film were similar enough that we could draw on popular culture for examples that we hoped would make our lectures more relevant to our students. Needless to say, we no longer enjoy this luxury. We need to continually remind ourselves of the fact that the defining experiences in our lives largely occurred before most of our current students were born. Thus, when referring to examples of moving eulogies, we used to cite Ronald Reagan's address to the nation after the explosion of the shuttle *Challenger* in 1986. Today's freshmen were born long after that event. In fact, for most of our students, using Reagan as an example of a speaker is no more a part of their life experience than talking about Franklin Roosevelt or Woodrow Wilson. For a discussion of how today's generation of college age students differs from previous generations, see the box "Speaking of . . . The Millennials."

Speakers should know not only the median age of their audience but also the range of ages and how those ages compare to their own. The age demography of the United States is changing at an accelerated rate; so is the demography of the classroom. At one time, college classrooms consisted of a relatively homogeneous group of 18- to 22-year-olds. Today's classroom comprises a much more diverse mix of students. For example, college classes in a state university in the 21st-century are likely to be of mixed ages. It's common for students to be as young as 17 or as old as 75. Many students are returning veterans of the wars in Iraq and Afghanistan. As a speaker, you need to take into account this demographic diversity in both preparation and delivery of your speech. You have to consider not only how 18- to 22-year-olds are likely to respond to your presentation, but also how continuing and reentry students are likely to respond. Likewise, you will also have to think through the response of students who may or may not be similar to you or other members of your audience. This makes it especially important that you compare your audience with yourself.

Some of the most effective speakers are similar but not too similar to their audience. Reentry students in their 40s can be somewhat intimidated by speaking to classes of 18- to 22-year-old classmates. Similarly, a 20-year-old asked to speak to a group of middle-aged people may feel uneasy. In situations where there is a big difference in age between speaker and audience, points of similarity can be stressed. For example, older students speaking to a younger audience can discuss their children, who might be the same age as the rest of the class. Similarly, younger persons facing an older audience can make reference to parents or grandparents in an effort to find a common thread linking them with the audience.

Gender and Biological Sex

Whether you agree that "men are from Mars and women are from Venus,"[22] you cannot deny that men and women often express themselves differently. As our discussion of masculine and feminine cultures illustrates, gender's influence on how people perceive themselves and others is a subject receiving considerable attention. As scholars such as Julia Wood point out, gender is much more than your biological sex.[23] Gender is the blend of social and cultural characteristics associated with maleness or femaleness in a particular culture. Individuals learn gender roles—the expectations their cultures have of them as males or females—in the course of growing up.

As you look out at an audience, you can usually tell who is male and who is female by such outward signs as dress and hairstyle. But unless you have more specific information, you cannot tell who is gay and who is straight, or who is in a committed relationship and who is single. Much gender-related information is probably beyond your knowledge in most public speaking situations.

Some audiences will be predominantly one sex or the other, and they may be the opposite of your own. Thus a male speaker facing a largely male audience is in a different situation than one facing a largely female or evenly mixed audience.

One of the first issues you will face is topic selection. For example, one of our students gave a speech about the dangers of breast enhancement surgery. She and the female members of the audience obviously had an interest in the topic. Why should the males care? She made a specific effort to include the men in her audience. She talked in terms of their girlfriends or wives, and made a strong plea to men to accept their mates as they are. Although this topic obviously had a greater direct relevance to the women in her audience, she was careful not to ignore her male audience members.

Ethnicity

Although closely related to culture, ethnicity is not the same thing. For example, in one of our classes recently, we had both a Japanese exchange student and a fifth-generation Japanese American. Both might appear outwardly to share the same ethnic background, but they identified with very different cultures. Geneticists will tell you that all of us can trace our ethnic roots to other places on the globe. The ethnic origins of many of your classmates may be significant to their self-concept. These same classmates may be actively involved in maintaining and passing on the traditions that define their ethnicity. Thus, if you are ignorant of the ethnic diversity present on your campus, you may inadvertently violate or be insensitive to one or more of these traditions. For example, although born in the United States, one of our students was very proud of her Filipino heritage. Knowing that was important to predicting how she would respond to certain topics, for example, the crisis that was occurring at the time in the Philippines, where hostages had been taken by a rebel group.

It is also important to recognize that many Americans have multiple ethnic backgrounds. Tiger Woods, who is Asian, African American, Native American, and Caucasian, is one of the most prominent examples of this trend. According to the 2000 U.S. Census, Woods is not alone. "About 2.4% of Americans, some 6.8 million people, reported themselves as belonging to more than one racial group."[24]

Geographic Origin

The varied makeup of today's audience is also reflected in the recent geographic origins of the audience members. One of our international students, when asked where she was from, said she was born in the USSR but lived in Kyrgyzstan without ever moving. Of course, when the Soviet Union fell, she became a citizen of a new country. Given that none of her classmates had ever heard of Kyrgyzstan, this student devoted an informative speech to telling us about her homeland.

Look around your campus. The chances are good that the population reflects national and regional demographic diversity. International student attendance at U.S. colleges and universities is at an all-time high. Faculties are becoming more international as well. To deny or ignore how this national diversity influences people's perceptions of each other, including how you are perceived as a public speaker, is foolish. The same can be said for the regional diversity reflected in your student body. Some campuses are near-mirror images of the region in which they exist. Others look more like international cities than like their regional environment.

A speaker can unknowingly offend audience members by using a reference that may be taken as a slight to their geographic home. When the rock group Lynyrd Skynyrd said, "I hope Neil Young will remember a southern man don't need him around," they were getting back at Young for lyrics they thought disparaged people in the South. Simply put, some people can be genuinely put off by speakers they perceive to be unfairly stereotyping or making light of their geographic roots. And it's not just southerners, it's also New Yorkers, not-so-laid-back Californians, and a few North Dakotans who were not too happy with the Coen brothers' portrayal of their region in the film *Fargo*.

Socioeconomic Status

The social grouping and economic class to which people belong is termed their **socioeconomic status.** Socioeconomic status is not always directly observable. Most universities want diversity in the social and economic backgrounds of their students. Thus your speech class may include students who come from impoverished backgrounds as well as students from affluent families. Although you can sometimes make inferences regarding the social status of your audience, these are not always reliable. For example, one of us once suggested to his class that a proposed tuition increase might lead to fewer minority students attending California universities. One minority student objected, pointing out that one

socioeconomic status
Social grouping and economic class to which people belong.

cannot assume that all minority students are necessarily too poor to afford higher tuition.

There is a strong relationship between socioeconomic background and the opinions audience members hold about topics ranging from health care to tax reform. Knowing the socioeconomic background of an audience, therefore, can inform us of other audience characteristics important to the preparation and delivery of our speeches.

Education

Socioeconomic status is closely related to level of education. In your public speaking class it is likely most students will have an educational background similar to your own—high school graduates in their first or second year of college. However, when you leave the classroom, you can expect audiences with more diverse educational backgrounds—from less than high school to those with advanced professional and graduate degrees. Whatever your situation, try to learn as much as you can about the educational background of your audience members and then choose material that is suitable.

Occupation

Demographic diversity is also reflected by the kind of work people do. On a residential campus, occupational roles are generally expressed in terms of major. At many schools, however, students are already involved in an occupation and pursuing a degree for purposes of advancement or career change. This is especially true of urban and metropolitan schools. One cannot always assume from outward appearances what a person's occupation or former occupation might be. For example, we recall one female student, barely five feet tall, who revealed in one of her speeches that she had been a truck driver for several years. Obviously, her perspective on many issues was affected by that experience. To assume she was uninformed about diesel technology, for example, would have been a clear mistake.

Occupations and coworkers influence how people see the world. Self-employed people, for example, probably see things differently than do people working in the public sector, at a large corporation, or in the home. Just as it is important for speakers to analyze age and social diversity, so it is important to respect the full range of occupations represented in audiences. As you get to know your classmates, you may be able to incorporate references to their majors or jobs when it fits your speech. For example, one student in our classes was a DJ. Other students often mentioned this when it fit with their speech topic, such as how to organize a special event. Audience members appreciate positive references to their occupations, and they can be offended by negative ones. For example, had a student made a derogatory remark about DJs, it could have alienated the audience member who earned his livelihood that way.

Religion

You need to consider religious diversity as a sensitive feature of your audience. At public colleges and universities, you can assume that almost every type of religious belief is represented. Even at universities like Notre Dame, which is affiliated with the Catholic Church, you will find diversity in the religious beliefs of groups of students. In some cases, a person's religion can be identified on the basis of apparel and appearance. Such cases include the Amish, Hasidic Jews, some Muslims, and Hindu Sikhs. Usually, religious affiliations will not be easily visible. You cannot tell a devout Catholic from an atheist by outward appearances.

In addition, the number of people expressing no religious affiliation nearly doubled between 1990 and 2009, from 8 percent to 15 percent. And the percentage identifying themselves as Christians dropped 10 percent.[25] These data indicate that speakers must be able to adapt to audience members who are nonreligious as well as those who represent a diverse range of religious beliefs.

We want to point out, however, that religious beliefs do not always predict actual attitudes. For example, despite official opposition by many churches to using human embryos for stem cell research, a Harris poll of more than 1,000 Americans revealed that "slightly more than 60% of Catholics and half of born-again Christians surveyed agreed that scientists should be allowed to use stem cells in their medical research."[26]

Perhaps the most important advice we can give about religious beliefs is to be tolerant and respectful of those who do not share your own views. A speech class is a captive audience. A speech that attacks one set of religious beliefs or seeks to proselytize class members is not appropriate for most colleges and universities. Thus you should always assume that there may be audience members who will be deeply offended by religious topics. This doesn't mean that the discussion of religion has no place in a public speaking class. We have heard more than a few good speeches that were successful in refuting common misconceptions about a specific religion or religious sect, describing the similarities between religions, and discussing the origins of certain religious practices. In every instance, however, these speeches were intended to inform audience members—not convince them of the "truth" of a particular religion.

Language

Finally, audience members may differ in terms of how they use language in their reference groups. Even people with a common native tongue often create a variation of their language that identifies them as a member of a specific reference group. Every generation of young people, for example, creates a shared vocabulary and syntax that distinguishes it from preceding generations. In the early 1950s college students referred to an object they liked as "real George." Generations that came later replaced *George* with *hip, cool, bitchin'*, and even *hella' bitchin'* in Northern California.

People of Mexican descent in the United States may refer to themselves as Mexican American, Chicano/Chicana, or Latino/Latina, depending on when they were born and where they were raised. And people of African descent may refer to themselves as Blacks or African Americans for similar reasons.

Language groups are not necessarily based on age or ethnicity, however. Special usage and vocabularies also can develop around an activity or interest. Surfers and sailboarders, snowboarders and skiers all have a vocabulary peculiar to their sports, as well as a way of using this vocabulary that is distinctive. The same can be said about computer hackers, photographers, serious backpackers, and white-water enthusiasts. What's more, these groups use their vocabulary not only to identify their own kind but also to differentiate themselves from others.

As the world becomes smaller and linguistic diversity grows even within the borders of the United States, it is important that speakers learn to adapt to their audience's linguistic background. According to the 2000 U.S. Census, 20 years ago only 1 in 10 Americans primarily spoke a language other than English, but today that number has reached nearly 1 in 5.[27] You may want to learn a few phrases in another language if you are speaking to an audience that doesn't share your primary language. Taking the time and making the commitment to learn another language signals to members of the language community that you are truly interested in them. President Obama's use of the traditional Arabic greeting "Assalaamu alaykum" (peace be upon you) in his speech in Cairo was greeted with applause and "resonated strongly among many Muslims."[28]

Individual Diversity

individual diversity
How individuals in an audience differ in terms of knowledge, beliefs, attitudes, values, motives, expectations, and needs.

For most public speakers, the most difficult aspect of audience diversity is predicting how individual members of the audience will respond to them and their message. What are some of the specific things you should look for in analyzing the individuals who make up your audience? **Individual diversity** is deeply embedded in people's knowledge, beliefs, attitudes, values, motives, expectations, and needs. What makes people truly unique is their individual diversity, which cannot be determined on the basis of their culture or demography alone. When you know people as individuals rather than simply as members of a culture or group, you can make far more precise predictions about how they will respond to your speeches and to you. You can also use this knowledge to plan your speeches and decide whether your purpose and goal are realistic.

One of the great advantages of most public speaking classes is that you will learn to know your audience members as individuals. In this class you will spend most of your time listening to your classmates give their speeches. If you actively listen to them, you will learn a great deal about what they know and think about the world around them. You can use this information as you prepare your own speeches.

Although many of your public speaking situations after college may not allow you to hear all of your audience members speak, you can endeavor to learn as much about them as individuals as possible before you speak. Even in situations where you face an audience "cold," you may be able to make certain assumptions about their interests and belief systems beforehand. For example, if you are asked to speak to the Lion's Club, it is useful to know in advance that they are concerned about raising funds to combat blindness and that they sponsor a public speaking contest for high school students. Any clues you can obtain about the individuals to whom you will be speaking can be valuable in crafting an effective speech.

Knowledge

One of the first things you'll want to know about your audience is what they know—about you and your topic. This is particularly important in selecting a topic for an informative speech. You have probably had the experience of listening to a speaker who simply tells you what you already know. Chances are you were impatient and bored. You have also probably had the experience of listening to a speaker who was almost incomprehensible because he or she used vocabulary you had never heard before, or assumed you had prior knowledge you didn't have about the topic.

Learn as much as you can about your audience's knowledge. Chances are there may be a range of knowledge on the topic you have chosen. If the difference in audience knowledge levels is too varied, preparing your speech may be very difficult. You will find yourself boring some members while losing others. For example, a speech on the federal reserve board may be old hat to economics majors but leave humanities majors mystified. If possible, speak on topics about which audience members are likely to have similar levels of knowledge. If you must rehash certain facts, at least try to put a new spin on them to keep the interest of well-informed audience members. In any event, you want to be sure you are the best-informed person in the room. It's embarrassing, to say the least, to be corrected on the facts by a member of your audience.

Beliefs

We all hold certain beliefs about a wide variety of topics. A **belief** is "an assertion about the properties or characteristics of an object."[29] Some beliefs are relatively obvious and undeniable. For example, we all (presumably) share a belief that the earth is round and revolves around the sun. On the other hand, some beliefs are controversial—for instance, those concerning life after death, abortion, and, as you can see in Exhibit 5.2, evolution. When you are dealing with matters on which people hold beliefs different from yours, you face a serious obstacle. You must either change their relevant beliefs or convince them that such beliefs are not relevant and not necessarily in opposition to your own point of view.

Social psychologist Milton Rokeach pointed out that some beliefs are more resistant to change than others.[30] Broadly speaking, there are three levels of beliefs—core, central, and peripheral. The beliefs most resistant to change are **core beliefs,** which can be divided into two types. Type A beliefs, or *primitive beliefs,* are learned by direct contact with the object of belief and reinforced by unanimous social consensus. A primitive belief would be that "death is inevitable." Type B, or *zero consensus,* beliefs are based on direct experience but do not require social support. These beliefs are also very resistant to change. For example, "I like myself" is a type B belief; it is not reinforceable by social consensus.

The next two types of beliefs are known as **central beliefs** and are still difficult to change. Type C beliefs are *authority beliefs.* For example, beliefs in the truth of the Bible or Torah or Qur'an would be a type C belief. Type Ds are *derived beliefs,* based on authorities' beliefs. For example, Muslims who believe they should abstain from drinking alcohol and eating pork are said to hold derived beliefs. Changing a type D belief requires an understanding of the type C belief from which it is derived. Thus a speaker might point to scripture to try to change a believer's views on a religious matter, but such an argument would have no impact on an atheist or a practitioner of a different religion.

The least central type of beliefs, type E, are called **peripheral beliefs.** For example, someone might like rap music, whereas another detests it. These are

belief
An assertion about the properties or characteristics of an object.

core beliefs
Primitive and zero consensus beliefs that are highly resistant to change.

central beliefs
Beliefs based directly or indirectly on authority.

peripheral beliefs
The least central type of beliefs, the easiest to change.

4:30

Exhibit 5.2

**Public Acceptance
of Evolution in
34 Countries, 2005**

Source: Figure from "Public
acceptance of evolution in
34 countries, 2005" by Jon
D. Miller et al from SCIENCE
313:765 (11 August 2006).
Reprinted with permission
from AAAS.

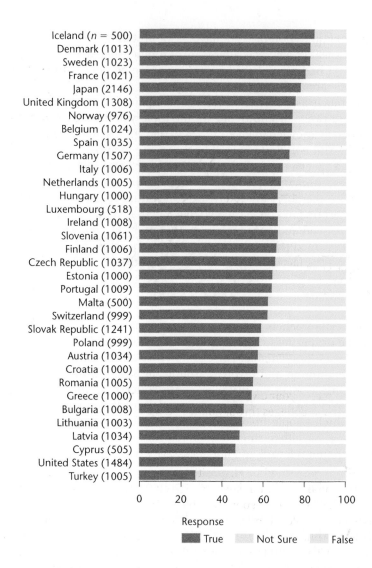

the most inconsequential of beliefs. Exhibit 5.3 illustrates the relationship among these levels of belief. Clearly, your chances of changing an audience member's core beliefs are far less than changing central or peripheral beliefs.

How can you learn what people believe? One way is simply to ask. In a speech about cell phone safety, for example, one student asked for a show of hands on how many of her classmates believed it was safe to use them while driving. Politicians and pollsters are always asking the American public what it believes about a variety of issues. Every year the Cooperative Institutional Research Program at UCLA sponsors a national study of thousands of incoming first-year college students. You may learn from such sources, in a general way at least, what audience members are likely to believe. For example, although in the general population there is widespread skepticism about global warming, UCLA's study of entering freshman in 2008 found a widespread belief in global warming. The study reports, "Close to half (45.3 percent) believe it is 'very important' or 'essential' to adopt green practices to protect the environment, while 74.3 percent believe 'addressing global warming should be a federal priority.'"[31] You might use this

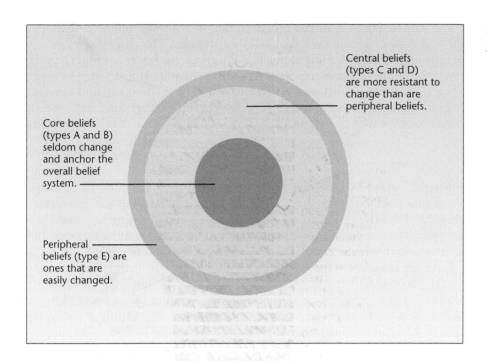

Exhibit 5.3
A Belief System

Central beliefs
(types C and D)
are more resistant to
change than are
peripheral beliefs.

Core beliefs
(types A and B)
seldom change
and anchor the
overall belief
system.

Peripheral
beliefs (type E) are
ones that are
easily changed.

information in one of your own speeches, knowing that the survey is representative of most students at colleges throughout the United States.

Attitudes

An **attitude** is "a learned predisposition to respond in a consistently favorable or unfavorable manner with respect to a given object."[32] Attitudes are not simply beliefs but rather ways of responding, based in part on beliefs. Over the course of our lives, we develop innumerable attitudes on everything from our favorite brand of soft drink to which political party (if any) we prefer. These attitudes affect how we respond to the messages we hear. Thus knowing your audience's attitudes toward your topic is crucial to your success as a speaker, as one speaker learned when she tried to challenge her classmates' aversion to eating a certain type of food—insects. Eating insects is rare in American culture, and most of her classmates groaned when they heard her topic. She attempted to convince her classmates that eating "bugs" actually could be healthy. Not everyone was convinced, but several of her classmates (and even the professor) ended up sampling her "mealybug chocolate chip cookies." Although not dramatically changing her audience's attitudes, the speaker did induce at least some class members to soften their strong attitude against this type of food.

How do you learn your audience's attitudes? Sometimes they are fairly predictable. Most Americans don't eat bugs. On the other hand, without asking, it's not easy to know what your classmates think about testing cosmetics on laboratory animals or how many of them are vegans. Never assume that all members of a particular group of people share the same attitudes: Not all Republicans think alike, any more than Democrats do. Nor do all members of a religion—whether Catholics, Protestants, Jews, Baptists, or Muslims—subscribe to exactly the same religious convictions.

attitude
A learned predisposition to respond in a consistently favorable or unfavorable manner with respect to a given object.

It is entirely possible, in fact probable, that in a diverse audience, individuals will have conflicting and even contradictory attitudes. The more you know about the predominant or prevailing attitudes of the group, the better are your chances of a majority of the audience responding positively to what you say in your speech. When an audience is fairly evenly divided, you need to attempt to find some middle ground. Finding areas of common agreement while recognizing and respecting differences of opinion is essential to dealing with an audience of mixed attitudes.

Values

values
Our most enduring beliefs about right and wrong.

One scholar describes **values** as "more general than attitudes, . . . enduring beliefs that hold that some ways of behaving and some goals are preferable to others."[33] Underlying someone's opposition to animal testing in research, for example, is both a belief about how animals are treated in doing research and a value system that believes all life is important, not just human life.

Rokeach classifies values as either terminal (ends in themselves) or instrumental (those that help achieve the ends we seek as humans).[34] Examples of terminal values include a comfortable life, an exciting life, a sense of accomplishment, a world at peace, a world of beauty, equality, family security, freedom, and happiness. Instrumental values are guides to behavior, the means to achieve the ends specified in the terminal values. Examples of instrumental values include ambitiousness, broad-mindedness, capableness, cheerfulness, cleanliness, courage, forgiveness, helpfulness, and honesty.

Although one might not always agree with Rokeach's classification—for example, honesty can certainly be viewed as an end in itself—the basic notion is useful. Some values are desirable in and of themselves, whereas others are instruments for achieving higher, terminal values. For example, forgiveness and courage may be seen as means to achieving a world at peace.

Values, particularly terminal values, are difficult to change because they are learned at an early age and widely shared among people. Values such as fairness, justice, life, patriotism, and so on are not only fundamental but also are taught to us in our most formative years. In fact, our basic value system probably is pretty well determined at a very young age, as Robert Fulghum points out in his best-selling book, *All I Really Need to Know I Learned in Kindergarten*.[35]

Speakers are best advised to appeal to known values shared by their audience rather than try to convince their audience to adopt new values. Some speeches don't just appeal to existing values, they seek to reinforce those values. A Fourth of July speech, a eulogy honoring a great hero, or an inspirational speech can be thought of as fulfilling a value-strengthening function. For the most part, speakers need to treat values as a given and build on them. For example, Martin Luther King Jr.'s "I Have a Dream" speech was not so much a call for new values as for Americans to live up to the values stated in the Declaration of Independence and the Bill of Rights.

Motives

Humans are motivated by a wide variety of desires, for example, popularity, financial security, love, peace, and so on. You should learn as much as you can about the likely motives of your audience relative to your topic. For example, a speaker at a graduation ceremony can assume that the audience is there to be

These antiwar protestors use the patriotic symbol of flag-draped coffins to show their opposition to the wars in Iraq and Afghanistan.

inspired and to receive diplomas. A lengthy speech on reform of the banking system would be inappropriate for this audience. On the other hand, a graduation speech focusing on the successes of graduates from the same school might be just what the audience wants to hear.

One specific type of motive concerns why your audience members are attending your speech. In most classroom situations, the answer is simple: because they have to. In those situations, you have to work harder at holding the audience members' interest and connecting to their needs than if they had come especially to hear you speak. In Chapter 8 we offer some suggestions that will help you connect with an audience and gain their attention. Even audience members who come to hear you need to have their attention held. It is easy to lose listeners and very difficult to recapture their attention, as any experienced speaker can testify.

Expectations

Closely tied to their motives for attending the speech are your audience's specific expectations. If audience members expect to be entertained, and you deliver a serious speech on the dangers of subprime lending, you are unlikely to receive a favorable reception. Similarly, if most audience members expect a serious lesson on a topic not to be taken lightly, you owe it to them to meet this expectation. It is usually wise to match your speech as much to the audience members' expectations as is possible while still achieving your goals.

Generally, speeches contrary to a majority of audience members' expectations may backfire or, at the very least, be apathetically received. For example, a few years ago on our campus, posters were plastered everywhere inviting students to attend a lecture by someone named "Josh" on "maximum sex." Needless to say, the room was packed. However, the audience was less than pleased when it turned out that Josh was a religious fanatic who had simply used the lecture title to draw a crowd.

Exhibit 5.4
Maslow's Hierarchy
of Needs

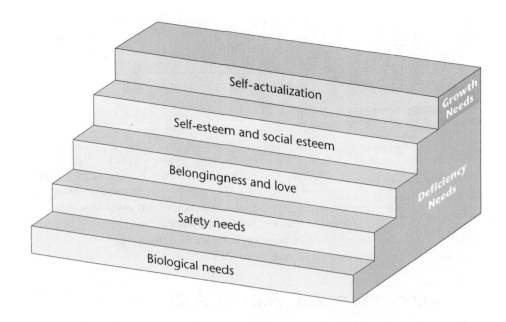

Exhibit 5.4
Maslow's Hierarchy
of Needs

Needs

deficiency needs
Basic human needs,
which must be satisfied
before higher-order
needs can be met. They
include needs for food,
water, air, physical safety,
belongingness and love,
and self-esteem and
social esteem.

growth needs
Higher-order human
needs, which can be
satisfied only after
deficiency needs have
been met. They include
self-actualization (the
process of fully realizing
one's potential),
knowledge and under-
standing, and aesthetic
needs.

Needs are physical and mental states that motivate us to behave in ways that lead to their satisfaction. Abraham Maslow wrote that we experience two sets of personal needs: deficiency needs and growth needs.[36] **Deficiency needs** are basic human needs. **Growth needs** are higher-order human needs. Maslow arranged these two sets of needs in the form of a hierarchy to show that our deficiency needs must be satisfied routinely before our growth needs become important to us.

As Exhibit 5.4 indicates, there are four sets of deficiency needs: (1) *biological needs,* such as food, water, and air; (2) *safety needs,* such as protection from physical harm; (3) *belongingness and love needs,* such as a child's need for the love of a parent; and (4) *self-esteem and social-esteem needs,* which involve believing in our self-worth and finding confirmation of that belief from others. Growth needs are not as straightforward as deficiency needs. They include self-actualization, knowledge and understanding, and aesthetic needs. Self-actualization is the most commonly discussed growth need. According to Maslow, *self-actualization* is the process of fully realizing one's potential. Self-actualized people not only understand themselves but also accept themselves for who they are and what they have achieved.

As you analyze your audience, consider how your speech can help audience members satisfy their likely needs. For example, many motivational speakers seek to help people satisfy their needs for self-actualization. On the other hand, someone selling home security equipment would appeal to safety needs.

Learning About Your Audience

The preceding discussion of audience diversity may seem overwhelming at first. After all, most of us have only a few friends whom we could describe in terms of all of the attributes of cultural, demographic, and individual diversity.

Fortunately, as a speaker, you do not need to know everything there is to know about your audience. Rather, focus your efforts on learning about those characteristics most relevant to your speech purpose. There are four basic ways to learn about audience members: observation, asking for information, doing a survey, and visiting online social networking sites such as Facebook.

Observe Your Audience

The most direct way to learn about audience members is by careful observation. In your own public speaking class, you will observe your classmates on a regular basis and particularly when they are speaking. You will learn a lot about their cultural background, demographic characteristics, and even their beliefs, attitudes, and values. If you are speaking to an audience outside your classroom, try to observe them in advance of your speech. Many demographic characteristics should be readily observable: age, sex, ethnicity, and so on.

Ask Someone Familiar With the Audience

If you cannot observe the audience for yourself, talk to someone who is familiar with it. In many cases you will be invited to speak by a member of the group. For example, the authors have spoken on numerous occasions to service organizations in our community. One of us was recently asked to speak to a group that helps senior citizens deal with Medicare and other health insurance issues. Knowing that helped the speaker to choose examples that would be directly related to the group's mission. Having had an elderly parent who spent time in a skilled nursing facility helped the speaker to relate to the organization's mission and understand its needs.

Survey Your Audience

In some cases you will have the opportunity to conduct a survey of your audience. This is one of the best ways to determine attitudes, values, beliefs, and knowledge levels, which are typically very hard to determine from mere observation. There is a danger of assuming that based on appearances your audience holds certain attitudes. A speaker may commit a major gaffe if he or she assumes attitudes based solely on culture or demographics.

Many professional speakers use survey data in designing their speeches. Your instructor may offer you the opportunity to survey your classmates prior to speaking. If so, avail yourself of the opportunity, but be sure to make the survey anonymous and brief. Too many questions will lead to no responses, and requiring respondents to identify themselves may inhibit candor. The box "Speaking of . . . Surveying Your Audience" provides an example of a survey by a student who plans to speak to the audience about cell phone safety. Notice that the questions focus on the use of cell phones while driving. In particular, this speaker wants to determine if the audience members think that by using hands-free headsets they are driving safely. If so, the speech will need to cite study results that claim that it's the distraction of a conversation more than the use of one hand that is the source of accidents.

1. Do you own a cell phone?   Yes _____   No _____   (if no, skip to question 6)
2. About how many hours a month do you use your cell phone? _____
3. Do you ever use your cell phone while driving?   Yes _____   No _____
4. If so, do you use a hands-free headset?   Yes _____   No _____
5. Do you ever text while driving?   Yes _____   No _____
6. Do you believe it is safe to use a cell phone while driving?
   Always ____   Never ____   Only with a hands-free headset ____   Only when not texting ____
7. What is your opinion on laws banning the use of cell phones while driving?

   _____ All cell phone use should be banned
   _____ Text messaging should be banned.
   _____ Cell phone use should be allowed only with a hands-free headset
   _____ There should be no restrictions on cell phone use while driving

Visit Social Networking Sites

Although we encourage you to be cautious, the chances are good that you can learn about your classmates by visiting online social networks such as Facebook.com, and professional networks such as LinkedIn.com. Should a classmate have a blog, you also could turn to it in search of information about his or her cultural, demographic, and individual background. Social networks such as the preceding have blurred the lines that once separated people's personal and public lives. Whereas you once would have had to interview people face-to-face to learn important details about their personal lives, you can now accomplish the same thing with a few clicks of your mouse. In fact, you may learn more about them than you need to know! And that brings us to an important point. Regardless of what you learn about individual audience members online, you should not use the information in a manner that will embarrass them. Further, be careful that you do not include information or photos in your own profile that could embarrass you. We saw one of our students humiliated when the campus newspaper published her picture in an embarrassing pose because one of the young men in the photo was a candidate for student office. Once on the Internet, any expectation of privacy is lost. You also should exercise care and avoid inferring too much about individual audience members on the basis of what you read and see online. This is especially true should you also find what you think is information about specific audience members through Google or Wikipedia.

Needless to say, the Web can be a tremendous source of information about potential audience members, whether or not they are in your class. Most organizations, including service groups such as Lions, Soroptimists, and Rotary have Web pages. Many of these Web pages also have links that will enable you to learn information about their individual members. Yet, as we'll discuss in Chapter 6, Web sites can be corrupted by the unscrupulous. Thus, you will want to exercise every caution when using information from a Web site to analyze audience members.

Confronting Constraints

We all face certain constraints on action. A **constraint** is a limitation on your choices. Among the common constraints you may face in giving your speech are the facts pertaining to the situation, legal constraints, ethical constraints, nature of the occasion, traditions, time, and resources. Let's examine each of these.

constraint
A limitation on choices in a rhetorical situation.

Facts Pertaining to the Situation

President John Adams observed that "facts are stubborn things."[37] Although some people seem oblivious to the facts governing their situation, sooner or later they must face reality. A speaker who hasn't done research is likely to be embarrassed by the lack of knowledge. As we noted earlier, part of preparing for a speech is to find out what it is that your audience knows, and make sure you know more. Furthermore, it is important to cite the sources from which you have learned your facts. Your audience will perceive you as a more knowledgeable speaker if you have solid sources for your facts.

Legal Constraints

We all must abide by certain legal constraints in our speaking. Libel and slander laws, for example, constrain certain types of speech. Other laws cover when and where groups may peaceably assemble. Some anti-abortion activists have been successfully prosecuted, for example, for blocking the entrances to abortion clinics. Although the First Amendment guarantees freedom of speech and assembly, these rights are not a license to do what you please.

Some speakers, however, have effectively challenged and even broken laws for a purpose. Nelson Mandela was willing to spend much of his life in jail to bring about the end of apartheid in South Africa. Ultimately, this self-sacrifice helped to sway world opinion against the White minority government of South Africa and led to Mandela's election as South Africa's president.

In your case, it is highly unlikely that you will choose to purposefully break the law to further the cause advanced in one of your speeches. Yet unless you check on the legal constraints relevant to your situation, you may accidentally break a law of which you are unaware. In our own experience, we've had students show up to class with everything from exotic beers to poisonous pets, both of which are illegal on our campus. We've learned, consequently, that it is necessary for us to check on the topics and plans of our students well before their time to actually speak. Check with your instructor before you unintentionally pit yourself against the law.

Ethical Constraints

We discussed ethical considerations for public speaking in detail in Chapter 3. At this point, we simply want to remind you of the fact that as a speaker and as a listener you will face ethical constraints. Although something may technically be legal, that doesn't make it ethical.

Nature of the Occasion

What is the nature of the occasion prompting you to speak? After the death of former president Ronald Reagan, his son Ron Reagan used the opportunity of his eulogy for his father to issue a thinly veiled attack against politicians who inject their religious preferences into political campaigns. The younger Reagan acknowledged that his father was a deeply religious man, but one who "never made the fatal mistake of so many politicians wearing his faith on his sleeve to gain political advantage. True, after he was shot and nearly killed early in his presidency, he came to believe that God had spared him in order that he might do well. But he accepted that as a responsibility, not a mandate. And there is a profound difference."[38] Some criticized the use of a solemn occasion such as this to raise a political issue; others applauded young Reagan's forthrightness at a time when the nation was watching.

You will most likely give speeches to classes during normal class times. Your audience is a captive one. Given that unavoidable fact, you must always decide whether your topic and presentation are appropriate to this context and occasion. One of our students made his classmates extremely uncomfortable by discussing his own first sexual experience. Such personal disclosure is inappropriate in a classroom setting. Similarly, vulgarity, profanity, and the like are obviously not suitable for the class. Even excessively casual slang is probably not appropriate for an academic environment. When you have a doubt as to the appropriateness of your speech for your class, it is always wise to check with your instructor.

Traditions

Many speeches are governed by tradition. Whereas this is not a major factor in most classroom speeches, it could be when you are called on to speak in situations outside the classroom. For example, many service clubs, such as Rotary or Lions, have a whole set of traditions that may seem puzzling to the outsider. For instance, there is a good deal of good-natured poking fun at certain members, "fines" are levied for infractions such as getting your name in the paper, and so forth. Major corporations, such as IBM and Apple, each have their own set of traditions. IBM is formal; Apple is much less so. In speaking to either group, therefore, you would want to reflect the degree of formality each expected in terms of dress, demeanor, and style of presentation.

Time

How much time do you have to give your speech? If you have been asked to speak for 5 minutes and you ramble on for an hour, the response will be predictably negative. On the other hand, imagine paying to hear an hour talk by a major public figure and having the speech end in 10 minutes. You need to know and respect time limits, as well as match how much information you cover in your speech to your allotted time. For instance, it is generally better to cover a narrow topic thoroughly than to try to cover a wide range of points superficially.

Time is also a factor to consider in your preparation. If you have a week to prepare a speech, you probably don't have time to line up interviews with far away sources. If you have a month, you probably do. You also will need time for practice. Public speaking deserves the same degree of practice as shooting free throws, swinging a golf club, or learning a new trick in gymnastics. Simply put, it cannot possibly be mastered without some degree of repetition. And this means committing time to practice as far in advance of the speech as possible. Relaxation techniques and other approaches to managing anxiety also require time to master.

Resources

Two questions are involved here. First, what resources do you have available to you? Resources include money, information sources, other people who might assist you, and the like. Second, what resources do you need to accomplish your speaking goal? If your resources match or exceed what you need, you are fine. If you lack the necessary resources, however, you must either redefine your goal or obtain more resources.

Suppose you are assigned to give a speech with at least three visual aids. How do you go about getting these? If you have enough money, you may be able to pay to have pictures enlarged to poster size or to have overhead transparencies prepared. If your classroom is equipped with a computer and projector, you may be able to use PowerPoint software to present part of your speech. If not, what alternative resources do you have? If you have a friend who is an art major, perhaps he or she can help you make posters. Whatever your situation, you need to give careful consideration to the resources you have or will need to obtain to achieve your goal.

Summary

www.mhhe.com/brydon7e

To evaluate your understanding of this chapter, visit our Online Learning Center Web site for quizzes and other chapter study aids.

In this chapter, we have provided the tools to analyze your audience and adapt your speech goals, both long- and short-term, to the audience and the situation. Here, we recap the four major areas to consider.

Analyze your audience in terms of cultural variables:

- Power distance
- Collectivism versus individualism
- Femininity versus masculinity
- Uncertainty avoidance
- Long-term orientation versus short-term orientation

Analyze your audience in terms of demographic characteristics:

- Age
- Gender and biological sex
- Ethnicity
- Geographic origin
- Socioeconomic status

- Education

- Occupation

- Religion

- Language usage

Analyze your audience in terms of individual diversity, including their:

- Knowledge

- Beliefs

- Attitudes

- Values

- Motives

- Expectations

- Needs

Adapt your goals to the audience and the total rhetorical situation. Consider the following constraints:

- Facts

- Legal constraints

- Ethical constraints

- Nature of the occasion

- Traditions

- Time

- Resources

Check Your Understanding: Exercises and Activities

1. Given the topic of alcohol abuse, how might you develop your speech presentation differently if your audience were made up of (a) high school students, (b) students your own age, (c) bar and tavern owners in your community, or (d) recovering alcoholics? In a short paper, explain how your approach and purpose would differ in each case.

2. Create a model of your belief system, including your core beliefs, authority beliefs, and representative derived beliefs, on one of the following topics: gun control, the importance of voting, abortion, same-sex marriage. What does your belief system say about how susceptible you are to being influenced on the topic selected?

3. Interview a student from another country who is studying at your university. What most surprised him or her about American culture? What would Americans be most surprised to know about his or her culture? Write a short paper or give a short talk about what you have discovered.

4. Learn as much as you can about the cultural, demographic, and individual diversity of your classmates. Construct a short questionnaire that will guide

you in preparing for an upcoming speech. After obtaining your instructor's approval, write a survey about your chosen topic. You might ask questions about what your audience members already know about the topic, their attitudes for or against your position, and their level of interest in the topic. Distribute the questionnaire to your classmates and collect their responses (anonymously, of course). Tabulate the results. For example, if your topic is banning the sale of handguns known as Saturday night specials, you might report that 60 percent of your classmates were familiar with the term, while 40 percent were not; that 50 percent agreed with a ban, 20 percent opposed one, and the remainder had no opinion; and that 30 percent felt gun violence was a major issue, while 70 percent did not. Based on these results, write a short paper on how you used this information to shape your speech. Also indicate how your plans for your speech may have changed based on the information from your survey.

Notes

1. Barack Obama, "2004 Democratic National Convention Keynote Address," 27 July 2004. [Retrieved from http://www.americanrhetoric.com/speeches/convention2004/barackobama2004dnc.htm, 15 October 2009.]

2. B. J. Reyes, "Punahou Left Lasting Impression on Obama," *Honolulu Star Bulletin,* 8 February 2007. [Retrieved from http://archives.starbulletin.com/2007/02/08/news/story02.html, 13 October 2009.]

3. Barack Obama, *Dreams From My Father: A Story of Race and Inheritance* (New York: Times Books, 1995).

4. Jeffery Ressner and Ben Smith, "Obama Kept Law Review Balanced," Politico.com, 23 June 2008. [Retrieved from http://www.politico.com/news/stories/0608/11257.html, 13 October 2009.]

5. Barack Obama, "Remarks by the President on a New Beginning," *The White House Office of the Press Secretary,* 24 June 2009. [Retrieved from http://www.whitehouse.gov/the_press_office/Remarks-by-the-President-at-Cairo-University-6-04-09/, 13 October 2009.]

6. Lloyd Bitzer, "The Rhetorical Situation," *Philosophy and Rhetoric* 1 (1968): 5. Bitzer further defines an exigence as "an imperfection marked by urgency; it is a defect, an obstacle, something waiting to be done, a thing which is other than it should be" (6). In this text we prefer to focus on the speaker's goal, which, strictly speaking, is to *overcome the exigence* present in the rhetorical situation.

7. Aristotle, *Rhetoric,* trans. W. Rhys Roberts (New York: Modern Library, 1954), 24.

8. Bitzer, "Rhetorical Situation," 8.

9. Haya El Nasser and Paul Overberg, "Index Charts Growth in Diversity Despite 23% Jump, Segregation Is Still Going on, Researchers Say," *USA Today,* 15 March 2001, 3A. [Lexis-Nexis, 5 August 2001.]

10. Geert Hofstede, *Cultures and Organizations: Software of the Mind* (London: McGraw-Hill, 1991), 14.

11. Hofstede, *Cultures and Organizations,* 14.

12. Peter A. Andersen, Myron W. Lustig, and Janis F. Andersen "Regional Patterns of Communication in the United States: A Theoretical Perspective," *Communication Monographs* 54 (1987): 128.

13. Hofstede, *Cultures and Organizations,* 262.

14. Hofstede, *Cultures and Organizations,* 260.

15. Hofstede, *Cultures and Organizations,* 261.

16. Hofstede, *Cultures and Organizations,* 53.

17. Hofstede, *Cultures and Organizations,* 261.

18. Hofstede, *Cultures and Organizations,* 262.

19. Hofstede, *Cultures and Organizations,* 263.

20. Hofstede, *Cultures and Organizations,* 261.

21. Hofstede, *Cultures and Organizations,* 262–63.

22. John Gray, *Men Are From Mars, Women Are From Venus: A Practical Guide for Improving Communication and Getting What You Want in Your Relationships* (New York: HarperCollins, 1992).

23. Julia T. Wood, *Gendered Lives* (Belmont, Calif.: Thomson Wadsworth, 2005).

24. Robert A. Rosenblatt, "Census Illustrates Diversity From Sea to Shining Sea; Population: Massive Surge of Immigration in '90s Makes Nearly One in Every Three U.S. Residents a Minority, Report Says. Trend Is Nationwide" [Lexis-Nexis, 5 August 2001] (*Los Angeles Times,* 13 March 2001, Part A; Part 1; Page 16).

25. Jon Meacham, "The End of Christian America," *Newsweek,* 4 April 2009. [Retrieved from http://www.newsweek.com/id/192583, 7 September 2009.]

26. Reuters News Service, "Six in Ten Americans Favor Stem Cell Research." [Yahoo News, http://dailynews.yahoo.com/h/nm/20010726/hl/stemcell_3.html, 26 July 2001.]

27. David Westphal, "More Speak Spanish in U.S.," *Sacramento Bee,* 6 August 2001, A12.

28. Brian Murphy, "A Nuanced Overture to Culture Skeptical of US Intent: Muslims See Signs of Hope in His Address," *Boston Globe,* 5 June 2009. [Retrieved from http://www.boston.com/news/world/middleeast/articles/2009/06/05/obamas_nuanced_overture_to_culture_skeptical_of_us_intent/, 15 October 2009.]

29. Sarah Trenholm, *Persuasion and Social Influence* (Englewood Cliffs, N.J.: Prentice-Hall, 1989), 6.

30. Milton Rokeach, *Beliefs, Attitudes and Values* (San Francisco: Jossey-Bass, 1968), 6–21.

31. Kathy Wyler, "Political Engagement Among College Freshmen Hits 40-Year High," *UCLA News,* 22 January 2009. [Retrieved from http://www.gseis.ucla.edu/heri/PDFs/press/pr01220808Freshman.pdf, 7 September 2009.]

32. Martin Fishbein and Icek Ajzen, *Belief, Attitude, Intention, and Behavior: An Introduction to Theory and Research* (Reading, Mass.: Addison-Wesley, 1975), 6.

33. Trenholm, *Persuasion and Social Influence*, 11, based on Rokeach, *Beliefs, Attitudes and Values*.

34. Milton Rokeach, "Change and Stability in American Value Systems, 1968–1971," in *Understanding Human Values: Individual and Societal*, ed. Milton Rokeach (New York: Free Press, 1979), 129–53.

35. Robert Fulghum, *All I Really Need to Know I Learned in Kindergarten* (New York: Ivy Books, 1988).

36. Abraham H. Maslow, *Motivation and Personality*, 2nd ed. (New York: Harper & Row, 1970).

37. John Adams used this phrase in a summation to a jury. You can read a more complete text at http://www.law.umkc.edu/faculty/projects/ftrials/trialheroes/HEROSEARCH5.htm.

38. Ronald Prescott Reagan, "Remarks by [Ronald] Prescott Reagan," 10 June 2004. [Retrieved from http://www.ronaldreaganmemorial.com/remarks _by_Prescott_Reagan.asp, 10 June 2004.]

PUTTING THEORY INTO PRACTICE

Research is essential to an effective public speech.

RESEARCHING YOUR MESSAGE

Objectives  www.mhhe.com/brydon7e

After reading this chapter and reviewing the online learning resources at www.mhhe.com/brydon7e, you should be able to:

- Conduct a search of the Internet to find support for a speech.
- Conduct systematic library research to find support for a speech.
- Conduct a meaningful interview with an expert on the topic of a speech.
- Record information in a usable form for your speech.
- Cite sources orally for your audience.

Key Concepts

abstract

blog

Boolean operators

Deep Web

fact

index

key word

online catalog

opinion

podcast

primary sources

research

RSS

secondary sources

subject heading

Surface Web

Twitter

URL

vidcast

wiki

"Genius is one percent inspiration and ninety-nine percent perspiration."

—THOMAS EDISON[1]

We have all had the experience of hearing speeches by well-respected speakers who never cite a single source. For example, the authors have heard Nobel Peace Prize winners Elie Wiesel and Mikhail Gorbachev speak. These speakers didn't need to say "according to an article in . . ." to show that they knew what they were talking about. We have also attended many lectures by less well-known speakers who, because of their expertise in a particular area, have not relied on other sources to document their claims.

For most of us, however, and certainly for students beginning their public speaking careers, it is important to use credible evidence from reliable sources to support what is said in our speeches. To do so requires **research:** the process of finding and evaluating supporting materials.

research
The process of finding and evaluating support-ing materials.

Why Do Research?

There are several reasons why research is important. First, unless we are relating firsthand experience, speeches that lack research can convey false or questionable information to an audience. Second, we have an ethical responsibility to provide good reasons to our audience for believing what we say. Without evidence, what assurance do our listeners have that our claims aren't simply made up? Third, unless our audience perceives us as knowledgeable, we are unlikely to convince them without documentation. Aristotle called such believability *ethos,* and contemporary researchers call it *source credibility*. Both agree that it is key to the art and science of public speaking. Our believability as speakers is enhanced by citing evidence from multiple sources in the body of our speeches.[2] Doing so requires research to uncover evidence from multiple sources. But there's a catch: We need to make sure that we research and orally cite sources that have weight with audience members and that listeners can readily check if they wish to. Telling an audience we pulled the evidence from some generic Web site just doesn't cut it.

We know that this is easier said than done. Hence, the remaining sections of this chapter will give you the tools not only to find information for your speeches but also to evaluate that information in a way that will enable you to convey it credibly to an audience.

Developing a Research Plan

Purposeful research begins with a research plan. And that plan begins with a thorough analysis of your rhetorical situation, as we emphasized in Chapter 5. Who will be your audience? What topics are of interest to them and you? What are your purposes—both general and specific?

For students in a basic speech class, some of these matters are predetermined. For example, your instructor and classmates are your audience. Depending on how far the term has progressed, you may have a clear idea of what topics interest them. But if it's early in the term, you may want to test-drive some ideas with classmates (we often have brainstorming sessions in class where different topics are discussed).

Your instructor may also predetermine the general purpose of a speech. You will typically be asked to give a speech to inform or persuade and will face some specific constraints, such as a time limit and visual aid requirements. Within those limitations, you will make a number of decisions that guide your research plan.

Given that your audience and general purpose are usually predetermined, you will need to decide on a topic for your speech. In Chapter 1 we discussed the standards for a good topic: it should be interesting to audience and speaker, appropriate to the situation and to the available time, manageable, and worthwhile. Once you have a topic, you need to decide what you want the audience to take away from your speech. Will they be able to do something they couldn't do before your speech? One of our students, for example, taught us the art of folding a fitted sheet (no, you don't just roll it up in a ball). Will the audience members be asked to change their attitudes about an issue? Another of our students gave a speech aimed at convincing her classmates to ditch their expensive bottled water and instead attach a simple water filter to their faucet and get pure water for pennies a glass. Whatever topic you pick, you need to be sure that information is readily available for your speech. Sometimes a promising topic will turn out to be too obscure or difficult to research in the time available. You will need to begin research early enough to allow yourself the time to shift topics if necessary.

Often it is not until after you have begun your research that you discover there is not enough information to meet the needs of your proposed presentation—or there is so much information that an entire lecture series would be required to adequately cover your topic. Be flexible and willing to enlarge or shrink the topic based on your research. One method for getting "the correct topic size" is by enlarging or contracting the time period covered. For instance, you may originally have wanted to speak about the history of U.S. immigration policy but found far too much information. Changing your topic to U.S. immigration policy since the 9/11 attacks would help reduce your presentation to a more manageable size.

The Goal: Reliable and Credible Evidence

At this point it is tempting to simply provide a laundry list of places to look for information: the Internet, the library, the daily newspaper, and so forth. We think this is actually backward. Before you start looking for evidence for your speech, we think you need to know what to look for. More specifically, you need to know what constitutes reliable and credible evidence. Reference librarians at our university developed a useful tool, which they nicknamed the CRAAP test, for assessing online information. The letters stand for *Currency, Relevance, Authority, Accuracy, and Purpose.*[3] We feel that it is useful for more than just Web sites. In fact, these are the hallmarks of credible evidence, whatever the source.

Currency

In today's world, things change at such a rapid pace that often yesterday's news is both stale and downright wrong. Whatever your topic, you want the most current, up-to-date information possible. One advantage of published sources is that the dates are usually apparent. With Web sites, you may not know when the information was created or modified. Some browsers allow you to access this information with a few steps. For example, in Internet Explorer click on the File menu option and then on Properties to determine the creation and modification date of a Web page. In Mozilla Firefox hold down the Control key, click somewhere on the page and choose "View Page Info." If you cannot determine the currency of information, you should not use it in your speech.

Tips and Tactics

Evaluating Currency

[handwritten: Currency → when was the info. published? Is it up to date?]

- When was the information published or posted? Has the information been revised or updated? Newspapers, books, periodicals, and many Web sites will provide this information. If it's not readily available, look for internal clues. For example, a Web site that speculates about whether Americans will vote for an African American for president is clearly out of date.
- Is the information current or out of date for your topic? If you are speaking about the Vietnam War, information from several years ago is probably fine. But if you want to discuss the current war in Afghanistan, information even a few days old may be out of date.
- Are the Web site links functional? One of the hints that a Web site is out of date is that it contains dead links.

Relevance

[handwritten: Relevance → If the information is actually the one you were looking for.]

Sometimes information is interesting but not really helpful in achieving your specific speech purpose. Suppose you are giving a speech on the sinking of the Titanic. Although he starred in the movie of the same name, Leonardo DiCaprio is not really relevant to the actual sinking of the Titanic. As we discuss how to conduct searches for information, we will give you some tools for narrowing things down to what is directly relevant to your purpose.

Tips and Tactics

Evaluating Relevance

- Does the information answer your question or need?
- Is this information at an appropriate level for your audience?
- Have you looked at a variety of sources before determining that this is one you will use? Is this the best source you can find to make your point?

Authority

[handwritten: Authority → Trusting the source/Author]

This is one of the most important things to look for in doing your research. Ultimately you need to convince your audience that they should trust the source. One of the most common complaints we get from students is that they don't know how to cite sources with an unknown author. Generally our response is: "Why should we believe anything from an unknown author?" Instead, find out who said it or at least what group or organization is responsible. Only then can you decide if it's worth including in the speech.

Evaluating Authority

- Who is the author/publisher/source/sponsor, and what are their credentials or organizational affiliations? Most books and periodicals will tell you something about the author. Also, a Google search (which we will discuss later) can often help you learn about a source. Clicking "About Us" or "Contact Us" on the Web page may help.
- What are the author's qualifications to write on the topic?
- Is there contact information, such as a publisher or e-mail address?
- Does the **URL** reveal anything about the author or source? For example, is the site a .com, .edu, .gov, .org, or .net? We will discuss these in more detail later in this chapter.

> **URL**
> Uniform Resource
> Locator: the address
> for Web sites, such as
> www.mhhe.com.

Accuracy

Even authoritative sources sometimes get it wrong. There's no surefire way to guarantee that information is accurate. Still, using sources that have a reputation for being reliable and truthful helps. Also helpful are different authoritative sources that offer evidence in support of the same conclusion: for example, a biochemist and a psychologist saying that there is chemical and behavioral evidence supporting the diagnosis of depression. If you can cite evidence from two sources that are usually opposed but agree on your claim, then you may convince even skeptics of the accuracy of your claim.

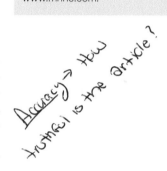

Accuracy → How truthful is the article?

Evaluating Accuracy

- Can you tell where the information comes from?
- Is the information supported by evidence such as footnotes or links to other verifiable sources?
- Has the information been reviewed or refereed by experts? A newspaper, for example, normally edits and checks sources before publishing a story; many Web sites do not.
- Can you verify any of the information using another source or from personal knowledge?
- Are there spelling, grammar, or typographical errors?

Purpose

Finally, a good researcher keeps in mind the stated and implied purpose of the source of information. Particularly on controversial topics, a source who has an axe to grind may be suspect.

Purpose? → Does the author state is own opinion or is he/she biase?

- What is the likely purpose of the information? A Web site touting a nutritional supplement is suspect if it invites you to click on a link to buy the product.
- Do the authors/sponsors make their intentions or purpose clear?
- Does the information seem unbiased, or is it merely opinion or propaganda? Does the language or tone seem unbiased and free of emotion?
- Are there obvious political, ideological, cultural, religious, institutional, or personal biases?

Where to Look for Supporting Materials

In the sections that follow, we will direct you to three primary places to find support for your speech: the Internet, the library, and personal interviews.

The Internet

Breakthroughs in information storage and retrieval have largely solved the physical limitations of the traditional bricks-and-mortar library. And personal computers in combination with the World Wide Web have made virtual libraries a reality for most college students and professors. If that were all there was to the story, our task in this chapter would be much simpler.

But as we know, there's more. The same technological breakthroughs that made virtual libraries possible have also eliminated many of the filtering processes that let valid information into and kept erroneous information out of every conceivable channel of communication, including speeches. In addition, the huge increase in the volume of resources has buried the researcher with information that needs to be evaluated.

The Internet is actually made up of two levels. The **Surface Web,** sometimes called the Open Internet, is searchable by Web search engines such as Google, Bing, and Yahoo. This part of the Internet often allows you free access to information. The other part of the Internet is the **Deep Web,** which is sometimes referred to as the Proprietary Internet. The Deep Web contains information in private databases that are accessible over the Internet but are not accessible by search engines. For example, some universities, government agencies, and other organizations maintain databases of information that were not created for general public access and do not allow search engines to index them. Other material on the Deep Web is from commercial publishers who require that you access it through a paid subscription or pay to view certain pages. Many traditional hard-copy materials such as newspapers, journals, magazines, dictionaries, and encyclopedias have been converted to electronic format and are sold via the Deep Web.

Why should you care about the Deep Web and the Surface Web? If you are using only the Surface Web for your research, then you may be locating only

Surface Web

(Open Internet) Web sites freely accessible to all users over the Internet.

Deep Web

(Proprietary Internet) Web sites accessible over the Internet only to authorized users and often at a cost.

information of limited value. The premium information that will add credibility to your presentation may only be available online through Deep Web databases. Information aggregators such as LexisNexis, Proquest, Factiva, and EBSCO package and resell commercially produced information via the Deep Web. Many college and local public libraries have subscriptions with such vendors, allowing you to search, view, and save expensive information for free.

How do you know if you have access to such Deep Web sources? Most library Web pages have guides that explain which premium online resources they provide. If you have a particular title in mind, such as the *New York Times* or *Economist,* you can check your library's online catalog to determine if a resource is available either in hard copy or electronically. These guides and catalogs may have "clickable" links that take you directly to the database containing your title.

It is easy to use the Internet to find information on a speech topic, but it is not as easy to tell which information is reliable and valid. As consumers of information, we must exercise our own critical faculties in assessing the information we receive from the Internet and even traditional sources, particularly when others rely on the information we use in a speech.

We recognize that most students begin their research with the Open Internet—so that is where we'll begin. In the process, let's see if we can improve the process of seeking evidence for your speeches. In the following sections, we provide specific advice on using a wide variety of Open Internet sources, including popular search engines (such as Google, Yahoo, and Bing), wikis (such as Wikipedia), podcasts, RSS feeds, user-powered news sites, YouTube, blogs, and Twitter.

Googling

As Google says on its Web site, "Google's mission is to organize the world's information and make it universally accessible and useful."[4] They certainly have mastered the goal of accessing a lot of information. Take a popular topic for student speeches: medical marijuana. We typed "medical marijuana" into the general Google search box and got over 3.6 million "hits." What can you do with over 3 million sources? And how would you know which ones are reliable and which are bogus? After all, medical marijuana is a controversial topic. Thus, Google's great power is also its greatest limitation.

Google, Yahoo, and Flickr are useful tools for locating materials for speeches.

Although Google does not use traditional Boolean operators (which we will explain shortly), its advanced search feature lets you include and exclude certain phrases and words from your search. Suppose we are interested in the effectiveness or efficacy of medical marijuana. We narrowed our search to sources that included the word *effectiveness* or the word *efficacy.* That cut the number of hits to a little over 1.6 million, still far too many to be useful.

To focus our attention on the most reputable sources, we next utilized "Google Scholar," a feature that searches various scholarly sources (peer-reviewed papers, theses, books, articles, and so on). Many of these sources are readily available on the Web; others may require subscriptions or membership. Don't automatically give up on sources that require access rights—you may be able to find them in your university library or through interlibrary loan. The advantage of using the Google Scholar tool is that the authority and accuracy of your research can be much more easily established for your audience. Using Google Scholar we found about 11,000 sources on the effectiveness or efficacy of medical marijuana. This included articles in such prestigious journals as the *Journal of the American Medical Association*. Also, we can limit the search to recent articles. Doing this cut our number of sources to about 5,000.

Using Google Scholar does not guarantee the quality of the sources you'll find, but it is certainly preferable to a general Google search. On the other hand, because it focuses on scholarly sources, it may not be as helpful in searching current topics.

But Beware . . .   We are big fans of Google. However, users need to understand something about how Google arranges results. For obvious reasons, Google refuses to disclose the exact methods by which it ranks results. This can lead to some startling results. To see how Google searches can go awry, see the box "Speaking of . . . When Google Misfires" on page 139. Users should also know that, in addition to the regular search results, Google also displays a number of sponsored links that are paid for by various Web sites—a source of revenue for Google. But their presence is no measure of their validity or reliability as a source; it merely indicates that they were willing to pay for advertising through Google.

Googling Sources   Before we leave the topic of Google, we want to suggest one additional way it can be a valuable research tool. Suppose you find an interesting article or Web site but there are no qualifications listed for the author. Sometimes a Google search of the author's name (or the name of the organization sponsoring the Web site) will help out. For example, in the "When Google Misfires" box, we mentioned the Martin Luther King Web site that was linked to a racist group that specifically recommended a book by David Duke. What if you had never heard of Duke? Well, Googling his name—in addition to leading you to his own Web site—takes you to articles about his role in the Ku Klux Klan and his visit to Iran for a conference on Holocaust deniers. If a person's credentials are not known to you, consider Googling the name. You may need to conduct an advanced search (especially if it's a common name), but being able to tell your audience your source's credentials is an important part of building your own credibility.

wiki

The Hawaiian word for "quick." A Web site that allows users to edit content easily and quickly—for example, Wikipedia.

Wikis

Wiki comes from the Hawaiian word for "quick."[5] The idea is that anyone can quickly make a change in an entry they find in a site like Wikipedia and the change will be instantly available to all users. No one demands that the user document or substantiate the edit. Wikipedia knows only the IP address of the computer used to post the information.

Unfortunately, not everyone who visits Wikipedia has good intentions, as the case of journalist John Seigenthaler Sr. illustrates. For 132 days in 2005, Wikipedia falsely reported that John Seigenthaler Sr.

> was the assistant to Attorney General Robert Kennedy in the early 1960's [*sic*]. For a brief time, he was thought to have been directly involved in the Kennedy assassinations of both John, and his brother, Bobby. Nothing was ever proven.[6]

As Seigenthaler recounts in an article for *USA Today,* no one knew who had posted the false accusations. Even a call to Wikipedia's founder, Jimmy Wales, failed to turn up the name of the perpetrator, because Wikipedia doesn't require contributors to reveal their identity. Further, because of the way the Internet is interconnected, Reference.com and Answers.com posted the same false accusation. Although the false information was eventually removed, this example illustrates that a claim isn't true just because it's found on the Internet. In 2009, Wikipedia recognized the dangers of such freewheeling contributions and announced that a layer of editorial review called "flagged revisions" will be added for articles about living people. Experienced volunteer editors will be required to approve any changes before they go live.[7]

In fact, sometimes even mainstream media mistakenly rely on unreliable Web sources. A Dublin University student, Shane Fitzgerald, was able to post a phony quotation on Wikipedia as a test to see how quickly it was picked up in the mainstream media. He made up a quotation and posted it within hours of the death of composer Maurice Jarre. The intriguing quotation– "One could say my life itself has been one long soundtrack"–was too good for those in the media to ignore. It quickly showed up on numerous newspaper Web sites throughout the world. Although Wikipedia quickly removed the phony quotation, a full month went by before the student revealed his hoax and newspapers started removing it from their online archives.[8]

One of the limitations of wikis, in addition to the ease with which they can be edited, is that they are at best a **secondary source.** Whenever possible, speakers should try to locate **primary sources** of information (original sources)

secondary sources
Information sources that rely on other (primary) sources rather than gathering information firsthand.

primary sources
Original sources of information.

139

Podcasts have become a useful source of information for researchers.

rather than a source that presents information that its authors did not gather firsthand. Wikipedia insists upon being *only* a secondary source; in fact, moderators will remove any information that is presented as original research.

At the same time, we think that wikis do have a role to play in your research. Rather than treating wiki articles as ends in themselves, use the external links and references in the articles to see if there are reliable sources that you can easily access. Wikipedia can be a good quick stop for statistics and factoids, and having the information may make it quicker to find the detail in question. For example, if we want to know the Academy Award–winning motion picture for a particular year, we can just go to Wikipedia, find the answer, and then follow the links in the article to a reliable source on Academy Award winners. If the wiki was wrong, we'll quickly find that out. It is also good for checking the reliability of other sources. It represents a consensus of many people. Thus, we suggest using sources such as Wikipedia as a way of locating other sources that can meet the tests of currency, relevance, authority, accuracy, and purpose.

Podcasts, Vidcasts, and RSS Feeds

podcast
An audio broadcast that has been converted to a digital format, such as MP3, for playback by a digital music player or computer.

vidcast
A video clip that is similar to a podcast. (Also called a "vcast," "vodcast," or "videocast.")

RSS (Really Simple Syndication)
A syndication format that aggregates updates to various news sites or blogs and transmits them to users.

With the widespread use of MP3 players and smart phones, such as Apple's popular iPod and iPhone, audio and video files can be transmitted over the Internet to anyone who is interested in accessing them. A **podcast** is an audio broadcast that has been converted to a digital format (such as MP3) for playback by a digital music player or computer.[9] A **vidcast** (also called a "vcast," "vodcast," or "videocast") is a video clip that is similar to a podcast.[10] Some universities make professors' lectures available in podcast or vidcast format. As this chapter was written, there were dozens of downloads available from Stanford University– everything from African American history to "Why Zebras Don't Get Ulcers." And that's just one university.

It's not only universities that have podcasts available. National Public Radio, the White House, TV networks, and major news sources like the *New York Times* all have podcasts or vidcasts readily available. The key, as with any other source of information, is how well it meets the CRAAP tests we've outlined.

RSS (Really Simple Syndication) is a format that aggregates updates to various news sites or blogs and transmits them to users.[11] For example, you can sign up for feeds from various news sources, even the White House. RSS is a form of "push technology": it pushes information directly to your desktop or smart phone. If you are doing ongoing research on a topic, then signing up for RSS feeds from reputable sources is a way to be sure you have current and relevant information from authoritative and accurate sources. The *New York Times*, for example, offers both podcasts and RSS feeds.

User-Powered News Sites

An interesting variation on search engines like Google and wikis are user-powered news sites. For example, Digg.com allows a user to post content that is then rated by other users. As their Web site explains: "Digg is a user driven social content website. . . . Well, everything on Digg is submitted by our community (that would be you). After you submit content, other people read your submission and Digg what they like best. If your story rocks and receives enough Diggs, it is promoted to the front page for the millions of visitors to see."[12] As of 2009, Digg.com averaged about 35 million different users a month.[13] Rather than relying on some editor to rank stories (as a newspaper would) or on a computer algorithm (as does Google), Digg relies on its users to post news stories and videos and then relies on other users to give their evaluation. You can search the news by topic and then arrange the results by most Diggs to find the articles that were found most useful by the community of users. You can link back to the stories that are most relevant to your topic and also give your own opinion as to whether or not you "Digg" it. Digg allows you to search by relevance (best match), recency (newest first), or "most dugg." One caution is that the most "dugg articles" are not always the most relevant. On the issue of global warming, for example, the best match as we were writing this chapter was a report on National Public Radio that global warming was irreversible.[14] On the other hand, the "most dugg" article on global warming was "10 steps to make sure you make the Digg front page," not exactly relevant to the topic. Digg.com is useful as a different way to search for information on topics, but you still have to assess whether or not the articles that it finds are from credible sources. A similar Web site primarily useful for science and technical news is slashdot.org.

YouTube

One of the most popular Web sites is YouTube. It allows users to post videos (often of themselves) on the site for anyone to view. Speakers using computer software, such as PowerPoint, often incorporate brief video clips into their presentation, and YouTube can be a source of videos on almost any topic imaginable. Most of the material on the site is entertaining or just odd, but some important videos have found their way onto this site. For example, Susan Boyle became an overnight sensation when the video of her singing "I Dreamed a Dream" was viewed by millions worldwide.

YouTube is a great source for finding video material for use in speeches or as background material. For example, a search for videos on global warming located everything from a National Geographic video explaining how greenhouse gases

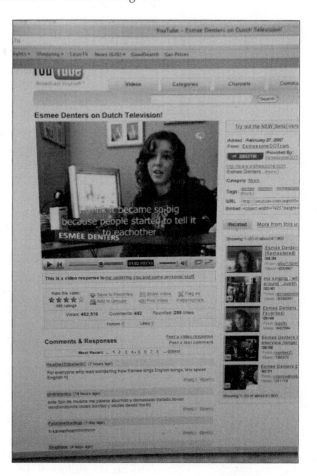

YouTube can provide video clips for use in speeches.

lead to global warming to a homemade video labeled "Global Warming Scam!" Just as with Wikipedia and other sources where the content is not screened for accuracy, the videos you find on YouTube are only as valid as their original source. That the Global Warming Scam video began with a "Space Monkey" and consisted of a guy in a ball cap ranting against Al Gore probably indicates it's not a very reliable source for a speech, whereas National Geographic would generally be considered a reliable source on scientific topics.

If you incorporate links to YouTube videos into a presentation, however, be sure to test them shortly before you speak. Videos are often removed from YouTube for a variety of reasons, including copyright violations. It is embarrassing to a speaker to click on the link to YouTube only to find the video is gone.

Blogs

Most of us are familiar with **blogs** (short for Web logs). They contain dated entries in reverse chronological order and can range from serious commentary by experts to mere "ranting and raving" by just about anyone with an opinion.[15] Many blogs have a strong persuasive component, especially those related to politics. However, they also tend to contain many links to more reputable mainstream media sources. Even blogs whose authors disagree with your point of view can be a valuable source of links.

The idea of using blogs in a speech brings us to an important distinction: fact versus opinion. A **fact** is something that is verifiable as true. An **opinion** is a judgment by someone that is subject to dispute. For example, as the *New York Times* reported, it is a *fact* that "Gov. Sarah Palin of Alaska abruptly announced on Friday [July 3, 2009] that she was quitting at the end of the month," but it was an *opinion*, to which many readers objected, that her speech was "an often-rambling announcement" or that her voice "seemed rushed and jittery."[16] Deciding whose opinions we should value is important in meeting the tests of authority dictated by the CRAAP test. The problem with blogs is that anyone can have one. We do not recommend citing blogs unless the source is clearly authoritative on the topic of your speech. Blogs often will have links to the biography or credentials of the blogger. A speaker must do more than cite the name of the blogger; the audience needs to hear why the blogger is a credible source on the topic.

One other aspect of blogs is that they are often the source for reports in traditional news outlets. If that is the case, such stories are really no more reliable than any other rumor. The danger is that if the news outlet relies on the blogosphere rather than developing its own sources, misinformation may be spread. An example of this occurred when a blog devoted to "outing" closeted gay politicians posted an item claiming that a well-known male politician had had sexual relations with at least three men (none of whom was named). A newspaper published the allegations along with the politician's denial. Nobody checked to see which version was true.[17]

Twitter

In the aftermath of the disputed elections in Iran in 2009 there was considerable buzz about the role of the social networking site **Twitter** in organizing the protests on the streets of Tehran. Many in the mainstream media ended up basing their reports on Twitter because the Iranian government had cut off traditional

blog (short for Web log)
A Web site that contains dated entries in reverse chronological order. They can range from serious commentary by experts to "ranting and raving" by people with no particular qualifications.

fact
Something that is verifiable as true.

opinion
A judgment by someone that is subject to dispute.

Twitter
A social networking service that enables users to send and read messages of up to 140 characters.

news sources. Although news organizations do their best to verify the information they receive, mistakes can be made. As was pointed out in the *New York Times*, "Nothing on Twitter has been verified. . . . And just as Twitter has helped to get out first-hand reports from Tehran, it has also spread inaccurate information, perhaps even disinformation."[18] For example, the *Times* points out that false tweets were posted that three million people protested in the streets, when the real number was in the hundreds of thousands. So although Twitter may be an interesting place to catch up on your friends or current events, it is not generally a reliable source for your speech research.

A Final Word About Evaluating Internet Information

The trickiest part of doing Internet research is knowing how to tell reliable from unreliable sources. You can tell a lot from a Web site's URL. Once you've used a search engine such as Google or Digg to locate possible Web sites, look at the URL for clues as to whether it is a legitimate source.[19]

- Is it a personal Web page? You can usually tell from the URL because it will often include a person's name following a tilde (~) or percent sign (%). If the server is a commercial Internet service provider, such as geocities.com, aol.com, or angelfire.com, this is another sign of a questionable source. For most speeches, personal Web pages should be avoided.

- What is the type of domain? Government sites are usually .gov, .mil, or .us. Educational sites are .edu. Nonprofit organizations are .org. The domains .com and .net are generally commercial. Look for the types of sites that are most appropriate for your speech topic. Government and educational sites are often the best place to begin for speeches on current events and issues.

- Who is the Web page's sponsor? For example, McGraw-Hill Higher Education publishes the Web site for this text (www.mhhe.com/brydon7e). One can safely assume that this is a reliable source of information about our text and its supporting materials. Look for pages sponsored by reputable organizations that have a direct bearing on your speech topic.

You should be aware that a .org domain is no guarantee that a site is noncommercial, and .edu is *not* a guarantee of scholarly content. Most university students can put a personal Web page up under their university's domain. Don't rely entirely upon the domain suffix, but consider it a minor tool in your CRAAP toolbox.

There are various sites that can evaluate Web resources. For instance, the Urban Legends Web site (http://snopes.com) is a terrific resource for determining the validity of commonly held ideas or theories. If you type in "Barack Obama birth certificate" in the search box at Urban Legends, you will get a detailed refutation of the often-repeated hoax that Obama wasn't born in Hawaii and that his birth certificate was forged. The Librarians' Internet Index (http://lii.org/) is also an excellent resource for locating reliable information on the free Web. The LII performs a similar filtering function for the Internet that librarians have traditionally provided for the patrons of brick-and-mortar libraries. Their mission statement declares: "The mission of Librarians' Internet Index is to provide a well-organized point of access for reliable, trustworthy, librarian-selected websites, serving California, the nation, and the world."[20]

The Library

It's common for us to meet students who have never set foot in the library on campus—but this doesn't mean that they haven't used the university's library resources. Today there are really two types of libraries available to students: the brick-and-mortar building; and the virtual library, available 24/7 from the convenience of a computer at home, on campus, or in an Internet café.

Even so, we require our own students to take a guided tour of the physical library. Some valuable resources for speeches reside only on the shelves of the library or in its special collections departments.

Research for a public speaking class will often involve a trip to the campus library. Although campus libraries vary in their extensiveness and degree of sophistication, the basic principles of a library search are the same whether in a physical or a virtual library.

The first step in using a library is familiarization. Most campus libraries feature in-person and online guided tours, handouts, and special seminars for groups interested in a particular area of research. Your instructor may have your class take a library tour or send you on a library scavenger hunt to familiarize you with the library. Whatever you do, though, don't wait until you are facing a speech deadline before familiarizing yourself with your library. If you didn't do it during your first few weeks on campus, make it a priority now.

We recommend the following four steps for library research whether in person or online.

Tips and Tactics

Four Steps of Library Research

1. Select key words.
2. Search the library catalog.
3. Search relevant indexes, abstracts, and other databases.
4. Consult reference sources.

Although each step isn't required every time for library research, it's useful to know about each step and how the steps are connected. Let's look at each in detail.

Select Key Words

key word
A word in the abstract, title, subject heading, or text of an entry that can be used to search an electronic database.

subject heading
A standard word or phrase used by libraries to catalog books or other publications.

Key words are significant ones taken from the abstract, title, subject heading, or text of an entry and used to search an electronic database.[21] They are like the combination to a safe: If we have the right combination, we can easily open the door; without it, our chances of opening the door are slim. Thus, the most effective library search begins with searching key words on the topic of interest.

In addition to key words, **subject headings,** developed by the Library of Congress, are standardized throughout libraries across the country. These headings often lead to sources we might otherwise miss. For example, suppose the topic we are interested in is the "three strikes law." We searched our university library's catalog for books on the topic and found three. However, the detailed record for the books revealed that the Library of Congress uses the subject heading *mandatory sentence.* Searching for that term yielded 21 books—a sevenfold increase. Although we normally begin our search using key words and phrases that seem logical, we check the official subject headings and try them as well. These can multiply our results several times over. Be aware, however, that not all databanks use Library of Congress subject headings. It is useful when using databases, such as those provided by EBSCO, to consult their thesaurus for appropriate key words.

Another hint for key word or subject searching is to use truncation and wildcard symbols. For example, at our university an asterisk (*) is used for these purposes. Thus, to search for *sentence, sentences,* and *sentencing,* we would type *sentenc** in the search box. The search engine will find all records with any string of characters following *sentenc.* Similarly, to search for both *woman* and *women,* the key word *wom*n* would do the job in most databases. However, some databases do not allow the use of truncation symbols within a word. Be sure to ask what characters your library uses as wild cards, as it varies from library to library and database to database.

online catalog
A computerized database of library holdings.

Boolean operators
Terms, such as *and, or,* and *not,* used to narrow or broaden a computerized search of two or more related terms.

Search the Library Catalog

Most libraries today use computerized online catalogs accessible from off campus as well as in the library building. An **online catalog** is a computerized listing of library holdings. Library catalogs are searchable by key words, subject, author, and title. When beginning a search on a topic, it is unlikely that we will know specific authors or titles. Thus, the key words search is the most likely basis for a search.

When using an online catalog or similar database for a key word search, use **Boolean operators.** These are terms, such as *and, or,* and *not,* used to narrow or broaden a computerized search of two or more related terms. Some databases and library catalogs will *assume* the Boolean operator *and* unless we supply another, while others will require us to type in *and* or *+.* For example, if we enter search words *human cloning* and the database assumes the *and,* it will locate all sources that use both the word *human* and the word *cloning* even if they are not used together. On the other hand, if the *and* is not assumed, the database may only locate sources where the phrase *human cloning* appears. Depending on our search needs, we need to determine which method is used in the library catalog. Check with a librarian at your school to learn whether you need to use Boolean operators, or experiment with different search combinations until you discover which way your library catalog operates. How Boolean operators can be used to broaden or narrow a search is shown in Exhibit 6.1.

Online library catalogs enable researchers to locate the materials they need in a fraction of the time it took using card catalogs.

Exhibit 6.1

Boolean Operators
Help Narrow or
Broaden a Search

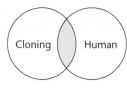

Cloning *AND* Human

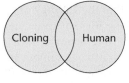

Cloning *OR* Human

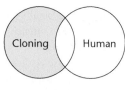

Cloning *NOT* Human

Tips and Tactics

Expanding Your Search

- When you locate a book or other source that is interesting, check to see what subject headings are used by the library to index the book in addition to the one used to find it. These subject headings can then provide new search terms to expand your search and locate additional sources on your topic.

- When visiting the stacks, do a little browsing as you find the specific books you have noted. Because books are shelved by subject, it is not unusual to find a book closely related to your topic that was overlooked. This serendipitous search for information often turns up better sources than those originally found.

- Follow the leads suggested by general books. The authors of books have done much of your work for you. A book's bibliography or footnotes lead to other sources. Read the more recent books first. In many ways, a researcher is like a detective looking for clues. A good general book on a topic is like a room full of clues. The author will have left fingerprints all over the place.

Search Relevant Indexes, Abstracts, and Databases

index
A listing of sources of information—usually in newspapers, journals, and magazines— alphabetically by topic.

abstract
A summary of an article or a report.

An **index** is an alphabetical listing of sources by topic of information—usually in newspapers, journals, and magazines that are not freely available via the open Internet. An **abstract** is a summary of an article or a report. Every topic you can imagine is classified in one or more specialized indexes. A good library has hundreds or even thousands of indexes related to specialized fields. Some indexes list and abstract articles in journals. Today, more and more indexes are available in the form of online databases. For example, a partial list of databases available through our university library is provided in Exhibit 6.2.

Whether your topic is art, science, religion, philosophy, or health and medicine, computerized databases can help you find reliable information. Your library will undoubtedly differ from ours in the available indexes. However, the basic search principles will be the same regardless of the index used.

Academic Search is an excellent source for searching scholarly and professional journals in the social sciences, humanities, and physical sciences. This database contains information on everything from astronomy to religion, law, psychology, and current events. Not only are citations and abstracts of articles available, but Academic Search also allows us to access the full texts of many articles. To search, we simply follow easy on-screen directions to enter appropriate search terms. The same Boolean operators we would use in an online catalog search can be used with most computerized databases. When we enter our search,

Database	Description of Coverage
Academic Search	More than 4,650 periodicals covering the social sciences, humanities, general science, multicultural studies, education, etc.
Biological Abstracts (BIOSIS)	Nearly 6,000 journals covered, representing agriculture, biochemistry, biotechnology, ecology, immunology, microbiology, etc.
Communication & Mass Media Complete	Scholarly and trade publications in communication and journalism/mass media; abstracts for several hundred titles, with full text available for more than 380 titles.
CQ Researcher	Full-text issues written in accessible language, including pros/cons, background info, the current situation, and references to other information sources on current affairs controversies.
LexisNexis Academic	Full text news, business, and legal information; includes newspapers, magazines, court opinions, laws, and law review articles.

Exhibit 6.2

Examples of Databases with Description of Coverage

a list of citations will be produced, and we mark the ones that interest us for viewing. Depending on the library's facilities, we may be able to print, copy to a flash drive, or even e-mail the results of our search.

Although databases such as Academic Search may initially seem to produce far too many results to be usable, a careful narrowing of the parameters of a search can lead to productive and easily accessible results. Although your library may not have this exact database, chances are it has a similar database that can access reliable published information on a wide variety of topics.

Of course, not every library has a physical or electronic copy of every journal listed in any given index or database. Thus you must compare the most promising articles from your search with your library's holding of journals. Some libraries provide listings of their journals. The online catalog may also list journals. You would look under the journal title, for example, to see if your library had a particular journal. Even if your library does not have it, you may be able to use interlibrary loan services to obtain a copy, if time permits. Also, some libraries subscribe to special services that enable them to have copies of journals not held in their collections faxed to the library for a nominal charge.

Consult Reference Sources

Frequently we need to find a very specific fact—for example, how much oil was produced in the United States in a certain year. We could search a dozen articles and never find that number. But a good reference book, such as the *Statistical Abstract of the United States,* puts that kind of information at our fingertips. For an online source of reliable government statistics, try the Web site http://www.fedstats.gov/, which bills itself as "the gateway to statistics from over 100 U.S. Federal agencies."[22] This site includes topics from A to Z, map statistics, links to various federal agencies, and even the ability to access the online version of the *Statistical Abstract of the United States.*

Perhaps we need a good quotation to begin or end our speech. Numerous books of quotations are available. Your library probably has books such as

Quotations

Bartlett's Quotations on its shelves. However, an easier way to find quotations is to go to Bartleby.com's Great Books Online at http://www.bartleby.com/, which includes thousands of quotations. For the first edition of this book, we were interested in a quotation frequently used by the late Robert Kennedy that went something like, "Some men see things as they are and say, why; I dream things that never were and say, why not." We expended several hours of library research tracking down the original source. For the sixth edition we used Bartleby.com, and in less than a minute we had found the original quotation. It is actually, "You see things; and you say 'Why?' But I dream things that never were; and I say 'Why not?' " The original source is George Bernard Shaw's play, *Back to Methuselah.* Ironically, although Kennedy used the quotation as a theme in his 1968 campaign for the presidency, the actual speaker of these words in Shaw's play is the serpent enticing Eve in the Garden of Eden.[23]

Numerous other reference books can be found in libraries, including encyclopedias, some of which are available online. Although the information in general encyclopedias is rather basic, a number of specialized encyclopedias are also available ranging from *Encyclopedia of Advertising* to *Violence in America: An Encyclopedia.*

There are countless other reference books available to track down information. For example, almanacs and yearbooks, such as *The World Almanac and Book of Facts* and *Information Please Almanac,* are useful sources of statistics and facts. Digests of information, such as *Facts on File* and *Editorial Research Reports,* are useful sources for information on current issues. Biographies, such as the *Who's Who* series, help you find out about the qualifications of various sources. Atlases are valuable in learning about the world. By consulting a current atlas, you can learn not only where a country is geographically but also important facts about it.

Interviews

We put off discussing interviews until now for a reason. It is tempting to go into an interview before researching the topic. In a sense, we expect the expert to write the speech. Although interviews with experts can offer useful information and may lead to other sources, they cannot substitute for doing our own research. Thus, an interview should be conducted only after doing a fair amount of research.

Finding potential interviewees on most topics is not difficult. At a university, most departments have experts on various topics. Often a call to the department asking if there is anyone familiar with your specific topic will elicit a name. In other cases, simply consult a department's course offerings. Someone who teaches a class on Middle Eastern studies, for example, most likely is an expert in that subject.

Another strategy is to contact organizations related to the topic and ask if someone there would be available to interview. For example, if we were researching the effects of secondhand smoke, the American Lung Association is a likely source of potential interviewees.

Sometimes we already know people who can help. We recall the case of one student who was speaking about a "miracle" weight-loss product. After calling the company's home office and getting the runaround, she contacted her local pharmacist. He informed her that the ingredients in the product were not capable of helping a person lose weight—in fact, they were potentially harmful. A brief interview with the pharmacist gave her information she would have had great difficulty finding on her own.

Once we have decided on a person to interview, we recommend the following basic guidelines for before, during, and after the interview.

Before the Interview

- Contact the potential interviewee well in advance. Explain the reason for the meeting and how much time it will take. If the person agrees to be interviewed, ask for a convenient time and place for a meeting (usually at the interviewee's place of business). If possible, confirm the appointment by e-mail.

- Do some general reading on the topic. Read at least a book or two and some recent articles, or visit relevant Web sites. This will provide a basis for framing questions and focusing on those things that cannot easily be found elsewhere.

- Prepare specific questions in advance. Ask open-ended questions, which will allow the interviewee an opportunity to talk at some length. Of course, be prepared to deviate from the planned questions as answers suggest other avenues to follow.

During the Interview

- Show up on time, dressed professionally, and ready to begin. Thank the person and explain how the interview will be used. Be sure to ask for permission to record the interview if this is desired. If an interview is by phone, there is a legal obligation to inform and gain consent from the other party to record the conversation.

- Using previous research as a guide, begin with general questions and then move to specific ones. Be sure to let the interviewee talk. Don't monopolize the conversation; doing so defeats the purpose of the interview.

- Ask the interviewee if he or she can suggest other sources of information— books, pamphlets, periodicals, or other experts. Often an expert will know of sources we never would have thought of ourselves. Sometimes the interviewee may even loan some relevant journals or other publications.

- Use the listening skills discussed in Chapter 4, especially being mindful, blocking out distracting stimuli, suspending judgment, using multiple channels, and taking effective notes.

- Either record (with permission) or take complete notes during the interview. Ask follow-up questions to make sure to get the essential points on paper. Quotations from the interview used in a speech must be accurate.

- When time is about up, ask the interviewee if there is anything he or she can add to what has been said. Perhaps there is some area that has been completely overlooked.

- Thank the interviewee again for his or her time and exit graciously.

After the Interview

- A follow-up thank-you letter is common courtesy.

- Transcribe the recording or notes while the interview is fresh in your mind. Notes that may have been clear at the moment will quickly fade from memory unless you flesh them out soon after the interview.

- Follow up on leads or other interviews suggested by the interviewee. Interviews provide a rich source of information and add credibility to your speaking. The fact that a speaker takes the time to speak directly to an expert shows concern for the audience. Further, the audience's perception of a speaker's expertise is enhanced by virtue of the interview. Be sure to let the audience know why the interviewee is a credible source on the topic.

Using Your Research

Preparing Bibliography, References, or Works Cited

Before beginning in-depth reading on a topic, prepare a preliminary list of the sources. Using either a computer word processor or small note cards (4 by 6 inches is a good size), list the following information about each source.

- For all sources: author(s), preferably by full name, if an author is listed; also include the author's qualifications on the subject matter.
- For books: exact title and the following facts of publication: location, publisher, and date.
- For periodicals: article title, periodical title, volume number, date, and pages.
- For government documents: the agency issuing the document as well as the document's full title, date, and publication information.
- For electronic resources: author, title, and publication information, as well as the e-mail address, Web site, or path by which the material was located and the date you retrieved it, which is very important as Web sites are constantly changing.

Always leave space to add information to each citation as you read the source.

All of this information is needed for the formal speech outline. It is easier to prepare the outline if this information is handy rather than having to go back to find it later. In Appendix A we provide samples of how to correctly cite sources according to the systems developed by the American Psychological Association (APA) and the Modern Language Association (MLA). Your instructor may require a different source citation system such as *The Chicago Manual of Style* or Kate Turabian's *A Manual for Writers of Term Papers, Theses, and Dissertations*. Regardless of the citation system used, the information listed above will be essential.

Recording Information and Avoiding Plagiarism

As you gather materials, it is essential to carefully and accurately record the supporting materials for a speech. In Chapter 7 we discuss the types of evidence you will want to record—facts, statistics, quotations from experts, and the like. It is important to record information in a way that ensures it will be honestly cited and represented in the speech. It is especially important that sources are apparent to audiences, as discussed in the box "Speaking of . . . Orally Citing Sources."

With the Internet, the temptation is to simply cut and paste material from the Web. This is simple and accurate, but there is one big downside. There is an increasing

SPEAKING OF . . .

Orally Citing Sources, by Christine Hanlon (from Nicholson Custom Edition)

Why Cite Sources?

There are several reasons why we should cite sources. According to Carol Bledsoe (former Coordinator of public speaking at University of Central Florida), there are three main reasons why we should cite sources:

- To establish credentials of the source and the data
- To enable the audience to retrieve the material
- To give credit to others

Establishing the Credentials of the Source and the Data

The first reason we should cite sources is to establish the credentials of the source and the data. If we, the audience, do not know why the source is credible, why should we believe that the information is valid? Let's take the following excerpt from a speech as an example:

> According to the CDC, there weren't any monkey pox cases in the United States until the 2003 outbreak.

The speaker has identified the CDC as the source of the data. Although many of us in the United States know that "CDC" is the acronym for Centers for Disease Control, you cannot assume that everyone is familiar with it. If you want to use the acronym for an organization, be sure to first identify what that acronym stands for. For example, state "the Centers for Disease Control, also known as the CDC . . ." Analyzing your audience will help you to determine if there is a time when you can break this rule. There will be times in the workplace when you will use acronyms. However, if you are ever in doubt, explain the acronym so your audience understands it.

Furthermore, there may be audience members who don't know what the CDC is. Be sure to briefly explain the purpose of the organization so your audience understands why the source is credible. Using this example, an appropriate explanation of the CDC could be, "The CDC is the United States' lead federal agency that investigates health problems and conducts research to prevent infectious diseases." Again, you want to analyze your audience to determine if an explanation is necessary.

Enabling the Audience to Retrieve the Material

By indicating where you found the information, you can enable the audience to retrieve the material. In the previous example, the speaker did not clarify where the information about the CDC was located. Was the information located on the CDC's official Web site or in a pamphlet distributed by the CDC, or did it come directly from a researcher who works for the CDC? To enable the audience to retrieve the material, speakers need to be clear about where the information can be found. Let's take some of these examples individually.

Where the information was found	Oral citation that enables the audience to retrieve the material
CDC's official Web site	"According to the CDC's Monkey pox factsheet posted online . . ."
CDC pamphlet	"The CDC's pamphlet entitled 'Tuberculosis: What you need to know' states that . . ."
Researcher who works for the CDC	"In a recent study, CDC researcher Jane Smith found that. . ."

Giving Credit to Others

It is important to give credit to others for their ideas. Many academics and scientists consider their ideas, their intellectual property, as their greatest contribution. There is even an international organization that works to uphold worldwide standards for intellectual property. According to the World Intellectual Property Organization (2004), "these works—intellectual property—are expanding the bounds of science and technology and enriching the world of the arts." If you use others' ideas during your presentation and fail to cite them, you are essentially *stealing* the ideas of others. There are two important reasons why you should orally cite your sources while presenting speeches, and they are both directly tied to credibility. Failing to cite a source can decrease your credibility, whereas orally citing a source can add to your credibility as a speaker.

There can be serious consequences for speakers who fail to orally cite their sources properly. First, they can be charged with plagiarism. Whenever students fail to orally cite a source in a speech, they are guilty of plagiarism. The reality is that there are consequences to plagiarism, whether or not it was intentional. The bottom line is always to orally cite your sources so you can avoid the situation altogether.

Christine Hanlon (M.A., University of Central Florida) is a public speaking instructor at the University of Central Florida's Nicholson School of Communication. She is also a past president of the Florida Communication Association. Her research interests include family violence and popular culture. She has presented scholarly papers at regional and national conferences for communication, sociology, women's studies, and popular culture associations. Additionally, she has published in past volumes of *Teaching Ideas for the Basic Communication Course*.

Adapted from Christine Hanlon, "Speaking of . . . Orally Citing Sources." Between One and Many, Nicholson School Edition, McGraw-Hill. Reprinted by permission of Christine Hanlon. **151** problem in society with the use of material written by others without proper attribution. *USA Today* dismissed a five-time Pulitzer Prize nominee, newspaper reporter Jack Kelley, when it was learned that he had plagiarized and fabricated numerous stories. As Blake Morrison of *USA Today* reports, there was "strong evidence Kelley fabricated substantial portions of at least eight major stories, lifted nearly two dozen quotes or other material from competing publications, lied in speeches he gave for the newspaper and conspired to mislead those investigating his work."[24] Numerous other highly publicized cases of plagiarism have damaged the careers not only of reporters but of many noted academics as well.

As professors, we've discovered numerous instances of plagiarism. In many cases the culprit was a downloaded bit of text that the student failed to properly cite in a speech or paper. For example, when asked to write a personal brief essay about her chosen major, one student simply downloaded the description of Communication Studies from another university's Web site. Presumably she knew we would recognize the language from our own Web site, so she cribbed her paper from a department elsewhere. The language didn't seem natural, so we did a simple Google search for some of the unusual phrases. The result was a clear case of plagiarism, which was reported to the university's authorities. Other students have cited the source in the References or Works Cited of their papers but have not indicated which words were direct quotes and which were their own words. In this situation, it's often sloppy recording during the research phase that is at fault. Plagiarism has become such a problem that many universities, including our own, subscribe to the plagiarism checking service Turnitin.com. This Web-based service checks papers submitted by students against both public Web sites and a database of millions of student papers.

How can students avoid this type of accidental yet potentially serious plagiarism? Here are some specific recommendations.

Tips and Tactics

How to Avoid Plagiarism

- Don't just automatically cut and paste from sources. Make notes in your own words about the main ideas.
- Keep printouts or photocopies. When doing the final draft of a speech or paper, be sure that any direct quotes are indicated by quotation marks and cited in the body of the speech or paper, not just in the Bibliography, References, or Works Cited.
- If a direct quotation is cut and pasted, use a different font to indicate that it is a direct quote. For example, once we have cut and pasted the quotation, we change the font color to red or put it in italics.
- Err on the side of full disclosure. A close paraphrase that is not cited is considered plagiarism, even if it's not a direct quote. If there's any doubt, it doesn't hurt to cite the source, both in the speech outline or manuscript and orally. For example, we discussed Robert Kennedy's paraphrase of the George Bernard Shaw quotation earlier in this chapter. Even though he didn't use the exact words, he would always say something like, "As George Bernard Shaw was fond of saying . . ." Citing sources is not a sign of weakness; rather, it enhances a speaker's credibility.

Summary

The process of researching to support your speech is like the process of inventing a new product: You need both a source of inspiration and the willingness to engage in hard work.

- Begin by developing a research plan.

- Choose an appropriate topic.

- Formulate a specific purpose you want to accomplish.

- Sources of information for your speech should meet tests of currency, relevance, authority, accuracy, and purpose.

Possible sources include:

- The Internet, but with particular attention to distinguishing authentic and reliable Web sites from questionable ones.

- Library resources, such as books, periodicals, and databases.

- Interviews.

Develop a recording system for both sources and data that avoids the danger of plagiarism and ensures accuracy. Be sure to cite sources orally for your audience.

www.mhhe.com/brydon7e

To evaluate your understanding of this chapter, visit our Online Learning Center Web site for quizzes and other chapter study aids.

Check Your Understanding: Exercises and Activities

1. Check your understanding of the American Psychological Association and Modern Language Association guidelines for source citations in Appendix A. Provide a correct source citation for each of the following hypothetical sources, using both APA and MLA guidelines:

   - A book with one author named Jack Smith, titled College Life, published in New York by University Press in 2010. How would your citation change if Smith were the editor of the book? How would you list a second author, John Q. Doe? How would you list a third author, Mary A. Smith?

   - An article titled Dorm Life in American Universities, by Peter Chu, published in the scholarly journal Universities and Colleges, volume 31, December 2010, pages 24–56.

   - A chapter by Jose Sanchez titled The Nine Lives Myth, appearing on pages 99–109 in the book Cat Stories, edited by Morris T. Katt, published by Feline Press in San Francisco, California, in 2010.

   - An article in Canine Magazine titled Snoopy and Me, by Charlie Brown, pages 56–57, on December 14, 2010, in volume 42. How would you list the article if no author were named?

2. Although the Internet is an invaluable source of information on almost any topic, it is also a notorious source of misinformation. As an exercise, try to locate the Web site of the Central Intelligence Agency (CIA). How many different Web sites did you find before locating the official page? How did you know when you were at the official site?

3. *Worksheet for speech topic choice.* One way to select an appropriate speech topic is to begin with an inventory of your own interests and those of your listeners as revealed by their self-introductions in class. Under each of the following headings, list at least three things that are important to you and to your audience.

	My interests	Audience interests
Hobbies	_____	_____
	_____	_____
	_____	_____
School	_____	_____
	_____	_____
Work	_____	_____
	_____	_____
Goals	_____	_____
	_____	_____

Situational factors _____

Nature of assignment _____

Time available _____

List of three possible topics _____

_____

_____

4. How would you go about determining on what subject Arthur L. Schawlow and Charles H. Townes are experts? (Hint: They won Nobel Prizes for their discovery.)

Notes

1. Gary Marin, "Genius Is One Percent Inspiration and 99 Percent Perspiration," *The Phrase Finder,* 2009. [Retrieved from: http://www.phrases.org.uk/meanings/146600.html, 18 October 2009.]

2. James C. McCroskey, "A Summary of Experimental Research on the Effects of Evidence in Persuasive Communication," *Quarterly Journal of Speech* 55 (1969): 169–176.

3. Adapted from Meriam Library, California State University, Chico, "Evaluating Information–Applying the CRAAP Test." [Retrieved from http://www.csuchico.edu/lins/handouts/eval_websites.pdf, 18 October 2009.]

4. "Company Overview," 2005. [Retrieved from http://www.google.com/intl/en/corporate/index.html, 7 January 2007.]

5. Chelsea Phua, "Web Site Has Scoop on Davis Community," *Sacramento Bee,* 10 December 2006, B4.

6. John Seigenthaler, "A False Wikipedia 'Biography,'" 29 November 2005, *USA Today.* [Retrieved from http://www.usatoday.com/news/opinion/editorials/2005-11-29-wikipedia-edit_x.htm, 5 January 2007.]

7. Noam Cohen, "Wikipedia Poised to Back Off from Do-it-Yourself Editing," *Sacramento Bee,* 25 August 2009, A4.

8. AOL News, "Fake Wikipedia Post Fools Some in Media," 12 May 2009. [Retrieved from http://news.aol.com/article/wikipedia-quote-hoax/475157, 2 July 2009.]

9. "Definition of Podcast," *PCMag.com Encyclopedia* (undated). [Retrieved from http://www.pcmag.com/encyclopedia_term/0,2542,t=podcast&i = 49433,00.asp, 9 January 2007.]

10. "Definition of Vidcast," *PCMag.com Encyclopedia* (undated). [Retrieved from http://www.pcmag.com/encyclopedia_term/0%2C2542%2Ct%3Dvidcast &i%3D56178%2C00.asp, 16 July 2009.]

11. "Definition of RSS," *PCMag.com Encyclopedia* (undated). [Retrieved from http://www.pcmag.com/encyclopedia_term/0,2542,t=RSS&i=50680,00 .asp, 9 January 2007.]

12. "What Is Digg?" 2006. [Retrieved from http://digg.com/about, 9 January 2007.]

13. Peter Guglielmetti, "The Digg Idea," *Reader's Digest,* August 2009, 48.

14. Richard Harris, "Global Warming Is Irreversible, Study Says," NPR, 7 July 2009. [Retrieved from http://www.npr.org/templates/story/story .php?storyId=99888903 7 July 2009.]

15. "Definition of Blog," *PCMag.Com Encyclopedia* (undated). [Retrieved from http://www.pcmag.com/encyclopedia_term/0,2542,t=blog&i=38771,00 .asp, 9 January 2007.]

16. Adam Nagourney and Jim Rutenberg, "Palin's Move Shocks G.O.P. and Leaves Future Unclear," *New York Times,* 3 July 2009. [Retrieved from http://www.nytimes.com/2009/07/04/us/politics/04palin.html?_r=1&sq =palin%20resigns&st=cse&scp=1&pagewanted=all, 11 July 2009.]

17. Edward Wasserman, "When Do Rumors in Blogosphere Rate Coverage?" *Sacramento Bee,* 19 November 2006, E3.

18. Noam Cohen, "Twitter on the Barricades in Iran: Six Lessons Learned," *New York Times,* 21 June 2009. [Retrieved from http://query.nytimes.com/ gst/fullpage.html?res=9C06E4DF1531F932A15755C0A96F9C8B63&scp =2&sq=twitter%20on%20the%20barricades&st=cse, 30 June 2009.]

19. Based on UC Berkeley–Teaching Library Internet Workshops, "Evaluating Web Pages: Techniques to Apply & Questions to Ask," 27 July 2004. [Retrieved from http://www.lib.berkeley.edu/TeachingLib/Guides/ Internet/Evaluate.html, 29 December 2004.]

20. "LII Selection Criteria," 2006. [Retrieved from http://lii.org/pub/htdocs/ selectioncriteria.htm, 20 January 2007.]

21. Adapted from Meriam Library, California State University, Chico, "Chico RIO: Research Instruction Online." [Retrieved from www.csuchico.edu/ lins/chicorio/glossary.html, 12 November 2004.]

22. See Fed Stats [http://www.fedstats.gov/].

23. Bartleby.com Great Books Online. [Retrieved from http://www.bartleby .com/73/465.html, 27 July 2004.]

24. Blake Morrison, "Ex-USA Today Reporter Accused of Plagiarism," *Sacramento Bee,* 20 March 2004, A8.

Supporting your speech with facts and figures helps make for an effective presentation.

SUPPORTING YOUR MESSAGE

Objectives

After reading this chapter and reviewing the online learning resources at www.mhhe.com/brydon7e, you should be able to:

- Recognize the three basic types of claims: fact, value, and policy.

- Explain the role of evidence in supporting a speech.

- Support a speech with examples that are relevant, sufficient, typical, and without counterexamples.

- Support a speech with verifiable facts from reliable and unbiased sources that are consistent with other known facts.

- Support a speech with numerical data from reliable, unbiased sources, including percentages, averages, and reliable polls.

- Support a speech with expert opinion, which is reliable and unbiased.

- Support a speech with clear and accurate explanations.

- Support a speech with vivid and accurate descriptions.

- Support a speech with narratives that have both probability and fidelity for your audience.

Key Concepts

claim

evidence

expert opinion

narrative

narrative fidelity

narrative probability

"Everyone is entitled to their own opinion, but not their own facts."

–SEN. DANIEL PATRICK MOYNIHAN[1]

Have you ever purchased a product that warns, "Requires some assembly"? If you have, then you also know what it's like to learn that the process described on the box is seldom as easy as described. Assembling the parts of your speech can also prove more difficult than you initially envisioned. After spending time in the actual or virtual library and systematically searching the Web, it's not uncommon to look at your notes and wonder how you will ever make sense of them in a speech. This chapter is designed to help you translate your research into a meaningful speech. When you break it down, every speech contains a series of **claims,** which are simply the conclusions that a speaker wants the audience to reach as a result of the speech. To support these claims, speakers need to present **evidence**–that is, facts, examples, expert opinion, numerical data, narratives, and the like, which support the claim.

Claims

We make three basic types of claims when speaking: factual, value, and policy. A *factual claim* states that something is true or false. Some facts are clear-cut: 2 plus 2 equals 4. Others aren't so easy to prove: Is the earth warming or not? The hallmark of factual claims is that they are theoretically verifiable. *Claims of value* make judgments about what is good or bad, right or wrong, moral or immoral. Much of the debate over so-called wedge issues such as same-sex marriage, stem cell research, and abortion concern value judgments. Finally, *claims of policy* are statements about what a person should do. Most persuasive speeches deal with claims of either value or policy, or both. Most informative speeches are primarily about claims of fact. As we look for evidence to support our speeches, we need to carefully assess the types of claims we plan to make. We also need to consider our audience. What facts do audience members already know or believe? What additional facts do they need to know? Will they accept the values implicit in our message? If we advocate policies, we need to base them on facts and values that are established in our speech. Thus research and audience analysis go hand in hand.

Evidence

To succeed as public speakers, we need to base our claims on facts and opinions. For example, whether we are teaching someone how to swing a golf club or persuading them to share our views on stem cell research, we need to do more than just offer our unsupported opinions. Audiences want us to provide evidence to support our claims. If a speaker says stem cell research could lead to a cure for diabetes, audience members are going to expect the speaker to tell them why and how. We can support a speech and answer the audience's desire for grounding in facts and reliable opinions using these methods:

- Examples
- Facts
- Numerical data
- Opinions

claim
A conclusion that a speaker wants an audience to reach as a result of a speech.

evidence
The facts, examples, expert opinion, numerical data, narratives, and the like, offered by a speaker in support of a claim.

Jared Fogel's dramatic weight loss made him a paid spokesman for Subway. However, his weight loss is not typical, nor was it solely the result of diet, as he also exercised regularly.

- Explanations
- Descriptions
- Narratives

Examples

An example is a specific instance that represents some larger class. We might cite a weight-loss program that worked for celebrities as a path for others to follow. The test of an example is whether it is actually representative of the larger category. To test whether an example is representative, we need to ask the following questions:

- *What is the relevance of the example to the larger category?* If our examples of weight loss were followed by subsequent weight gain, they probably aren't very relevant to those who want to lose weight for good. Thus, celebrities such as Charles Barkley or Kirstie Alley, who regained the weight they lost, are probably poor examples for a speech on weight loss.

- *Are there enough instances to support the generalization?* We all know the story of Subway spokesman Jared Fogel, who lost well over 200 pounds on Subway sandwiches. Isolated examples are not sufficient to prove that eating subs will cause the pounds to melt off.

- *Is the example typical of the larger category?* We should avoid atypical examples. As Subway admits on their own Web site, "Individuals lost weight by exercising and eating a balanced, reduced-calorie diet that included SUBWAY® sandwiches with 6 grams of fat or less. Their results are not typical."[2] In fact, most weight loss plans have a similar disclaimer, usually in fine print, about their testimonials.

- *Are there counterexamples that disprove the generalization?* A counterexample is one that contradicts the generalization. Whereas several examples can only suggest the truth of a generalization, even one example to the contrary can disprove it. Thus, to argue that eating Subway sandwiches will definitely lead to weight loss is easily disproved—for every Jared, there are numerous Subway patrons who tip the scales at far more than their ideal body weight. In short, although Jared's story may be inspirational, by itself it is not sufficient to prove the effectiveness of his particular diet plan.

Facts

A fact is something that is verifiable as true. It is a fact that there are 50 states in the United States. As former baseball great Yogi Berra might say, "You can look it up." On the other hand, the statement that Texas is the best state in which to live is not a fact, though it may be widely believed by Texans.

We noted earlier that a fact is one of the three types of claims we may make in a speech. But facts are also the building blocks of a speech. For each claim we make, there are likely other claims of fact that will support that claim.

A fact, of course, is only as good as the source of that fact. To evaluate a fact, ask the following questions:

- *Does the fact come from a reliable source?* Encyclopedias, almanacs, authoritative books, and scholarly articles are usually reliable. On the other hand, if the "fact" comes from someone who has a clear bias about the topic, we should be suspicious. For example, many Internet sites claim to state facts, such as that extraterrestrials exist or that there are "black ops helicopters" constantly spying on us. Just because something is on the Internet, we shouldn't assume that it is true, as we illustrated in Chapter 6.

- *Is the fact verifiable?* We should be suspicious of facts that are difficult to verify. For example, estimates of certain types of crime, such as rape, vary because so many rapes go unreported. Thus the number of reported rapes is multiplied by some factor assumed to represent the number of unreported rapes for every reported one. However, these numbers are impossible to verify for the very reason that the unreported rapes are, by definition, unverifiable. Although these estimates may be useful, they are not facts in the sense of being verifiable.

- *Is the fact the most recent available?* Until 2001, statistics about the federal budget projected a large annual surplus. Yet as this book is being written, these projected surpluses have been replaced by deficits measured in trillions of dollars. A speech built around the existence of budget surpluses would clearly be out of date.

- *Is the fact consistent with other known facts?* Facts do not stand alone. We should be suspicious of alleged "facts" that seem to be inconsistent with other known facts. For example, many tobacco manufacturers once claimed that nicotine is not addictive. However, not only the surgeon general but also anyone who has tried to give up smoking can tell you that such a "fact" is suspect. We should double-check sources for possible error and be particularly careful with *secondary sources,* which rely on another source rather than gathering the information firsthand. As we noted in Chapter 6, it is always better to look at *primary sources,* which are the original sources of information, because there may be honest mistakes in transferring information from one source to another. Finally, we should keep in mind what facts the audience already knows. If our facts are inconsistent with what the audience believes to be true, we first have to convince them that ours are more reliable if we are to have any success.

Numerical Data

Numerical summaries of data, such as percentages, averages, and statistics, are valuable when used judiciously in our speeches. These can be a rich source of information; yet they can also be confusing and misleading. For example, an American automobile manufacturer announced a survey showing that its cars were preferred overwhelmingly to foreign cars. However, it turns out that the company included only 200 people in its survey, none of whom even owned a foreign car.[3]

Numbers that seem authoritative but are of dubious value constantly bombard us. When considering using numerical data ask yourself:

- *Is the source reliable and unbiased?* The tip-off to the problem with the survey on foreign versus American cars is that it was sponsored by an American car company. Numbers found through general searches of commercial, individual, or organizational Internet sites are often suspect. On the other hand, those found in official sources, such as www.fedstats.gov, are less likely to be biased, because this site collects official government data. However, even official government estimates can prove wildly off base. Look for numbers that are corroborated by multiple sources, particularly when the issue is controversial.

- *What are the percentages based on?* Speakers often toss out percentages without telling us what the percentage really means. Just because something is up or down a certain percentage doesn't really mean anything unless you know the base of the percentage. For example, between 2007 and 2009 the stock market fell approximately 50 percent from its all-time high. The Dow Jones Industrial Average peaked at 14,164 on October 9, 2007. By February 7, 2009 it had dropped over 50 percent to 7062.[4] The market began to recover later in 2009. But it would need to rebound 100 percent to completely make up the 50 percent drop from its peak. The reason is that the 50 percent fall was based on twice the base from which the recovery would be calculated. Sound confusing? It is. The point is that we need to be sure we understand what percentages are based on before relying on them to prove a point.

- *What type of average is being used?* We often hear about the average family, student, taxpayer, and so on. In reality, average has several meanings. One of the most frequently reported numbers is the mean. Although easily computed, the mean is often misleading because it is commonly distorted by numerical extremes. Consider a newspaper report stating that the average (mean) salary for new college graduates is $40,000 a year. That doesn't mean a majority of college graduates are paid $40,000 a year. It simply results from adding the salaries paid to all college graduates surveyed and dividing that sum by the number of graduates in the sample, resulting in the mean (the arithmetic average). The number likely has been distorted by graduates in engineering, computer science, and information systems management, who, though few in number, start at salaries two to three times as much as their more numerous counterparts in the liberal arts and social sciences. The most telling number is the *median,* which is the midpoint in a distribution of numbers. Knowing the median tells us that half of the numbers in the distribution are larger, and half are smaller.

- *Are the numbers based on a poll?* A meaningful poll calls participants, not the other way around. Based on sophisticated sampling techniques and random selection, a national poll can predict a presidential election with about a 4 percent margin of error. But when our Internet provider, local television station, or newspaper conducts an "unscientific poll," in which people record their views, the results are meaningless. Only people who are interested in the topic will respond, and some polls even allow multiple responses. In short, such polls are worse than worthless because they undermine confidence in legitimate polls.

- *Were unbiased questions asked?* One poll asking whether disposable diapers should be banned was preceded by a statement that disposable diapers account for only 2 percent of trash in landfills. Not surprisingly, 84 percent of those polled felt disposable diapers should not be banned.[5]

- *Was the sample representative?* A representative sample is absolutely necessary for a poll to be reliable and valid. A representative sample is one made up of people who possess the same attributes as the people in the population from which the sample is drawn. A class of economics majors, for example, is hardly representative of the typical college's student population.

  There are many ways to obtain a representative sample, but the most common way is to randomly select people from the population in which we are interested: for example, college students between the ages of 18 and 25. A properly designed survey gives everyone in the population being surveyed an equal chance to be included. Generally speaking, the larger the sample randomly drawn from a population, the more representative the sample.

  The complexities of sampling theory are beyond the scope of this book. Even so, we want to emphasize that the value of any poll depends on sampling. Thus, at a minimum, we should never accept a poll at face value. We need to find information about the sample on which the results are based.

- *Are the differences in the poll greater than the margin of error?* Good pollsters report the margin of error. Keep in mind that the margin of error increases as the sample gets smaller. Whereas the margin of error for a sample of 1,067 people is about plus or minus 3 percent, for 150 people the margin of error is about plus or minus 8 percent.[6] Suppose a poll has a margin of error of plus or minus 4 percent. This means that if the poll shows a political candidate ahead of her opponent by 51 to 49 percent, she could be ahead by as much as 55 to 45 percent, or behind by 47 to 53 percent—or any number in between. When only subgroups of a larger sample are

Numerical Data

Tests for using numerical data

- Know the source—is it unbiased and reliable?

- Know what percentages are based on—it is misleading to compare percentages from widely differing bases.

- Know the kind of average used—was it the mean (average) or the median (midpoint)?

- For polls, know what questions were asked—were they fair and unbiased?

- Know how a poll's sample was chosen—is it representative?

- Consider the margin of error—do the differences exceed it?

considered, there are even more chances for error. So when you see a poll that says it surveyed 1,000 voters with a margin of error of plus or minus 4 percent, realize that a subgroup (say African American women) is a small fraction of the total and carries a far larger margin of error.

This list of questions is not meant to discourage you from using numerical data. They can be a powerful form of support. The key is to know what your numbers mean and how they were collected, and to avoid biased sources and questionable sampling techniques. Most important, you need to adequately explain your numbers to your audience so that they will have confidence in the claims you are making. Useful tests for numerical data can be found in the box "Speaking of . . . Numerical Data."

We must be careful, however, not to overwhelm our audience with numbers. To make numerical data meaningful, we suggest rounding off information presented orally. For example, rather than saying, "The Dow closed at 11,997.7," we could simply say, "The Dow closed today just below 12,000." Comparisons are also useful. For example, let's say a speaker wants the audience to visualize how much land would be needed to produce corn for ethanol in order to significantly reduce our dependence on foreign oil. The speaker could say it will take 90 million acres to produce the corn. That sounds like a lot, but few of us can really visualize an acre, let alone 90 million of them. On the other hand, it turns out that 90 million acres is an area roughly the size of the state of Montana. For an audience, such a comparison would be much more meaningful than raw numbers. Finally, consider using charts, graphs, and other visual aids to express numerical data, as shown in Exhibit 7.1 and discussed in Chapter 12.

Opinion

We all have opinions on all sorts of topics. One of the authors loved *Brüno* and the other hated it. Some people love hip-hop, others can't stand it. The list of topics on which we have opinions is endless. As speakers, we may want to share our opinions with our audience. However, unless we are recognized experts on a topic, our opinion is unlikely to carry any weight with audience members. After all, why should they give any more weight to our opinion than to their own?

Sometimes speakers have special qualifications that enable them to use their own opinions as support for their speech. For example, a student whose mother

Exhibit 7.1
Visual aids such as pie charts help audiences visualize numerical data.

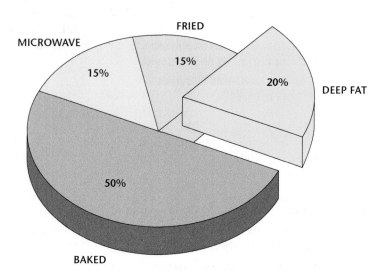

Cooking Methods

had terrible complications from breast implant surgery spoke in one of our classes. Her speech was short on quotes from experts but was still very powerful because she told the story of her mother's suffering in a convincing way. If we intend to use our own opinions as support in a speech, we need to be sure to explain to the audience why our opinions are worth considering.

More common than personal opinion in supporting a speech is **expert opinion**—a quotation from someone with special credentials in the subject matter. Quotations from experts, whether gathered from a personal interview or from written sources, can be a persuasive way of supporting your points. However, you need to ask four basic questions about expert opinion:

expert opinion
A quotation from someone with special credentials in the subject matter.

- *What is the source's expertise?* How do you know this person is an expert? Try a Google search or look at biographical sources (such as *Who's Who*), if you do not know who the person is. Look for marks of expertise, such as academic credentials, official positions, or references from other authorities. Finally, make sure your source is an expert in the subject matter of your speech. It is important to explain to your audience why the person you are quoting is an expert they should believe.

- *Does the expert have a reputation for reliability?* How accurate have the expert's previous statements been? If someone has a record of either false or mistaken statements in the past, it is misguided to rely on that person's statements today.

- *Is the source unbiased?* If a source has a vested interest in one side of a topic, his or her opinions are automatically suspect. Your audience needs to be assured that you are not relying on sources that have an axe to grind.

- *Is the source credible for the audience?* No matter how many academic credentials or awards someone has, if your audience distrusts that person, they will not be impressed when you quote the source in your speech. For example, although Al Gore shared a Nobel Prize, citing him in a speech to skeptics of global warming, who do not find him credible, is likely to undermine the audience's perceptions of your own credibility. So the more carefully you have analyzed your audience, the better informed you will be in selecting sources they will believe.

Explanations

An explanation is an account, an interpretation, or a meaning given to something. Detailed explanations may prove useful in a speech. But to be effective, explanations must meet three tests:

- *Is the explanation clear?* A complex or unclear explanation may only confuse your audience. One way to clarify an explanation is to use comparisons and contrasts. Thus, someone might explain a nuclear power plant by comparing it to a teakettle whose source of heat is a nuclear reaction.

- *Is the explanation accurate?* An explanation that is clear is not necessarily complete or correct. Make sure the explanations provided are as complete and accurate as possible, given the limitations of the speech situation.

- *Is the explanation interesting?* Unfortunately, explanations can be boring to an audience, particularly if they are highly technical. One way to overcome this problem is to make sure there are specific, vivid examples that make the explanations come to life. For example, melting ice in a glass to illustrate the way melting glaciers might affect sea level is more interesting than just giving a technical explanation of the relationship between sea ice and sea level.

Descriptions

A description is a word picture of something. For example, you might describe a place you have visited or researched. Consider the following statement from a speech by one of our students, Chalsey Phariss: "Imagine a place where the rivers are flowing, the sun is shining, and the fun is unlimited, where there is never a dull moment, and the freedom of the outdoors will captivate your mind." This description leads into a speech about the "Lake of the Sky," Lake Tahoe.[7]

Descriptions should meet the following tests:

- *Is the description accurate?* Descriptions can be tested for accuracy by comparing them with the thing being described. Thus, for the Tahoe example, looking at pictures of the lake or visiting it would help verify the description.

- *Is the description vivid?* To hold an audience's attention, we need to paint a word picture. Calling Lake Tahoe by its Native American name, "Lake of the Sky," is much more vivid than simply describing the blueness of the water. Photographs and other visual materials, which are discussed in Chapter 12, can sometimes supplement descriptions in a speech.

Storytelling is a favorite way to bring families closer together and share the experiences of one generation with the next.

Narratives

narrative

An extended story that is fully developed, with characters, scene, action, and plot.

A **narrative** is an extended story that is fully developed, with characters, scene, action, and plot. Narratives sometimes provide an effective way of driving home a point to an audience. An effective narrative builds gradually from the beginning, through conflict, to a climax. The conflict is then resolved, and the ending of the story often ties back into the beginning. It is important to maintain suspense in telling a story. If you begin by giving away the "punch line" or climax, the audience will not be captivated by the story. So, unlike many speeches, when we assign a storytelling or narrative speech, we urge our students not to state the thesis or moral of the story in the introduction. It should emerge from the story as it unfolds.

Narratives can be more than a useful supporting tool for a speech; in some cultures narrative is an organizing principle of speaking. We were in the audience when actor-activist Edward James Olmos spoke at our university. His speech was largely a series of stories—about his career, his family, how people of different cultures can come to understand one another. Award-winning rhetorical scholar Walter Fisher has argued, in fact, that human beings are fundamentally storytellers. Fisher believes that reasoning is done in the form of narrative. Even if you don't accept Fisher's narrative paradigm, it is undoubtedly the case that a well-told story, real or fictional, can captivate an audience. Fisher claims that two basic tests apply to narrative reasoning:[8]

narrative probability

The internal coherence or believability of a narrative.

- *Does the narrative have probability?* **Narrative probability** is the internal coherence or believability of a narrative. Does a story make sense in and of itself? If you've seen the *Back to the Future* trilogy, you may have wondered how there could be two Doc Browns and two Marty McFlys and even two DeLorean time machines at the same time and place. Setting aside Doc's explanations of the space-time continuum, trying to sort out the paradoxes and inconsistencies of time travel is one sure way to a gigantic headache. When using a narrative to support a speech, it needs to be clearly plausible to the audience for it to be believed.

Stephen Glass was caught fabricating stories for the *New Republic* when his story on hackers didn't ring true.

- *Does the narrative have fidelity?* **Narrative fidelity** is the degree to which a narrative rings true to real-life experience. Even if a story makes sense internally, it may not make sense in terms of the real world. For example, consider the case of Stephen Glass, a writer for the *New Republic* who was caught making up stories out of whole cloth. In fact, the story that exposed his fabrications was uncovered by an online publication, *Forbes Digital Tool,* because the details of Glass's account of a youthful hacker outsmarting a powerful Silicon Valley company did not ring true for those familiar with technology. For example, the alleged Web site of this multi-million-dollar cutting-edge technology company was an amateurish-looking AOL site, and the "hacker's convention" Glass described took place at a location that was closed on the very day he claimed the convention occurred. Because the details of his story lacked fidelity, Glass's lies were exposed. Once one story unraveled, it soon turned out that most of what he had written for the *New Republic* was fabricated. The *New Republic*'s investigation revealed that Glass had fabricated at least 27 of 41 articles. The case became the basis of a 2003 motion picture entitled *Shattered Glass.*[9]

narrative fidelity
The degree to which a narrative rings true to real-life experience.

When we tell a story to an audience, we should let them know if it is true or hypothetical. Either type of story needs to ring true to the audience's own experience if it is to have impact. For a speech to have impact, the narratives need to have probability and fidelity.

Narratives can stand alone, as in a storytelling speech, which is one of the first assignments we give our students. For an example of a storytelling speech, see the box "In Their Own Words: Storytelling Speech" to read a speech by Kristin Wilhelm describing a rather unusual situation she confronted during Thanksgiving break when she was home alone. As you read or watch this speech, ask if it meets the tests of narrative probability and fidelity previously discussed.

 www.mhhe.com/brydon7e

To view a video of Kristin Wilhelm's storytelling speech, click on the Speech Coach link in our Online Learning Center Web site and go to Segment 7.1.

Storytelling Speech

by Kristin Wilhelm

It is Thanksgiving break and my roommates Krissy, Lauren, and Karrisa had all gone home. Meagan and I had the lovely opportunity of working all break, or should I say, we had no choice but to stay and work or else we'd be fired. When I woke up that first Monday morning of break, imagined my day, my list of to-dos: work, work, homework, I would have never imagined I'd be running down the street, barefoot, in my pink teddy bear pajamas, with my wet hair wrapped up in a towel and holding a knife.

So that Monday, when I got home from a long day at work, tired and smelling like the mocha I spilled on my pants, I was just ready to get home and relax. I knew Meagan wasn't going to be getting home until late because she was working long hours, so I had it all planned out, a night to myself. I'd come home, take a shower, eat some dinner, and probably fall asleep while watching some random movie or some trashy MTV show.

So after I got home, I took a shower, walked downstairs, started boiling some water, you know, getting my pasta ready to go. And as I was picking out my favorite pasta sauce, I started hearing some rattling noise coming from the back door. I was thinking, maybe I'm a little delusional, long day at work, making coffee for 8 hours straight, a little tiring. And then again, I heard a shaking of the door, like someone was trying to fiddle with the lock to get in. Now I was really freaking out because customer after customer was telling me all day long that student homes were being broken into. I was thinking, great, my lucky day. This is my house. I'm the one student who gets robbed at this house . . . this block, and so I go and I peer into my roommate's room, look at the window, you know, hoping that it's my roommate, not anyone else, hoping that she came home early. But what do I see, but a roughly 40-year-old man, bald, black leather jacket, working on the doorknob. At this point, I screamed on the inside, ran into the kitchen, grabbed the largest kitchen knife I could find—of course, not knowing what I'd do with it—I just thought I'd need it. Ran as quickly and as quietly as I could, outside to my neighbor's house.

At this point, keep in mind that I was in my pajamas, my wet hair was wrapped up in a towel, and I was carrying a knife. I hadn't even met my neighbors at this point, and I was going to be banging on their doors. So I went, I was banging . . . I ring the doorbell; no answer, great, just my luck. Went to the next house, did it again. Luckily an old man answered the door and asked me if I was okay. At this point, I was hysterically crying and probably sounded like, sounded a little something like this: "Oh, my god, my house is being broken into, please help me, I don't know what to do." Yeah, I was freaking out. So he offered, he invited me in and we

Kristin Wilhelm
George Rogers

called the police. Now being the curious old man that he was, he wanted to go check out the situation. So we go, walk across the street. We're standing across the street looking down my driveway where you can see my back door. The man is still standing there, trying to get in. He must have not been a good robber if this was the case because he should have been in and out already. But anyways, all of a sudden, four police cars came swirling around the street, stopped with no audible sound, they all got out, the police officers unholstered their guns, started doing hand signals and talking on their walkie talkies like they do in the movies. They had their guns stiffly pointed at the assailant, running down the driveway, yelling, "Freeze, put your hands in the air." The man came walking out yelling, "It's okay, it's okay, I'm Kris's dad."

My jaw dropped. Literally hit the concrete. I had called the police on my roommate's dad. I didn't even know what to do. All I remember is running over to him, giving him a hug, and trying not to stab him in the process. Sprinting back inside, all the while hearing the police officers complaining about how they didn't get any action that day. Running in, putting the knife safely back in the drawer, and going upstairs to eat my overcooked pasta.[10]

Story credit—Krissy Raymond adapted by Kristen Wilhelm.

Summary

There are three basic types of claims:

To evaluate your understanding of this chapter, visit our Online Learning Center Web site for quizzes and other chapter study aids.

- Claims of fact deal with statements that are verifiable.

- Claims of value deal with statements about right or wrong, good or bad, moral or immoral.

- Claims of policy state that something should be done.

Many types of evidence are effective in supporting speeches:

- Examples should be relevant, of sufficient quantity, typical, and without significant counterexamples.

- Facts should be from a reliable source, verifiable, recent, and consistent with other known facts.

- Numerical data should be from a reliable and unbiased source. Know what percentages are based on and whether the mean or median is being cited. Polls should be based on fair questions, should be taken from a representative sample, and should report the sample size and margin of error.

- Expert opinion should come from a subject matter expert who is reliable, unbiased, and viewed as credible by your audience.

- Explanations should be clear and accurate.

- Descriptions should be accurate and vivid.

- Narratives should have probability (coherence) and fidelity for the audience.

Check Your Understanding: Exercises and Activities

1. A speaker arguing that we should buy American products presents the following example: "I purchased a Hyundai last year. Since I purchased it, I have had nothing but trouble. I think this proves that you should buy American!" Compare this example with the tests of examples discussed in this chapter. Which of the tests does it fail to meet?

2. How would you go about verifying the "fact" that the leading causes of death in the United States are heart disease, cancer, and infectious diseases? What sources would you consult? Are these in fact the three leading causes of death?

3. Obtain a recent poll (one that appears in an article in, for example, *USA Today* or *Newsweek*). Does the poll meet the tests of numerical data outlined in this chapter? How large was the sample, and what was the margin of error? Did differences in the poll exceed the margin of error? What, if anything, does the article on the poll not tell you that you need to know to properly interpret the poll?

4. Compare the results of a poll based on a large representative sample (such as can be found at Gallup.com) with an Internet poll on the same topic. Are the results similar? Which is more reliable, and why?

169

Notes

1. FactCheck.org, 2004. [Retrieved from http://www.factcheck.org, 5 August 2004.]

2. "Jared's Statistics," Subway.com, 2009. [Retrieved from http://www.subway .com/subwayroot/MenuNutrition/Jared/jaredStats.aspx, 10 July 2009.]

3. Cynthia Crossen, "Lies, Damned Lies—and 'Scientific' Studies," *Sacramento Bee,* Forum, 24 November 1991, 1–2. [Reprinted from the *Wall Street Journal.*]

4. "The Dow Jones Industrial Average December 31 1974–June 30, 2009," *Privateer Market Letter,* 30 June 2009. [Retrieved from http://www .theprivateer.com/chart/dow-long.html, 8 July 2009.]

5. Crossen, "Lies, Damned Lies—and 'Scientific' Studies."

6. Robert S. Erikson and Kent L. Tedin, *American Public Opinion: Its Origins, Content, and Impact,* 7th ed. (New York: Pearson Longman, 2007), 30.

7. Chalsey Phariss, "Lake Tahoe," speech delivered at California State University, Chico, 18 April 1998.

8. Walter R. Fisher, *Human Communication as Narration* (Columbia: University of South Carolina Press, 1987).

9. Billy Ray (director), *Shattered Glass,* Lions Gate Entertainment, 2003.

10. Story credit—Krissy Raymond adapted by Kristen Wilhelm.

A key to gaining your audience's attention is to open your speech with impact.

INTRODUCTIONS, TRANSITIONS, AND CONCLUSIONS

Objectives  www.mhhe.com/brydon7e

After reading this chapter and reviewing the online learning resources at www.mhhe.com/brydon7e, you should be able to:

- Construct an effective introduction for your speech.
- Open your speech with impact.
- Connect with your audience in the introduction to your speech.
- Focus on a clear thesis statement for your speech.
- Preview the main points of your speech.
- Utilize appropriate transitions from one point to the next in your speech.
- Construct an effective conclusion for your speech.
- Summarize the main points of your speech.
- Close your speech with impact.

Key Concepts

aphorism

call to action

primacy-recency effect

proverb

rhetorical question

> "You never get a second chance to make a first impression."
>
> *–Head and Shoulders Shampoo Ad*

As we thought about how to best approach the topic of organization over two chapters, we ended up facing an organizational problem of our own. Should we begin at the beginning—with the introduction to the speech—then move to the body, and finally the conclusion? Should we begin with the heart of the speech— the body or main points—and save the introduction and conclusion for later? Would it make more sense to discuss introductions and conclusions after we have shared methods to organize the main points you hope to make, including the supporting material you found in your research? Or would it make more sense to begin with the beginning of the speech, realizing that unless a speaker captures an audience's attention initially, it is unlikely that the speech will succeed?

The reality, of course, is that a speech grows as an organic whole, in many ways taking on a life of its own. Sometimes we begin at the beginning. Something in our research or thinking about the topic suggests a powerful introduction from which the rest of the speech logically grows. At other times we struggle with the introduction and decide to put it aside while we write the body of the speech. Then we discover somewhere in that body the key to an effective introduction. In short, there is no one sure way to construct a speech.

Ultimately, we decided to start with the parts of a speech that the audience is most likely to remember—the beginning and the end. We've all heard the adage that you never get a second chance to make a first impression. It's said that in a job interview, the decision to hire or not is often made in the first five minutes. A speech is similar—audiences decide early whether or not they are interested in the speaker and the topic. It is very difficult to recover from a weak introduction, for much the same reason that some job interviews are effectively over before they ever get past the handshake.

Thus, this chapter and the one that follows should be considered as a whole. You will undoubtedly end up revising or rewriting an introduction once you have written the body of your speech. And it won't be possible to write the preview and summary parts of the introduction and conclusion until you've settled on your main points.

If our combined experience listening to and evaluating students told us that they seldom have problems with opening and closing their speeches, we would not need to devote a full chapter to introducing and closing a speech. That, however, has not been the case. Instead we have consistently found that far too many students treat introductions and conclusions as if they were the least important part in the art and science of public speaking.

The truth of the matter is that 2,000 years worth of writing and research tell us that depending on how it is presented, what we *first* hear and see has a better chance of being remembered than what immediately follows. The same writing and research also suggests that, depending on how it is presented, what we *last* hear and see may be more readily remembered than what immediately preceded it. What's more, this **primacy-recency** effect, as it is commonly called, shows up in research on classroom learning, interpersonal communication, and public speaking.[1] Simply put, how you open and close your speech influences your audience just as your communication behavior influences the first and last impression you create when first meeting someone or being interviewed for a new job. Blow it and chances are you will neither see these people again nor be offered the job.

Thus, in the pages that follow we hope to accomplish three related tasks. First, we want to show you a manageable list of alternatives you can choose from to open your speeches so that they create a positive impression and enlist your

primacy-recency effect
The tendency for people to remember and be most influenced by what they hear either at the beginning or at the ending of a speech.

audience's attention to your topic. Second, we want to show you some simple but important transitional techniques you can use to smoothly and effectively move from the opening of your speech to its body, and from the body of your speech to its close. Finally, we want to help you with your conclusions, making sure you have reserved enough energy to close your speech with the same kind of impact with which it began. We'll start, however, by revisiting a subject that has to be considered when deciding on how to open your speech.

The Rhetorical Situation

Recall from Chapter 5 that the rhetorical situation reflects nearly everything about the speech transaction we need to consider in preparing and delivering speeches—for example, the audience, the nature of the occasion, speaker goals, and any physical as well as psychological constraints we face. The rhetorical situation once again reminds us that the speech transaction involves a system of interdependent variables, arrayed so that a change in one can affect all the others. Speaking inside a church, mosque, or temple is not the same as speaking inside a public establishment where Rotarians or Soroptomists meet weekly. By the same token, speaking at a gathering to memorialize a person is not the same as speaking to graduating seniors at a commencement ceremony.

The point here is simple. The manner in which you introduce a speech and close it needs to reflect the fact that you have taken into account the rhetorical situation that presented itself to you. Ignoring this simple but instrumental lesson is usually a recipe for disaster.

Introducing the Speech

Introductions do more than simply reveal the topic of your speech. When carefully constructed and well delivered, introductions also serve to overcome distractions competing for an audience's attention, promote audience and speaker rapport, and communicate a framework that makes it easier for an audience to follow and stay tuned-in to a speaker's message. Said another way, effective introductions:

- Open a speech with impact to enlist the audience's undivided attention.
- Clearly communicate the thesis of the speech.
- Connect the speaker's topic with the self-interest of audience members.
- Preview the speech so that audience members can more easily follow the speech as it unfolds.

effective intro

Let's look at each of these functions in the detail it deserves.

Open With Impact

The kind of stimuli competing for your audience's attention has increased in recent years. Clock-watching and whispered conversations in the back of the room used to be a speaker's (or professor's) chief competition for an audience member's attention. Today text messaging and other smart-phone activities have been added to the list. After President Obama's first speech to a joint session of the House and Senate, for example, it was discovered that more than a few members of the two legislative bodies were texting or tweeting the entire time the president spoke.

Text messaging and tweeting are a technological form of rudeness teachers and students alike are all too familiar with. Hardly a class period goes by when we don't notice one or more students staring down at blazing thumbs as we do our best to teach or listen while a student makes an earnest effort to deliver an interesting speech. Although many students may think or claim that they can both text and listen at the same time, the research on "multitasking" is unequivocal: They cannot.[2]

Still, barring the unlikely ban on cell phones in the classroom or an unanticipated surge in people recognizing just how rude and condescending this behavior is while another person speaks, text messages, tweets, and other mobile device activities are likely to be a continued source of irritation in our classrooms. It's up to us, therefore, to do everything in our power to encourage audience members to pay attention to us instead of their smart phones.

That said, the following opening and its variants are the standard for far too many speakers:

"Today I'm going to talk about . . ."

The fact that they are common, however, should not be interpreted as evidence of their effectiveness. Aside from the fact that such openings are too weak to enlist an audience's attention, they also tell the audience that the speaker was too lazy to invest the time and practice needed to develop any one of a number of more powerful methods available for opening a speech with impact.

Stories

There are few methods for opening a speech more powerful than a well-told story. There is an important reason for this. Stories and storytelling, as the eminent scholar Walter Fisher writes, have played an extraordinary role in human development. Stories enabled preliterate people to share and pass on the personal and cultural lessons necessary to their survival. And even though writing and mass printing eventually made it possible for people to share these lessons without the benefit of face-to-face contact, storytelling remained the most important literary form for doing so. It should come as no great surprise, then, that we have been conditioned over time to be more attentive to speakers who open with a story than those who immediately introduce their topic or begin with their thesis statement.

Stories can be used effectively for most, if not all, of the speech purposes discussed in this book. Effectively shared, a story can be used with speeches intended to inform, persuade, and entertain. As we pointed out in our discussion of narratives in Chapter 7, the key is making sure that the stories we share meet two criteria: (1) narrative probability and (2) narrative fidelity.

Mark Twain, for example, was a gifted speaker in addition to being a gifted writer. Nearly a century before the term *motivational speaker* became part of our cultural vocabulary, Twain was paid thousands of dollars for his speeches. One chief reason was that Twain could make even the tallest tale seem believable or at least plausible.

Given this framework, the story you tell to open a speech can be drawn from published literature, popular culture, your personal experience, or the experiences of others you know personally. Whatever its source, however, you must try to make sure the story is:

- Appropriate to the rhetorical situation.
- Relevant to your topic.
- Connected to the interests of your audience.
- Delivered convincingly.

Consider the following example excerpted from a commencement speech delivered by Apple cofounder Steve Jobs. It is introduced with a personal story and the lesson he learned from it when he was similar in age to his audience.

> When I was 17, I read a quote that went something like: "If you live each day as if it was your last, someday you'll most certainly be right." It made an impression on me, and since then, for the past 33 years, I have looked in the mirror every morning and asked myself: "If today were the last day of my life, would I want to do what I am about to do today?" And whenever the answer has been "No" for too many days in a row, I know I need to change something.[3]

This personal disclosure meets most of the criteria for opening a speech with impact. This is especially apparent when you add the next paragraph:

> Remembering that I'll be dead soon is the most important tool I've ever encountered to help me make the big choices in life. Because almost everything—all external expectations, all pride, all fear of embarrassment or failure—these things just fall away in the face of death, leaving only what is truly important. Remembering that you are going to die is the best way I know to avoid the trap of thinking you have something to lose. You are already naked. There is no reason not to follow your heart.[4]

Jobs juxtaposes life and death in his story by sharing a personal experience he had when he was close to the age of the graduates in his audience. He links the story to his thesis, risk taking, and then connects the thesis with a list of external expectations that nearly all of us can relate to at one or more stages of our life. Jobs's introduction is still a good illustration of how we can all draw on our personal experience to make our introductions more likely to enlist the highly selective attention of our audience. That listeners make a decision to focus on some people and messages to the exclusion of others. Jobs's introduction also shows how the opening of a speech can be used to bridge the indivisible divide that can undermine the speech transaction when the speaker and audience represent very different generations.

Humor

As our former student, TV producer, comedy writer, and novelist Russ Woody, talks about in the box "Speaking of . . . . Writing Humor," stories are but a single way to use humor to introduce a speech. When Russ spoke to the graduating class of our university a few years ago, he began with some self-deprecating humor: "Look . . . I write sitcoms for a living, so don't expect much. Which means . . . basically, I'm gonna tell a few jokes, hit a few well-worn platitudes, and try to sell you a Dodge minivan."[5] But you need to be very careful in this regard. Regardless of the type and form of humor used, what you find funny may not strike your audience as funny. Irony, whether conveyed in a one-liner, joke, or anecdote, is often misperceived by audience members. The same is true of satire and sarcasm. Thus, humor needs to be audience-tested before you choose to use it to open your speech.

SPEAKING OF . . .

Writing Humor? by Russ Woody

As a college student, Russ Woody excelled in an event called "Speech to Entertain." Not only was humor Russ's hobby, it became his profession. Russ began his writing career at MTM productions, where he wrote episodes for shows such as *Newhart*, *St. Elsewhere*, and *Hill Street Blues*. For two years he was a producer and writer for *Murphy Brown*, for which he received an Emmy in 1990. He received a Golden Globe as co-executive producer of *Cybill*. He has also served as a consulting producer for *Foxworthy* and *The Middle*, and was co-executive producer of *Becker*. Russ recently published his first novel, *The Wheel of Nuldoid*. We asked Russ to do the impossible: explain writing humor in 250 words or less. Here is the result.

Russ Woody
Joe Woody

Writing Humor?

by Russ Woody

Two-hundred fifty words on how to write humor? Gee, can't I just whack myself in the forehead with a ball-peen hammer? Trying to explain humor is a little like trying to wrest a ripe banana from an immense and bitter gorilla. If not handled correctly, you can end up looking rather foolish.

With that in mind, "Hello, Mr. Gorilla . . ."

The fact of the matter is, humor is more difficult to write than drama. Because, while both humor and drama rely heavily on emotional content, humor is much more difficult to break down mechanically. Therefore it's more difficult to construct initially. It's relatively easy to figure out what makes a person sad or angry or uneasy or embarrassed or happy. Yet it is, for the most part, difficult to say why a person laughs.

So I guess the first thing you've got to do is figure out what type of humor appeals most to you. Monty Python, Andrew "Dice" Clay, The Naked Gun, Murphy Brown, Full House, Spy Magazine, Mad Magazine, Saturday Night Live. Whichever it is, find it. Then—study it. Watch it, read it, take it apart, figure out how it's constructed, how it's set up, how it pays off—figure out the dynamics of humor. (Which will make it terribly unfunny when you do, but that's the perpetual hell comedy writers live in.) For instance—one of my favorite jokes of all time is in one of the Pink Panther movies where Peter Sellers goes into a hotel and approaches a man at the desk who has a dog sitting beside him. Sellers says,

"Does your dog bite?" The guy says no. So Sellers reaches over to pat the little pooch, and it tries to rip his arm off. Sellers then looks to the guy and says, "I thought you said your dog didn't bite?" The guy says, "It's not my dog."

I love that joke because every element of it is real, and nobody involved thinks it's funny. The man was quite correct in his literal interpretation of Sellers's question. Sellers is more than a little annoyed at the man for misunderstanding what seemed to be a logical and straightforward question. And the dog is just pissed off. In a more general sense, one person becomes a victim because the other is a stickler for precise wording. It is extreme focus on one character's part and vulnerability on the other character's part. In a way, it's like the movie The In-Laws, with Peter Falk and Alan Arkin. Falk is intensely focused on his job with the government, which in turn makes Arkin's life a living hell. (If you've seen the movie, you know what I'm talking about—if you haven't, go see it, because I'm coming up on two-fifty pretty fast here, so I can't get into it.)

When you've taken enough jokes and stories apart, you may start to get an idea of how to construct your own. That's when it gets really tough. Just be sure you always remember the one, underlying key to writing humor—oops, outta time.

Reprinted by permission of Russ Woody.

Refer to the Rhetorical Situation

A third and potentially powerful way to introduce your speech involves referring to the rhetorical situation itself. Recall that the rhetorical situation includes things such as the occasion and the audience. Needless to say, many of history's most memorable introductions *and* speeches have been given in circumstances dictated by the rhetorical situation. Obvious examples include, but are not

IN THEIR OWN WORDS

Oprah Winfrey Speaks at Duke University

Consider how Oprah Winfrey used a reference to the rhetorical situation in her commencement address at Duke University on Mother's Day 2009. She made specific reference not only to the occasion, but also to one of the graduates, who just happened to be her godson:

Oh, yes, I'm going [to] have everyone call me Doctor now. Thank you, President Brodhead. Ladies and gentlemen and graduates, and especially to all the mothers here—will all the mothers stand so we can say Happy Mother's Day? Happy Mother's Day to you. What a great day to celebrate mothers. You love me still, even though I'm a doctor now?

Well, I wanted to just say, first of all, thank you for the doctorate degree, and I'm so happy to be here, and I'm here because someone I love is graduating today, my godson, William Bumpus, the son of Will Bumpus and my best friend, Gayle. You know, William never wants people to know that he knows me, and his sister, Kirby, never did either. I'm like the crazy aunt they keep in the attic, and they let me out to do commencements, so here I am.

Oprah Winfrey speaking at Duke University.

Source: Office of News and Communications, Duke University, Oprah Winfrey's Commencement Address at Duke, 12 May 2009. [Retrieved from http://news.duke.edu/2009/05/winfrey_address .html, 31 July 2009.]

---

limited to, Lincoln's Gettysburg Address, Dr. Martin Luther King's "I Have a Dream" speech, and President Ronald Reagan's "Mr. Gorbachev, Tear Down This Wall" speech at the Brandenburg Gate in Berlin.

Many of life's predictable milestones require us to speak publicly. Examples range from joyful occasions such as a 50th wedding anniversary, to the most solemn of ceremonies, such as a memorial service. As demonstrated in the box "In Their Own Words . . . Oprah Winfrey Speaks at Duke University," it is both natural and appropriate to draw your introduction from these significant occasions.

Aphorisms, Proverbs, and Quotations

We realize that it's not always possible to introduce your speech with a story, humorous bit, or reference to the rhetorical situation. Your instructor's requirements, including time constraints, may preclude the possibility of telling a story. We acknowledge the fact that speaking to fulfill an assignment in a college classroom, moreover, is not the typical kind of rhetorical situation that inspires speakers to make it a focal point of their speeches. As a result, you may want to explore the possibility of introducing your speech with an aphorism, proverb, or quotation that strikes you as sufficiently powerful to gain your audience's attention.

Aphorisms are usually brief statements that ring true with our experience. More often than not, they convey a hard-to-deny principle or imply a lesson.

aphorism
A brief statement embodying a principle or lesson.

179

CONSIDERING DIVERSITY

Cross-Cultural Proverbs

After dark all cats are leopards.—*Native American Proverb* (Zuni)

An army of sheep led by a lion would defeat an army of lions led by a sheep.—*Arab Proverb*

Better to light a candle than to curse the darkness.
—*Chinese Proverb*

Cuando amor no es locura, no es amor. (When love is not madness, it is not love.)—*Spanish Proverb*

Don't dig your grave with your own knife and fork.
—*English Proverb*

Those who sleep with dogs will rise with fleas.—*Italian Proverb*

Vision without action is a daydream. Action without vision is a nightmare.—*Japanese Proverb*

The wise man has long ears and a short tongue.
—*German Proverb*

Source: Confucius Institute, *Quotes and Sayings*, 2009. [Retrieved from http://www.quotesandsayings.com/proverbial.htm, 16 October 2009.]

"The shortest distance between two points is a straight line," "Look before you leap," and "It's easier to catch flies with honey than with vinegar" are but a few examples of aphorisms that might well begin a speech.

Proverbs are similar to aphorisms in the sense that they typically teach a lesson, often one that speaks to our foremost values and beliefs. Religious texts are one of the most common and widely used sources for finding proverbs relevant to your planned speech. So too are cultural but nonreligious texts written by people regarded as especially wise. Confucius and the Buddha both used proverbs to make a point. The box "Considering Diversity: Cross-Cultural Proverbs" illustrates a few of the wide range of proverbs that can be located using a simple Internet search.

Though very similar to aphorisms and proverbs, quotations can, but don't always, teach a lesson. Some quotations can be anonymous. If a quotation is attributable to a prominent person, this can add to its impact on an audience. In addition to conveying a lesson, quotations also can be used to startle or provoke an audience at the beginning of your speech. Imagine speaking to a group of avid fans of Rush Limbaugh and opening your speech with the following quotation from the philosopher John Stuart Mill:

> "Conservatives are not necessarily stupid, but most stupid people are conservatives."[6]

Conversely, imagine introducing a college graduation speech with the following quotation from the philosopher-mathematician Bertrand Russell:

> "Men are born ignorant, not stupid; they are made stupid by education."[7]

Of course, startling or provoking an audience with a quotation should do more than simply enlist the audience's attention. Ideally it should serve the larger purpose of the speech. If it doesn't, we will eventually lose our audience no matter how startled or provoked audience members were as we began.

Posing a Question or Series of Questions

We are not great fans of introducing speeches with a single question, rhetorical or otherwise. **Rhetorical questions,** which audience members are not expected to answer out loud, are often misused and ineffective, in our experience. For a beginning speaker, however, using a question or series of questions to introduce a speech and gain the audience's attention is certainly worth considering. We have listened to many beginning speakers who have used a single question or series of questions that

usually for beginning speakers

proverb
A short, commonly used saying that expresses a well-known truth, often with a religious or moral aspect.

rhetorical question
A question that the audience isn't expected to answer out loud.

180

not only introduced the topic of their speech but also did so with observable impact on the audience. Typically these students asked questions linked to their own and their audience members' experience. As the following examples from actual student speeches illustrate, moreover, they commonly involved personal emergencies and crises, humor owing to embarrassment, and life lessons worth passing on:

- "How many of you think you could administer CPR in an emergency situation? How many of you have actually had to use CPR in an emergency situation? How many of you who had to use CPR, did so with someone you dearly loved?"
- "Have you ever done something so embarrassing that you thought you would never live it down?"
- "What would it take to radically change the direction of your life? Winning the lottery? Meeting your perfect match? How about living in another country, where you are reminded every single day of just how lucky you are?"

When we work with students who introduce their speeches with a question or questions, we encourage them to prompt audience members to raise their hands in response, by raising their own hands as they ask the question. This helps audience members appropriately respond, which is one of the most common problems when a question or series of questions introduces a speech. Instead of audience members attempting to guess about how they should respond, they are shown how to respond by the speaker using a simple gesture.

Startling Statements

Humans are attracted naturally to surprising, startling, and unusual events. A truly surprising or startling statement delivered appropriately can provoke the audience and enlist its undivided attention. For example, a student in our class began her speech by describing horrible symptoms of Lyme disease: "Imagine pain so severe you are writhing in agony, headaches so intense you feel as though your head is going to explode, legs that ache so bad you can't even walk, and being so tired you can't get up to go to the bathroom."[8] Then she revealed that she has had those very symptoms since she was eight years old. The audience was immediately drawn, not only by the terrible symptoms described, but also by the fact that she had personal credibility on the topic of Lyme disease. Further, because the object of her speech was to inform her classmates on how to prevent getting the disease themselves, they were highly motivated to listen.

Tips and Tactics

Ways to Open With Impact

Effective ways to open a speech with impact include:

- Telling a story
- Using appropriate humor
- Referring to the rhetorical situation
- Aphorism, proverb, or quotation
- Posing a question or series of questions
- Startling statement

[handwritten margin note: opening w/ Impact]

Focus on Your Thesis Statement

Once you have involved your audience by opening your speech with considerable impact, the next recommended step is to state your thesis. Generally, your thesis statement discloses to the audience (1) the purpose of your speech and (2) the central idea driving that purpose. When novice speakers mistakenly begin their speeches with "Today I'm going to talk to you about the physical and environmental benefits you will enjoy as a result of becoming a vegetarian," they are actually making their thesis statement. The risk they run when doing so is unnecessarily turning their audience off because the topic may be shopworn or one with which many audience members disagree. Typically, then, we recommend to our students that they make their thesis statement only after they have won their audience's attention with their opening. We also emphasize that this is especially true if their purpose is persuasive and their topic is controversial.

Unless you are a skilled and practiced public speaker who can always pull an audience back into your speech, you do not want audience members asking themselves "What's the point?" midway or later in your speech. With few exceptions, therefore, declaring the thesis of your speech immediately after your opening is a good rule of thumb.

Connect With Your Audience

One of the most common mistakes we make when we are experts on a topic is to assume that its significance is as obvious to others as it is to us. As a result, we fail to see the need to demonstrate why they should be interested in the topic. Just so you know, we college professors are as guilty as anyone in making this assumption.

We've learned over the years that as teachers *and* public speakers we have an obligation to connect what we find important and interesting to the personal and professional lives of our students or audience members. We also have found that we need to make the connection as explicit as possible, given the increased diversity of experience so characteristic of today's classrooms.

There is more than one way to connect with an audience. For example, an audience that feels connected to you personally will be much more responsive to your speech, even if audience members remain dubious about the personal or professional relevance of the content of your speech. Thus, it is in your self-interest to make clear the similarities in attitudes, beliefs, values, and background you share with your audience.

Ideally you want to make both a personal connection with your audience and a connection between the content of your speech and audience member needs. If you have been thorough in the research that led you to your topic, making this latter connection should not be that difficult. After all, who is better equipped to identify and relate to the needs of audience members than a student colleague?

Finally, during your introduction especially, you need to do your best to connect nonverbally with audience members. This means making sure that you know the introduction of your speech well enough that you can maintain eye contact with individual audience members as you tell a story, draw on the rhetorical situation, relate an aphorism, proverb, or quotation, or begin with a question. As we will discuss in Chapter 11, managing your nonverbal communication

Computer projection can help a speaker's organization become clear to the audience.

behavior is key to your success as a public speaker. To reiterate, nowhere is this fact more important than in your introduction. It constitutes not only your audience's first impression of you but also the one that will most affect their evaluation of what follows.

Preview Your Speech

Previewing the body of your speech is an exercise in one of human communication's most important functions: uncertainty reduction, a concept we introduced to you when discussing the common dimensions of culture in Chapter 5. As we explained, whole cultures vary when it comes to tolerating uncertainty. What's true of entire cultures also is true of individuals. Some people can live with lots of uncertainty in their lives, while others become anxious if their personal lives are not planned to the minute. Students who ask "What's going to be on the test?" or worse, "Will (fill in the blank) be on the test?" are attempting to have their instructor reduce the anxiety they feel because of their uncertainty.

Previewing the main points from the body of a speech serves the same function as behavioral objectives and student learning objectives, which should be familiar to most students in your audience. They enable the learner, or in this case the audience member, to build a framework for recognizing well in advance what is most important in a speech. This makes it easier for listeners to follow along and avoid guessing about what deserves their utmost attention.

A preview can also benefit the speaker, providing what educational psychologists call cognitive organizers. This is simply their way of saying that your preview will reinforce the sequence in which you organized the body of speech, and thereby help you to stay on track as you progress from the introduction to the body of the speech, and from the body of the speech to its conclusion.

In previewing your speech, however, it is important not to become too mechanical or trite. For example, it is not particularly interesting to tell an audience: "My first main point is . . . , my second point . . . , and my final point is . . ." Although such a preview is clear, it is not particularly engaging for an audience. Having opened with impact, try to preserve that positive impression by previewing your points in an interesting and creative manner. Speakers often organize the main points of the speech alphabetically. So as a preview a speaker might say: "We're going to cover the ABCs. In this case A stands for Attitude, B for Behavior, and C for Control."

Transitions

Rare is the college student who can truthfully say, "I've never listened to a lecture that wasn't logically organized and easy to follow." To the contrary, your authors can recall sitting in classes both large and small where we couldn't predict one sentence to the next from certain professors. We enjoy spontaneity of thought and the occasional digression from the subject at hand as much as anyone, but we also know that when lectures needlessly meander and frequently digress from the topic, it drives most students nuts.

Given what we've said about the importance of previewing the body of your speech, it should come as no great surprise that we encourage our own students to learn and use transitional words and phrases in their speeches. Used effectively, transitional words and phrases become verbal signposts that help your audience recognize and follow the progression of your speech. *Signposts* can be used in at least three ways to improve the transaction between speaker and audience.

Internal Summaries

In the speech class, public speeches seldom exceed 15 minutes. In the professional world, however, oral presentations are seldom that short. As a general rule of thumb, the longer a speech goes on or the more ground it covers, the more necessary it is for the speaker to consider providing the audience with one or more internal summaries. In a sense, internal summaries allow the audience "to catch its collective breath" and link where they've been with where they're going. Using internal summaries as a transitional device is fairly simple, as the following examples show.

> "Before we go any further, let's briefly review the main points we've already covered."

> "Now that we have looked at the role of one, genetics, and two, environment, it's possible to move on to how these two relate to evolutionary psychology."

"The big idea I've tried to share so far in my speech is that being ignorant is not the same as being dumb. I based this claim on two facts, both of which deserve repeating."

Connections

The parts to a well-constructed speech should be interdependent rather than independent. A good introduction should set the table for what follows, the second main point should logically follow the first, and the conclusion should reinforce everything that preceded it. Signposts are useful in making these interdependent connections between and among the parts of your speech more obvious to your audience. The following examples show how you can use signposting words and phrases in your speech to (1) connect the introduction, body, and conclusion, (2) connect the components within the speech, and (3) use your conclusion to reinforce the connections made.

"Mark Twain's quote is a good introduction to the topic of my speech."

"This story doesn't just introduce my subject, it speaks as well to the three main ideas I want to first preview and then expand on."

"My second point is based on the first."

"In conclusion, let me first repeat the three main points we just covered."

"To conclude, I'd like to take you back to the introduction of my speech and reinforce the lesson it teaches."

Speech Progression

In addition to the preceding, it's also a good idea to use transitional words and phrases as temporal signposts. By that, we mean signposts that clearly let the audience know where we are in our speech and how close we are to finishing. While it's important to use words and phrases that allow us to smoothly move through the parts of our speech, it's equally important for us to use words and phrases that tell the audience we are leaving one part of the speech and beginning another—for example, "Now that I've introduced my main points, let's look at the first one in more detail." Audience members should not have to guess where you are in your speech or how much longer you expect them to listen.

The above is particularly true as you transition from the body of your speech to its conclusion. Have you ever been in an audience that guessed wrongly that a speaker had finished, when in reality the speaker had paused a little too long? It's embarrassing, isn't it? With rare exception, premature applause is the result of the audience getting lost in a speech. What's more, the audience is lost because the speaker has failed to let them know where he or she was in the speech's progression. To ensure that it doesn't happen to you, plan on using words or phrases that will make "where" you are in the progression of your speech abundantly clear to your audience. The following tips and tactics should prove helpful in this regard.

By permission of John L. Hart FLP and Creators Syndicate, Inc.

Tips and Tactics

Techniques for Transitional Statements

- *Refer to preceding and upcoming ideas.* "Now that you know what computer viruses are, I'll discuss how to prevent their spread to your computer."

- *Enumerate key points.* "First, never assume that a program from a friend or computer bulletin board is virus free."

- *Give nonverbal reinforcement.* Changes in vocal inflection signal a change is coming. Movement can signal a transition. Some speakers physically move from one place to another while speaking in order to emphasize that they are moving from one point to the next. Others hold up fingers to indicate the number of points.

- *Use visual aids to reinforce transitions.* Moving to the next PowerPoint slide or putting up a new transparency clearly signals to the audience that you are moving on. It's also a way to help you remember the sequence of your speech.

- *Use words that can cue the audience that you are changing points:* Next, another, number, moving on, finally, therefore, and in summary.

Concluding Your Speech

In a conversation with some of our colleagues in the English Department, we discovered a shared frustration. Student essays, like student speeches, all too often conclude "not with a bang but a whimper." Having expended so much energy on the introduction and main body of their work, students seem to have little or nothing to say of note in their conclusion.

One of the most important things to remember is to avoid making your conclusion an afterthought. Your topic and the research you've gathered to support it should still be relatively fresh and personally interesting.

Although your introduction creates an initial audience impression of you and your speech, your conclusion will be most prominent in the minds of audience members once you retake your seat. Concluding a speech on a memorable high note can help speakers in at least two ways. First, a memorable conclusion can turn the audience's favorable impression following the introduction into a lasting impression. Second, a memorable conclusion can help the speaker favorably impress audience members at the end of a speech, even if the audience's initial impression of the speaker was neutral or negative. Recall from the beginning of the chapter what the research tells us about primacy and recency. We tend to remember most what we see and hear first or last.

Given this reminder, effective conclusions are a lot like effective introductions. Instead of focusing on an audience's attention, however, your conclusion should be focused on their retention of the information you've conveyed or the claims that you have made. That said, an effective conclusion to a speech should:

- Respect the time your audience has already given you.
- Briefly summarize or repeat your most important points.
- Close with as much or more impact than when you began.

Time

If you have done your job well, "in conclusion" shouldn't leave your audience cheering. The absence of applause when you announce that you are about to conclude, however, doesn't mean that you can go on for another ten minutes. In fact, one of the worse things a speaker can do is to prematurely lead the audience to believe a speech is near its end and then introduce content that the speaker failed to preview in the introduction.

As a rule of thumb, your conclusion should take approximately the same amount of time as your introduction, or a little less. This is in keeping with our conviction that you should value your conclusion every bit as much as your introduction. Taking three minutes to introduce your speech and thirty seconds to conclude it says just the opposite. Simply put, you want to avoid devaluing your speech with an abrupt and hastily delivered conclusion.

Having said that, however, a word of caution is in order. How much time you take to conclude your speech ultimately depends on the evolution of the rhetorical situation as you progress through the parts of your speech. As you gain in experience and confidence as a public speaker, you will learn to monitor the rhetorical situation for changes even as you speak. For example, you'll learn to recognize and adapt to informative nonverbal cues from audience members, including the amount of time you had planned for conclusion.

Summarize Your Speech

Summarizing your speech is a natural complement to previewing your speech. A summary should be clear, concise, and without embellishment. A summary can revisit your speech in its entirety or simply restate the main points in the body of the speech. For example:

"In closing, I began with the nursery rhyme about sticks and stones will break your bones but words will never hurt you. I said it teaches a false lesson, and supported this claim with three main points. They were . . ."

"To sum up, I believe that as currently configured California is ungovernable. I provided you with the reasons I believe this to be the case. First . . ."

Again, the key to a good summary is brevity. You want to gently remind your audience members about what you covered—not beat them over the head with it.

Close With Impact

This topic brings us full circle. As was the case with opening your speech, you have choices in deciding how to close it. These choices include the ones we covered much earlier (stories, humor, the rhetorical situation, aphorisms, proverbs, quotations, startling statements, and questions), as well as closing with a call to action. In some cases you may take questions at the end of your speech, a topic we'll discuss in detail in Chapter 16. However, that comes after the formal conclusion of the speech and should not be a substitute for closing the speech with impact.

Story

Stories can be just as powerful at the end of your speech as they were in the beginning, assuming they meet the criteria we listed on page 176. You might choose to close your speech with a story different from the one with which you opened it. Many speakers, though, return to their initial story to reinforce its lessons, draw out new ones, or to reveal something about the story that the speaker withheld from the opening, such as the identity or gender of the story's author or narrator. What matters most here is that your choice is relevant and adds rather than detracts from your speech.

Aphorism, Proverb, or Quotation

Of course, there needn't be perfect symmetry in the opening and close of your speech. You can open with a story and close with an aphorism, proverb, or quotation, or vice versa. You also can close by answering the questions you posed in your opening, if it makes sense to do so.

Reference to the Rhetorical Situation

Not surprisingly, reference to the nature of the rhetorical situation may be your best choice to close your speech. In fact, the occasion at which you are speaking may be so compelling that to choose otherwise would undermine your effectiveness. Although we are sure that there are exceptions, most politicians are astute enough to know that there are certain rhetorical situations that demand nonpartisanship. Imagine public reaction, for example, to a politician concluding a speech at the Tomb of the Unknowns on Veteran's Day with a call to vote for his or her party in the next election.

Return to Opening

One of the most effective ways to close a speech is to return to the beginning—to come full circle. Not only does this remind the audience of the introduction, it also gives the speech a sense of closure. For example, we recall a speech that described the effects of a plane crash using the classroom as a stand-in for the cabin of a plane. The speaker began his speech by pointing to various members of the class and telling them how they fared in what we all assumed was a hypothetical crash. At the end of the speech, however, he revealed that the crash he was describing wasn't hypothetical at all. Each of the students in the class represented a real passenger in a real plane crash. By ending on this note, he drove home the idea that each of us is directly affected by the steps airlines take to improve passenger safety.

Call to Action

While a **call to action** at a solemn memorial service would be unusual, it is hardly uncommon for a public speaker to close a speech in this manner. President Kennedy's famous admonition from his inaugural address, "Ask not what your country can do for you—ask what you can do for your country," wasn't the last thing he said in his speech, but it is the line from his closing remarks that had the most lasting impact on people.

Whether a call to action is direct, as when an evangelical minister calls people to come forward to be saved, or indirect, as when a student speaker asks other students to volunteer in the community, it can be difficult to make a call to action successfully. There is always the very real possibility that when a speaker calls on the audience to take direct action, no one in the audience will comply. If the call is indirect, moreover, how will the speaker know that audience members were sufficiently influenced to follow up on the call?

Closing with a call to action works best when the speaker provides the audience with the means to comply. This might take the form of a petition audience members need only sign, a written pledge, or a sign-up sheet that requires not just audience members' names but contact information as well. We had a student who, seeking to convince audience members to broaden their dietary perspective and eat things they normally would reject, offered cookies made with insects for her audience to eat at the end of her speech. A measure of the speech's success was that most class members ate the cookies.

This speaker's t-shirt makes a direct appeal for action—to earn students' votes in an election.

call to action
A request by the speaker, usually at the end of a speech, for the audience to take specific actions to fulfill the speech's purpose.

Tips and Tactics

Ways to Close With Impact

Effective ways to close a speech with impact include:

• Story
• Aphorism, proverb, or quotation
• Reference to the rhetorical situation
• Return to opening
• Call to action

www.mhhe.com/brydon7e

To view a video with examples of introductions and conclusions, click on the Speech Coach link on our Online Learning Center Web site, and go to Segment 8.1.

 www.mhhe.com/brydon7e

To evaluate your understanding of this chapter, visit our Online Learning Center Web site for quizzes and other chapter study aids.

Summary

To make a positive first impression, the introduction to a speech should:

- Open with impact
- Focus on the thesis statement
- Connect with the audience
- Preview the body of the speech

Effective openings may include:

- A story
- Humor
- Reference to the rhetorical situation
- An aphorism, proverb or quotation
- A thought-provoking question or series of questions
- A startling statement

Use transitional statements to help the audience follow the organization of the speech.

The conclusion to a speech should:

- Summarize the main points of the speech
- Close with impact

Ways to close with impact include:

- A story
- An aphorism, proverb, or quotation
- Reference to the rhetorical situation
- Return to opening
- Call to action

Check Your Understanding: Exercises and Activities

1. Consider the following speech introductions. Rewrite them to fit the "open, focus, connect, and preview" model suggested in this chapter.

   a. Today, I'm going to talk to you about pit bulls. I got attacked last week by a pit bull, and I think they are really dangerous. Something's got to be done!

   b. Have any of you ever thought about going snowboarding? I really like to snowboard, and that's what my speech is going to be about.

   c. I think capital punishment is wrong. What if somebody who was innocent got killed? I'm going to persuade all of you that life without parole is a better way to go.

2. Previews, summaries, and transitions often have a tendency to be boring and mechanical. Suggest alternative ways of phrasing the following:

   a. My three main points are: (1) Too many Americans fail to recycle, (2) recycling is easy, and (3) recycling can save you money.

   b. Now that I've discussed my first main point, that we still face a threat of terrorism, I will move to my second main point, how to combat it.

   c. In summary, my three main points were the history of coffee, how it's grown, and how to brew a perfect cup.

3. Consider the following closing for a speech on gun control. How could it be rewritten to have more impact?

   If we pass gun control, as the old saying goes, "When guns are outlawed, only outlaws will have guns."

Notes

1. J. Murphy, C. Hofacker, and R. Mizerski, "Primacy and Recency Effects on Clicking Behavior," *Journal of Computer-Mediated Communication* 11, no. 2 (2006), article 7. [Retrieved from http://jcmc.indiana.edu/vol11/issue2/murphy.html.]

2. Helene Hembrooke and Geri Gay, "The Laptop and the Lecture: The Effects of Multitasking in Learning Environments," *Journal of Computing in Higher Education* 15 (September 2008): 46–64.

3. Steve Jobs, "You've Got to Find What You Love," Commencement Address to Stanford University, 12 June 2005. [Retrieved from http://www.graduationwisdom.com/speeches/0014-jobs.htm.]

4. Jobs, "You've Got to Find What You Love."

5. Russ Woody, "Commencement Address," delivered at California State University, Chico, 23 May 1998.

6. Jone Johnson Lewis, *Stupidity Quotes,* 2009. [Retrieved from http://www.wisdomquotes.com/cat_stupidity.html.]

7. Jone Johnson Lewis, *Stupidity Quotes.*

8. Shelby Anderson, "Lyme Disease," speech given at California State University, Chico, 12 May 2008. An outline of this speech appears in Chapter 9, and a video is available online at www.mhhe.com/brydon7e.

Visualizing organization can help an audience follow your message.

ORGANIZING MESSAGES: HELPING AUDIENCES LISTEN

Objectives  www.mhhe.com/brydon7e

After reading this chapter and reviewing the online learning resources at
http://www.mhhe.com/brydon7e, you should be able to:

- Develop an organizational strategy geared to your audience and purpose.
- Refine the specific purpose of your speech.
- Organize the body of your speech.
- Recognize organizational patterns used across diverse cultures.
- Prepare a formal outline for a speech to your class.

Key Concepts

alphabetical pattern

categorical pattern

causal pattern

comparative advantages pattern

extended narrative pattern

formal outline

Monroe's motivated sequence

problem–solution pattern

spatial pattern

spiral pattern

star pattern

stock issues pattern

subpoint

supporting point

time pattern

two-sided refutational pattern

wave pattern

> "Every discourse, like a living creature, should be so put together that it has its own body and lacks neither head nor feet, middle nor extremities, all composed in such a way that they suit both each other and the whole."
>
> —PLATO

If organizing your thoughts into an effective speech were easy, there would be no need for professional speechwriters. If all gifted speakers were also great speechwriters, this would be doubly so. But that's not the case; and it's one of the reasons why six-figure salaries are paid to people like Peggy Noonan, who wrote some of President Reagan's most memorable speeches, and Bob Shrum, whose speechwriting talents helped the late Senator Edward Kennedy craft some of his most memorable phrases.

In Chapter 1 we said that public speaking is a highly refined extension of many of your everyday communication skills. That doesn't mean, however, that a public conversation between you and a friend is the same thing as a public speech between you and an audience of your peers. During a conversation we often speak in a random and seemingly disorganized fashion. We freely jump around topics, modify opinions, and clarify what we mean to say on an "as needed" basis. Normally we have no reason to formally structure our messages, which are by nature spontaneous and unpredictable, verbal as well as nonverbal.

As we move from informal conversation to speeches in public, however, the "rules" for effective communication start to change. Listeners want structure from speakers. They want to know where speakers plan on taking them, including a verbal road map that alerts them to important points along the way. They also don't want to have to guess whether they have reached the destination the speaker promised. Thus, we need to construct a speech that not only is interesting but also helps the audience follow what we say and make sense of our message. This means developing an organizational strategy for the content of our speech that increases the chances that the audience will understand us as we intend to be understood.

This chapter focuses first on the need to match your organizational strategy to the rhetorical situation you face—specifically, your audience, the occasion, and your purpose for speaking. Second, we introduce and explain specific organizational strategies from which you can choose. Third, we look at some practical criteria that should help you fully develop the organizational strategy you choose. Finally, we show you how you can adapt the principles of formal outlining to make the process of organizing your speech more manageable.

Refocusing on the Audience, Occasion, and Specific Purpose

A lesson we repeatedly share with our own students is one we first learned as college debaters: What speakers think they know about a topic is inevitably turned on its head once they thoroughly research the topic. Thus, a topic that initially strikes you as simple and straightforward becomes far more complex and nuanced once you dig in and do the kind of research necessary to construct a credible speech. As a result, usually you have no choice but to (1) revisit and reassess the rhetorical situation, (2) determine whether your initial analysis needs to be revised, and (3) decide how you can best use what you have learned in choosing a strategy to organize your speech. This process typically begins by weighing what your research has taught you relative to the audience and occasion you will face.

Consider the case of organ donation. It's exactly the kind of topic that many people, including beginning speech students, regard as significant but also fairly simple and straightforward. How can anyone take issue with what amounts to "the gift of life"? As it turns out, lots of people oppose organ donation. Further, their reasons are as diverse as the society to which we all belong. Some people oppose organ donation on religious grounds, others because they don't want to "pull the plug" on perchance a miracle of modern medicine, and still others because they think the system of determining the recipients of the donated organs is biased in the direction of the very rich.

Another lesson we may learn from our research is that the fit between our topic and the speech occasion is not a good one. The calendar is full of days and even months that may not mean much to you but are very meaningful to people who might be members of your audience. Examples include holy days and months for the religious and cultural dates of significance for many ethnic groups. It is the speaker's obligation to make sure that the topic and the issues it implies reflects such sensitivities. It is not a matter of "political correctness" but of respect. Not everyone celebrates Christmas morning with opening presents, for example, including many Christians. To assume that everyone in your audience will immediately relate to your planned introduction, in which you will ask audience members to recall the feeling of anticipation they experienced as a child on Christmas morning, may work against you.

When your research reveals new information relative to your audience and the speech occasion, it doesn't mean that your only choice is to find another topic. Although in rare instances that may be your best option, more typically such a discovery means you may have to modify the specific purpose of your speech.

Determining Your Specific Purpose

Recall from Chapter 1 that your instructor more often than not assigns the general purpose of a classroom speech: for example, constructing and delivering an informative speech. Determining the specific purpose of your speech, however, is typically up to you. To reiterate, the specific purpose of a speech involves the goal or objective a speaker hopes to achieve with a given audience. On a very general level you may be required to inform your audience on a topic of your choosing. But on a specific level, your purpose may be to demonstrate how the information you've gathered from your research can be applied in daily life.

In the same vein, you most likely will be assigned a speech where the general purpose

Audiences attending tea party protests in 2009 responded favorably to speakers who sought to persuade them that expansion of government programs was wrong and unfavorably to those who favored more government spending.

George Rogers

is to persuade your audience. Determining what "persuading your audience" actually means, however, will greatly depend on what your research suggests you can reasonably expect to achieve, given the audience and the occasion. Persuading people merely to listen to a viewpoint contrary to their own, for example, is not nearly as tough as persuading them to change their viewpoint. Thus, going into your research, your specific purpose may be "to change your audience's viewpoint." Coming out of your research, though, you may conclude that you would be better served by changing your specific purpose to persuading your audience to at least listen to your contrary view.

Patterns of Organization: Form and Function

Once you are certain about your specific purpose, you need to look for a pattern of organization that helps you realize your goal. You'll find that some patterns of organization are better suited to realizing your specific purpose than other patterns. The following ones, for example, reflect the rhetorical roots of the art and science of public speaking and were initially conceived to help speakers organize their speeches for persuasive effect.

Rhetorical Patterns of Organization

Monroe's Motivated Sequence

Monroe's motivated sequence
A five-step organizational scheme, developed by speech professor Alan Monroe, involving (1) attention, (2) need, (3) satisfaction, (4) visualization, and (5) action.

Professor Alan Monroe has developed what we call **Monroe's motivated sequence** for organizing the content of a speech. His sequence has been introduced and taught to students for 75 years.[1] It covers an entire speech from beginning to end with five, interdependent steps: (1) *attention*, (2) *need*, (3) *satisfaction*, (4) *visualization*, and (5) *action*.

To begin with, Monroe's sequence alerts speakers to the fact that an audience's *attention* is far from guaranteed. To achieve our specific purpose, we have to first enlist the audience's attention with our introduction. Failing to do so is not an option, because the remaining four steps depend on successfully completing the first. The second step, *need*, reflects the work of both rhetoricians and humanistic psychologists. Few things are as motivational as an important need that demands satisfaction, whether it is as basic as food or as abstract as the pursuit of happiness. When we tap into an existing need or create one that hadn't occurred to an audience, we can then take the next step by linking our message to the *satisfaction* of the unmet need. This is where a specific plan of action is presented to meet the need aroused in the audience. Monroe's fourth step, *visualization*, echoes what we said about this technique in Monroe's fourth step, visualization, carries over to actual behavior. Visualization done properly carries over to actual behavior. Thus, if we can verbally and nonverbally facilitate visualization among audience members, this increases our chances of realizing our specific purpose. The last step in Monroe's motivated sequence, *action*, is also the most difficult to successfully negotiate. Moving an audience to act in accordance with what we suggest is seldom accomplished with a single speech. This is especially true in a college classroom, where students can be stingy with verbal and nonverbal feedback.

Thus, Monroe's approach works best in the classroom when we urge audience members to take some action that doesn't require a major commitment.

Obviously, Monroe's approach is best suited to persuasive presentations. Because informative speaking generally kicks off a persuasive campaign, however, we can easily see the motivated sequence being adapted to an informative presentation. A speaker could (1) show audience members why they need the information being presented, (2) connect the presentation to satisfying the need, and (3) help the audience visualize the process. The speaker could then conclude with information about applying the content that's been shared.

Problem–Solution Pattern

Instead of raising a need and then suggesting the best way to satisfy it, speakers using this second rhetorical pattern call the audience's attention to a significant problem and the best way to solve it. This strategic pattern of organization is not only common but easily applied to many of today's most pressing topics. Using the **problem–solution pattern,** a speaker divides the organization of the speech. The first half introduces the audience to the problem by establishing (1) why the problem is harmful, (2) why it is significant, and (3) its root cause. The second half of the speech is then devoted to the solution to the problem. The speaker (1) describes the solution for the audience, (2) demonstrates its feasibility, and (3) then shows why the solution is advantageous to audience members.

Stock Issues Pattern

Closely related to the problem–solution pattern, and also well suited to persuasive speeches, is the **stock issues pattern.** Based on the model of deliberative debate, this pattern addresses four key questions: (1) How serious is the problem? (2) Who is to blame? (3) How should the problem be solved? and (4) Is the solution worth the cost? In debate, these four stock issues are referred to as (1) ill, (2) blame, (3) cure, and (4) cost. The so-called burden of proof, moreover, requires that speakers present the audience with persuasive evidence for all four issues.

Causal Pattern

The **causal pattern** of organization is less elaborate. It is often useful in persuasive presentations where you need to cut to the chase because of time constraints. It also can be used in some informative speeches where you want to demonstrate the effects that typically follow a known cause: for instance, the drop-off in fine and gross motor skills when you drink too much alcohol.

While it's possible to construct a persuasive speech that moves from effects to cause, most speakers opt to move from cause to effect(s). For example, the speaker might try to persuade audience members to adopt a practice that produces positive effects or avoid one that produces negative outcomes. Recently, for instance, it has been widely published that many people are deficient in vitamin D because they don't get enough sunlight. Too much ultraviolet radiation from sunlight, however, is the leading cause of skin cancer in the United States. Thus, one speaker could argue that you should get at least 15 minutes of unprotected exposure to the sun each day to maximize your body's production of vitamin D, but another speaker might follow with a warning that the

problem–solution pattern
A pattern of organization that analyzes a problem in terms of (1) harm, (2) significance, and (3) cause, and proposes a solution that is (1) described, (2) feasible, and (3) advantageous.

stock issues pattern
A four-point pattern of organization that is based on (1) ill, (2) blame, (3) cure, and (4) cost.

causal pattern
A pattern of organization that moves from cause to effect or from effect to cause.

recommended 15 minutes shouldn't be used as an excuse to avoid the use of sunscreen or risk a sunburn by trying to "tan."

Whether the effects are positive or negative, however, the speaker who chooses this pattern needs to anticipate and prepare for a simple fact: Causal relationships in nature and in human behavior are seldom simple. Causal relationships in which there is a single cause are almost nonexistent. For example, although there is abundant scientific evidence to support the claim that climate change is largely the result of human-generated carbon emissions, no credible scientist would claim that carbon emissions are the sole cause of climate change.

Speakers who opt for this pattern also need to make sure that they have not confused correlation with causation. Many phenomena in nature and human behavior are related. That doesn't mean that one *caused* the other. Self-esteem and academic success are moderately related, but high self-esteem doesn't cause academic success.

Two-Sided Refutational Pattern

two-sided refutational pattern

A pattern of organization that involves (1) introducing the topic and thesis statement, (2) presenting arguments and evidence supporting the thesis, (3) acknowledging arguments against the thesis, (4) refuting these arguments, (5) restating arguments and evidence supporting the thesis, and presenting the conclusion.

The **two-sided refutational pattern** is ideally suited to persuasive speeches where speakers expect audience members to be exposed to counterpersuasion in the immediate or near future. In today's world it is a virtual certainty that anything you say in a persuasive speech will be disputed at a later date, if not immediately following your speech. The two-sided, refutational pattern of organization requires that speakers anticipate the counterpersuasive arguments the audience is most likely to hear. These counterarguments are then included in the speech and refuted. Speakers using this pattern typically organize their speech in the following manner.

1. Introduce the topic and the thesis statement.
2. Present arguments and evidence that support the thesis statement.
3. Acknowledge that not all people agree, and introduce common arguments these people make.
4. Refute these arguments.
5. Briefly restate the arguments and evidence in support of the thesis statement, and present the conclusion.

When speakers both state and then refute common arguments from the "other side" of an issue, they also provide their audience with the means to refute these exact or similar arguments in the future. Research shows that audience members who hear a two-sided, refutational speech are not nearly as susceptible to counterpersuasion as audiences who hear only the speaker's point of view.[2]

Comparative Advantages Pattern

The preceding patterns of organization usually require speakers to take on the status quo (present system) and provide an alternative that is fundamentally different from it—for example, proposing to eliminate the current system of auto liability insurance and replace it with a no-fault auto insurance system. This is easier said than done. Most people are predisposed to resist fundamental change. What's more, many people are perfectly content with principles, practices, and products they think work just fine, as expressed in the cliché "If it ain't broke, don't fix it."

Many things that work do not work well. They might not need to be completely replaced, but we all benefit when they are improved. Many of the products and practices we all enjoy today are improvements on products and practices we once found quite functional. Examples include diagnostic tools in medicine such as magnetic resonance imaging, ergonomic workstations in places of business, the virtual library you can access online at your school, and your smart phone. You could "get by" without any of these improved technologies. But are you willing to go back because the technologies they improved on were not broken?

The **comparative advantages pattern** of organization is based on this logic. Rather than demanding that you take on the status quo, it enables you to take the more audience-friendly approach of demonstrating how the status quo can be improved, in three steps. First, you describe the current state of affairs relative to your topic. Second, you propose a plan of action. Third, you show how this action will make the lives of audience members even better if they agree to the action.

To see a comparison of how these rhetorical patterns compare to one another, see the box "Speaking of . . . Rhetorical Patterns of Organization Compared" on pages 200–201, which shows how the topic of prevention of skin cancer can be approached in different ways.

> **comparative advantages pattern**
> A pattern of organization based on the idea that things can be better even if they are not currently harmful.

Conventional Patterns of Organization

The preceding patterns have deep roots in the study and practice of rhetoric. Although they can be modified to suit nearly any speech purpose, they are most commonly used to organize a persuasive speech. We now turn to a handful of conventional alternatives to the preceding ones: (1) alphabetical, (2) categorical, (3) spatial, (4) time, and (5) extended narrative. These patterns are often used to teach expository writing, so you may have had practice in using them to organize essays. For this reason, plus the fact they are so straightforward they need little elaboration, we will be brief.

Alphabetical

The **alphabetical pattern** is a common and useful tool many speakers use to organize a speech. It is familiar and easily followed by most audience members. Typically, the main points or body of the speech are organized so that

> **alphabetical pattern**
> Main points are in alphabetical order or spell out a common word.

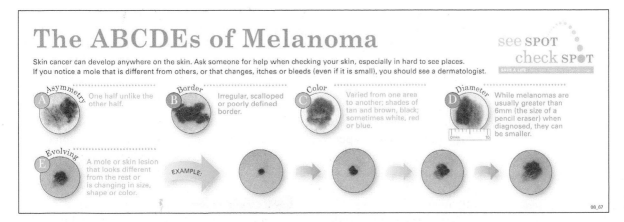

Alphabetical organization is used by the American Academy of Dermatology to illustrate how to spot the deadly skin cancer melanoma.

Rhetorical Patterns of Organization Compared

The following compares and contrasts the rhetorically based patterns of organization we've presented, using a single example of a speech on the prevention of skin cancer. This example should further help you decide which pattern of organization is best suited to the speeches you have been assigned.

Monroe's Motivated Sequence

I. *Attention*: Skin cancer is increasing at an alarming rate among college-age students and is the leading cause of death among college-age women.

II. *Need*: People in general, and college-age women specifically, need to protect themselves from skin cancer and its potentially lethal effects.

III. *Satisfaction*: According to the American Dermatological Association, skin cancer is the most easily prevented form of cancer.

IV. *Visualization*: Prevention begins with recognizing visible changes in moles and freckles or previously unnoticed spots and growths that are asymmetrical, exhibit irregular borders, vary in color, and/or are about the size of a pencil eraser.

V. *Action*: The best way to do this is with a partner, each of you examining the other's entire body for these signs, not just the skin that is routinely exposed. Should you notice something suspicious, immediately see a dermatologist or other physician.

Problem–Solution

I. *Problem*: Skin cancer is the fastest growing and most easily prevented type of cancer in the United States.

A. *Harm:* Untreated, skin cancer can lead to death or disfigurement.

B. *Significance*: 2 million new cases of skin cancer are diagnosed each year in the United States.

C. *Cause*: Harmful ultraviolet radiation from excessive exposure to the sun is the leading cause of skin cancer.

II. *Solution*: People practicing comprehensive sun protection best achieve skin cancer prevention.

A. *Described*: Comprehensive sun protection includes sunscreen, sunglasses, and a wide-brimmed hat.

B. *Feasibility*: Wearing sunscreen, sunglasses, and a wide-brimmed hat are easy to do.

C. *Advantages*: Longevity and younger-looking skin your entire life; millions of dollars in saved health costs for the U.S. population.

Stock Issues

I. *Ill:* Skin cancer in the United States is growing at an alarming rate.

II. *Blame*: Most skin cancers are caused by ultraviolet radiation from the sun.

III. *Cure*: The same skin cancers are easily prevented if people practice sun-safe behavior.

IV. *Costs*: Whereas medical interventions to treat skin cancer are expensive, the routine practice of sun safety costs pennies on the dollar.

letters correspond to words or form an acronym (*MADD* for *Mothers Against Drunk Driving*). For example, dermatologists encourage people not only to examine themselves and their partners for potential skin cancers, but also to use the letters A-B-C-D-E in the process. These five letters correspond to the observable characteristics of skin cancers people should look for in their self-examinations of moles or suspicious spots on the skin: asymmetry, border irregularities, color variation, diameter, and evolving.[3] A speaker could easily adapt the American Dermatological Association's A-B-C-D-E system to organize an informative speech about recognizing potential signs of skin cancer.

categorical pattern
A pattern of organization based on natural divisions in the subject matter.

Categorical

Speakers commonly use the **categorical pattern** to organize speeches where there are natural divisions in the subject matter. Biology, botany, and geology immediately come to mind. Animals can be divided into mammals, reptiles, or birds. Plants can be categorized as annual or perennial. Rocks can

Causal

I. *Cause(s):* The leading cause of skin cancer in the United States is excessive ultraviolet radiation from the sun.
II. *Effects:* Preventable forms of skin cancer owing to excessive ultraviolet radiation from the sun:
   A. Can lead to disfigurement from surgery.
   B. Can lead to premature aging.
   C. Are a preventable burden on the health care system.

Two-Sided Refutational

(Side One)

I. *Introduce topic and thesis statement:* For the people most susceptible to skin cancer—fair-skinned people with light hair and eye color—there is no such thing as a safe tan.
II. *Support topic and thesis statement:* According to the American Dermatological Association, fair-skinned people with light hair and eye color should follow these guidelines:
   A. Strictly limit their unprotected time in the sun to avoid sunburning.
   B. Apply and reapply sunscreen every 3 hours when they cannot avoid the sun.
   C. Wear a wide-brimmed hat and ultraviolet protective sunglasses.

(Side Two)

III. *Acknowledge opposition and common arguments:* People holding a contrary point of view, including the indoor tanning industry, make the following arguments:
   A. Exposure to the sun is essential to the production of vitamin D.
   B. The use of indoor tanning beds is a good substitute for people who live in climates with limited sunshine.
IV. *Refutation:* Scientific research refutes these claims.
   A. Even fair-skinned people with light hair and eyes need no more than 15 minutes of unprotected exposure, 3 to 5 times a week, to produce needed amounts of vitamin D.
   B. The ADA also points out that for people who live in climates with limited sunshine, food and supplements containing vitamin D are a better and cheaper alternative to tanning beds.
V. *Restatement and support:* To conclude, the scientific evidence shows that for fair-skinned people with light hair and eyes there is no such thing as a safe tan, and that they need only minimal unprotected exposure to the sun for needed vitamin D.

Comparative Advantages

I. *Describe the status quo:* Currently skin cancer screenings are voluntary, thus many melanomas aren't detected until they become life-threatening.
II. *Propose a plan of action:* Free skin cancer screenings should be made available at convenient locations, such as pharmacies and walk-in clinics.
III. *Advantage:* More skin cancers will be detected early, and more lives will be saved.

be categorized as igneous, sedimentary, or metamorphic. When using this pattern, however, we need to be careful that we don't create false categories. What works well for animals, plants, and rocks may be inappropriate for people. Much social and ethnic prejudice is rooted in the invention of false categories and forcing people into them. Tony Soprano is no more representative of all Italian men, for instance, than Katie Couric is representative of major network news anchors.

Spatial

Speakers can also use a **spatial pattern,** based on physical space and geography, to organize their speeches. An informative speech on the spread of a contagious disease, for example, could be organized on the basis of population density in a city. In the case of a pandemic, the same speech might be organized around the country of origin and the subsequent path of the disease as it spread throughout the world.

spatial pattern
A pattern of organization based on physical space or geography.

TV meteorologists often use a spatial pattern to explain the weather.

Time

Many speech topics are best organized in a simple **time pattern;** examples include informative speeches focusing on an event of historical significance or on a process. You can organize your speech so that it describes not just the event itself, but what took place before and after the event as well. You also can use the increments of time to impress upon your audience the magnitude of the process you describe—for example, how long it takes a plastic water bottle or plastic diaper to decompose in a landfill.

Extended Narrative

An **extended narrative** is a pattern of organization based on the tradition of storytelling. People are predisposed to respond favorably to stories because their organization is usually quite familiar, with a clear beginning, middle, and end. Although brief stories are often told to illustrate or reinforce the main points of a speech, an extended narrative embodies a speaker's specific purpose in a single story.

When asked what the secret was to his success, the late Don Hewitt, who created the highly rated and long-running *60 Minutes* program, answered with four little words: "Tell me a story."[4] Skillfully told stories can convey an important lesson or simply entertain an audience. Again, it depends on what the speaker hopes to accomplish. Stories tend to be less threatening than speeches that confront issues head-on. As a result, storytelling is a favored organizational strategy, especially in low-context cultures, where speakers go to great lengths to ensure that they do not cause audience members to "lose face."

Conventional Patterns of Organization Compared

The following compares and contrasts the conventional patterns of organization we've presented, using a single example of a speech on the prevention of skin cancer. This example should further help you decide which pattern of organization is best suited to the speeches you have been assigned. You can also compare this to the rhetorical patterns illustrated earlier on the same topic.

Alphabetical

I. Skin cancer prevention begins with your A-B-C-D-E.
   A. *A* stands for asymmetry.
   B. *B* stands for irregular borders.
   C. *C* stands for changing and uneven color.
   D. *D* stands for diameter, meaning anything the diameter of a pencil eraser or larger.
   E. *E* stands for evolving, meaning a skin lesion that changes over time.

Categorical

I. There are three categories of skin cancers.
   A. Basal cell skin cancers
   B. Squamous cell skin cancers
   C. Melanoma skin cancers

Spatial

I. Your skin examination should be systematic. Proceed in this order:
   A. Head and neck
   B. Back and upper torso
   C. Arms and hands
   D. Legs and ankles
   E. Feet and toes

Time

I. It was once thought that skin cancer was a rare disease and of little concern to the average person.
II. Beginning in the latter part of the 20th century, skin cancer became epidemic as the ozone layer was depleted and more people moved to sunny climates.
III. In the future, skin cancer rates should decline as preventative measures, such as sunscreen and protective clothing, are more widely adopted.

Extended Narrative

I. My skin cancer story has a beginning, middle, and no end.
II. It starts with my partner noticing a suspicious spot behind my earlobe, seeing a dermatologist, and a bioscopy.
III. The middle of my story is about the scare I got when the bioscopy tested malignant and I was diagnosed with an *in situ* melanoma.
IV. The reason it has no complete end is because even though the Mohs surgery I had showed that the malignancy had not spread, I am now committed for the rest of my life to skin checkups every 6 months and pale but healthy skin owing to my sun-safety routine.

To see a comparison of how these conventional patterns compare to one another, see the box "Speaking of . . . Conventional Patterns of Organization Compared," which shows how the topic of prevention of skin cancer can be approached in different ways.

Organic Patterns of Organization

With the exception of storytelling, the patterns we have discussed thus far are rooted in the traditions of Western civilization. They reflect the deductive method of science and are decidedly linear. Increasingly, however, we find that many of our students would prefer to construct their speeches using an organizational pattern that is less lockstep in form and function.

As the diversity of our culture grows and evolves, it's good to know that there are alternative patterns we can choose from to organize our speeches. These alternatives may better suit us personally or better suit our audience and the

Exhibit 9.1

Wave Pattern
Martin Luther King Jr. used a wave pattern in his speech.

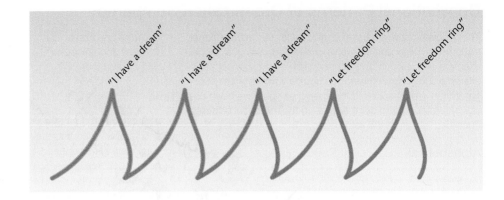

rhetorical situation we face. Communication scholar Cheryl Jorgensen-Earp, for example, suggests that there are alternative, organic patterns of organization preferred and proven effective by women and people of color. They are the wave, the spiral, and the star.[5]

Wave

wave pattern
A pattern of organization in which the basic theme, often represented by a phrase, is repeated again and again, much like a wave cresting, receding, and then cresting again.

The **wave pattern** is highly rhythmic. It mimics its namesake in the sense that it builds, crests, and recedes to build again. Often heard from the pulpit of many African American churches, the skilled speaker's words metaphorically wash over the audience and then recede to form the next wave. Although there are always exceptions, speakers who choose this pattern usually feature a recurrent theme in their speeches, treating it much like a musical refrain or musical bridge.

Dr. Martin Luther King Jr. used the wave to great effect in more than one speech. He is most remembered, however, for the speech that took its title from its recurrent refrain, "I have a dream." Dr. King complemented this most remembered phrase with another as the speech closed—"Let freedom ring." Exhibit 9.1 illustrates the wave pattern of speaking.

Spiral

spiral pattern
A pattern of organization that employs repetition of points, with the points growing in intensity as the speech builds to its conclusion.

The **spiral pattern** is the second organic template Jorgensen-Earp suggests you consider. It too repeats points, but each point grows in intensity as the speech builds to its pinnacle at the conclusion. We had the privilege of being in the audience as one of our former students, Dr. Rick Rigsby, used the spiral pattern in a motivational speech presented to faculty, current students, and distinguished alumni of the School of Communication. A powerful, charismatic, and nationally prominent motivational speaker, Rick said that what he knew about life he learned from the death of Trina, his wife and the mother of their two children. Rick went on to relate what Trina told him and the lesson it taught even as she lay dying from metatastic breast cancer. "She told me that it isn't how long you live but how you lived that mattered."

As the speech progressed, Rick returned to this theme again and again, each time with more emotional intensity. At the end of his speech he asked the audience this question: "How are you living?" Thus he spiraled to a climax that had been foreshadowed throughout the speech. Exhibit 9.2 illustrates the spiral pattern of organization.

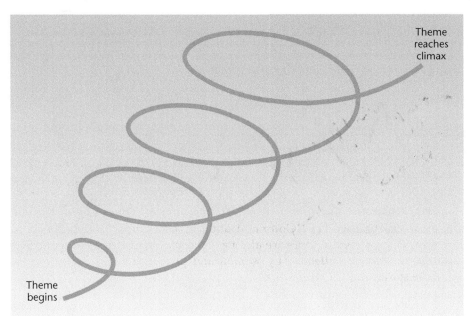

Exhibit 9.2
Spiral Pattern
Each point in a spiral
pattern repeats the theme
with greater intensity.

Star

A third organic pattern identified by Jorgensen-Earp is the **star pattern.** In this case the main points speakers wish to make grow from a central idea. All of the points of the star are of equal importance in this pattern. Thus, speakers can present them in any order they choose to support the common theme that encircles the star and holds the speech together.

For audiences accustomed to hearing speakers who use a linear pattern of organization, the star pattern can take some getting used to. For example, actor and community activist Edward James Olmos spoke at our university several years ago. As we listened, the speech initially seemed like a random list of stories and anecdotes. But a more careful analysis shows that each of his stories was really a point on a star, with the central message being "We are all one gang." Exhibit 9.3 illustrates the star pattern.

star pattern
A pattern of organization
in which all of the points
are of equal importance
and can be presented in
any order to support the
common theme.

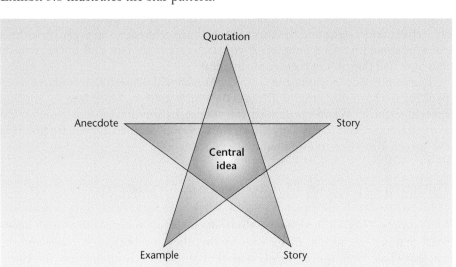

Quotation

Anecdote

Story

**Central
idea**

Example

Story

Exhibit 9.3
Star Pattern
In a star pattern all points
grow from a central idea.

Organizational Patterns

Any of the patterns we've discussed could be used to fulfill any speech purpose. However, certain patterns seem more suitable than others for one or two purposes. This table highlights the patterns most likely to be useful for each speech purpose.

Pattern	Informative	Persuasive	Entertaining
Rhetorical Patterns			
Motivated Sequence	X	X	
Problem–Solution		X	
Stock Issues		X	
Causal	X	X	
Two-Sided Refutational		X	
Comparative Advantages		X	
Conventional Patterns			
Alphabetical	X	X	X
Categorical	X	X	X
Spatial	X		
Time	X		X
Extended Narrative	X	X	X
Organic Patterns			
Wave	X	X	X
Spiral	X	X	X
Star	X	X	X

As a speaker, carefully consider both the audience members' cultural backgrounds as they affect their organizational preferences and your own cultural affinity for certain patterns of organization. Although cultural diversity provides the opportunity to expand the ways in which speeches may be organized, these patterns should be used only when you are certain of your skill in this respect and how well they fit the rhetorical situation.

The box titled "Speaking of . . . Organizational Patterns" summarizes the patterns we have discussed and suggests which patterns work best for various speech purposes. Whatever pattern you choose, be sure it is appropriate for your audience, topic, and purpose. Sticking with one pattern for all the main points of the speech also helps to avoid audience confusion.

Organizing the Body of the Speech

As Plato suggested in this chapter's introductory quotation, every speech needs parts that are "composed in such a way that they suit both each other and the whole." Thus, your speech needs a well-organized body to support the thesis statement and achieve your purpose. Carefully thought-out main points, subpoints, and supporting points will provide that organization.

Once you have refined the specific purpose of a speech, formulated the thesis statement, and decided on the appropriate pattern of organization, you can tackle organizing the body of the speech. In the preceding chapter we discussed introducing and concluding your speech. At this point in the process, it is important to review your tentative introduction to revise it in light of the pattern of organization that you have selected. Transitional statements or signposts and the conclusion also need to be created or revised at this time.

The body of your speech is typically made up of three levels of supporting information. The first level is composed of the main points you want to make in support of your thesis statement. The second level consists of subpoints that support and illustrate the main points. The third level is made up of supporting points, which help to illustrate the subpoints you've introduced. These levels are interdependent, meaning they have a reciprocal influence on each other. Thus, if one level appears to be at odds with the others, it probably won't make logical sense to your audience and you'll need to change it.

Main Points

As we discussed briefly in Chapter 1, the key ideas that support the thesis statement of a speech are the *main points*. They should fully develop the thesis statement. As a result of understanding these points, your audience should be informed, persuaded, or entertained in accordance with your specific purpose. We want you to remain mindful of the following five guiding principles as you organize the body of your speech.

Tips and Tactics

Guidelines for Developing Main Points

- Limit the number of main points.
- Focus each main point on developing the thesis statement.
- Construct main points so that they are parallel in structure.
- State main points as simply as the subject will allow, limiting each main point to one idea.
- Give all main points balanced treatment.

Number: Why Less Is More

We cannot emphasize enough the importance of limiting your speech to a manageable and memorable number of main points. Aside from the fact that you should anchor your speech to at least two main points (if there is only one main point, then that is, in effect, the same as the thesis statement, and the subpoints are in fact the main points), there is no magical formula on the exact number of main points you should have. We tell our own students that a good rule of thumb, for classroom speeches especially, is to shoot for three main points. We also request that they limit themselves to no more than five main points, regardless of the topic or purpose of the speech.

Our reasons are straightforward. First, limiting yourself to between three and five main points requires you to exercise self-discipline in distinguishing between main points in support of your message and subpoints that support your main points. Second, it shows that you respect and appreciate the information-processing limits of your audience. Your speech is likely to be embedded in a barrage of other messages to which your audience has previously attended during the day. Finally, by limiting your speech to between three and five main points you also are far more likely to stick to the time constraints required by your instructor.

Obviously some topics do not fit into a predetermined number of pigeonholes. As the number of main points in your speech increases, though, it will become more difficult for you to manage your speech. It could also become more difficult for your audience to follow your speech. If you begin to think that you cannot do justice to your topic and purpose with three or four main points, you may want to ask yourself whether you are trying to cover too much ground in a single speech or confusing subpoints with main ones.

Main points should have enough weight to stand on their own and be easy to distinguish from each other. Subpoints are derivative and play a supporting rather than starring role in your speech. This should become more obvious as we now turn to the relationship between your main points and the focus of your speech.

Focus on the Thesis

Your main points should fully develop your thesis statement without going beyond the focus of the speech. For example, if you're speaking about trends in contemporary music, your thesis statement might be "Pop music is more diverse than ever." In support of your thesis statement, your main points might be as follows:

  I. Pop music is multinational.
 II. Pop music is multicultural.
III. Pop music is multilingual.

If you added a fourth main point, *Pop music is political,* however, you would have strayed beyond the territory implied by your thesis statement. The thing to remember and put into practice, then, is twofold: (1) Make sure you include enough items of information to fully support your thesis statement, while (2) also making sure that you include only those items that directly support your thesis statement. Your goal is to fulfill the promise of your thesis statement at the conclusion of your speech—no more, no less.

Parallel Structure

Because main points form the essence of a speech, they should be clear, concise, and memorable. One technique to help achieve this is to construct main points in parallel fashion. Which of the following examples of main points would work best for our pop music speech?

Example 1

   I. Today's pop music comes from all over the world.
  II. Many cultures are represented in today's pop music.
 III. The language of pop music is no longer simply English.

Example 2

   I. Pop music transcends individual countries.
  II. Pop music transcends individual cultures.
 III. Pop music transcends individual languages.

Obviously the second example is easier to remember. The repetition of the phrase "Pop music transcends individual . . ." in all three main points stresses the focus of this speech. We want to be clear that mere repetition is not the same as parallel structure. What is important is that in constructing the main points, a key phrase or concept begins each point. Repeating words randomly throughout the speech is not the same thing as having a parallel structure for your main points.

Simplicity Versus Complexity

When you read a confusing sentence or stumble on an unfamiliar word, you can stop and reread the sentence or look up the meaning of the word. An audience, however, has only one chance to process information as it is shared. Main points need to be phrased so that they are (1) comprehensible and (2) understood as intended. This can be tricky, especially when your topic involves complicated or abstract subject matter. Although you don't want to oversimplify the content of your speech, you also don't want it to sail over the heads of audience members. Concise and simple language makes the structure of a speech clear and needn't reduce the richness of its content. Compare the following two examples from a speech on AIDS:

Example 1

   I. AIDS is transmitted through unprotected sexual relations, including
      homosexual and heterosexual encounters.
  II. AIDS is transmitted when drug users, often desperate for their next fix,
      share dirty needles.
 III. AIDS is transmitted by the exchange of blood, such as in a transfusion or
      between a mother and her unborn child.

Example 2

   I. AIDS is transmitted by unprotected sex.
  II. AIDS is transmitted by sharing needles.
 III. AIDS is transmitted by blood.

Which of the two do you think the audience will remember? Main points should be as simple as the subject will allow.

   Closely related to the point of simplicity of main points is the requirement that each main point should focus on only one main idea. To the extent that a single point incorporates several different ideas, it will lack simplicity and may confuse an audience.

Balance/Symmetry

A consistent finding of cultural anthropologists is that people all over the world have a decided preference for balance and symmetry in their evaluations of people, places, and things. Whether this finding carries over to the body of your speech is an empirical question we cannot answer. Intuitively, however, we think it makes perfect sense to strive for balance and symmetry as you develop the main points in your speech. For example, if one main point dominates the time you've been allotted for your speech, your audience is likely to dismiss what comes later as an afterthought. The audience also may think that they missed something, or worse, you left something out that you intended to say.

Subpoints

subpoint
An idea that supports a main point.

Don't let the word *subpoint* mislead you into thinking that the following discussion is less important than the preceding one. **Subpoints** are to main points what main points are to the thesis statement. Much of what we said about main points also applies to the subpoints you introduce in support of your main points. You need to limit their number, keep them in balance with the entire body of the speech, and state them in easily understood language.

Subpoints illustrate the statement you make with a main point. For example, you cannot afford to assume that when you state, "Pop music transcends national boundaries," it will be as obvious to your audience as it is to you. You must provide your audience with information that supports what your main point asserts. For instance:

[main point]
[subpoint]
[subpoint]
[subpoint]

I. Pop music transcends national boundaries.
   A. Shakira is from Brazil.
   B. Fergie is from Great Britain.
   C. Christina Agulera is from the United States.

You need at least two but probably no more than five subpoints to support one main point. If a main point is not divisible into at least two subpoints, it probably isn't really a main point.

Supporting Points

supporting point
An idea that supports a subpoint.

Not all speeches require a third level of support. The more sophisticated your speeches become, however, the more likely it is you will need to offer **supporting points.** In this case the supporting point expands on what is implied in your subpoint. Returning to our example of pop music, your main point, subpoints, and supporting ones might look like this:

[main point]
[subpoint]

[supporting point]
[supporting point]

II. Pop music transcends cultures.
   A. African American and Caribbean cultures are well represented in today's pop music.
      1. Hip-hop music has obvious ties to African American culture.
      2. Reggae and SKA have obvious ties to Caribbean culture.

Each supporting point could be further subdivided, but such a detailed substructure probably would lose the audience. For a normal classroom speech, it is

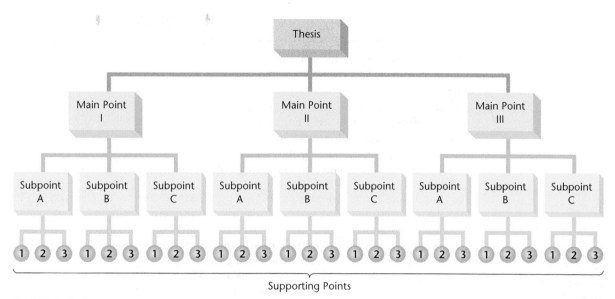

Exhibit 9.4
Relationship of Points in a Traditional Speech

unlikely there will be time to develop points beyond this level. If we must further subdivide a supporting point, we use lowercase letters in the outline as follows:

II. Pop music transcends cultures.   *[main point]*
    A. African American and Caribbean cultures are well represented in   *[subpoint]*
        today's pop music.
        1. Hip-hop music has obvious ties to African American culture.   *[supporting point]*
            a. The rhythms are African American.   *[further support]*
            b. The music fuses elements of rhythm and blues, soul, and rap. *[further support]*
        2. Reggae and SKA have obvious ties to Caribbean culture.   *[supporting point]*
            a. Bob Marley continues to be popular.   *[further support]*
            b. As does his son Ziggy.   *[further support]*

Exhibit 9.4 illustrates the relationship among various levels of support in a speech.

Preparing the Formal Outline

If the preceding discussion reminds you of the lessons you've been taught about the importance of outlining an essay or term paper before writing it, you are one step ahead of us. As is the case with essays and term papers, outlines can be a valuable tool for turning the rough structure of a speech into a precisely organized one. Creating a formal outline also can help you see the whole of your speech, not just its interdependent parts.

Given this framework, a **formal outline** is a template used to prepare and bring into manageable focus the details of a speech from beginning to end. It also is one in a series of steps in which speakers begin to reduce the details of their speech to a skeleton they will flesh out when they present the speech.

 www.mhhe.com/brydon7e

To help you prepare your speech outline, go to our Online Learning Center Web site and click on the Outline Tutor link.

formal outline
A detailed outline used in speech preparation, but not, in most cases, in the actual presentation.

There are two basic types of outlines. *Phrase* or *key word outlines* are meaningful to the speaker but probably would not make a lot of sense to anyone else. For example, a speaker might prepare the following outline for her own use:

Intro: Tell story

  I. Rock music
 II. Volume
III. Deafness

Conclusion: Same story 10 years later

Because this outline probably would make sense only to the speaker, beginning speakers are frequently expected to prepare a *complete-sentence outline*. In this type of outline, speakers include a full statement indicating what each main point and subpoint covers. All the parts of the speech are included, even transitions. Generally a formal outline should include the following:

- The specific purpose, stated as an infinitive phrase (to . . .), describing exactly what the speaker wants the speech to accomplish.
- Three sections–labeled *introduction, body,* and *conclusion*–each separately outlined and beginning with the Roman numeral "I."
- The introduction, including opening, thesis statement, connection with the audience, and preview.
- The body, including main points, subpoints, supporting points, and further support, and, if your instructor requires them, transitions (in parentheses) between the main points.
- The conclusion, including a summary and a close.
- A bibliography, called "References" or "Works Cited" (depending on whether you use APA or MLA style). Specific quotations or facts drawn from a source should also be cited in the main outline. Of course, you should check with your instructor about the specific outlining requirements, if any, for your class. Some instructors prefer a different source citation system than the ones discussed in this text. Appendix A provides a guide for source citation using APA and MLA formats.

Outlines typically use a standard outline notation, which indicates the levels of subordination of points:

  I. Main point
    A. Subpoint
      1. Supporting point
        a. Further support

Any subdivision should include at least two matching points. Thus an "A" subpoint implies there should also be at least a "B." Supporting point "1" should be matched by at least a "2," and further support "a" should be followed by at least a "b." Many instructors prefer that outlines be written in complete sentences, at least through the level of subpoints. This provides a clear idea to your instructor of what you are going to say. Divide separate ideas into different sentences. An "outline" using paragraph form really is an essay with outline notation scattered throughout. Thus, the following is not really in outline form:

I. The first men on the moon were Americans. Neil Armstrong stepped out first. He was followed by Buzz Aldrin. At the same time, Michael Collins orbited the moon.

This paragraph could be turned into the following outline:

I. The first men on the moon were Americans.
   A. Neil Armstrong stepped out first.
   B. He was followed by Buzz Aldrin.
   C. At the same time, Michael Collins orbited the moon.

Notice how each sentence is placed in a separate point. The more general statement is the main point, and the specific instances are subpoints.

Some aspects of an outline do not need to be in complete-sentence form. For example, a speaker who wants to list the components of a larger whole, such as ingredients or tools, could use an outline like this:

   1. Cigarette smoke has three components:
      a. Carbon monoxide
      b. Nicotine
      c. Tar

You need to use judgment, therefore, when you are asked to write a complete-sentence outline. Use complete sentences for your main points and subpoints and anywhere the meaning would not be clear if not expressed in complete-sentence form. The box "In Their Own Words: Sample Speech Outline: Lyme Disease by Shelby Anderson" follows the suggested format.

We require our own students to prepare a complete-sentence outline of their speech far enough in advance that we can read it and provide them with feedback before they finalize their speech. How your instructor treats the topic of outlining may vary slightly or even significantly. What we recommend, therefore, should be checked for compatibility with what your instructor requires.

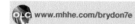

To view a video of Shelby Anderson's speech, click on the Speech Coach link on our Online Learning Center Web site, and go to Segment 9.1.

Looking Ahead

Remember, the outline you create is only the first step in a series of steps that help you move from organizing to delivering your speech. As you negotiate these steps, you should become increasingly familiar with the content of your speech and the organized sequence you plan to follow as you share your content with your audience. Just how familiar you become in this respect, however, will depend on the level of your commitment to your speech and your instructor's expectations about how you should present your speech. For example, will your instructor expect you to deliver the speech extemporaneously, relying on the briefest of notes? Or will you be expected to deliver the speech from memory? A formal complete-sentence outline is sometimes required of beginning speakers as part of the preparation process. Speaker's notes, usually placed on small cards or pages, can be used when presenting the speech. We will have much more to share with you in this regard when we take on the topic of delivery in Chapter 11.

IN THEIR OWN WORDS

Sample Speech Outline

LYME DISEASE
by Shelby Anderson

Specific Purpose: To educate the audience about Lyme disease and how it can affect them.

I. **Open with Impact:** Imagine pain so severe you are writhing in agony, headaches so intense you feel as though your head is going to explode, legs that ache so bad you can't even walk and being so tired you can't get up to go to the bathroom.
   A. Imagine your life changing in an instant.
   B. When I was eight years old my life changed forever when I became ill with Lyme disease.

Shelby Anderson
George Rogers

II. **Thesis:** Lyme disease is a debilitating, devastating disease that is prevalent all over the United States.

III. **Connect:** Lyme disease is in Chico, in Bidwell Park, and in your very own backyard.
   A. It is important for you to know about Lyme disease and how it can affect you.
   B. It is important for you to know how to protect yourself from Lyme disease.

IV. **Preview:** Today I am going to educate you on Lyme disease.
   A. Transmission.
   B. Signs and symptoms.
   C. Treatment.
   D. Prevention.

Body

I. **Main Point:** Lyme disease is a bacterial infection caused by a tick bite.
   A. This bacteria is in the form of a spiral-shaped spirochete (Todar, 2007).
      1. Also known as Borrelia burgdorferi.
      2. The bacteria is transmitted to tick via a mouse, during the tick's larvae stage ("Lymenet Guide," n.d.).
   B. There are three common types of ticks that carry Lyme disease, although many different types can also transmit the bacteria (Fearn, 2007).
      1. The Deer Tick, also known as the Black-Legged Tick.
      2. The Western Black-Legged Tick, which is a relative of the Deer Tick.
      3. The Lone Star Tick.

(Transition: Now that you know about the history and transmission of Lyme disease, I am going to tell you about the symptoms of the disease.)

II. **Main Point:** Lyme disease is known as the "Great Imitator" because it can mimic so many other diseases.
   A. Initially Lyme disease presents itself with flu-like symptoms (Burrascano, 2005).
      1. Body aches, sore throat, fever, fatigue and other flu-like symptoms.
      2. Another sign of disease are Erythema migrans (EM), which is a "bullseye" rash.
         a. Rash will begin four days to several weeks after a bite.

      b. If you have this rash you have Lyme disease, however fewer than half of people with Lyme disease had this rash.

    3. Most people with Lyme disease do not remember a bite.

  B. Lyme disease can lead to variety of symptoms (Burrascano, 2005).

    1. Severe joint and muscle pain.

    2. Fatigue.

    3. Headaches, light and sound sensitivity.

    4. Neurological issues.

    5. Gastrointestinal issues, anxiety.

    6. Facial paralysis (Bell's Palsy).

    7. Cardiovascular problems.

    8. If left untreated Lyme disease can lead to neurological disorders, crippling arthritis, blindness, deafness, psychiatric or psychological disorders, or death (Fearn, 2007).

(Transition: This leads me to my third point, the diagnosis and treatment of Lyme disease.)

III. **Main Point:** The longer a patient has been ill with Lyme disease, the longer the duration of treatment and the more aggressive the treatment (Burrascano, 2005).

  A. Diagnosis of Lyme disease is diagnosed clinically (Burrascano, 2005).

    1. Current tests for Lyme disease are not reliable.

  B. There is no one cure for Lyme disease, but antibiotics are used in treating Lyme disease (Burrascano, 2005).

  C. If diagnosed and treated early, recovery from Lyme disease is very likely (Burrascano, 2005).

    1. If erythema migrans or symptoms are present, treatment is a must.

    2. After a tick bite, the person should be treated with oral antibiotics for 4 to 6 weeks.

    3. Disease that is not caught early can lead to chronic Lyme disease (Burrascano, 2005).

      a. Often requires months to years of aggressive, high dose, long-term, intravenous antibiotics.

      b. Usually requires a combination of antibiotics.

(Transition: Lyme disease is a horrible disease which is why prevention is a must.)

IV. **Main Point:** Prevention is key since ticks love the environments that we love.

  A. Ticks are found in woodlands, fields, meadows, yards, and other green places (Fearn, 2007).

    1. Found in tall grass, gardens, wood piles and rock walls.

    2. Abundant where mice are found.

  B. Protect yourself against tick bites ("Lymenet Guide," n.d.; California Department, n.d.).

    1. Wear light colored clothing, long sleeves and pants.

    2. Use tick repellants with DEET on your skin and premethrin on your clothes.

    3. Stay on paths when hiking.

    4. Keep pets on flea and tick control.

  C. Check your entire body for ticks and remove the tick properly if found ("Lymenet Guide," n.d.; California Department, n.d.).

    1. If a tick is found remove it with fine tweezers.

      a. Grab as close to skin as possible.

      b. Do not squeeze the body, apply Vaseline, use a match, or use alcohol to remove the tick.

    2. Send ticks in for testing.

Conclusion

I. **Summary:** Now you know the devastating effects of Lyme disease caused by a measly, little tick.
   A. The transmission of Lyme disease.
   B. The signs and symptoms of Lyme disease.
   C. Treatment of Lyme disease.
   D. Prevention of Lyme disease.

II. **Close with Impact:** The next time you are having fun at Upper Bidwell Park, just remember that it's not the mountain lion you should be afraid of, but the poppy seed sized tick that you probably will never see.

References

Burrascano Jr., J. J. (2005, September). *Advanced topics in Lyme disease, 15*. Retrieved from http://www.lymenet.org/drbguide200509.pdf

California Department of Health Services Vector-Borne Disease Section. (n.d.). Ticks and prevention against tick bites. Retrieved from http://www.cdph.ca.gov/healthinfo/discond/Documents/Smalltickposter.pdf

Fearn, D. W. (2007, April). Lyme disease and associated diseases the basics, 5. Retrieved from http://www.lymepa.org/html/the_basics_-_description.html

Lymenet guide to Lyme disease. (n.d.). Retrieved from http://library.lymenet.org/domino/file.nsf/bbf2f15334c1f28585256613000317cc/eee9f15bfb66a105852567c700120022?OpenDocument

Todar, K. (2007). *Borrelia burgdorferi* and Lyme disease. *Todar's online textbook of bacteriology.* Retrieved from http://www.textbookofbacteriology.net/Lyme.html

 www.mhhe.com/brydon7e

Summary

Reaching your audience as intended with a speech is no easy task. It demands a strategic pattern of organization. Choosing a strategic pattern of organization should be based on:

- Reassessing the rhetorical situation you face following research on your topic.

- Refining the specific purpose you plan to achieve.

- Knowledge of the strategic patterns of speech organization from which you can choose.

Strategic patterns of organization with strong ties to the rhetorical history of the art and science of public speaking include:

- Monroe's motivated sequence

- Problem–solution

- Stock issues

- Causal

- Two-sided refutational
- Comparative advantages

More conventional patterns of organization include:

- Alphabetical
- Categorical
- Spatial
- Time
- Extended narrative

Organic patterns that are neither linear nor based on Western tradition include:

- Wave
- Spiral
- Star

After choosing an appropriate strategic pattern for organizing your speech, the next step is to organize the body of the speech, composed of:

- Main points, which support the thesis statement.
- Subpoints, which support main points.
- Supporting points, which bolster subpoints.

When organizing the body of the speech, keep in mind five guiding principles:

- Limit the number of main points, which automatically limits subpoints and supporting points.
- Focus each main point on developing the thesis statement.
- Construct main points so that they are parallel in structure.
- State main points as simply as the subject will allow, limiting each to one idea.
- Give all main points balanced treatment.

Depending on your instructor's requirements, use a formal outline to finalize the organization of your speech.

- Complete-sentence outlines are preferred to phrase or key word outlines.
- Remember that your outline is not normally used for your presentation, but is part of the preparation process.
- Speaker's notes can be used when presenting the speech.

Check Your Understanding: Exercises and Activities

1. View a speech on our Online Learning Center Web site at www.mhhe.com/brydon7e. Using the format described in this chapter, construct a complete-sentence outline of the speech. How closely did the speech seem to follow the steps indicated in the chapter? Was the speech easy to outline? If not, how could the speaker have made the organization clearer?

2. Analyze an ad in a magazine, newspaper, or Web site to see whether it uses a problem–solution, causal, or motivated-sequence pattern. If it does, explain how each step is fulfilled. If it doesn't, discuss how the ad might be modified to fit one of these organizational patterns.

3. Following is an outline of a speech. After the outline you'll find a list of points in scrambled order. Your task is to match the appropriate sentence from the scrambled list with the points in the outline. This may be done as an individual or a group exercise, depending on your instructor's preference.

Specific purpose: _____

Introduction
   I. Open with impact: _____
  II. Focus on the thesis statement: _____
 III. Connect with your audience: _____
 IV. Preview: _____

Body

   I. Main point: _____
      A. _____
      B. _____
      C. _____

(*Transition:* _____)

  II. Main point: _____
      A. _____
      B. _____
      C. _____

(*Transition:* _____)

 III. Main point: _____
      A. _____
      B. _____
      C. _____

Conclusion

   I. Summarize: _____
      A. _____
      B. _____
      C. _____
  II. Close with impact: _____

Scrambled list:

1. Use fresh bread, preferably whole grain.

2. Use a quality jelly or jam, made without artificial additives.

3. Use either plain or chunky peanut butter.

4. You must have the necessary ingredients.

5. Fold the wax paper neatly around the sandwich.

6. Place the sandwich in a paper bag.

7. Use a biodegradable wrapper, such as wax paper, rather than plastic wrap.

8. You need to package the sandwich to take to school.

9. Put the two slices together.

10. Spread the first slice with peanut butter.

11. Spread the other slice with jelly or jam.

12. You need to assemble the sandwich.

13. To inform the class how to make a peanut butter and jelly sandwich.

14. First make sure you have the necessary ingredients.

15. Finally, wrap the sandwich.

16. Second, assemble the sandwich.

17. Enjoy your lunch and go to a movie with the money you've saved.

18. You can save money and eat better.

19. Today you will learn how to make the perfect peanut butter and jelly sandwich.

20. Are you tired of spending $5 for a greasy hamburger and fries?

21. Making a peanut butter and jelly sandwich involves three basic steps: having the ingredients, assembling the sandwich, and packaging the sandwich.

22. After you have the ingredients, you need to make the sandwich.

23. Unless you are eating it immediately, the sandwich must be wrapped to stay fresh.

24. To review, there are three steps:

Notes

1. Alan Monroe, *Principles and Types of Speech* (New York: Scott, Foresman, 1935). See also the most recent edition: Kathleen M. German, Bruce E. Gronbeck, Douglas Ehninger, and Alan H. Monroe, *Principles and Types of Public Speaking,* 17th ed. (Upper Saddle River, NJ: Allyn & Bacon, 2010).

2. James C. McCroskey, Thomas J. Young, and Michael D. Scott, "The Effects of Message Sidedness and Evidence on Inoculation Against Counterpersuasion in Small Group Communication," *Speech Monographs* 39 (1972): 205–212.

3. American Academy of Dermatology, "ABCDEs of Melanoma Detection," 2010. [Retrieved from http://www.aad.org/public/exams/abcde.html.]

4. Paul Wilner, "Broadcast News," *Monterey County Weekly,* 27 August–2 September 2009, p. 15.

5. Cited in Clella Jaffe, *Public Speaking: A Cultural Perspective* (Belmont, Calif.: Wadsworth, 1995), 187–192. Based on a telephone interview by Jaffe with Jorgensen-Earp, as well as the latter's unpublished works.

Stephen Colbert treats his audience to a segment titled "The Word" on his popular show *The Colbert Report*.

CHAPTER

10

LANGUAGE: MAKING VERBAL SENSE OF THE MESSAGE

Objectives  www.mhhe.com/brydon7e

After reading this chapter and reviewing the online learning resources at http://www.mhhe.com/brydon7e, you should be able to:

- Construct examples that illustrate the power of language to shape thought.
- Analyze your audience's cultural, demographic, and individual diversity and make effective language choices based on that analysis.
- Use inclusive and immediate language, avoiding marginalizing, totalizing, and sexist language.
- Use credibility-enhancing language, avoiding verbal qualifiers and grammatical errors.
- Use visual, auditory, and kinesthetic speech to enhance your speeches.
- Use metaphors, similes, analogies, and rhythmic speech to enhance your speeches.
- Vary language intensity in your speeches.
- Use concrete words and phrases, as well as consistent, simple, and oral language.
- Use transitional phrases in your speeches to enable your audience to follow your organization.
- Avoid slang and perceived obscenities that could offend audience members.

Key Concepts

analogy

antithesis

credibility-enhancing language

immediate language

inclusive language

language

language intensity

linguistic relativity hypothesis

marginalizing language

metaphor

receiver-centric

sexist language

simile

totalizing language

verbal qualifiers

"How can I tell what I think until I see what I say?"

—EDWARD MORGAN FORSTER[1]

Whether or not satirist extraordinaire Stephen Colbert took a course in general semantics while attending Northwestern University, we cannot say. But it's clear that he understands the importance of words and language and skillfully uses them to skewer those naive enough to believe that, "Sticks and stones may break their bones but words will never hurt them." With tongue firmly in cheek, for example, Colbert treats viewers of his hit show on Comedy Central to a feature he calls "The Word." During the inaugural show of the *Colbert Report,* he even introduced his audience to a word of his own invention: "Truthiness."

According to Colbert, truthiness is a condition that describes people who base their opinions on gut reaction rather than the reasoning and evidence demanded by models of argument. Truthiness is a product of what people feel intuitively, rather than reason logically. Thus, a person in a state of truthiness might say, "I don't know . . . I just *feel* like I can trust the guy," rather than, "I trust him because he's given me repeated examples that I can."

Although truthiness was named word of the year by the dictionary folks at Merriam-Webster in 2006, it remains to be seen whether it becomes a part of people's accepted vocabulary. Even so, it illustrates a point we will make repeatedly in this chapter. Language is a living and dynamic feature of the communication landscape. The words we choose to express ourselves change. They change because the evolving world in which we live requires it.

This chapter links words and language to the art and science of public speaking. Our goal is twofold. First, we want to demonstrate how people use words and language to shape the world we see and think about. Second, we want to show how you can use words and language to breathe life into your speeches so that audiences can share the world you see and think about. Topics we will cover include:

- How words and language relate to what we see and think
- How understanding words and language assist us in audience analysis
- And how we can actually use language to make our speeches instruments of understanding and influence.

Word Power

language
The rule-governed word system we use to verbally commmunicate.

Language is the rule-governed word system we use to verbally communicate. Stripped to the barest of essentials, words are symbolic substitutes for the things they represent. The word *chair* is not the actual thing, for example, but a symbolic representation of it. And the word *love* is not the emotion that prompts us to use it in conjunction with someone about whom we care deeply. Yet the power these "symbolic substitutes" have in shaping what we think or feel about persons, places, and things can be mind-boggling.

There is considerable evidence, for example, that words "frame" how we see the world and how we interpret our experience. Knowing this, people who hope to influence us choose specific words and phrases to maximize the chances that we will interpret their messages as *they* intend them to be interpreted. When successful, such people shape both the meaning we give to words and phrases and how we react to their referents.

As a case in point, the words and phrases politicians repeatedly use to describe themselves and define issues are no accident. They are the result of consultants, focus groups, and surveys of people just like us.

A good example of the preceding involves the recurring debate in congress over the federal tax levied on a family's inheritance. Even though less than one percent of all families are touched by this tax, it became a hot-button issue among unaffected voters when politicians and talk show hosts started calling it "the death tax." The term was actually coined by Dr. Frank Luntz, a highly paid consultant to the Republican party and the author of *Words That Work*. So successful was Luntz's advice that many people continue to mistakenly believe that their surviving families will be unjustly taxed at life's end. Says Luntz, the book's subtitle—"It's Not What You Say, It's What People Hear"—is "the most important single line that I have ever written."[2] Luntz realizes that the meaning of a word is not in the intent of the speaker, but in how it is understood by the listener. Not to be outdone, Democrats have turned to Emory University psychology professor Drew Weston, author of *The Political Brain,* to help them shape their messages. Here is one of Weston's suggestions: "Instead of using euphemisms like 'pro-choice' and 'reproductive health,' . . . liberal candidates might insist that it is un-American for the government to tell men and women when to start a family or what religious beliefs to follow, arguments that test well in focus groups with conservatives and independents."[3]

We are not suggesting that you should model your use of words and phrases after that of people who put politics above principles. However, we do want you to critically examine the relationship between words, phrases, and thought. We also want you to examine how you can use your knowledge of audience analysis to choose words and phrases for your speeches that will help share your vision with individual audience members. This process begins with the difficult task of assessing the role language plays in your general life, and the role it can potentially play in the preparation and delivery of your speeches. For example, before reading any further, respond to the Self-Assessment box "Language Mindfulness" on page 224, which concerns: (1) how you use language and (2) how you respond to others' use of language.

If you carefully read and truthfully responded to the statements in the self-assessment box, your summed score should reveal the degree to which you are aware of how your language can affect others, and how others' language can affect you. The higher your score, the more mindful you are in using language. While clichés, slang, and colloquialisms are usually okay in a conversation with friends, they are inappropriate in a job interview. They also should be avoided or only used with a specific purpose in your speeches. When you adapt your language to people and situations or switch from informal to formal language, it shows that you are mindful of this fact.

Your reaction to others' language also is an indication of how flexible or inflexible you are in giving meaning to words and phrases. Some people are **receiver-centric**—easily turned off to a speaker's language. Receiver-centric audience members apply a very narrow range of meaning to words. Without consulting either the speaker, other audience members, or considering how the

receiver-centric
A person's assumption that the meaning he or she gives to a word or a phrase is its exclusive meaning.

context comes into play, receiver-centric audience members force their meaning on the message. Words can, and very often do, have diverse meanings depending on the context in which they are used and the life experiences of those using them; you can read about this in the box "Speaking of . . . Linguistic Relativity." What's more, the speech transaction is not a one-way street where the speaker or the audience member controls meaning. Simply said, the more we know about the nuances of words and language, the better equipped we are to make good use of them in conversation and speeches. Similarly, the more we know about words and language, the better equipped we will be as audience members in formulating a thoughtful impression of what a speaker is trying to say.

Language and Audience Analysis

Having seen that words and language color people's perception and experience, we can now examine the relationship between language and the three types of diversity (cultural, demographic, and individual) introduced in Chapter 5. Understanding the connections between language and diversity is crucial to effective speaking because today's audience is more diverse than ever.

Linguistic Relativity

What is true of individual words is even more true of the language you speak. Whether you speak English, French, Spanish, or Russian makes a difference in how you experience and interpret the world. According to the **linguistic relativity hypothesis,** introduced more than 40 years ago by cultural anthropologist Benjamin Whorf, what we perceive is influenced by the language in which we think and speak. Different languages lead to different patterns of thought.[1]

Whorf formulated this hypothesis while studying the Native American language of the Hopi. He discovered there are no words in their language for the concept of incremental time: no seconds, no minutes, and no hours.

Thus it would never occur to the Hopi that someone could be half an hour early or late for a visit, because they have no words for the concept.

Each language has certain concepts that cannot be easily expressed in other languages. The expression "something was lost in the translation" doesn't mean part of a statement was literally lost as it was translated from one language to another. It means an identical idea couldn't be found in the second language, so part of the statement's original meaning was diminished.

[1]Benjamin Lee Whorf, *Language, Thought, and Reality* (New York: Wiley, 1956).

> **linguistic relativity hypothesis**
> The idea that what people perceive is influenced by the language in which they think and speak.

Language and Cultural Diversity

Recall from Chapter 5 that *cultural diversity* is multidimensional, including audience characteristics such as individualism/collectivism and masculinity/femininity. Knowing something about the dimensions of culture reflected in the audience is essential to choosing appropriate language for a speech.

One of the authors, for example, had the opportunity to attend an IBM recognition event where former NFL quarterback Joe Theismann was one of the keynote speakers. Theismann's audience included many people from IBM operations in the Far East and Latin America, both of which are largely collectivistic in outlook. Although most North Americans in the audience responded positively to Theismann's speech, not everyone did. His remarks were perceived as egotistical and self-aggrandizing by people from such places as Japan, Taiwan, Singapore, Argentina, and Venezuela. As one person from Buenos Aires remarked, "You would have thought American football was an individual sport listening to him [Theismann]—that he won the Super Bowl single-handedly. Does he know a word other than I?"

All too often speakers choose language appropriate to their culture, but not necessarily to the cultures of their audience members. Like Theismann, they naively assume that what is good enough for their culture is good enough for everyone's. Of course, this kind of thinking is not only inaccurate, it is arrogant.

Even commonplace language choices, such as what name to call a person, can be influenced by culture. In many, such as those that use the Spanish language, strangers are not addressed informally, and certainly not by their first names. A salesperson, for example, who addresses a potential client by his or her first name may, unintentionally, offend that person. Yet this is commonplace in the United States. The best advice is to ask people how they prefer to be addressed rather than automatically assuming that they want to be on a first-name basis.

As we discussed in Chapter 5, Geert Hofstede's dimensions of culture include differences in how cultures deal with issues of power, uncertainty, and the like.

Last year, people skied on champagne powder, windblown pack, groomed, corn snow, cold smoke, frozen granular, firm, good crud, bottomless powder, sugar, machine tilled, crust, hero powder, buffed snow, man made, corduroy, ball bearings, velvet, cut up powder, spring snow, ballroom, and acre after acre of virgin powder.

[Eskimos may have more words for snow, but we have more lifts.]

THE ASPENS
SNOWMASS · BUTTERMILK
ASPEN MOUNTAIN

Aspen Central Reservations 1-800-262-7736 Snowmass Central Reservations 1-800-332-3245.
The Aspen Skiing Company Hotels: The Little Nell, The Snowmass Club 1-800-525-6200.

This ad uses words to describe snow conditions rich in imagery for skiers and snowboarders but meaningless for those not involved in these sports.

Courtesy Hal Riney & Partners Inc.

For an example of how such dimensions are related to the languages we use, see the box "Considering Diversity: Language, Culture, and Airline Safety."

Language and Demographic Diversity

Recall from Chapter 5 that *demographic diversity* is reflected in the groups to which people belong and with which they identify. This includes such characteristics as nationality, race and ethnicity, gender, and religion. Demographic diversity also includes social and economic class, the region of the country that people call home, and the generation to which people belong.

CONSIDERING DIVERSITY

Language, Culture, and Airline Safety

Best-selling author Malcolm Gladwell tells the story of how an airline with one of the worst safety records in aviation became one of the safest, largely by changing the language spoken by its pilots and crew.[1]

Between 1988 and 1998, Korean airlines had one of the worst safety records of any major airline. It was seventeen times more dangerous to fly than United. The U.S. Army would not even allow its troops to fly Korean Air.

On Hofstede's power distance index, South Korea was second only to Brazil in the deference paid by subordinates to superiors. Further, the Korean language has six levels of conversational address, and a crewmember would not dare to use a familiar or intimate form with a pilot. This could lead to tragedy when a pilot was headed for danger. For example, on August 5, 1997, Korean Air Flight 801 flew into a mountain trying to execute a visual landing in a storm despite the first officer's comment to the captain, "The weather radar has helped us a lot." What he meant was they were in danger of crashing and they needed to switch from a visual approach and rely on radar. But with the power difference embedded in his culture, he dared not use language that would imply the captain had made an error. In fact, he used what's called "mitigated speech," which relies on the receiver to understand what is implied in the message. This is in contrast to Western languages that have a "transmitter orientation," where the onus is on the speaker to communicate clearly and unambiguously.

The upshot of the investigations of this and the other Korean Air crashes was the hiring of David Greenberg of Delta to run flight operations. He instituted a policy that required all flight crews to be proficient in English and conducted all training in English. Greenberg decreed: "The new language of Korean Air was English . . ."[2] In Gladwell's words, "Greenberg wanted to give his pilots an alternate identity. . . . They needed an opportunity to step outside those [cultural] roles when they sat in the cockpit, and language was the key to that transformation."[3]

The result: Since 1999, Korean Air has had an unblemished safety record. Today, it is one of the safest airlines in the world.

[1]Malcolm Gladwell, *Outliers: The Story of Success* (New York: Little, Brown, and Co., 2008), 177–223.
[2]Gladwell, *Outliers,* 218.
[3]Gladwell, *Outliers,* 219.

Demographic diversity, although always important in a speaker's audience analysis, has become even more so. Today's college classroom is likely to be populated by people with a variety of different demographic backgrounds. Race and ethnicity, as cases in point, are often an important part of today's audience diversity.

How we refer to a specific racial or ethnic group can have a strong impact on the individual members of that group in our audience. For example, when Anglos speak to a gathering of English-speaking people of Mexican descent, they need to choose the appropriate language in referring to the audience. Scholars Mario Garcia and Rodolfo Alvarez suggest that people of Mexican descent in the United States constitute several rather than a single demographic group.[4] Two such reference groups are Mexican Americans and Chicanos/Chicanas. The Mexican American group comprises people who immigrated from Mexico to border states, such as California and Texas, following World War II. According to Garcia and Alvarez, people who consider themselves Mexican Americans are generally older and more conservative than those who identify themselves as Chicanos or Chicanas, who are generally younger and more militant.

Chicanos and Chicanas came of age in the 1960s and gained some attention in the 1970s. They perceived Mexican immigrants who wanted to assimilate with the predominant Anglo culture as sellouts. To distinguish themselves from the Mexican American group, Chicanos and Chicanas adopted specific patterns of behaving, including their own code words. The list of code words included *vendido* (sellout) and *socios* (the old boy network). Today, members of this demographic group sometimes refer to each other as *veteranos* (veterans). Thus,

The 2006 Sundance Film Festival award winner, *Quinceañera,* tells the story of a young Latina girl, Magdalena, who becomes pregnant on the brink of her 15 birthday and is cast out by her parents, forcing her to live in a very different culture than that of her middle class upbringing.

referring to Chicanos/Chicanas as Mexican Americans in a speech could prove inappropriate even though you were trying to be responsive to ethnicity. As speakers, we need to learn as much as possible about the language preferences of our audiences. Otherwise, we may inadvertently lose at least some of them.

The varied preferences of Spanish-speaking people apply to many other demographic groups as well. Some African Americans prefer being referred to as Black. And though they may be too polite to tell you so, the Chinese, Hmong, Japanese, Korean, Laotian, and Vietnamese prefer being referred to by their ancestral origins rather than being categorized as Asian.

As speakers, we cannot afford to overlook the demography of our audience in choosing language. How we refer to people who identify themselves with specific demographic groups and the words we use in talking about the demographic groups themselves will influence not only how the content of our speech is received but audience perceptions of our credibility as well.

Language and Individual Diversity

Choosing appropriate language for a speech doesn't stop with a consideration of cultural and demographic diversity. We also must consider and evaluate *individual diversity,* which reflects such factors as personal views on the meaning of gender, sexual orientation, and religious beliefs. The fact that someone is Catholic, Jewish, Muslim, Hindu, or Protestant, for example, doesn't tell us much about the diversity of beliefs held by people who consider themselves members of one of these religious groups. Moreover, religious beliefs are only one element of the individual diversity of our audience. Consequently, before choosing the language with which to construct a speech, we will also have to explore other individual beliefs, attitudes, and values of the people in our audience.

As a case in point, think about an audience of people who describe themselves as Christians. Such people are extraordinarily diverse in what they believe individually. Some think the Bible is to be taken literally as the word of God; others believe the Bible should be interpreted metaphorically. In the same vein, Orthodox and Reformed Jews frequently disagree about religious practices, as do Sunni and Shiite Muslims. Knowing this kind of information in advance is essential for speakers who want the language of their speech to be effective.

Remember, the words and sentences with which we construct the speech will influence the meaning of our speech in the minds of the audience members. We want to control this process as much as possible. Thus, doing our homework about the relationship between language and diversity as it reflects our speech transaction is a matter of common sense, not political correctness.

Tips and Tactics

Language and Audience Diversity

- Be mindful of how words and phrases can shape meaning.
- Consider how you use words to "frame" debates and discussions.
- Actively search for information about the role of language in cultures other than the one with which you most identify.
- Exercise caution when labeling demographic groups . . . don't assume that there is a one-size-fits-all word for people in ethnic or religious groups.
- When possible, use words and language that reflect the individual diversity in your audience.

Use Language Effectively

Let's assume that we have thoroughly analyzed how audience diversity should be reflected in our choice of words to construct our speech. We are now ready to begin writing the outline of our speech with language that will enhance our credibility with the audience and create a high degree of mutual understanding. There are a number of guidelines to follow in this process. The first rule is to choose language appropriate to the rhetorical situation. The second rule concerns choosing language that makes every member of our audience feel included in our message. This is known as inclusive language, as opposed to marginalizing or totalizing language, concepts we will explain shortly. The third rule concerns choosing language that will enhance rather than undermine audience perceptions of our competence and trustworthiness as a speaker.[5] The fourth rule concerns using language to its fullest potential to involve our audience in the speech. The fifth rule focuses on using language that will help us manage our speech, and help our audience understand what we want to communicate.

Use Language Appropriate to the Rhetorical Situation

The language of a speech needs to reflect the overall rhetorical situation we face, not just audience diversity. In addition language also should be appropriate to the context in which we find ourselves. We've learned that we can face the same or similar audience in very different contexts. For example, we have given speeches honoring a retiring colleague to an audience that also has listened to us speak in opposition to a policy proposed by the university administration. Although the audience was the same, our rhetoric, in style and in substance, was different.

Along the same lines, language should reflect the purpose of a speech and the goal we hope to achieve. An informative speech demonstrating how to read a company's annual report requires language very different from a persuasive speech advocating the replacement of the company's Board of Directors.

Use Inclusive Language

The next rule in choosing the words of a speech is to use language that is inclusive. **Inclusive language** helps people believe that they not only have a stake in matters of societal importance but also have power in this regard. Inclusive language doesn't leave people out of the picture because of their gender, race, ethnicity, age, religion, sexual orientation, or ability.

Inclusive language is an important aspect of being civically and civilly engaged by recognizing that we are all part of a larger community. Put another way, inclusive language doesn't marginalize people.

Marginalizing language diminishes people's importance and makes them appear to be less powerful, less significant, and less worthwhile than they are. Marginalizing language also appeals to biases audience members may hold consciously or subconsciously.

At the same time, inclusive language doesn't totalize people.

Totalizing language defines people on the basis of a single attribute, such as race, ethnicity, biological sex, or disability. In a speech, the following statements would exemplify totalizing:

"John's a victim of cystic fibrosis."

"Don't forget that Susan's wheelchair bound!"

"The Howards' baby is physically challenged."

Each of these statements could be well-meaning and intended to demonstrate the speaker's sensitivity to people with disabilities. Yet what each statement does in reality is call attention to a single attribute among audience members and treat the attribute as if it were the only thing about audience members that truly counts. People are more than their disability. Speakers need to use language that acknowledges that people are complex individuals.

According to the Disability Support Services on our campus, persons with disabilities prefer the following descriptors to the first set we listed for you:

"John has cystic fibrosis."

"Don't forget that Susan uses a wheelchair."

"The Howards' baby has a disability."

Thus, we want to remind you of Lincoln's admonition: "'Tis better to be silent and be thought a fool, than to speak and remove all doubt."[6] When in doubt about words and their consequences, consult an authority.

inclusive language
Language that helps people believe that they not only have a stake in matters of societal importance but also have power in this regard.

marginalizing language
Language that diminishes people's importance and makes them appear to be less powerful, less significant, and less worthwhile than they are.

totalizing language
Language that defines people exclusively on the basis of a single attribute, such as race, ethnicity, biological sex, or disability.

Of course, it is not just people with disabilities who are stereotyped. Stereotyping occurs when people make generalizations about a whole group of people and then apply those generalizations indiscriminately to anyone from that group. Generally, these stereotypes are negative–think of blonde jokes. However, positive stereotypes can be erroneous too–not everyone who wears glasses is smart. Just because someone belongs to a particular group of people is no guarantee that he or she shares all the attributes commonly associated with that group.

People in different professions, of different ethnicities, and with different sexual orientations, to name just a few categories, are frequently the subject of stereotypic language. The competent speaker avoids such stereotypes.

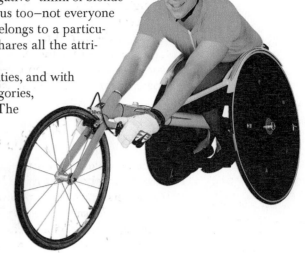

This athlete disproves stereotypes about persons with physical disabilities.

Sexist language is language that stereotypes gender roles–for example, terms such as *housewife* and *fireman*. Why is sexist language a problem? It conveys, intentionally or not, a stereotype of certain roles and functions, based on biological sex. When the head of an academic department is referred to as a chair*man*, a member of the U.S. House of Representatives is called a congress*man,* and a flight attendant on an airplane is known as a steward*ess,* it is clear which roles are held to be "male" and which ones "female." An effective public speaker avoids sexist language.

One of the easiest ways to unintentionally convey sexism is to use singular pronouns in the masculine form. For years, speakers and writers excluded women from their examples involving a single person, saying such things as "If a person is strong, he will stand up for himself."

If we have no other choice in constructing examples to illustrate our speech, we can do one of two things with regard to singular pronouns. First, we can say "he or she" or "she or he" in conjunction with a singular verb. Second, we can use "she" in some cases and "he" in others. Yet both of these alternatives are awkward, and neither is likely to please everyone in our audience. Thus, we suggest a third alternative: Use plural nouns and pronouns when constructing examples to make the speech more vivid, involving, and inclusive. Instead of saying, "If a person is strong, he will stand up for himself," say, "Strong people stand up for themselves."

It is not just biological sex that can lead to language that stereotypes people. Consider also language that pigeonholes people in terms of their sexual orientation. Unless a person's sexual orientation is directly related to the topic in question, our best advice is to avoid mentioning it, as it is likely to be perceived as totalizing language. It should go without saying that words that denigrate or are offensive to gays, lesbians, bisexuals, and transgendered persons should be avoided.

Finally, inclusive language is **immediate language;** it reduces the perception that people are psychologically distant from each other–with little or nothing in common. Remember the example of Joe Theismann? His use of the personal pronoun "I" actually made him seem more distant from members of the audience. Inclusive language emphasizes the fact that a speaker and audience are

sexist language
Language, including terms such as *housewife* and *fireman,* that stereotypes gender roles.

immediate language
Language that reduces the psychological distance that separates speakers and audience members and stresses that speech is a transaction.

IN THEIR OWN WORDS

"We, the People" *by Barbara Jordan*

We are dedicated to keeping the memory of Barbara Jordan alive. Recipient of the Presidential Medal of Freedom, Congresswoman and State Senator from Texas, she was arguably one of the most gifted speakers of the 20th century. Many experts regard her keynote address to the Democratic Convention in 1976 as the top political speech in modern history. Here is a brief excerpt of her statements during the debate on the impeachment of President Nixon in 1974:

We, the people. It is a very eloquent beginning. But when that document was completed on the 17th of September in 1787, I was not included in that "We, the people." I felt somehow for many years that George Washington and Alexander Hamilton just left me out by mistake. But through the process of amendment, interpretation and court decision I have finally been included in "We, the people."[1]

Two decades later, Jordan was asked to head the United States Commission on Immigration Reform. Testifying before the very congressional committee of which she was once a member, Jordan echoed her words from long ago:

I would be the last person to claim that our nation is perfect. But we have a kind of perfection in us because our founding principle is universal—that we are all created equal regardless of race, religion or national ancestry. When the Declaration of Independence was written, when the Constitution was adopted, when the Bill of Rights was added to it, they all applied almost exclusively to white men of Anglo-Saxon descent who owned property on the East Coast. They did not apply to me. I am female. I am black. But these self-evident principles apply to me now as they apply to everyone in this room.[2]

[1]"Barbara Jordan: A Passionate Voice," *Sacramento Bee*, 18 January 1996, A16.
[2]Jerelyn Eddings, "The Voice of Eloquent Thunder," *U.S. News and World Report*, 29 January 1996, 16.

a collective rather than two separate entities. For example, the late Barbara Jordan not only used immediate language in her distinguished political career, she also spoke eloquently about inclusive speech. Both facts are featured in the box "In Their Own Words: We, the People," printed above.

Lest you think otherwise, inclusive language is not the same as the politically correct language talk show hosts justifiably satirize. Inclusive language is firmly rooted in the ethical principles we introduced in Chapter 3. Consider inclusive language in terms of Immanuel Kant's categorical imperative. Have you ever had someone use language to purposely hurt you? Did you think the language was justified or mean-spirited?

We need to think through what motivates us to use certain words and phrases before we use them. We also need to weigh the possible consequences of these words and phrases before speaking them. And we need to ask ourselves ahead of time, how would we interpret and respond to words and phrases if they or their equivalents were directed at us?

Less Immediate	More Immediate
I Me You Them	We Us
I think It's my opinion I know	Wouldn't you agree? How many of us believe . . . ?
Tell Show Explain	Share Look at
Talk to	Talk with

Exhibit 10.1
How to Say It More Immediately

We are not saying that you must avoid critical words and phrases in your verbal characterizations of people. We are simply asking you to put the shoe on the other foot to first measure how you think you would respond in similar circumstances.

Tips and Tactics

Inclusive Language

1. Inclusive language avoids defining people on the basis of their gender, sexual orientation, disability, racial, ethnic, or religious identity. Inclusive language uses terms such as *humankind* rather than *mankind, athlete* rather than *woman athlete,* and *friend* rather than *Islamic friend.*

2. Inclusive language reflects the self-referents used by the members of a minority group; for example, *gay* or *lesbian* rather than *homosexuals* and *person with a disability* rather than *disabled person.*

3. Inclusive language is immediate. As you can read in Exhibit 10.1, it's about *we* rather than *me* and *us* rather than *you and I.*

Use Credibility-Enhancing Language

In Chapter 3 we discussed credibility in terms of the relationship between ethical conduct and perceptions of the speaker's trustworthiness. Here we want to emphasize that credibility also depends on whether audience members perceive that a speaker is a competent source of information. Does the speaker appear to know what he or she is talking about?

How speakers use language influences perceptions of competence in the eyes of audience members. For example, a number of researchers have documented that there is a difference between "powerful" and "powerless" speech.[7] Powerless speech is characterized by the use of language such as hedges (I *kind of* agree with you), qualifiers (I *could* be wrong), hesitations (uhs and ums), and tag questions

(That's right, *isn't it?*). On the other hand, powerful speech is fluent and direct and avoids these types of phrases. Messages containing a significant amount of powerless language produce lower ratings of a speaker's competence and attractiveness, whereas powerful speech produces higher ratings on these dimensions.

Therefore, the third rule to follow in constructing the text of our speech is to use powerful, **credibility-enhancing language,** words that emphasize rather than undermine audience perceptions of our competence. Language that enhances perceptions of competence avoids verbal qualifiers.[8] **Verbal qualifiers** erode the impact of what we say in a speech.

Beginning speakers often use verbal qualifiers without thinking of them as such. They say, for example:

> "It's just my opinion, but . . ."
>
> "You'll probably disagree, but . . ."
>
> "This is my belief, but you may think otherwise."
>
> "I'm pretty sure, though I could be wrong in stating . . ."
>
> "Of course, your opinion counts at least as much as mine."

Credibility-enhancing language emphasizes the significance of what we say in a speech. Whether giving an informative, persuasive, or testimonial speech, we should be the expert on the subject or person. Not only does this require that we do our homework, it also requires that we choose language that illustrates the fact. Using language such as the following is one way of accomplishing this without appearing to be a "know-it-all" to the audience.

> "Ten years of research as summarized on the NASA Web site demonstrates that . . ."
>
> "For the past four summers, I've been involved with . . ."
>
> "I recently was certified to . . ."
>
> "Scholars such as the late Carl Sagan tell us . . ."

Each of these statements begins with a phrase that emphasizes the speaker's credibility. They imply that through either research or experience, the speaker knows his or her subject well. We should not exaggerate claims beyond what we know to be true, but we should take full credit for the facts as we know them. This is not to say that we should never qualify what we say. In persuasive speeches, especially, the evidence may demand that we temper the claims we make. It is unethical to make an absolute claim in a persuasive speech when the evidence only partly supports the claim. This is another reason for conducting research on the topic prior to constructing a speech.

There are other ways to use language to increase the audience's perception of our competence. Some of the best are also the most obvious. They include using correct grammar, correct pronunciation, and correct usage of a word. Although we can get away with grammatically incorrect language in conversation, it usually sticks out like a sore thumb when speaking in public.

Grammar

Like it or not, grammar affects how others see us. In an otherwise effective speech on educational reform, for example, former president Bush asked his audience, "Is your children learning?" He meant to say, "Are your children

---

credibility-enhancing language
Words that emphasize rather than undermine audience perceptions of a speaker's competence.

verbal qualifiers
Words and phrases that erode the impact of what a speaker says in a speech.

learning?" Although this was but a single grammatical mistake, it became the most memorable part of the speech in terms of what was written and said about it afterwards.

Some of the most common grammatical mistakes we hear in our own students' speech are double negatives, incorrect subject-verb agreement, and inappropriate slang.

A double negative occurs when someone uses a negative to modify another negative. As in mathematics, a negative times a negative is actually a positive. Thus, "No one never works around here" really means that there is no person who "never works." That suggests people really do work—the opposite of what the speaker intended.

Incorrect subject-verb agreement occurs when a plural subject is matched with a singular verb or vice versa. Avoid such sentences as "We is going to the movies."

Finally, unless they are essential to the speech, certain expressions common in everyday conversation are inappropriate in a speech. Many speech teachers object in particular to the overuse of "you know," "you guys," and "like." It is irritating to hear, "You know, like, I really mean it, you guys."

This is far from a complete list of grammatical pitfalls for the speaker. A speech is not as formal as written English. Although you traditionally are not supposed to end a sentence with a preposition, it is not uncommon to hear someone say, "I know what it's all about." The best advice we can give is that if you are in doubt about any grammatical issues, consult someone who is knowledgeable and ask his or her advice, or check a grammar handbook or style manual, such as Strunk and White's *The Elements of Style*.

Pronunciation

It is easy to mispronounce a word, especially when it is a word we do not routinely use or have heard others use incorrectly. For example, how do you pronounce the word *nuclear*? Many people, including those in positions of authority, pronounce it "nuk-u-lar." The correct pronunciation is "nuk-le-ur." How do you pronounce the word *vehicle*? Many people pronounce it "ve-hick-ul." The correct pronunciation is "ve-ik-ul." Mispronunciation of words may seem a picky point to you. Yet when speaking before an educated audience, mispronunciation is one of the surest ways to be perceived as incompetent.

Mispronunciation of words can lead to problems other than your competence being undermined. One of the most significant involves meaning. Frequently, for example, people say "assure" when they mean "ensure." Assuring your child that she is safe is not the same as ensuring the safety of your child. *Assure* and *ensure* mean two different things.

Usage

Incorrect usage of a word is another credibility-detracting issue we want to caution you about. We hear many students who confuse the words *except* and *accept*. We also hear students use the terms *irregardless* and *orientated* when what they really mean is *regardless* and *oriented*. Again, this may strike you as picky on our part. But it's not. When we hear people use words inaccurately, it opens the door for us to question their credibility in areas other than language as well.

Truthfulness

Perceptions of a speaker's credibility are not just based on audience perceptions of the speaker's competence. Audiences also must believe that the speaker is trustworthy. As a result, speakers need to make sure that the words they use to make a point are borne out by their actions. Saying one thing and doing another has a way of catching up with people. This is especially true in an age of You-Tube, Facebook, and *The Daily Show*. More than a few college students have had the words on their résumés contradicted by their actions on either Facebook or YouTube. And more than a few politicians have been caught by Jon Stewart and his staff saying one thing and doing something completely opposite.

Tips and Tactics

Credibility-Enhancing Language

1. Avoid qualifiers such as *I'm pretty sure* or *I'm kind of certain.* Instead, assert yourself with statements such as *I'm convinced, I strongly believe,* or *I am of the firm belief.*

2. Avoid tag questions that make it seem as if you are uncertain. For example, instead of saying, "I think this is a problem but you may not," say, "This is a problem for all of us." Avoid saying, "I believe we have no other choice, what do you think?" Instead, say, "Wouldn't you agree that we have no other choice?"

3. Don't be afraid to interject experience or training that gives you expertise or insight to your topic. Personal experience is a powerful form of evidence in the eyes of the audience. Share with your audience the fact that "I've now been rock climbing for over three years"; or "Proper nutrition is not only something I try to practice, it's a subject in which I've taken two courses"; or "This past year marked my tenth year of being smoke free."

4. Use familiar words. When we are not familiar with a word, we are more prone to mispronounce or misuse it. If the listeners are unfamiliar with the word, they will fail to understand our meaning even when the word is used correctly. Our best advice is to stick to words that are familiar to both the audience and speaker.

5. Use a dictionary so that when you do incorporate a word you do not routinely use in your speech, you can find out the word's denotative meaning and phonetically correct pronunciation. Some online dictionaries have audio pronunciations. Watch out for words that sound similar but mean different things, such as *except* and *accept, access* and *assess,* or *ask* and *axe.* Also watch out for words that are spelled and pronounced alike but may have different meanings depending on usage (homonyms). For example, the word *quail* can be used in reference to a type of bird or in reference to cowering in terror.

6. Don't use language that plays fast and loose with the truth.

Use Language to Its Fullest Potential

Language, as the surprise-hit documentary *Wordplay* shows, is food for the mind. In fact, there is increasing evidence that using language to its fullest potential can help thwart degenerative diseases such as Alzheimer's. Thus the fourth rule, using language to its fullest potential in your speeches, will feed your brain at the same time it makes you a better speaker.

Of the many ways you can use language, we encourage you to first take advantage of:

- Language appropriate to the diverse ways audience members process information.
- Language that shows and tells what you hope to share in your speech.
- Language that is rhythmic.
- Language that varies the intensity of your speech.

Visual, Auditory, and Kinesthetic Speech

In the 1980s Professor Howard Gardner introduced the idea that not all people process information the same way. He also pointed out that whether people process what they are being taught depends on whether it is conveyed to them through a channel appropriate to their "preferred" style of information processing.[9]

Research shows that some people need to see a lesson, others need only to hear it, and still others need to become immersed in the subject matter. These three styles of learning are technically called visual, auditory, and kinesthetic. The obvious way for a speaker to deal with these three is to augment a speech with visual aids, speak audibly and clearly, or involve the audience in demonstrations or other hands-on experiences. Yet sometimes options one and three are impossible for a speaker.

To get around this fact, author and corporate trainer Loretta Malandro encourages her clients to connect metaphorically with the varied learning styles present in most audiences. Exhibit 10.2 on page 238 suggests a number of specific visual, auditory, and kinesthetic words that help the audience better process a speech.

Although we may not be able to literally show our audience members prejudice, we can connect with visual learners by

- asking them to envision a world free of hate,
- drawing a picture of racism or sketching out an example for them, or
- making a hazy concept such as affirmative action crystal clear so that they can see the problem.

Although we may not be able to let them literally feel our thoughts, we can connect with audience members who need to experience some things by asking them to imagine

- what racism feels like,
- that a problem is a giant weight pressing down on them, or
- how oppressed people hunger for freedom.

Exhibit 10.2
Words Linked to Vision,
Hearing, and Touch

VISUAL WORDS			
Focus	Graphic	Watch	Colorful
Bright	Illustrate	Vision	Glimpse
Show	Color	Brilliant	Look
Pretty	See	Evident	Sight
Envision	Picture	Sketch	Shining
Draw	Hazy	Oversight	Hidden
View	Peek	Clearly	Notice
Clear	Imagine	Perspective	

AUDITORY WORDS			
Listen	Ringing	Compliment	Pardon
Hear	Resonate	Loud	Sound
Discuss	Yell	Silent	Request
Declare	Told	Shout	Whispering
Implore	Call	Talk	Quiet
Acclaim	Assert	Noisy	Ask
Harmony	Profess	Orchestrate	
Petition	Noise	Address	

KINESTHETIC WORDS			
Feel	Terrified	Hunger	Contact
Pressure	Burdensome	Doubt	Nurture
Hurt	Firm	Shocking	Emotion
Get the point	Tense	Heavy	Graceful
Experience	Touchy	Touch	Sensual
Longing	Pushy	Concrete	Weighty problem
Wait	Shatter	Irritated	

And though we may not be able to literally produce the sound of abused children for our audience members, we can connect to auditory learners by asking them:

- whether they hear what we are trying to say,
- to imagine what it's like to live in a world where they cannot speak out for themselves, or
- to imagine the mournful sound of children crying.

The point is simple. Not everyone in the audience will respond in a like manner to the words we speak. Thus, to maximize audience members' receptivity to what we say, we must make every effort to use expressive words that reflect their different styles of information processing.

Words That Show and Tell

One of the best ways to respond to the diverse styles of information processing in your audience, is to combine the preceding suggestions with language that helps you show *and* tell your audience what's on your mind. For example, metaphors, similes, and analogies help audiences see and listen to your speech.

Metaphor is one of the most powerful sources of expressive language. A metaphor is a figure of speech in which a word or phrase literally denoting one kind of object or idea is used in place of another to suggest a likeness or an analogy between them. It's one thing, for example, to say that a corporation is "polluting the environment." It's quite another to say that the same corporation is "raping virgin timberland." To say that "freedom is an open window" or that "music unshackles the mind and spirit" would be metaphorical. Metaphors provide an audience with a kind of linguistic break from the expected. Thus, just when audience members may be losing interest in a speech, a phrase or word can grab them by the lapels and help them "see" what we are trying to say.

Metaphors should fit the topic. For example, sports metaphors are often used in the popular media to describe political contests. Thus, a political candidate who does well in a debate "hits a home run," whereas a less successful candidate "strikes out." Sometimes a desperate politician is said to "throw a Hail Mary pass," while the favored candidate is said to "sit on a lead." Be careful, however, not to mix metaphors. It sounds odd to say, "He scored a touchdown while steering the ship of state through troubled waters." Metaphors can add spice and interest to a speech, but they must be used appropriately.

Simile is a form of figurative language that invites a direct comparison between two things that are quite different. A simile usually contains the word *like* or *as.* "Sharp as a tack," "tight as a snare drum," and "pointed as an ice pick" are examples of simile. Similes can also be used effectively to "show" the audience what we are attempting to communicate.

Similes differ from metaphors in that they explicitly state the comparison, whereas metaphors imply it. Similes are useful, therefore, in making a comparison very clear to the audience. For example, a speech on preventing sexually transmitted diseases might use a simile such as "Having unprotected sex is like playing roulette with a 357 Magnum." On a topic such as drunk driving, you might say, "Drunken drivers are like unguided missiles."

Analogies are extended metaphors or similes. Analogies can be effective in helping an audience imagine something you are trying to describe. In an informative speech on writing a basic software program, for example, one of our students used a cooking recipe to help students follow along. In another informative speech, we had a student describe fly-fishing for wild trout as analogous to chasing butterflies with a net.

Our use of metaphor, simile, and analogy in speeches is limited only by our imagination. What's more, we can get ideas for their effective use from listening to other speakers and from reading both fiction and nonfiction works.

Rhythmic Speech

Rhythm is part of the natural order. We often hear people speak about the "rhythm of life" or the "rhythm of the season." Perhaps this is the reason we are so easily drawn to beating drums and chanting people. In any case, the best speakers know that a speech needs rhythm every bit as much as does the DJ at a

metaphor

A figure of speech in which words and phrases that are primarily understood to mean one thing are used in place of another to suggest likeness or an analogy between them. Race car drivers, for example, may have to "wrestle with" a car that is difficult to control.

simile

Invites the listener to make a direct comparison between two things or objects that are quite different, such as "my roommate lives like a pig in slop" or is "dumb as a rock."

analogy

An extended metaphor or simile. Suggesting that the rebuilding of Iraq is much like rebuilding Germany and Japan after World War II is an analogy.

dance club. To create rhythm, speakers commonly use alliteration, parallelism repetition, and antithesis.

Alliteration is the repetition of the same initial sound in a series of words. You may recall that the Wizard of Oz loved alliteration, referring to the Tin Man as a "**c**linking, **c**lanking, **c**lattering **c**ollection of **c**aliginous junk," and the Scarecrow as a "**b**illowing **b**ale of **b**ovine fodder!"[10]

One of the most famous alliterations of American political history came from former vice president Spiro Agnew, who called his opponents in the media "nattering nabobs of negativism." The power of alliteration comes from the way it sticks in audience members' minds. The danger is that if the alliteration seems forced, it may be memorable, but ineffective.

Parallelism is the "similarity of structure in a pair or series of related words, phrases, or clauses."[11] It helps the audience remember our key ideas and fulfills their expectations for symmetry. For example, consider Jesse Jackson's words: "Today's students can put dope in their veins or hope in their brains. If they can conceive it and believe it, they can achieve it. They must know it is not their aptitude but their attitude that will determine their altitude."[12] Not only is the structure similar, the use of rhyming words (*dope-hope, veins-brains*) and the use of alliteration (*aptitude, attitude, altitude*) give the statement its power.

Parallelism can extend to the construction of the main points of a speech when each main point begins with the same or similar phrase. In many respects that's what occurs when a speech follows the wave pattern, discussed in Chapter 9. When Martin Luther King Jr. began a series of main points with "I have a dream . . . ," he was using parallelism. The use of parallelism helps audiences anticipate the points to come and remember them when the speech is over. However, be careful to use parallelism that fits the speech. If not, it will seem forced and artificial.

Repetition is the use of the same words repeatedly in a speech to drive home a point. Unlike parallelism, in which the same phrase is used only to build each main point, repetition uses a word or phrase repeatedly throughout the speech to emphasize the essential point that the speaker seeks to convey. If you recall the words by Barbara Jordan in the box on page 232, you will note that the phrase "We, the people" is repeated three times in one short excerpt. Her theme is clearly conveyed by that one phrase, taken from the U.S. Constitution.

Antithesis involves the use of opposites. In addition to adding another rhythmic element to a speech, language that links opposites can add intensity and even urgency to a speech. History is replete with speeches that feature antithesis and range from Jesus' declaration that the "last will be first" to President Theodore Roosevelt's promise to "speak softly and carry a big stick."

Another example of antithesis is the contemporary use of the term "Chicken Hawk." It has commonly been applied to describe militaristic politicians who advocate the use of the armed forces, even though these politicians have never served in the armed forces in peacetime much less during war.

Language Intensity

The degree to which words and phrases deviate from neutral affects **language intensity.** The intensity of words varies along a continuum ranging from relatively neutral to highly intense. For example, *savory* and *delicious* are more intense than *tastes good.* By the same token, the phrase *I find you attractive* is not nearly as intense as *you rock my world.* Intense language is much more likely to

antithesis
The use of opposites, e.g., light–dark.

language intensity
The degree to which words and phrases deviate from neutral.

enlist the attention of the audience than neutral language. We can increase language intensity by using action words and humorous language. We can also increase intensity with metaphor and simile, which we have already discussed.

Action Words Try to use words that are exciting and action oriented. For example, which do you find more involving, "The speech was well received" or "The speech was a knockout"? What about "He got mad" versus "He went ballistic"? How about "dunk" versus "monster slam" or "excited" versus "out-of-control"? Action words and action-loaded metaphors help listeners picture what you say.

Humor In Chapter 8 we talked about using humor to open a speech. The guidelines for using humor we discussed there apply to this discussion as well. Humor should be appropriate and relevant to our topic or the occasion and mindful of the diversity in our audience.

Although humorous language can increase the intensity of a speech, not all speakers are well suited to using it. Some people really can't tell a joke. If you count yourself in this latter group, don't try being something you are not. On the other hand, if humor is customary to your communication style, use it to your advantage. Poke fun at yourself but not at your audience. Tell a joke you have successfully told before, if appropriate. And share humorous anecdotes you have shared before if they suit your speech purpose.

Contrast and Action A final way to intensify language is to incorporate contrasting phrases and words that suggest action. In discussing the irrationality that often grips the minds of people when going to war, German philosopher Friedrich Nietzsche wrote, "How good . . . bad music and bad reasons sound when we march against the enemy."[13] Nietzsche's simple contrast between good and bad is much more effective in making war seem illogical than any extended discussion would have been.

Manage Language Effectively

Finally, consider some guidelines for managing language effectively. This involves using language that helps audience members understand the intended meaning of our message and avoids unneccessarily alienating audience members. We offer several guidelines to achieve those goals.

Define Terms

As discussed in Chapter 4, words have denotative and connotative meanings. If we look in the dictionary for the definition of a word, the first entry we will find is the most agreed-upon meaning for the word when the dictionary was published. This is also the denotative meaning of the word.

Connotative meanings for a word evolve over time. Usually, connotative meanings are given birth by groups of people bound by some collective purpose or activity. The word *nose* means the tip of the board to surfers, for example, but also may refer to the fragrance of a newly opened bottle of wine to the connoisseur.

Because words have both denotative and connotative meanings, we must be careful in our assumptions about shared meaning with an audience. We should never assume that the meaning we most commonly assign to a word will always be the same for our audience. When in doubt, then, it is in everyone's interest to define our terms in the course of our speeches.

Be Careful With Colloquial Words and Idioms

Our everyday conversations are liberally peppered with colloquial words and idioms. The temptation to use them in formal speech and writing is understandable. Even so, they should be avoided. Conversational colloquialisms such as "gonna," "gotta," or "wanna" undermine audience perceptions of credibility. Sarah Palin's use of colloquialisms, such as "You betcha," was a gold mine for comic Tina Fey, who mercilessly (and many would say unfairly) satirized the vice presidential nominee in 2008. For the non-native speakers in your audience, they are also likely to be meaningless.

This happens even more so with idioms. These figures of speech have highly idiosyncratic use and meaning. While we may know what it means when someone gets "antsy" or is "all ears," non-native speakers probably would be baffled by the term and expression. Because idioms also can be regional, native speakers also can be confused in this regard. For example, whereas Southern Californians are likely to think of the word "ramp" as an entrance or exit from the freeway, a Southern West Virginian, upon hearing the word, is more likely to think of a pungent plant that is the focus of festivals in the spring.

Use Concrete Words and Phrases

Speakers do not always use language to enlighten an audience. Sometimes speakers intentionally use language to keep their audience in the dark. Political consultants will tell reporters that a candidate misspoke rather than said something stupid. Military spokespeople will tell an audience that collateral damage occurred rather than candidly admit innocent civilians were injured or killed. And the spokesperson for a company will announce to the general public that it is "right sizing" the workforce, when it would be more accurate to say 1,000 employees were losing their jobs.

We do ourselves and our audience a favor when we speak in concrete language. Concrete language consists of words and phrases that increase the chance of our audience interpreting the meaning of our message as intended. Put another way, concrete language is void of words and phrases so abstract that each person in our audience can walk away from the speech with a different interpretation of what was said.

The easiest way to make language concrete is to use words our audience recognizes and routinely uses; for example, *cat* instead of *feline*, *sneaky* rather than *surreptitious*, *book* rather than *tome*, and *abusive* rather than *vituperative language.* We can also make our language more concrete by providing our audience with details that will clarify our intended meaning. For example, instead of saying a person is tall or short, give the person's actual height. Rather than describing someone as a criminal, detail the nature of his or her crime or criminal record.

And rather than arguing that someone is either conservative or liberal, provide the audience with detailed evidence of the person's voting record.

Use Oral Language

The language in our speeches should look and sound more like the language of conversation than the language of written discourse. However, the language in our speeches needs to be a refined version of that used when conversing. We should strive to use language in our speeches that is grammatically sound and clearly enunciated. By the same token, we should feel free to use contractions more liberally in a speech, split all the infinitives we want, and end a thought with a preposition. Spoken thought and written sentences are similar but not identical. It's a good idea to read aloud and even record a speech. We can then listen critically to what we have said, and check to make sure that it sounds like we are conversing with rather than formally talking to our audience.

Keep It Simple

Less is often more in a speech. By that we mean simple words and simple sentences are usually better than polysyllabic words and compound, complex sentences. "Ask not what your country can do for you . . . but what you can do for your country," is much easier to hear and understand than the following:

> It's important that each of you gives some thought to the kinds of demands that you make on your government, and at the same time begin to think about the meaning of sacrifice, and what you possibly could do to help out your government and elected leaders.

When possible, it also is important to avoid jargon our audience may not fully understand. Although the term "cognitive dissonance" is fine when speaking to a group of psychologists, the term "buyer's remorse," which is a form of cognitive dissonance, is better suited to a general audience. If we find that there is no substitute for jargon, we must define the jargon in concrete terms for our audience.

Use Transitional Words and Phrases

Still another technique to manage a speech is to make effective use of transitions, which we explained in Chapter 8. We've repeatedly emphasized how important it is to let our audience know where we are going with our speech. You know from your own experience in taking lecture notes that it's much easier to follow an instructor who uses verbal transitions that alert you to changes in direction or clearly link one thought to another. You need to do the same for the members of your audience.

Transitional words and phrases tell our audience we are about to make a shift in direction. They also serve to verbally link our thoughts as we speak. It's always a good idea to let the audience know that there is a sequence to our message–"Let's consider three important issues"–and then to remind the audience where we are in that sequence–"Having covered the first issue, let's now look at the second."

It's also a good idea to let the audience know that the speech is about to end by using transitional words and phrases such as *lastly, to summarize, to conclude,* and *in closing.* Audiences are likely to grow impatient if they think a speech will never end.

Be Consistent

Because we are more accustomed to using informal language, making the switch to the oral language required in a speech can be difficult. One behavior we have observed with our own students when they speak is a form of *code switching*. This simply means that they sometimes switch back and forth between the language of public speaking and the language of informal conversation. For example, in the beginning of their speech they avoid colloquialisms and carefully enunciate their words. As they move further into their speech and feel more relaxed, though, they sometimes fall back into an informal style full of clipped words, idioms, and slang. Simply put, the language we use should be consistent through-out our speech. It's okay to be conversational in tone; it's not okay to treat our audience to language more appropriate to the street.

Avoid Slang Words and Perceived Obscenities

We subscribe to the adage, "when in doubt . . . leave it out." Slang words such as "dude" or "dawg" have their place. Normally, that place is not the classroom where you are learning and mastering the art and science of public speaking. If you are unsure about a word and whether it qualifies as slang, ask your instructor!

Also try to avoid words that may be perceived as obscene. We are not prudes in this respect. But we have learned personally over the years that obscenities are truly in the eye of the beholder. Words we regard as mild at worse have proven highly offensive to some of our students. How do we know? Because these students have felt offended enough to tell us outside of class.

In addition to avoiding slang and profanity, remember to use inclusive language, avoiding totalizing, marginalizing, and sexist words that can offend your audience. Ultimately, effective public speakers carefully analyze the rhetorical situation they face and use language that is appropriate to that situation and sensitive to preferences of the audience.

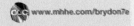 www.mhhe.com/brydon7e

To evaluate your understanding of this chapter, visit our Online Learning Center Web site for quizzes and other chapter study aids.

Summary

Although words alone can't break our bones, words are powerful symbols and should be treated as such. In recognition of this fact, keep the following in mind as you construct your speeches:

- Language is symbolic and influences the process of perception.

- Language reflects the multiracial, multiethnic, multicultural audience of today.

- Effective language is inclusive rather than marginalizing, totalizing, or sexist.

- Effective language enhances your audience's perception of your credibility.

- Effective language connects with the visual, auditory, and kinesthetic styles of processing information present in your audience.

- Effective language takes advantage of devices such as metaphor, simile, alliteration, antithesis, parallelism, and repetition.

- Intense language includes use of action words, humor, and words showing contrast and action.

- To manage language effectively, define terms, be careful with colloquial words and idioms, use concrete words and phrases, use oral language, keep language simple, use transitional words and phrases, be consistent, and avoid slang and obscenities.

Check Your Understanding: Exercises and Activities

1. Rewrite the following paragraph using inclusive language:

   When a speaker begins his speech, the first thing he must do is thank the chairman of the group for the opportunity to speak to his group. As we know, the quality that separates man from the animals is the ability to speak. Regardless of his job, a man must know how to speak clearly. Similarly, a woman must know how to impart language skills to her children. Thus, every speaker is urged to use language to the best of his ability.

2. Write five transitional statements without using the following words:

   first (second, third, etc.)

   therefore

   next

   finally

   in conclusion

3. Company X has an internal policies manual that is written in marginalizing language. As an employee of the company, you find the language disturbing and believe the language in the manual should be changed. Write a letter to the head of the documents division explaining why you believe such changes are necessary and why you believe the changes will enhance the image of the company. (Thanks to Dr. Madeline Keaveney for suggesting this exercise.)

4. Exclusive language is marginalizing and biased. Provide an inclusive-language alternative for each of the following, or state under what conditions the term might be appropriately used in a speech. [Adapted from Rosalie Maggio, *The Bias-Free Word Finder: A Dictionary of Nondiscriminatory Language* (Boston: Beacon Press, 1991).]

actress	meter maid
airline stewardess	mother
businessman	majorette
craftsmanship	Mrs. John Doe
doorman	old wives' tale
executrix	waitress
goddess	

Notes

1. W. H. Auden and L. Kronenberger, *The Viking Book of Aphorisms* (New York: Dorsett Press, 1981), 238.

2. Deborah Solomon, "The Wordsmith," *New York Times Magazine,* 24 May 2009, 17.

3. Shaila DeWan and Robbie Brown, "A Psychologist Helps Repackage Democrats' Message," *New York Times,* 29 October 2008. [Retrieved from http://www.nytimes.com/2008/10/30/us/politics/30message.html?_r=1&ref=politics&oref=slogin, 10 October 2008.]

4. Earl Shorris, Latinos: *A Biography of the People* (New York: Norton, 1992), 95–100.

5. Julia T. Wood, ed., *Gendered Relationships* (Mountain View, Calif.: Mayfield, 1996), 39–56.

6. Michael Moncur, *The Quotations Page,* 2007. [Retrieved from http://www.quotationspage.com/quote/844.html, 21 September 2009.]

7. See, for example: W. M. O'Barr, *Linguistic Evidence: Language, Power, and Strategy in the Courtroom* (New York: Academic Press, 1982); James J. Bradac and Anthony Mulac, "A Molecular View of Powerful and Powerless Speech Styles: Attributional Consequences of Specific Language Features and Communication Intentions," *Communication Monographs* 51 (1984): 307–319.

8. H. Giles and J. Wiemann, "Language, Social Comparison, and Power," in *Handbook of Communication Science,* ed. C. R. Berger and S. H. Chaffee (Newbury Park, Calif.: Sage, 1987).

9. Howard Gardner, *Intelligence Reframed: Multiple Intelligences for the 21st Century* (New York: Basic Books, 1999).

10. Michael E. Eldenmuller, *American Rhetoric: Rhetorical Figures in Sound,* 2001–2009. [Retrieved from http://www.americanrhetoric.com/figures/alliteration.htm, 18 September 2009.]

11. Richard Nordquist, "Parallelism," *About.com,* 2009. [Retrieved from http://grammar.about.com/od/pq/g/parallelismterm.htm, 21 September 2009.]

12. Nordquist, "Parallelism."

13. Auden and Kronenberger, *The Viking Book of Aphorisms,* 359.

Agree or disagree with her political views, few can deny that former governor, Sarah Palin is a dynamic speaker.

DELIVERY:
ENGAGING YOUR AUDIENCE

Objectives  www.mhhe.com/brydon7e

After reading this chapter and reviewing the online learning resources at
www.mhhe.com/brydon7e, you should be able to:

- Describe how to adapt your style of delivery to the audience and the
  rhetorical situation.
- Describe when manuscript, memorized, impromptu, or extemporaneous methods of delivery are most appropriate to a speech.
- Define nonverbal behavior and distinguish it from verbal behavior.
- Describe the relationship between delivery and the interdependent
  codes of the nonverbal system:
  - the environment
  - appearance and posture
  - voice
  - facial expressions and eye contact
  - gestures and body language
  - touch
  - time
- Recognize the functions these codes perform in the delivery of a
  speech, including:
  - Regulating the transaction between speaker and audience.
  - Substituting for a verbal symbol such as a word.
  - Reinforcing the verbal dimension of a speaker's message.
  - Increasing immediacy.

Key Concepts

communication orientation

emblem

environment

impromptu delivery

manuscript delivery

memorized delivery

nonverbal behavior

performance orientation

proactive delivery

self-adapting behaviors

vocalized pauses

zone of interaction

"What people do is frequently more important than what they say."

—EDWARD T. HALL
anthropologist[1]

"He had one of those rare smiles with a quality of eternal reassurance in it that you may come across four or five times in life. It faced, or seemed to face, the whole external world for an instant and then concentrated on you with an irresistible prejudice in your favor. It understood you just as far as you wanted to be understood, believed in you as you would like to believe in yourself."[2]

F. Scott Fitzgerald, the American novelist and screenwriter, used the preceding passage to introduce the central character in perhaps his most famous book, *The Great Gatsby*. The passage conveys the impression the novel's narrator Nick Carraway forms as he meets Jay Gatsby for the first time.

We use it to introduce this chapter for a simple reason. The most memorable public speaking transactions are those in which individual members of the audience believe the speaker's attention and message are focused exclusively on them. What's more, we have encountered innumerable cases where people described this experience in language similar to, if less eloquent than, Fitzgerald's, saying such things as, "I felt like I was the only person in the auditorium and she was speaking directly to me."

At its best the public speaking transaction should not only make us think about a topic but also leave us with the impression that the speaker was trying to personally connect with us as individuals. To do so, however, speakers must realize and act on the fact that their effectiveness depends on both *what they say* and *how they say it*. This chapter is intended to complement Chapter 10. It focuses on the role delivery plays in distinguishing a public speech from a written essay. It also presents an overview of the functional role nonverbal communication plays in the process of delivering a speech, including the impression you make with audience members before, during, and after you have presented it.

 www.mhhe.com/brydon7e

To view a video illustrating different delivery styles, click on the Speech Coach link on our Online Learning Center Web site, and go to Segment 11.1.

Delivery and the Rhetorical Situation

There is no single method and style of delivery required to effectively speak. Each of the ones we first introduced in Chapter 1 and revisit here must be adapted to the rhetorical situation. This means that the method and style of delivery that you choose should be:

- Appropriate to the situation
- Appropriate for the audience
- Well suited to your overall communication skills and specific strengths as a public speaker.

Choosing an Appropriate Method of Delivery

Manuscript Delivery

manuscript delivery
A mode of presentation that involves writing out a speech completely and reading it to the audience.

Manuscript delivery involves writing out the speech completely and reading it to the audience. This method may be the best choice when an audience requires precise information or our words will be quoted by others. Any time we use a manuscript, our eye contact, movement, and gestures are restricted. If a manuscript must be used, therefore, learn it well. Practice repeatedly so that you do not have to look down often. Mark up the manuscript with notes to yourself, and underline or highlight main ideas. Also, be sure pages are numbered so that

Barack Obama has been criticized by many for his overreliance on a TelePrompTer in delivering speeches.

they will not get out of order. Use a large typeface and double or even triple spacing. Manuscript speaking is more difficult than most people realize. Success depends on practice and skill in converting words on a page into a living speech.

An electronic version of manuscript speaking involves the use of a TelePrompTer. To avoid the appearance of reading verbatim from a written speech, public figures, newscasters, and actors frequently use a TelePrompTer instead of a written manuscript. The text is not visible to the audience, although the speaker can see it. Thus, nonverbal contact with the audience is potentially better than with a manuscript.

As is the case with any technology, skill in using a TelePrompTer varies. The best TV newsreaders and personalities, for example, seem to be speaking off the cuff rather than reading copy that is being revealed to them as they report the day's events or talk about an issue. Some are so good at using a TelePrompTer that we may forget that they are reading from copy.

No doubt president Obama wishes that were the case when he uses one. Even his supporters have criticized him for what many see as his noticeable reliance on a TelePrompTer regardless of the context in which he is speaking. Thus, a TelePrompTer, no matter how skillfully used, has the potential to undermine rather than enhance a speaker's effectiveness, depending on the situation and audience addressed.

Memorized Delivery

A speaker using **memorized delivery** writes out the speech and commits it to memory before presenting it without notes. Most audiences don't expect a memorized speech unless they are watching a professional speaker, an actor delivering lines in a play, or a student competing in a speech tournament. Although memorization allows the speaker's eye contact, movement, and gestures to surface naturally, it does so at a price—a speaker may forget parts of a speech, and this method requires a greater investment of time than any other method.

memorized delivery
A mode of presentation in which a speech is written out and committed to memory before being presented to the audience without the use of notes.

If you must write a speech to be memorized, keep the organization simple and memorable. A good rule of thumb is to memorize the speech in small chunks. Practice reciting your speech from the beginning through as far as you have it memorized. The repetition of earlier parts will help fix them in your mind. Don't panic if you forget a part of the speech. Try to ad-lib for a bit, and often the next section will come to mind. Finally, try to make your delivery of the speech sound as spontaneous and unrehearsed as possible.

Impromptu Delivery

There will inevitably be times when you will be expected to give a speech using **impromptu delivery**–a spontaneous, unrehearsed method of speaking. Usually these short speeches are given in response to someone who asks you to say a few words, make a toast, or respond to an inquiry in class or at work. No one knows better than you the chances that you'll be asked to say a few words at a social occasion or in a professional setting. With this in mind, we offer the following suggestions:

Forewarned is forearmed.   If there is even the slightest chance you'll be asked to speak, you should prepare in advance. Does this mean that you should write out a speech? Not really. Simply anticipate what you might be asked to say based on the context in which you'll find yourself. This will, at the very least, enable you to mentally rehearse your response. Should you not be asked to speak, you'll only be better prepared for the next time one of these occasions pops up.

Get organized.   The thing that impresses people the most about people who speak effectively off the cuff is organization. One of the most effective patterns for organizing an impromptu speech is to (1) introduce the points you want to make, (2) expand on the points, and (3) conclude with a summary of those points. This harks back to the "Tell 'em what you're going to tell 'em, tell 'em, and then tell 'em what you told 'em" sequence introduced in Chapter 1. Consider a classroom example. The instructor asks, "What's your take on the effects of rap lyrics on violence?" One student responds: "I have two points to make about the effects of rap. First, the effects are exaggerated. Second, most people who think rap affects violence are clueless about modern music. So what I'm saying is they're making a mountain out of another molehill." Notice in this example that the first sentence not only previews the points being made but also restates in modified form the question asked. The two points are made and then summarized in the final sentence. Compare this response with another hypothetical, but typical, student response: "I don't know . . . I guess I disagree. It's just a bunch of people who are out of it coming down on alternative music. Get a life, you know?" This response is both disorganized and equivocal, bringing us to our next tip.

Take a position.   Few of us are impressed with people who are wishy-washy. When someone asks a speaker, "What's your opinion?" we think the speaker is obligated to give it. On the other hand, if a speaker has not yet formulated a clear-cut opinion, an audience would much rather hear the person say, "I'll get more information and I'll get back to you" than hem and haw in response to such a query.

Use powerful language.   Powerful language goes hand in hand with the preceding guidelines. Recall that powerful language avoids the use of unnecessary qualifiers and vague questions. Powerful people say such things as "My opinion is firm" or "My experience leads me to the unequivocal belief that . . ." Powerful people do not say, "I could be wrong, but I think . . ." or "I believe it's okay, do you?" Impromptu speaking is tough enough without undermining your authority with powerless language.

Hitchhike.   It's sometimes effective to begin an impromptu message with what others have already said on the matter. This hitchhiking technique shows that you have been actively listening. It also acknowledges the contributions of others, even when you disagree with what they've said. For example, "Bill's point that this situation demands caution is well taken, but I must respectfully disagree for a couple of reasons." You also might say, "Let me summarize what's been said thus far, and then I'll add my two cents worth." Again, this kind of bridge tells your audience you are tuned in *and* organized.

Use stories and anecdotes.   If you know a story or an anecdote that contains a lesson that is both relevant and straightforward, by all means use it as a basis for your impromptu speech. Organizational culture often gives rise to stories about people and events that can be used in an impromptu speech. Some stories and anecdotes are generally known and can be applied to almost any point you choose to make. The real power of Aesop's fables, for instance, is that each contains multiple lessons you can apply to life. The same is true of many well-known children's stories, such as *Goldilocks and the Three Bears* and *The Boy Who Cried Wolf.*

Bookmark reference works on your computer.   Impromptu speaking is a matter of when, not if. Thus, we recommend to our own students that they spend some time surfing the Web for sites that specialize in quotations, anecdotes, and even jokes that have widespread application. We also recommend that, in the process, they look for examples that are either familiar or likely to ring true to their audience's experiences.

Extemporaneous Delivery

For most students who are still learning to give a speech, extemporaneous speaking remains their best choice. As we explained in Chapter 1, extemporaneous delivery combines careful preparation with spontaneity. Brief notes, rather than a manuscript or outline, are used. This enables the speaker to maintain eye contact, move freely, gesture, and adapt to audience feedback. Some speakers dispense with using a lectern altogether and simply hold their notes in one hand. (Avoid holding them in both hands, as this restricts the ability to gesture.)

Today's audiences are more likely to expect and appreciate the extemporaneously delivered speech than other methods of delivery. Just as it allows the speaker to remain in contact with the audience, so does it allow the audience to remain connected to the speaker. Audience members not only can give feedback to someone speaking extemporaneously but also can assess the degree to which their feedback registers with the speaker.

SPEAKING OF . . .

Performance versus Communication Orientation

By Jim Katt

Accomplishing your speaking goals can be facilitated or harmed by your orientation to delivering a speech. Many speakers take a **performance orientation,** *putting undue pressure on themselves by seeing their presentation as a performance and seeing their audience as a group of critics, just waiting for the speaker to make an oratorical mistake. For speakers with a performance orientation, perfection is the goal (Motley, 1997).*

Most of you, at one time or another, have watched television coverage of women's gymnastics at the Olympic Games. This competition may represent the epitome of a performance orientation. Let's use the vault as an example. These amazing young athletes speed down the runway, spring from the vault, and literally fly through the air while executing a dizzying sequence of twists and turns. You say to yourself, "How can anyone do those things?" But then the color commentator states gravely, "Well, she had excellent elevation, but she bent her knee on her take-off, over-rotated on her third twist, and had her toes over-pointed on her landing; the judges will take off points for each of these and she'll be effectively out of the competition." In other words, her lifetime of practice and preparation have all been for naught because when it counted most, she was less than perfect. The quest for perfection is cold-hearted.

Some speakers imagine their presentation requires the same type of perfection. They feel their audience is just waiting to criticize them, and that any imperfection will result in total failure. But that simply isn't true. Audiences aren't subtracting (or awarding) style points. The only real concern audiences have is that listening to the presentation is worthwhile for them. They are hoping to learn something, or to feel something, or to be inspired to do something, and it is doubtful they will even notice your mistakes unless your mistakes are so egregious or frequent that they interfere with your speech being worthwhile.

A more helpful orientation is a **communication orientation,** *where your focus as a speaker is simply to achieve your communicative goals (Motley, 1997). It gets back to what we discussed earlier: helping your audience to know or understand something differently, stirring your audience to feel about something differently, or motivating your audience to do something differently than they did before. If you accomplish your communicative goals, your presentation is a success, and no one will remember whether or not you "over-rotated."*

Another attitude that will help you maintain a communication orientation is thinking of your speech as merely an expanded version of the type of conversation you have every day with friends, family, or at work. When you have something you want to share—a great movie experience, your latest tale of road rage, your take on how to make

Instead of thinking of a presentation as a performance, imagine it to be more like an expanded conversation you have every day with friends or co-workers.

the perfect peanut butter and jelly sandwich, or the latest juicy gossip—you talk about it in conversations with others. While you're telling your story, you are doing most of the talking and your co-conversationalists are acting as your audience. You become part of their audience when they are telling their stories. Making a presentation is not fundamentally different. Over 70 years ago, public speaking scholar James Winans offered the following advice:

> *I wish you to see that speech-making, even in the most public place, is a normal act which calls for no strange, artificial methods, but only for an extension and development of that most familiar act, conversation. Should you grasp this idea you will be saved much wasted effort and unnecessary worry and effort (as cited in McCroskey, 2001, p. 274).*

In spite of the fact that Winan's advice has been often repeated, many speakers still see public speaking from a performance orientation. For them, speech delivery is a terribly difficult process, one at which they are destined to fail. If we instead see public speaking as the natural extension of the conversations we engage in daily, we realize we are not attempting something new and dangerous, we are just enlarging what we already know how to do. One scholar put it simply, "Public speaking is enlarged conversation. It should be enlarged enough to fill the room" (Brigance, 1961).

Brigance, W. N. (1961). *Speech: Its techniques and disciplines in a free society* (2nd ed.). New York: Appleton-Century-Crofts.

McCroskey, J. C. (2001). *An introduction to rhetorical communication* (8th ed.). Needham Heights, MA: Allyn & Bacon.

Motely, M. T. (1997). *Overcoming your fear of public speaking.* Boston, MA: Houghton Mifflin.

Speaking extemporaneously typically involves some form of notes. Perhaps the most common form is the note card. Before we say anything specific about preparing and using note cards, we want to warn you against the most common mistake we see in their use. Instead of each card highlighting a few points, students sometimes end up with 10 or more cards that outline their speech in its entirety. This is not extemporaneous speaking!

That said, note cards should be thought of as a primitive visual aid, intended to prompt you rather than be read. If your instructor permits notes, then we refer you to the following tips and tactics for preparing and using them in your speeches.

Tips and Tactics

Preparing Speaker's Notes

- *Use bright colors and large, bold lettering.* This will make the notes easier to see.
- *Use no more than five or six lines per note card if cards are used.* If too much is crammed on one card, it will be confusing.
- *Put each part of a speech on a separate card or page.* For example, the introduction might go on one, the body on another, and the conclusion on a third.
- *Number the cards or pages.* It is easy to lose track of your place while speaking. One way to help prevent this from happening is to number each card or page.
- *Write on only one side of a card or page.* Writing on both sides compounds the chances of losing your place.
- *Highlight main ideas.* Just like highlighting key passages in books, highlight the points you wish to emphasize.
- *Use notes to make comments to yourself.* It is perfectly appropriate, for example, to write prompts on notes. For example, write "O.H." to remind yourself to show an overhead at that point in the speech.
- *Don't try to write out the speech word for word.* This only encourages reading the speech rather than presenting it in a conversational manner. The only exception to this rule would be exact quotations, facts, or statistics, which obviously need to be written out.

Speaker's notes contain all the same ideas as the complete outline, but the words are designed to cue you to what comes next. Practice is needed to speak from these notes and still be assured of covering all the ideas in the original outline. Successful speakers practice prior to an actual presentation and you should follow their example. No matter how good the organization seems, it is only as good as the speaker's ability to deliver it. That takes practice. And practice doesn't mean running through the speech the night before or, even worse, the morning of the presentation. It means devoting significant amounts of time to practicing the speech until you have internalized its basic organization.

Extemporaneous speaking is not without drawbacks. Notes can restrict the speaker's range of gestures and can be distracting when waved about while

This student uses note cards that she has highlighted for quick reference.

speaking. Finally, speakers can get carried away with notes, writing down so many words that the notes almost become a manuscript. (See Exhibit 11.1 on page 257 for a summary of the modes of delivery.)

The Situation and the Audience

If you have a choice in the matter, the method and style of delivery you choose for your speech should reflect the dictates of the situation. Your choice also should reflect what you have learned about the diversity of your audience. Consider first the significance of the situation and the potential consequences of misstating or mistakenly leaving something out of your speech. More than a few politicians have spoken extemporaneously in a situation where they would have been far better off reading from a prepared manuscript. vice president Joe Biden, for example, is notorious for putting his foot in his mouth with his off-the-cuff remarks.

Consider next the expectations of audience members, given both the situation and their diversity. While an informal, extemporaneous style of delivery is

Mode of Delivery	Advantages	Disadvantages
Manuscript	Accuracy Precision May be quoted	Loss of eye contact Written rather than oral style Easy to lose place
Memorized	Keeps eye contact with audience Freedom of movement	Easy to forget Appears "canned" Extensive preparation required Lack of spontaneity
Impromptu	Spontaneous Maintains eye contact with audience Adaptable to situation	Lack of time to prepare Can be anxiety arousing Can be embarrassing if speaker fails to anticipate possible questions
Extemporaneous	Combines preparation and spontaneity Can maintain eye contact Adaptable Allows for accuracy in wording where necessary	Excessive use of note cards can inhibit spontaneity Poor use of note cards can limit ability to gesture

Exhibit 11.1
Advantages and Disadvantages of Delivery Modes

both expected and appreciated by many audience members here in the United States, this is not universally true. Northern European audiences, for example, expect speakers in business, politics, and higher education especially to deliver prepared content in a more formal style. Finally, consider and prepare for the fact that a method and style of delivery that has worked to your benefit with past audiences may not work for the more diverse ones you inevitably will face as your life evolves.

Nonverbal Communication: Making the Most of Your Delivery

Nonverbal behaviors combine to constitute a wordless, but not silent, dimension of communication. Nonverbal behavior has the potential to make verbal behavior more meaningful, but nonverbal behavior also can serve to confuse us in our attempts to interpret the words we hear.[3]

Given this framework, nonverbal behaviors generally fall into a set of interdependent and functional codes that make communication in general and public speaking specifically a more robust system of expression. Before we turn our attention to these codes and functions in detail, however, we first want to briefly explain why the nonverbal dimension of communication is not analogous to the verbal dimension we described in Chapter 10.

nonverbal behavior
A wordless, but not silent, system of communication.

The Difference Between What You Say and How You Say It

Recall from Chapter 10 that language is the rule-governed word system we use to verbally communicate. It is the same system we use to write an essay or construct a full-sentence outline of our speech. When in doubt about a rule or the meaning of a word, we have the luxury of turning to an accepted source for clarification, such as a guide to grammatical rules and syntax or a dictionary. Generally speaking, this is not the case with the nonverbal dimension of communication. Although it is true that a limited number of nonverbal behaviors, either alone or in combination, mean pretty much the same from one culture to the next, these are exceptions. Briefly, then, we want to highlight some of the most important characteristics that distinguish the nonverbal dimension of communication from its verbal counterpart.

Nonverbal Behavior Is Continuous

Verbal behavior, composed of words, is discrete. This means verbal behavior can be divided into distinct elements: nouns, verbs, and adjectives. These elements of composition are governed by complex rules, dictating how they should be combined in your speech to form phrases, clauses, and sentences. Each word has a denotative meaning that can be found in the dictionary. Words must be arranged in a precise manner to convey the intended meaning. For example, the words *I am happy* must be arranged in that order to convey the intended meaning. To say "Am I happy" changes the statement to a question or an exclamation. To say "Happy am I" seems odd to English speakers. When words with agreed-on meanings are used in a specified order, the meaning of the verbal behavior is apparent as in this example. This is not so with nonverbal behavior, which is continuous rather than divisible.[4]

Consider the physical expression of happiness as you speak. What the audience sees is a complex message that involves the entire face. The muscles of the face contract, affecting the eyebrows, the corners of the mouth, and the corners of the eyes. Unlike verbal behavior, these involuntary movements cannot be broken down into compositional elements. The eyes, for example, do not convey "I" while the eyebrows say "am" and the mouth represents "happy." You cannot re-arrange the components to convey a different meaning, as you can with "I," "am," and "happy." There are no highly defined rules of grammar to explain the meaning conveyed by these facial expressions. Only the total, continuous combination of these elements can constitute the nonverbal expression of happiness.

The Simultaneous Use of Multiple Channels

Returning to the example of expressing happiness, nonverbal behavior also involves the simultaneous use of multiple channels.[5] For example, try conveying an emotional expression, such as happiness, anger, sorrow, or bewilderment, through a single channel of communication, such as your mouth or eyes or hands. You'll soon see that it is difficult, if not impossible. At the same time you'll recognize that we use these multiple channels simultaneously rather than sequentially.

Spontaneity of Nonverbal Behaviors

As the preceding characteristics might lead you to believe, another distinguishing characteristic is that "true" nonverbal behavior is largely spontaneous. With the possible exception of so-called Freudian slips, when people unintentionally say what they really mean, verbal behavior is planned behavior.[6] We consciously think about the words we speak and write, though we do so with such speed it may not occur to us that we are doing it.

Smiles, gestures, and body language most often occur at a subconscious level. To put it another way, these nonverbal behaviors are "natural." And this is the chief reason we are predisposed to accept them as authentic expressions of what a person is thinking and feeling. Does this mean that nonverbal behaviors can never be scripted? The answer is both yes and no. Gestures and the like can be scripted as nonverbal complements to the content of a speech. Unless they are rehearsed to the point that they become a part of your overall nonverbal repertoire, however, your audience will probably perceive them for what they are—part of a script rather than an authentic expression of what you are thinking and feeling. That's why, as you will read a bit later, we caution our own students against forcing themselves to use gestures that feel unnatural and awkward, especially when they speak.

Delivery and the Nonverbal Communication System of Codes

Recall that a system is a collection of interdependent and interrelated components. A change in one component will produce changes in them all. The nonverbal system has as its components several interdependent codes of behavior that profoundly affect the delivery of a speech. Our overview of these codes and their relationship to effective delivery begins on a macro level, focusing first on the environment and second on your overall appearance and posture. We then move on to the more micro level of nonverbal codes, discussing the significance of the voice, eyes and face, gestures and movement, touch and time.

The Environment

For our purposes, **environment** refers to the physical surroundings as you speak and the physical distance separating you from your audience. Both surroundings and physical space have an undeniable impact not only on your delivery but also on how the speech is perceived by your audience.

The physical characteristics of the room in which you speak—for example, lighting, temperature, comfort, and aesthetics—will influence both you and the audience physically and psychologically.[7] A bright, aesthetically neutral room that is neither sterile nor plushly decorated, and in which the temperature is 68 degrees, will have a much different overall impact on the speech transaction than a room that is dimly lit, richly furnished, and 75 degrees. Whereas in the first, both speaker and audience are likely to be alert and attentive, the second might prove so comfortable that neither the speaker nor the audience is sufficiently aroused for the transaction. Thus you would have to plan your delivery accordingly. Whereas a "normal" pattern of delivery probably would be

environment
The physical surroundings as you speak and the physical distance separating you from your audience.

appropriate in the first environment, you likely would need to put extra energy and enthusiasm into the delivery to succeed in the second.

A second environmental consideration is the physical layout of the room. We have been in situations where student presentations were hindered by pillars supporting the roof, by the width and length of the room, and by immovable objects such as tables. Sometimes speakers have no alternative but to do the best they can in such situations. As a result, they move more than they had planned, abandon visual aids that would prove impossible for the entire audience to see, or enlarge and exaggerate their gestures.

At other times, however, you will have the opportunity to physically arrange the room in which you will speak. You might change the position of a lectern, arrangement of a stage, and configuration of an audience. Given this opportunity, experienced speakers will arrange the environment in concert with their style of delivery. Speakers who have a traditional style of delivery may prefer a lectern, perhaps an overhead projector or laptop immediately to their side, and an elevated stage from which to speak. Speakers who are much less formal in their style of delivery may want the room to be arranged so that they can move from side to side or even up and down its length.

Traditional and informal styles of delivery can be equally effective. However, the room layout consistent with the traditional style is more restrictive than its counterpart, in two ways. The first concerns the **zone of interaction,** the area in which speakers can easily make eye contact with audience members (Exhibit 11.2). The second concerns the amount of space physically separating speakers from their audience.

The zone of interaction is limited to the range of the speaker's peripheral vision. The immediate zone of interaction between a speaker and the audience diminishes

zone of interaction
The area of an audience in which speaker and audience members can make eye contact.

Exhibit 11.2

Zone of Interaction in the Traditional Room Setting

Where people are seated in rows and the speaker is stationary, eye contact between speaker and audience is limited to the shaded area. The speaker must turn to make eye contact with those outside the shaded area.

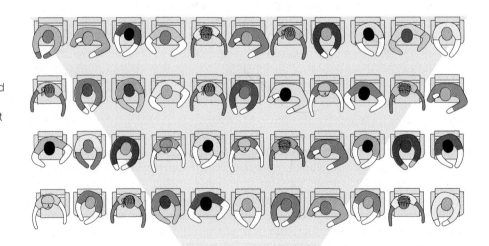

Lectern

Stationary speaker

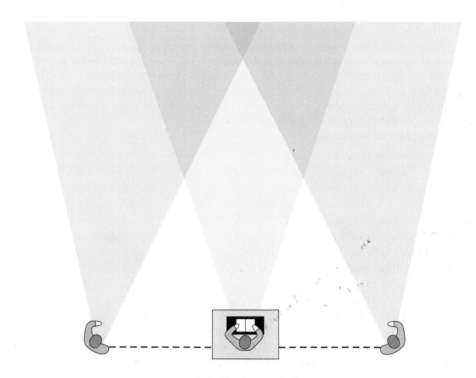

Exhibit 11.3
**Shifting the Zone
of Interaction With
Movement**
Changing positions can
increase the perception
of inclusiveness as well
as add energy to your
speech.

as a room gets larger. To compensate for this fact, speakers have two choices. Either they can shift the zone of interaction by looking from side to side, or they can physically move from one point to another when they deliver their speeches. This latter choice is illustrated in Exhibit 11.3. Obviously, in a very large room the traditional style of delivery limits you to looking from side to side in the attempt to shift the zone of interaction. This means that you cannot help but ignore part of your audience part of the time.

The traditional style of delivery also allows less flexibility in manipulating the physical distance separating speakers from their audiences. Whereas a speaker who moves about the room can reduce or increase distance physically as well as psychologically, a relatively stationary speaker is restricted to the latter. Thus, for those who prefer stationary delivery, eye contact becomes their primary agent for managing audience perceptions of immediacy.

To summarize, the relationship of the speaking environment to delivery is significant. Not only does it influence your style of delivery, it also influences how you are perceived by your audience. Experienced public speakers try to plan the delivery of their speeches accordingly. When faced with a "tough room," for example, they know that the arousal level of their delivery will need to increase if they are to reach their audience. Inexperienced speakers, on the other hand, all too often play "victim" to their speaking environment. Instead of surveying and planning for the environment, they simply deliver their speech as if the environment were of no consequence to them. As a student of public speaking, you know what's good and bad about the layout of the classroom in which you must speak. Thus you, too, should plan your delivery accordingly. The box "Speaking of . . . Seating Arrangements" discusses another factor you should consider when planning your delivery.

SPEAKING OF . . .

Seating Arrangements

Can the physical seating arrangement have an impact on both your speech and the manner in which it is perceived? Yes—a very dramatic one. So you should think about your goals as a speaker and the physical layout of the room in which you will speak. Traditional rows will focus attention exclusively on you. A horseshoe arrangement, however, allows audience members to make eye contact with each other. And speaking at the head of a conference table not only narrows the zone of interaction but also puts a physical barrier between you and your audience. Which of these arrangements do you think would most likely encourage audience feedback and participation? Why?

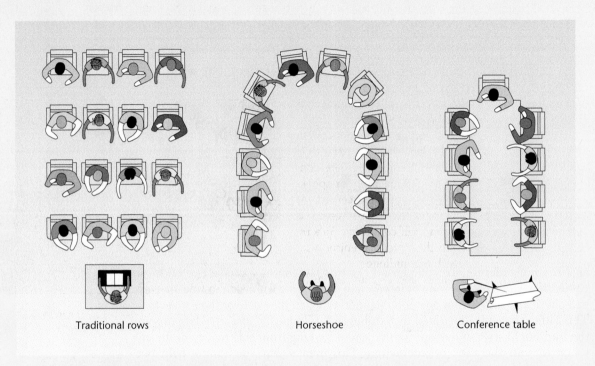

Traditional rows   Horseshoe   Conference table

Tips and Tactics

The Speaking Environment

- Check out the room in which you'll speak well in advance. Take note of the seating arrangement, availability of lectern, and availability of equipment necessary for any media you will be using.
- If permissible, consider changing the environment to better reflect your speech purpose and style of delivery.
- Rehearse your planned movements, including how you will use any equipment necessary for your presentational media.
- If possible, try to set the room temperature to between 68 and 70 degrees. Check lighting at the same time.

Appearance and Posture

According to communication expert Dale Leathers, "Our visible self functions to communicate a constellation of meanings which define who we are and what we are apt to become in the eyes of others."[8] These "others" are the people with whom we come into contact, including the members of our audieces.

Appearance often has a disproportionately significant effect on audience perceptions of a speaker's message and delivery.[9] Speakers never get a second chance to make a first impression with an audience. First impressions are based largely on appearance, including posture, body type and height, skin and hair color, and clothing and accessories.

The significance of appearance to public speaking can be measured in at least two ways. The first involves audience members' first impressions. The second involves how people perceive themselves as a result of their appearance and the impact this perception has on their self-confidence and delivery.

Audience members use appearance initially to make judgments about a speaker's level of attractiveness and degree of similarity to themselves. The consequences of this judgment are far-reaching for speakers. Research shows that speakers perceived as attractive by audience members also are perceived as smart, successful, sociable, and self-confident. As a result, speakers who fall into this category enjoy a favorable first impression with the audience.

Yet appearance influences more than an audience's initial impression of a speaker. Appearance also can have a very real effect on a speaker's self-confidence. Research tells us that speakers who feel

Inappropriate dress and nonverbal behavior can seriously damage a speaker's credibility with an audience.

Business casual dress is appropriate for most public speaking situations.

Some public speaking situations call for formal business attire.

they appear attractive report greater self-confidence than those reporting otherwise.[10] Keeping up your appearance under conditions of uncertainty, moreover, also has been shown to moderate the effect of uncertainty on self-esteem.[11]

Although some facets of your appearance and their impact on audience perception are outside your control—for example, body type and height—you can improve your posture, dress, and grooming with little effort or expense. Simply said, your dress should be appropriate to the situation. Obvious as this advice may seem, it is frequently ignored by students in public speaking classes. All too often they show up to speak dressed as if they had thought little about the appropriateness of their attire. Their attitude, as reflected in their dress, seems to be saying, "It's just a speech class."

Posture is obviously related to overall appearance. Posture is vital to your delivery and the manner in which it is received. People make all kinds of attributions about speakers on the basis of their posture, ranging from how confident a speaker is to how seriously the speaker takes the topic and the situation. Consequently, you will want to guard against an audience making an incorrect attribution about you because you slouched, folded your arms across your chest, stood with one hand on your hip, or put your hands in your pockets.

Because the norms governing appropriate posture vary across cultures, there are no hard-and-fast rules for speakers to follow. Still, given what we know generally about the culture of the beginning public speaking class, there are some steps you can follow to achieve a good posture for delivering your speeches. Remember that the more you slouch and shrink posturally, the less likely it is that you will be perceived as powerful. Remember as well that posture influences the mechanics of your voice. Standing with shoulders back stretches the diaphragm and opens the air passages. That's one reason opera singers invariably have good posture. It helps them use their voice to full effect.

Consider an analogy. Good students know what the research suggests about the relationship between the appearance of a term paper and the mark it receives. Frequently, it's the difference between a minus or a plus in their grade. Good students, therefore, go to some length to make sure that their papers not only conform to the requirements but "look" impressive as well.

The same relationship may exist between appearance and the marks students receive on their speeches. Inappropriate attire or careless grooming will never add points to a speech; moreover, there is a chance they will unnecessarily detract from such things as the speaker's perceived competence. Although we do not recommend formal business attire for most classroom speeches, we urge you to consider a form of attire often called "business casual." For both men and women, business casual could include a polo shirt or sweater, slacks, and shoes you would normally wear in an office. Appropriate dress confers status on you and shows respect for your audience.

Tips and Tactics

Guidelines for Posture While Delivering a Speech

- Find your center of balance. Usually this means standing with your feet apart at about shoulder width.
- Pull your shoulders back, sticking your chest out and holding your stomach in.
- Keep your chin up and off your chest.
- Initially let your arms rest at your sides with palms open, which will allow you to gesture easily as you speak.

Your Voice

Before we talk about what makes voices as unique as fingerprints, we want to reemphasize the fact that what you say and how you say it are not the same thing. The spoken word has two dimensions. One dimension is content—the words themselves and the way they are configured to form sentences. The other dimension is vocalic—the sound that shapes the meaning the spoken word conveys to the audience. Consider the sentence *I love you.* By changing the pitch, volume, and inflection of your voice as you utter the sentence, you can actually alter the meaning the sentence conveys to another person. It can be sensuous or sincere, for example, depending on the tone of voice with which it is spoken.

In a sense, words are like musical notes, and the voice is like an instrument. In the hands of a skilled musician, notes are not simply played but are shaped. Skilled guitarists playing the same notes can produce quite different sounds, depending on how they bend or agitate the strings with their fingertips. Skilled speakers do much the same thing with the pitch, tempo, and rhythm of their voices.

To gain better control of your voice, you need to know how sound is produced and how it can be manipulated. You also need to appreciate the role articulation plays in the process of shaping this sound so that it is meaningful to your audience. Finally, you need to accept the fact that you are better off speaking in your own voice than trying to imitate someone else's voice.

The production of sound in the voice is fairly straightforward. You take in air and expel the air through the trachea across your vocal cords, which are contained in the larynx (voice box), and then across your teeth, tongue, and lips. Variations in the amount of air expelled, the positioning of the vocal cords, or the placement of the teeth and tongue and position of the lips will result in variations in the sounds produced. Shallow breathing and the rapid expulsion of air across the vocal cords, for example, will produce a much different sound than breathing deeply and then slowly expelling the air. In the first case your voice is likely to be described as feminine and in the second masculine, even though neither is necessarily true. The basic mechanical operation of the voice, however, is not as important to the topic at hand as are the characteristics of the voice. These include volume, pitch, range, rhythm, and tempo.

Volume

How loudly you project your voice is a consequence of both the amount of air you expel when speaking and the force with which you expel it. For example, try to speak loudly without first taking a fairly deep breath. Surprising, isn't it? Some examples of people capable of speaking with great volume are actor/talk show host Oprah Winfrey, talk radio's Rush Limbaugh, actor James Earl Jones (the person you hear saying "CNN"), and Soundgarden singer Chris Cornell. On the other hand, people with more soft-spoken voices include actor George Clooney, TV news anchor Diane Sawyer, and singer Norah Jones.

You need not be loud to be heard. What's more, speaking in a consistently loud voice is likely to grate on the ears of your audience. You want to *project* your voice, not break eardrums with it. The key is to vary the volume of your voice depending on the impact you hope to have with your audience. Sometimes lowering the volume of your voice will draw in your audience, whereas a sudden increase in volume may startle your audience. As a public speaker, you need to

Chris Cornell of Soundgarden is known for his powerful voice.

have enough volume to be heard by your audience. But that can vary tremendously depending on the size of your audience, the room in which you are speaking, and the availability of a microphone. Seasoned speakers prepare differently depending on these factors. That is to say, they vary the volume with which they practice depending on where and with whom they will be speaking. You should do the same thing. Practice your speech as if you were delivering it in the classroom where you will speak, to an audience equivalent in size to your actual class. When you actually do speak to your class, moreover, look for feedback about volume in the faces and posture of audience members. If those in the back of the room are leaning forward or look puzzled, you may need to raise your volume. On the other hand, if people seated in the first row are leaning back in their seats, you may be speaking too loudly.

Pitch

The degree to which your voice is high or low is its pitch. A person who sings bass has a low pitch, whereas a person who sings soprano has a high pitch. The bass knob on your stereo controls the lower pitch, the treble knob controls the higher pitch. Pitch is a key to vocal inflection, and effective speakers vary their pitch to shape the impact of their words. They may lower pitch to sound more serious or raise it to convey a sense of urgency. Control of pitch depends not only on their skill as a speaker but on the natural range of their voice as well.

Range

The extent of the pitch, from low to high, that lies within your vocal capacity is known as range. Just as a piano has a tremendous range in pitch, some speakers have a great vocal range. On the other hand, some speakers are like an electric bass guitar, which no matter how well played, does not have much range. As a speaker, you need to make the fullest use of your normal conversational vocal range. That means you first need to discover the bottom and top of your own vocal scale.

To get a sense of how pitch and range control the inflection in your voice, audio-record yourself. Recite the alphabet beginning in your normal voice. Then raise your pitch with each new letter until your voice cracks. Next do the same thing, but lower your voice as you recite. Play back the recording and note where your voice begins to break as you go up and then breaks as you go down. This will give you an audible idea about the limits of your vocal range, as well as at what pitches your voice sounds relaxed and natural. Then practice varying your pitch within this relaxed and natural range, using the audio recorder to further get in touch with the natural range of your pitch.

Rhythm

Think of rhythm as the characteristic pattern of your volume, pitch, and range. Perhaps you have heard someone describe a speaker's voice as "singsong." This means the speaker's voice goes consistently up and then down in pitch, almost as if the person were talking to a small child.

Some speakers use predictable rhythm to great effect. Many evangelical preachers have a decided rhythm in their sermons. The Reverend Jesse Jackson is an easy target for comedic impersonators because of the predictable rhythm with which he takes his audience up, and then pauses before taking them down. Jackson heightens this effect with his inflection and frequent use of alliteration, which we discussed in Chapter 10.

Tempo

The rate at which you produce sounds, or how quickly or slowly you speak, will influence how you are perceived. Tempo also tends to vary across and even within cultures. In the United States, for example, speech in the South is relatively slow in tempo, whereas on the East Coast tempo is accelerated. This is readily apparent if you compare the speaking voices of Jeff Foxworthy, who is from the South, and Jon Stewart, who is from New Jersey.

Because tempo varies, you have to use good judgment in terms of how quickly or slowly you speak. Doing either to the extreme can turn off your audience. An excessively rapid pace can be perceived as a sign of nervousness. An excessively slow pace may suggest that a speaker is not well prepared. Researchers have found that audiences tend to associate moderate to fast rates of speaking with speaker competence.[12] Other researchers have noted a ceiling to that effect, however, meaning that too fast a rate of speaking can backfire.[13] In addition, when audiences perceive speech rates to be similar to their own, they are more likely to find speakers socially attractive and to comply with their requests.[14] The best advice is to moderately vary your tempo. Not only will this accommodate the different preferences of individuals in your audience, it will also enhance the overall effectiveness of your message.

Your tempo is also affected by pauses. Sometimes a brief moment of silence can convey much to an audience. Pausing just before delivering a crucial word or phrase helps grab the audience's attention. Pausing after you've made an important point gives it time to sink in. Used judiciously, pauses can be an effective rhetorical device. It is also better to pause a moment than to fill the air with "ums," "uhs," and "you knows," which are really vocalized pauses. The best way to control disfluencies such as these is to practice your speech until it is second nature.

Articulation

If you expect an audience to understand what you are saying, you need clear articulation, which refers to the distinctness with which you make individual sounds. You may have experienced the frustration of listening to someone who sounds mushy, failing to distinctly vocalize sounds. A common articulation problem comes from either running together differing sounds or dropping parts of a word: *goin'* instead of *going, wanna* instead of *want to,* or *whatcha doin'?* in place of *what are you doing?* A good way to test your articulation is to audio-record your speech and listen critically to yourself. If you find a consistent articulation problem or set of problems, you may want to find out if your college or university offers a course in voice and articulation. Sometimes drama or theatre department courses in voice for performers can be of assistance. Severe articulation problems are often best treated by a speech pathologist. But for most students in public speaking classes, exercising care, practicing, and slowing down are the keys to being understood by the audience.

In Chapter 10 we emphasized the importance of using words correctly. This is a good place to reemphasize the fact. As you practice articulating words, make sure that you are also pronouncing them correctly. "Nu-ku-lar" is still wrong, no matter how well you articulate it.

As we said in Chapter 10, mispronounced words tend to undermine audience perceptions of a speaker's credibility. This is true whether the mispronunciation involves a term unique to a profession or the name of a person or place. Medical terms such as *hemangioma* can tie up the tongue of even the most articulate speaker. So, too, can place names such as Mexico's Cacaxtla or the last name of recognized football star Troy Polamalu.

For some words, the correct pronunciation is as close as a dictionary. In addition, some online dictionaries (such as the one at www.howjsay.com) let you type in a word and hear it pronounced. For terms and names like those in our example, however, a dictionary may be no help at all, and the advice of an expert is required: a physician, an authority on Central America, or the person whose surname you will otherwise murder. The time for such consultation is well in advance of the day you are scheduled to speak. Until the correct pronunciation becomes a habit, you cannot be sure that you will be able to speak terms as they are intended to be spoken. That requires repetition and lots of practice using the terms in your speech.

In the final analysis, judgments about the relationship between the qualities of your voice and the quality of your delivery will depend on the preceding characteristics operating in concert. Important as pitch or tempo may be on their own, it is their collective impact with range and rhythm that most counts.

Speaking in Your Own Voice

With these qualities of voice in mind, let's now turn to your voice specifically. Are you pleased with the way it sounds and complements your overall delivery? No matter how you answer this question, it is just as important for you to find your own voice as a speaker as it is for authors to find their own voice when they write. We mention this need to find your own voice with good reason. When public speaking students are advised to make better use of their voice in their delivery, all too often they take this to mean they must change their voice to some ideal. The ideal, moreover, is usually thought to be the voice of a television or radio personality.

We don't encourage you to imitate the vocal delivery of someone who hosts a game show, reads the news, or introduces music videos. Instead, we encourage you to experiment with your voice; for example, record your attempts to convey varying emotions in your voice, listen to yourself, and then repeat the process. This kind of exercise will let you hear what your vocal strengths and weaknesses are. In the process, be realistic but not unfairly harsh about how you think you sound. Chances are, what you think you hear is much different from what others hear. Finally, recognize that, important as it is, your voice is but a single component of your overall delivery. Not all good speakers have tremendous "pipes." For example, the *Today Show*'s Matt Lauer and *Good Morning America*'s Robin Roberts are both engaging, but their voices would hardly be described as rich in timbre. Further, if you were to listen to a number of highly paid motivational speakers, you would see that this is the case with them as well. All of us tend to underutilize the full potential of our voices. What ultimately counts, then, is whether we're willing to do the hard work necessary to rectify this fact.

Tips and Tactics

Improving Your Voice

Like it or not, people will make judgments about you based on the way you sound. Although we want you to be comfortable with your voice, the following tips may help you if you think something about your voice needs to be changed.

- *Relaxation:* More than one problem with voice can be solved by monitoring tension in your vocal apparatus. Nasality, shrillness, screeching, and excessive rate of speech are often a consequence of tension or stress. The same relaxation techniques can alleviate the impact of tension or stress on your voice.
- *Vocal variation:* Audio-record yourself. If you find, as a result of monitoring your recording, that greater vocal variation is needed, pick out someone whose vocal characteristics you admire and repeatedly listen to the person. Then try to adapt that person's vocal variation to your own voice. Repeat this process while using an audio recorder.
- *Being heard:* Have a friend monitor your speaking volume. When you speak too softly, tell your friend to raise an index finger within your view. Use this signal to increase the volume of your voice. The goal is to be easily heard, even in the back of the room.

Your Eyes and Face

Although today's technology makes it possible to see our online communication partner using a Web cam, many e-mail and Internet chat room users still use emoticons (or symbols) such as a smiley face to add emotion to their messages. Such symbols are designed to approximate what would be communicated through the eyes and face in normal conversation.

The eyes have been called the windows to the soul. Perhaps, then, it is only fitting that many people also believe eye contact is the single most important variable in delivering a speech. The eyes connect speaker and audience. The eyes also tell the speaker and the audience much about each other.

To repeat, in mainstream North American culture, people generally use eye contact to make judgments about:

- Whether a person is competent
- Whether a person can be trusted
- Whether a person is approachable.

Competence and trustworthiness are two key components of a speaker's credibility; that is, the degree to which a speaker is perceived as believable. Generally, the more a speaker makes eye contact with audience members, the more the speaker will be perceived as credible. Because credible speakers are also likely to have more influence with an audience, it only makes good sense for the speaker to maintain as much eye contact as possible with an audience.

Eye contact also has the power to reduce physical distances psychologically. When we make and sustain friendly eye contact with people at a distance, it makes us feel "closer" to each other. It also helps to make people appear attractive and open to dialogue. As was the case with competence and trustworthiness, this is clearly to a speaker's benefit.

But there is yet another reason for maintaining eye contact with an audience. Eye contact is an important source of audience feedback. In North America, for example, an audience will use eye contact to let the speaker know the degree to which it is engaged. Speakers can then use this feedback to make decisions about whether they need to modify their speech to gain the audience's attention.

Having established its importance to delivery, let's talk about how you can optimize the positive effects of eye contact. First, recognize that you cannot fake eye contact! People know you are looking directly at them or looking only at the tops of their heads. Second, some eye contact is better than no eye contact at all. Ideally, however, eye contact works best when you look at individual members of the audience as you speak. This type of eye contact personalizes a public message. All too often, people think eye contact means looking at the audience members as a group, beginning with those in the center seats, and then turning to those seated to our right or left. To the contrary, effective eye contact means making every person in the room feel as if you are speaking only to him or her.

Eye contact works best when it is complemented with appropriate facial expressions. The face and eyes, for example, can communicate happiness, surprise, fear, anger, disgust, contempt, sadness, or interest. The face and eyes can also modify the intensity of any of these nonverbal expressions of emotion.[15]

Just as you can use metaphor to manipulate language intensity, you can use your face and eyes to intensify your delivery. In most cases, you intensify what you say in this manner with little or no conscious thought. As you grow angry, for example, the muscles in your face tense and your eyes narrow spontaneously. The purveyor of bad news can make things even worse by accentuating it with the face and eyes.

You can also use your face and eyes to neutralize the message you deliver. Based on an analysis of your situation, you may know that at least some members of the audience will disagree with your views. Suppose you are in a class situation that requires you to deliver a persuasive speech. If your topic is truly controversial, you can reasonably predict that not everyone in your audience

Can you identify the meanings of these facial expressions?

will agree with everything you say. Although you may not be able to win them over, you also don't want to alienate them. As a result, you may want to use your face and eyes to neutralize some of the more contentious and evocative points you wish to make.

In a sense, what you give an audience in your face and eyes will determine what you can expect to get back from that audience. An intensely worded argument accompanied by the delivery of an equally intense message in the face and eyes invites the same from those who differ with you. On the other hand, using the face and eyes to neutralize the message improves your chance of a more favorable response from your audience. The city of Palo Alto, California, took this to an extreme when it considered a guideline that would have discouraged city council members from using facial expressions to show their disagreement, frustration, or disgust at meetings. The idea behind the guideline was that it would promote civility and defuse conflict among council members and between council members and constituents during public meetings. Good intentions, however, do not always make for good policy. The guideline was unworkable because it is nearly impossible to suppress nonverbal expressions of underlying feelings. In addition, the guideline violated council members' First Amendment rights.[16]

To close, keep in mind that what we have suggested here is based on mainstream North American norms, especially in the corporate world. Remember that many cultures frown upon the sustained and focused eye contact that most North Americans value. Members of many Asian cultures, for example, view such eye contact as rude and even hostile. Both speakers and audience members should keep this in mind. As a speaker, recognize that when international students and those outside the mainstream appear uncomfortable or don't return your attempts to make eye contact, it may be the result of their culture. As an audience member, realize that your expectancies about eye contact may be at odds with the norms of students from cultures other than your own.[17]

Tips and Tactics

Using Your Eyes and Face

- Always face your audience when speaking; avoid turning your back to the audience unless absolutely necessary.
- Make eye contact with people before you begin. Maintain eye contact by meeting the gaze of individual audience members in all parts of the room.
- Avoid excessive eye contact with one person; for example, your instructor.
- Don't be afraid to be expressive with your face.

Gestures and Movement

You've heard the expression "Different strokes for different folks." Nowhere is it more applicable than to the subject of gestures and movement relative to delivery. Although president Ronald Reagan neither moved nor gestured very much when he spoke, he became known as the "Great Communicator." Thus, before we say a single word about how much or how little you should gesture or move as you speak, we want to say this: Your gestures and your movements as you grow as a public speaker should be a refined reflection of what you do naturally. We'd much rather see speakers gesture and move less as an authentic complement to their everyday communication style, than force themselves to increase the number of gestures they make or move about a room.

A gesture helps this speaker make her point.

As is the case with the eyes and face, gestures and movements also can be used to intensify or lessen the emotional impact of verbal messages. Many gestures, for instance, serve as *affect displays;* that is, they visibly communicate feelings. Placing both of your hands over your heart when you explain how important a subject is to you is an example. So, too, are clenched fists, open palms held face up, or lightly slapping the side of the face.

Touch

Touch, which is by far the most intimate and reinforcing of the nonverbal dimensions, can affect your delivery in at least two ways.[18] The first involves **self-adapting behaviors,** which are distracting touching behaviors that speakers engage in unconsciously.

In arousing situations, people frequently touch their face, hair, or clothes without realizing it. Just as frequently they touch some convenient object. They may squeeze the arm of a chair, roll their fingers on a tabletop, trace the outside edge of a glass with a fingertip, or mistake the top of a lectern for a conga drum. They do these things unconsciously.

Because public speaking is arousing, it can provoke these self-adaptive forms of touch. Further, they can needlessly detract from your delivery. Tugging at an earlobe, rubbing the outside of your upper arm, or jingling the change in your pocket won't help your delivery. Neither will pounding on the lectern with the palms of your hands or rocking it from side to side.

The second way touch can affect your delivery concerns other people. At some point it's likely that your presentations will involve close contact with other people. Corporate trainers spend much of their lives giving informative presentations that involve audience participation. The same can be said for sales managers, teachers, attorneys, and practitioners of public relations. Touch very often comes into play in these scenarios. Sometimes it's as simple but as important as shaking a person's hand. At other times it may involve guiding someone by the hand, patting someone on the back, or even giving a more demonstrative tactile sign of approval. At the same time, you must avoid touch that can be interpreted as inappropriate. For example, there have been several widely reported cases of schoolteachers accused of inappropriately touching students. Unwelcome touching can, in fact, be grounds for accusations of sexual harassment.

self-adapting behaviors
Nonverbal behaviors used to cope with nervousness; for example, touching oneself or grasping the sides of a lectern with one's hands.

Time

The final nonverbal code to think about relative to delivery is time. As journalist Michael Ventura writes:

> Time is the medium in which we live. There is inner time—our personal sense of the rhythms of time experienced differently by each of us; and there is imposed time—the regimented time by which society organizes itself, the time of schedules and deadlines, time structured largely by work and commerce.[19]

First, time varies from one individual to the next. Research confirms what you no doubt long ago suspected. Each of us has an internal body clock that regulates not only when we sleep but also peak performance when we're awake. Some people perform best from early to midmorning, some during the middle of the day, and others late at night. What is true of performance in general, moreover, is true of public speaking specifically. During our time awake, there are periods when our speaking abilities peak, depending on our individual body clock. Most of us know from our own experience that we either are or are not very alert in the early morning or late afternoon. To the extent possible, attempt to schedule a speaking time when you know your mind and body will be alert.

Time affects your delivery in other ways as well. The time limits you face as a speaker can have an impact on your delivery. If you try to cover too much material, time limits may cause you to hurry your delivery. Conversely, if you find that you're about to finish your speech under the minimum time requirement of an assignment, you may slow down your delivery in an attempt to meet the time requirement. Time also plays an obvious role in your "timing" of a joke or sharing a story for dramatic effect. Neither technique is likely to be successful, as any entertainer will tell and show you, if your "timing is off."

Because the norms that govern the use of time vary across cultures, how quickly or how slowly you deliver your speech may be a consideration. A relatively speedy style of delivery may be well received in New York City; in parts of the South and Southwest it may be received as evidence of the "little time" you have for an audience. Conversely, a slow rate of speech, which some mistakenly confuse with the speed at which a person thinks, may prove irritating to audience members whose culture is fast-paced.

Finally, whether you are "on time" or late, not only for a speech but just in general, affects your credibility in our North American culture. People who are on time are perceived as efficient and courteous, both of which affect perceptions of competence and trustworthiness. People who are routinely late give the impression they are disorganized and not especially considerate of the time needs of an audience. This is very true of both your classmates and your instructor.

The Functional Roles Nonverbal Codes Play in Delivery

Given the preceding overview we can now turn to the specific functions nonverbal codes perform as you deliver a speech. They are:

- Regulating the transaction between speaker and audience
- Substituting for a verbal symbol such as a word or phrase
- Reinforcing the verbal dimension of a speaker's message
- Increasing immediacy.

Regulating the Transaction

Earlier we discussed how you could reconfigure a speaking environment or move about it to change the zone of interaction—the area in which eye contact between speaker and audience is maximized. Here we want to talk about how both the speaker's and audience members' nonverbal behavior can regulate the degree to which the speech transaction achieves its general purpose.

The primary mechanism by which all communication transactions are regulated is feedback. Unlike in the case of conversation, feedback in the transaction between speaker and audience is predominantly nonverbal. With rare exception it is channeled through eye contact and facial expressions, body language, gestures and movement, and voice. It's just as important for speakers to know what to look for in the audience as it is for them to know how to use their delivery skills to control what the audience is telling them.

In highly individualistic cultures such as the United States, speakers may focus most on feedback from individual audience members, discounting the meaning and significance of what the entire audience's feedback is telling them.[20] This is especially true if the speaker interprets the feedback as negative—for example, two or three audience members leaning back rather than forward in their seats, appearing distracted or bored in their facial expression and eyes, or engaging in what we call leave-taking behavior (glancing at text messages or stuffing note-taking materials into a backpack). Thus, a few audience members can have a disproportionate and unrepresentative influence on our delivery, making us unjustifiably anxious, prone to rushing the rate of our speech and making mistakes.

Our tendency to pay more attention to the feedback of the few rather than the many is both contrary to the practice of speakers in collectivistic cultures *and* illogical. As speakers we need to survey the entire audience for feedback rather than let a few audience members' feedback regulate what we say and how we say it. We also need to recognize the fact that this scenario is not a one-way street.

We have the power to regulate an audience's feedback as well. We simply need to recognize and interpret it accurately and then modify our delivery accordingly. We can change the rate of our delivery and the urgency in our voice, move closer to the audience, make direct eye contact with inattentive audience members, and use gestures that prompt an audience to raise hands in response to questions we raise. There is no guarantee that such changes in delivery will regulate the transaction in the speaker's favor, but you'd be surprised to see just how effective these proactive changes are when used by skilled speakers.

Gestures can help regulate the flow of interaction.

Substituting for a Verbal Symbol

Have you ever seen entertainers and politicians raise their hands and motion in the attempt to stop an audience's continued applause? They are using a nonverbal cue as a substitute for a verbal one. In many circumstances, such a nonverbal cue is both more appropriate and more effective than a verbal one. An icy stare shot in the direction of someone talking as you speak is likely to be less disruptive, for example, than politely asking the person to be quiet. Shrugging your shoulders, reaching out with open palms, and raising your eyebrows, moreover, may more clearly communicate your bewilderment than actually saying you're puzzled by something.

The speeches of the best public speakers are usually rich in emblems. An **emblem** is a nonverbal behavior that can be directly translated into words and phrases and may replace them.[21] For example, it's now widely understood that

emblem
A nonverbal symbol that can be substituted for a word.

An emblem, such as the "peace sign," can take the place of a verbal message.

when a person holds up his or her hand to an ear with the thumb and little finger extended and the other fingers curled under, it means "call me." Emblems must meet the following criteria:

1. The emblem means something specific to the audience members.
2. The emblem is used intentionally by the speaker to stimulate meaning.
3. The emblem can be easily translated into a few words.

Reinforcing Your Message

A third and common function performed by nonverbal behavior is reinforcement of the content of your speech. You can reinforce what you say verbally with *complementary* nonverbal behaviors, nonverbal behaviors that purposefully *contradict* the words you say, and those that serve to *repeat* what you verbally communicate. Consider first how something as simple as a smile can complement what you tell your audience. A generous and genuine smile as you thank your audience for inviting you to speak, for example, is much more reinforcing than the words standing on their own. Making individual eye contact with audience members as you ask them for their attention has a similar effect.

A less common method of reinforcing the intent of your words is to contradict the literal meaning nonverbally. Rolling your eyes as you tell an audience how much you respect your opponent in a debate will leave audience members with little doubt about how you really feel about him or her. You can also use your voice to contradict your words, as many actors do in the role of Marc Antony in Shakespeare's play *Julius Caesar.* In Antony's eulogy of Caesar, the line "But Brutus was an honorable man" is delivered in a voice that drips with sarcasm. Antony's point, of course, is that Brutus was anything but honorable.

Finally, you can reinforce a verbal message with nonverbal behaviors that make the words redundant. This can be very useful in using your fingers to alert audiences to the fact that you are transitioning from your first to second point in a speech or in reminding audience members in your summary that you covered three points in the body of your speech.

Increasing Immediacy

Your delivery also will be more effective with nonverbal behaviors that increase the perception of immediacy between you and your audience. Immediacy concerns how psychologically close or distant people perceive each other, as well as the degree to which they perceive each other as approachable.[22]

SPEAKING OF . . .

Delivery and ELM Factors

By Jim Katt

Some speech teachers have a list of specific public speaking "no-no's" involving the delivery of a speech. For example, one training method is to have everyone in the audience rap on the table each time an "um" or "ah" slips out of the speaker's mouth. Apparently, this helps speakers break the habit of using **vocalized pauses** *(the official name for um's and ah's). Some teachers promote some very specific rules for gesturing, demanding different types of gestures for specific speaking situations and suggesting that the use of any other type of gesture would be* wrong. *Other delivery "no-no's" might include: moving around too much, or not moving around enough; exhibiting poor posture while speaking; or failing to vary the pitch and volume of one's voice. The problem is that concentrating on not breaking these oratorical rules can lead to a performance orientation. If we have adopted a communication orientation, we can see that all of these delivery issues are examples of sender variables, which from an Elaboration Likelihood Model perspective, would be considered peripheral cues. The ELM suggests that when a topic is perceived to be relevant, the audience's focus is drawn away from these behaviors in favor of the message itself. This might lead us to believe that as long as our audience is motivated, delivery doesn't matter. But as you may recall from our discussion of the ELM, there are two factors that determine whether audience members are likely to engage in effortful processing of a message. The relevance of the message provided* **motivation** *to process, but the other factor is* **ability**—*the audience must be able to process the message. This is where delivery comes in. While good delivery cannot make an audience more able to process your message, poor delivery can interfere with message processing. If delivery faults are severe enough or frequent enough to be distracting, they may act as a hindrance to the audience's ability to elaborate on the message—even a*

relevant message. We have all endured presentations from speakers who have a bad habit of saying "ah" or "um" before practically every phrase they utter. If the audience perceives the message to be relevant, they may listen through the vocalized pauses for a while, but eventually the constant barrage of ah's and um's draws their attention away from the message and becomes a barrier to message processing. So, the problem is not that throwing in an occasional vocalized pause is an oratorical sin. However, when the ah's and um's are frequent enough to be distracting, they can interfere with message processing"

Even delivery elements that are normally considered "good" can be distracting when overused. For example, by moving around a bit while speaking you can foster a sense of closeness with your audience. Some speakers, however, pace back and forth quickly and constantly, creating the impression that they may wear out a portion of the floor. In these cases, there is a danger the audience will focus on the pacing instead of the message. If other bodily movements, such as shifting your weight, fiddling with your ring, or pushing back your hair, occur only occasionally during your presentation, they probably won't even be noticed by your audience. But if they occur over and over while you speak, there is a good chance your audience will be focused on your movements rather than your message.

How to avoid a distracting delivery? Rather than worry about all the distracting things you might be doing (most of which you probably do not have a problem with that), ask a friend to give you a report on your delivery the next time you make a presentation. If your friend identifies distracting behaviors in your delivery, work on eliminating them. Perhaps the best delivery advice is the simplest: do those things that help you accomplish your communicative goals and avoid doing those things that get in the way.

Generally the perception of immediacy between people is desirable because people who are perceived as immediate are also perceived as friendly and approachable, stimulating, open to dialogue, and interpersonally warm.

Because public speaking normally takes place in a setting that arbitrarily puts physical distance between speakers and their audiences, speakers usually have to reduce this physical distance psychologically. You can do this in at least two ways. The first, which we discussed at length in Chapter 10, involves the use of immediate language. The second is to make your delivery more nonverbally immediate.

The easiest and most effective way to make the delivery more immediate is through nonverbal channels. Eye contact is the perfect medium. Even when people are separated by substantial physical distance, eye contact enables them to bridge this distance in a psychological sense. The best public speakers, for example, are often the ones who make you feel as if they are speaking to you, and only you, with their eyes as well as their voices.

Eye contact is not the only medium, however, through which you can achieve greater immediacy with your audience. Immediacy can also be achieved with facial expressions such as a smile, with a conversational rather than condescending tone of voice, and by standing beside or in front of the lectern instead of appearing to hide behind it.

Taking a Proactive Approach

proactive delivery
Taking the initiative, anticipating, and controlling variables that will affect speech delivery.

Knowing something about the nature and functions of nonverbal behavior should assist you in making your speech delivery proactive rather than reactive. To engage in **proactive delivery** means that a speaker takes the initiative and anticipates and controls for as many variables as possible rather than merely reacting to them. Reactive delivery is like the boxer who only counterpunches. This wait-and-see attitude is rarely the mark of a championship boxer, and it can be disastrous for even the most seasoned public speaker. The guidelines that follow should help you ensure that your nonverbal behavior enhances, rather than detracts from, the delivery of your speech.

Tips and Tactics

Guidelines for Proactive Speech Delivery

1. *Take control of your environment.* Regardless of when or where you are speaking, you are responsible for making sure the environment suits your purpose and delivery style. This means checking out and modifying the environment well ahead of the time you are scheduled to speak. Check on the configuration of seats and whether or not they need to be rearranged. Check on the lighting, including its operation if you need to darken the room. Check on the equipment available, including projectors, screens, video monitors, and computers. During your check, make sure you know how to operate equipment if you plan on using it. If you are using a microphone, make sure you have rehearsed with it and have done a thorough sound check.

2. *Rehearse.* You will never be comfortable with your delivery until you are first comfortable with the content of your speech. If you have to "overly think" about content as you speak, then it will impede your ability to complement your message nonverbally. When you are comfortable to the point that your speech becomes second nature, your facial expressions, gestures, and movements will become natural extensions of your message. Rehearsing content, therefore, paves the way for proactive delivery.

3. *Take control of your appearance.* Dressing appropriately is one of the easiest ways to enhance initial impressions of you as the medium of your message. Think about the possible effects of apparel, such as the baseball cap that seems to be attached to your scalp, the baggy shorts you prefer, or the saying on your favorite T-shirt.

4. *Use natural gestures.* Make a video of your practice. Check on your gestures. Do they appear natural and complement your delivery, or do they appear forced and detract from your spoken message?

5. *Time your speech.* Do this more than once and on video if you can. Note your timing and the degree to which the rate at which you speak facilitates the

Assessing Your Personal Style

Most of us have a personal style of communicating. Read each response and record whether you Strongly Agree (SA), Agree (A), Neither Agree or Disagree (N), Disagree (D), or Strongly Disagree (SD) with the statement.

1. I think people see me as bland.   SA A N D SD
2. I think people find me entertaining.   SA A N D SD
3. I think I'm a little introverted.   SA A N D SD
4. I show what I'm thinking and I'm feeling in my facial expressions.   SA A N D SD
5. I try and conceal my true feelings from others.   SA A N D SD
6. I gesture a lot.   SA A N D SD
7. I think I make a memorable impression.   SA A N D SD
8. I dislike conflict.   SA A N D SD
9. I'd like to be a performer.   SA A N D SD
10. I prefer that others take the lead in conversations.   SA A N D SD

Statements 1, 3, 5, 8, and 10 are associated with people who are cautious about communicating and avoid arguing. People who tend to agree with these items generally would be less demonstrative in their nonverbal behavior than people who tend to agree with items 2, 4, 6, 7, and 9. These items reflect people who are fairly dramatic in their nonverbal behavior.

The best speakers are ultimately those who are flexible enough to adapt their personal style to the rhetorical situation. That kind of flexibility typically evolves with time and practice. Become comfortable with what comes to you naturally. People who force facial expressions and gestures, for example, are less effective because such a forced style is usually perceived as "canned" and phony.

---

mood you want to communicate to your audience. Also, remind yourself that your practice time probably will be longer than when you speak before your audience.

6. *Avoid self-adapting behaviors.* During practice, watch out for self-adapting behaviors such as playing with your hair, tugging on a finger, cracking knuckles, licking your lips, and hiding your hands. Self-adapters such as these will call attention to themselves and undermine perceptions of your power and self-confidence. Before you speak, empty your pants pockets of loose change and keys, and leave pencils and pens at your desk.

Discovering Your Personal Style

A class in public speaking shouldn't be looked on as an episode of *Extreme Makeover*. All of us have a personal "style" of communicating that has been evolving over the course of our lives. Our goal is to help you develop and adapt your personal style to the demands of the public speaking transaction, both now and in the future. This involves teasing out the elements of your personal style that can work for you when you speak, and modifying elements of your personal style that may be undermining your ability to truly shine.

There is no one method of delivery that works best, regardless of a speaker's skills set or the rhetorical situation at hand. Some speakers have a dramatic style characterized by a high level of energy. They contort the expression on their face, freely gesture, and gracefully move as they speak. Other speakers are nearly deadpan but still highly effective. As we recommend in the Self-Assessment box "Assessing Your Personal Style" on page 279, build on the style of delivery that comes most naturally to you and don't mimic a style unsuitable to you.

 www.mhhe.com/brydon7e

To evaluate your understanding of this chapter, visit our Online Learning Center Web site for quizzes and other chapter study aids.

Summary

You have choices about how to best deliver your speech. The bottom line, however, is that you should choose a method that is appropriate for the rhetorical situation, the audience, and your overall communication skills and strengths as a public speaker.

• Speakers may choose from four methods of delivery: manuscript, memorized, impromptu, and extemporaneous.

• Extemporaneous speeches are commonly delivered using speaker's notes.

• Nonverbal behaviors are a wordless, but not silent, system of communication.

• Unlike language, nonverbal communication is continuous, makes use of channels of communication simultaneously, and is spontaneous.

• Specific codes of the nonverbal communication system that influence delivery include the environment, physical appearance and posture, voice, eyes and face, gestures and movement, touch, and time.

• Important functions of nonverbal communication in the delivery of speeches include regulating the transaction between speaker and audience, substituting for a verbal symbol such as a word or phrase, reinforcing the verbal dimension of a speaker's message, and increasing immediacy.

• Speakers are encouraged to take a proactive approach to delivery and to find their personal style.

Check Your Understanding: Exercises and Activities

1. Observe a speaker outside of your class. Keep track of the number of times the speaker (a) changes the zone of interaction, (b) moves away from the lectern, and (c) gestures. On a scale of 1 to 10, with 10 being the high end, rate the speaker in each of these areas. Compare and discuss your observation and ratings with those of other students. See if a pattern emerges.

2. Make two blank copies of the personal style scale you filled out in the Self-Assessment box on page 279. The next time you speak, ask two class members to fill out these scales in terms of how they perceive your communication style. Compare their assessments with yours. Do they agree? If they

do not agree, discuss the differences they see in your style relative to how you see yourself. Also see if you can isolate specific nonverbal behaviors that may help you explain any perceived differences.

3. On a scale of 1 to 10, how confident are you as an audience member in your interpretations of a speaker's nonverbal behavior? Using the same scale, how confident are you as a speaker in your audience's interpretation of your nonverbal behavior? If you responded as most people do to these two questions, you'll notice a discrepancy. We are more confident in our own interpretative abilities than those of our audience. Nonverbal communication research indicates that all of us are more confident in our ability to decode nonverbal behavior than we should be. This research also shows that this is especially true in terms of decoding nonverbal behaviors we associate with truthful rather than deceptive public speakers. Most of us, in fact, are lousy at deception detection. Discuss with other people in class the implications of this research for the transaction between speakers and audiences.

4. Have someone loosely tie your hands behind your back or try to keep your hands clasped behind your back. Now, standing in front of the class, try to give audience members directions from where you are standing to your exact residence. What lessons about the relationship between nonverbal communication and delivery can be learned from this frustrating exercise? Be specific. Write down at least three and share them with your class.

5. Differences in nonverbal norms, as well as differences in communication styles and patterns, are common across cultures. Choose two or three mainstream North American norms for nonverbal behavior—for example, eye contact, gesturing, and time. Interview a student or faculty member from a culture other than your own about how these communication behaviors differ in his or her culture. Write a short paper summarizing your findings.

6. Explain why sign language is a *verbal* behavior, whereas vocal variation in pitch, rate, tempo, and the like are *nonverbal* behaviors, even though sign language is not vocalized and vocal variation is.

7. Explain why nonverbal behavior is continuous, uses multiple channels simultaneously, and is spontaneous, and how these characteristics distinguish it from the language of your speech.

8. Review the six guidelines for proactive delivery. Before your next speech, develop a plan to use at least three of these guidelines to improve your delivery skills in that speech.

9. Ask a classmate to apply Exercise 1 to your next speech. Talk with the classmate afterward about the relationship between his or her observations and the overall effectiveness of your delivery.

10. How would you describe your public speaking style? Is it a dramatic or understated style? Is it formal or informal? Ask some of your classmates to choose five adjectives they would use to describe your style of speaking. Compare their adjectives with five of your own. If you take advantage of this exercise, there is a good chance it will at least suggest a visual image of the style you communicate to others as you speak. You can then use this image to refine your style of speaking.

Notes

1. Edward T. Hall, *The Silent Language* (Greenwich, Conn.: Fawcett, 1959), 15.

2. F. Scott Fitzgerald, *The Great Gatsby* (New York: Charles Scribner & Sons, 1925).

3. Peter A. Andersen, *Nonverbal Communication: Forms and Functions,* 2nd ed. (Long Grove, Ill.: Waveland Press, 2008). See also M. L. Knapp and J. A. Hall, *Nonverbal Communication in Human Interaction,* 6th ed. (Belmont, Calif.: Wadsworth, 2006).

4. Andersen, *Nonverbal Communication: Forms and Functions,* 3–29.

5. Andersen, *Nonverbal Communication: Forms and Functions,* 3–29.

6. Andersen, *Nonverbal Communication: Forms and Functions,* 3–29.

7. R. Sommer, "Man's Proximate Environment," *Journal of Social Issues* 22 (1966): 60.

8. D. Leathers, *Successful Nonverbal Communication: Principles and Practices* (New York: Macmillan, 1986).

9. K. E. Lewis and M. Bierly, "Toward a Profile of the Female Voter: Sex Differences in Perceived Physical Attractiveness and Competence of Political Candidates," *Sex Roles* 22 (1986): 1–11.

10. L. A. Malandro, L. Barker, and D. A. Barker, *Nonverbal Communication,* 2nd ed. (New York: Random House, 1989).

11. Benedict Carey, "When All You Have Left Is Your Pride," *New York Times,* 6 April 2009.

12. George B. Ray, "Vocally Cued Personality Prototypes: An Implicit Personality Theory Approach," *Communication Monographs* 53 (1986): 266–76.

13. Richard L. Street and Robert M. Brady, "Evaluative Responses to Communicators as a Function of Evaluative Domain, Listener Speech Rate, and Communication Context," *Communication Monographs* 49 (1982): 290–308.

14. David B. Buller and R. Kelly Aune, "The Effects of Speech Rate Similarity on Compliance: An Application of Communication Accommodation Theory," *Western Journal of Speech Communication* 56 (1992): 37–53.

15. P. Ekman and W. V. Friesen, *Unmasking the Face: A Guide to Recognizing Emotions from Facial Expression* (Englewood Cliffs, N.J.: Prentice-Hall, 1975). See also P. Ekman, W. V. Friesen, and S. Ancoli, "Facial Signs of Emotional Expression," *Journal of Personality and Social Psychology* 39 (1980): 1125–34.

16. Nicole C. Wong, "Palo Alto May Relent—It's OK to Frown," *Sacramento Bee,* 18 April 2003, A6.

17. Andersen, *Nonverbal Communication: Forms and Functions,* pp. 42–44, 84.

18. Stephen Thayer, "Close Encounters," *Psychology Today* 22, no. 3 (1988): 31–36. See also A. Montague, *Touching: The Significance of the Skin* (New York: Harper & Row, 1971).

19. Michael Ventura, "Trapped in a Time Machine With No Exits," *Sacramento Bee,* 26 February 1995, C1.

20. A. Timothy Church, Cheryl A. Anderson-Harumi, Alicia del Prado, Guy Curtis, Junko Tanaka-Matsumi, José Valdez Medina, Khairul A. Mastor, Fiona White, Lilia A. Miramontes, and Marcia S. Katigbak, "Culture, Cross-Role Consistency, and Adjustment: Testing Trait and Cultural Psychology Perspectives," *Journal of Personality and Social Psychology*, 95, no. 3 (September 2008): 739–55.

21. Andersen, *Nonverbal Communication: Forms and Functions,* 31–54.

22. Andersen, *Nonverbal Communication: Forms and Functions,* 31–54.

chapter 12

EFFECTIVE USE OF VISUAL AIDS

— Dr. Jim Katt

Objectives

After reading and discussing this chapter, you should be able to:

- Define the term *visual aid* from a functional perspective

- Identify the strengths of visual aids and describe the ways that visual aids can help you communicate with your audience more clearly

- Describe the characteristics of effective visual aids

- Understand the advantages and disadvantages of the various types of visual aids

- Demonstrate the use of PowerPoint™ in a way that establishes the proper relationship between you and your visuals

- Incorporate underused techniques when using PowerPoint™ in your speech

Key Concepts

Animation effects

"B" key

Bullet lists

Fonts

Labels

Legibility

Objects and models

Overhead transparencies

Pass-around visual aids

Posters and flip charts

PowerPoint

Reveal

Titles

Visual aids

Visual aids can make or break your presentation. This chapter explores how the effective use of presentation aids can enhance a presentation, enhance your own credibility, and increase your audience's understanding, acceptance and retention of your message. When you are making a presentation to an audience, your audience has five senses with which to receive your message. Of the five, three have limited use in public speaking: touch, taste, and smell. Yes, there have been presentations where the audience was able to feel the texture of the fabric sample that was passed around, or was treated to some tasty samples of Greek pastry, or got a whiff of freshly baked bread, but most of the time speakers use the channels of sound and sight. Of course having something worthwhile to say, crafting sound rhetorical arguments, and creating a well-organized, compelling message are important aspects of any presentation. But no matter how well-conceived, your message won't be effective unless you can effectively translate it into sounds and sights. This chapter focuses on the visual part of your presentations.

Defining Visual Aids

Today, visual aids seem to pop up in almost every speech. PowerPoint slides, flip charts, diagrams, objects, and video clips increasingly find their way into presentations. These visual augmentations are supposed to help the presenter deliver the message to the audience. Unfortunately, visual aids are often poorly conceived and fail to help speakers communicate more clearly. In fact, they often get in the way of an otherwise clear presentation. But used well, visual aids can enhance the effectiveness of a presentation. While your most important visual is yourself, our discussion will focus on the use of *other* visual elements in your speeches. But it is appropriate to be reminded of the importance of ourselves as visuals, because we want to be sure the other visuals don't take attention away from the most important element in your presentation–you.

visual aids

Visual elements that help your audience receive your message

Visual aids are visual elements that help (aid) your audience in receiving your message. It is important to remember that the visual aid, whether it takes the form of an object, a poster, or some sort of projected image, is not the message, and not the messenger; it is just your helper. If, when speaking, you treat the visual aid like it is more important than you, your audience may begin to feel that it *is* more important than you. It is unfortunate when that happens, because ultimately they would have been able to relate more to you, the person, than they will ever relate to your object, your poster, or your projected image.

Using Visual Aids

Visual aids can help or hurt your presentation. There are several ways visual aids, if used effectively, can assist you in getting your message across:

Attract Audience Attention

Visuals attract the audience's attention. Hold up an object or project a slide and all eyes will be on it. For a speaker, this is a two-edged sword. Drawing your audience's attention away from their daydreaming or looking around the room is a good thing, but drawing your audience's attention away from you, the presenter, is only worthwhile if the visual they are drawn to conveys (or helps to convey) your message. This is one reason it is unwise to display visual aids throughout the entire speech. When you need to draw attention to something visual, use a visual aid. The rest of the time, put the visual aids away and let the audience pay attention to the presenter.

Emphasize Key Points

Because visuals draw attention, they can be used to emphasize key concepts. When your audience can see as well as hear certain key points, they are likely to remember them (Katt, Murdock, Butler, & Pryor, 2008; Vogel, Dickson, & Lehman, 1986). A well-constructed **bullet list** can help your audience see your main points and how they relate to one another. A compelling photograph may stay in your audience's memories far longer than your words. But it's important to realize that this effect can backfire if overused. We have all fallen victim to presenters who have almost the entire text of their speeches written out on PowerPoint slides or overhead transparencies, and then proceed to read to us what we are seeing on the screen. This technique fails for several reasons. First, everything in the speech can't be a key point. Someone once noted that there cannot be peaks without valleys. The same logic goes for messages. If you were composing a written message you might bold a key word, for emphasis. But if you bold *all* the words, you end up emphasizing nothing. Secondly, the audience can read for themselves, so it's patronizing to read to them. Finally, when everything is on the screen, the audience gets the idea that *you* aren't very important, since you don't seem to add any value to the transaction. When that happens, you throw away the high-touch impact of your presence. And if you don't add anything to the presentation, you're wasting your audience's time. You could have emailed your slides to them, if that's all you had. Judicious use of visuals for emphasis can be effective in helping your audience know and remember those key concepts.

bullet list
listing your key ideas can help your audience see your main points and how they relate to one another

Show the Relationship between Points

When you read a book, there are sentences, and paragraphs, and sections, and chapters to help you know how the information goes together. When you listen to someone speak, it can be difficult to know what goes with what. There are some aural things (like using clear transitions and signposts) that you can do to make the organization of your speech clearer to your audience. Visuals can also be used for this purpose. A concise list of points, for example, provides a visual indication of how one point relates to the next. If you reveal the points one at a time as shown in Exhibit 12.1, it can further help your audience realize when you are moving from one point to the next.

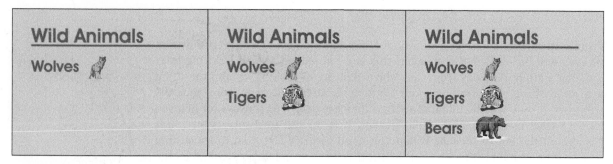

Exhibit 12.1
Revealing one bullet at a time helps make your speech clearer to your audience

As we said earlier, be careful when designing PowerPoint slides. Too many bullet lists or wordy and hard to read bullets can confuse the audience; or worse, put them to sleep. In a later section we will discuss how to design effective PowerPoint bullets.

Simplify Numeric Information

Most people learned numbers visually. We learned to recognize them visually, and we learned to add, subtract, multiply, and divide them visually. So it's little wonder that when we receive a barrage of numeric information orally, it is difficult to follow. When hearing numeric data, many people resort to mentally visualizing the numerals to make sense of them. Properly designed visual aids like the ones shown in Exhibit 12.2 can make things easier on our audiences. Either by showing them the numbers, or by providing a graphic representation of the values the numbers represent, speakers can make life easier for their audiences, and be more effective presenters.

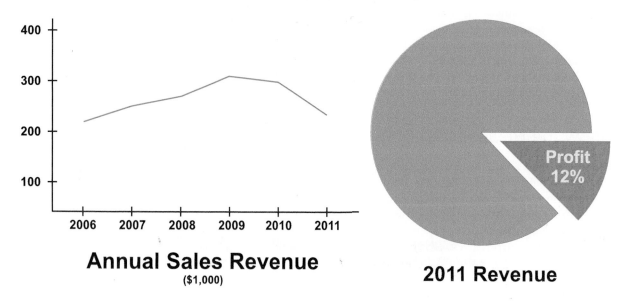

Exhibit 12.2
Graphic representation of numeric data helps your audience make sense of the information

Make Examples More Specific

Perhaps your speech is about your camp counselor who first got you interested in astronomy and inspired you to work hard, get good grades, and go to college to become a rocket scientist. There would be stories to tell and touching anecdotes to include in your speech, but a photograph of that counselor (maybe even one with you in the shot), would go a long way in helping your audience feel like they *knew* that person, instead of just knowing some things about her.

Exhibit 12.3

A picture can take a general idea and quickly make it specific

Perhaps it is not a technique that works for every speech, but sometimes a well-placed picture can take an example from general to specific in a hurry. I once heard a young woman give a speech about her job driving a huge, off-road dump truck at a coal mining site. She mentioned several times that the truck was very large, but it wasn't until she showed the picture (Exhibit 12.3) of her standing next to the truck (the top of her head came only to the middle of the wheel) that the audience really got a sense of how large the truck really was. Saying "large" provided a general idea; showing the truck, with her as a reference, made it specific.

Illustrate Difficult-to-Describe Objects or Scenes

Some things are just difficult to put into words. If you wanted to describe a location on the other side of the campus, you could talk about how to get there, or what it was near, or where it was relative to some central feature of the campus—or you could show them a campus map like the one in Exhibit 12.4 showing all the landmarks and highlighting the location. Some things are just easier to show than to tell; that's where a good visual aid can be a real helper.

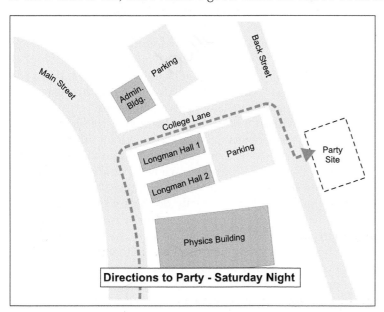

Exhibit 12.4

Maps can quickly illustrate locations that are difficult to describe

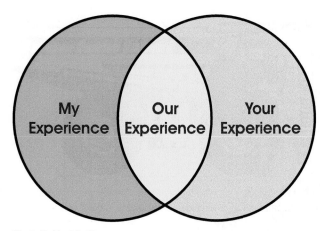

Exhibit 12.5
Drawings can simplify complex concepts

Illustrate Symbolic Relationships

A drawing or diagram is often symbolic rather than literal. Suppose you were giving a speech about interpersonal communication and you needed to describe the importance of each person's experiences as they relate to the shared experiences between two people in a relationship. You could talk it through, but it is a fairly abstract concept that might become clearer if you introduced a diagram that helped your audience visualize the concept.

Of course people don't literally walk around with big circles of experience that intersect other people's circles, but the circles provide a symbolic way of representing the experiential relationship.

So visual aids can help speakers attract an audience's attention, emphasize key points, show relationships between points, simplify numeric information, make examples more specific, illustrate things that are difficult-to-describe, or create symbolic relationships. But this isn't always the case. Frequently, speakers employ visual elements that fail to accomplish any of these functions. In an attempt to avoid having that happen to us, let's examine some of the characteristics of effective visual aids.

Characteristics of Effective Visual Aids

Effective Visual Aids Are Visible

Of course, it wouldn't make any sense to have an invisible visual aid, but some speakers create visual aids that might as well be invisible because they are not *large* enough, or not *legible*. Ideally, visual aids are not just visible; they are *easy* for the audience to see. If the visuals involve text, the letters must be large enough for everyone to see easily. We recommend that projected visuals (either PowerPoint or overhead transparencies) be set in no less than 24-point type. That means that *all* text, even captions, labels, and citations, should be at least 24-point. If you are creating a poster or flip chart, the "correct" size will depend on how large the room is. For small rooms (seating 30 people or fewer) a minimum text size of 1½ inches is suggested, with titles at least twice as large (Hamilton, 1996).

If your visual aid is an object, it needs to be large enough for all to see. One sure way to annoy your audience is to hold up a small object and then say, "Well, you probably can't see this, but…." Besides the obvious dysfunction of a visual aid the audience can't really see, the act of showing them the "too small" object can send the unintended message that you really don't care that much about whether or not the audience receives your message clearly. And if they get the idea you don't care, there really isn't any reason for them to care either. If the thing you are talking about is too small, figure out a way to enlarge it for your audience. Often, the easiest method is to find (or take) a digital picture of the object and make the image into a PowerPoint slide. In that case, you might still show the actual object, so they can see how small it is, but use the PowerPoint slide to allow them to visually examine the object.

**Mint Mark
(Denver Mint)**

A PowerPoint slide of a small object can help your audience see it in detail

Today, most college students have grown up with computers and graphic programs like PowerPoint. It wasn't that long ago when the most common student visual aid was created with poster board and markers. That put a lot of pressure on the creator to write legibly, so the audience could actually read what was written on the poster. One would think computers would solve the legibility problem, but presenters have found new, computerized ways to make even computer-generated visuals illegible. The PowerPoint section of this chapter will cover this issue at some length, but at this point, let's remind ourselves that increasing the **legibility** of your visual aid is not about making text *possible* to read; it's about making it *easy* to read. Decorative fonts or font colors that don't contrast with the background will reduce legibility. Many fonts available in PowerPoint, such as Old English or script fonts are illegible (along with green text over a blue background).

legibility
The ease with which something can be read

Effective Visual Aids Are Non-Distracting

A good visual aid can draw the audience's attention to key points, but a poor visual aid can draw their attention away from the speaker's message. Some speakers allow their visual aids to be more disruptive than instructive. This unfortunate situation can be avoided by following two guidelines.

First, keep the visual aid out of sight when not in use. Suppose your speech included a reference to a complex optical illusion. What if, at the beginning of your speech, you set up an easel with a poster-sized image of the illusion and then started in on your introduction? Do you think the audience would be paying attention to what you were saying? Most of them would be engossed in the picture, trying to figure out how the illusion works. In this case, your visual serves as a distraction rather than an aid. The solution is to keep it out of sight until you are ready to use it. In the case of a poster on an easel, just bring a sheet of white poster board to cover the visual until you're ready for it. If you are using an overhead transparency, leave the projector turned off until its time comes. If you are using PowerPoint, display a black slide or use the "B" key (as explained later in this chapter). When you are finished referring to your visual, put it back out of sight, using the same method.

Second, keep the visual aid in your possession if at all possible. There may be occasions where a **pass-around visual aid** is necessary, but try to avoid those situations. The pass-around visual aid inevitably draws attention away from the presentation as it snakes its way through the audience. And from the perspective of the individuals in the audience, the pass-around is received too early or too late for everyone except the lucky one or two who happen to have it exactly when it's being referred to.

pass-around visual aid
Can draw attention away from the presentation

Effective Visual Aids Are Simple and Clear

Because visuals naturally draw attention, it is important to have the attention focused on something that helps communicate your message. Sometimes speakers include too much visual information and leave their audience confused instead of enlightened. As the story goes, someone viewed one of Michelangelo's sculptures, a stunning lion, just after the artist had completed it. The observer asked Michelangelo how he was able to create such a beautiful lion from a block of stone. The artist thought a moment, and then said he studied the blank stone until he could "see" the lion inside it. Then, he continued, it was simply a matter of removing all the stone that wasn't the lion. Of course! That explains why everyone who is skillful with a chisel can't create timeless art. It only works for those who can "see the lion." A student gave a speech on jet engines. He explained that there were really only five major components of a jet engine: the air intake, compressor, combustion chambers, turbine, and the exhaust nozzle. That seemed simple enough to his audience. Then he projected an overhead slide that must have been copied from an aircraft repair manual. The illustration showed every nut, bolt, and washer in a commercial airliner's jet engine, along with part numbers and arrows to connect the part numbers to the parts. It was an incredibly complex visual. As the speaker frantically pointed to various areas in the mass of parts that he claimed corresponded to the five basic components, the audience became confused, quickly gave up trying to understand, and soon tuned out the speaker and his message. Metaphorically speaking, this speaker was guilty of displaying the block of stone and expecting his audience to see the lion within. Good visual aids have nothing extraneous that needs to be chipped away. Good illustrations show the elements that are being explained and nothing else.

Showing the audience more than you are prepared to explain is, at the least, an annoyance, and, at the most, reason for them to give up on your message altogether.

Air Intake **Combustion Chamber** **Nozzle**

Compressor **Turbine**

Exhibit 12.6
Good illustrations only include the elements you want to discuss

Effective Visual Aids Serve a Communicative Purpose

Some students include visual aids in their presentations because their professor has required them to do so. While adherence to the requirements of the assignment is a good thing, a visual aid that has no communicative purpose is not. Remember the definition at the beginning of the chapter: visual aids are visual elements that help your audience receive your message. If your visual aid doesn't help get your message across, it is not really a visual *aid*. A student who presented a speech about his job building and selling computers held up a computer mouse at the end of his speech. He said, "By the way, here's a mouse. Most of the computers I sold came with a mouse." What communicative purpose did that visual serve? Was there nothing else in his message that could have been communicated more effectively with the help of a visual aid? During the course of his speech, he mentioned that the systems he built offered more features for less money than the brand-name computers. He might have created a visual that pictured one of his computer systems next to a brand-name system. He could have listed the pertinent specifications of each along with the prices, reinforcing his claim that the computers he built were a better value than the brand-name computers. That sort of visual aid would have served a communicative purpose. The mouse did not. In this case, it didn't even fulfill the requirement to have a visual aid–his professor refused to give him credit for a non-functional visual aid.

Types of Visual Aids

Objects or Models

Often, showing your audience "the thing" that you are talking about goes a long way toward making your speech more effective. This is where using a real object can be very effective. Of course, some things are too large or too small, but many objects are portable enough to bring with you and still large enough to see. Often, objects can be used effectively with other visuals. For example, if you were giving a speech that included describing the parts located on the motherboard of a computer, for example, you might bring in an actual motherboard, so your audience gets a sense of its overall size, and also have a series of projected pictures that show the individual parts, which would be too small for them to see on the motherboard. Objects can be helpful in a *literal* sense (such as showing the audience how big the motherboard is) or in a *symbolic* sense.

A student speaking about his job as a server in a restaurant used a waiter's wallet (the leather or plastic folder containing the bill that servers bring to the table) as a symbol of ongoing feedback from customers that is reflected by the size of the tips. "Some employees are evaluated once a year," he said. "Servers are evaluated every day, and the results show up here, in this wallet." The audience members already knew what the wallet looked like, so it wasn't informative in the usual sense, but the speaker made it into a symbol of the evaluative nature of tips. Each time he referred to one of the customer service aspects of his job, he held up the wallet, reminding the audience that being a waiter (and earning tips) is all about customer service. It was an effective–and symbolic–visual.

If the real object is too large, too expensive, or too dangerous to bring with you a model or facsimile may be the answer. The space shuttle is too large, too expensive, and too dangerous to bring with you, but a model of the space shuttle might provide a more compelling visual than a picture of it. The young woman who spoke about the huge truck she drove couldn't bring the truck, but the picture she brought got her message across. Also, beware of safety regulations, particularly for college presentations. When you give that speech about bow hunting, you'll want to bring in a *picture* of your cross bow and leave the real thing at home.

Posters or Flip Charts

Posters and flip charts are only useful for relatively small audiences, but they have some advantages. They are inexpensive, they do not require special lighting, and they are completely low-tech, so they aren't subject to the technical problems that often plague PowerPoint presentations. They do have problems of their own, however. First, if the posters or flip charts are hand drawn, care must be taken to make them legible—not just decipherable, but *easy* to read. As we mentioned previously, text should be no smaller than 1½ inches high and titles should be at least twice as large. Second, some thought needs to go into how they are going to be supported (literally, what's going to hold them up). Poster boards balanced on the chalk tray of a blackboard will almost always fall down in the middle of your presentation. In the same manner, masking tape doesn't really stick to a chalkboard—at least not for long. Some tapes can also damage paint or wall coverings, which leaves you making a bad impression with whoever is hosting the event. Pushpins are effective, providing you bring them and there is a "pinable" surface available. Easels also work well, if the visual is stiff enough not to bend over during your speech. The biggest reason speakers have poster support problems is that they fail to carefully think through the issue *before* their speeches. This isn't rocket science, just one of those cases where an ounce of prevention really *is* better than a pound of cure. Finally, posters should look *professional.* If it looks like an elementary school student scribbled it together moments before your speech, your credibility can be damaged.

Overhead Transparencies

The venerable overhead transparency projector is often scornfully viewed by speakers who increasingly prefer to use projected computer images like Power-Point. While it is true that presentation software has many advantages over its low-tech predecessor, there are still some merits in using overhead transparencies. First, transparencies can be projected effectively in rooms that are too bright for computer video projectors to work properly. The most important advantage, however, is dependability. About the only thing that can go wrong with the overhead projector is the bulb burning out. Many projectors have spare lamps built into them, making them extremely dependable. Even though projecting PowerPoint is hardly cutting-edge technology, there is a lot that can go wrong. Murphy's Law suggests than anything that *can* go wrong *will* go wrong, so overhead transparencies provide fewer opportunities for Murphy to interfere with your speech. Many professional speakers who use PowerPoint as their primary presentational aid carry overhead transparencies of key slides just in case disaster strikes.

Although overhead transparencies are not used very much these days, it is still a good idea to know how to use this old, but reliable visual aid. There are "Tips for Projecting Overhead Transparencies" listed at the end of this chapter. You would do well to read the tips carefully, just in case you ever find yourself needing to make a low-tech presentation.

Tips and Tactics

Projecting Overhead Transparencies

There are a few things to bear in mind when using overhead transparencies. First, when creating the transparencies, follow the same rules for text visuals that you would for designing PowerPoint slides. This includes trying to keep the text size at least 24 point. Speakers will sometimes photocopy a page of a book onto a transparency. This almost always makes a poor visual, with text so small that the audience either cannot read it or will not be willing to put forth the effort to read it. Projecting a bad visual doesn't make it a good visual–it just increases the number of people who can see that it's bad.

The overhead projector will project either a landscape or portrait slide, but nearly all screens are oriented for landscape, so compose your slide in the landscape format. Also, be careful with colors. Many of the inks used in inkjet printers are opaque rather than translucent. Since light must shine through the transparency for a color to be projected, opaque colors end up looking black when projected. The best practice is to test your slides prior to your presentation.

Getting the projector positioned and focused is a fairly simple matter, but should be taken care of prior to your speech. The following hints and a little practice should be all you need to use an overhead projector effectively.

- **Image size**–is determined by the distance of the projector from the screen (the farther away, the larger your image will be). Be sure the projector is far enough away to produce an image that is big enough to be seen by everyone.

- **Focus**–is adjusted by the knob near the lens-head. Check focus prior to your presentation.

- **Vertical position of image**–The lens-head tilts to allow you to move the image up or down on the screen. Adjust tilt prior to your presentation.

- **Orientation of slide**–If you are standing behind the projector (your back to the screen), place the slide on the glass with the same orientation as if you were reading it (upper left at the upper left, etc.).

- **Position slide with the projector OFF**–Whenever possible, turn the projector off to position or change slides. Spare your audience the distraction of watching you set up the next slide.

- **Avoid "giant hand"**–Using your finger to point to things on the transparency can have a King Kong effect. If it is necessary to point to items on the slide, use a pencil, pen or other small pointer.

- **Eye contact**–Avoid turning toward, or talking to, the screen. Maintain eye contact with your audience.

- **Find a good place to stand**–You'll want to avoid standing in the projector beam (and thus casting a distracting shadow on the screen), or blocking part of your audience's view. This is one of the biggest disadvantages of overhead projector use. It is often difficult to find a place that doesn't obstruct someone's view. Stepping back to a position next to the screen is often the only solution–if you are using speaker's notes, be sure to take them with you when you step back.

- **Turn the projector off**–when not in use.

PowerPoint

Presentation software, such as Microsoft's PowerPoint, has become a standard tool of the workplace, something everyone is expected to know how to use–like word-processing or email. In many ways, this is a good thing. Visual information that was once displayed on poster boards, flip charts, or overhead transparencies now can be easily and clearly presented with the help of PowerPoint or one of the competing presentation software packages. A well-designed set of PowerPoint slides can provide visual support to a spoken message and allow the speaker to devote only a minimal amount of his or her attention to displaying the visuals.

PowerPoint is a tool, and like any tool, it can be misused. The experienced carpenter can use saws and chisels to create fine furniture. However, those same tools, badly used, can turn good lumber into worthless scraps of wood. In the realm of carpentry, even the less-than-skillful carpenter generally realizes his or her mistakes and doesn't try to assemble the mis-crafted pieces into furniture. Unfortunately, in the realm of presentations, ill-fashioned PowerPoint slides often fail to go to into the trash and instead become part of the presentation–to the detriment of both presenter and audience. Are there any among us who have not been the victims of some of the following varieties of PowerPoint abuse?

- Speakers who include nearly everything they say on the slides, and spend most of their "presentation" reading the slides to the audience
- Speakers who turn their backs to their audiences, face the screen, and read the slides

There are many ways that PowerPoint can distract from your message

- Presentations where every new bullet point or graphic object flies into view in a distracting, annoying manner
- Presentations where the annoying fly-ins are accompanied by even more annoying sound effects
- Speakers who turn the lights out on themselves, their voices becoming disembodied, mystery narrators for their slides
- Text slides that are difficult to read because the text is too small, they are too wordy, poorly laid out, or the color of the lettering blends into the background
- Illustrations, charts, and graphs contain so much information that it is difficult to find the point of the message

Using PowerPoint Effectively

There are many books and Web sites that explain how to create slides and operate PowerPoint software, but very few resources offer guidance on how to effectively integrate PowerPoint visuals into a presentation. The remainder of this chapter concerns using PowerPoint effectively and avoiding PowerPoint abuse.

Who Is the Presenter and Who Is the Helper?

One way to avoid PowerPoint abuse is to be clear about your role and PowerPoint's role in your presentation. It is easy, and sometimes more comfortable, to think of PowerPoint as the presenter and you as the helper/technician/projectionist, but to do so relinquishes the power of face-to-face communication. You are the human being–the living, breathing, thinking, feeling person who can relate to and communicate with other humans in much a more powerful way than any arrangement of ones and zeros and pixels. You are the speaker–the communicator, the person in charge of the presentation. PowerPoint can be a great helper, but be careful not to let it take over your role as presenter. Here are some things you can do to help keep you and PowerPoint in a proper relationship.

Maintain Eye Contact with Your Audience

During your presentation, maintain eye contact with your audience, not with your PowerPoint slides. It's okay to sneak a quick peek at the screen every so often, just to make sure it's working, but when you find yourself looking at the screen most of the time and at your audience only occasionally, you are (nonverbally) telling your audience that PowerPoint is the presenter and you are just the narrator. Keeping your eyes off the screen is easier said than done. When all of your audience is looking at the screen, it is tempting to join them. But when you do so, you relinquish your role as the presenter. Fight the temptation.

Show Visuals Only When They Add Something to Your Speech

Realize that you do not have to display an image on the screen at all times. It's okay to turn the screen off when you don't need it. In fact, building in some PowerPoint down time during your speech is desirable. After all, the PowerPoint images are usually larger and more colorful than you are. It is easy for your audience to become immersed in what's on the screen behind you and forget about *you*. Actors refer to this process as being "upstaged." In a theater, the part of the stage closest to the audience is referred to as downstage, while the area farthest away from the audience is upstage. If, while an actor is delivering lines downstage, actors behind him capture the audience's attention by making distracting movements, the distracters are guilty of "upstaging" the actor. A good director will not allow that to happen. When you are making a presentation, you are your own director, and you need to be careful not to allow yourself to be upstaged by your own PowerPoint.

Building in some time where PowerPoint is dark allows your audience to re-connect with you, the presenter. Because it is so easy to create PowerPoint slides, presenters often include slides that are not really necessary. Did you ever use poster board and markers to create a visual aid for some high school or middle school presentation? In those cases, would you ever go to the trouble of preparing a poster that said "Introduction" to hold up during the first part of your presentation? Most of us would not, yet speakers using PowerPoint do it all the time. In doing so, they not only miss an opportunity to connect with their audience, they demonstrate to their audience that the images shown on the screen may not be all that important. If the audience gets the idea that *you* aren't very important (because you are constantly being upstaged by PowerPoint), and that your PowerPoint isn't very important either (because information like "Introduction" isn't really useful), they will likely tune you *and* your PowerPoint out, and let their minds wander elsewhere.

The solution is to display PowerPoint images only when they add something to your speech. The rest of the time, when a visual aid is not essential to your message, turn PowerPoint off and take advantage of having your audience's undivided attention. Techniques for making PowerPoint "fade to black" are discussed later in this chapter.

Draw Attention to the Content, Not the Package

Your audience only has a limited amount of attention. The more they divide their attention, the less of it is focused on any one thing. While you are making a presentation, you want your audience to be attending to your *message*. What you say and do is an important part of your message, so you want your audience to be paying attention to *you*. But it's actually a little more complicated than that. What if you were giving a presentation on wireless widgets and decided to wear an orange and purple striped jump suit? That would certainly get your audience's attention, but would they be paying attention to your wireless widgets or your wardrobe? In fact, all of the attention they gave to your outfit would be attention that did *not* go to your message. So you want your audience to pay attention to the parts of "you" that are your message, and not be distracted by other aspects of "you."

The words and images on your PowerPoint slides are also part of your message, but presenters often make the mistake of dressing their messages up in ways that draw attention to the package instead of the content. When text or images fly onto the screen from all directions, the movement is at best distracting and at worst distracting *and* annoying. Either way, the audience is paying attention to the animation effect instead of the content. I find it troubling that the newer versions of PowerPoint have included a category of animation effects labeled "exciting." Do we really want the method by which our content appears on the screen to be exciting? Wouldn't it be more effective if our *content* was the exciting part? Art curators know how to frame paintings and photographs in ways that draw the viewers' attention to the picture, not the frame. Speakers using visuals must strive to accomplish the same result.

Use **animation effects** with extreme caution. For most situations, choose "appear" as the desired effect. If you simply must have things fly in, choose one of the subtle moves and use that same move throughout your presentation. Mixing up animation effects encourages your audience to pay attention to the effects–attention that would be better directed to the message.

animation effects
the use of animations should be minimal and consistent

PowerPoint also allows you to have sound effects accompany slide changes or animation effects. Although many presenters become infatuated with sound effects, the inclusion of sound rarely helps communicate the message and often distracts and annoys the audience. Sound effects should only be used on those rare occasions when they help convey the message. Using sounds as attention-getters only draws attention away from you and your message.

Make Your Visuals Easy for Your Audience to Receive

Some experts suggest that effective visuals should be designed so the viewer can absorb the information in no more than six seconds (Hamilton, 1996). This means text slides must be easy to read. Many authors have written lists of guidelines for creating PowerPoint text slides, most of which come down to limiting the amount of text and presenting it in the most easy-to-read manner. To that end, I suggest the following:

- use a maximum of six lines of text per slide   *6x6 Rule!*
- use a maximum of six words per line
- use a minimum of 24 point text
- use phrases, not sentences
- use upper- and lowercase type
- use simple typefaces (fonts)

Paying attention to these simple rules will result in slides that are legible. If, when a slide appears on the screen, it looks like it will require some mental energy to decode the information, audience members are likely to either fall into a reading mode (which necessitates ignoring the aural message), or simply tune out the visual altogether. Either way, the visual aid is not aiding the communication process. On easy-to-read text slides, the information jumps off the screen, and the audience does not feel they have to exert significant mental effort to interpret it.

Slides with graphics should also be comprehensible in six seconds. One common mistake that results in difficult-to-comprehend graphics is the inclusion of too much information. Charts and graphs are efficient ways of displaying a lot of information, but we must be careful not to display more than the audience can reasonably comprehend. A single chart that makes several points can be difficult for audiences to follow. One chart that illustrates one point is usually a better way to go. Also, most presentations do not require a lot of charts and graphs (although that doesn't stop some speakers from including them anyway). Pick just one or two that clearly illustrate the points being made.

Illustrations and diagrams can also suffer from information overload. Illustrations downloaded from the Internet often include more detail than the presenter intends to cover. While it is tempting to use the overloaded illustration and just ignore the extraneous information, there is a good chance that your audience will be distracted by the unexplained items. A good rule of thumb is never to show something you are not going to talk about. This might mean a little extra work. You may have to apply some electronic "White-Out" to the unwanted items, or you may have to create a new, simplified diagram or illustration. Expending the extra effort, however, is a good habit to acquire.

titles

describe the general
focus of a graphic slide

labels

identify specific elements
of a graphic slide

Presenters are rarely accused of being too clear, and displaying unsuitable images may convey to your audience that you do not value them sufficiently to create graphics that might actually help them understand and remember your message.

Effective graphic slides are also well identified. This includes **titles**, which tell the audience what they are looking at in general, and **labels**, which identify and call attention to specific items within the slide. PowerPoint makes it easy to highlight elements electronically, eliminating the need for presenters to use fingers, sticks, or laser pens to point out items while presenting. Highlighting and labeling are excellent examples of how PowerPoint's drawing and animation features can be used to focus the audience's attention on the message rather than distract from it. When using complex graphics, it is also possible to have Power-Point *reveal* portions of the graphic one at a time, so that the audience does not have to try to comprehend the entire graphic all at once. Some tips for labeling and highlighting are provided later in this chapter.

The bottom line is that when your visuals are unclear or difficult to comprehend, your audience is faced with the decision of either devoting a lot of attention to your visuals (at the expense of attending to your oral message), or tuning out your visuals (which usually involves tuning you out as well). In either case, the PowerPoint has taken over your presentation.

Underused PowerPoint Techniques

The techniques described in the following section are ways to really make PowerPoint work for you. A detailed tutorial is provided at the end of this chapter to help you master each technique.

Making PowerPoint "Fade to Black" during a Presentation

It is difficult to make PowerPoint actually "fade," but it is easy to have the screen go dark. As we discussed earlier, there are often times when visuals aren't required, and it would be better to give PowerPoint a rest. Having the screen go black accomplishes just that, and there are two techniques for achieving a black screen.

Create a Black Slide

A black slide is a slide with a black background and no text or graphics. When you project it, there is nothing to project, so the effect is the same as if you have turned the projector off. At the end of this chapter there are instructions for creating a black slide–it's not difficult. Many presenters begin their presentations with a black slide. This allows them to connect with their audience during the introduction of the presentation. Later, when a visual image is required, a simple slide advance will display the first image. Black slides work best when you have places in the presentation where you *know* you want to give PowerPoint a rest. Inserting the black slide will make it impossible for you to forget to give the graphics a break.

Use the "B" Key

Sometimes, in the course of making a presentation, you might want to go to black in a place where you had not planned to do so. The more spontaneous way to achieve a black screen is simply to touch the "B" key (the letter "B" on the keyboard, just above the middle of the space bar). It's easy to remember–"B" for black or "B" for blank. When you touch the key, the screen goes black. When you touch it again, your slides come back on, just where you left off. Be aware that this feature only works when you are in the presentation (slide show) mode.

Whether you do so by using black slides or the "B" key, giving PowerPoint some time off during your presentation is a good idea. The slides you show will be more effective if you show only the slides that add something to your presentation.

Using Custom Animation for Your Bullet Lists

As we said in an earlier section, revealing points in a list one at a time will help your audience realize when you are moving from one point to the next. This also keeps your audience from reading ahead and pondering the points you have not yet covered. One useful feature of PowerPoint is the ability to have your bullet points revealed one at a time. Sometimes you may have a list that has main points and sub points:

- Main Point 1
- Main Point 2
    - Sub Point 2.1
    - Sub Point 2.2
    - Sub Point 2.3
- Main Point 3

You may want the sub points to be revealed along with the main point, or you may want each sub point revealed separately. The custom animation feature in PowerPoint allows you to choose the way that helps you present your message most clearly. Before your next speech, practice using custom animations to create bullet lists as shown in the tutorial at the end of the chapter . If the default settings are not helpful for your presentation, change them. Remember, you are in charge.

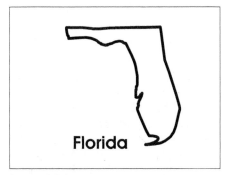
Original Slide

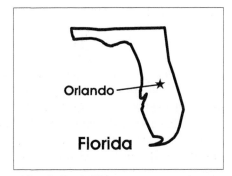
Highlighted Slide

Exhibit 12.7
Highlighting a slide is a simple technique to clarify your message

Highlighting Portions of a Slide

Earlier we talked about the need to highlight or point out specific elements on a picture or diagram. There are a number of ways of accomplishing this, but the instructions at the end of this chapter offer one of the more foolproof methods that does not require a lot of advanced PowerPoint knowledge. You can use this highlighting technique on charts, graphs, pictures, or diagrams. You can also add labels to go along with your highlights.

For example, if you are talking about the State of Florida, you might display a simple map (as shown above). When you want your audience to know where Orlando is located, you might add a star to highlight the location and a label to make it clear what you are highlighting. This simple technique uses the power of PowerPoint to help make your message clearer.

PowerPoint Recap

The use of PowerPoint can either help or hinder your presentation. It is a wonderful tool that can help you create and present effective visuals, but it can also be used to produce distracting images that overload and annoy your audience. How you use it is your decision, but bear in mind that **you** are the presenter and PowerPoint is your helper. This means **you** (not PowerPoint) are the most important element in your presentation. This means PowerPoint can (and should) go away when it's not needed. This means your slides must be designed in ways that emphasize the content, not the package. This means your audience should never feel like they are the victims of PowerPoint abuse.

Final Thoughts on the Effective Use of Visual Aids

Whatever type of visual aids you use, it is important to practice your speech with the visual aids–preferably in the location where you will be speaking. Whether your plan is to hold up an object, use a poster on an easel, project overhead transparencies, or utilize PowerPoint, practice can make the difference between success and failure. We have all witnessed presentations where problems with visuals not only distracted the audience, but distracted the speaker. Objects that prove to be unexpectedly difficult to hold, posters that slide off their easels, overhead transparencies that are projected upside-down (or backwards), or PowerPoint files that the computer refuses to read are the sorts of occurrences that every speaker dreads. But, in most cases, these potential disasters can be avoided with a little preparation. Lack of preparedness can add unnecessary stress to your speaking situation. Visual elements that you have practiced using, that you feel confident using, can help *reduce* anxiety. Do yourself and your audience the favor of practicing your presentation with your visual aids.

Visual aids can make your speeches more interesting, more memorable, and more effective–or not. The key is making the visual elements help you communicate your message more clearly. Don't fall into the trap of including visual elements just because everyone else has visuals, or because they're fun, or because you hope they will make your speech seem more professional. Let form follow function. Use visuals when they help your audience receive your message clearly, and put them away when they do not.

Summary

In this chapter, you learned the following:

- Visual aids can help you communicate more effectively by

  - Attracting audience attention
  - Emphasizing key points
  - Showing the relationship between points
  - Simplifying numeric information
  - Making examples more specific
  - Illustrating difficult-to-describe objects or scenes
  - Illustrating symbolic relationships

- To be effective, visual aids must be visible, non-distracting, simple, and serve a communicative purpose.

- While the most important visual element in your presentation is *you*, other visual elements include objects, models, posters, flip charts, and overhead transparencies. All require thought, planning, and caution.

- Presentation software, such as PowerPoint, when used with care, can add value to your presentation; however, it's important to remember that *you* are the presenter and PowerPoint is the helper.

Check Your Understanding: Exercises and Activities

1. Think about the visual aids you see speakers use when making presentations in your classes or at work. How do they help or hinder your learning?

2. Next time you encounter a speaker using visual aids (a professor, fellow student, business presenter) pay attention to the use of visuals. Are there points during the presentation where the visuals help make something more clear, compelling, or memorable? Are there other times when the visuals detract from the message? Which happens more often?

3. Think about a presentation you saw that annoyed you. What advice from this chapter could have helped the presenter make a more effective (less annoying) presentation?

References

Brigance, W. N. (1961). *Speech: Its techniques and disciplines in a free society* (2nd ed.). New York: Appleton-Century-Crofts.

Hamilton, C. (1996). *Successful Public Speaking*. Belmont, CA: Wadsworth.

Katt, J., Murdock, J., Butler, J., & Pryor, B. (2008). Establishing best practices for the use of PowerPoint as a presentation aid. *Human Communication. 11,* 193-200.

Vogel, D., Dickson, G., & Lehman, J. (1986). *Persuasion and the role of visual presentation support: The UM/3M study* (MISRC-WP-86-11), Minneapolis, MN: University of Minnesota, Management Information Systems Research Center.

PowerPoint Tutorial: Practicing Effective Visual Aid Techniques

How to Create a Black Slide in PowerPoint (Office2010™ version)

These instructions will vary slightly depending on which version of PowerPoint you are using, but the basic technique remains the same.

1. Create a new, blank presentation (File>New>Blank Presentation>Create).

2. If you are not already in the slide editing, or "normal" view, click the "View Tab" and then the "Normal" button.

3. Right click on a blank area of the slide, a menu will appear.

4. From the menu, choose "Format Background." A dialog window will appear.

5. In the "Fill" options, click "Solid Fill" and "Hide background graphics."

6. Next, click the "Fill Color" icon. Color selection boxes will appear. Click the black box, then click "Close." You will be returned to the "Normal" view

   Caution: Do *not* click "Apply to all," as this will turn all of your slides black.

   You have created a black slide. To create additional black slides, go into the "Slide Sorter" view, and select (single click) your black slide. While holding down the "Control" key, drag your existing black slide to wherever you need an additional black slide. PowerPoint will place a copy of your black slide in the new location, and leave the original where it was.

How to Customize Bullet List Animations (Office2010™ version)

PowerPoint makes it fairly easy to set up the animations, although the exact instructions differ from version to version. The instructions below should give you the basic idea.

1. Create a new, blank presentation (File>New>Blank Presentation>Create).

2. A newly created slide will appear. Right click on a blank area of the side, a menu will appear; click "Layout" to reveal a selection of layouts; chose "Title and Content."

3. Click where it says "Click to add text" and type a bullet list with several bullet points and a couple of sub points. To create a bullet list with sub points, press the *Tab* key before typing the first word of the sub point. PowerPoint will automatically indent and add a "sub" bullet. (To return to another main point, press *Shift + Tab*.)

4. Select the "Animations" tab, choose "Add Animation" A list of effects should below the "Add Animation" button.

5. In the "Entrance" group, click on "Appear."

6. You'll notice that numbers appear in boxes to the left of each of your bullet points. These indicate which items will appear on each successive click. (All of the items labeled "1" will appear on the first click, all of the items labeled "2" on the second click, etc.) If you want each point and its sub points to appear at the same time, skip to step 13.

7. If you want each point and each sub point to appear separately, click on "Animation Pane" (to the right of "Add Animation"); the animation pane should appear on the right of you PowerPoint desktop.

8. Activate the drop-down menu by right clicking on the first item, then select "Effect Options..." which will open a new window.

9. In the new window, select the "Text Animation" tab.

10. Select "By 2nd Level Paragraphs" in the Group text drop-down menu, click OK.

11. Notice that the boxes have been re-numbered, indicating that each sub point now requires a separate click.

12. Note: If the numbers in the boxes do not reflect the order of appearance you desire, click on the double down-arrowhead (just below the left side of the first item in the "Animation Pane"). This will allow you to view the controls for each of your bullet points and change them to suit your needs.

13. To test the animation, select the "Slide Show" tab; choose "From Current Slide."

How to Highlight Portions of a PowerPoint Slide (Office2010™ version)

The exercise below will highlight some text, but the same technique can be used for any visual.

1. Create a new, blank presentation (File>New>Blank Presentation>Create).

2. On the newly created slide, click where it says "Click to add title." Type your first name, middle initial and last name. *Note: if your slide doesn't have a box with "Click to add title," right click on a blank area of the side, a menu will appear; click "Layout" to reveal a selection of layouts; chose "Title Slide," then click where it says "Click to add title" and type your first name, middle initial and last name.*

For the sake of practice, let's assume that you wanted to call attention to your middle initial in a presentation. The following steps show how to highlight the initial.

3. Enter the "Slide Sorter" view of PowerPoint (View>Slide Sorter).

4. Click on the thumbnail of the slide you just created. If not already present, a box should appear around the slide, indicating you have selected it.

5. While holding down the Control Key, click on the slide, drag to the right, and release. You should now have two copies of your slide.

6. Double-click the second slide. This should take you to the "Normal" view.

7. Select the "Insert" tab and click on the "Shapes" button. Lots of options appear. Under "Lines" select the leftmost line tool – its icon is a diagonal line.

8. Position your cursor just under the left side of your middle initial.

9. Click and drag to the right, underlining your initial, and release. A line should appear. (Don't be concerned that it is not very attention-getting. We'll work on that.)

10. Your line should have little circles on each end, indicating that it is "selected." If it is not selected, select it by single-clicking on the line.

11. Select the "Format" tab and then click on "Shape Outline" and then select "Weight." Click on "6 pt." Your line should become thicker.

12. Next, go back to the "Shape Outline" menu and click on a bright color, like red. You should now have a thick, red line below your middle initial.

13. In the "Slides" display at the left side of your PowerPoint desktop, notice that you have two slides that are identical except that the second one has your middle initial underlined.

14. Select the "Slide Show" tab and then click "From Beginning." Your first slide should appear in full-screen, presentation mode.

15. Press the spacebar once to advance the slide and notice what happens. You are advancing to the next slide, but because everything except the underline is the same, it appears that the underline has been added to the original slide.

This is a very basic example of highlighting. There are other drawing tools besides the line tool. For example, you could use the rectangle tool or the oval tool (Insert > Shapes > Basic Shapes > Oval) to highlight something. *Tip: When you create closed shapes like ovals and rectangles, PowerPoint defaults to drawing a filled (colored-in) object. To remove the fill, click on the shape to select it, then select the "Format" tab, click "Shape Fill," and choose "No Fill."*

Alternatively, it is possible to make highlights and labels "appear" by using animations, but often it is easier and quicker to simply copy the slides and add the highlights to the copies. The copy technique is also more likely to work correctly on all versions of PowerPoint, while animations sometimes work differently from one version to another.

CONTEXTS FOR PUBLIC SPEAKING

Teachers use the skills and principles of informative speaking on a daily basis.

INFORMATIVE SPEAKING

Objectives  www.mhhe.com/brydon7e

After reading this chapter and reviewing the online learning resources at www.mhhe.com/brydon7e, you should be able to:

- Explain the relationship between informative speaking and persuasion.

- Explain how to adapt your informative speeches to audiences with diverse learning styles.

- Illustrate how informative speaking can be used in your other classes, at work, and in your community.

- Prepare an informative speech that is audience involving, appropriate, accessible, and potentially life enriching.

- Prepare informative speeches that explain, instruct, demonstrate, or describe processes, concepts, and skills.

Key Concepts

audience accessible

audience appropriate

audience involving

informative speaking

learning styles

"Those who can't do, teach. Those who can't teach, teach gym."

—WOODY ALLEN[1]

Woody Allen's tongue-in-cheek play on the idea that people who teach do so only because they would fail in "the real world" is funny. The fact that so many people, especially critics of the teaching profession, accept what the original quote implies is contrary to the experience of nearly every parent who has ever attempted to teach a son or daughter to drive a car, wield a tennis racket, or play a musical instrument. Teaching, in the best sense of the term, requires more than competence in the subject matter or the skill taught. It also demands the ability to transfer the competence and skill to others.

This chapter focuses on informative speaking. Whether the intent of informative speaking is to explain a process, describe a system, or demonstrate the benefits people can expect from following a speaker's advice, the transaction between speaker and audience is undeniably similar to the process of effective teaching.

Informative speaking is the process by which a speaker presents an audience with new information or a new perspective on old information. Put another way, the goal of informative speaking is audience learning. An effective informative speaker needs to master several skills, which we will look at in this chapter. These skills include:

- Understanding the relationship between informative speaking and persuasion.
- Understanding the relationship between informative speaking and audience analysis, including diversity of learning styles.
- Understanding how you are likely to give informative presentations throughout your life: in the classroom, the workplace, and the community.
- Making informative speeches involving, appropriate, accessible, and potentially life enriching for the audience.
- Putting theory into practice in speeches that explain, instruct, demonstrate, or describe.

informative speaking
The process of presenting an audience with new information or a new perspective on old information.

Informative Speaking and Persuasion

Although informative and persuasive speeches are nearly always treated separately in books like this one, the relationship between the two speech purposes can be confusing. Some argue that the relationship clearly is dichotomous: informative speeches educate, whereas persuasive speeches change minds and behavior. Others argue that the lines between informative and persuasive speaking have become so blurred that they are interchangeable.

Our position is based on a simple premise. An informative speech is not worth giving unless it is designed to reasonably ensure that it won't go in one ear and then right out the other. What good, for example, is an informative speech on wearing a helmet while biking, skiing, or snowboarding if it doesn't increase the probability of the audience seriously considering the information? Similarly, what good is to be gained by an informative speech on preventive health practices such as using sunscreen regularly if it has no motivational value for an audience?

Instead of looking at the relationship between informative and persuasive speeches as a dichotomous one, we want you to think about the two in terms of a continuum (Exhibit 13.1). On one end of the continuum is knowledge; on the

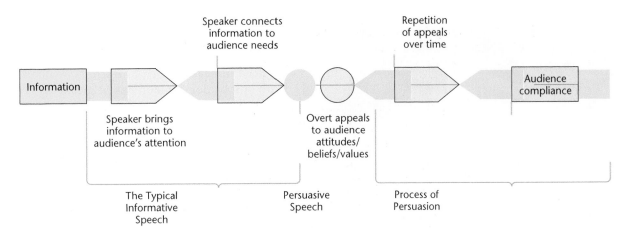

Exhibit 13.1
Continuum of Informative to Persuasive Speaking

other end is behavior. Given the poles of this continuum, persuasion is seldom the result of one powerful speech delivered by a singularly credible and charismatic speaker. More typically, persuasion is a process comprised of a series of interdependent messages over time. In the so-called real world, this process—this campaign—begins with someone or some agency providing people with information designed to stimulate them. This information, then, is used as a base from which a more explicitly persuasive campaign can be built to influence people.

At the same time, we recognize that messages primarily intended to persuade are often couched in the language of information. Infomercials, for example, are designed to make it look like the host is providing the audience with an "educational service," whether the topic is weight loss or pet stains on the carpet. Of course, the studio set and pitch are a ruse to deceive the gullible into buying the product being persuasively pitched.

As you select your speech topics, you need to be aware that simply calling a speech informative is no guarantee that it will be received by your audience as free of persuasive intent. Thus, before you choose a topic for an informative speech, be sure to ask yourself whether your ultimate goal is really to just present the facts and information necessary to educate them, or rather to affect people's attitudes and behaviors. Speeches that focus primarily on the latter goals are more appropriately delivered as persuasive speeches. When in doubt about the appropriateness of a topic, our advice is always to ask for feedback from your instructor.

Informative Speaking and Audience Analysis

Given our suggestions thus far in the book, it should come as no surprise that we want you to carefully analyze your audience as you prepare your informative speech. Obviously you need to consider the individual, group, and cultural makeup of an audience as you select your topic, decide on a specific purpose, and organize your informative speech. Rather than belabor what should now be obvious to you, however, we want to refocus on the diverse learning styles likely to be present among audience members.

Effective informative speaking requires adapting to a range of learning styles. This teacher involves one of his students in teaching the class.

learning styles
Differences in the way people think about and learn new information and skills.

Not everybody thinks in a linear or "logical" fashion. Some people can simply read a book and absorb the information, whereas others need to hear and see to learn. Still others learn best by doing. Good public speakers recognize these differences and appeal to as many styles as possible.

There are, of course, many useful ways of categorizing how people learn information, such as this list of diverse **learning styles:**[2]

- *Auditory linguistic:* Learning by hearing the spoken word.
- *Visual linguistic:* Learning by seeing the printed word.
- *Auditory numerical:* Learning by hearing numbers.
- *Visual numerical:* Learning by seeing numbers.
- *Audio-visual-kinesthetic combination:* Learning by hearing, seeing, and doing in combination.
- *Individual:* Learning when by oneself.
- *Group:* Learning in collaboration with other people.
- *Oral expressive:* Learning by telling others orally.
- *Written expressive:* Learning by writing.

Teachers confront this variety of learning styles every day. Many teachers use a combination of methods—individual and group work, written and oral assignments, print and visual materials—in an effort to adapt to the variety of learning styles in their classrooms. You can do much the same in an informative speech.

Given your time and resources, it makes no sense to suggest that you try to assess the preferred learning style of each and every member of your audience. Not only would such a recommendation be unrealistic, it generally is not necessary. You can make an earnest effort to adapt to the diverse learning styles you can expect among audience members by taking advantage of the multiple channels of communication available to you. Posters, overhead transparencies, or PowerPoint slides are excellent ways to reinforce visually what you say orally. Distributing a handout *after* a speech can help visual learners retain what was said. It helps to provide the audience with an opportunity to use as many senses as possible to process the message. If parts of the presentation can be seen, heard, and even touched, odds increase that the message will sink in.

For example, we had a student give an informative speech on using acupressure to relieve stress. By instructing the class to press on certain points on their bodies, the speaker allowed the audience to use their sense of touch to understand what was being said. Other speakers have appealed to their audience's sense of taste. We frequently have international students speak about a food unique to their culture and bring samples for the audience to try. We have also seen student speakers involve their audiences in a group exercise to better appreciate the subject on which they are speaking—for example, one speaker asked fellow students to model the simple yoga poses he first demonstrated, and a blind student spoke with the room dark for part of her speech, so that sighted students might better appreciate what she experiences when listening to a lecture.

Informative Speaking Throughout the Life Span

Informative speaking is probably the form of public speaking you're most likely to be called on to do throughout your life. One of the chief reasons is that informative speaking is used in so many settings, including the classroom, the workplace, and the community.

Informative Speaking in the Classroom

Two time-honored traditions in the college classroom are the term paper and the oral report. Although most students have at least passing familiarity with the elements of a good term paper, many students don't make the connection between the elements of a good oral report and the process of informative speaking.

An oral report basically is an informative speech. Thus, by putting to use what you know about informative speaking, you will be able to give oral reports that are both substantively and stylistically more effective than those of your classmates.

Viewing the oral report as an opportunity to speak informatively has several advantages. First, it provides you with an organizational framework for constructing your report. Second, it reminds you that you have an audience for your report whose background and learning styles must be taken into account. Finally, it forces you to think about how relevant the information in your report is to both your instructor and student colleagues.

Informative Speaking in the Workplace

No matter what you plan on doing to make a living, the odds are great that you will need to make informative presentations. What's more, the more successful you become in your chosen career, the more likely it is you will be required to give informative presentations. Although you won't necessarily have to speak to large numbers of people, you can reasonably expect to speak to groups of people you work with or lead.

While you may not think you are being evaluated when you speak at work, companies often use these "little" presentations to gauge your suitability for promotion to the managerial ranks or higher. Regardless of your career path, moreover, each rung you climb on the corporate ladder typically means you can expect to speak informatively more often rather than less.

Informative Speaking in the Community

You can reasonably expect to speak informatively with members of your community in at least one of two capacities: as a representative of your employer or as a concerned citizen. Private, as well as public, enterprises are justifiably concerned about their image within their local community. Many opinion polls show that the public is increasingly suspicious of the motives of private enterprise and increasingly dissatisfied with the performance of public agencies. It's not uncommon, therefore, for these organizations to make themselves available to service groups, such as Rotary International, the general public, or a citizens' group organized around a specific cause.

Some businesses have a person whose job is company spokesperson; large corporations may even have whole departments dedicated to public relations. Many organizations, however, have come to expect anyone in management to serve as an informative speaker to the community. In fact, private corporations, such as IBM, and public agencies, such as the police or fire department, may actually write such community service into their managers' job descriptions. Thus, just because you currently perceive your intended career as low profile, that doesn't necessarily make it so.

Finally, you may one day want or need to speak informatively as a private citizen. If you live in a community where cable television is available, your city council meetings probably are televised on your community access channel. If you tune in, you will see ordinary citizens making informative presentations at these meetings. Topics can range from the environmental impact of a new housing development to excessive noise from student housing. If you watch several of these presentations, you will probably conclude that very few of the speakers have much training in public speaking; people who do have training are easy to spot.

Your days as a public speaker will not be over once you've completed this class. Given what we've said here, in fact, you should now realize they are just beginning.

Message Keys of Effective Informative Speaking

Given that informative speaking is so common across the life span, you might think that people in general would be better at it. Yet you needn't be as old as your authors to have been put to sleep more than a few times by a boring lecture, policy presentation, or training seminar. So what makes one speaker's presentation so informative and stimulating that we want to learn more about what we initially thought was a boring topic? And why does another speaker's presentation leave us cold from beginning to end? Is the reason (a) the speaker, (b) the topic, (c) the message, (d) our perceptions, or (e) all of the above? Because the public speaking transaction is an interdependent system, the answer, of course, is (e) all of the above.

Research over the past two decades suggests that the likelihood of an audience's perceiving information as relevant and conducive to learning depends significantly on the degree to which they find it involving, appropriate, accessible, and potentially life enriching.[3]

Audience Involvement

Information is worthless unless people pay attention to it. As with any speech, informative speeches need to be **audience involving.** The history of the world is full of examples of great ideas, practices, and products that failed because no one paid much attention to them. One of the first things you'll want to ensure, then, is that your topic and speech get the audience involved.

Novelty is the quality of being new and stimulating. It can be useful in gaining an audience's interest. Just as plants are heliotropic, we human beings are stimulatropic. Whereas plants continuously orient themselves toward the Sun to activate the process of photosynthesis, we continually orient ourselves toward new sources of stimulation.

Although novelty alone is not enough to sustain an informative speech, it certainly can make a speech more effective. Research has documented the fact that the perception of novelty heightens selective exposure, selective attention, and selective retention of information. People are more likely to seek out, pay attention to, and remember novel information. The most obvious way to get the benefit of novelty in an informative speech is to choose a topic that is new for the audience. You are much more likely to captivate the audience members with the unfamiliar than with the mundane. Novelty, however, shouldn't be confused with the obscure. For example, whereas computer software for accountancy probably would be an obscure topic for most audiences, the fact that the software could save us money on our income taxes might be a novel topic.

Another way to use novelty to your advantage is in the construction of the message. Even though the rule of thumb is to structure a speech so that the audience can predict what comes next, this is not an unbending rule. Sometimes it is to your advantage to violate the expectancies of an audience. Writers, for example, sometimes begin with a story's end and then backtrack. Similarly, a skilled speaker could start a speech with what normally would be considered its conclusion and build backward.

Novelty in your delivery can also work to your advantage when speaking informatively. Audiences, for instance, generally are accustomed to speakers who are relatively stationary. Movement may add needed novelty to your presentation. In addition, some of our suggestions about the nonverbal dynamics of delivery in Chapter 11 will help introduce novelty to a presentation, as will some of the media discussed in Chapter 12.

Finally, for listeners to become fully involved with an informative speech, they need to find it enjoyable. One of the most involving experiences of a visit to a national park, for example, is to go on a tour with a knowledgeable guide who can inform us with facts and anecdotes we might not otherwise learn, as Yosemite Tour Guide Jack Peters points out in the box, "Speaking of . . . Learning and Enjoyment," on page 316.

Audience Appropriateness

Although novelty can increase the chances of an audience initially paying attention, the information you share also needs to be compatible with what audience members believe is appropriate to the occasion. If your topic immediately turns the audience off, the audience also will tune you out.

SPEAKING OF . . .

Yosemite tour guide Jack Peters

Consider what Jack Peters, a Yosemite National Park tour guide, has to say about his experience as an informative presenter:

Like many people before me I wandered into Yosemite National Park for a visit and ended up living and working there. My degree in economics didn't really prepare me to be a tour guide, so I started from the bottom up in my training. First I listened to, and sometimes copied, other people's tours until I developed my own narrative style and informational content. In my line of work, style and substance often share equal importance as communication tools. If the guests relate to you personally, that is how you present the material; they will be more receptive to and retain more of the information you put forward. The inevitable question at day's end is "did you enjoy the tour?" rather than "what did you learn?" Learning and enjoying do not have to be mutually exclusive, as we all know.

The importance of communication should be self-evident. The better we communicate, the more we understand about our world, and ultimately, ourselves. So I just go up to that microphone and let 'er rip!

---

audience appropriate
Informative topic and speech that are perceived as compatible with the audience members' belief systems.

Early in this book we said that communication is perceptual and that the process of perception is selective. Basically, people perceive what they choose to perceive. **Audience appropriateness** is the audience's perception that a message is compatible with their belief systems—their attitudes, beliefs, values, and lifestyle. All too often, speakers fail to take appropriateness into account when choosing topics and constructing their informative speeches.

Consider how you might approach an informative speech on stem cell research for two different audiences. The first audience is composed of family members of people with diseases such as Alzheimer's, Parkinson's, and diabetes. The second is a religious group whose members believe that life begins at the moment of conception. The first group is likely to be hopeful that embryonic stem cell research can provide a cure for their loved ones. The second is likely to oppose any research that could lead to the destruction of what they believe is human life. A speech virtually the same would engender quite different reactions from these two groups. In approaching the second group, you need to make it clear that your intent is not to attack their deeply held religious beliefs. You might qualify the information in the speech with statements such as these:

"I realize that for many people the whole issue of stem cell research raises ethical concerns, and I am mindful of these concerns."

316

"Putting aside our religious views for the moment, let me describe what we know about the potential benefits of stem cell research."

"Regardless of how you feel about this issue, I'd like you to put yourself in the shoes of someone who has just learned his or her young daughter has been diagnosed with juvenile diabetes and faces a lifetime of insulin shots, with potentially fatal complications."

The point is that information that is potentially incompatible with audience members' worldviews can be made appropriate if it is presented in a way that acknowledges their point of view.

Audience Accessibility

Audience members cannot benefit from information that they cannot grasp. An **audience accessible** informative speech is one that the audience readily understands. Suppose, for example, that you are a biology major and you want to inform an audience about mapping the human genome. Should you use words peculiar to your major? Should you use the same approach with an audience of beginning speech students as you would with a group of seniors in a biochemistry class? Of course not.

Research tells us that one of the quickest ways to turn off an audience is to unnecessarily complicate a topic. You don't have to avoid complex topics for your informative speeches. In fact, they are likely to be both novel for the audience and interesting for you to research. The goal is to make complex topics easily grasped and compelling.

An excellent way to reduce the complexity of a speech is through analogies or comparisons. Explain a complex process, for example, by comparing it with a common process based on the same principle. A statistician we know, for example, was having a tough time getting students to truly understand the concept of representative sampling—that is, selecting a relatively small sample of people (say, 400) to survey but then applying the survey results to the entire population from which the sample was drawn (say, 10,000). He finally found an analogy that seemed to work for 95 percent of his students:

> How many have you had blood drawn as part of a physical? Okay; how much blood did they draw, one or two of those small vials? When you met with your physician, did she tell any of you that your blood sample indicated your cholesterol was too high, within limits but still a little high, or just right? Did you believe her? Why? They didn't test every pint of blood in your body.

Visual aids can also be helpful in reducing complexity. For example, we recall a speech about a complex carbon molecule in which the speaker used a Tinkertoy model to show what the molecule looked like. The speaker also used an analogy, calling the molecule a "soot ball," to help the audience visualize what it would be like.

One final way to make sure your topic and content will be readily grasped is to clearly define any terms that may be unfamiliar to some or all of them. For example, suppose you heard a speech on bovine spongiform ecephalopathy. Unless the speaker explained that this was commonly known as mad cow disease, you would likely be lost and probably disinterested. Even more obscure are speeches that only use acronyms, or letters representing key words. For example,

audience accessible
Content the audience is able to understand, regardless of its complexity.

a speech on BSE would be confusing at best if the audience did not know that it was the official acronym for mad cow disease. Furthermore, whatever term is used for the disease, it needs a fuller definition, explaining that it is a chronic, degenerative disorder of a bovine's central nervous system.

Life Enrichment

When we introduced the tools you need to get started on your first speech, we talked about the importance of connecting with your audience. If they are to learn, audience members need to know explicitly why it is in their interest to listen to what you have to say.

When we connect with our audience, we are in effect saying, "My topic and message are potentially life enriching." Life enrichment can take the form of valuable information or suggestions to improve behavior. Don't think that just because you have a good idea, people will necessarily see what you see. History is replete with good ideas, the proverbial better mousetrap, that are collecting dust for want of the public's attention. Consider two examples from Everett M. Rogers's classic work, *The Diffusion of Innovations*.[4]

If you have studied the history of science, you may recall that the disease scurvy, caused by a deficiency of vitamin C, was a serious problem for sailors on long voyages. As early as 1601, it was found that sources of vitamin C effectively inhibited scurvy. Yet it took almost 200 years for the British Navy to put this finding to use on its ships and almost 75 years more for sources of vitamin C to be made available on commercial ships.

We needn't look back 200 years, however, for a good example. Consider preventive health practices. Hardly a day goes by in which we are not bombarded by informative messages intended to help us become healthier. Yet in spite of such messages and their promise that we will feel better and live longer if we don't smoke, exercise, and watch our diet, millions of people ignore them.

Never assume that audience members will recognize they have something to gain personally or professionally from a speech. What may be perfectly obvious to you, however, may be just the opposite for your audience. Consider a case with which you already have some experience—college classes. Regardless of the subject matter of their classes, most college professors believe that the information they have to share is absolutely essential to every student's intellectual well-being. So secure are they in this belief, in fact, some seldom spend any time convincing students that there are "good reasons" for their being in the professor's class.

Occasionally, this oversight doesn't much matter—for example, when students are taking a course in their major. Students listen because they know they "have to learn" what is being taught, regardless of how well it's being taught. This is seldom the case, though, when they find themselves in a required course outside their major. "Why do I need a course in art history?" complains the computer science major, while the chemistry major asks, "Why do I need a class in public speaking?"

Just as teachers have an obligation to connect their course to the professional aspirations of students, speakers have the same kind of obligation to their audiences. It's not enough that their information is perceived as involving or appropriate by their audience. Their information—their speech—must also be readily perceived as enriching audience members' lives.

Trevor Morgan's speech on bees and beekeeping outlined in this chapter explains that bees are essential to the production of about one-third of all the food we eat. Rather than treating bees as pesky insects, he hopes his listeners will learn to appreciate how bees enhance our lives.

Putting Theory Into Practice

Now that we have covered some of the principles related to conveying information to an audience, it's time to plan your own informative speech. This section offers some practical suggestions for how to give an informative speech. We discuss five ways to inform an audience: explanation of a process, explanation of a concept, instruction, demonstration, and description. Your speech may employ more than one of these modes. And the list is not exhaustive. Nevertheless, these five categories should be a useful way of thinking about how to translate the principles of informative speaking into an actual speech.

Speeches That Explain a Process

www.mhhe.com/brydon7e

To better understand an informative speech explaining a process, click on the Speech Coach link on our Online Learning Center Web site, and go to Segment 13.1 to view Trevor Morgan's speech on bees.

One of the primary functions you may wish to accomplish in an informative speech is to explain a process. Technically, a *process* is a continuous phenomenon without an obvious beginning or end. Examples of processes are plentiful in science and include photosynthesis, erosion, and osmosis. Because true processes are complex and often hidden from our ordinary senses, their explanation requires genuine creativity from a speaker. At a minimum, you must break down the process into increments that the audience can readily comprehend. If the process involves a specialized vocabulary, you also need to define terms for the audience. Because the process also may be invisible, you may have to create visuals that approximate the process.

The key to explaining a process is to find the right complement of language and visual media for your audience. This involves finding the best analogies, metaphors, and similes to start. You can then complement these elements of language with static visual media such as overheads or dynamic visual media such as animated PowerPoint slides or even the actual objects themselves. You can review an outline of a speech explaining a process in the box "In Their Own Words: Sample Informative Speech Outline—Bees and Beekeeping" by Trevor Morgan on pages 320–321.

Speeches That Explain a Concept

Although not as difficult to explain as a process, a concept demands care on the part of the speaker who chooses to explain it. A *concept* is a symbolic abstraction that pulls together a class of objects that share common attributes. The word *ball*, for example, is also a concept that can be applied to baseballs, basketballs, soccer balls, golf balls, racketballs, squash balls, and volleyballs. Although different in size and purpose, these types of balls share at least one common attribute: They are round.

The key to explaining a concept is to describe the essential attributes that distinguish it from other concepts. How is a democracy different from a republic?

IN THEIR OWN WORDS

Sample Informative Speech Outline

BEES AND BEEKEEPING
by Trevor Morgan

Specific Purpose: To discuss a different side of bees and beekeeping that is less well-known to most people.

Trevor Morgan

Introduction

Notice how the speaker both gains attention and connects with the audience.

I. **Open with Impact/ Connect with Audience:** A show of hands: How many people do not like or are even scared of bees?

II. **Thesis Statement:** Due to the majority of people being unfamiliar with bees, bees tend to get a bad reputation that I hope to change.

The three-point organization is clearly previewed and easy to follow.

III. **Preview:** I am going to discuss types of bees, species, and pollination.

Body

I. **Main Point:** There are three main types of bees: queen bee, drone bee, and the worker bee.

A. Queen bee:

The speaker provided notations to himself about using visual aids.

1. Head of all bees in a colony. (Visual Aid)
2. Colony would not function properly without her.
3. Longer body than the worker bee.
4. Main job in hive is to lay eggs—up to 3,000 eggs a day.
5. Only stings other queen bees—not people; multiple stings.

B. Drone bee:
1. The only male bee—doesn't have a stinger.
2. Only takes about twenty-five flights in its life.
3. Specially designed for mating only with the queens.
4. Very lazy. When the mating process is over, the worker bees kill the drone because it is no longer productive.

C. Worker bee:
1. The powerhouse of the hive.
2. Does all the work and carries out all the functions in the hive.
3. Undeveloped female that is unable to lay eggs.

The speaker not only cites his source, he held up the book at this point.

4. They have pollen baskets used for pollination (Morse, 1975).
5. They do not act as individuals—they work together.

(Transition: Now that you know the three main types, I'll discuss some species.)

II. **Main Point:** There are hundreds of different species of bees.
   A. There are African, Italian, Irish, Yugoslavian, etc., but I'll discuss two main types of bees.
   B. The African Bee:
      1. Originated in Africa and smuggled into the United States.
      2. Very aggressive and attacks in large numbers. (Visual Aid)
      3. Africanized bees cannot survive Northern California winters.
   C. The Italian Bee:
      1. Most common around this area.
      2. Very gentle bee compared to the African bee. (Visual Aid)

(Transition: Now that you know two different types of species, I'm going to discuss the important topic of pollination.)

III. **Main Point:** Pollination by bees is very important.
   A. The honeybee is the most important insect in pollination of agricultural crops.
   B. Without a doubt, the honeybee is far more important and valuable to humankind as a pollinator than as a honey producer.
   C. Approximately one-third of our food supply is either directly or indirectly dependent on bee-pollinated plants (Root, 1983).
   D. Two main types of flower pollination:
      1. Nectar pollination.
      2. The transfer of stamen (male) pollen to the pistil (female).

Conclusion

I. **Summarize:** Now you know:
   A. Types of Bees
   B. Species
   C. Pollination
II. **Close with Impact:** So the next time you see a bee flying around your dorm room or your car, instead of squishing it, just remember how important bees are and let it go.

References

Africanized honeybee range in U.S. (picture). (n.d.). Retrieved from http://www.stingshield.com
Morse, R. (1975). *Bees and beekeeping.* New York: Cornell University Press.
Root, A. (1983). *The abc and xyz of bee culture.* Ohio: A. I. Root Company.

The speaker uses clear transitional statements.

At this point, the speaker held up a box with about 5,000 bees in it.

The significance of this topic to our lives is stressed and a source is cited. He refers to the book as the bible of beekeeping.

Closing statement directly connects to the audience.

The United States is a republic, yet most people refer to it as a democracy. A good informative speech would not only explain why this is the case but also point out the specific attributes that distinguish a republic from a democracy.

In selecting a topic for a speech that explains a process or a concept, keep in mind that the topic should be relevant to the audience, something they are capable of understanding, and something you can explain in the time allotted. Although the theory of relativity is highly relevant, explaining it in a 5- to 10-minute speech is a tall order.

Making sure your topic and content are within your audience's reach is particularly important in speeches that explain. Recall that one way to reduce complexity for an audience is to use an analogy. Consider the use of analogy in this excerpt from the speech by Jonathan Studebaker found in Chapter 1:

> Like I said, I'm a nice person. I'm cheerful, I'm energetic. Okay, so I have a disability. I was born with osteogenesis imperfecta, a disease which causes my bones to be fragile. Have you ever accidentally dropped a glass on the floor? What happens? It breaks. Well, my bones kinda break like glass, which is why I tell people, when you carry me, treat me like your best crystal.[5]

The use of a simple analogy of bones to glass helps the audience understand a disease most of us cannot even pronounce. For Jonathan's purposes—to introduce himself and explain his disability—that is the extent of the technical information his audience needs to know.

As was the case with processes, explaining a concept may demand a visual reference. Imagine an entrepreneur explaining the concept behind a new Web site she's pitching to a group of potential investors. How successful do you think she will be if her explanation is based on words alone?

During your college career, you will undoubtedly be called on to explain something to an audience, if not in your public speaking class, then in another setting. Similarly, in the professional world, it is common for people to be called on to explain everything from a new product idea to why the last quarter's sales were so bad. Using the principle of accessibility can help you enhance your explanations.

Speeches That Instruct

Informative speaking can also be used to instruct an audience. The key to instruction is to provide new information the audience can put to use, or a new perspective they can bring to bear on old information. Modern educational theory emphasizes observable behavioral objectives; that is, after receiving instruction, students should be able to show that they have mastered the subject, either by answering questions or by engaging in some activity.

Involving the audience is important to speeches that provide instruction. Unless the information in a speech presents new information or a *fresh perspective* to your audience, all you have done is bore them with what they already know. For example, speeches on how to ride a bike or how to pack a suitcase are unlikely to provide anything new to an audience. However, even new topics can be perceived as irrelevant by large portions of an audience. For example, a speech on how to wax your skis is old news to experienced skiers but irrelevant to nonskiers in the class.

So, the key to speeches that instruct is to provide new, yet relevant information to your audience, or at least a new perspective on such information. That

SPEAKING OF . . .

The Pitchmen and Pitchwomen

Although their ultimate goal is to persuade us to order the product pitched, it's the demonstration of the product that hooks all of us into paying attention to Vince Offer's spiel for Sham Wow, Ron Popeil's can cook anything Showtime Rotisserie, or Susan Powter's sweat-drenched exercise infomercial asking us to "stop the insanity." Although multiple takes and digital editing have helped to make their seemingly extemporaneous pitches and simultaneous demonstrations appear flawless, that wasn't always the case. Before the proliferation of cable channels that made pitch people and their products a 24/7 broadcast phenomenon, all but a few were doing live demonstrations in front of real audiences at State Fairs, Flea Markets and Swap Meets. Getting to the big leagues where they can show their skills at slicing and dicing or making stains and odors disappear, as the reality show *Pitchmen* demonstrates, only happens to the best in the breed.

Source: "Top Infomercial Stars of All Time," WalletPop.com. 2009. [Retrieved from http://www.walletpop.com/specials/profiles-of-tv-product-pitchmen, 9 November 2009.]

Billy Mays was one of the most successful pitchmen of all time.

means using the novelty of your topic to involve people while pointing out how learning the information can be life enriching.

Speeches That Demonstrate How to Do Something

Speeches with a demonstration are closely related to those that provide instruction, but the speaker actually shows the audience how to do something. Further, a good demonstration allows the audience to try out what is being demonstrated, either immediately or at the conclusion of the demonstration.

A good example of demonstration speeches can be found on television infomercials or on shopping channels such as QVC. TV pitchman Billy Mays, for example, became famous and wealthy by demonstrating everything from OxiClean to the garden weasel. You can read about prominent examples of people who make their livings by demonstrating products in the box "Speaking of . . . The Pitchmen and Pitchwomen."

A demonstration speaker needs to provide audience members with enough information to do the activity on their own or with information on where to obtain further instruction so that they can try out the activity. For example, although no one can master karate from just listening to a single speech, or even a series of speeches, a demonstration of karate moves can spur an audience member to seek out individual instruction in the martial arts. In fact, many martial arts studios make a practice of giving demonstrations in schools and at public events as a way of recruiting new students.

323

Teaching cooking requires hands-on demonstration as it is practiced at the Luis Irizar cooking school in Spain.

Topics for speeches that demonstrate need to be chosen with care. A complex, difficult task cannot be adequately demonstrated in a few minutes. There can even be the danger of making people think they know how to do something based on a speech when in fact they do not. Few of us could do CPR, for example, based on simply watching a speaker demonstrate the activity. We need the opportunity to try it out (perhaps on a life-size doll) before we can know if we can do it. On the other hand, another lifesaving technique, the Heimlich maneuver, is often the subject of demonstration and can be learned in a reasonably short time.

The key to making a demonstration effective is careful planning. Late night comedy shows purposely make a mockery of this advice in the name of entertainment. If you plan to demonstrate a process in your speech, rehearse it carefully. Also, it is sometimes useful to prepare various steps of the process in advance. Watch any cooking show demonstration on TV. The onions are already chopped, the flour is already sifted and measured, and an example of the finished product is near at hand. You don't want the audience drifting off as you measure ingredients or sift the flour. Providing a written recipe in a handout or as a visual will save a lot of time and let the audience focus on watching the demonstration. In short, a demonstration requires extra preparation.

In addition, be sure that the demonstration is an accurate representation. If you misinform an audience, you have done more harm than good. Depending on what you are demonstrating, you might even be inviting injury to the audience members or someone else. Make certain, therefore, that you can accurately demonstrate the process in the time allowed.

Finally, make sure the demonstration is visible to the audience. A demonstration speech on making sushi, or small origami paper figures, may initially seem like a good idea. Unless there is a way to magnify the demonstration so that all the audience can see what you are doing, making sushi or origami figures isn't a very good idea.

Speeches That Describe

Another function of informative speeches is description. Using visuals can obviously enhance a descriptive speech. Not only can visuals be useful; you may also want to provide a word picture of the subject. Consider the following description of a familiar character, Mickey Mouse, provided by student speaker Jennie Rees:

> They designed him using a circle for his head and oblong circles for his nose and snout. They also drew circles for his ears and drew them in such a way that they appeared to look the same any way Mickey turned his head. They gave him a pear-shaped body with pipe-stem legs, and stuffed them in big, oversized shoes, making him look like a little kid wearing his father's shoes.[6]

Can't you almost picture Mickey from that description? Visual language is key to effective description.

Explaining a process such as . . .	Explaining a concept such as . . .
• Climate change • How hydrogen can power cars • How solar panels convert sunlight into electricity • How West Nile Virus is transmitted • How exposure to UV rays causes skin cancer	• Credit card fees and how they can accumulate • A type of art; for example, impressionism • The nature of a disease; for example, muscular dystrophy • Compound interest and how a small amount invested over time can grow • Musical harmony
Demonstrating how to . . .	**Describing . . .**
• Grow your own herbs • Fill out the EZ1040 income tax form • Fly fish • Give CPR • Prepare your favorite food • Properly protect yourself from injury while skiing	• A visit to Rio de Janeiro • The most unforgettable person you ever met • The weaknesses in airport security allowing hijackers to take over planes • The beauty of Yosemite National Park • The judging of an Olympic sport such as gymnastics
Instructing how to . . .	
• Reduce your carbon footprint • Select the best wines to accompany different foods • Maintain a healthy body weight • Improve your gas mileage	• Reduce your risk of getting the flu • Recognize the symptoms of binge drinking • Improve your sleep habits • Study more effectively

Exhibit 13.2
Possible Speech Topics for Informative Speeches

Examples of speech topics for each type of informative speech are offered in Exhibit 13.2.

A Hard Truth

Even though we have categorized informative speeches into the preceding five types, in practice informative speeches more often than not include elements of each. Instruction demands explanation, description, and, sooner or later, demonstration of the process, concept, practice, or skill on which the speech is focused.

Tips and Tactics

Informative Speaking

When putting an informative speech together, you need to do the following:

• Use words that appeal to the different learning styles of audience members.
• Use techniques that make the speech involving, appropriate, accessible, and potentially life enriching.

• Establish whether the speech purpose is to explain a concept or a process, instruct, demonstrate, or describe.

• Maximize observability through the use of appropriate visual aids.

One Final Word

If a word could be used to summarize the difference between an outstanding and less successful informative speech it would have to be *enthusiasm*. There is simply no substitute for your enthusiasm for your topic and the pleasure your audience senses that you receive from talking about it. Enthusiasm is contagious. When you are enthused, it is hard for your audience to avoid sharing your enthusiasm. Obviously, this fact reminds us of an additional one: Your success with informative speaking depends upon a carefully selected and researched topic you care about!

 www.mhhe.com/brydon7e

To evaluate your understanding of this chapter, visit our Online Learning Center Web site for quizzes and other chapter study aids.

Summary

Informative speaking is the process of presenting an audience with new information or a new perspective on old information.

• Learning is the goal of informative speaking.

• Informative and persuasive speaking are two opposite ends of a continuum.

• It's important that the individual learning styles of audience members be reflected in the verbal and nonverbal content of informative speeches.

• Informative speeches are common in the classroom, the workplace, and the community.

• Successful informative speeches are involving, appropriate, accessible, and potentially life enriching for the audience.

• Informative speeches can be used to explain, instruct, demonstrate, or describe processes, concepts, and skills.

Check Your Understanding: Exercises and Activities

1. Develop an outline for a brief speech in which you inform an audience about a topic with which you are personally familiar. Then show how you would adapt the speech to each of the following learnings styles: Auditory linguistic, visual linguistic, auditory numerical, visual numerical, and audio-visual-kinesthetic combination.

2. Come up with at least two possible topics each for speeches that explain, instruct, demonstrate, and describe. Do some topics seem to fall naturally into one category? Are there other topics that might be used for more than one type of speech?

3. What is your preferred learning style? To find out, go to http://www.engr
.ncsu.edu/learningstyles/ilsweb.html and take the "Index of Learning Styles
Questionnaire" developed by Barbara A. Solomon and Richard A. Felder of
North Carolina State.

Notes

1. Woody Allen, *Good Reads,* 2009. [Retrieved from http://www.goodreads
.com/author/quotes/10356.Woody_Allen.]

2. P. Friedman and R. Alley, "Learning/Teaching Styles: Applying the Prin-
ciples," *Theory Into Practice,* 23 (1984): 77–81. Based on R. Dunn and
K. Dunn, *Teaching Students Through Their Individual Learning Styles: A Practical
Approach* (Reston, VA: Reston Publishing, 1978).

3. Michael D. Scott and Scott Elliot, "Innovation in the Classroom: Toward a
Reconceptualization of Instructional Communication" (paper presented at
the annual meeting of the International Communication Association, Dallas,
Texas, 1983).

4. Everett M. Rogers, *Diffusion of Innovations* (New York: Free Press, 1983).

5. Jonathan Studebaker, "Speech of Self-Introduction: Who Am I?" The full
text appears in Chapter 1.

6. Jennie Rees, "Informative Speech: Mickey: A Changing Image," California
State University, Chico, 1992.

PERSUASIVE COMMUNICATION

— *Dr. Burt Pryor*

Objectives

After reading this chapter, you should be able to:

- Define the concept of persuasion

- Discuss the influence of the Elaboration Likelihood Model

- Discuss how the central and peripheral routes allow persuasion to occur

- Understand the effect of source, message, channel, and receiver on receivers' likelihood to elaborate.

- Define the three types of persuasive effects.

- Explain how one-sided versus two-sided messages, inoculation theory, use of statistical and story evidence, and fear appeals can make messages more persuasive.

- Understand how source characteristics, message-related peripheral cues, and sequential request strategies influence persuasion.

Key Concepts

Central route processing

Conformity effect

Door-in-the-face

Elaboration Likelihood Model

Extended Parallel Process Model

Foot-in-the-door

Forewarning

Inoculation Theory

Low-ball

One-sided messages

Peripheral cues

Peripheral route processing

Persuasion

Scarcity strategy

Selective exposure

Sequential-request strategies

Source credibility

Source expertise

Two-sided non-refutational messages

Two-sided refutational messages

Wear-out point

Why the Study of Persuasion is Important

Persuasion is so much a routine part of our lives that most of us are probably not aware of its pervasiveness unless it is called to our attention. Literally everyone is in the business of persuasion. If you were to keep a log of every persuasion attempt that you encountered in a given day as a persuader, receiver, or observer, you would soon realize the necessity of having that log available wherever you went. Think of those who practice persuasion professionally: advertisers, attorneys, politicians, educators (including the authors of the message you are reading right now), clergy, salespeople (including telemarketers), media consultants, managers, coaches–even engineers. The list is practically endless. We receive direct mail ads on a daily basis, the so-called "junk mail." Pratkanis & Aronson (2001) reported that adults are exposed to an average of 750 television ads per week. We are also bombarded with advertising through other media, including newspapers, magazines, radio and the Internet. When we are driving in our cars, the persuasive messages on the radio, billboards, and bumper stickers permeate our consciousness. Even our clothing carries persuasive messages. Hats and T-shirts display the logos and slogans of manufacturers, and our casual clothing is commonly decorated with designer labels. Add to this the daily interpersonal influences involving parents, couples, children, friends, and relatives, and one begins to see that we humans are constant participants in this process we call persuasion. Because of its central role in our daily lives, it is an understatement to say it makes sense to study persuasion. A better understanding of the persuasion process, from the perspectives of both the persuader and the one being persuaded, will have far-reaching personal and professional benefits.

Defining the Concept of Persuasion

Persuasion

The process by which attitudes or behaviors are influenced as a result of receiving a message

Persuasion is the process by which attitudes or behaviors are influenced as a result of receiving a message (Anderson & Pryor, 1992). However, definitions of persuasion vary according to whether they recognize *unintentional influence* as persuasion. For example, let's assume you plan an "informative" presentation about recycling programs, including their costs and benefits. Though your purpose may only be to inform, it is quite plausible that your discussion about the long-term benefits of recycling on the environment may influence your audience's attitudes and even their behaviors involving recycling. So, your "informative" message might also persuade the receivers. A broad definition of persuasion might include this type of unintentional persuasion.

Narrower definitions of persuasion typically limit what we call persuasion to situations that include an intentional persuader. It should be noted that those who espouse the "intentional" model of persuasion do not argue that people's minds and behaviors are never changed without an intentional persuader. They just believe that attitude or behavior change without an intentional persuader should not be classified as persuasion. Most of the research on persuasion works from this narrower definition of persuasion.

It is also important to distinguish between *coercion,* which is based on reward and punishment power and receivers' lack of perceived choice, and persuasion, which is based on information power. The statement, "Give me your money, or I will shoot you" allows the receiver little choice in light of the punishment for refusing to give up the money. The lack of perceived choice is what separates persuasion from coercion. So, if you are thinking that a gun threat is pretty persuasive, it isn't. It is, however, pretty coercive.

This chapter focuses on strategies that persuaders can implement to increase their odds of success. The strategies are derived from systematic research conducted by social scientists over the past few decades that has led to a better understanding of cause-effect relationships in persuasion. These relationships center on how various characteristics of the source (as speaker or as writer), message, channel, and receiver influence persuasive effects. We will begin by examining some of these relationships within the framework of the most comprehensive theory yet developed in the field of persuasion, the Elaboration Likelihood Model, also known as the ELM (Petty & Cacioppo, 1986).

The Elaboration Likelihood Model

As suggested by its name, the Elaboration Likelihood Model (ELM) predicts the likelihood that receivers will "elaborate" (that is, process, think about, evaluate) a message under various circumstances. The ELM suggests that people want to make "correct" decisions about how to respond to persuasive messages, but cannot possibly scrutinize every persuasive message that comes their way. Sometimes we engage in effortful, elaborative processing; other times, we may choose not to mentally elaborate on the message. According to the ELM and its research findings, the two major determinants of the extent to which receivers engage in message elaboration are their *motivation* and *ability* to process the message. Those who are motivated (they really *want* to process a message) and are able (they *can* process a message) tend to engage in elaborative message processing. Those who lack motivation or ability tend to process the message superficially.

Two Routes to Persuasion: Central and Peripheral

The ELM identifies two main routes to persuasion–the **central route** and the **peripheral route**. Essentially, the central route involves persuasion achieved by the quality of the arguments in the message, while peripheral route persuasion occurs when receivers are influenced by factors other than argument quality (e.g., speaker expertise or attractiveness). The ELM holds that receivers will focus on the message arguments to the extent that they are both *motivated* and *able* to process the message. Central route persuasion, then, relies on high message elaboration.

On the other hand, to the extent that receivers are lacking in either motivation or ability to process the message, persuasion will succeed or fail based on factors outside the message. These are called *peripheral cues*. As demonstrated earlier, we are inundated with persuasive messages on a continual basis. We simply do not have the time or energy to thoroughly process every message that comes our way, lest we pull our cars to side of the road to make sure we carefully consider every billboard. Think of it as literally "paying" attention: it costs us time and energy to process a message. Consequently, we use decision rules, or mental shortcuts, in response to many persuasive messages, particularly those we perceive as low in relevance or consequence for our daily lives. We often quickly accept or reject persuasive appeals, from advertisements to issues of

central route processing
Persuasion achieved by the quality of the arguments in a message

peripheral route processing
Influence based upon factors outside of the quality of the message

The Elaboration Likelihood Continuum

Low Elaboration Likelihood	High Elaboration Likelihood
Receiver lacks motivation or ability	Receiver has motivation and ability

Peripheral Route	Central Route

Cursory examination of peripheral cues	Elaborative processing of arguments
Peripheral factors more important than arguments	Argument quality most important
Short-term persuasion	Longer lasting persuasion
Susceptible to competing messages	Resistant to competing messages

Exhibit 14.1
The central/peripheral routes to persuasion are not an either/or relationship. Instead, they represent a continuum.

national scope, on the basis of peripheral cues–such as whether or not we like the speaker, or how expert we perceive the speaker to be–without even examining the arguments the speaker presents.

It is important to note, though, that the central-peripheral distinction represents a continuum, not an "either/or" relationship. It is not a matter of using one route or the other exclusively, but of relying more on the central route than the peripheral route in some situations, and more on the peripheral route than the central route in others.

What ELM Research Offers Persuaders

The ELM has spawned a body of research about how numerous factors affect the likelihood of message elaboration. The research has shown two main advantages of central route over peripheral route persuasion. Because it is more grounded in substantive attitude and belief modification than persuasion achieved through the peripheral route, central route persuasion is (1) longer lasting, and (2) more resistant to subsequent competing messages (Petty & Cacioppo, 1986). Since receivers will process the message more thoroughly when they are using the central route, it makes sense that a speaker must use high quality arguments to be successful.

Consider a situation where receivers are highly motivated and able to scrutinize the message, but the message contains weak arguments. For example, "We should raise the drinking age to 23 because several prominent politicians think it is a good idea and some think it will curb alcohol sales." If the audience consists of college age people, the persuader would likely be better off if they processed the message *less* thoroughly, because thorough processing of weak arguments only accentuates receivers' negative responses to the message. The critical point here is that strategically increasing receivers' attention to a set of arguments is not always a good thing. It's a good idea only if the receivers perceive the arguments to be strong.

Central Route Factors: Things That Make Elaboration More Likely

We have already stated that receivers engage in effortful information processing (elaboration) of a message when they are both motivated and able to do so. This section introduces some of the factors that have been shown to make elaboration more likely. These include characteristics of the source/speaker, elements of the message, the use of multiple channels, and the attitudes and perceptions of the receivers. Once we've examined the research, we will explore some practical applications you can use as a persuader.

Source Characteristics

Source expertise

Source expertise refers to receivers' perceptions of the source's (persuader's) knowledge, qualifications, and competence. Although source expertise has its most direct impact on persuasion as a peripheral cue (discussed in detail later in this chapter), it can affect receivers' motivation to engage in elaborative processing of the message. Source expertise has little effect on information processing of highly relevant messages because receivers are already motivated to process the message; however, some studies (e.g., Petty & Cacioppo, 1984) have shown that expert sources increase receivers' motivation to process messages when issue relevance is moderate or ambiguous. Petty & Cacioppo (1986) explain that when receivers are not sure whether a message merits their attention, "characteristics of the message source can help a person decide if the message is worth thinking about" (p. 206).

> **source expertise**
> Receivers' perceptions of the persuader's knowledge, qualifications and competence

Number of Sources and Arguments

The relationship between attention and stimulus variety has been well documented in social science research. Vernon (1962, p. 183) concluded from early research that "normal consciousness, perception, and thought can be maintained only in a constantly changing environment." Harkins and Petty (1981) examined the effects of multiple sources/multiple arguments on receivers' message processing and attitude change. In this study, participants listened to messages from one speaker or from three speakers that utilized one argument or three different arguments. The combination of three speakers, each with a *different strong argument*, produced more positive thoughts about the issue and more persuasion than any of the other conditions. Harkins and Petty concluded that each time the participants heard the voice of a new speaker making a strong argument (changing stimulus) they were re-stimulated to process the message. Because the arguments were strong, increased attention to the message resulted in more favorable thoughts and more persuasion. The ELM would predict that, had the arguments been weak, the increased processing brought by multiple sources would increase receivers' negative thoughts and, therefore, decrease persuasion.

Listeners are more likely to process a message from an expert source.

It has been said that variety is the "spice of life." This research suggests that adding a little of that spice to your presentation might help motivate your audience to more thoughtfully process your message.

Message Characteristics

ELM research has identified several message characteristics that affect receivers' motivation and ability to process information. Among those that have received research attention are *forewarning* of persuasive intent and message *repetition*.

Forewarning and Resistance to Persuasion

You have probably heard someone say that "forewarned is forearmed." In other words, if we know something is coming, a hurricane, cutback in work hours, or the need to make repairs on a declining old car, we will be more likely to prepare for it. In the case of persuasive messages, this statement should be amended to say that forewarned is forearmed, but only if (1) the issue is personally relevant to the receiver, (2) the message is intended to change attitudes (not create or reinforce attitudes), and (3) the receivers have at least a few minutes to arm themselves. Sometimes we receive warnings that we are soon to be the target of a persuasion attempt. A friend may warn you that a mutual acquaintance plans to talk to you about joining a pyramid business scheme; your mother may alert you that she and Dad want to sit down with you to discuss your progress toward graduation; a company may alert you that a salesperson will be "in your area" next week. The ELM research shows that these warnings can render you more, or less, susceptible to influence, depending on the three factors listed above.

One important study showing how forewarning can increase resistance to persuasion was done by Petty and Cacioppo (1977). In this study, participants listened to a live class presentation in which a speaker, identified as a psychologist from the testing center, presented strong arguments for initiating comprehensive exams as a graduation requirement. Since a previous survey had shown that students were against this policy change, the message constituted an attempt to change attitudes. In various classes, the students were either informed (warned) about the persuasive intent of the impending presentation five minutes prior to the speaker's arrival, told of the intent as the speaker was introduced, or not warned at all.

Only the group that received the five-minute warning resisted being persuaded. The data showed that they had spent the time following the warning thinking of counterarguments to the anticipated presentation. The forewarning had motivated them to do so. For this group, forewarned was forearmed. Since the participants who were warned immediately prior to the presentation had no time to develop their defenses, they were persuaded, along with the unwarned group, by the strong arguments.

Forewarning and Increased Persuasion

At other times, forewarning may lead to increased persuasion. For example, *when issue relevance is low*, receivers are less motivated to devote efforts to building ammunition to defend against the anticipated message. This is particularly true in interpersonal situations where friendship and harmony may take priority over rejecting someone's influence attempt on a topic of low importance (see Cialdini, Levy, Herman, Kozlowski, & Petty, 1976). Another situation where forewarning may increase persuasion is when the relevance of the issue is high but the position taken is consistent with the receiver's attitude. Under such circumstances, the ELM would predict that the warning would cause receivers to experience mostly positive thoughts in anticipation of the message, leading to increased susceptibility to attitude reinforcement.

Message Repetition

Persuaders often use repetition for purposes of clarifying, reminding, or reinforcing message effects. This tactic is most common in advertising, where the same commercial airs repeatedly until it reaches the **wear-out point** for its audience. Virtually all persuaders – the clergy, attorneys, parents, teachers and students – employ message repetition in their efforts to influence listeners. ELM research, including its applied studies in advertising, has yielded consistent results on the effects of message repetition on information processing and persuasion. With messages that initially produce positive responses to a set of strong arguments (for example, in a novel, clever commercial) the repetition effects follow an inverted U-shaped pattern. That is, positive thoughts and persuasion increase up to a wear-out point, then decrease as receivers begin to tire of the message. Wear-out points vary, largely as a function of the complexity and

wear-out point
The point at which a repeated persuasive message loses its effectiveness

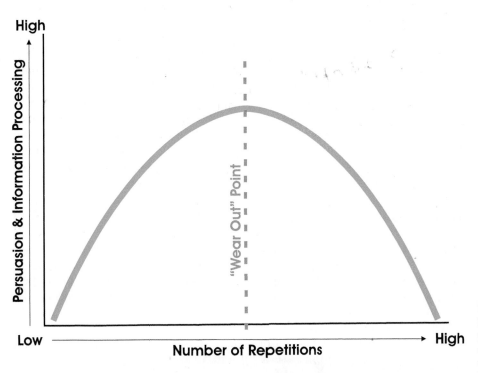

The Effects of Argument Repetition

Exhibit 14.2
Positive thoughts and persuasion increase up to a wear-out point, then decrease as receivers begin to tire of the message.

novelty of messages, but the pattern does not. At some point, even the cleverest commercial begins to lose its appeal.

In an experiment by Cacioppo and Petty (1979), participants listened to strong arguments that advocated increasing tuition to facilitate hiring more faculty, offering more classes, and other student-oriented improvements. Each participant listened to the message one, three, or five times. Participants who heard the message once generated mostly positive thoughts and were influenced by the strong arguments. Attitude change and the number of positive thoughts increased in the three-repetition condition, but decreased with five repetitions. Petty and Cacioppo reasoned that repeating the message three times increased receivers' ability to think about the strong argument, but five repetitions was too much, causing feelings of boredom and tedium.

A subsequent study by Petty and Cacioppo (1985) showed that three repetitions of weak arguments increased receivers' negative thoughts and reduced attitude change. Repetition of the weak arguments gave participants more opportunity to recognize just how weak the arguments were.

Channel Options

Information processing is also affected by whether the message is transmitted through written or spoken channels. Research (e.g., Chaiken & Eagly, 1976) indicates that when messages are complex, written versions are more persuasive than spoken versions. This finding has been attributed to greater comprehension of complex or difficult material when receivers can process (read) the message at their own pace. In ELM terms, the written channel increases receivers' ability to process the message; however, one does not have the opportunity to slow down or revisit material when they are listening to a speaker. Since the receivers' re-reading of material is actually a form of message repetition, one could infer from this research that, when dealing with complex spoken messages, using an alternate channel to provide some form of repetition might increase the audience's ability to elaborate on the message. When messages are spoken, however, it isn't usually possible for listeners to slow down or revisit material. This research suggests that speakers using an alternate channel (such as a PowerPoint® slide or a brief handout summary at the end of a presentation) as a form of repetition in complex spoken messages might increase the audience's ability to elaborate on the message.

Receiver Characteristics and Information Processing

Receiver's Initial Position

The receiver's initial position on a topic determines which of three types of persuasive effects are possible. The three main types of persuasive effects are (1) creating a new attitude, (2) reinforcing an existing attitude or behavior, and (3) changing an attitude and/or behavior.

When the receiver has had no previous exposure to a topic, the effects of a persuasive message are to **create a new attitude**. The new attitude may also lead to new behavior. Examples of this type of persuasion include consumers seeing an advertisement for a new product, jurors hearing initial evidence in a court case, or employers interviewing a job candidate or seeing a candidate's resume

The three types of persuasive effects are:
- create a new attitude
- reinforce an existing attitude or behavior
- change an attitude or behavior

for the first time. The new attitudes toward the product, defendant, or job candidate will likely affect the receiver's behaviors when making a decision about purchasing the product, voting for guilt or innocence, or hiring the applicant.

The majority of persuasive messages that we pay attention to involve the second type of persuasive effect: **reinforcement of an existing attitude**. This is because people tend to place themselves in environments where others' viewpoints and messages coincide with their own attitudes. Republicans would usually rather listen to Republican candidates for office; Democrats prefer listening to Democrats; we attend to messages that reinforce our own religious views; we'd rather watch our favorite team play while surrounded by supporters of that team. People attend church, political rallies, and fundraisers for a favored charity, knowing that the persuasive messages they will hear will be reinforcing, consistent with their own views. Social scientists refer to our tendency to place ourselves in "like-minded" situations as **selective exposure**. This may be seen as a defense mechanism that helps us avoid the psychological discomfort of listening to messages that conflict with our views.

selective exposure
The tendency to place ourselves in environments with others who think as we do

The third type of persuasive effect involves **attitude or behavior change**. Despite our preference for information that supports our views, we often come into contact with competing views. You might hate minivans, but you will have a difficult time avoiding every minivan commercial. You might disagree with a television host's position on a political candidate, but you watch the show because you do like the featured guest's views. When receivers are exposed to competing views, they sometimes engage in selective attention as a defense. In other words, receivers can still avoid a message by not paying attention to it. Message positions that are in conflict with listeners' attitudes must overcome the selective attention barrier. As you will see in the following sections, there are numerous strategies that can be used to motivate receivers to attend to a message.

Receiver's Involvement (Relevance)

Perhaps the most important determinant of the amount of effort audience members will expend to process a message is their involvement in the issue. When receivers perceive that a message is personally relevant and that the information being presented has useful or important implications for their lives, they tend to pay close attention, processing the information carefully and discerning the strengths and weaknesses of the arguments. This has been shown in numerous experiments. Let's examine one experiment by ELM researchers Petty and Cacioppo.

Petty and Cacioppo (1979) developed persuasive messages of high quality and low quality that argued for instituting required senior comprehensive exams. The high quality message contained eight strong arguments. The low quality message contained eight weak arguments. The participants in the experiment were asked to listen to either the high or low quality message and then complete a questionnaire on which they recorded their attitudes toward

People will listen to messages they perceive as personally relevant.

the issue. They were also tested to determine how much effort they had put into processing the messages.

Half of the participants (in both the high and low quality conditions) were told the exams were being considered for their university (high involvement). The other half were told the exams were being considered for a different, far-away university (low involvement). Participants who were led to believe *they* would be the ones taking the exams evaluated the messages more carefully. Because the message was personally relevant, they were motivated to pay close attention. Accordingly, they were very aware of the weaknesses in the low quality message, but also very aware of the strong points in the high quality message. Responses to the questionnaire showed that these highly involved participants responded more positively to the strong message, and were more persuaded than participants who thought the exams were intended for students at another university. But, the highly involved participants listed a greater number of negative thoughts and were *less persuaded* than the participants with low involvement when the arguments were of low quality.

It is important to note that it is the audience's *perception* of relevance, not the "actual" relevance of the message that counts when it comes to providing motivation to elaborate. In the examples cited above, it is unlikely that perceptions differed from reality; comprehensive tests being considered for *your* university are relevant to you and you would be unlikely to perceive otherwise. Conversely, comprehensive tests being considered for some other university would have nothing to do with you and you would be unlikely to perceive the topic as relevant. But what about all of the topics that are potentially relevant to your audience, but not necessarily perceived to be relevant? For example, it may be true that climate change *should* be relevant to everyone, but many do not perceive it to be relevant. Although the research is still evolving in this area, Katt (2004) found that for some topics, even a single statement explaining why a topic is relevant can increase receivers' perceptions of relevance, and based on previous ELM research, we would expect increased perceptions of relevance to be accompanied by increased elaborative message processing.

Tips and Tactics

Increasing Message Elaboration

- You should consider ways to ensure you are perceived as a knowledgeable and expert **source** in both formal and informal persuasion situations. Perceptions of your expertise will directly enhance message effects mostly *when issue relevance is low* for receivers.

- An important indirect effect of source expertise occurs *when issue relevance is moderate.* Under these conditions, your demonstrated expertise will motivate receivers to process the message more actively. By this point, you should know what that means for the impact of argument quality: Anything that increases receivers' active processing of the message also *increases the importance of argument quality.* The perceived relevance of most issues is likely to vary from person to person. For example, a presentation on the value of mastering a second language may be highly relevant to some audience members, but moderately or minimally relevant to others. It seems reasonable to suggest that many issues will not be seen as particularly high or low, but will fall into the moderate relevance range for some receivers. For such receivers, your demonstrated expertise will enhance the motivation to process the message.

- Consider presenting the actual arguments of *multiple sources*, rather than relying on just one source. This not only varies the stimulus but also has the potential to increase **message** credibility by showing the **receivers** that several different **sources** have independently arrived at a similar position or conclusion. So, it is advantageous to cite several different, respected sources to reinforce your argument.

- If you were planning to try to change receivers' attitudes on an issue important to them, you would not want them to have prior knowledge of your intent. Whether it takes the form of telling audience members about your topic or even inadvertently displaying your PowerPoint® slides while setting up for a presentation, **forewarning** could provide the chance for receivers to build defenses in the form of thoughts that are negative to your purpose. On the other hand, it is probably best to reveal your intent in advance of presenting a message that will coincide with receivers' attitudes.

- Organizing persuasive messages to provide moderate **repetition of strong arguments** is an effective strategy. One way to apply this strategy is to introduce or preview strong arguments in an introduction, develop them in the body of the presentation, and then include them in a summary. Although there is no formula for calculating the best use of repetition, it is likely that the wear-out point will be higher for messages that are complex or novel.

- Use **alternate channels** to provide repetition. While you would rely primarily on the spoken channel in a presentation, repetition can be accomplished by reinforcing your message with presentational aids, such as Power-Point or other means of displaying key points in written form. Assuming your message is of high quality, such repetition should produce an increase in receivers' positive thoughts and persuasion. Of course, too much repetition can bore or annoy your audience, so you should be careful not to overdo it.

- In planning your message, consider your receivers' **initial position** on the issue. Will you be attempting to create a new attitude, reinforce an existing attitude, or change an existing attitude? Note that the same message has the potential to produce all three effects, depending on the controversial level of the issue and a given receiver's initial position.

- Receivers' perceptions of the **relevance** of your message may be the most important factor in determining their **motivation to elaborate** on your message. Perceptions of relevance will increase your listeners' motivation to process the message, but be sure your message contains high quality arguments. Speakers who pique listeners' interests, but then provide weak arguments that cause listeners to rehearse negative thoughts in their minds, are likely to succeed only in increasing opposition to their position.

Argument Quality: How to Plan a Strong Message

Our discussion of the persuasion research has so far centered on characteristics of the SMCRE Model (*source, channel, receiver, and message*) that affect the likelihood receivers will actively process the message. In reviewing the ELM research, we saw that if you increase receivers' processing by employing one or more of these characteristics, the receivers will be persuaded based primarily on the quality of your arguments. Increased processing leads to more persuasion when the arguments are strong, but decreased persuasion if the arguments are weak. The arguments used in the ELM research were all pre-tested to validate that the strong arguments elicited mostly positive thoughts from receivers and the weak arguments produced mostly negative thoughts. But what was it about the "strong" messages that made them stronger than the "weak" messages? We must look at research outside the ELM for answers to this question.

Research on *one-sided versus two-sided messages, inoculation theory, use of statistical and story evidence, and fear appeals* has identified strategies that can make a message more persuasive. While the research in these areas has not been conducted within the ELM framework, the ELM would suggest that effective message strategies would have their greatest impact when motivation and ability (and thus the likelihood for central route processing) are high.

One-sided versus Two-sided Messages

Message-sidedness:

One-sided messages provide only the arguments that support your message;

two-sided nonrefutational messages provide counter-arguments but do not refute those arguments;

two-sided refutational messages provide and refute counter-arguments

Suppose a university board of directors sought to create positive public perceptions regarding a tuition increase. In terms of the "**message-sidedness**" research, the board could develop a campaign based on any of three strategies. These include the **one-sided, two-sided nonrefutational**, and **two-sided refutational approaches**. One-sided messages provide only the arguments that support one's position, never acknowledging competing views. If the board was to adopt the one-sided strategy, they would cite all the benefits the tuition hike would provide to students, e.g., more summer classes, more parking facilities, availability of more sections of required classes at varied times of day.

Alternatively, they would go one step further by using use the two-sided nonrefutational approach. Here, the board would continue to emphasize the benefits of the increase, but would also present reasons why some constituents may react negatively to it, e.g., "Some may feel the increase is too much, but let's look again at what you get for your money." Notice that the opposing view (counterargument) that the increase is too much was not directly refuted. The two-sided nonrefutional strategy identifies opposing views, then tries to overcome them with additional one-sided arguments. Research has generally shown two-sided nonrefutational strategies to be less persuasive than one-sided messages. One possible explanation for this is that identifying competing arguments but failing to show they can be refuted lends additional credence to those competing views.

The two-sided refutational approach has been shown to be the most effective of the message-sidedness strategies (see Allen, 1991; O'Keefe, 1999). Were the board to adopt this message strategy in their efforts to influence public perceptions, they would not only identify specific competing arguments, but would also attempt to directly refute them. For example, after acknowledging that some may feel the proposed increase is too much, they might compare the increase with rising costs of products and services, the cost of living index, or higher tuition rates at other schools as evidence that the higher tuition rate is still a bargain in today's market.

Inoculation Theory: Resistance to Persuasion

As the above heading states, this section deals with *resistance* to persuasion, not persuasion. Much of the work on resistance to persuasion has been conducted within a theory known as Inoculation Theory (McGuire, 1964; see Szabo & Pfau, 2002 for a review and analysis of research on this theory). This research is closely related to the message-sidedness research, as it deals with the effectiveness of one-sided versus two-sided refutational messages in conferring resistance to subsequent counter-persuasion. Going back to the tuition increase issue, let's assume that the board of directors used the one-sided strategy, giving only the arguments in support of the increase. Let's assume further that in the days and weeks following the release of their messages, the target audience is exposed to competing views from other sources. Even if the board's campaign had been successful in inducing somewhat favorable perceptions regarding the increase, they would not have prepared receivers to resist the "counterattacks." Would these same audience members have been better able to resist the counter-persuasion had the campaign identified and refuted the arguments they subsequently heard? The research tells us that they would.

Two-sided refutational messages "inoculate" receivers, making them better able to resist counter-persuasion similar to the way that a biological inoculation helps us to better resist certain diseases. The research findings show that receivers who are first given a two-sided refutational message rate subsequent, opposing arguments as less credible than receivers who are first exposed to a one-sided message (see Pryor & Steinfatt, 1978, for further explanation).

Evidence: Statistics versus Stories

As you might expect, the research has shown clearly that citing evidence to support one's claims increases persuasiveness (Maurin, 2000). The two main types of evidence are statistical and story evidence. Statistical evidence is usually based on averages or percentages from a sample of many, while story evidence is based on a single case. For example, if you were trying to persuade a person or group about the need for organ donations, you could support your contention by providing statistics showing the national shortage of available organs, or you could develop a story about a person who went through a long and life-threatening wait for an organ transplant. While statistical evidence may be seen as more valid than a single story, receivers may be more attentive to an interesting story that supports a point. The question of whether statistical or story evidence is most effective has been extensively researched. Some studies have concluded that statistical evidence is superior (e.g., Hoeken, 1999), some show an advantage for story evidence (e.g., Koballa, 1986), while still others (e.g., Krupat, Smith, Leach, & Jackson, 1997) report no difference. At this point, the best conclusion is that both types of evidence are more effective than no evidence, but there is no consistent advantage to one over the other.

Fear Appeals

The use of fear appeals as a persuasive strategy is a common practice. Advertisers suggest that if we fail to buy the their brand of tires, we are risking the safety of our families, anti-cigarette ads depict the dire consequences of

Fear appeals require a convincing threat and an effective solution.

Extended Parallel Process Model
persuasiveness of a fear appeal hinges on receivers' parallel processing about the threat and the solution offered in the message

nicotine addiction, and public service ads ("Click it or ticket") threaten that the police will be ticketing us if we are caught not wearing our seatbelts. Parents, managers, and relationship partners sometimes resort to threats in their efforts to persuade. Do fear appeals work? The answer is not a simple yes or no, but the research does provide guidelines about how best to use fear as a persuasion tactic.

Though researchers have been interested in fear appeals for decades, the most consistent and useful findings have grown out of a theory developed by Witte (1992) known as the **Extended Parallel Process Model** (EPPM). The EPPM holds that the persuasiveness of a fear appeal hinges on receivers' parallel processing about the threat and the solution offered in the message. According to the EPPM, receivers assess the threat in two ways, including (1) the severity of the consequences of not following the source's recommendations and (2) the likelihood that they, personally, would fall prey to those consequences. Receivers are also said to consider the solution quality in two ways, including assessments about (1) whether the recommended solution would work, and (2) whether they are capable of following the recommendation. Research has been supportive of the theory (see, for example, Regan, 2001; Witte, Cameron & McKeon, 1998).

An example may help clarify the EPPM terminology. Mass media campaigns on various health and safety issues sometimes incorporate fear appeals. Assume that such a campaign uses a fear appeal strategy in an effort to persuade people to 'always wear seatbelts'. Following the EPPM guidelines, the messages would need to demonstrate both the *likelihood and severity* of the threat. Statistical evidence could be used to show receivers (1) the likelihood that they will be involved in a car crash at some point in their lives, and (2) the possible increased severity of the consequences of being in a crash while not wearing a seatbelt. The severity issue could be demonstrated with story and statistical evidence (and perhaps some photos). If the messages are successful in convincing receivers of the severity and likelihood of the threat, the ultimate persuasiveness of the campaign will depend on also convincing the receivers that (1) seatbelts do work to reduce injury and (2) they are capable of wearing a seatbelt every time they travel by car. Such a campaign may have to deal with misconceptions ("I'll be trapped in my seatbelt in a bad crash") and concerns ("Seatbelts wrinkle my clothes") by using two-sided refutational arguments.

Tips and Tactics

Building Strong Arguments

Inoculation theory
Two-sided refutational messages "inoculate" receivers, making them better able to resist counter-persuasion

- Should you use a **one-sided** or **two-sided** message? The research evidence is clear. Your best strategy is to *use the two-sided refutational strategy* in a persuasive speech. You may need to do some research to identify the potential counterarguments and how best to refute them, but your efforts should enhance the persuasiveness of your speech.

- **Inoculation theory** suggests that knowing both sides of an argument makes one less susceptible to being "un-persuaded." Speakers who use two-sided refutational messages not only make their message more persuasive but also increase their listeners' resistance to counter-persuasion. One-sided messages do not prepare receivers to resist counter-arguments.

- Though the research has focused primarily on whether **statistical** or **story evidence** is more persuasive, the best approach might be to use both. This would take advantage of both the interest value of story evidence, and the validity value of statistical evidence. In any case, you will be more persuasive if your claims are supported by evidence.

- Notice the next time you hear **fear appeals** whether the Extended Parallel Process Model (EPPM) guidelines seem to be met. This will help you understand and apply the EPPM. If you are planning to use fear in a persuasive presentation, make sure that you carefully consider each of the four steps in the model. It is essential that you provide a high quality solution, meaning that receivers are convinced both that the solution will work, and that they are capable of applying the solution. When these two requirements for a high quality solution are met, receivers are more likely to engage in *danger control* by adopting the solution. Research has also shown that when fear is aroused without a high quality solution, receivers may defensively avoid thinking about the message (see Regan, 2001). There is psychological discomfort in being shown a problem for which no good solution is given. Consider a physician who uses a fear message in an effort to motivate obese patients to follow a certain diet. If the patients believe that the diet is good, but they personally could not stick to it, the fear message could cause the patients to avoid dealing with the problem (*fear control*).

Peripheral Route Persuasion Cues

As we discussed earlier, when listeners lack either the motivation or the ability to engage in effortful processing of a message, they will rely more on simple decision rules, called peripheral cues, to determine responses to persuasive messages. These cues act as decision shortcuts. In most situations, you should make the case for the relevance of your topic and then back up your position with strong arguments, hoping your receivers will take the trouble to engage in elaborative processing and rely primarily on the central route react to your message. But even your best efforts cannot guarantee that each message recipient will focus on your arguments. At least part of their attention will fall on peripheral cues, so it is also important to make those elements of a speech as persuasive as possible. The peripheral cues that will be covered in this section include *characteristics of the source, message-related peripheral cues, and compliance-gaining strategies* that place the receiver in a position of reliance on decision rules.

Source Characteristics

Credibility

Source credibility has been defined as "the image held of a communicator at a given time" (Andersen & Clevenger, 1963, p. 59). This definition captures two important characteristics of the concept. First, any source of information will hold varying levels of credibility for different receivers, depending on how those receivers evaluate the expertise and character of the source. While one receiver

> **Source Credibility**
> The image held of a communicator by a receiver at a given time

may believe that a certain presidential candidate is extremely competent and of high moral character, others may question that candidate's competence, character, or both. The words "image held" in this definition mean that the receiver assigns source credibility. The second important feature of the definition is contained in the words "at a given time." This phrase makes the point that a speaker's credibility can fluctuate over time even in the eyes of the same receiver. If a star athlete or politician behaves in a way that you feel shows bad character, your assessment of that person's character may be lowered. If a physician misdiagnoses your illness, you may revise you evaluation of that physician's expertise. Research has identified expertise (competence) and character (trustworthiness) as the two main components of speaker credibility (see, for example, McCroskey, 1966). From these examples, you can see that speaker credibility, including both the expertise and character components, is a dynamic variable, with the potential for favorable and unfavorable fluctuations.

Both the competence and character dimensions of source credibility have been shown to affect persuasion (for a review of this research, see O'Keefe, 2002). Petty, Cacioppo, and Goldman (1981) demonstrated that source effects have their greatest impact when issue relevance is low. Consistent with ELM predictions, when participants in the experiment thought the issue advocated in the message *would not* affect them (low relevance), they were more influenced by source expertise (the peripheral cue) than by the argument quality. Because the receivers thought they would be unaffected by the issue they put less effort into processing the message. As a result, they were not as tuned in to the strengths and weaknesses of the arguments. Instead, the participants with low involvement used source expertise as a shortcut to determine their responses to the message. As you should now be able to predict, the receivers who thought the issue *would* affect them (high relevance) were motivated to carefully process the message and were more influenced by the quality of the arguments than by speaker expertise. Because they engaged in effortful processing, they noticed the quality of the arguments and were more persuaded by strong arguments than weak arguments.

But how can you build your credibility as a speaker? Strategies for developing receivers' perceptions of expertise and character may be classified as message factors or delivery factors.

Building Credibility through Message Factors

The strategies outlined in the previous section on argument quality will help you demonstrate your expertise on the issue at hand. For example, using good evidence and two-sided messages will show that you are communicating from a position of knowledge and understanding regarding the topic. If you are not an expert on your topic, citing your sources lets your receivers know that you are relying on those who are experts. Informing receivers of your own issue-relevant experience is another effective message strategy for enhancing your expertise. For example, if you were attempting to convince someone that yoga is an excellent workout option, your expertise would be judged higher if you were a yoga instructor, or had been practicing yoga over a period of time, than if you had limited experience with yoga.

Regarding character ratings, research has also shown that when the position you take appears to be self-serving, receivers may question your sincerity. One of your authors witnessed a student speech that compared the virtues of various vacuum cleaners. The speaker consistently portrayed one of the brands as superior to the others. When questioned by the class following the speech, it was revealed that the speaker currently held a sales job with that company. Research on "vested interest" has shown that speakers are viewed as more trustworthy when they appear to speak from unbiased positions (see, for example, Peters, Covello, & McCallum, 1997).

Building Credibility through Delivery Factors

Regarding spoken presentations, certain delivery characteristics also affect ratings of speakers' expertise. Monotone speech (Addington, 1968), and nonfluent speech, including vocalized pauses, such as "um," "uh," and "you know," word repetitions, and pronunciation corrections (Bledsoe, 1984), appear to damage ratings of speakers' expertise. Studies have shown that maintaining eye contact with the audience throughout most of the speech has a favorable impact on expertise ratings (see, for example, Wagner, 1999).

Research also shows that certain delivery characteristics are related to ratings of a speaker's trustworthiness. Pearce and Conklin (1971) reported that a conversational delivery style produced higher ratings of honesty and trustworthiness than a highly dynamic style. The authors speculated that extreme levels of dynamism, marked by wide variations in pitch and loudness, might lead to perceptions of affectation and manipulative intent. Late-night infomercials are filled with examples of this. Accordingly, the more moderate levels of dynamism that define the conversational style evoke more favorable ratings of a speaker's genuineness and trustworthiness. Too little dynamism, as exhibited in monotone speech, lowers ratings of a speaker's trustworthiness (Addington, 1968). As was the case with expertise, research shows that nonfluencies and lack of eye contact are detrimental to ratings of trustworthiness.

Source Attractiveness

Research indicates that physical attractiveness correlates positively with persuasiveness. Cialdini (2001), cites "halo effects" as one explanation. "Research shows that we automatically assign to good-looking individuals such favorable traits as kindness, honesty, and intelligence (p. 148)." Whether the issue is getting the best paying jobs (Hamermesh & Biddle, 1994), a jury's decision on a defendant (see Downs & Lyons, 1990), or dating preferences in speed-dating contexts (Kurzban & Weeden, 2005), both males and females show a bias for attractive others.

In one study, Chaiken (1979) measured the effects of attractiveness on persuasion by looking at the success of 68 college student speakers in persuading their peers to support a new policy regarding the university's food plan. Judges rated the attractiveness

People are more likely to be persuaded by someone they consider attractive.

of each speaker, based on photographs and videotaped speeches. Chaiken reported that the 34 most attractive speakers were significantly more persuasive than the 34 least attractive speakers, regardless of whether the receivers were male or female. This result is consistent with other research on the topic (see Knapp & Hall, 2002). Research has also shown that attractive people tend to be more liked (see O'Keefe, 2002). Increased liking appears to be another reason why attractive people have more social influence than less attractive people.

Clothing also contributes to perceptions of attractiveness. Since dress has been shown to affect ratings of both competence and character, it follows that dress can serve as a peripheral persuasion cue. Mills and Aronson (1965) used clothing and makeup to make a female speaker appear attractive (fashionable clothing and make-up), or unattractive (poorly fitted clothing, no make-up). Though the speaker and speech were the same in each case, the attractive condition obtained greater persuasion. Similar findings have been reached in other studies (see Knapp & Hall, 2002).

Source Similarity

Source similarity is another important peripheral cue. Research has consistently demonstrated that similarity breeds liking (see O'Keefe, 2002). For example, Byrne (1961) asked participants to complete a questionnaire about their beliefs on various issues, and then evaluate another participant on the basis of their responses to the questions. The evaluators' responses showed a distinct preference for others who displayed beliefs that were highly similar to their own. Concluding from research on the connection between similarity and liking, Cialdini (2001) stated "those who want us to like them so that we will comply with them can accomplish that purpose by appearing similar to us in a wide variety of ways" (p. 150). Like all peripheral cues, we would expect attractiveness and similarity to be less important when the receivers are engaged in elaborative processing, but because central and peripheral routes are not mutually exclusive, we would do well to pay attention to any factors that may affect our persuasiveness.

Tips and Tactics

Peripheral Source Characteristics

- If your message is perceived to be relevant and understandable, your receivers will be more likely to focus more on your **message** (central route) than on peripheral factors such as your appearance, your credibility, or their perceptions of you being likeable or similar to them. But, even in high relevance situations, they will pay *some* attention to the peripheral elements, so you would do well to consider them.
- You can build your **credibility** in the eyes of your receivers with high quality messages and good delivery. Conscientious preparation of the message content and practice are necessary in delivering presentations. Practice until you can deliver your message fluently, while maintaining eye contact with the audience throughout most of the presentation.

- In cases where receivers do not perceive your message as relevant, they may use your **appearance** as a peripheral persuasion cue. The research tells us that in such situations, a neat, clean appearance with appropriate dress will contribute to your credibility and persuasiveness.

- Persuaders can take advantage of the peripheral cue effects of **similarity** and **liking** by demonstrating what they and the audience have in common. Similarities in dress, demographics, experiences, and interests have all been shown to contribute to liking (Cialdini, 2001).

Message-Related Factors as Peripheral Persuasion Cues

Conformity Effect

Asch (1951) published a series of experiments on what he called the conformity effect. In Asch's experiments, participants were asked to look at several straight lines projected on a screen. Each participant was asked to pick out which lines were the same lengths. When performing this task alone, everyone correctly identified which lines were the same lengths. In another treatment however, participants were asked the same question after they witnessed others (who were secretly in collusion with Asch) give a wrong answer. Nearly all participants who witnessed one or two others give the wrong answer still answered correctly themselves, but an amazing thing happened when the number of people giving the same wrong answer reached three. At that point, one-third of the participants "conformed" by giving the same wrong answer. Subjects no longer trusted their ability to judge line lengths when their perceptions were threatened by the judgments of three others. No additional conformity effects were observed as the number of confederates was further increased. Summing up this and other research on the conformity effect, Cialdini (2001, p. 100) concluded: "Whether the question is what to do with the empty popcorn box in a movie theater, how fast to drive on a certain stretch of the highway, or how to eat the chicken at a dinner party, the actions of those around us will be important guides in defining the answer."

Scarcity

Persuasion practitioners, particularly in the areas of marketing and advertising, are constantly telling us that certain offers or opportunities will be available only until a specified deadline, or that supplies are limited in regard to a certain item. These familiar strategies are applications of the "scarcity principle" that Cialdini (2001) argues is a powerful compliance motivator. In Cialdini's words, "...opportunities seem more valuable to us when they are less available" (p. 205). Consider a difficult to find toy at Christmas, a rare coin, a ticket to a sold-out event, or a soon-to-expire 20%

Shoppers can be persuaded to compete for items they believe to be scarce.

off coupon. Realization of the scarcity of the opportunity and the possibility of losing it seems to increase perceptions of the desirability of that item or opportunity. Stories of the frenzied behavior of shoppers on quests for limited supply bargains are common around the holidays and at liquidation sales at stores that are going out of business.

The use of time and supply limits are so commonplace in advertising that we may not even be aware of the tug on our purchasing intentions and behavior, but the effects are undeniable. Viewers of television shopping channels routinely respond to time limits and a continually decreasing supply of the item. Faced with a 1:00 P.M. deadline, Macy's customers annually rush to use discount coupons on the Friday after Thanksgiving. Car dealership sales events "end at the close of business on Sunday," and price reductions on a multitude of products, services, and opportunities are advertised with time and/or quantity limits. Scarcity effects can even be fatal, as witnessed at Wal-Mart's day after-Thanksgiving sale in 2008. About 2000 people waited outside the Wal-Mart doors before the advertised 5:00 A.M. opening on that day. Among the bargain priced, limited supply items they would compete for that day were plasma televisions, digital cameras and a $9 *Incredible Hulk* DVD. When the doors opened, the crowd's fervor to claim the sale merchandise was so strong that a 34-year-old Wal-Mart employee was trampled to death, and at least four other people, including a pregnant woman, were taken to the hospital with injuries. One woman who witnessed the incident reported that when the shoppers were told the store was closing because of the death, people began yelling that they had been in line since Thanksgiving morning. "They just kept shopping," she said (Long, 2008). Research has supported the stark anecdotal evidence of the power of scarcity effects. For example, Worchel, Lee, and Adewole (1975) asked participants to taste a chocolate chip cookie from a jar containing either two or 10 cookies. Participants rated the cookies more positively when they were aware they were getting one of just two remaining cookies. The bias for the two-cookie condition increased when it was presented in a slightly different way. This time, a jar of 10 cookies was taken away and replaced with a jar of two cookies. Witnessing the dwindling supply of cookies apparently caused the participants to value them even more.

Compliance-Gaining Strategies

Compliance-gaining strategies are 'sequential request' persuasion techniques that rely on decision rules, not quality arguments, for their success. Persuasion practitioners employ these techniques when the main goal is to elicit desired behaviors (compliance) rather than to change attitudes. An understanding of three compliance techniques is valuable for persuaders and potential persuadees.

Foot-in-the-Door (FID) Strategy

The FID strategy is so labeled because the speaker tries to get a "foot-in-the-door" by making a simple, small request. Once the receiver complies with the small request, the persuader attempts to capitalize on the initial commitment by getting the receiver to agree to a second, larger request. The first request is a tactic to increase the chances of getting compliance with the real behavior that the persuader wants. The effectiveness of this strategy has been documented in numerous experiments (see Cialdini, 2001). For example, Freedman and Fraser (1966) showed that California homeowners were more likely to agree to place a four-by-six foot "Be a Safe Driver" sign on their front lawns to support Safe Driver Week if they had previously agreed to sign a petition or display a window sticker in support of the cause. The FID strategy is predicated on the premium people place on remaining consistent with their commitments, a principle most of us learn from our parents early in life. If we make a commitment to do something, we are taught, it is our responsibility to keep it. Persuasion practitioners take advantage of this belief with the FID strategy. In one application of this strategy, Sherman (1980) reported a 700% increase in American Cancer Society collection volunteers by individuals who, a few days earlier, had answered 'yes' to a survey question that asked them to predict what they would say if asked to donate three hours of their time to this organization.

Many salespeople use compliance-gaining strategies to persuade potential customers.

Door-in-the-Face (DIF) Strategy

The DIF strategy employs the opposite sequence of requests. Practitioners first ask for a large "favor" that they know will be refused. The goal is to then get the receiver to compromise by agreeing to a smaller request. Research has shown DIF to be an effective technique. For example, Cialdini and Ascani (1976) reported that college students who had previously denied a request to donate blood regularly for two years were more likely to agree to donate blood once than students who were simply asked to donate once. Various explanations have been offered for the effectiveness of DIF, including perceptual contrast (the second request seems smaller when you are first exposed to the large request), guilt about refusing the first request, or compromise. The effects are probably best explained by a combination of these factors.

Low-Ball Strategy

Another compliance strategy that relies on the power of commitment is called the low-ball technique. In this strategy, the persuader tries to elicit a commitment from the receiver before revealing all of the "costs." For example, after inducing a customer to commit to a deal at a certain price, a car salesperson might add on a dealer fee of several hundred dollars. Or, you might agree to assume an office with a school organization, only to find out afterwards that the job requires far more time than you thought. The research indicates that your initial commitment makes it less likely that you will reverse your decision. For example, Cialdini, Cacioppo, Bassett, and Miller (1978) obtained greater compliance from students asked to participate in a 7:00 a.m. experiment when they obtained a commitment to participate before informing the students of the time than when students were told "up front" of the early starting time.

Tips and Tactics

- Even when you do everything you can to increase your receivers' motivation and ability to engage in elaborative processing of your message, there may be some who are unwilling to expend the mental effort and are looking for a shortcut to help them decide whether or not to accept your position. Available research suggests several elements that might serve as mental shortcuts for those who are unwilling, or unable, to thoroughly process the message:

- People have a tendency to go along with the crowd. You may be able to employ the **conformity effect** by citing evidence that a majority of others who are similar to your receiver(s) have complied with your request. For example, in helping with a blood donation campaign on campus, you may be able to show prospective donors that numerous similar others (students, members of fraternities/sororities, certain majors, etc.) have already signed up to donate.

Conformity effect
People will question their own perceptions when presented with the judgements of others

- The **scarcity strategy** refers to messages that alert receivers of time or quantity limitations regarding the availability of a product, service, or opportunity. Persuasion practitioners can often find ways to apply the strategy to fit their own circumstances. For example, one student who worked at a movie rental store reported that DVD rentals of certain movies lagged when there was too much supply. In the eyes of at least some customers, if all 12 copies of a movie were still on the shelf, the movie must not be very good. This student reported that re-arranging the "supply" so that it appeared that only a few of the 12 copies were still available produced an increase in rentals. It appears the movies were viewed as more desirable when the apparent dwindling supply made the loss of the opportunity more preeminent, just like the cookies in the Worchel et.al. (1975) experiment. Note that this application takes advantage of both the scarcity and conformity strategies.

- We have all experienced each of these **sequential request strategies**, as both persuaders and as the ones being persuaded. Your agreement to complete a brief telephone survey may have led to your compliance with a request for an "obligation-free" trial of a product or service (**foot-in-the-door**); your refusal to loan a friend $50 may have resulted in a $20 loan (**door-in-the-face**); and you have probably agreed to help out on a project that later required a much larger commitment than you were initially led to expect (**low-ball**). You may be able to design ways to apply one or more of these techniques. For example, in a presentation, you might ask audience members to promise themselves they will take certain actions (private commitment), or you might ask for a public commitment, such as signing a petition. In any case, you must keep ethical considerations in mind when using these compliance strategies. The same strategy (FID, for example) can be used for ethical purposes–persuading your out-of-shape friend to visit the fitness center just once, or unethical purposes–the drug dealer who convinces your nephew to try cocaine "just one time."

SPEAKING OF...

Six Principles of Influence

Robert Cialdini is not just a highly respected scholar; he is also an in-demand public speaker who frequently presents his message to gatherings of CEOs, Wall Street traders, international diplomats, and fellow academics. He speaks about what he knows best—the how and why of influence. His advice is grounded in theory and research but also is easy to grasp and put into practice.

Cialdini suggests that people have been conditioned over thousands of years of civilized life to respond positively to six simple principles embedded in the concepts of reciprocity, liking, authority, social support, scarcity, and commitment.

Reciprocity

The saying "You scratch my back, and I'll scratch yours" illustrates reciprocity A reciprocity-based appeal can work in one of two ways in a persuasive speech. Candidates for political office often promise to give something in return for a person's vote. They may promise to reciprocate by proposing legislation, supporting a specific bill, or voicing a concern of their constituency.

Another common way reciprocity is used in a persuasive speech is when the speaker calls on the audience to reciprocate. During homecoming week, as a case in point, the school president may appeal to alumni for financial support. The appeal is usually couched in terms of "giving something back to the institution that gave you so much."

Reciprocity appeals are effective because people are conditioned from an early age to return favors, gifts, and services. Reciprocity is a norm. Thus, when people receive a promise or are asked to return something received, the conditioned response is to reciprocate in kind.

Liking

Appeals based on liking are commonly used in persuasive campaigns. Politicians, for instance, enlist stars from film and music to speak persuasively on their behalf. The assumption is that if a star is well liked, the feeling may be generalized to the candidate endorsed by the star. Liking is a staple of advertisers, who employ well-known people as spokespersons for a product. It's not that the celebrities are experts on the product, but they are well liked by the public. Thus, if well-liked figures Tiger Woods and LeBron James wear Nikes, the hope is that the public will also like the product.

Authority

Research shows that some people are predisposed to comply with the requests of individuals and institutions perceived as authoritative. Examples of these authoritative sources range from members of law enforcement and the clergy to federal agencies such as the military. Thus, a speaker attempting to encourage a group of conservative Catholics to voice their opposition to stem cell research might use the words of the Pope as an appeal. Similarly, a politician speaking to veterans might rely on an endorsement received from a military hero to win the audience's vote in the election.

Social Support

An appeal based on social support is nothing more than an appeal based on numbers. There's a tendency among people to think that if enough folks say something is so, then it must be so. Thus, product advertisers tout their product as "the number-one seller in its class" in an effort to convince consumers that their product must be the best. Research shows that when people are confronted with an appeal supported by large numbers, they are much more likely to be persuaded by the appeal–to jump on the bandwagon, so to speak. In a sense, they accept social support as a form of grounds for the argument.

Scarcity

The appeal to scarcity is based on the law of supply and demand. It is a maxim in economics that when demand exceeds supply, the value of the commodity increases. Thus,

Celebrities such as Tiger Woods are effective in promoting products because they are well liked by the public.

an appeal based on scarcity is also one based on relative value. As is the case with reciprocity, authority, and social support, people are conditioned to believe that something that is scarce is valuable enough to demand their attention. Persuasive speeches about the environment frequently use scarcity as the basis of appeal. For instance, the ecological benefit of the rain forests is made even more valuable when the speaker tells the audience that the world's rain forests are disappearing at an alarming rate.

Commitment

One of the most powerful methods of persuasion is the appeal to commitment. In the aftermath of September 11, 2001, millions of Americans made the commitment to donate blood. Even when the blood banks were overwhelmed with more donors than they could take, people were encouraged to pledge that they would come back at a later date when blood supplies needed replenishment. When people make even small commitments as a result of a persuasive message, the principle of psychological consistency comes into play. This principle tells us that we all feel pressure to keep our attitudes, beliefs, and values consistent with our commitments. If an appeal to commitment leads a person to write a letter, to volunteer, or to sign a petition, it increases the chances that the person's attitudes, beliefs, and values will reflect the commitment. In some cases, action may actually precede changes in attitude, reversing the normal order of persuasive goals.

To reiterate, the appeals you make in your persuasive message should reflect your goal and your audience. Not all audiences jump aboard the bandwagon after hearing an appeal based on social support. There are those who steadfastly refuse to get on a bandwagon, no matter how many other people have already done so. Choosing the right appeals to flesh out your persuasive message, therefore, is part science and part art.

Summary

The results of a large body of research help us understand the process of persuasion and provide strategies for increasing our effectiveness as persuasive communicators.

The Elaboration Likelihood Model helps us understand that people who have sufficient motivation and ability tend to engage in effortful processing of messages.

- This message scrutiny results in their reacting positively to strong arguments and negatively to weak arguments.

- Whether we are attempting to persuade an audience of one or many, we would do well to create relevant and understandable messages that proffer the strongest possible arguments to increase the likelihood for elaboration.

The likelihood for elaboration can also be influenced by

- source factors (expertise and use of outside sources)

- channel factors (the use of the visual channel to enhance the audience's ability to process the message)

- message factors (forewarning and repetition)

- receiver factors (their initial position or their level of involvement with the topic)

- Of these, receivers' perceptions of the relevance of the message may be the most important determinant of the likelihood for elaboration.

Receivers who engage in elaborative processing are persuaded mainly by strong arguments.

We also discussed strategies for making messages strong:

- The appropriate use of one- and two-sided messages

- The use of statistical or anecdotal evidence

- The use of fear appeals

Because the central/peripheral distinction is not an either-or proposition, and we cannot be sure that all receivers will be sufficiently motivated and able to process a given message, we should also pay attention to peripheral cues.

- Credibility, attractiveness, and similarity are some of the source characteristics that may serve as peripheral cues.

- The message can also contain elements that may serve as peripheral cues, such as appeals to our audience's need for conformity, perceptions of scarcity, and the use of sequential request strategies.

Check Your Understanding: Exercises and Activities

1. Analyze several television advertisements for different products for the use of central and peripheral route strategies. Which route seems to be emphasized in each advertisement? Evaluate the potential effectiveness of each ad for high and low involved receivers.

2. Think of one example for each of the following peripheral cues in which you were a participant as a persuader or receiver: similarity, conformity, scarcity, FID, DIF, low-ball.

3. Follow up on the list of tips we gave for assessing and enhancing perceptions of your credibility. List the specific factors you believe make you credible about the topic of your persuasive speech. Then describe how you plan on using these specific factors so that they will sustain the audience members' perceptions of your credibility as you deliver your speech.

4. Identify a television ad that you believe represents a fear appeal. Evaluate its effectiveness with reference to Witte's concepts of perceptions of the severity and likelihood of the threat and solution quality. Do you think the ad would result in *fear control* or *danger control* for the majority of people?

5. Develop a 2-sided refutational strategy for a persuasive speech topic.

References

Addington, D. (1968). The relationship of selected vocal characteristics to personality perception. *Speech Monographs*, 35, 492–503.

Allen, M. (1991). Meta-analysis comparing the persuasiveness of one-sided and two sided messages. *Western Journal of Speech Communication*, 55, 390–404.

Andersen, K., & Clevenger, T., (1963). A summary of experimental research in ethos. *Speech Monographs*, 30, 59–78.

Andersen, S., & Pryor, B. (1992). *Speech fundamentals: A contemporary approach*. Needham Heights, MA: Ginn Press.

Asch, S. (1951). Effects of group pressure upon the modification of and distortion of judgment. In H. Guetzhow (Ed.), *Groups, leadership, and men*. Pittsburgh: Carnegie.

Bledsoe, D. (1984). *Nonfluencies and distraction theory: A proattitudinal approach*. Unpublished masters thesis, University of Central Florida.

Byrne, D. (1961). Interpersonal attraction and attitude similarity. *Journal of Abnormal and Social Psychology,* 62, 713–715.

Cacioppo, J. T. & Petty, R.E. (1979). Effects of message repetition and position on responses, recall, and persuasion. *Journal of Personality and Social Psychology*, 37, 97–109.

Cacioppo, J. T. & Petty, R.E. (1982). The need for cognition. *Journal of Personality and Social Psychology,* 42, 116–131.

Cacioppo, J. T. & Petty, R.E. (1984). The need for cognition: Relationship to attitudinal processes. In R. McGlynn, J. Maddux, C. Stoltenberg, and J. Harvey (Eds.), *Social perception in clinical and counseling psychology*. Lubbock: Texas Tech Press.

Cacioppo, J. T. & Petty, R. E. (1985). Central and peripheral routes to persuasion: The role of message repetition. In A. Mitchell & L. Alwitt (Eds.), *Psychological processes and advertising effects*. Hillsdale, NJ: Erlbaum.

Chaiken, S. (1979). Communicator physical attractiveness and persuasion. *Journal of Personality and Social Psychology*, 37, 1387–1397.

Chaiken, S. & Eagly, A.H. (1976). Communication modality as a determinant of message persuasiveness and message comprehensibility. *Journal of Personality and Social Psychology*, 39, 752–766.

Cialdini, R. (2001). *Influence: Science and practice.* Boston: Allyn and Bacon.

Cialdini, R., & Ascani, K. (1976). Test of a concession procedure for inducing verbal, behavioral, and further compliance with a request to give blood. *Journal of Applied Psychology*, 61, 295–300.

Cialdini, R. B., Levy, A., Herman, P., Koslowski, L & Petty, R.E. (1976). Elastic shifts of opinion: Determinants of direction and durability. *Journal of Personality and Social Psychology*, 34, 663–672.

Cialdini, R. B., Cacioppo, J. R., Bassett, R. & Miller, J. A. (1978). The low-ball procedure for producing compliance: Commitment then cost. *Journal of Personality and Social Psychology*, 36, 463–476.

Downs, A.C., & Lyons, P.M. (1990). Natural observations of the links between attractiveness and initial legal judgments. *Personality and Social Psychology Bulletin*, 17, 541–547.

Freedman, J., & Fraser, S. (1966). Compliance without pressure: The foot-in-the-door technique. *Journal of Personality and Social Psychology*, 4, 195–202.

Hamermesh, D. S., & Biddle, J.E. (1994). Beauty and the labor market. *American Economic Review*, 84, 1174–1194.

Harkins, S. G. & Petty, R. E. (1981). The multiple source effect in persuasion: The effects of distraction. *Personality and Social Psychology Bulletin*, 7, 627–635.

Hoeken, H. (1999). The perceived and actual persuasiveness of different types of inductive arguments. In F. van Eemeren, R. Grootendorst, J. Blair, & C. Willard, (Eds.), *Proceedings of the fourth international conference of the International Society for the Study of Argumentation* (pp. 353–357). Amsterdam: Sic Sat.

Katt, J. (2004, November). *Influencing perceptions of relevance*. Paper presented at the annual conference of the National Communication Association, Chicago, IL.

Knapp, M., & Hall, J. (2002). Nonverbal communication in human interaction. Fort Worth: Harcourt Brace.

Koballa, T. (1986). Persuading teachers to reexamine the innovative elementary science programs of yesterday: The effect of anecdotal versus data-summary communications. *Journal of Research in Science Teaching*, 23, 437–449.

Krupat, E., Smith, R., Leach, C., & Jackson, M. (1997). Generalizing from atypical cases: How general a tendency? *Basic and Applied Psychology*, 19, 345–361.

Kurzban, R., & Weeden, J. (2005). HurryDate: Mate preferences in action. *Evolution and Human Behavior*, 227–244.

Long, C. (2008). Sought: Wal-Mart shoppers who trampled NY worker. *Associated Press*, http://news.yahoo.com/s/ap/20081129/ap_on_re_us/wal_mart_death/print;_ylt=Aqy5vJg…

Maurin, P. (2000). *The effects of statistical and story evidence on attitude change*. Unpublished masters thesis, University of Central Florida.

McCroskey, J. C. (1966). Scales for measurement of ethos. *Speech Monographs*, 33, 65–72.

McGuire, W. J. (1964). Inducing resistance to persuasion: Some contemporary approaches. In L. Berkowitz (Ed.), *Advances in experimental social psychology*, (Vol.1). New York: Academic Press.

Mills, J., & Aronson, E., (1965). Opinion change as a function of the communicator's attractiveness and desire to influence. *Journal of Personality and Social Psychology*, 1, 173–177.

O'Keefe, D. (1999). How to handle opposing arguments in persuasive messages. A meta-analytic review of the effects of one-sided and two-sided messages. *Communication Yearbook*, 22, 209–249.

O'Keefe, D. (2002). *Persuasion: Theory and research*. Thousand Oaks, CA: Sage.

Pearce, W. B. & Conklin, F, (1971). Nonverbal vocalic communication and perceptions of a speaker. *Speech Monographs*, 38, 235–241.

Peters, R., Covello, V., & McCallum, D. (1997). The determinants of trust and credibility in environmental risk communication: An empirical study. *Risk Analysis*, 17, 43–54.

Petty, R. E. & Cacioppo, J. T. (1977). Forewarning, cognitive responding, and resistance to persuasion. *Journal of Personality and Social Psychology*, 35, 645–655.

Petty, R. E. & Cacioppo, J. T. (1979). Issue involvement can increase or decrease persuasion by enhancing message-relevant cognitive responses. *Journal of Personality and Social Psychology*, 37, 1915–1926.

Petty, R. E. & Cacioppo, J. T. (1984). Source factors and the elaboration likelihood model of persuasion. *Advances in Consumer Research*, 11, 668–672.

Petty, R. E. & Cacioppo, J. T. (1984). The effects of involvement on responses to argument quality and quantity: Central and peripheral route to persuasion. *Journal of Personality and Social Psychology*, 46, 69–81.

Petty, R. E. & Cacioppo, J. T. (1986). *Communication and persuasion: Central and peripheral routes to attitude change*. New York: Springer-Verlag.

Petty, R. E., Cacioppo, J. T., & Goldman, R. (1981). Personal involvement as a determinant of argument-based persuasion. *Journal of Personality and Social Psychology*, 41, 847–855.

Pratkanis, A. & Aronson, E. (2002). *The age of propaganda: The everyday use and abuse of persuasion*. New York: W.H. Freeman & Co.

Pryor, B. & Steinfatt, T. M. (1978). The effects of initial belief level on inoculation theory and its proposed mechanism. *Human Communication Research*, 4, 217–230.

Regan, N., (2001). *Fear appeals and health communication: The effects of threat and efficacy on intentions to modify behavior*. Unpublished masters thesis, University of Central Florida.

Sereno, K. K. & Hawkins, G. J. (1967). The effects of variations in speakers' nonfluency upon audience ratings of attitude toward the speech topic and speakers' credibility. *Speech Monographs*, 34, 58–64.

Sherman, S. (1980). On the self-erasing nature of errors of prediction. *Journal of Personality and Social Psychology*, 39, 211–221.

Szabo, E., & Pfau, M. (2002). Nuances in inoculation: Theory and applications. In J. Dillard & M. Pfau (Eds.), *The persuasion handbook: Developments in theory and practice.* Thousand Oaks, CA: Sage.

Vernon, M. (1962). *The psychology of perception*. Baltimore: Penguin Books.

Wagner, T. (1999). *Effects of various levels of speakers' eye contact on receivers' assessments of the speaker and the speech.* Unpublished masters thesis, University of Central Florida.

Witte, K. (1992). Putting the fear back in fear appeals: The extended parallel process model. *Communication Monographs*, 59, 329–349.

Witte, K., Berkowitz, J., Cameron, K., & McKeon, J. (1998). Preventing the spread of genital warts: Using fear appeals to promote self-protective behaviors. *Health Education and Behavior*, 25, 571–585.

Cable TV hosts, such as Glenn Beck of Fox News Channel and Keith Olbermann of MSNBC, have been criticized for using rhetoric that inflames rather than informs their viewers.

CHAPTER 15

THINKING AND SPEAKING CRITICALLY

Objectives 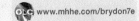 www.mhhe.com/brydon7e

After reading this chapter and reviewing the online learning resources at www.mhhe.com/brydon7e, you should be able to:

- Explain the difference between verbal aggressiveness and reasoned argument.
- Evaluate the soundness of arguments using the Toulmin model of reasoning.
- Identify and refute common fallacies of argument.

Key Concepts

ad hominem

arguing in a circle (begging the question)

backing

critical thinking

distorted evidence

fallacy

false analogy

false dilemma

grounds

halo effect

hasty generalization

hyperbole

loaded language

misleading statistics

mistaking correlation for cause

non sequitur

post hoc, ergo propter hoc

pseudoreasoning

qualifier

rebuttal

red herring (smoke screen)

slippery slope

stereotyping

straw person

unsupported assertion

verbal aggressiveness

warrant

> "It is better to debate a question without settling it than to settle a question without debating it."
>
> —JOSEPH JOUBERT[1]

One of the unintended consequences of the proliferation of cable TV news channels is that there is not enough "real news" to fill their 24/7 broadcast cycle. As a result, there has been a corresponding proliferation of airtime devoted to the kind of political rhetoric that is more likely to inflame than inform the viewing audience on issues of the day. Without naming names, the hosts and guests of these "political forums" have made a mockery of civic engagement and civil discourse, promoting shoddy thinking and giving unjustified importance to the opinions of people whose only qualification seems to be the ability to talk nonstop. As Professor Kathleen Hall Jamieson of the University of Pennsylvania's Annenberg Public Policy Center states:

> The rhetoric becomes more shrill, more strident. It becomes hysterical and hyperbolic. . . . One thinks that it's appropriate to ridicule the other side, to demonize the other side. One stops calling it ridicule and demonization. One starts to think that that's how we talk politics.[2]

To compound matters, much of what people take away from these broadcasts finds its way onto the Internet. As a result, anyone with access to a computer and an Internet connection is free to not just pass along the misinformation received from cable TV programming, but also promote and reinforce the misleading arguments it contains.

This chapter is about the need for all of us to think critically about the arguments we construct and make, as well as the need to apply critical thinking skills to the genuine and pseudo-arguments directed at us. We focus on the significance of critical thinking to speakers and audience members, as well as the public at large. In the process, we point out the difference between the verbal aggressiveness seen and heard in the popular media and the reasoned arguments necessary in a civil society. We introduce a model of argument that can help us in both constructing and evaluating sound arguments. And we use that model to identify several types of unsound arguments.

Critical Thinking and the Speech Transaction

critical thinking
The process of making sound inferences based on accurate evidence and valid reasoning.

Critical thinking is the process of making sound inferences using accurate evidence and valid reasoning to guide you. Critical thinking skills are important to both speakers and listeners. As speakers, understanding how to think critically about arguments is the first step in constructing sound arguments and then applying them to our transactions with audience members. As listeners, understanding the process of critical thinking helps protect us from being duped by unsound arguments that at first glance seem reasonable. Furthermore, the importance of critical thinking goes far beyond our immediate needs as speakers and listeners.

When we use the tools necessary to logically dissect the merits of an argument, we may learn in the process that these tools also can reveal a truth we keep hidden: the fact that we are frequently just as guilty of unsound reasoning as the people with whom we disagree. In a very real sense, the ability to think critically and apply what we learn is essential if we are to become a community of civically minded and civilly engaged decision makers.

Verbal Aggressiveness Versus Reasoned Argument

Civic engagement demands a civil tongue. A civil tongue should not be confused with a "politically correct" one. Legitimate differences of opinion among people on important topics and issues need to be openly expressed and debated. The decisions we make about these issues usually benefit from this process.

Expressing sound arguments and then debating them in an open forum, however, should not be confused with the verbally aggressive behavior so often seen or heard on political talk shows. In his book *Arguing Constructively,* communication scholar Dominic Infante defines **verbal aggressiveness** as a personality trait.[3] More-over, he highlights research that reveals that verbally aggressive people use derision rather than sound arguments to try and assert their superiority in a debate. Most commonly, verbally aggressive people attack their opponents' identity instead of their arguments.

Verbal aggressiveness can lead to hostility and a failure to think rationally.

verbal aggressiveness The trait of attacking the self-concept of those with whom one disagrees about controversial claims.

Needless to say, it is much easier to dismiss someone as a blathering idiot or as subhuman than it is to try and refute his or her claims with sound arguments of our own. It doesn't take much critical thinking either. Keep this in mind as we now turn to the relationship between critical thinking and the elements that make up a sound argument.

A Model of Argument
Constructing a Sound Argument

So what is it that makes and distinguishes a sound argument from a questionable one? To better answer this question we want you to take a look at the box, "In Their Own Words: Point-Counterpoint—To College or Not to College?" It features excerpts from two student speeches that make competing claims about the very process in which you are engaged: pursuing a college degree. After you have read these excerpts or viewed the online speeches from which they were taken, we'll show you how they can help us answer this basic question.

IN THEIR OWN WORDS

Point-Counterpoint—To College or Not to College

Greg Shafer
George Rogers

Greg Shafer, a student in our honors public speaking course, provoked serious discussion in the class with his speech, "Quit School Today." Although the audience was made up of honors students, whom you might expect to be highly committed to college, several students said the speech made them really think about their choices. On the other hand, Arjun Buxi, a recent graduate of our program, presented a counterargument in his speech, "Mind on College." Full transcripts are in Appendix B, and videos of each are at the Online Learning Center.

QUIT SCHOOL TODAY
by Greg Shafer

. . . I propose that the amount of money, effort, and time put into obtaining a four-year college undergraduate degree could be better spent elsewhere, and for many it is not only an unwise financial investment, it is also detrimental to their self-image and to their future prospects. . . .

First of all, let's talk about whether or not college is a worthy investment. Now, we can all agree that college graduates make a substantial amount more money than high school graduates. This is undisputable and I'm not here to argue that fact. However, if you look closely at the numbers, it's not always the case. For example, the average cost of attending a public four-year university is $76,000. For any reasonable person, that's a sizable amount of money, especially for kids our age. Most of us are having our tuition and housing paid by either our parents or the government or a combination of the two. Also, this is just for attending a public university. For private universities or for upscale universities the cost is going to be much, much greater.

In addition, the average earnings of a college graduate more than a high school graduate after 40 years is approximately $400,000. Now this is a sizable amount of money; this is true. However, if you look at it, over 40 years, that's not really that great of a return. In fact, the rate of return is approximately 4.42 percent. Now if you took the same amount of money, the same $76,000, and put it in a sound investment portfolio for stocks, you would get something more along the lines of a 6 or 7 percent rate of return, conservatively. Compared with this 4.42 percent, it's not that much money. In addition, you have to consider that this is just the average. For every student that makes this amount of money or more, there's another student who makes this amount of money or less. For every successful engineering student or physics major, there's a philosophy or art history student who's making less. . . .

Here is a list of famous college dropouts. [See Exhibit 15.1.] Now, we have this stigma in our heads that's instilled in us since we first attended elementary school that in order to be successful, you have to have a college degree. You have to work hard; you have to get at least your undergraduate or your masters to be successful. Here's a list of people who are wildly successful by anyone's standards, who either never attended college, dropped out part way, or dropped out and then returned several years later. On this list you'll see politicians, entrepreneurs, businessman, performers, . . . artists, all of who are wildly successful. This just shows that a person with drive, ambition, and personal discipline is able to be successful regardless of whether they have a college degree or not. . . .

Employers are looking for people with practical job skills. They're looking for people with connections and they're looking for people who have job experience. A lot of graduates will leave college without these skills. It's imperative that we get these skills to be able to function in the real world. In the real working environment, we have to make sure that we have something to contribute. . . .

Startlingly, 40 percent of 2 million freshman admissions each year will not finish college in four years. It will take five, six, even seven years to complete their degree. Each year that's

362

another 10, 20 thousand dollars of debt that they might be incurring. Even more startlingly, 45 percent of admitted freshmen will never graduate, no matter how much time they spend in college. That's terrifying. Think about it, what if you attend school for five or six years and the money just runs out; you never get your degree; you have nothing to show for all the money and time that you have wasted. This is terrifying. We have to make sure that we know what we're getting into. . . .

Famous College Drop Outs

- Bill Murray
- David Bowie
- David Byrne
- Andrew Carnegie
- Winston Churchill
- Ellen DeGeneres
- Michael Dell
- Charles Dickens
- Walt Disney

- Thomas Edison
- Albert Einstein
- F. Scott Fitzgerald
- Henry Ford
- Benjamin Franklin
- Bill Gates
- Steve Jobs
- George Gershwin
- John F. Kennedy

Exhibit 15.1

This slide was used in Greg Shafer's speech to illustrate that many rich and famous people had dropped out of college.

Greg Shafer

MIND ON COLLEGE
by Arjun Buxi

. . . The first question then is, what is the cost of college? How much does it really cost? All right, we look up College Board.com, here is what they say. On average, a private college, four-year college, will cost you about $25,000 to $26,000 a year. Okay, how about a four-year public college like Chico State? About $6,000 to $7,000 a year. Oh, what about a JC, a two-year college? Maybe $2,000 to $3,000. Do you see the gradations here? There's a lot of leeway—a lot of money to be spent or a lot of money to be saved. It's up to us.

But just while I'm on the subject of JCs, Gladieaux and Perna did a study in 2005. You know what they found out? That if you go to a JC before you go to a four-year school, you are only one-third as likely to borrow a single cent in student loans. That's a thought.

Then the question is, well okay, maybe I can afford college, but then does it pay me back? Is it worth it? Here's why. David Leonhardt of the New York Times. . . . He did a quick study in 2007 and here's what he found out. Median income if you were a high school grad, you're looking at . . . about $27,000 a year. . . . Let's move on—high school grad, college dropout, $33,000 a year. Still looking better. Oh, but wait, here it gets better. If you've finished your degree and you're a full college grad, you earn an average of $47,000 a year. That's a jump of $20,000 for just having the degree. But I'm not even done yet. The Bureau for Labor Statistics 2008, October, a government body, did a few number samplings of their own and here's what they found out. That of the labor force of that time, the kids that had just a high school diploma, only 27 percent of

Arjun Buxi
George Rogers

363

them even had a job to begin with. But a college grad, 55 percent of all college grads had a job. And then, when you add the fact that we mentioned before of them earning almost twice as much, we're looking at some real holiday dividends here. And then don't forget, that if $20,000 is the average boost for a college degree, it's also the average debt. So, already it starts paying itself off. . . .

Let's talk about what the degree [means] to us, does it really come across as useful? You might hear these comments. For example, I hear, well maybe, maybe my degree is, you know, not really related to what I'm going to do. My major has nothing to do with my job. But hold back. The University of Washington, Seattle, what do they tell us? They tell us, that's exactly what it's supposed to be. It's not supposed to be specific, not unless you're an engineering major or a medical major, something more technical. But the general stuff, social sciences and liberal arts, it's supposed to be general, it's designed that way to give us maximum spectrum of jobs to look into. That's opening up opportunity, opening up the mind. . . .

Before I end . . . I wanted to address one last comment that you hear a lot. Well, you can get rich without going to college, right? You can get famous without going to college, right? You know what, I did a Google search. There's actually a Web site called collegedropoutshalloffame .com and you're absolutely right. I'm not going to sugarcoat it. Yes, you can get rich without college. Yes, you can get famous without college. But are these metrics—rich and famous— are these really what we want to judge success by? Whatever happened to thinking about other things, about other people, about self-actualization where you treat other people differently as a result of your knowledge, where you treat the world and you see the world differently as a result of your knowledge. Pursuing knowledge for knowledge's sake. Whatever happened to that?

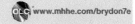

To view videos of speeches by Greg Schafer and Arjun Buxi, click on the Speech Coach link in our Online Learning Center Web site and go to segments 15.1 and 15.2.

grounds
The evidence a speaker offers in support of a claim.

warrant
The connection between evidence (grounds) and claim.

These speeches are well above average in content and delivery. But how do we know whether the arguments Greg and Arjun make are sound? Are the extraordinarily successful college dropouts Greg cites to support his argument (see Exhibit 15.1) typical of college dropouts or are his examples really "outliers," a term Malcolm Gladwell uses to describe people far removed from the norm?[4] Similarly, how do we know whether the statistical average Arjun uses to support his competing claim is to be trusted, when statisticians tell us the average can be highly misleading?

Questions like these are the perfect segue to a model of argument that is used in many college classrooms to explain what distinguishes an argument that is sound from one that is logically flawed. Developed by philosopher Stephen Toulmin, the basic model features three interdependent parts.[5] The first is the *claim,* which we defined in Chapter 7 as a conclusion a speaker wants an audience to accept. Greg and Arjun's competing assertions about the relationship between a college education and its consequent value for a student are examples of claims.

Next come the **grounds** to support the claim, which we will refer to by the more commonly accepted term *evidence.* Greg used Bill Gates and Steve Jobs as evidence to support his claim. Arjun used, among other things, statistical evidence on the relationship between education and salaries in support of his competing claim.

The third, and sometimes most confusing, part of Toulmin's model, is called the **warrant.** It is the logical connection between a speaker's claim and the evidence offered in its support. Although these connections can be obvious, speakers all too often imply them rather than spell them out for audience members. As a result, the warrant connecting a claim and the evidence a speaker offers in support of it may not always be perceived by audience members.

Backing, qualifiers, and rebuttals flesh out Toulmin's model of argument. **Backing** is a type of evidence, but it serves a different function than evidence that directly supports a claim. Backing bolsters the warrant that connects a claim and the evidence offered to directly support the claim. Backing can make the warrant more explicit in the minds of audience members. By choosing and then limiting his examples to the most visible and richest college dropouts, for instance, Greg begged the question of whether or not his examples were generalizable to the experience of the average college student. Clearly Greg needed better backing for his warrant; for example, he might have shown that what is true of people like Gates and Jobs also is true of many lesser known but successful college dropouts across the career spectrum.

The next part of Toulmin's complete model is the **qualifier,** which specifies how likely it is that the claim is true. Because the claim we make in an argument is better expressed as a probability than as an absolute, it only makes good sense for speakers to acknowledge the fact that there are exceptions to the claim as stated. No doubt you can find numerous instances in Greg's and Arjun's speeches where they could have used qualifiers to good effect.

Finally, the perfect argument is seldom seen in practice. In addition to the many bits and pieces of sound evidence that typically qualify our arguments, there is also a good chance that there is a **rebuttal,** evidence at hand, or that can be tracked down, to refute at least part of what we claim. In Chapters 9 and 14 we introduced and then reinforced the fact that it's a good idea in persuasive speeches to organize and present a two-sided message. Rather than ignore counter-arguments that realistically might occur to audience members, we urge students to use these arguments to their advantage. In doing so, they might improve their chances not only of audience members accepting their argument, but also of inoculating listeners against similar rebuttals they are likely to hear in the future.

Using Toulmin's Model of Argument

Given the preceding framework, as depicted in Exhibit 15.2, we can use Toulmin's model to test the soundness of our own arguments as well as those made by others. To do so, however, we need to first look at the common practice of **pseudoreasoning.** It occurs when people make or accept an argument that at first glance seems reasonable, but when put under the microscope of critical thinking proves to be based on a fallacy. Philosophers Brooke Noel Moore and Richard Parker define a **fallacy** as "an argument in which the reasons advanced for a claim fail to *warrant* acceptance of the claim."[6] Put another way, a fallacy is an argument in which the claim made has not been proven by the evidence or there is a deficiency in the warrant connecting the evidence to the claim.

The fallacies on which pseudoreasoning feeds are antithetical to critical thinking and the case we have been making for improving the quality of arguments

backing
Evidence that directly supports a warrant.

qualifier
An indication of the level of probability of a claim.

rebuttal
An exception to or a refutation of an argument.

pseudoreasoning
An argument that appears sound at first glance but contains a fallacy of reasoning that renders it unsound.

fallacy
An argument in which the reasons advanced for a claim fail to warrant acceptance of the claim.

Exhibit 15.2
The Toulmin Model
of Argument

Toulmin, Stephen Edelson, INTRODUCTION TO REASONING, 2nd Edition. © 1984. Reprinted by permission of Pearson Education, Inc., Upper Saddle River, NJ.

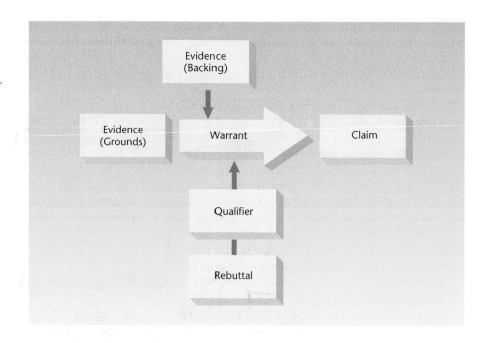

both in and outside the classroom. As a result, critical thinking demands that you learn to recognize the most common types of fallacies you will see and hear people use in the attempt to "prove" their point.

Fallacies Associated With Evidence

As we discussed in chapters 7 and 14, sound evidence is essential to a sound argument. As a rule of thumb, the evidence we use to construct or evaluate an argument should be relevant, of sufficient quantity, and typical. Examples should be typical and representative. Facts should come from a reliable source and be verifiable, recent, and consistent with other known facts. Statistical data should be based on a representative or defined sample and published by a reliable and unbiased source. If statistical data are based on a survey, its contents and method of administration should be reported. If evidence is attributed to an expert, then the credentials establishing the expert's credibility need to be documented. Further, anything about the expert that might bias the expert's opinion should be disclosed. Explanations should be clear and accurate. Descriptions should be accurate and vivid. Narratives should have probability (coherence) and fidelity to the real world. That said, the three most common mistakes speakers and listeners make in this regard involve unsupported assertions, evidence that has been distorted, and misleading statistics.

Unsupported Assertion

unsupported assertion
A claim without any evidence to support it.

Unsupported assertions are a staple of TV and radio talk show pundits. An unsupported assertion is a claim without any evidence whatsoever offered in its support. For example, both Greg and Arjun make claims about what employers

BEWARE OF SPEAKERS BEARING GIFTS...

© 1997 McGraw-Hill Higher Education/Kevin Opstedal

want. Neither speaker provides any verifiable sources for these claims. What's more, unless they can demonstrate rather than simply assert that they are experts on a topic, there's no reason to accept their claims as evidence of anything other than their personal opinions.

Distorted Evidence

Evidence is easily distorted, particularly in a digital age where images can be electronically manipulated, unrelated documents and publications can be cut and pasted together, and such distortivons can be passed along in threads and emails as if they were reliable and valid.

Distorted evidence typically is the result of significant omissions or other changes that alter the intent of the source from which it was taken. It is just as common as the unsupported assertion. For example, we are all familiar with movie ads that show selected quotes from a critic's review that seem to recommend a film, when in fact the quote was lifted out of context from a 300-word review in which the film was slammed.

Unlike the unsupported assertion, which should be obvious to critical thinkers, evidence that has been intentionally distorted or even completely fabricated is not so easily detected. This is particularly true, moreover, if is delivered by a source perceived to be credible. Thus, if you are either considering using or accepting evidence, you need to be sure that you have the tools necessary to track down its authenticity.

distorted evidence
Significant omissions or changes in evidence that alter its original intent.

A couple of excellent sources for finding distorted evidence are the Web sites factcheck.org, sponsored by the Annenberg Center for Public Policy, and the Urban Legends site, Snopes.com. For example, Snopes.com unmasked a bogus quotation allegedly from a commencement address by Oracle founder Larry Ellison, who supposedly told the graduating class of Yale University that they were "losers" who had wasted their time getting a diploma. In fact, Ellison gave no such speech; it was the invention of satirist Andrew Marlatt, writing for the SatireWire Web site.[7] Snopes.com even provided a link to the original source.

Misleading Statistics

misleading statistics
Statistics that are incomplete or based on faulty data.

In Chapter 7 we introduced you to a variety of types of numerical data that can be used to support a claim. Statistical data are often the source of unsound arguments. **Misleading statistics** are incomplete or based on faulty data. We don't need to repeat all of the types of tests of numerical data here, but we do want to call your attention to a particularly onerous form of statistical manipulation—the misleading average.

Although both Greg and Arjun frequently cite averages such as the costs of college and the earnings of graduates versus nongraduates, their statistics often don't tell the whole story. For example, neither tells us how their estimates for "average" costs for college were figured. Greg tells us that the average cost of attending a public university for *four years* is $76,000. Arjun prefers to cite the *one-year* cost of a public four-year school, which he claims is $6,000 to $7,000 a year. Simple math tells us that four times $7,000 is $28,000, not $76,000. Something is wrong here.

The problem is that neither speaker tells us what their figures for average college costs include. We suspect Greg is including the costs of such things as room and board and books, along with tuition, at both public and private schools. Arjun is most likely only including tuition. Like apples and oranges, these statistics are not really comparable.

No doubt you can find other examples of statistics in their speeches that are not fully explained or that are not really comparable with those offered by the other speaker. The key here is to make sure you clearly explain your statistics and demand the same from other speakers when you are a listener.

Fallacies Associated With Claims

Sometimes fallacies are an inherent feature of the claim itself. The two fallacies discussed in this section center on the relevance of the claims to the thesis of the speech and whether the claims are, in essence, used to prove themselves. We need to guard against these fallacies both in our speeches and as we listen to the speeches of others.

red herring (smoke screen)
An irrelevant issue introduced into a controversy to divert attention from the real issues.

Red Herring

Sometimes called a *smoke screen,* a **red herring** is an irrelevant claim introduced into a controversy to divert attention from the real issues. Debates over public issues are well known for the use of red herrings. One of the most commonly used and emotionally charged red herrings, repeatedly used in the history of the United States, involves the charge of socialism. People whose self-interest was threatened by the legislation proposing the National Parks System, for example, wanted nothing to do with arguments about the need to protect the nation's greatest natural wonders for all citizens and future generations, or the fact that the wilderness was disappearing at an incredible rate of speed. As a result they tried to turn the debate into one about the merits of capitalism versus the evils of socialism.

The same red herring was reintroduced in the 1940s debate on Social Security, the 1960s debates on civil rights and on Medicare, and during the most recent debate on health care reform. In each of these cases, opponents to what was being proposed tried to frame the debate in terms of two competing economic philosophies rather than in terms of the issues that had given rise to the legislation.

Arguing in a Circle

Another common fallacy is the use of a claim to prove its own truth. **Arguing in a circle,** sometimes called *begging the question,* occurs when the argument proves nothing because the claim in need of proof also is the only evidence offered in its support. Consider the following quotation from nationally syndicated columnist George Will: "Intelligent people agree that, absent immediate radical action regarding global warming, the human race is sunk." Why accept this claim? ". . . because those who do not agree are, definitionally, unintelligent."[8] Although such clear-cut expressions of question begging are rare, when distilled to their essence, many arguments do, in fact, beg the question. Be careful, then, anytime you find yourself beginning an argument or listening to one that starts out claiming something like "All true patriots support . . ." or "Only fools believe. . . ."

arguing in a circle (begging the question) An argument that proves nothing because the claim to be proved is used to prove itself.

Fallacies Associated With the Warrant

Recall that the warrant logically connects evidence with the claim it is intended to support. While a warrant may be so obvious to an audience that it needn't be stated explicitly, we urge our students to exercise caution in this regard. This means providing backing for the warrant as we construct our own arguments, and demanding backing for the warrant when listening to someone else's argument.

Pseudoreasoning thrives in an environment where people assume that the warrant in an argument is so obvious that no backing is needed. Consider the almost sacrosanct argument that deficit spending by the federal government is bad. Many reputable economists would say that whether deficits are good or bad depends on the circumstances. For example, referring to the current time of economic recession and multiple overseas wars, Nobel Prize winner Paul Krugman writes, "In fact, you could argue that the worst thing we can do for future generations is NOT to run sufficiently large deficits right now."[9] Deficit spending in perpetuity may be bad, but deficit spending may also be necessary during tough economic times and times of war.

Different types of warrants provide different ways of connecting evidence to the claim it is intended to support. The six most common types of warrants are authority, establishing a generalization, applying a generalization, comparison (analogy), causal, and sign. Each type of warrant is vulnerable to particular fallacies. Learning to recognize these fallacies can help us determine if a warrant is suspect. If it is, then we should ask the speaker to back the warrant with evidence showing the warrant is sound.

Authority Warrants

When we use authority warrants, we are really saying that the reason the claim should be believed is because someone we perceive to be an authority says that it is true. Some people are actually predisposed to accept without question the claims of people and agencies they perceive as legitimate authorities. Authority warrants are subject to the tests of expertise, qualifications, trustworthiness, lack of bias, and reliability.

Given the generation to which your authors belong, we still believe in a mantra we first heard in the mid sixties: *Question Authority.* Simply put, it's not a bad idea to either question authorities or politely ask that they provide evidence to substantiate their claims. This is particularly so if we find ourselves automatically assigning authority to people because their biases reflect our own. Remember Cialdini's implied admonition in Chapter 14 that looking or sounding like an authority doesn't make one an expert.

When using an authority warrant in your own arguments, chances are good that your audience may not be familiar with the source's qualifications. As a result, you'll need to provide *backing* for your authority warrant: for instance, bolstering your source's credibility using techniques such as those described in Chapter 14.

There are two common fallacies we hear in conjunction with an authority warrant. The first fallacy involves giving undue credit to an authority. The second involves an attack on the authority's persona rather the soundness of the argument.

Halo Effect

halo effect
The assumption that just because you like or respect a person, whatever he or she says must be true.

The **halo effect** is typically a consequence of liking, which we discussed in Chapter 14. If we like someone, we are more susceptible to the person's influence. What's more, intense liking can make us susceptible to the person's influence even when it is against our own interest or better judgment. In politics, for example, the halo effect is frequently extended to the officeholders we support during and after the election. The reach of the halo effect in this respect may extend well beyond the person's time in office or life span. Historians, for example, are far more critical of Presidents Kennedy and Reagan than are the remembrances of their supporters and champions. If you don't believe us, try and find a Democratic or Republican prime-time convention speech in which Kennedy's or Reagan's ghost does not loom large.

Regardless of the underlying reasons, liking people should give them no more credibility on a topic or issue than their credentials justify. For example we enjoy Janeane Garofalo's stand-up comedy routine. The fact that she's a good comic, however, doesn't make her an expert on foreign policy or justify her being treated like one on cable TV and talk radio, where she frequently pontificates on the subject. We are not implying that her views are necessarily wrong. Rather, we are saying that her fame as a comedian gives her no specific expertise or qualifications to discuss foreign policy beyond that of any other ordinary citizen.

Ad Hominem

Ad hominem means "against the person." Attacking people rather than the soundness of their arguments is one of the most common fallacies associated with authority warrants. If you are in a debate and your opponent follows the argument you present with an attack on your identity, the opponent is guilty of the ad hominem fallacy.

Frequently this fallacy simply substitutes name calling or worse for sound reasoning. Some people become lightning rods in this regard. Examples that immediately come to mind are, in no particular order, filmmaker Michael Moore and actor Alec Baldwin, on one side, and Rush Limbaugh and Bill O'Reilly, on the other. We've heard Baldwin's detractors call him a child abuser and wife beater. Al Franken called Rush Limbaugh a "big fat idiot" and used the slur in the title of one of his books. No doubt you can think of many other examples. Civility is a virtue that's becoming increasingly rare in our public discourse. Ad hominem arguments and name calling only debase the public dialogue.

ad hominem
Attacking the person rather than the soundness of his or her argument.

Tips and Tactics

Evaluating Authority Warrants and Associated Fallacies

- Is the authority an expert in the area under discussion?
- Has the speaker adequately documented the qualifications of the authority?
- Is the authority trustworthy and unbiased?
- Is the authority acting on reliable information?

Generalization-Establishing Warrants

Every time you hear or read about the results of an opinion poll, you are being provided with a working example of a warrant that asks you to generalize a sample of opinion to the entire population from which the sample is drawn. Speakers argue much the same when they use specific and limited numbers of examples and statistics to draw general conclusions. For example, Greg Shafer uses a number of well-known celebrities to attempt to prove that a college degree isn't necessary for success. The fallacy most commonly associated with this type of warrant is readily exposed when the instances cited are unrepresentative of the generalization claimed. Whether as a speaker or listener, the tests are the same: relevance, sufficiency, typicality, overgeneralization, and negative example.

Hasty Generalization

Hasty generalization usually occurs in one of two conditions. Either there are too few instances to support a generalization or the instances are unrepresentative of the generalization. But how do we determine that such instances are both sufficient in number and representative to avoid this fallacy? Once again, consider Greg's speech and argument relative to the first test: Are the examples cited relevant to his claim? With the exception of those who later returned to college and completed their degree, the people in Greg's examples did, in fact, drop out of college. What about the second and the third tests: Are there sufficient examples to establish his claim, and are they typical? In total, Greg cites the names of 18 people—not an overwhelming list. Further, many are entertainers (Bill Murray, David Bowie, Ellen Degeneres), writers (F. Scott Fitzgerald), or artists (George Gershwin, Walt Disney). These are not exactly common career paths, and more people fail than succeed in them, regardless of whether they drop out or complete college.

So did Greg avoid making a hasty generalization? That's a judgment call, but one could certainly make the case that he overgeneralizes. This is particularly apparent when the last test is applied to Greg's warrant: Are there significant negative examples? The answer, of course, is an emphatic yes. The key here is to limit generalizations to the extent that they are justified by the evidence. Greg's argument would have been far sounder had he used this key.

Tips and Tactics

Questions to Ask When Evaluating a Generalization

- Is the evidence relevant to the claim?
- Is there sufficient evidence to establish the claim?
- Is the evidence typical of the larger population?
- Is overgeneralization avoided?
- Are there significant negative examples?

Generalization-Applying Warrants

If we know a generalization is true, we can apply it to a specific instance and reach some valid conclusions about that specific instance. This is something we do on a daily basis. We comply with the traffic regulation that requires us to come to a full stop for a red light at a controlled intersection, look left and right before attempting to cross a busy highway on foot, or yield to a pedestrian who has entered a crosswalk.

Applying generalizations we believe to be true to specific instances works well in this traffic scenario, but we need to exercise caution when we attempt to apply an established generalization to specific people or complicated issues. Generalization-applying warrants are subject to the tests of applicability, exceptions, substantiation, and classification. Consider fallacies owing to inappropriate stereotypes and the false dilemma.

Danica Patrick has effectively broken through stereotypes about the role of women in a sport normally thought of as "male only."

Stereotyping

The most common fallacy associated with warrants that apply established generalizations to specific instances is known as **stereotyping.** This fallacy assumes that what is considered to be true of a larger class is necessarily true of particular members of that class. Consider our former student and friend Jonathan Studebaker, whom you learned about in Chapter 1. Jonathan spent most of his adult life speaking to school-age children about the importance of not stereotyping people because they have a disability.

> **stereotyping**
> The assumption that what is considered to be true of a larger class is necessarily true of particular members of that class.

False Dilemma

Another common fallacy associated with applying an established generalization is to create a **false dilemma,** that is, a generalization that implies there are only two choices when nothing could be further from the truth. A true dilemma requires proof that we have only two choices in a matter. True dilemmas also are fairly uncommon. Consider the following telephone call to our local newspaper that was printed in a daily feature called "Tell it to the ER."

> **false dilemma**
> A generalization that implies there are only two choices when there are more than two.

They Should Fight Child Abuse

I'd like to talk to the pro-lifers about abortion. They want to stop abortion so bad and they take their time to do it. Why don't they take the same painstaking time to help fight children being killed by dads and moms when they get a very light sentence?[10]

From "Tell It to the ER" in CHICO ENTERPRISE-RECORD, 13 March 1992, p. 2A. Reprinted by permission of Chico Enterprise-Record.

Needless to say, being pro-life (or anti-abortion) doesn't preclude being against child abuse. The caller created a dilemma where none existed. Extreme as this example may strike you, the false dilemma is commonly heard in debates that are characterized by both high complexity and uncertainty. Under such conditions people are susceptible to oversimplifying the issues on which the debate is focused. Sometimes this is an innocent attempt to make the issues more manageable. As is the case with pseudosurveys that purport to be interested in our opinion, however, it also can be an attempt to deceive us into believing we can only be "for or against" abortion, health care reform, job creation, the environment, clean energy, business, or immigration reform. It's not that simple, is it?

Tips and Tactics

Questions to Ask When Evaluating Applications of a Generalization

- Does the generalization apply to all possible cases?
- Are there exceptions to the generalization? If so, does the specific case fall within one of the exceptions?
- Is the generalization substantiated?
- Does the specific instance fall clearly within the category specified by the generalization?

Comparison (Analogy) Warrants

Reasoning based on a comparison warrant claims that because two cases are similar in some known respects, they are also similar in some unknown respects. These arguments are called comparisons or, more commonly, analogies. War is a commonly used analogy. The war on poverty and the war on drugs, for example, were both declared nearly a half century ago, and the analogies are still in use to this day.

The issue here is not whether analogies can be useful in connecting a claim with evidence to support it, but whether there is good fit between the analogy and the argument being made. Briefly, then, let's look at some types of analogies commonly used as warrants, as well as the fallacy most likely to result from comparisons that are poorly reasoned.

A *literal analogy* claims that two different instances are really similar. For example, a lot of people compared September 11, 2001, to December 7, 1941 (the date on which Pearl Harbor was bombed). This is certainly a literal comparison—both were attacks on U.S. soil by foreign enemies (Hawaii was not yet a state, but it was a U.S. territory at the time of the attack).

A *figurative analogy*, on the other hand, is a device of language used to enhance the effectiveness of a speech. A figurative analogy clearly seeks to establish some similarity between the two items being compared, but no one could reasonably argue that they are really alike. Saying that September 11 was like being sucker-punched is not literally comparing two things that are the same. In the first instance, thousands died and the nation was plunged into war. In the second instance, about all that is hurt is the victim's pride. There's nothing wrong with figurative analogies—they can add a lot to a speech—but they don't constitute proof in the same way that literal analogies can. There is no logical force to such arguments.

Powerful analogies need to meet two important criteria. First, the similarities between the events compared need to outweigh their dissimilarities. Second, their similarities, rather than their dissimilarities, should be most relevant to the claim being made.

False Analogy

The most common fallacy associated with comparison warrants is the **false analogy.** This occurs when two things that are not really comparable are compared as if they were essentially the same. For example, we were forced into a debate on our campus wherein a prominent administrator and former professor claimed that our campus's requirement for a public speaking course should be abolished. In more than one public forum, the critic of the course argued, "Our students have been talking since they were two-years old. Do they need a whole course focusing on a skill they've been practicing for 16 years or longer?"

Talking, as you have presumably learned in this class, is not analogous to giving a public speech. Public speaking is both an art and a science and has been the focus of serious scholarship for over 2,000 years. It also is ranked near the top of desirable skill sets in decades' worth of surveys investigating what corporations desire most in their employees.

false analogy
The comparison of two different things that are not really comparable.

Tips and Tactics

Questions to Ask When Evaluating Comparisons or Analogies

- Are only literal analogies used for proof?
- Do the similarities outweigh the differences?
- Are the similarities more relevant than the differences to the claim being made?

Causal Warrants

Reasoning based on a causal warrant claims that a cause will produce or has produced an effect. This is a natural form of reasoning that we use all the time. We learn that if we stay up all night and cram before a test, we are so groggy in the morning that we can't focus. The cause—too little sleep—produces an effect that's the opposite of what we intended—doing well on the test. We can reason either from a known cause to a predicted effect or from a known effect to a suspected cause. Using the first kind of reasoning, proponents of the theory that humans cause global warming claim that burning fossil fuels raises the level of CO_2 in the atmosphere and thus warms the planet. On the other hand, one can reason from a known effect back to what caused the effect. Opponents of global warming often agree the planet is getting warmer, but point to previous eras of global warming in prehistoric times to argue that natural cycles are to blame for current warming trends.

Causal arguments can be successfully and persuasively made. For example, there is considerable scientific evidence to support claims that tobacco is harmful to our health, and few independent scientists dispute the harmfulness of the product. A speaker relying on such experts and scientific studies would be on solid ground. Often a speaker is best advised to make causal arguments when they can be buttressed by expert testimony and scientific studies.

Causal warrants are subject to several tests. First, the cause and effect must be reasonably related to one another. Second, other causes for the effect need to be ruled out, and other effects that result from the same cause need to be acknowledged. Finally, we should avoid assuming that just because one event precedes the other, they are causally related. The two most common fallacies associated with causal warrants involve claiming a cause after the fact (post hoc) and the so-called slippery slope.

Post Hoc

Warrants dealing with effect-to-cause reasoning frequently are guilty of what is technically known as the **post hoc, ergo propter hoc** fallacy ("after the fact, therefore because of the fact"). Once again our local newspaper provides us with an example of this fallacy. Following the end of a California drought, the paper published a letter in which the author claimed the drought's welcomed end owed to the prayers of the people of the small town of Paradise. The letter writer even referred to them as "God's chosen helpers." Far be it from us to disparage anyone's faith, but clearly the drought was going to end sometime. Just because this small community's prayers were followed by rain doesn't mean that's why the drought ended. Simply put, the fact that one event follows another doesn't prove a causal relationship.

Slippery Slope

Warrants that reason from a known cause to a projected effect are susceptible to the **slippery slope** fallacy. This fallacy is committed when people argue that one undesirable event will automatically lead to a series of equally, if not more, undesirable events. Such a domino effect, as it has frequently been called, has been used to argue against the decriminalization of marijuana, lowering the legal age to drink alcohol to 18, gay rights, and providing all U.S. citizens with guaranteed health care.

The slippery slope imagined by those opposing the preceding propositions can border on the absurd. Marijuana can be a gateway drug, for example, but most recreational users don't end up addicted to heroin or resorting to crime to support their habit, as many have argued over the course of decades. The passage of the Medicare bill in the 1960s did not lead to socialized medicine, as some argued it would, although it is ironic that many who have most benefited from its passage used the same argument against a government-sponsored health option in 2009. This does not mean, however, that there is no such thing as a slippery slope. This is especially true when a person's health is in crisis. A staph infection in the hospital can quickly lead to a slippery slope that includes organ failure and then death.

Tips and Tactics

Questions to Ask When Evaluating Causal Reasoning

- Is the cause related to the alleged effect?
- Are there other causes of the effect?
- Are there other effects from the same cause?
- Has the time sequence been mistaken for cause (post hoc fallacy)?

Sign Warrants

Reasoning using a sign warrant infers the presence of an unobserved phenomenon from the presence of an observed one. For example, if you have a high fever, cough, and trouble breathing, a doctor may infer you have influenza. Although it would be necessary to take a swab and send it off for testing to confirm the diagnosis, most physicians will likely prescribe antiviral medicines such as Tamiflu based on these symptoms.

Reliable signs are not always easy to find. In testing sign reasoning, ask how reliable such signs have been in the past. Your doctor's experience over time helps equip her or him to distinguish between the signs of flu and other similar illnesses. The second test is to look for conflicting signs. Although the cough and fever may signify flu, other symptoms might point to a very different cause, such as pneumonia. Finally, one needs to be sure not to confuse a mere coincidence or correlation for a cause-and-effect relationship.

Mistaking Correlation for Cause

The most common fallacy associated with sign reasoning is **mistaking correlation for cause.** A correlation simply means that two things occur in conjunction with each other, without regard to their cause. Both Arjun and Greg acknowledge that completing a college degree is correlated with higher income. Both seem to assume there's a causal relationship. Although Greg questions whether the additional income is worth the cost and time spent, he doesn't seem to deny that college grads on the whole make more income throughout their lives.

However, a possibility that neither speaker considers is that they may have mistaken a correlation for a causal relationship. Perhaps those who have more money, better family connections, more talent, and so on are the very people most likely to go to college. It is possible that college completion is correlated with high income for the same reasons that life expectancy and other variables correlate with socioeconomic status—coming from high-income families might make completing college more likely, rather than completing college causing higher income. The only way to really know would be to compare two sufficiently large and randomly drawn groups of people from the same socioeconomic background—one group that went to college, and the other that didn't. If there is a difference in income between the two groups, then you would have reason to infer causation.

> **mistaking correlation for cause**
> The assumption that because one thing is a sign of another, they are causally related.

Tips and Tactics

Questions to Ask When Evaluating Sign Reasoning

- Are the signs reliable indicators of the claim?
- Are there conflicting signs?
- Has a correlation been mistaken for a cause?

Fallacies Associated With Qualifiers

As we noted previously, a qualifier indicates the level of probability of a claim. Some arguments are virtually certain to be true, whereas others have a much lower degree of certainty. It is unusual for speakers to own up to the fact that their arguments are at best about probabilities. Yet knowing how likely it is that the speaker's claim is true is important in deciding whether to act on the basis of that claim. Depending on the nature of the argument, a qualifier can make a big difference. For example, in a criminal trial, the claim that the defendant is guilty must be true "beyond a reasonable doubt," a phrase that acts as the qualifier of the argument for guilt. Thus, a very high degree of certainty is required before a jury can convict someone of a criminal offense. On the other hand, in a civil case the standard is "a preponderance of evidence." That is, if it is more likely than not that the defendant wronged the plaintiff, the judgment should go to the plaintiff. Because of the difference in the level of proof required, someone found not guilty in a criminal trial can still be sued in civil court.

We need to know what level of proof our audience will expect. As with virtually every other aspect of public speaking, the success of our reasoning depends on careful analysis of the audience. As listeners, we should also be clear about what level of proof we need before accepting a claim. Many of the fallacies of reasoning associated with qualifiers are a result of overstating or distorting the degree of certainty with which the arguer has supported his or her claim. Two such common fallacies are the use of loaded language and hyperbole.

loaded language
Language that triggers strong emotional and negative responses.

hyperbole
An exaggeration of a claim.

Loaded Language

Language that triggers strong emotional and negative responses is termed **loaded language.** Depending on the specific characteristics of our audience, what we might consider neutral language may in fact carry strong emotional connotations. The cable TV and talk radio shows we referenced in the opening of this chapter are replete with examples of loaded language. Phrases like "death panels" and "Republicans want you to die quickly"[11] show that both sides of the political spectrum can be guilty of this fallacy.

Of course, effective persuasion often requires vivid, intense, and expressive language, as we discussed in Chapter 10. There is a fine but important line between language that is necessarily vivid and language that is so "loaded" that it distorts the reasoning being presented. There is no hard-and-fast rule that can be applied here. Speakers and listeners need to exercise their judgment in evaluating the use of language.

Avoiding hateful language is essential to rational discussion about controversial issues.

Hyperbole

Hyperbole is an exaggeration of a claim. Rather than properly qualifying a statement, the person engaged in hyperbole exaggerates the claim in question. When boxer Muhammad Ali declared himself to be "the greatest," it may have been an effective way to build interest in his fights, but it was certainly an exaggeration of his prowess, especially because he didn't limit his claim to the boxing ring. Other examples of hyperbole include the use of such terms as *superstar, greatest ever,* and *megahit.* It often seems as if it is not enough anymore to be a star, to be great, or to have a mere hit. Hyperbole ends up cheapening the currency of language, inflating claims, and devaluing more moderate language.

Fallacies Associated With Rebuttals

The rebuttal to an argument is an exception to or refutation of an argument. For example, Arjun seeks to refute what he takes as the basic premise of one of Greg's arguments—that the measure of success is fame and fortune. He states "Yes, you can get rich without college. Yes, you can get famous without college. But are these metrics—rich and famous—are these really what we want to judge success by?" Greg, on the other hand, seeks to refute the assumption that college is the best place to learn. He states, "And if you don't know what interests you, if you don't know what you're passionate about, spend this time to figure that out. It's not worth it to spend all this time in college to find that you hate what you've studied for all this time." Thus both speakers offer rebuttals to commonly held assumptions about the role of college.

Rebuttals too can be flawed. A fallacy can occur when a speaker misanalyzes an opponent's argument in order to refute it more easily.

Straw Person

The **straw person** fallacy occurs when someone attempts to refute a claim by misstating the argument being refuted. Rather than refuting the real argument, the other side constructs a "person of straw," which is easy to knock down. This is not to be confused with a legitimate two-sided presentation, where the opposing view is accurately characterized and then refuted. Rather, the straw person argument deliberately misrepresents the opponent's point of view in a way that makes it appear to be ridiculous or absurd.

For an example of a straw person argument, one need only turn to cable TV opinion shows where the other side is falsely represented as everything from fascists who want to take total control of the lives of average citizens to uncaring capitalists who will sacrifice anything to make a buck.

straw person
An argument made in refutation that misstates the argument being refuted. Rather than refuting the real argument, the other side constructs a person of straw, which is easy to knock down.

The Non Sequitur: An Argument That Does Not Logically Follow

Until now we've looked at each component of an argument as a separate source of fallacies. Of course, we also have to look at the argument as a whole. Even if the evidence is true, the warrant believable, and so on, an argument that doesn't hang together logically is still fallacious. Thus, the final fallacy of reasoning we examine is the non sequitur.

A **non sequitur** is an argument that does not logically follow from its premises. In Toulmin's terms, there is no logical connection between the claim, the evidence, and the warrant used to support the claim. Consider the example of a person who called in this opinion to a newspaper:

non sequitur
An argument that does not logically follow from its premises.

No Wonder Welfare Is So Popular

I'd like to thank the person who dropped the two little black lab-mix puppies off at the golf course some time in the week of Jan. 28. What irresponsible person caused others to try to find homes for these dogs? It's amazing people don't take responsibility for their actions and cause other people to. No wonder everybody's on welfare.[12]

From "Tell It to the ER" from CHICO ENTERPRISE-RECORD, 16 February, 1992, p. 2A. Reprinted by permission of Chico Enterprise-Record.

SPEAKING OF . . .

Pseudoreasoning: The Fallacies

Fallacies Associated With Evidence

unsupported assertion: A claim without any evidence to support it.

distorted evidence: Significant omissions or changes in evidence that alter its original intent.

misleading statistics: Statistics that are incomplete or based on faulty data.

Fallacies Associated With Claims

red herring (smoke screen): An irrelevant issue introduced into a controversy to divert attention from the real issues.

arguing in a circle (begging the question): An argument that proves nothing because the claim to be proved is used to prove itself.

Fallacies Associated With Authority Warrants

halo effect: The assumption that just because you like or respect a person, whatever he or she says must be true.

ad hominem: Attacking the person rather than the soundness of his or her argument.

Fallacies Associated With Generalization-Establishing Warrants

hasty generalization: A fallacy that occurs when there are too few instances to support a generalization or the instances are unrepresentative of the generalization.

Fallacies Associated With Generalization-Applying Warrants

stereotyping: The assumption that what is considered to be true of a larger class is necessarily true of particular members of that class.

false dilemma: A generalization that implies there are only two choices when there are more than two.

Fallacy Associated With Comparison (Analogy) Warrants

false analogy: The comparison of two different things that are not really comparable.

Fallacies Associated With Causal Warrants

post hoc, ergo propter hoc ("after the fact, therefore because of the fact"): The assumption that because one event preceded another, the first event must be the cause of the second event.

slippery slope: The assumption that just because one event occurs, it will automatically lead to a series of undesirable events even though there is no relationship between the action and the projected events.

Fallacy Associated With Sign Warrants

mistaking correlation for cause: The assumption that because one thing is a sign of another, they are causally related.

Fallacies Associated With Qualifiers

loaded language: Language that triggers strong emotional and negative responses.

hyperbole: An exaggeration of a claim.

Fallacies Associated With Rebuttals

straw person: An argument made in refutation that misstates the argument being refuted. Rather than refuting the real argument, the other side constructs a person of straw, which is easy to knock down.

Additional Fallacy

non sequitur: An argument that does not logically follow from its premises.

Aside from stereotyping people on welfare as irresponsible and hyperbolizing in claiming that "everybody's on welfare," this argument has absolutely no link between its evidence (the two dogs abandoned at the golf course) and its claim (that this irresponsibility is symptomatic of people on welfare).

You can review the preceding fallacies in the box "Speaking of . . . Pseudoreasoning: The Fallacies." We encourage you to do so often. Although fallacies and the pseudoreasoning they feed on may strike you as fairly harmless, they can and do undermine civic engagement. They also lead to poor judgments that can negatively affect our unalienable rights to life, liberty, and the pursuit of happiness.

Summary

Reasoning and critical thinking are important both in constructing good arguments and in listening to others' arguments.

Verbal aggressiveness is the trait of attacking the self-concept of those with whom one disagrees.

Grounds for an argument consist of evidence supporting a claim.

Fallacies associated with defective evidence are:

- Unsupported assertions
- Distorted evidence
- Misleading statistics

Claims may contain the following fallacies:

- The red herring
- Arguing in a circle

Warrants link grounds and claims by means of:

- Authority
- Establishing a Generalization
- Applying a Generalization
- Comparison
- Cause
- Sign

Backing is evidence that supports the warrant and is especially important in cases where the audience is either unfamiliar with the warrant or unconvinced of its truth.

One fallacy associated with generalization-establishing warrants is the hasty generalization.

Fallacies associated with authority warrants are:

- The halo effect
- Ad hominem

Fallacies associated with generalization-applying warrants are:

- Stereotyping
- False dilemmas

One fallacy associated with comparison warrants is the false analogy.

Fallacies associated with causation warrants are:

- Post hoc, ergo propter hoc
- Slippery slope

 www.mhhe.com/brydon7e

To evaluate your understanding of this chapter, visit our Online Learning Center Web site for quizzes and other chapter study aids.

One fallacy associated with sign warrants is mistaking correlation for cause.

Qualifiers are an indication of the level of probability of the claim. Fallacies associated with qualifiers are:

- Loaded language
- Hyperbole

A rebuttal is an exception to or refutation of an argument. A common fallacy found in a rebuttal is the straw person.

The non sequitur is a fallacy that occurs when an argument does not logically follow from its premises.

Check Your Understanding: Exercises and Activities

1. Find a public argument, such as a blog posting, a letter to the editor, a political or product advertisement, or an editorial. Identify the claim being made and the evidence on which it is based. Is the warrant explicitly stated? If not, determine the implied warrant. What evidence, if any, is offered as backing for the warrant? Is the argument adequately qualified? Are there possible rebuttals to the argument? Are any fallacies present?

2. Find an example of each of the following types of arguments in a publication: authority, establishing a generalization, applying a generalization, comparison, cause to effect, effect to cause, and sign. Which of these arguments is the strongest logically, and which is the weakest? Explain your answer in terms of the tests of reasoning outlined in this chapter.

3. Pick an advertisement from any medium—for example, television, the Internet, magazines, newspapers, or direct mail. In a brief paper, identify at least three fallacies used in the advertisement. Define each fallacy in your own words. Cite the specific example of each fallacy from the ad, and explain why the example meets the definition. Finally, highlight the fallacies on a copy of the ad and attach the copy to your paper.

4. Analyze the arguments presented for and against staying in college by Greg Shafer and Arjun Buxi. The full transcripts of their speeches are available in Appendix B, and the videos of their speeches are at the Online Learning Center at www.mhhe.com/brydon7e. Do you detect any fallacies in these speeches? Which speaker presents the strongest argument for his case? How could their arguments have been strengthened? Write a brief paper or make a short speech presenting your conclusions.

Notes

1. Joubert Quotes, *Brainy Quote,* 2009. [Retrieved from http://www.brainyquote .com/quotes/quotes/j/josephjoub377081.html, 13 November, 2009.]

2. "TV, Radio Talkers Shaping Political Discourse in U.S.," *The News Hour with Jim Lehrer* (transcript), 4 November 2009. [Retrieved from http://www .pbs.org/newshour/bb/media/july-dec09/talkers_11-04.html.]

3. Dominic A. Infante, *Arguing Constructively* (Prospect Heights, Ill.: Waveland Press, 1988).

4. Malcolm Gladwell, *Outliers: The Story of Success* (New York: Little, Brown, & Co., 2008).

5. Stephen Toulmin, Richard Rieke, and Allan Janik, *An Introduction to Reasoning,* 2nd ed. (New York: Macmillan, 1984).

6. Brooke Noel Moore and Richard Parker, *Critical Thinking,* 5th ed. (Mountain View, Calif.: Mayfield, 1998), 476, italics added.

7. "Questionable Quotes: Oracle of Truth," *Snopes.com,* 24 September 2007. [Retrieved from http://www.snopes.com/quotes/ellison.asp.] You can read the original satirical piece at http://www.satirewire.com/news/0006/satire-ellison.shtml.

8. George Will, "No Climate for a Change Treaty," *Chico Enterprise-Record,* 8 November 2009, 5A.

9. Paul Krugman, "The Conscience of a Liberal: Crowding In," *New York Times,* 28 September 2009. [Retrieved from http://krugman.blogs.nytimes.com/2009/09/28/crowding-in/.]

10. "Tell It to the ER," *Chico Enterprise Record,* 13 March 1992, 2A. Reprinted by permission.

11. Jonathan Allen, "Grayson, GOP Wants You to Die," *Politico.com,* 29 September 2009. [Retrieved from http://www.politico.com/news/stories/0909/27726.html.]

12. "Tell It to the ER," *Chico Enterprise Record,* 16 February 1992, 2A. Reprinted by permission.

This class is just the beginning of your public speaking career.

CHAPTER
16

SPEAKING BEYOND
THE CLASSROOM

Objectives  www.mhhe.com/brydon7e

After reading this chapter and reviewing the online learning resources at
www.mhhe.com/brydon7e, you should be able to:

- Present a speech of introduction.

- Present or accept an award.

- Make a speech of commemoration.

- Make a speech to entertain.

- Make a wedding toast.

- Present an elevator pitch.

- Handle a question-and-answer session.

- Lead or participate in a small group discussion.

- Recognize symptoms of groupthink and take measures to avoid it.

- Effectively participate in panel discussions in a small group.

- Recognize the potential benefits of a career in public speaking.

Key Concepts

agenda

elevator pitch

eulogy

group

groupthink

panel discussion

speech of acceptance

speech of commemoration

speech of introduction

speech of recognition

speech to entertain

"You've been giving your attention to a turkey stuffed with sage;
you are now about to consider a sage stuffed with turkey."

—WILLIAM MAXWELL EVARTS (1818–1901)
American statesman, speaking after a Thanksgiving dinner[1]

Dragon's Den requires contestants to make a pitch to venture capitalists to get their projects funded.

Have you ever seen an episode of *Dragon's Den*? First broadcast in the United Kingdom, there is now a U.S. version of this TV reality show dedicated to the big dreams of inventors and entrepreneurs alike. Participants selected for the show are given the opportunity to "pitch" their concept or product to a panel of venture capitalists in the hope of obtaining the funding necessary to take it to the next level.

Dragon's Den showcases a type of public speaking that was once largely confined to Hollywood. You pitched a concept for a film or TV show to people with the power to "green light" the concept to begin the process of making it a reality. Today, however, mastery of the art of the pitch is necessary to anyone who hopes to see an idea take wing, whether it's an internal proposal for a new version of a company's smart phone, a plan to market the phone, or the methodology necessary to measure customer satisfaction with the phone following its launch.

Like everything else, the transaction between speaker and audience is evolving. Although we feel safe in saying that public speaking will remain a primary medium through which we carry out some of our culture's most important customs and rituals, it would be dishonest for us to say that the lessons and skills that we've shared in the past 15 chapters will never need to be modified and adapted to rhetorical situations we haven't anticipated.

Our purpose in this last chapter is twofold. First, we want to emphasize the fact that this book and the course in which you are enrolled have begun the process of preparing you to meet predictable challenges you'll face when required to speak during times of joy and personal satisfaction, as well as times of duress and even grief. Second, we want to demonstrate that the same skills that will help you meet these conventional challenges can be generalized well beyond their original scope, whether you need an effective "elevator pitch" or need to lead a team at work.

SPEAKING OF . . .

The Wedding Toast

Whereas 40 percent of people express fears about presenting a public speech, 97 percent report that they are fearful over the prospect of being asked to give a wedding toast. One potential consequence of this fact is that unrehearsed and poorly thought-out wedding toasts have become the rule rather than the exception. Wedding planner Deborah McCoy describes some of them in her book *The World's Most Unforgettable Weddings*. They range from simply incoherent toasts by maids of honor, to raunchy and obscenity-laced stories about the bachelor party by best men.

Simply put, there is no excuse for dishonoring a bride and groom with a terrible toast. And this is especially true of a best man or maid/matron of honor. The idea is to honor the couple—not get a laugh, or worse, at their expense.

Here are some tips for making an appropriately memorable wedding toast:

1. Consult with the couple about what they expect from you.

2. Learn about who will be in attendance and take into account their diversity in age, education, and experience.

3. Talk to the wedding planner if it's an option.

4. Make it short, sweet, and memorable for the right reasons.

5. Prepare, including finding an appropriate story, anecdote, or quote that celebrates the event.

6. Rehearse.

7. Hold off on the champagne until after you've given the toast.

8. Speak clearly and loudly enough for all to hear.

9. Face the bride and groom, but don't turn your back on guests.

10. Ask the guests to join "with you" in your toast.

Source: J. Freedom du Lac, "Burnt Toasts: Bad Taste Seems to Be Rigueur at Many Weddings," *Sacramento Bee,* June 17, 2003, E1–2.

One of the most common speeches we will give is the wedding toast.

Rituals and Special Occasions

No matter how much the world changes and the tools with which we communicate evolve, certain rituals and customs regarding speaking public are not about to suddenly disappear from the rhetorical landscape. With the possible of exception of a speech in which you are *expected* to entertain an audience, there are rituals and special occasions for public speaking you cannot altogether dodge. They range from the deceptively simple and short art of proposing an apropos toast to the much more challenging task of eulogizing someone whose life made yours more meaningful. With respect to the former, we offer some helpful tips in the box "Speaking of . . . The Wedding Toast."

As we have repeatedly emphasized throughout this book, the chances of any speech succeeding begins with an analysis of the rhetorical situation. This is doubly so, however, in the case of rituals and special occasions, whether your purpose is to honor newlyweds with a toast, introduce a guest speaker or honoree, graciously accept an award, or thank a group of people who have gathered to honor your own achievements. Consider the seemingly simple task of a short speech in which you have been asked to introduce a featured guest at work, a service club such as the Rotary, or a representative from the national college fraternity or sorority with which you are affiliated.

Speech of Introduction

speech of introduction
A speech that briefly sets the stage for an upcoming speaker.

A **speech of introduction** should briefly set the stage for an upcoming speaker or a featured guest. Typically you and the audience know the purpose of the occasion. Where people drop the ball in such situations involves their commitment to learn enough in advance about the background of the speaker or guest to make a proper introduction. Speeches of introduction are designed to meet two objectives. The first is to enlist the audience's attention and interest, and the second is to reinforce or induce the audience's perceptions of the speaker or guest's credibility. You cannot achieve either of these without knowing something about the person's biography. As a result, it is common for this person or the one who extended the invitation to provide you in advance with background information, such as a brief biographical sketch. Such sketches provide highlights about the person you can then use to enlist your audience's interest and establish the speaker or guest's credentials.

Time and again, we've seen this information ignored by otherwise competent and responsible people tasked with an introduction. In more than a few cases, in fact, the speaker admits a lack of preparation, telling the audience he or she didn't get a chance to become familiar with the biography of the person about to be introduced. So the speaker ends up fumbling through the introduction by reading the biographical sketch for the first time. This is, quite simply, inexcusable. What's more, it embarrasses all parties involved, beginning with the introducer. The key, then, is preparation and practice when tasked with a speech of introduction. Begin by familiarizing yourself with the person's biographical sketch well in advance of the event. If you haven't been provided with one, make a point of getting one. Learn the highlights of the sketch well enough it deliver the introduction extemporaneously—and deliver it like you mean it!

Tips and Tactics

Guidelines for a Speech of Introduction

- *Be brief.* The audience came to hear the speaker, not the introducer. A one- or two-minute introduction is sufficient for most speech situations. For a particularly lengthy or formal speech situation, the introduction might be longer, but in no case should it exceed about 10 percent of the speaker's time (six minutes out of an hour, for example).
- *Don't steal the speaker's thunder.* Although you want to prepare the audience for what is to come by focusing their attention on the topic, you should not discuss the substance of the speech topic. Again, the audience wants to hear the speaker's views on the topic, not yours. Your job is to create an appetite for the upcoming main course, not fill up the audience with hors d'oeuvres.

- *Be prepared: Work with the speaker in advance.* It is best to talk to the speaker or a representative about your role as introducer. Are there specific points to be stressed? Is there anything the speaker wants to avoid? Some speakers may even want to preview your introductory remarks or may provide written suggestions for you.

Speech of Recognition

The elements of a good speech of introduction also apply to speeches of recognition. A **speech of recognition** presents an award honoring an individual. Although audience members frequently know something about the person being recognized, this isn't always the case. Thus, you may need to connect the narrative of the honoree's life, including the purpose for the award, to the lives of audience members. To do so, you must make sure that you are not only well acquainted with the honoree, but also sufficiently knowledgeable about the audience's composition that you can predict how this mutual familiarity can best be communicated to connect the two.

Speech of Acceptance

There are rituals and occasions where we are the object of attention and must find a way to respond that is both gracious and appropriate to the situation. According to most of the sports writers and broadcasters who listened to Michael Jordan's acceptance speech at his induction to the National Basketball Association Hall of Fame, the game's greatest player fell short on both counts. As one writer put it, "This wasn't a Hall of Fame induction speech, but a bully tripping nerds with lunch trays in the school cafeteria. He had a responsibility to his standing in history, to players past and present, and he let everyone down."[2]

A **speech of acceptance** expresses thanks to the people responsible for presenting it, as well as those who helped the honoree achieve the very thing that led to the award—for example, friends and family or coworkers and teammates. In many cultures, calling attention to ourselves is considered to be in bad taste, even though the research on nonverbal communication suggests that spontaneous expressions of pride may not be conscious. Many of us have been taught this norm. Even so, there are times in our lives when we cannot help being the center of attention. One of them is when we are singled out publicly for some recognition or award. For some, this becomes a dilemma. On one hand, they know they need to accept the recognition or award in a fashion that recognizes and pays tribute to those responsible. On the other hand, they don't want to appear as if they expected the recognition or award and prepared their remarks well in advance of the event. All too often, therefore, they do not prepare or rehearse their response and end up appearing humble but tongue-tied. Most audiences would prefer to hear someone accept recognition in a fashion that is both gracious and articulate, even if it was obviously prepared in advance. Being well spoken does not mean that we are self-absorbed or glib.

A good speech of acceptance should serve four functions. First, it should be either brief or within the time constraints imposed by the situation, as when you are one of several people being recognized. Second, it should be genuine and heartfelt. Audience members can typically tell by the speaker's nonverbal

speech of recognition
A speech presenting an award honoring an individual.

speech of acceptance
A speech expressing thanks for an award or honor.

behavior whether expressions of gratitude are sincere. Third, it should recipro-cate the recognition by praising the people or group who have singled you out. Fourth, it should engender liking. People like people who like them. It's well worth the effort to make audience members feel liked and attractive.

Rather than rehash everything we've said about the characteristics of an effective speech, simply review and put to good use what you've already learned about the speech transaction: Open with impact, connect the occasion to the needs of your audience, use content that is appropriate to the occasion in your message, and close your speech so that you leave your audience with an impression that is favorable and memorable.

Speech of Commemoration

A **speech of commemoration** is slightly different from one of recognition. Very often it centers on an event of cultural significance, such as a turning point in the nation's history or an episode of collective sacrifice. Famous examples well worth revisiting online include the written accounts of Lincoln's Gettysburg Address and video of Ronald Reagan's speech commemorating the 50th anniversary of D-Day, the day when U.S. soldiers stormed the beaches of Normandy to begin the liberation of France from Nazi Germany during World War II.

The fact that few of us are likely to find ourselves speaking from the same platform as Lincoln or Reagan doesn't mean that we will never find ourselves in the position of commemorating an event or a life. Adult children are expected to speak in commemoration of their parents' 50th wedding anniversary, just as parents are expected to speak in commemoration of their grown children's wedding.

The speech of commemoration that we often dread, but that in some respects is one of the most important we will ever make, is a **eulogy,** typically

Senator John McCain is joined by other former POWs as he prepares to deliver a eulogy for retired Vice Admiral William P. Lawrence, who was also a POW in Vietnam.

delivered shortly after a person's death. The eulogy is a ritual as old as recorded time itself and an important custom in most cultures. Writing and delivering a eulogy can be trying. It also can prove an uplifting and empowering narrative for the living. For example, when Earl Spencer eulogized his sister, Diana, Princess of Wales, he spoke lovingly of her as "the very essence of compassion, of duty, of style, of beauty. All over the world she was a symbol of selfless humanity, a standard-bearer for the rights of the downtrodden, a very British girl who transcended nationality, someone with a natural nobility who was classless, who proved in the last year that she needed no royal title to continue to generate her particular brand of magic."[3]

Speech to Entertain

When the great British actor Donald Wolfit lay on his deathbed, he was reputedly told by a young actor, "Sir Donald, after a life so filled with success and fame, dying must be hard." His reply has become famous: "Dying is easy . . . Comedy is hard."[4] True or false, it's hard to argue with the admonition. It is not easy to be funny, one of the chief functions expected of a speech to entertain. Sometimes called "after dinner speaking" because it's frequently delivered following a meal, a speech to entertain is more than just a string of jokes or a comedy monologue. A **speech to entertain** makes its point through the use of humor. Because not everyone is capable of being funny, self-awareness may be the most important criterion to consider.

Jon Stewart at the 2006 Academy Awards.

speech to entertain
A speech that makes its point through the use of humor.

Before you even think about this type of speech, answer this: Do you think you're funny? Better yet: Do you have good reason to believe that people in general think you can be funny? Assuming the answer is yes to the last question, a speech to entertain needs to meet the criteria all effective speeches must meet, beginning with the fact that it should reflect the situation and the audience.

Subjects

Every year the Washington Press Corps hosts a dinner for the president of the United States. Every year the organizers invite a personality to present an after dinner speech. Examples include Don Imus during the Clinton administration, Stephen Colbert during the Bush administration, and most recently Wanda Sykes, who spoke at the first event honoring president Obama.

It probably comes as no great shock to you that at each of the preceding occasions the speakers managed to offend someone in the audience. Don Imus didn't make a friend of president Clinton, because his speech contained numerous and thinly veiled references to Clinton's affair with White House intern Monica Lewinsky. Although Stephen Colbert's satire was more cerebral, his skewering of president Bush's intelligence failed to enamor him with Republicans in the audience. And Wanda Sykes's speech, which for the first time introduced racial humor, managed to upset both black and white audience members.

You need to pay attention to the topic you select for a speech intended to entertain. The topics that work best are also the ones you have a great deal of experience with, including some notion about how you can appropriately relate this experience to your audience. Keynote speakers at the National Convention of Alcoholics Anonymous, for example, can predict with some certainty that self-effacing humor about the stupid things they did while under the influence will resonate with their audience. Could the same be said, however, if they were speaking at the National Convention of Mothers Against Drunk Driving? A little common sense goes a long away in determining topics that are fair game or taboo relative to the situation and makeup of the audience.

Organization

Typically a speech to entertain needn't rigidly conform to any of the specific patterns of organization introduced in Chapter 9. If there is a preferred organizational pattern for speeches meant to entertain, it is the narrative. Storytelling, as many gifted and highly paid professional speakers demonstrate, is ideally suited to entertaining an audience. With its familiar beginning, middle, and end, both speaker and audience know which direction the speech is headed.

Narratives have the potential to transport audience members to the events the story describes. The reason the stories Chris Rock shares work so well is because audience members can see themselves in the scenarios he describes, whether they focus on parenting, lovers' quarrels, or the absurd events of everyday life. The same can be said of many other comedic storytellers, including Jeff Foxworthy. Foxworthy's trademark setup ("You might be a Redneck . . .") works so well because we either know someone who fits the description supplied or find elements of ourselves in it.

Sources of Humor

What we find funny may be at odds with what you find funny. Humor that is obvious to one person, moreover, may go unnoticed by another. For example, a recent study of college students who described themselves as conservatives, found that these students thought Stephen Colbert's comments were meant to be taken seriously.[5] So we are not about to tell you how to be funny in terms of the content you select or the style in which it is delivered. The following is a list of traditional sources of humor that some, but not all, people have drawn from in the attempt to entertain.[6]

- *Exaggeration.* Will Ferrell and Adam Sandler have made a living off exaggeration. In their character sketches, such as Ferrell's portrayal of stock car driver Ricky Bobby or Sandler's hockey-stick-wielding golfer Happy Gilmore, both go way over the top to make a point.
- *Incongruity.* Two objects that under normal circumstances would never be connected are incongruous. For example, pairing Jim Carey with the

normally serious Jeff Daniels in the movie *Dumb and Dumber* was, in and of itself, incongruous. The oddity of casting them together made the film funnier than it might have been had Carey been paired with another actor known for physical comedy.

- *Attacking authority.* Making fun of authority figures is a staple of humor. Matt Stone and Trey Parker have gotten rich off making parents, teachers, self-important movie stars, religion, politicians, talk show hosts, and the federal government look ridiculous. But in addition to making us laugh in this respect, their attacks on authority figures also make a point about hypocrisy. The same can be said for *Family Guy* creator Seth McFarlane, *Beavis and Butthead*'s Mike Judd, and the Godfather to all animated TV satire, *The Simpsons'* Matt Groening.

- *Sarcasm.* Used skillfully, sarcasm is another traditional source of humor (particularly when directed against sources of authority). David Spade, Dennis Leary, and Lewis Black all use sarcasm to great effect. So does Bill Maher. The downside to sarcasm is that many people just don't get it, confusing it with mean-spirited nastiness. This is especially so if audience members believe the sarcasm is unfairly directed at a person they potentially find sympathetic. Thus, it can easily backfire, in particular with less than sophisticated audiences.

- *Irony.* In Mike Judd's film *Idiocracy,* the narrative is set up with a simple premise: Smart people produce fewer children than dumb ones, both now and in the future. The irony is found in the future Judd depicts, where the dumbing-down of the population has created a trash-filled landscape and led to the election of the Ultimate Fighting champion as president of the United States.

- *Self-deprecating humor.* Few sources of humor are as safe or as appreciated by an audience as the fun we poke at ourselves. Self-deprecating humor not only negates the risk of audience alienation associated with sarcasm and attacks on authority figures, it can make the famous and highly accomplished appear downright ordinary. When actors George Clooney and Brad Pitt allow themselves to be portrayed as dorks in a Coen Brothers' film, they endear themselves to their audience. A good example of the power of self-deprecating humor was put on display by Hall of Fame quarterback Terry Bradshaw at a speech in Sacramento, California. Bradshaw was appearing at a forum for business leaders and found himself in the company of, among other luminaries, Colin Powell. Bradshaw remarked to the audience as he opened his speech, "I have no clue about why I was invited to speak here today. I made my living by putting my hands under another man's butt."[7]

- *Delivery.* Humor is driven by a combination of content and delivery. For instance, two people can tell an identical joke, and only one will lead an audience to laugh. A deadpan delivery may work for one speaker but prove disastrous for another. There is, in other words, no single style for delivering a speech intended to entertain people. If you have evidence that you can pull off what may be the most difficult of all types of speeches to deliver, the chances are your style only needs to be refined rather than made over.

Transferring Your Skill Set to Other Settings

The elevated status of public speaking in ancient civilizations has had an undeniable effect on the study of the speech transaction ever since. As a consequence, those of us who study and teach public speaking all too often confine both what we think about the subject and the examples that follow to life's largest rhetorical arenas—for instance, politics. We've tried to avoid leaving you with the impression that models of effective speaking can be found only in these largest of life's arenas. Still, we want to try one more time to show you how common and important the skill set we've focused on is in everyday rhetorical venues.

The Elevator Pitch

Much as e-mail changed both the way we communicate and the language used to construct messages, the effects of text messaging on communication and language may be even greater. While the debate on the nature of these effects is just beginning, the effect of text messaging on the pace and duration of the communication transactions between people is undeniable in at least one respect: They start and end in a hurry.

The trend for saying what you need to say in the least amount of time possible is nowhere more evident than in the elevator pitch, a form of public speaking that derives its name from the average time it takes to get on and off a mechanical elevator. In about 300 or fewer words, the ideal **elevator pitch** takes 30 seconds to provide an audience with a broad overview of a concept, product, or practice. It evolved during the dot.com frenzy as a means for angel investors and venture capitalists to hear as many proposals in the shortest time possible so that they could distill the ones they perceived as having the greatest promise. For good or bad, it has become the standard speech format in many industries, most notably information technology.

Thankfully, the 30-second format has been modified to accommodate the fact that it is nearly impossible to do justice to a worthwhile proposal in less than a minute. Imagine, for example, the delegates assembled in Philadelphia at the Continental Congress in July 1776 telling Thomas Jefferson that he had 30 seconds to explain the Declaration of Independence, or Franklin Delano Roosevelt telling Einstein that he had 30 seconds to explain nuclear fission and its implications for the outcome of World War II.

One-, two-, and three-minute elevator pitches share elements in common, including six basic questions that they need to answer:

1. What is the concept, product, or service?
2. What is the need the concept, product, or service satisfies?
3. What is the revenue model?
4. Who are the people on the team?
5. Who are the competitors?
6. What are the differentiators that give you a competitive advantage?

The key to an effective elevator speech is to be brief, but thorough enough to ensure that the essence and significance of the concept, product, or practice gets

elevator pitch
A thirty-second to 3-minute speech designed to introduce and enlist interest in a concept, product, or practice.

through to the listener. Every sentence uttered must both be high in impact and connected to the self-interest of each audience member.

The goal of an elevator pitch is to enlist enough interest to get you to the next level of the process. Usually this means audience members have questions they want to ask you in the effort to better understand the concept, product, or service. As anyone who has watched an episode of *Dragon's Den* will tell you, audience members also may ask questions that challenge your assumptions about the very worth of the concept, product, or service you propose.

Handling the Q & A

Many speeches, not just successful elevator pitches, are followed by question-and-answer sessions. Here are some basic guidelines for handling the question-and-answer period following a speech:[8]

Controversial filmmaker Michael Moore takes audience questions.

Courtesy of The Orion

- *If this hasn't been prearranged, announce at the outset that you will take questions at the end of your speech.* Unless you have no choice, under no circumstances take questions during the speech, as it will cause you to lose control of the situation. When audience members know they will have the opportunity to ask questions at the end of the speech, they will be able to think about them as you speak.

- *Know far more about the substance of your speech than what you specifically share in the speech itself.* You need to know more than you cover in the speech if you are to take questions. If you expect a hostile audience, it is a good idea to anticipate their toughest questions and prepare answers in advance.

- *Restate questions if they cannot be heard by all or strike you as unclear.* If you are speaking with a microphone, someone asking a question from the audience probably cannot be heard. Restating the question not only allows everyone to hear what was asked, it also allows you time to think of an answer. If a question is wordy, hostile, or imprecise, try to rephrase it in a way that neutralizes some of the problems with the question.

- *Answer questions directly with facts to back up your answers.* This requires you to be fully prepared. However, if you don't know the answer, just say so. You can always promise to obtain the facts and get back to the questioner at a later date. It is better to admit you don't know an answer than to be proved wrong because you tried to bluff your way through an answer.

- *Depending on the circumstances, take questions from different audience members.* Don't let yourself get into a debate or an argument with one audience member. Insist that everyone who has a question gets a chance to ask it before you return to a previous questioner. Choose questioners from different parts of the room so that everyone feels he or she will get a chance.

- *Be brief.* Answer questions as succinctly as possible and move on to the next question. Overly long answers bore the audience and frustrate others who want to ask questions.
- *If appropriate and in your control, announce when you are near the end of the Q&A.* When you sense the audience growing restless, the questions have become repetitive, or you are near the end of your allotted time, simply announce that you can take only one or two more questions.
- *If given the opportunity at the end of the Q&A, restate the focus of your speech and summarize its essential points.* This is your chance to get in the last word and remind the audience of the basic theme of your speech. Depending on the situation, you may want to make yourself available for informal discussion after the speech.

Small Groups

group

Three or more individuals who are aware of each other's presence, share a purpose for the group's formation, and engage in communication transactions.

Facets of the skill set that makes one an effective public speaker can be transferred to the inevitable task-oriented groups and teams you may be a member of or lead both now and in the future. A **group** normally consists of three or more individuals who are aware of each other's presence, share a purpose for the group's formation, and engage in communication transactions.

What's good about groups also can be what is bad about them. For example, when groups are assigned a collective task, the hope is that the group will manage it more effectively than any single group member could working alone. What frequently happens in practice, however, is that individual group members

Small group meetings are common in all walks of life.

use this fact to excuse themselves from taking personal responsibility for undesirable group outcomes, such as failing to solve a problem given to the group. As you probably know from your own experience with school-related group work, one or two group members can end up carrying the entire load group members were supposed to share.

Given this caveat, the skill set needed to construct and deliver a good speech has significant carryover to the skill set group members need to solve problems, achieve goals, and share the results of their deliberations when required to do so. Examples of the most important skills in this overall set are the abilities to critically think, understand the situation as well as the constraints that characterize it, and understand the cultural, demographic, and individual differences among group members. Groups also must know how to conduct the research important to an assigned task, and be able to support the decisions made to complete the task.

Leading a Task-Oriented Group

With the exception of loosely defined social groups, leaderless groups are virtually nonexistent in business, education, and government. Leaders may be designated by a manager or they can emerge from the group. Regardless, a leader in name only is no leader at all.

Although leadership styles may vary, leaders are expected to empower group members intellectually and move them along procedurally. Meeting the first expectancy is what truly separates an effective from an ineffective leader. Roles can be assigned and responsibilities distributed to group members, but that doesn't necessarily mean that they will embrace either. To gain group members' compliance, the leader of a group must be perceived as competent and trustworthy, the operational definition of source credibility, a term discussed in Chapter 14.

It's also the leader's job to systematically move the group from point A to point B, including developing an agenda, keeping face-to-face discussions on track, asking probing questions, summarizing progress, and transitioning from one agenda to the next. The leader usually calls the next face-to-face meeting and also connects the assignments and responsibilities of group members during the interim to the agenda of the next meeting. Finally, all group members share a responsibility for avoiding the folly of groupthink.

Developing an Agenda

A group without an agenda is one that will fail, fall short, or take twice as long to meet its responsibilities. The **agenda** defines the purpose and direction the group takes for a single meeting as well as for an entire project. It may involve defining a problem, mapping out the steps necessary to solve it, and establishing the criteria that will be used in weighing possible solutions. Yet it also can be as simple as mapping out the sequence of topics that the group needs to discuss in a single meeting. Regardless of its scope, however, a sound agenda is a reflection of the critical thought that a group brings to bear on a problem, and it is every bit as important to a group's success as sound organization is to a speech's success. What's more, a sound agenda can be, and often is, based on some of the same patterns for organizing a speech we introduced in Chapter 9.

agenda
Something that defines the purpose and direction a group takes for a single meeting as well as for an entire project.

Keeping Groups on Task

What transpires when group members meet face-to-face is a direct consequence of what took place when they last met and the task-oriented work that occurred in between. When group members fail to complete their assignments or do so halfheartedly, the quality of face-to-face interaction will suffer proportionately. In the "real world," it is the leader's duty to keep group members on task between and during face-to-face meetings. Anyone who has ever wasted time being party to a group that is unprepared to work face-to-face at a scheduled meeting will thank the true leader who, rather than muddling through the allotted meeting time, brings the real issue to the surface then and there.

Probing Questions

There are many types of questions leaders can and should use to probe the intellectual contributions group members bring to the table. Four of the most important are questions asking for information, interpretation, suggestions, and procedure. A *question of information,* for example, could ask group members to report on the research they were assigned at the last meeting. *Questions of interpretation* seek clarification. They probe respondents to expand on the results of their research, including gray areas that may have been uncovered. Because a leader's influence emanates from perceptions of credibility, it's always a good idea to ask for leaders to enlist the input of the group. For example, leaders can ask for *suggestions* about where to turn next or how to fill in holes that remain in the group's investigation of the problem. Unless group members also believe that such solicitations will be taken seriously, a leader is better off not asking for the group's input. Finally, *procedural questions* can serve multiple purposes. Asking a group whether it's time to move on, for instance, is both a question and a suggestion in cases where the group has bogged down or a single group member simply refuses to let go of an issue the rest of the group has moved past.

Summarizing and Transitioning to Other Points

As we pointed out regarding your speeches, summaries and transitional devices such as signposts are highly functional. At some point it will become apparent that the group is moving in a specific direction. Although not everyone may agree on every point, as the leader you can try to summarize those points on which everyone agrees, thus defining which issues need further exploration. By the same token, as a leader you are obligated to make sure that a group has reached consensus and that all viewpoints have been sufficiently aired and debated. For example, think how differently things might have turned out had president Lyndon Johnson paid serious attention to the dissenters in his cabinet when he committed hundreds of thousands of U.S. troops to what Secretary of Defense Robert McNamara later admitted was an unwinnable war in Vietnam fought over false assumptions.[9]

Setting the Agenda for the Next Meeting

Assuming the group's task has not been completed, the next action is to agree on a time and place for the next meeting, group member tasks that need to be completed, tasks necessary to the agenda, and items for the next meeting. This should be done deliberately and without haste, even when people clearly show signs indicating they are ready to leave the meeting.

Avoiding Groupthink

Whether you lead a group or take your membership in a group seriously, we would be remiss if we didn't alert you to the fact that even the most well-intended groups are susceptible to the folly and fallout from **groupthink**.[10] In a very real sense, groupthink is the result of unsound reasoning and most often occurs in highly cohesive groups.

Groupthink is characterized by eight symptoms that alone and in combination erode the ability of group members to reason critically:

1. The illusion of invulnerability.
2. Unquestioned belief in the group's moral superiority.
3. Collective rationalizations.
4. Stereotypical and condescending views of people outside the group.
5. Pressure to conform.
6. Self-censorship.
7. The illusion of consensus.
8. "Mind-guards" who protect the leader from dissenting points of view.

Examples of powerful groups exhibiting these symptoms that should have been painfully obvious are historically significant. Victims of groupthink include the closest advisors to numerous presidents, the top directors of important governmental agencies, and the chief officers of powerful international corporations. Consider the following examples of historically significant groups that fell victim to groupthink. NASA's launch of the doomed space shuttle *Challenger* occurred despite the best advice of the engineers who created the space shuttle's solid booster rockets not to launch the *Challenger*. The spectacular failure to first prevent and then contain the Deep Water Horizon oil spill was a result of a series of faulty decisions by BP and its subcontractors. Finally, consider the top advisors in the Bush administration who told the president that Iraq would be economically self-sufficient within a year after the overthrow of Saddam Hussein. These and many other examples are well-documented cases of ignoring critics and hunkering down as a group—classic symptoms of groupthink with tragic consequences.

Given just how susceptible to groupthink the movers and shakers in the world have proven to be, it's safe to assume that the groups we either lead or participate in are not immune to the phenomenon. It's in our self-interest, therefore, to look at the tips and tactics that should help us avoid groupthink.

groupthink
A mode of thinking where highly cohesive group members become so insulated from outside criticism and so convinced of their own moral superiority, they lose their capacity to think critically.

Tips and Tactics

Guidelines for Avoiding Groupthink

- Play the role of devil's advocate and encourage others to do so.
- If you lead the group and members feel beholden to you, probe them for ideas but don't prejudice the group with your views.
- Bring in outside experts to voice opposite points of view.

- Have an outside and completely independent group work on the problem.
- Reward rather than discourage dissent.
- Don't fall prey to impulsive decisions hastily implemented.

Panel Discussions

panel discussion
An extemporaneous group discussion held for the benefit of an audience.

A **panel discussion** is an extemporaneous group discussion held for the benefit of an audience. In a panel discussion, as in a speech, it is important that the group has a clear outline of the topics to be covered, and that members are adequately prepared. The advantage of a panel discussion is that it is a blend of preparation and spontaneity. Members should feel free to comment on one another's points, ask questions, and openly discuss points throughout the presentation.

A panel discussion requires a leader to act as the *moderator* of the presentation. The moderator calls on members and keeps the discussion on track. Members who want to comment on another member's statement should wait to be recognized by the moderator. A panel discussion is more formal than a normal private group discussion.

Most panel discussions also provide an opportunity for audience members to ask questions. This can occur as the group moves through its outline or can be held as a *forum* period at the end of the panel presentation.

The outline for a panel discussion is similar to that of a speech; however, some modifications need to be made. Here is an example of a panel discussion outline on the topic of secondhand smoke:

Bill Main is a Certified Speaking Professional who earns between $6,500 to $9,500 for speaking engagements. He has clients throughout the nation and is considered to be in the top 3 percent of professional speakers.

George Rogers

I. Introduction of topic and group members.
II. Is secondhand tobacco smoke harmful?
III. What is being done to limit exposure to secondhand smoke?
IV. What is causing these efforts to fall short?
V. Recommendations for new regulations on smoking in public places.

Ideally, each member should be able to offer comments on each of these topics, rather than having one member prepared on each topic. A panel discussion should be a true discussion, not a series of individual presentations.

Public Speaking as a Career

There is one other type of true public speaking that we decided was best left to the close of this chapter and our book: the type for which you get paid. For example, if you took the time to visit the National Platform Speaker Association, you would open yourself to a world of possibility hidden from most people. Every year corporate America, as well as the hundreds of national and regional associations that represent nearly every career path conceivable, spend millions of dollars on speakers tasked with informing and entertaining employees and

IN THEIR OWN WORDS

SPEAKING TO IMPACT!
by Rick Rigsby, PhD

Dr. Rick Rigsby is president and CEO of Rick Rigsby Communications and founder of Rick Rigsby Ministries. With over 200 engagements annually, Dr. Rigsby presents to diverse audiences ranging from Fortune 500 corporations to churches around the world. He is a featured speaker at the Promise Keepers national events and speaks at chapel services for numerous teams in the National Football League. A former award-winning communication professor at Texas A&M University, Dr. Rigsby continues to serve as chaplain for the Aggies football team. We asked him to discuss how his training and experience as a public speaker have impacted his life:

Dr. Rick Rigsby

The ability to speak passionately, powerfully, and persuasively will inspire people and offer you opportunities for a lifetime. My professional success is contingent on the ability to speak with precision, power, and authority. And so is yours!

As a motivational speaker, I must be my very best every time I take the stage. I cannot afford to be average or kind of good. I must be inspiring, motivating, provocative, knowledgeable, moving, and credible. In other words, I must make an IMPACT . . . and not just an impression.

I learned the value of rhetoric at an early age, realizing that through the use of language, tone, timing, and intent, I could summon the power to make people laugh, cry, or think. Moving from the streets of the San Francisco Bay Area to the college classroom, I learned formally about the rich tradition of rhetoric. I fell in love with the process of communication and the potential to influence lives through the power of the spoken word.

My education would serve me well—first during an exhilarating career as a television news reporter in Northern California. Eventually, I would attend graduate school earning a master's degree from my alma mater, California State University, Chico, followed by time at the University of Oregon where I earned a doctorate. I spent two decades teaching college students the power of communication and how the spoken word works to establish and maintain every contour of life.

As president of my own professional speaking organization, I use every communication lesson learned to insure that I am at the top of my game. With over two hundred engagements a year, and a stable of speakers that I am responsible for training, it is critical that I model the art of effective communication. Such an accomplishment would not be possible without my teachers—from Socrates, Plato, and Aristotle in Greece to Brydon and Scott at Chico State!

During a 30-year career built on the study and practice of oratory, I know how to use words to decrease my distance from my audience—thus creating a more intimate environment more conducive to listening and learning. I know how to be rhetorically bilingual—how to speak to both the head and the heart. Most of all I know how to engage audience members—whether 50 or 5000!

The art of persuasion is a learned behavior. If you are willing to learn, prepare your presentations, and practice your craft . . . you may find yourself one day standing in front of thousands and making millions! Are you ready? Well, what are you waiting for? Continue reading and discover how you can learn to move mountains . . . by making an impact with words!!!!

"Speaking to Impact" by Dr. Rick Rigsby. Reprinted by permission.

association members. Some of the people paid to speak are famous, as a consequence of their role in life and achievements, but the chances are good that a majority of these speakers are people who are completely unfamiliar to you. One of them is Dr. Rick Rigsby, featured in the box "In Their Own Words: Speaking to Impact!"

A Parting Thought

Not long ago we attended an event where distinguished alumni spoke to undergraduates at a career forum. They represented a wide spectrum of positions in business, civil service, education, engineering, entertainment, and science. Although we expected the few who had graduated with degrees in communication to talk about the role of public speaking in their success, we were most gratified by the fact that so many others echoed what they had to say. They were unanimous in letting students know that whatever their plans following graduation, they shouldn't pass on the opportunity to take a class in public speaking.

These alumni reinforced something we have learned from our experience. Sooner or later, successful college graduates move beyond the narrow confines of the professional path for which they were initially trained. The salesperson becomes the sales manager; the computer engineer becomes the CEO; the TV writer becomes an officer in the writers' guild; and the ecologist becomes a lobbyist. Chief among the responsibilities that both precede and follow such turning points is skill in the art and science of public speaking—making the necessary connection between one and many.

 www.mhhe.com/brydon7e

To evaluate your understanding of this chapter, visit our Online Learning Center Web site for quizzes and other chapter study aids.

Summary

Rituals and special occasions give rise to different types of speeches, including:

- Speeches of introduction

- Speeches of recognition

- Speeches of acceptance

- Speeches of commemoration

- Speeches to entertain

The skill set you develop as a public speaker in its most conventional sense, easily transfers to less conventional settings and even small group communication and panel discussions.

An increasingly common but unconventional type of public speaking is called the elevator pitch, which is usually between 30 seconds to a few minutes in length and is dedicated to proposing a concept, product or service.

Successful elevator pitches as well as other types of speeches can lead to a question and answer session that requires extra preparation from a speaker.

Group leaders and members frequently rely on many of the same intellectual tools and skills as public speakers. Among the tasks of group leaders and members are:

- Developing an agenda

- Keeping the group on task

- Asking probing questions

- Setting the agenda for the next meeting

- Avoiding groupthink.

Panel discussions, which are similar to both groups and speeches, also involve elements of the speech transaction, including the need to base research on an analysis of the situation and audience, organized messages, effective delivery and sound reasoning.

Careers in public speaking can be both satisfying and lucrative.

Check Your Understanding: Exercises and Activities

1. Your best friend is getting married, and you will be asked to say a few words at the wedding. Prepare your toast. Do the same thing for a wedding anniversary, a baptism, and a bar or bat mitzvah.

2. Think of a special award for one of your classmates. Write a speech of recognition for presenting the award.

3. Track down several quotations and anecdotes that are general enough to be used as an opening or a closing for a speech of acceptance or a speech of recognition. There are numerous Web sites devoted to finding quotations. One of our favorites is www.brainyquote.com/. In addition, there are numerous print sources you can turn to. For example:

   Clifton Fadiman, ed., *The Little Brown Book of Anecdotes* (Boston: Little, Brown, 1985).

   Edmund Fuller, ed., *2,500 Anecdotes for All Occasions* (New York: Avenel Books, 1980).

   James B. Simpson, ed., *Simpson's Contemporary Quotations: The Most Notable Quotes Since 1950* (Boston: Houghton Mifflin, 1988).

4. A speech of nomination can make or break the nominee's chances for being elected to office. Speeches of nomination are more common than you may think. Social clubs such as fraternities and sororities, business and professional associations such as the Soroptomists, Rotary, or local Bar are all examples. On a separate sheet of paper, list and explain what you think are the essential characteristics of a speech of nomination. Then see if you can find a published example of a speech of nomination that conforms to your criteria. Mark the conforming examples on a copy of the speech with a highlighter and share your analysis with classmates.

Notes

1. Edmund Fuller, ed., *2,500 Anecdotes for All Occasions* (New York: Avenel Books, 1980), 135.

2. Adrian Wojnarowski, "Jordan's Night to Remember Turns Petty," *Yahoo Sports,* 12 September 2009. [Retrieved from http://sports.yahoo.com/nba/news?slug=aw-jordanhall091209&prov=yhoo&type=lgns.]

3. "I Stand Before You . . . ," *Newsweek,* 15 September 1997, 24.

4. Rabbi Yaakov Asher Sinclair, "The Last Laugh," *Ohrnet,* 2002. [Retrieved from http://ohr.edu/ohrnet/5762/shmos/teruma.pdf.]

5. Heather L. LaMarre, Kristen D. Landreville, and Michael A. Beam, "The Irony of Satire: Political Ideology and the Motivation to See What You Want to See in The Colbert Report," *International Journal of Press/Politics,* 14, no. 9 (2002): 212–31. [Retrieved from http://hij.sagepub.com/cgi/content/abstract/14/2/212.]

6. Adapted from Jack Perella and Steven R. Brydon, "Speaking to Entertain," in *Intercollegiate Forensics: A Participant's Handbook,* ed. T. C. Winebrenner, 42–46. © 1992 Northern California Forensics Association.

7. Sam Stanton, "Clinton Remains Topic A at Cal Expo Speechathon," *Sacramento Bee,* 10 October 1998, A23.

8. Some of these guidelines are based on a pamphlet by Robert Haakensan, *How to Handle the Q&A* (Philadelphia: Smith Kline & French Laboratories, Department of Public Relations, n.d.).

9. *The Fog of War,* director Errol Morris with Robert S. McNamara, Sony Pictures Classics, 2003.

10. Irving R. Janis, *Groupthink,* 2nd. ed. (Boston: Houghton-Mifflin, 1983).

Appendix A

Guide to Source Citations

AMERICAN PSYCHOLOGICAL ASSOCIATION (APA) STYLE

For more information on citing sources in APA or MLA style, go to the Online Learning Center.

The following information is based on the *Publication Manual of the American Psychological Association,* sixth edition (second printing), 2010, and on their Web site, www.apastyle.org. Please note that there are several changes in APA style from the earlier editions. Hanging indents (not tabs) are to be used in the references list, titles should be *italicized* rather than underlined, and the citation of online sources has changed to use a DOI (digital object identifier) where available, rather than the URL. It is also no longer necessary to state the date of retrieval, unless you are citing a source (such as a wiki) where the material is subject to change.

It is important that you fully document the sources of information you use in preparing a speech outline. Cite the source in parentheses in the body of the outline by name and date. Include page numbers for quotations or specific facts—for example: (Jones, 2010, p. 1). If there are two authors, use both names separated by & (Jones & Smith, 2010, p. 1). For three to five names, cite all of the names (Jones, Smith, & Chavez, 2010, p. 1). Use the abbreviation et al. if there are six or more authors (Jones et al., 2010, p. 1). If there is no author, cite the title (or shortened version), date, and page if there is one (*Fear of Public Speaking,* 2009, p. 1).

Include a list titled "References" at the end of your outline. Always include the author, date, title, and facts of publication. Personal communications, such as letters, phone calls, e-mail, and interviews, are cited only in the text, not the reference list: for example, J. Q. Jones (personal communication, April 1, 2010). The format varies depending on the type of work referenced.

Here are some of the most common types of works you may use in a speech. Notice that APA style does not place quotation marks around the titles of articles or book chapters. Also, titles of books and articles are not capitalized, except for the first word, the first word following a colon, and proper names. Periodical titles are capitalized. Authors are listed by last name first, followed by first and sometimes middle initials. However, editors are cited with their initials first, followed by the last name.

Books

Single Author

Freeley, A. J. (1990). *Argumentation and debate: Critical thinking for reasoned decision making* (7th ed.). Belmont, CA: Wadsworth.

Multiple Authors

Germond, J. W., & Witcover, J. (1989). *Whose broad stripes and bright stars?* New York, NY: Warner Books.

Corporate Author

American Psychological Association. (2010). *Publication manual of the American Psychological Association* (6th ed.). Washington, DC: Author.

Government Document

Department of Health and Human Services. (1989). *Smoking tobacco and health: A fact book.* (DHHS Publication No. CDC 87-8397). Washington, DC: U.S. Government Printing Office.

Chapter in a Book

Steeper, F. T. (1978). Public response to Gerald Ford's statements on Eastern Europe in the second debate. In G. F. Bishop, R. G. Meadow, & M. Jackson-Beeck (Eds.), *The presidential debates: Media, electoral, and policy perspectives* (pp. 81–101). New York, NY: Praeger.

Periodicals

Weekly Magazine

Alter, J. (1988, September 26). The expectations game. *Newsweek, 112,* 16–18.

If the author is unknown, you would list the article as follows:

The expectations game. (1988, September 26). *Newsweek, 112,* 16–18.

Scholarly Journal (in print) Divided by Volume Numbers

Vancil, D. L., & Pendell, S. D. (1984). Winning presidential debates: An analysis of criteria influencing audience response. *Western Journal of Speech Communication, 48,* 63–74.

This means the article was published in 1984, in volume 48 (which is italicized), on pages 63–74, and that the pages are numbered continuously throughout the volume. If the pages of each issue are numbered by the issue instead of the volume, you will need to also include the issue number (not italicized) in parentheses after the volume number, as shown below:

Vancil, D. L., & Pendell, S. D. (1984). Winning presidential debates: An analysis of criteria influencing audience response. *Western Journal of Speech Communication, 48*(1), 63–74.

Newspaper

Rosentiel, T. H. (1988, October 14). Minus a Dukakis home run, Bush is called winner. *Los Angeles Times,* p. A25.

If the author is unknown, you would list the article as follows:

Minus a Dukakis home run, Bush is called winner. (1988, October 14). *Los Angeles Times,* p. A25.

Pamphlet (published by author)

American Diabetes Association. (1987). *Diabetes and you.* Alexandria, VA: Author.

Online Sources

As computer sources multiply, the citation format has been evolving. APA guidelines ask that you include the type of medium and the electronic information necessary to permit retrieval. You should consult the APA Web site at www.apastyle.org for the most recent information on how to cite Internet resources. Here are examples based on the sixth edition of the APA *Publication Manual.*

Internet Articles Based on a Print Source Taken From a Library Subscription Database

Many databases provide assistance in how to cite sources. For example, if you click on the *help* link in the upper right corner of an EBSCOhost database citation, it will take you to a menu that includes a link to *styles of citation*. EBSCOhost provides examples for APA as well as numerous other citation styles. However, some database systems are not accurate, so don't rely on them exclusively.

Freeman, T., Sawyer, C. R., & Behnke, R. R. (1997). Behavioral inhibition and attribution of public speaking state anxiety. *Communication Education, 46,* 175–187. Retrieved from Communication and Mass Media Complete database.

Scholarly Journal (from an online database with a DOI—Digital Object Identifier)

Yang, Y., Gillingwater, D., & Hinde, C. (2005). A conceptual framework for society-oriented decision support. *AI & Society, 19,* 279–291. doi:10.1007/s00146-004-0314-1

Note: You do not type a period at the end of the DOI. If there is no DOI, type "Retrieved from" and the home page URL or the name of the database from which the article came. "DOI" is not capitalized in the actual citation.

Article in an Online Newspaper

Baker, P. & Hulse, C. (2009, December 29). U.S. had early signs of terror plot, Obama says. *The New York Times.* Retrieved from http://www.nytimes.com

Because article URLs often change once a newspaper archives the article, include only the newspaper's home page URL. Do not underline or put a period after the URL.

Article in an Internet-Only Journal

The URL is required in addition to normal publication information. Because a period can be confused with the dot (.) of a URL, there is no period at the end of the URL. Also do not underline the URL.

Guzley, R., Avanzino, S., and Bor, A. (2001, April). Simulated computer-mediated/video-interactive distance learning: A test of motivation, interaction satisfaction, delivery, learning & perceived effectiveness. *Journal of Computer Mediated Communication, 6.* Retrieved from http://jcmc.indiana.edu/vol6/issue3/guzley.html

Internet Document, No Author Identified

Begin with the title of the Web document in *italics,* the date of last update (if known) and a retrieval statement. You can find the date of many Web pages, even if they are not listed on the page itself, by going to the *File* menu and selecting *Properties* in Internet Explorer (PC version) or right-clicking on the page and selecting *Page info* in Firefox.

Fear of public speaking: The fear that blocks careers. (2009, November 23). Retrieved from http://www.anxietycoach.com/fear-of-public-speaking.html

If no date is available, use (n.d.) in place of the date.

Fear of public speaking: The fear that blocks careers. (n.d.). Retrieved from http://www.anxietycoach.com/fear-of-public-speaking.html

All references are listed in alphabetical order by authors' last names, regardless of type, at the end of the speech outline. Works listed by title, where the author is not known, are placed alphabetically by title. For an example of a reference list using APA style, see the outline in Chapter 9 on page 216.

MODERN LANGUAGE ASSOCIATION (MLA) STYLE

This section is based on *The MLA Handbook for Writers of Research Papers,* seventh edition, 2009. Although there are numerous similarities between APA and MLA style, there are also many differences. For example, you may cite sources in parentheses in the actual body of the outline, as you do with APA, but use only the author's name and the page number, not the date (Jones 1). Notice that in MLA style you do not separate the name and the page number by a comma, nor do you use "p." before the page number. MLA also allows you to incorporate the name of the author in your text and cite only the page numbers in parentheses. For example: John Jones tells us that "secondhand smoke is deadly" (1). Notice that the ending punctuation comes after the page number in this example.

If more than one author has the same name, include first initial (A. Jones 1). If there is more than one author, use names separated by "and" (Jones and Smith 1), (Jones, Smith, and Chavez 1). If there are more than three names, use et al. (Jones et al. 1) If there is more than one work by an author, use the name and a short title (Jones, *Stagefright* 1). If there is no author, use the short title and page number (*Stagefright* 1).

Include a list titled "Works Cited" at the end of your outline. References need to point to the specific source in your Works Cited list. Always include the author, title, facts of publication, and date. Personal communications are included in the Works Cited list, unlike in APA style. For example, an interview would be cited as follows: Jones, John Q. Personal interview. 1 Apr. 2010.

There are several changes from previous editions of the *MLA Handbook*.[1] In summary they are:

- Titles are no longer <u>underlined</u>, they must be *italicized*.

- No more URLs unless you think a reader would need the URL in order to find the source. However, we suggest you consult your instructor for his or her preference in this regard.

- All journal citations now require an issue number, even if they are paginated continuously by volume.

- Every entry should indicate the publication medium (print, Web, DVD, etc.) at the end of the entry. However, if it is a Web source, the medium is followed by the date of access.

- New abbreviations are used: N.p. for no publisher, n.d. for no date, and n. pag. for no page.

Below are some of the most common types of works you may use in a speech. Notice that MLA style places quotation marks around the titles of articles or book chapters. Titles of books and periodicals should be *italicized,* which is a change from previous editions that permitted underlining. Also, titles of books, articles, and periodicals are capitalized. First authors are listed by last name first, followed by full first names and sometimes middle initials. If there is more than one author, the remaining authors are listed by first name first. Finally, the date comes at or near the end of the citation, not right after the author's name, as in APA style.

[1]Purdue OWL. "MLA Formatting and Style Guide." *The Purdue OWL.* Purdue U Writing Lab, 23 Sep. 2009. [Retrieved from http://owl.english.purdue.edu/owl/resource/557/01/.]

Books

Single Author

Freeley, Austin J. *Argumentation and Debate: Critical Thinking for Reasoned Decision Making.* 7th ed. Belmont: Wadsworth, 1990. Print.

Multiple Authors

Germond, Jack W., and Jules Witcover. *Whose Broad Stripes and Bright Stars?* New York: Warner Books, 1989. Print.

Corporate Author

American Psychological Association. *Publication Manual of the American Psychological Association.* 6th ed. Washington: American Psychological Association, 2010. Print.

Government Document

United States. Dept. of Health and Human Services. *Smoking Tobacco and Health: A Fact Book.* Washington: GPO, 1989. Print.

Chapter in a Book

Steeper, Frederick T. "Public Response to Gerald Ford's Statements on Eastern Europe in the Second Debate." *The Presidential Debates: Media, Electoral, and Policy Perspectives.* Eds. George F. Bishop, Robert G. Meadow, and Marilyn Jackson-Beeck. New York: Praeger, 1978. 81–101. Print.

Periodicals

Weekly Magazine

Alter, Jonathan. "The Expectations Game." *Newsweek* 26 Sep. 1988: 16–18. Print.

If the author is unknown, you would list the article as follows:

"The Expectations Game." *Newsweek* 26 Sept. 1988: 16–18. Print.

Scholarly Journal

Vancil, David L., and Susan D. Pendell. "Winning Presidential Debates: An Analysis of Criteria Influencing Audience Response." *Western Journal of Speech Communication* 48.1 (1984): 63–74. Print.

This means that the article was published in 1984, volume 48, number 1, on pages 63–74, and is found in print. Note that the issue number is required in MLA even if the volume is numbered continuously.

Newspaper

Rosentiel, Tom H. "Minus a Dukakis Home Run, Bush Is Called Winner." *Los Angeles Times* 14 Oct. 1988: A25. Print.

If the author is unknown, you would list the article as follows:

"Minus a Dukakis Home Run, Bush Is Called Winner." *Los Angeles Times* 14 Oct. 1988: A25. Print.

Pamphlet (published by author)

American Diabetes Association. *Diabetes and You.* Alexandria: ADA, 1987. Print.

Online Sources

MLA has numerous differences from APA in citing Internet-based sources. Include both the name of the Web site in *italics* and the name of the Web site publisher in plain text. If there is no publisher, use n.p. to indicate that. Follow with date of publication, Web as the medium, and the date of access. Here are some examples:

Internet Articles Based on a Print Source From a Library Subscription Database

Cite online journal articles in the same fashion as print, but add the database name in italics and list the medium of publication as Web and end with the date of access.

Freeman, Terri, Chris R. Sawyer, and Ralph R. Behnke. "Behavioral Inhibition and Attribution of Public Speaking State Anxiety." *Communication Education,* 46.3 (1997): 175–187. *Communication and Mass Media Complete.* Web. 30 December 2009.

Article in an Online Newspaper

Peter Baker and Carl Hulse, "U.S. Had Early Signs of Terror Plot, Obama Says." *New York Times.* New York Times, 29 Dec. 2009. Web. 30 Dec. 2009.

This means the article appeared on the *New York Times* Web site, published by the New York Times, on Dec. 29, 2009 on the Web and was accessed on December 30, 2009.

Article in an Internet-Only Journal

Ruth Guzley, Susan Avanzino, and Aaron Bor. "Simulated Computer-Mediated/ Video-Interactive Distance Learning: A Test of Motivation, Interaction Satisfaction, Delivery, Learning & Perceived Effectiveness." *Journal of Computer Mediated Communication,* 6.3 (2001): n. pag. Web. 30 Dec. 2009.

Internet Document, No Author Identified

Begin with the title of the article or page, followed by the name of the Web site (*italicized*), the publisher of the Web site, the date the Web site was last updated, the medium, and your date of retrieval. You can find the date of many Web pages, even if they are not listed on the page itself, by going to the *File* menu and selecting *Properties* in Internet Explorer (PC version) or right-clicking on the page and selecting *Page info* in Firefox.

"Fear of Public Speaking: The Fear That Blocks Careers," *Anxietycoach.com.* Anxiety Coach. 23 Nov. 2009. Web. 30 December 2009.

If there is no date for the article, use n.d.

"Fear of Public Speaking: The Fear That Blocks Careers," *Anxietycoach.com.* Anxiety Coach. n.d. Web. 30 December 2009.

Some instructors may also require the URL or, for hard-to-find sources, you may wish to include it as shown below:

"Fear of Public Speaking: The Fear That Blocks Careers," *Anxietycoach.com.* Anxiety Coach. 23 Nov. 2009. Web. 30 December 2009. < http://www.anxietycoach.com/ fear-of-public-speaking.html >.

As with APA, a complete list of sources—called "Works Cited"—in alphabetical order by author (if none, use title) should follow the text. If more than one work by the same author is included, replace the author's name with three hyphens (---) in all listings after the first. For an example of Works Cited using MLA style, see Appendix B, page 416.

Appendix B

Speeches for Analysis

The following two speeches are excerpted in Chapter 15. The complete transcripts are presented here. Greg Shafer takes the position that students who don't really know why they are in college should drop out, at least for a while, and figure out what their purpose really is. He argues that many of the reasons commonly given for attending college don't hold up under scrutiny. Arjun Buxi takes the opposite point of view. He argues that college graduates end up far better off than those who drop out, that the costs of college don't have to be overly burdensome, and that there are more reasons to complete a college degree than just to achieve fame and fortune.

As you review these speeches, answer the following questions:

- How strong is the evidence cited by each speaker? Are the sources clearly cited and are they authoritative and unbiased?

- What warrants or assumptions do the speakers make about their audience members' reasons for attending college? Do you agree with these assumptions? If not, how does that affect your acceptance of their arguments?

- Does either speaker commit any fallacies of reasoning? If so, how does that affect your view of his credibility as a speaker?

- Does either speaker succeed in changing your mind about the importance of a college education? If so, why are you persuaded?

QUIT SCHOOL TODAY

by Greg Shafer

Why are you here? Seriously, think about it: What are you doing here? This isn't just a clever rhetorical device that I'm using to start my speech. I want you to seriously consider what you are doing here in college.

If you're like most American students today, your thought process follows something like this: I'm in this class so that I can graduate; I'm going to graduate so I can get my degree; I'm getting my degree so that I can get a good job or into a good master's program; so that I can make money; so that I can be happy. The tragedy is how many students have the same process. The lie is that you have to go through the first four to get to number five.

I propose that the amount of money, effort, and time put into obtaining a four-year college undergraduate degree could be better spent elsewhere, and for many, it is not only an unwise financial investment, it is also detrimental to their self-image and to their future prospects.

So, initially when I choose this topic, I picked it as a joke. I didn't think I would seriously believe it in the end. But after I started to do some research, I began to convince myself. So allow me to show you what I found doing my research.

First of all, let's talk about whether or not college is a worthy investment. Now, we can all agree that college graduates make a substantial amount more money than high school graduates. This is undisputable and I'm not here to argue that fact. However, if you look closely at the numbers, it's not always the case. For example, the average cost of attending a public four-year university is $76,000. For any reasonable person, that's a sizable amount of money, especially for kids our age. Most of us are having our tuition and housing paid by either our parents or the government or a combination of the two. Also, this is just for attending a public university. For private universities or for upscale universities the cost is going to be much, much greater.

In addition, the average earnings of a college graduate more than a high school graduate after 40 years is approximately $400,000. Now this is a sizable amount of money; this is true. However, if you look at it, over 40 years, that's not really that great of a return. In fact, the rate of return is approximately 4.42 percent. Now if you took the same amount of money, the same $76,000, and put it in a sound investment portfolio for stocks, you would get something more along the lines of a 6 or 7 percent rate of return, conservatively. Compared with this 4.42 percent, it's not that much money. In addition, you have to consider that this is just the average. For every student that makes this amount of money or more, there's another student who makes this amount of money or less. For every successful engineering student or physics major, there's a philosophy or art history student who's making less. Additionally, this is assuming that these graduates have a 100 percent debt financing. Now, a lot of students are going to go to college and not have the money to pay for it, but they think that by going, they'll be able to pay off their debts. They're going to take out tons of student loans, they're going to go to these private universities that promise them that they are going to make the money back after they get their degree. This, unfortunately, is not the case. A lot of students end up going through college with a serious amount of student loans and debt that they will be paying off for several years, even their entire lifetime.

Here is a list of famous college dropouts [see Exhibit 15.1]. Now, we have this stigma in our heads that's instilled in us since we first attended elementary school that in order to be successful, you have to have a college degree. You have to work hard; you have to get at least your undergraduate or your master's to be successful. Here's a list of people who are wildly successful by anyone's standards, who either never attended college, dropped out part way, or dropped out and then retuned several years later. On this list you'll see politicians, entrepreneurs, businessman, performers, politicians I already mentioned, artists, all of who are wildly successful. This just shows that a person with drive, ambition, and personal discipline is able to be successful regardless of whether they have a college degree or not.

College is essentially a business. The college's goal is to convince students that it is in their best interest to invest time and money in their institution. In that way they may convince students that by obtaining this degree they'll make money in the future, which may or may not always be the case. We, as consumers in the college industry, have to watch our money. We have to make sure that the amount of investment that we are putting into college is going to be returned. Unfortunately, this is not always the case. Let's look at this number. A 1997 survey by the United States Department of Education's National Center for Education Statistics found that four years after attaining a bachelor's degree, 55 percent of graduates were in jobs related to their major field of study. This is from the United States Bureau of Labor Statistics. Now, 55 percent, that seems like a decent statistic when you look at, but look at it in reverse. This means that 45 percent of graduates are in jobs unrelated to the field of study four years after graduating. Let's take it to a personal level. Everyone on this side of the room, in eight years, will be doing something completely unrelated to what they're studying now. I don't know about you, but that seems wildly inefficient to me. I don't want to spend four, eight, maybe even longer, these years of my life—these best years of my life when I'm young, unattached—obtaining a college degree that will not benefit me in the future. We have to be . . . seriously consider about how we spend our money in college and our time.

Employers are looking for people with practical job skills. They're looking for people with connections, and they're looking for people who have job experience. A lot of graduates will leave college without these skills. It's imperative that we get these skills to be able to function in the real world. In the real working environment, we have to make sure that we have something to contribute. A lot of graduates will leave college without these . . . without these skills.

Startlingly, 40 percent of 2 million American freshman admissions each year will not finish college in four years. It will take five, six, even seven years to complete their degree. Each year that's another 10, 20 thousand dollars of debt that they might be incurring. Even more startlingly, 45 percent of admitted freshmen will never graduate, no matter how much time they spend in college. That's terrifying. Think about it, what if you attend school for five or six years and the money just runs out; you never get your degree; you have nothing to show for all the money and time that you have wasted. This is terrifying. We have to make sure that we know what we're getting into.

So, here's my solution. If you're exactly sure what you want to do with your life right now, if you know that you're going to have to have a college degree to obtain the employment that you want, by all means stay here. Work as hard as you can, try not to incur too much debt, and hope that you've chosen a field that will pay off in the future. However, if you're not entirely sure what you want to do with the rest of your life; if you're not entirely sure why you are even at college or what you should be studying, I suggest this: just quit. Simply quit school, leave for a year or semester, you can always come back if you need to. While you're gone, I suggest you use the time wisely. Do something you've always wanted to do. This is a picture of a fishing boat. I think it would be really cool to work on a fishing boat, learn practical skills, learn how to react in the real world to real-world situations. Show employers that you're creative, you're counter-intuitive, and that you can decide for yourself what's important in life. Volunteer in . . . with an organization that you care about. Go overseas, work with kids, learn how to work in the field of study that interests you. And if you don't know what interests you, if you don't know what you're passionate about, spend this time to figure that out. It's not worth it to spend all this time in college to find that you hate what you've studied for all this time. Go somewhere. I'm sure everyone here has someplace that they've always wanted to go. Save up, work hard, get a job, save up, and go wherever that is you want to go. This is a picture of a castle in the Ukraine, which is relatively inexpensive to travel to. If you're creative and you work hard, you can go wherever you want to go. I suggest that you spend this time to go places that you want to go, do things that you want to do, learn skills that you want to learn.

Like I said, college is a business. Its goal is to convince us that it's worth our time and money to attend the institution. It's our responsibility to decide for ourselves whether or not it's worth our investment. We need to be careful about what we are doing with our lives and with how we are spending our youngest years. Right now we're more [un]attached than we've ever been before and will ever be again. We need to make sure that we are using this time wisely and that it's going to pay off in the future. So, we really need to think about what we are doing here in college. I'll leave you with this warning: If we cannot summon the will to decide for ourselves what is important, if we cannot shed the fear of an unknown future for the sake of a more adventurous present, if we cannot forsake the safety and institution of our current lives for the higher ideals of self-satisfaction and personal knowledge; then our lives will never transcend mediocrity, and we will not know the powers of the great. Thank you very much.

Works Cited

Dohm, Arlene, and Watt, Ian. "College At Work: Outlook and Earnings for College Graduates, 2000–10." *Occupational Outlook Quarterly,* Bureau of Labor Statistics, Fall 2002. Web. 7 April 2009.

Karlgaard, Richard. "Is College Worth it?" *Forbes.com.* Forbes, 27 March 2006. Web. 7 April 2009.

Kim, Brian. "Top Ten Reasons Why College Graduates Can't Get a Job." *BrianKim.net.* N.p., 2006. Web. 7 April 2009.

Kremer, John. "The College Dropouts Hall of Fame." *The College Dropouts Hall of Fame.* N.p., 2009. Web. 7 April 2009.

Robertson, Michael, and Donaldson, Tina. "Is College Worth it?" *Robertson Education Empowerment Foundation.* Robertson Education Empowerment Foundation, 6 Dec. 2006. Web. 7 April 2009.

Twohey, Megan. "Is College Worth it?" *Chicago Tribune.* Chicago Tribune, 14 Oct. 2008. Web. 7 April 2009.

Williams, Walter E. "Is College Worth it?" *Townhall.com.* Salem Web Network, 27 August 2008. Web. 7 April 2009.

Source: Transcribed from a speech given at California State University, Chico, on May 15, 2009.

MIND ON COLLEGE
by Arjun Buxi

"Let me take you to a place, where the mind is without fear and the head is held high, and knowledge is free . . ."

But it's not. No it isn't. That's part of the reason why I'm here today, ladies and gentlemen. Let's talk about this.

Hi, my name is Arjun, and I had a few questions you know about college and college degrees, some concerns and worries as a student. Let's talk about them, maybe a few questions I had, maybe you could have some answers. Like, for example, what do I do about tuition, all those student loans, how do I pay them off. Well, what about the second one—how about, is my degree useful? What is it meant for? And finally, what is the real meaning of college? Why are we here?

Now, since this is the pursuit of truth, let's talk about the most basic thing—the money. It is the most stressful thing, I know. So, let's talk about that. Kathy Kristof of Forbes.com tells us a real nice sob story. Joel Kellum is this kid, history major, the private college, let's not say which one, happy-go-lucky guy. Wants some money for tuition, go takes out a student loan, everything seems fine 'till he graduates and then the money is due. Nothing new about that—that's how we do it. But here's the problem. They're charging him 12 percent compound interest and he didn't know that. He thought it was a subsidized government loan. No, no no. It's a Sallie Mae corporate unsubsidized loan with all these lovely hidden fees and charges that he had no clue about. So we can't really pity him. He didn't ask how much the interest was for, he didn't know when it was due, he didn't know how it was compounded—semiannually, annual, monthly, no clue. And then there was his wife's loans and all the things in between and poor Joel is looking at $200,000 in debt. But freeze, let's not pity him so quickly. Step aside, look at the facts. It's a $60,000 loan that he took out, and according to David Leonhardt of the *New York Times,* that's three times the average amount that any of us would take out or should take out as a loan. Mistake number one. Mistake number two, Joel didn't know the rate of interest nor how much it was compounded, and nobody's going to tell you. It's a loan shark business out there. He didn't know it was a corporate loan and once that was in place all the dice [*sic*] had been dealt. He was done.

But the question is, why should this happen to everybody? Why should this happen at all? Let's look at some possible answers, let's see what we can do differently. The first question then is, what is the cost of college? How much does it really cost? All right, we look up, College Board.com, here is what they say. On average, a private college, four-year college, will cost you about $25,000 to $26,000 a year. Okay, how about a four-year public college like Chico State? About $6,000 to $7,000 a year. Oh, what about a JC, a two-year college? Maybe $2,000 to $3,000. Do you see the gradations here? There's a lot of leeway—a lot of money to be spent or a lot of money to be saved. It's up to us.

But just while I'm on the subject of JCs, Gladieaux and Perna did a study in 2005. You know what they found out? That if you go to a JC before you go to a four-year school, you are only one-third as likely to borrow a single cent in student loans. That's a thought.

Then the question is, well okay, maybe I can afford college, but then does it pay me back? Is it worth it? Here's why. David Leonhardt of the *New York Times,* we're back to him. He did a quick study in 2007 and here's what he found out. Median income if you were a high school grad, you looking at about, oh I don't know, about $27,000 a year, not too bad, not to shabby. Let's move on—high school grad, college dropout, $33,000 a year. Still looking better. Oh, but wait, here it gets better. If you've finished your degree and you're a full college grad, you earn an average of $47,000 a year. That's a jump of $20,000 for just having the degree. But I'm not even done yet. The Bureau for [*sic*] Labor Statistics 2008, October, a government body, did a few number samplings of their own and here's what they found out. That of the labor force of that time, the kids that had just a high school diploma, only 27 percent of them even had a job to begin with.

But a college grad, 55 percent of all college grads had a job. And then, when you add the fact that we mentioned before of them earning almost twice as much, we're looking at some real holiday dividends here. And then don't forget, that if $20,000 is the average boost for a college degree, it's also the average debt. So, already it starts paying itself off.

Okay, we're taking a breath now. The money doesn't seem so bad already. But you know what, let's talk about the practical start. Let's talk about what the degree [means] to us, does it really come across as useful? You might hear these comments. For example, I hear, well maybe, maybe my degree is you know not really related to what I'm going to do. My major has nothing to do with my job. But hold back. The University of Washington, Seattle, what do they tell us? They tell us, that's exactly what it's supposed to be. It's not supposed to be specific, not unless you're an engineering major or a medical major, something more technical. But the general stuff, social sciences and liberal arts, it's supposed to be general, it's designed that way to give us maximum spectrum of jobs to look into. That's opening up opportunity, opening up the mind.

The second comment that I get a lot is well, okay, but then I'm not doing anything really practical, right, it's all theory? Well, number one, you know, you do need a little theory to do the practical, it's a start and then there's a finish to it. Well, let's not go there. There's something called internships and more and more majors, including mine, Communication Studies, require them to be a full-time major and to graduate with that degree. It's in the cards, you gotta do it. And more and more employers look at them as gold points if you apply for a job. Wow, you did an internship, fantastic. Let's hire you. I'm not even done yet. Here is even more practical stuff for you. Just do a quick Google search. Type in something like "entry level management training," something generic. You'll get a huge list of companies: Target, Walmart, WaMu, CSX, Cintas, L' Oreal, Anheiser Busch (the Budweiser guys–don't drink kids). And all these companies have these laid out, designed, clear-cut programs for entry-level jobs for college grads. They don't want you to know everything when you get out of college. They're going to teach you how to work in their factories, in their workplaces. That's how they do it. But here's the catch. In those job profiles, if you look a little closely, they do require something of you. They require interpersonal skills, they require people skills, they require thinking rational skills, cognitive skills. And what is all that about? Human development. And that's exactly–human development–is exactly what college is all about.

With that, let's come to the final point. What does college really mean? Go back with me to the meaning of the word. Dictionary.com, what does it say? A place for people to come together, people of like mind for a common purpose. What is that common purpose? The pursuit of truth, the pursuit of knowledge, in one word, inquiry. And what better place to do it? Where people you know and like and people you don't know and maybe don't like, all come together, sharing of minds, engagement. And what's the next step? With engagement comes empowerment, comes democratic values. That's the second core thing that we need to look at with a college degree. We need to know that the positive social and political change that every citizen in this country makes starts right here. The opening of the mind and the galvanizing of the people into a way that, yes, we need to do something about our country; we need to fix a few things. This is where that spark begins. And with all this comes the culmination of self-actualization–the reaching of a higher level of thinking. And that comes because of critical thinking. Critical thinking, according to the centerforcriticalthinking.org, is the ability to think about thinking and then to evaluate its strengths, evaluate its weaknesses, and take it, as I said before, to a higher level—improved kind and qualities of thinking. This is what college is really all about.

Before I end off, I wanted to address one last comment that you hear a lot. Well, you can get rich without going to college, right? You can get famous without going to college, right? You know what, I did a Google search. There's actually a Web site called collegedropoutshalloffame.com and you're absolutely right. I'm not going to sugarcoat it. Yes, you can get rich without college. Yes, you can get famous without college. But are these metrics—rich and famous—are these really what we want to judge success by? Whatever happened to thinking about other things, about other people, about self-actualization where you treat other people differently as a result of your knowledge, where you treat the world and you see the world differently as a result of your knowledge? Pursuing knowledge for knowledge's sake. Whatever happened to that?

Ladies and gentlemen, we've learned a few things today. I've think we've learned how we can actually handle our money better and not be burdened by debt too much when it comes to school. I've think we've learned a little bit about how our college degree can be practical, can be useful, can take us somewhere we need to go. And I hope, I really do hope, we've learned the real meaning of college.

But let me leave you with this thought. Let's go back to the beginning, the poem I was quoting: "Where the mind is without fear and the head is held high, and let the mind be led forward into ever widening thought and action and into that heaven of freedom let us awake."

Thank you.

References

College. (n.d.). *Dictionary.com unabridged.* Retrieved from Dictionary.com website: http://dictionary.reference.com/browse/college

College enrollment and work activity of 2008 high school graduates. (2009, April 28). *Bureau of Labor Statistics.* Retrieved from http://www.bls.gov/news.release/hsgec.nr0.htm

College costs–Average tuition cost. (2009). *The College Board.* Retrieved from http://www.collegeboard.com/student/pay/add-it-up/4494.html

Center for Critical Thinking. (1996). *Three definitions of critical thinking.* Retrieved from http://www.criticalthinking.org/University/univlibrary/library.nclk

Education and democracy. (2008, May 6). *America.gov: Engaging the world.* Retrieved from http://www.america.gov/st/democracyenglish/2008/May/20080609223034eaifas0.935177.html

Gladieaux, L., & Perna, L. (2005, May). Borrowers who drop out: A neglected aspect of the college student loan trend. *The National Center for Public Policy and Higher Education.* Retrieved from http://www.highereducation.org/reports/borrowing/borrowers.pdf

Kristof, K. (2009, February 2). The great college hoax. *Forbes.* Retrieved from http://www.forbes.com/forbes/2009/0202/060.html

Leonhardt, D. (2009, September 27). The college calculation. *The New York Times*. Retrieved from http://www.nytimes.com

Tagore, R. (2009). Mind without fear. *Gitanjali*. Retrieved from http://www .schoolofwisdom.com/gitanjali.html UW advising-Majors and careers

The college dropouts hall of fame. (n.d.). *College dropouts hall of fame.com*. Retrieved from http://www.collegedropoutshalloffame.com/

UW advising–Majors and careers (n.d.). *University of Washington at Seattle*. Retrieved from http://www.washington.edu/uaa/gateway/advising/majors/ intro4.php

Source: Transcribed from a speech given at California State University, Chico, on October 28, 2009.

Glossary

A

abstract A summary of an article or a report.

ad hominem Attacking the person rather than the soundness of his or her argument.

agenda Something that defines the purpose and direction a group takes for a single meeting as well as for an entire project.

alphabetical pattern Main points are in alphabetical order or spell out a common word.

amoral The process of communication is ethically neutral.

analogy An extended metaphor or simile. Suggesting that the rebuilding of Iraq is much like rebuilding Germany and Japan after World War II is an analogy.

antithesis The use of opposites, e.g., light–dark.

aphorism A brief statement embodying a principle or lesson.

arguing in a circle (begging the question) An argument that proves nothing because the claim to be proved is used to prove itself.

attitude A learned predisposition to respond in a consistently favorable or unfavorable manner with respect to a given object.

audience accessible Content the audience is able to understand, regardless of its complexity.

audience appropriate Informative topic and speech that are perceived as compatible with the audience members' belief systems.

audience diversity The cultural, demographic, and individual characteristics that vary among audience members.

audience involving Gaining the audience's attention through an informative topic and speech.

B

backing Evidence that directly supports a warrant.

belief An assertion about the properties or characteristics of an object.

blog (short for Web log) A Web site that contains dated entries in reverse chronological order. They can range from serious commentary by experts to "ranting and raving" by people with no particular qualifications.

Boolean operators Terms, such as *and, or,* and *not,* used to narrow or broaden a computerized search of two or more related terms.

C

call to action A request by the speaker, usually at the end of a speech, for the audience to take specific actions to fulfill the speech's purpose.

captive audience Listeners who have no choice about hearing a speech.

categorical pattern A pattern of organization based on natural divisions in the subject matter.

causal pattern A pattern of organization that moves from cause to effect or from effect to cause.

central beliefs Beliefs based directly or indirectly on authority.

central route processing Persuasion achieved by the quality of the arguments in a message.

central route processing Receivers mentally elaborate on the elements of your message and carefully scrutinize your arguments and evidence.

Channel The means through which the message is sent.

claim A conclusion that a speaker wants an audience to reach as a result of a speech.

collectivistic cultures Cultures that discourage individual assertiveness and stress group harmony.

Communibiology The study of the biological bases of human communication.

Communication Apprehension Fear and avoidance of communication with other people.

comparative advantages pattern A pattern of organization based on the idea that things can be better even if they are not currently harmful.

Conformity effect People will question their own perceptions when presented with the judgments of others.

Connotative meaning The implied meaning of a word based upon its use within a given context.

constraint A limitation on choices in a rhetorical situation.

content (of messages) The essential meaning of what a speaker wants to convey.

core beliefs Primitive and zero consensus beliefs that are highly resistant to change.

credibility The degree to which an audience trusts and believes in a speaker.

credibility-enhancing language Words that emphasize rather than undermine audience perceptions of a speaker's competence.

critical thinking The process of making sound inferences based on accurate evidence and valid reasoning.

cultural diversity Differences among people in terms of beliefs, customs, and values—in a sense, their worldview.

D

decoding The process by which a code is translated back into ideas.

Deep Web (Proprietary Internet) Web sites accessible over the Internet only to authorized users and often at a cost.

deficiency needs Basic human needs, which must be satisfied before higher-order needs can be met. They include needs for food, water, air, physical safety, belongingness and love, and self-esteem and social esteem.

demographic diversity Variations among people in terms of such attributes as socioeconomic background and level of education.

demographics Basic and vital data regarding any population.

Denotative meaning The literal or explicit definition of a word.

distorted evidence Significant omissions or changes in evidence that alter its original intent.

door-in-the-face Persuasion strategy that asks for a large commitment then gains compliance by asking the receiver to compromise by agreeing to a smaller request.

E

elaboration The degree to which a receiver scrutinizes a message.

Elaboration Likelihood Model Model of communication that predicts the likelihood that receivers will engage in effortful thinking (elaborative processing) depends on their *motivation* and *ability* to process the message.

elevator pitch A thirty-second to 3-minute speech designed to introduce and enlist interest in a concept, product, or practice.

emblem A nonverbal symbol that can be substituted for a word.

encoding The process by which ideas are translated into a code that can be understood by the receiver.

Environment The physical surroundings as you speak and the physical distance separating you from your audience, The situation or context in which the transaction takes place.

environmental reinforcers Factors within our environment that contribute to our fear of speaking.

ethos The receiver's perception of a sender's competence, trustworthiness, and goodwill; credibility.

eulogy A kind of commemorative speech about someone who has died that is usually given shortly after his or her death.

evidence The facts, examples, expert opinion, numerical data, narratives, and the like offered by a speaker in support of a claim.

expert opinion A quotation from someone with special credentials in the subject matter.

extemporaneous delivery A mode of presentation that combines careful preparation with spontaneous speaking. The speaker generally uses brief notes rather than a full manuscript or an outline.

extended narrative pattern A pattern of organization in which the entire body of the speech is the telling of a story.

Extended Parallel Process Model Persuasiveness of a fear appeal hinges on receivers' parallel processing about the threat and the solution offered in the message.

F

fact Something that is verifiable as true.

fallacy An argument in which the reasons advanced for a claim fail to warrant acceptance of the claim.

false analogy The comparison of two different things that are not really comparable.

false dilemma A generalization that implies there are only two choices when there are more than two.

feedback Audience member responses, both verbal and nonverbal, to a speaker.

foot-in-the-door Persuasion strategy in which the speaker gains compliance with a small request then asks the receiver to agree to a second, larger request.

forewarning Informing the receiver of the persuasive intent of a message before offering an argument.

formal outline A detailed outline used in speech preparation, but not, in most cases, in the actual presentation.

G

general purpose The primary function of a speech. The three commonly agreed-upon general purposes are to inform, to persuade, and to entertain.

Generalized Anxiety Feelings of anxiety associated with communication in nearly all situations.

Genetic Contributors Combinations of inherited tendencies that may exert influences on our behavioral preferences.

grounds The evidence a speaker offers in support of a claim.

group Three or more individuals who are aware of each other's presence, share a purpose for the group's formation, and engage in communication transactions.

groupthink A mode of thinking where highly cohesive group members become so insulated from outside criticism and so convinced of their moral superiority, they lose their capacity to think critically.

growth needs Higher-order human needs, which can be satisfied only after deficiency needs have been met. They include self-actualization (the process of fully realizing one's potential), knowledge and understanding, and aesthetic needs.

H

halo effect The assumption that just because you like or respect a person, whatever he or she says must be true.

hasty generalization A fallacy that occurs when there are too few instances to support a generalization or the instances are unrepresentative of the generalization.

hyperbole An exaggeration of a claim.

I

immediate language Language that reduces the psychological distance that separates speakers and audience members and stresses that speech is a transaction.

impromptu delivery A spontaneous, unrehearsed mode of presenting a speech.

inclusive language Language that helps people believe that they not only have a stake in matters of societal importance but also have power in this regard.

index A listing of sources of information—usually in newspapers, journals, and magazines—alphabetically by topic.

individual diversity How individuals in an audience differ in terms of knowledge, beliefs, attitudes, values, motives, expectations, and needs.

individualistic cultures Societies that stress individual assertiveness over group harmony.

informative speaking The process of presenting an audience with new information or a new perspective on old information.

Inoculation theory Two-sided refutational messages "inoculate" receivers, making them better able to resist counterpersuasion.

interdependence A relationship in which things have a reciprocal influence on each other.

invention The creative process by which the substance of a speech is generated.

K

key word A word in the abstract, title, subject heading, or text of an entry that can be used to search an electronic database.

Kinesics The study of body movement and facial expressions.

L

labels identify specific elements of a graphic slide

language The rule-governed word system we use to verbally communicate.

language intensity The degree to which words and phrases deviate from neutral.

Learned Helplessness A person feels unable to predict whether a behavior will result in a reward or punishment, therefore he or she avoids the behavior all together if possible.

learning styles Differences in the way people think about and learn new information and skills.

legibility the ease with which something can be read.

linguistic relativity hypothesis The idea that what people perceive is influenced by the language in which they think and speak.

listening The process of receiving, attending to, and assigning meaning to aural and visual stimuli.

loaded language Language that triggers strong emotional and negative responses.

logos Logical appeals.

long-term goals Those ends that we can hope to achieve only over an extended period of time.

low-ball Persuasion strategy in which the speaker tries to elicit a commitment from the receiver before revealing the full cost of the commitment.

M

main points The key ideas that support the thesis statement of a speech.

manuscript delivery A mode of presentation that involves writing out a speech completely and reading it to the audience.

marginalizing language Language that diminishes people's importance and makes them appear to be less powerful, less significant, and less worthwhile than they are.

memorized delivery A mode of presentation in which a speech is written out and committed to memory before being presented to the audience without the use of notes.

Message The meaning produced by communicators, The message the speaker *intends* to send.

Message-sidedness: One-sided messages provide only the arguments that support your message.

metaphor A figure of speech in which words and phrases that are primarily understood to mean one thing are used in place of another to suggest likeness or an analogy between them. Race car drivers, for example, may have to "wrestle with" a car that is difficult to control.

misleading statistics Statistics that are incomplete or based on faulty data.

mistaking correlation for cause The assumption that because one thing is a sign of another, they are causally related.

Monroe's motivated sequence A five-step organizational scheme, developed by speech professor Alan Monroe, involving (1) attention, (2) need, (3) satisfaction, (4) visualization, and (5) action.

N

narrative An extended story that is fully developed, with characters, scene, action, and plot.

narrative fidelity The degree to which a narrative rings true to real-life experience.

narrative probability The internal coherence or believability of a narrative.

Negative Self-talk Destructive self-criticism

non sequitur An argument that does not logically follow from its premises.

nonverbal behavior A wordless, but not silent, system of communication.

O

online catalog A computerized database of library holdings.

opinion A judgment by someone that is subject to dispute.

P

panel discussion An extemporaneous group discussion held for the benefit of an audience.

pathos Emotional appeals.

perception The process by which we give meaning to our experiences.

peripheral beliefs The least central type of beliefs, the easiest to change.

peripheral cues Factors outside the message that act as decision rules and allow receivers to accept or reject persuasive appeals without examining the argument.

peripheral route processing Influence based upon factors outside of the quality of the message.

peripheral route processing Receivers give brief attention to the message without elaborated thought.

Persuasion The process by which attitudes or behaviors are influenced as a result of receiving a message.

pervasiveness Communication takes place wherever humans are together because people tend to look for meaning, even when a message is not deliberately sent.

podcast An audio broadcast that has been converted to a digital format, such as MP3, for playback by a digital music player or computer.

Positive self-talk The use of positive coping statements instead of negative self-talk.

post hoc, ergo propter hoc ("after the fact, therefore because of the fact") The assumption that because one event preceded another, the first event must be the cause of the second event.

preview A forecast of the main points of a speech.

primacy-recency effect The tendency for people to remember and be most influenced by what they hear either at the beginning or at the ending of a speech.

primary sources Original sources of information.

proactive delivery Taking the initiative, anticipating, and controlling variables that will affect speech delivery.

Proactive Imagination The process of visualizing yourself having a successful communication experience.

problem–solution pattern A pattern of organization that analyzes a problem in terms of (1) harm, (2) significance, and (3) cause, and proposes a solution that is (1) described, (2) feasible, and (3) advantageous.

proverb A short, commonly used saying that expresses a well-known truth, often with a religious or moral aspect.

pseudoreasoning An argument that appears sound at first glance but contains a fallacy of reasoning that renders it unsound.

Q

qualifier An indication of the level of probability of a claim.

R

rebuttal An exception to or a refutation of an argument.

receiver-centric A person's assumption that the meaning he or she gives to a word or a phrase is its exclusive meaning.

Receivers The audience to whom the message is delivered.

red herring (smoke screen) An irrelevant issue introduced into a controversy to divert attention from the real issues.

relational component (of messages) The combined impact of the verbal and nonverbal components of a message as it is conveyed.

research The process of finding and evaluating supporting materials.

rhetorical question A question that the audience isn't expected to answer out loud.

rhetorical situation A natural context of persons, events, objects, relations, and an exigence [goal] which strongly invites utterance.

RSS (Really Simple Syndication) A syndication format that aggregates updates to various news sites or blogs and transmits them to users.

S

scarcity strategy Realization of the scarcity of the opportunity and the possibility of losing it seem to increase perceptions of the desirability of that item or opportunity.

secondary sources Information sources that rely on other (primary) sources rather than gathering information firsthand.

selective exposure The tendency to place ourselves in environments with others who think as we do.

self-adapting behaviors Nonverbal behaviors used to cope with nervousness; for example, touching oneself or grasping the sides of a lectern with one's hands.

self-talk Silent communications with oneself that influence one's perceptions of reality.

sequential request strategies Persuasion strategies that rely on a series of decision rules, not quality arguments, to gain compliance or elicit desired behaviors.

sexist language Language, including terms such as *housewife* and *fireman,* that stereotypes gender roles.

short-term goals Those ends that we can reasonably expect to achieve in the near term.

signposts Transitional statements that bridge main points.

simile Invites the listener to make a direct comparison between two things or objects that are quite different, such as "my roommate lives like a pig in slop" or is "dumb as a rock."

slippery slope The assumption that just because one event occurs, it will automatically lead to a series of undesirable events even though there is no relationship between the action and the projected events.

socioeconomic status Social grouping and economic class to which people belong.

Source Credibility The image held of a communicator by a receiver at a given time.

source expertise Receivers' perceptions of the persuader's knowledge, qualifications and competence.

Source The person initiating the communication.

spatial pattern A pattern of organization based on physical space or geography.

specific purpose The goal or objective a speaker hopes to achieve in speaking to a particular audience.

speech of acceptance A speech expressing thanks for an award or honor.

speech of commemoration A speech that calls attention to the stature of the person or people being honored, or emphasizes the significance of an occasion.

speech of introduction A speech that briefly sets the stage for an upcoming speaker.

speech of recognition A speech presenting an award honoring an individual.

speech to entertain A speech that makes its point through the use of humor.

spiral pattern A pattern of organization that employs repetition of points, with the points growing in intensity as the speech builds to its conclusion.

star pattern A pattern of organization in which all of the points are of equal importance and can be presented in any order to support the common theme.

stereotyping The assumption that what is considered to be true of a larger class is necessarily true of particular members of that class.

stock issues pattern A four-point pattern of organization that is based on (1) ill, (2) blame, (3) cure, and (4) cost.

straw person An argument made in refutation that misstates the argument being refuted. Rather than refuting the real argument, the other side constructs a person of straw, which is easy to knock down.

subject heading A standard word or phrase used by libraries to catalog books or other publications.

subpoint An idea that supports a main point.

supporting point An idea that supports a subpoint.

Surface Web (Open Internet) Web sites freely accessible to all users over the Internet.

symbol Something that stands for or suggests something else by reason of relationship or association.

system A collection of interdependent parts arranged so that a change in one produces corresponding changes in the remaining parts.

Systems Model of Listening Characterizes listening as more than simply the interaction of a sender and a receiver.

T

thesis statement A single declarative sentence that focuses the au fdience's attention on the central point of a speech.

The three types of persuasive effects are: create a new attitude, reinforce an existing attitude or behavior, change an attitude or behavior.

time pattern A pattern of organization based on chronology or a sequence of events.

titles describe the general focus of a graphic slide.

totalizing language Language that defines people exclusively on the basis of a single attribute, such as race, ethnicity, biological sex, or disability.

transaction An exchange of verbal and nonverbal messages between two or more people.

Twitter A social networking service that enables users to send and read messages of up to 140 characters.

two-sided nonrefutational messages provide counter-arguments but do not refute those arguments.

two-sided refutational messages provide and refute counter arguments.

two-sided refutational pattern A pattern of organization that involves (1) introducing the topic and thesis statement, (2) presenting arguments and evidence supporting the thesis, (3) acknowledging arguments against the thesis, (4) refuting these arguments, (5) restating arguments and evidence supporting the thesis, and presenting the conclusion.

U

unsupported assertion A claim without any evidence to support it.

URL Uniform Resource Locator: the address for Web sites, such as www.mhhe.com.

V

values Our most enduring beliefs about right and wrong.

verbal aggressiveness The trait of attacking the self-concept of those with whom one disagrees about controversial claims.

verbal qualifiers Words and phrases that erode the impact of what a speaker says in a speech.

vidcast A video clip that is similar to a podcast. (Also called a "vcast," "vodcast," and "videocast.").

visual aids Visual elements that help your audience receive your message.

voluntary audience Listeners who choose to hear a speaker.

W

warrant The connection between evidence (grounds) and claim.

wave pattern A pattern of organization in which the basic theme, often represented by a phrase, is repeated again and again, much like a wave cresting, receding, and then cresting again.

wear-out point The point at which a repeated persuasive message loses its effectiveness.

wiki The Hawaiian word for "quick." A Web site that allows users to edit content easily and quickly—for example, Wikipedia.

Z

zone of interaction The area of an audience in which speaker and audience members can make eye contact.

Photo Credits

Index

Clinton, Hillary, 104
clothing, 263
collectivism *vs.* individualism, 99
collectivist cultures, 41, 101
colloquial words, 242
commemoration speeches, 390
commitment, 114, 197, 264, 388
communibiology, 39
communication
  advances our life-agenda, 53–54
  amoral, 53
  ethics of, 63–65
  pervasive, 52
  variables
    channel, 57, 58–59
    environment, 57, 59
    least control, 60
    message, 57, 58
    most control, 60
    receiver, 57, 59
    source, 57, 58
communication apprehension (CA),
    38–39
  anxiety, 37–38
  causes of, 39–41
  and class selection, 42
  and college graduation, 42–43
  effects of, 42–43, 45–46, 48
    kinesics, 45
    positive self-talk, 43–44
    positive visualization, 44–45
  and grades, 42
  research, 43
  and standardized test scores, 42
communication orientation *vs.*
    performance orientation, 254
communication transaction, 83
communicative purpose, 293
comparative advantage patterns,
    198–199
comparison warrants, 375
competence, 55, 229, 233–236, 264, 267,
    270, 274, 310
compliance-gaining strategies, 348–349
comprehensive listening, 75
concept speeches, 319–322
conclusions, 7, 158, 186, 371–372
  aphorism, 188
  call to action, 189
  proverb and quotation, 188
  return to beginning, 188–189
  rhetorical situation, 188
  steps in
    closing with impact, 22
    summarizing, 187
  stories and, 188
  time, 187
concrete words, 242
conformity effect, 347
Confucius, 106, 180

connections, transitioning to, 185, 224,
    362, 365, 377, 413
connotation, 378
constraints, 8, 94–95, 121, 133, 175, 179,
    187, 208, 389, 397
content, message, 10–11, 13, 30, 107,
    138, 141–143, 178, 182, 187, 194,
    196–198, 209, 213, 228, 257, 259,
    265, 271, 276, 278, 316–317, 322,
    364, 366, 390, 392–393
content-oriented listening style, 78–79
context. *See also* rhetorical situations
  audience and, 13–14
contrast words, 9, 11, 165, 241
controversial issues, 8
conventional patterns, 199, 203, 207
copyright, 102, 142
core beliefs, 113–115
CRAAP test, 133, 140, 142
credibility. *See also* ethos
  of search engines, 136–137
  of speaker, 15
credibility-enhancing language,
    233–234, 236
credit, financial, 106, 151, 168, 234, 325,
    370
critical listening, 75–76
critical thinking. *See also* arguments
  fallacies, 7–8, 360–361, 365–366, 405,
    409, 417
cross-cultural proverbs, 180
cultural diversity
  adapting to, 106
  demographic, 106
    age, 107–108
    education level, 110
    ethnicity, 108–109
    gender and biological sex, 108
    geographic origin, 109
    language, 111–112
    occupation, 110
    religion, 110–111
    socioeconomic status, 109–110
  dimensions
    collectivism and individualism, 101
    femininity and masculinity,
      102–104
    long-term and short-term
      orientation, 104, 106
    power distance, 100–101
    uncertainty avoidance, 104
  individual
    attitudes, 115–116
    beliefs, 113–115
    expectations, 117
    knowledge, 112–113
    motives, 116–117
    needs, 118
    values, 116
  language and, 225–226

organization and, 209
cultural factors, 41
cultures, 94, 99–101, 103–104, 106, 108,
    166, 183, 202, 209–211, 225, 229,
    264, 267, 272, 274–275, 389, 391.
    See also cultural diversity
currency of information, 134

D

databases, 18, 136–137, 144–147, 407
debates, 368–369, 373
decoding, 10, 12, 72
Deep Web, 136–137
deficiency needs, 118
delivery. *See also* nonverbal
    communication
  and ELM factors, 277
  factors, 345
  humor and, 392–393
  methods of, 25–26, 250–257
  personal style of, 279–280
  self-assessment, 279
  of speech, 277
  use of
    body, 23, 25
    face and eyes, 23
    voice, 22–23
demographic diversity, 106–107,
    109–110, 226–228
demonstration speeches, 323
derived beliefs, 113
descriptions, message support, 165, 314,
    366
descriptive speeches, 324
discriminative listening, 75
distorted evidence, 367–368, 380
diversity, 12, 180. *See also* cultural
    diversity; individual diversity;
    individual entries, e.g., audience
    diversity
  considering
    cross-cultural proverbs, 180
    language, culture and airline safety,
      227
domains, Internet, 143
door-in-the-face (DIF) strategy, 349
dress, 25, 108, 122, 264

E

ecological fallacy, 43
education, 110
elaboration, 60
  strategies, 85
Elaboration Likelihood Model (ELM),
    60, 277, 330, 331
  ability, 61–62
  central route processing, 60–61
  motivation, 61–62
  peripheral cues, 60–61

kinesics, 45
kinesthetic speech, 237
knowledge, 112–113, 118

L

labels, 300
language, 237–241. *See also* analogies
  credibility-enhancing, 233–236
  diversity, 227
  inclusive, 230–233
  intended meanings and, 241–242
  intensity, 240–241, 270
  loaded, 378
  oral language, 243–244
  self-assessment, 224
  summary, 244–245
leaders, 7, 105, 243, 393, 397–398
learned helplessness, 40
learning styles, 237, 310–313, 325
Leathers, Dale, 263
legal constraints, 121
legibility, 291
Lewis, Thomas R., 393
Librarians' Internet Index (LII), 143
libraries, 144–148
Library of Congress, 144–145
lines of communication, 9
linguistic relativity hypothesis, 221, 225
listening
  appreciative, 76–77
  audience, 86–87
  comprehensive, 75
  critical, 75–76
  decoding, 72
  discriminative, 75
  and gender, 83–84
  hearing, 73
  LSP-16, 77
  process of, 74
  selective attention, 73
  skills, improving, 84–86
  SMCRE model, 72
  styles, 77, 80–81
    action-oriented, 78
    content-oriented, 78–79
    elaboration strategies, 85
    and empathy, 82–83
    people-oriented, 78
    and personality, 81
    time-oriented, 79
  systems model of, 74
  therapeutic, 75
Listening Styles Profile-16 (LSP-16), 77
literal analogies, 374
loaded language, 378
logos, 54, 97
long-term goals, 96, 106
long-term *vs.* short-term orientation,
  104–106
love needs, 118

low-ball strategy, 349–350
LSP-16. *See* Listening Styles Profile-16
  (LSP-16)
Lustig, Myron, 100
lying. *See* ethics
Lyme disease, 181, 213

M

main points, 21–22, 187, 199–200, 202,
  207–208
Malandro, Loretta, 19, 32, 237–238
manuscript delivery, 250–251
marginalizing language, 230
Martin, Mary, 116, 138–139
masculinity *vs.* femininity, 102–104
Maslow, Abraham, 118
MBIT™. *See* Myers-Briggs Type
  Indicator (MBIT™)
McCain, John, 8, 390
media. *See* presentational media
memorized delivery, 251–252
memory, 95
messages, 11, 95, 165
  characteristics of, 334–336
  factors, 345
  part of
    content, 11
    relational component, 11
  variables, 57, 58
message-sidedness, 340
metaphors, 221, 239, 241, 319
Mill, John Stuart, 180
Millennial Generation, 107
misleading statistics, 368
mistaking correlation for cause, 377,
  380
mitigated speech, 227
MLA. *See* Modern Language
  Association (MLA)
models, visual aids, 293–294
Modern Language Association (MLA),
  150, 153, 212, 405, 408–410
Monroe, Alan, 196–197, 200
Monroe's motivated sequence, 196–197,
  200, 206
Moore, Brooke Noel, 98, 365, 371, 395
Morales, Edna
  public speaking and, 4–5
Morgan, Trevor, 105, 319–320
motivation, 61–62, 331
motives, 116–117
movements, 23. *See also* gestures
Myers-Briggs Type Indicator
  (MBIT™), 81

N

narrative fidelity, 167
narrative probability, 166–167, 176
narratives, 166–167, 176–177, 188, 253,
  392. *See also* extended narratives

National Communication Association
  (NCA), 63–64
nature of the occasion, 122
NCA. *See* National Communication
  Association (NCA)
negative self-talk, 44
networking sites, social, 119–120
Nichols, Ralph G., 151
non sequiturs, 379–382
nonverbal behaviors, defined, 257
nonverbal communication. *See also*
  appearance
  environment and, 259–262, 278
  eyes/face and, 270–271, 277–278
  functional roles of
    immediacy, 276–278
    transaction, regulating, 274–275
    verbal symbol, 275–276
    words message, reinforcing, 276
  gestures/movement and, 12, 23,
    273, 278
  in introductions, 183
  overview, 257–258
  proactive, 278, 280–281
  time and, 273–274
  touch and, 273
  for transitions, 186
  verbal communication *vs.*, 257, 259
  voice and, 22–23
    articulation, 267–268
    pitch, 266
    range, 266–267
    rhythm, 267
    speaking in, 268–269
    tempo, 267
    volume, 265–266
note cards, 255–256
novelty, 315
numerical data, 161–163

O

objects, 293–294
obscenities, 244
observations, 119
occupations, 6–7, 110, 400–401
Olmos, Edward James, 166, 205
one-sided messages, 340–341
online catalogs, 145
opinions, 142, 163–164
organic patterns, 203
  spiral pattern, 204
  star pattern, 205–206
  wave pattern, 204
organization. *See also* organization
  strategies; patterns of
  organization
  of conclusions, 22, 186–187
  of introductions, 175–184, 207
  overview, 5, 250, 259, 274, 394
  steps, 19